The Whole Works of King Alfred the Great
by Alfred (King of England)

Copyright © 2019 by HardPress

Address:
HardPress
8345 NW 66TH ST #2561
MIAMI FL 33166-2626
USA
Email: info@hardpress.net

The whole works of King Alfred the Great

Alfred

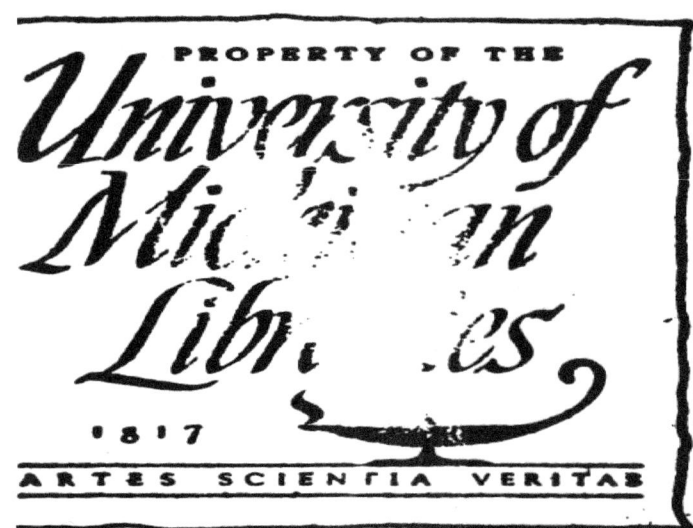

THE WORKS
OF
KING ALFRED THE GREAT.

11581

THE WHOLE WORKS

OF

KING ALFRED THE GREAT:

WITH

PRELIMINARY ESSAYS

ILLUSTRATIVE OF THE HISTORY, ARTS, AND MANNERS, OF THE NINTH CENTURY.

Volume II.

LONDON:
BOSWORTH & HARRISON, 215, REGENT STREET.
1858.

828
A392
tA39
1858
cop.2

AN ENGLISH TRANSLATION OF
KING ALFRED'S
ANGLO-SAXON VERSION
OF
THE HISTORIAN OROSIUS.

INTRODUCTION.

In the time of king Alfred, OROSIUS was so well known as an historian, that his name was commonly used instead of the title of his work. This is evident, from Alfred's first sentence.—" Here beginneth the book which men call Orosius." This compendious history of the world [1] from the creation to the year A. D. 416, written by Orosius, continued to be held in the highest esteem, from the days of Alfred to the invention of printing, for it was selected one of the first works to be committed to the press. The first edition appeared in Germany, so early as 1471.[2] After this, numerous editions [3] were published by the most celebrated printers. It must be interesting to know the origin of a work, that has attracted so much attention, and been highly valued for so many ages—a work chosen by the first man of his age, our GLORIOUS KING ALFRED, as a book worthy to be translated by him into Anglo-Saxon—the English of his day—to teach his people history. The origin and intention of this work will be best shewn by a short biographical account of Orosius, its author.

PAULUS OROSIUS was a learned Spanish presbyter, born in the latter part of the fourth century, at Tarragona,[4] on the coast of the Mediterranean. He was educated in Spain; but, being a young man of great talents, the information to be acquired in his

---

[1] Ab initio mundi usque in præsentem diem [A. D. 416]: Havercamp's Orosius 4to, Leyden 1767, l. vii, c. 43, p. 587. Apparently the same book published in 1738, with only a new title page.

[2] Impressus is liber est . . . Augustæ a. 1471, per Johannem Schuszler. Haver. p. xii. In the same page of Haver. the date is 1470: . . Florentissimæ urbis Augustæ . . anno a partu virginis Mariæ salutifero millesimo quadrigentesimo et septuagesimo; circiter Junii nonas septimas.

[3] Fabricius says: Prela multum sudavit. Haver. adds: Sæpissime prela fatigavit Orosius, p. xiii.

[4] Tarraconensem esse Orosium non dubitat Don Paolo Ignazio de patria Orosii edita Hispanice Barcinone 1702, Fol. libro quadrigentarum paginarum, Fabricius, liber iv, c. 3.

own country did not satisfy his inquiring mind. He had energy enough to overcome any difficulty in the acquisition of knowledge; he did not, therefore, hesitate to go to Africa, to benefit by the instruction of S. Augustine, bishop of Hippo Regius, one of the most able and voluminous writers of that age. There is great difficulty in ascertaining how long Orosius remained in Africa, under the instruction of S. Augustine, before he returned to Spain. Some suppose that Orosius did not arrive in Africa before A. D. 414, when the Spanish bishops, Eutropius and Paul, sent him to consult S. Augustine about the nature and origin of the soul and several abstruse points of doctrine, which were held by the Priscillianists and the Origenists. Orosius, about that time, wrote on the subject,—" Consultatio sive Commonitorium Orosii ad Augustinum de errore Priscillianistarum et Origenistarum." In answer to which, S. Augustine published—" Ad Orosium contra Priscillianistas et Origenistas." These are both in the works of S. Augustine.

In A. D. 415, S. Augustine recommended Orosius to proceed to Palestine, that he might consult S. Jerome on some particulars as to the origin of the soul, which Augustine could not satisfactorily explain. Jerome was then living at Bethlehem, and engaged in translating the scriptures from the Hebrew and Greek originals into Latin, which is the present vulgate or authorized version of the Roman Catholics. S. Jerome was the most learned man, and the most profound critic of the early church. The deference paid by Augustine, in sending Orosius to Jerome for a solution of what was too difficult for himself, is a proof of the high estimation, in which he held S. Jerome's talents and learning. This letter of introduction, S. Augustine sent, in his treatise, De ratione animæ, by Orosius to S. Jerome, to whom it was most respectfully dedicated. The letter is so honourable to them all, and so descriptive of Orosius, that part of it, at least, ought to be inserted.

"S. Augustine to S. Jerome.—Behold, there has come to me a religious young man, in catholic peace a brother, in age a son, in rank a co-presbyter, Orosius—of active talents, ready eloquence, ardent application, longing to be, in God's house, a vessel useful for disproving false and destructive doctrines which have killed the souls of the Spaniards much more grievously, than the barbarian sword their bodies. He has hastened to us from the ocean shore—expecting from report, that he might learn from me, whatever he wished of those matters he desired to know; but he has not reaped the fruit of his labour. First, I desired him not to trust much to fame respecting me: next, I taught him what I could; but what I could not, I told him where he might learn, and I advised him to come to you. In which matter, on his having willingly and obediently acceded to my advice or command, I have asked him, on his coming from you, that he would take us, on his way home."⁵

S. Jerome thanks Augustine, in his answer, for the dedication and for sending a copy of the book by so celebrated a man as Orosius, whom he gladly received, on account of his merits, as well as from the introduction of S. Augustine.⁶

That Orosius should have gained the respect and esteem and the high praise of two men, like Augustine and Jerome,—the most eminent of their day for talents and learning, is a proof that he was a man of no ordinary ability, and acquirements. But Orosius was as estimable for his disposition and character, as he was respected for his talents and erudition. Look at his conduct and his writings.—He was a man of great liberality, and benevolence, considering every country his home⁷ and every man his brother. Though zealous for the truth, and ready, at all times, to defend what he believed to be true, he never descended to uncharitable personalities, or gave way to hostile feelings even against his most bitter opponents.⁸ He had no desire to enter upon disputed points, being a humble and practical christian⁹; but if drawn into discussion, it was his first wish to shew a friendly regard for the person of his opponent, and then to bring his strongest arguments against his errors. Under the influence of these feelings he first came to Africa,¹⁰ and afterwards went into Palestine.¹¹

When Orosius was in Palestine, Pelagius and his disciple Cælestius, were there, disseminating their doctrines,¹² with great zeal. Orosius was called to oppose them in a synod, held at Jerusalem July 30th, A. D. 415, before John, bishop of that

---

5 Haver. p. XXVIII, and XXXV.—S. Augustine's works, letter 165.—Du Pin's Bibliotheca Patrum; or, A new History of Ecclesiastical writers, Folio, London, 1693, century Vth, vol. III, Part I, p. 156.

6 Virum honorabilem Orosium, et sui merito, et te jubente suscepi. S. Jerome's works, letter 94.—Du Pin, vol. III, Pt 1, letters 92 and 94, p. 94.

7 Orosius says of himself,—Inter Romanos, ut dixi, Romanus, inter Christianos Christianus, inter homines homo. . . . Utor temporarie omni terra quasi patria. Haver. l. v, c. 2; p. 289.

8 Odisse me fateor hæresim, non hæreticum. Haver. p. 634.

9 Vos me participem certaminis vestri esse voluistis, ut auxiliator non auctor accederem. Latebam siquidem in Bethleëm, ignotus, advena, pauper. . . . Traditus a patre Augustino, ut timorem Domini discerem, sedens ad pedes Hieronymi: inde Hierusalem vobis accersentibus vocatus adveni. Dehinc in conventum vestrum una vobiscum, Joanne episcopo præcipiente, consedi. Haver. p. 590.

10 Nunc me, inquam . . . Africa excepit pace simplici, sinu proprio, jure communi. Id. l. v, c. 2, p. 288.

11 See the last two paragraphs in page 11, and note 9.

12 " Pelagius mihi dixit, docere se, hominem posse esse sine peccato, et mandata Dei facile custodire, si velit." Respondit Pelagius, " Hoc et dixisse me et dicere, negare non possum." Haver. p. 591.——" Ego dixi hominem sine peccato." Id. p. 600.——Ecce

city.[13] He then wrote his celebrated treatise, which he modestly calls, "Apologia contra Pelagium de arbitrii libertate." It is appended to his History.[14]

Orosius remained in Palestine till the close of 415, for he was induced by Heros, bishop of Arles, and Lazarus, bishop of Aix, to present a memorial against Pelagius at the council,[15] held at Diospolis,—the Lydda of Holy Scripture,—on the 20th of December in that year.

Orosius returned from Palestine to Africa, in accordance with his promise,[16] to visit his friend S. Augustine, bishop of Hippo Regius, before he bent his course homeward to Spain. This must have been in 416; for, in the autumn of that year, Orosius presented to the African council of Milevis [17] the letters of Heros and Lazarus against Pelagius.

Rome was captured and pillaged in A. D. 410, by Alaric king of the Visi-Gothi, Wisi-Gothi or West-Goths, also known by the name of Mœso-Goths, from their residence in Mœsia.[18] These Mœso-Goths were Christians, under the guidance of Bishop Ulphilas, a man of great learning and piety, who, with the view of leading them to the fountain of his doctrine, translated the New Testament from Greek, between A. D. 360 and 380, into the language of the Mœso-Goths—the pure German of that period. It is the earliest specimen of High-German now in existence, and prevailed in the south or high part of Germany, as the Old-Saxon, the nearest relative of the Anglo-Saxon, did in the north or low and flat part of that country.[19] Great moderation and forbearance were manifested by Alaric the Visi-Gothic king and his army in taking Rome. Orosius gives a detailed account of the mercy shewn to the Romans by the king of the West-Goths.[20] Alfred epitomized this detail in the following simple style: "Alaric, the most Christian and the mildest of kings, sacked Rome, with so little violence, that he ordered no man should be slain,—and that

---

Pelagius, qui ausus est profiteri, se esse sine macula atque peccato, Id. 601.——Homo qui hoc potest, Christus est. Id. 603.

13 See the latter part of note 9.—Du Pin's History of Ecclesiastical Writers, Fol. London 1693. vol. III, Pt 1, p. 221.

14. Haver. pp. 588—634.

15 Tom. II Conc. p. 1529.—Landon's Manual of Councils, p. 207—209.—Dupin, vol. III, Pt 1, p. 221, 222.

16 Augustinus rogavit eum (Orosium) ut abs te [Hieronymo, JEROME] veniens per nos ad propria remearet. Haver. p. XXXV.

17 Tom. II, Conc. p. 1537.—Landon, p. 410.—Du Pin, vol. III, Pt I, p. 222:—also p. 157, S. Augustine's 175th letter.

18 Bosworth's Origin of the English and Germanic Languages, VII, 2, 6, 7, 9. p. 114—116.

19 Id. II, 4, p. 13: V, 1—10, p. 81—83.

20 Haver. l. VII, c. 39, p. 573—575.

nothing should be taken away, or injured, that was in the churches. Soon after that, on the third day, they went out of the city of their own accord. There was not a single house burnt by their order."[21]

This sacking of Rome, however, afforded the Romans a pretence for accusing Christianity of being the cause of the affliction and ruin, which had befallen the empire. These heathens asserted that Christianity had been injurious rather than beneficial to mankind, alleging, that, before the coming of Christ, the world was blessed with peace and prosperity; but that, since they had changed their old religion for Christianity, victory had entirely forsaken the Romans, and both their glory and empire had declined; for, the gods, filled with indignation to see their worship neglected, and their altars abandoned, had visited the world with those plagues and desolations, which were still on the increase."[22] S. Augustine wrote his celebrated treatise, "The city of God," to shew the absurdity of this assertion, and to prove, by historical facts, how much the world had been ameliorated by revelation. This work, in defence of Christianity, appears to have been immediately commenced by S. Augustine: it is full of matter and profound erudition. It naturally occupied much of his thoughts, and was a subject of discussion with his friends, especially with Orosius. A man, so full of zeal as Orosius, would soon enter warmly into the subject, and he was readily induced, at the request of his friend, to write a work to prove from the facts of general history, what S. Augustine had shewn from the history of the Church—the city of God—that the preaching of 'peace on earth and good will toward men' could never be the cause of increasing the misery of mankind. This is the origin of the compendious History of the world by Orosius. It is written, on Christian principles, as a defence or an apology of Christianity. The tone pervading the work is that of a Christian, impressed with a proper sense of justice and humanity, deprecating ambition, conquest and glory, gained at the expense of human blood and human happiness.

This History of Orosius was undertaken at the request of S. Augustine and dedicated [23] to him. Orosius commenced writing about A. D. 410, when Honorius was emperor of the West, and when S. Augustine had finished ten books of his City of God.[24]

---

21 See this translation of King Alfred's Orosius, b. VI, c. 38, § 1.

22 Mosheim's Eccl. Hist., Cent. V, Pt 1, c. II, § 2.

23 Præceptis tuis parui, beatissime pater Augustine. Haver. p. 1. Totum tuum [est], quod ex te ad te redit, opus meum. Id. p. 3.

24 Hanc historiam conscripsit Orosius, nimirum post Romam captam sub Honorio Imperatore, anno Christi CCCCX. Quum ergo Augustinus jam decimum de Civitate Dei perfecisset, atque jam undecimum conscriberet, tum Orosius noster hæc scribere aggressus

Part of it was composed in Africa," and it was probably finished about A. D. 416, at which date the work closes.

The highest authorities continued to speak, in the strongest terms, in favour of this History. From many others, one only is here quoted. Pope Gelasius the First, in a council of seventy bishops, held at Rome in A. D. 494, praised Orosius as a most learned man, who had, with wonderful brevity," written a work against heathen perversions.

The reputation of this History was so great, in the time of King Alfred, that he determined to transfer the substance of it from the original Latin into Anglo-Saxon, for the benefit of his subjects; but in doing this, he often imitated rather than translated, and frequently added new illustrative clauses, and sentences of his own, and occasionally new paragraphs. At other times, he abridged what appeared to him less important, and passed over what was not to his purpose. Thus, by omitting the last four chapters of the fifth book, and the first three with a few others in the sixth, the king brought the substance of the fifth and sixth books of the original Latin, into the fifth book of his Anglo-Saxon work. Alfred's sixth book is, therefore, the seventh of Orosius, in which most of the chapters are much abridged, and the last three omitted. Alfred did not think the dedication and the first chapter of Orosius adapted for his subjects, he did not therefore insert them; but he still kept up a unity of design in his work, as will appear from the following short sketch of it.

In book I, he gives a geographical description of the whole world, then known, with a summary of general history from the earliest period to the building of Rome, A. M. 3251, and B. C. 753—Book II, after a reference to the creation, and the four great empires, describes the foundation of Rome, the wars of the Romans and Sabines, the affairs of Cyrus, Darius, Xerxes, Leonidas, etc. and concludes with the capture of Rome by the Gauls, A. M. 3608, and B. C. 396—Book III speaks of the affairs of the Lacedæmonians, Persians, Romans, Gauls, Carthaginians, Latins, Mæcedonians, etc. and ends with the death of Seleucus about the year A. M. 3714, and B. C. 290—Book IV contains the history of Rome from the wars of Pyrrhus to the fall of Carthage, A. M. 3853, and B. C. 151.—Book V, including the Vth and VIth books of Orosius, comprises the period from the taking of Corinth to the birth of our SAVIOUR, A. M. 4004.—Book VI,—the VIIth of Oro-

est. Fabricius. Haver, p. 4, note 24.—SEE, also, this edition of Alfred's Orosius, B. VI, c. 37, § 1.
25 Nunc me Africa excepit. Haver. l. V. c. II, p. 288.
26 Orosium, virum eruditissimum, collaudamus, quia valde necessaria adversus paganorum calumnias ordinavit, miraque brevitate contexuit. Haver. p. XXVIII.—Dupin, Tom. III, Pt II, p. 175, and 180.

sius,—recapitulates the succession of the four great empires, and continues the history of Rome from the accession of Tiberius Cæsar, A. D. 14 to A. D. 416, A. M. 4420, including an account of the greatest event of the age, the taking and sacking of Rome by Alaric in A. D. 410.

In the first book especially, Alfred introduced much new matter and added considerably to the geography of Europe.

These geographical additions prove that he had recourse to original sourses for information. He then left his author and stated, from the best authorities of his age, all the particulars of Europe, that he could collect, filling up the chasm between the time of Orosius, the commencement of the fifth century, and his own, the end of the ninth century.

This is the only geography of Europe, written by a contemporary, and giving the position of the Germanic nations, so early as the ninth century.

Besides this geography of Europe, composed by Alfred, the king inserts the very interesting voyages of Ohthere a Norwegian navigator and of Wulfstan. Ohthere, "wishing to search out how far the land lay due north, or whether any man dwelt to the north," [27] sailed by the coast of Norway round the North Cape into the White-Sea; [28] and afterwards into the Baltic. [29] Wulfstan's voyage was confined to the Baltic. [30] These voyages were written by the king, from the relation of these intrepid navigators; for, in the narration, Wulfstan uses a pronoun of the first person plural. [31]

The simplicity of the narration bears the impress of truth, the former beginning thus :—" Ohthere told his lord, King Alfred, that he dwelt north-most of all the northmen." [32]—Ohthere was a man of great wealth, [33] and his strict adherence to truth in his narrative may be concluded, from his refusing to vouch for any thing, of which he could not bear personal testimony. He says: "The Biarmians told him many stories both about their own land, and about the countries, which were around them; but *he knew not what was true, because he did not see it himself*." [34]

These important additions and separate essays of King Alfred, are very interesting, as his original composition; and valuable, because they contain information relative to the geography of Europe, not otherwise to be obtained, and because they are authentic pictures of the manners and of the political condition of a great part of the north, in the ninth century. The following literal English translation, from the Anglo-Saxon of King Alfred,

27. See b. I. c. 1, § 13.   28. Id. § 14—17.   29. Id. § 18, 19.   30. Id. § 20—23
31. Id. § 20.   32. Id. § 13.   33. Id. § 15.   34. Id. § 14.

is, therefore, not a mere translation of what Alfred selected from Orosius; but an English version of the king's own Anglo-Saxon additions and essays, with his abridgement, and occasional amplification, of the most interesting parts of the compendious universal History of Orosius. The most striking of these will be pointed out, in brief notes at the foot of the page, and a reference made to the original Latin of those parts, which Alfred condensed, translated, imitated, paraphrased or enlarged; for he did not hesitate to adopt any of these plans, when he thought that he could improve the work, and make it more useful for his people. These short notes are only intended for the general reader; they, for the most part, give the result of investigations, rather than a detail of the reason or authority for arriving at that result.

If then new views be given, or old opinions advanced, apparently without satisfactory evidence being adduced, it is hoped that judgment will be suspended, till the reformed Anglo-Saxon text shall be printed, with an appendage of various readings, and more ample notes.—

JOSEPH BOSWORTH.

ETWALL, UTTOXETER,
MARCH 16th, 1852.

CONTENTS.[1]

BOOK I.

Here beginneth the book, which men call OROSIUS.

CHAPTER I.

How our elders divided all the globe into three parts, § 1, 5.—[2] [The boundary of Asia, § 2, 6.—of Europe, § 3.—of Africa, § 4.—of India and Parthia, § 7.— of Babylonia, Mesopotamia, Palestine, Armenia, Syria, Phœnicia etc. § 8.—of Egypt § 9.—of the south of Asia, § 10.—Extent of Alfred's

---

1 The original Latin work of Orosius has no part of this Table of Contents; the whole of it, therefore, must be the composition of the Anglo-Saxon translator, for it is contained in both the Anglo-Saxon manuscripts now existing, the Lauderdale, and the Cotton, said to be written in the ninth and tenth centuries. See Preface to King Alfred's Anglo-Saxon Version.

2 What is placed between the brackets is not in Anglo-Saxon: it is inserted to complete the Table of Contents.

GERMANIA, § 11.—of the East Franks, Bavarians, Bohemians, Frisians, Danes, Angles, Old-Saxons, etc. § 12.—The first voyage of Ohthere § 13.—of the Biarmians § 14.—Ohthere a rich man, § 15.—of the country of the Northmen, § 16.—Of Sweden, § 17.—Ohthere's second voyage, § 18. He sails into the Baltic, § 19.—Wulfstan's voyage, § 20.—Customs of the Esthonians, concerning the dead, § 21.—Horse races, § 22. Of keeping the dead, § 23.—Of Greece, § 24.—Of Italy, § 25.—Of Gallia Belgica, § 26.—Of Spain, § 27.—Of Britain, § 28.—Extent of AFRICA, § 29, 30, 31.—Of Byzantium, Carthage, Numidia, § 32.—Islands in the MEDITERRANEAN, § 33.—The Cyclades or Dodekanista, § 34.—Of Sicily, § 35.—Of Sardinia, § 36.—Of Corsica, § 37.—The Balearic Islands, § 38.]

CHAPTER II.

How Ninus, king of Assyria, first began to reign over the men of this world, § 1.—And how, after him, Semiramis, his queen, with great severity, and profligacy, seized the government, § 2. 3.

CHAPTER III.

How the fire from heaven burnt up the land, on which the two cities, Sodom and Gomorrah, were built, § 1, 2.

CHAPTER IV.

How the inhabitants of Candia and Scarpanto fought with each other, § 1.

CHAPTER V.

How the righteous man, Joseph, saved the people of Egypt from the seven year's great famine by his wisdom; and how they afterwards, according to his appointment, gave every year the fifth part of all their fruits to their king as tribute, § 1, 2.

CHAPTER VI.

How in Achaia, there was a great flood in the days of king Amphictyon, § 1, 2.

CHAPTER VII.

How Moses led the people of Israel from Egypt over the Red sea, § 1, 2.

CHAPTER VIII.

How, in one night, there were fifty men slain in Egypt by their own sons; § 1.—and how Busiris, the king, commanded to sacrifice all the strangers, who visited him, § 2; and about the contention of many other people, § 3, 4.

Chapter IX.

How the Cretans and Athenians, people of Greece, fought with each other, § 1, 2.

Chapter X.

How Vesoges, king of Egypt, would subdue both the south part which is Asia, and the north part, which is Scythia, § 1.—And how two noblemen were banished from Scythia, and about the women, who are called Amazons § 2.—5.—And about the Goths whom Pyrrhus, the cruel king of Greece, and Alexander the Great, as well as Julius, the emperor, dreaded, § 6.

Chapter XI.

How Helen, the king's wife, was taken in the city of Lacedæmon § 1, 2.—And how king Æneas went with an army into Italy, § 3.

Chapter XII.

How Sardanapalus was the last king of Assyria, and how Arbaces, his chief officer, deceived him, § 1, 2.—And how the women upbraided their husbands, when they wished to flee, § 3.—And how the brass-founder formed an image of a bull for the prince, § 4, 5.

Chapter XIII.

How the Peloponnesians and Athenians fought with each other, § 1.

Chapter. XIV.

How the Lacedæmonians and Messenians fought with each other, on account of the offerings of their maidens, § 1—3: § 4.

Book II : Chapter I.

How Orosius said, that our Lord created the first man very upright and very good, § 1.—And about the four empires of the world, § 2—6.

Chapter II.

How the brothers, Remus and Romulus, built the city of Rome in Italy, § 1—3.

Chapter III.

With what wickedness, Romulus and Brutus dedicated Rome, § 1—4.

Chapter IV.

How the Romans and Sabines fought with each other, § 1—4. And how Cyrus was slain in Scythia, § 5—8.

Chapter V.

How king Cambyses despised the Egyptian idols, § 1.—And concerning the wars of Darius, § 2.—And of Xerxes and Leonidas, § 3—9.

Chapter VI.

And how a wonder was shewn to the Romans, as if the heavens were burning, § 1—5.

Chapter VII.

How the people of Sicily were fighting with each other, § 1—2.

Chapter VIII.

How the Romans beset the city Veii, ten years, § 1—And how the Senonian Gauls (Galli Senones) stormed the city Rome, § 2—6.

Book III: Chapter I.

How a disgraceful and crafty peace was made between the Lacedæmonians and Persians, § 1—6.

Chapter II.

How there was an earthquake in Achaia § 1 : § 2.

Chapter III.

How the great pestilence was in Rome, at the time of the two Consuls, § 1, 2—And how Marcus Curtius plunged into the yawning earth, § 3.

Chapter IV.

How the Gauls ravaged the Roman territories to within three miles of the city, § 1.

Chapter V.

How the Carthaginian ambassadors came to Rome, and offered peace, § 1 ; § 2—5.

Chapter VI.

How the Romans and Latins fought with each other, § 1. And how a nun (vestal virgin) was buried alive, 2—3.

Chapter VII.

How king Alexander, uncle of the great Alexander, fought with the Romans, § 1. And how Philip, father of the great Alexander, took the sovereignty of Macedonia, 2—5. And chose Byzantium for his Capital, 6—7, 8.

Chapter VIII.

How the place, Furculæ Caudinæ, became well known for the disgrace of the Romans, § 1, 2 : 3.

Chapter IX.

How the great Alexander took the sovereignty of Macedonia, § 1—5.—And how he told a certain priest to say, according to his wish, who was his father, 6.—And how he overcame king Darius, 7—9 : 10—18.—And how he himself was killed with poison, 19, 20.

Chapter X.

How, under two consuls, four of the strongest nations wished to overcome the Romans, § 1—2.—And how the great pestilence was at Rome, 3.— And how they told them to fetch Æsculapius, the magician, with the magical snake, 4 : 5, 6.

Chapter XI.

How, under two consuls, the Samnites, and the Senonian Gauls became enemies of the city Rome, § 1.—And how, after Alexander's death, his generals ended their lives in strife, 2—12.

Book IV : Chapter I.

How the Tarentines saw ships of the Romans sail on the sea, when they were playing in their theatre, § 1—6.

Chapter II.

How the many evil wonders happened in Rome, § 1, 2.

Chapter III.

How milk was seen to rain from heaven, and blood to spring from the earth, § 1 : 2, 3.

Chapter IV.

How a great plague came upon the Romans, § 1.—And how Caperone, the nun (vestal virgin) was hanged, 2.—And how the townspeople of Carthage sacrificed men to their gods, 3.

Chapter V.

How Himilco, king of the Carthaginians, went with an army into Sicily, § 1.—And how a certain man, Hanno, was yearning for power, 2.—And how the Carthaginians heard, that the great Alexander had stormed the city Tyre, 3 : 4, 5.

Chapter VI.

How the people of Sicily and Carthage fought with each other, § 1.—And how the Romans beset Hannibal, king of the Carthaginians, 2, 3.—And how Collatinus, the consul, went with an army to Camarina a town of Sicily, 4—And how the Carthaginians fixed again that the aged Hannibal should fight against the Romans with ships, 5.—And how the Romans went into Africa with three hundred and thirty ships, 6.—And how Regulus, the consul, killed an immense serpent, 7.—And how Regulus fought with three Carthaginian kings, in one battle, 8, 9.—And how Emilius, the consul, went into Africa with three hundred ships, 10, 11.—And how Cotta, the consul, ravaged Sicily, 12.—How two consuls went into Africa with three hundred ships, and how in the time of three consuls Asdrubal, the new king, came to Lilybæum in the island [of Sicily,] 13 : 14.—And how Claudius, the consul, went against the Carthaginians again, 15.—And how Caius, the consul, went into Africa and was cast away in the sea, 16.—And how Lutatius, the consul, went into Africa with three hundred ships, 17.

Chapter VII.

How the immense fire happened at Rome, § 1.—And how the Gauls withstood the Romans, 2.—And how the Sardinians made war on the Romans, as the Carthaginians advised them, 3.—And how Orosius said, that he was come to the good times, of which the Romans afterwards boasted much, 4.—And how the Gauls warred against the Romans, and the Carthaginians did so, on the other side, 5.—And how two consuls fought with the Gauls, 6, 7, 8.—And how many wonders were seen, 9.—And how Claudius the consul, slew thirty thousand Gauls, 10.

Chapter VIII.

How Hannibal, king of the Carthaginians, beset Seguntum, a

city of Spain, § 1.—And how Hannibal, king of the Carthaginians, broke over the Pyrenean mountains, 2.—And how Scipio, the consul, fought with the Spaniards, 3.—And how, many wonders happened at that time, 4.

Chapter IX.

How Hannibal deceived two consuls in their battle, § 1.—And how the Romans appointed a dictator, and Scipio as consul, 2.—And how the Romans sent Lucius, the consul, into Gaul, with three legions, 3, 4 : 5, 6.

Chapter X.

How Marcellus, the consul, went with a fleet against Sicily, § 1 : 2—6.—And how Hannibal fought against Marcellus the consul, three days, 7.—And how Hannibal stole upon Marcellus, the consul, and slew him, 8.—And how Asdrubal, Hannibal's brother, went from Spain into Italy, 9 : 10, 11.—And how peace was granted to the Carthaginians by Scipio, the consul, 12.

Chapter XI.

How the second war of the Romans was ended, § 1.—And how Sempronius, the consul, was slain in Spain, 2 : 3—5.—And how Philip, king of Macedon, killed an ambassador of the Romans, 6 : 7.—And how the Macedonian war arose, 8.—And how Emilius, the consul, overcame Perseus, the king, 9.

Chapter XII.

How the greatest fear came upon the Romans, from the Celtiberians, a people of Spain, § 1 : 2, 3.

Chapter XIII.

How the third war of the Romans, with the king of the Carthaginians, was ended, § 1—5.

Book V : Chapter I.

How Orosius spoke about the boast of the Romans, how they overcame many people; and how they drove many kings before their triumphs towards Rome § 1 : 2, 3.

Chapter II.

How, in one year, the two cities, Carthage and Corinth, were destroyed, § 1.—And how Veriatus, the shepherd, began to reign in Spain, 2, 3.—And how Claudius, the consul, routed the

Gauls, 4 : 5—7.—And how Mancinus, the consul, concluded a peace with Spain, 8.—And how Brutus, the consul, slew sixty thousand Spaniards, 9.—And how a child was born in Rome, 10.

Chapter III.

How the Romans sent Scipio into Spain, with their military force, § 1—3.—And how Gracchus, the consul, contended with the other consuls till they slew him, 4.—And how the slaves contended with their masters, 5.

Chapter IV.

How Lucinius, the consul, who was also chief priest of the Romans, went with an army against Aristonicus the king, § 1.—And how Antiochus, king of Asia, wished for the severeignty of the Parthians, 2.—And how Scipio, the best officer of the Romans, complained of his hardships to the Roman senators, 3.—And how the fire of Etna ascended, 4 : 5.

Chapter V.

How the Romans afterwards ordered Carthage to be rebuilt, § 1.—And how the consul Metellus subdued the pirates, 2.

Chapter VI.

How Fabius, the consul, overcame Bituitus, king of the Gauls, § 1.

Chapter VII.

How the Romans contended with Jugurtha, king of the Numidians, § 1, 2.

Chapter VIII.

How the Romans fought with the Cimbri, and with the Teutones, and with the Ambrones, § 1.

Chapter IX.

How the Romans began to raise contention (civil war) among themselves, in the fifth year, that Marius was consul, § 1, 2.

Chapter X.

How there was deliberate war, over all Italy, in the sixth year that Julius Cæsar was consul, § 1 : 2—4.

Chapter XI.

How the Romans sent Sylla, the consul, against Mithridates, king of the Parthians, § 1 : 2—4.

Chapter XII.

How the Romans gave seven legions to Julius, the consul, § 1—3.—And how Julius beset Torquatus Pompey's general, in a fortress, 4, 5,—And how Julius fought with Ptolemy three times, 6—9.

Chapter XIII.

How Octavianus seized upon the empire of the Romans, against their wish, § 1 : 2, 3.

Chapter XIV.

How Octavianus Cæsar shut the door of Janus, § 1—4.

Chapter XV.

How some Spaniards were adversaries to Augustus, § 1 : 2, 3 : 4, 5.

Book VI : Chapter I.

How Orosius spoke about the powers of the four chief empires of this world, § 1—7.

Chapter II.

How Tiberius Cæsar succeeded to the empire of the Romans, after Augustus, § 1—3.

Chapter III.

How Caius was emperor four years, § 1—4.

Chapter IV.

How Tiberius Claudius succeeded to the empire of the Romans, § 1—4.

Chapter V.

How Nero succeeded to the empire of the Romans, § 1.

Chapter VI.

How Galba the emperor succeeded to the government of the Romans, § 1, 2.

Chapter VII.
How Vespasian succeeded to the empire of the Romans, § 1.

Chapter VIII.
How Titus succeeded to the empire of the Romans, § 1.

Chapter IX.
How Domitian, brother of Titus, succeeded to the empire of the Romans, § 1.

Chapter X.
How Nerva succeeded to the empire of the Romans, § 1—3.

Chapter XI.
How Adrian succeeded to the empire of the Romans, § 1, 2.

Chapter XII.
How Antoninus Pius succeeded to the empire of the Romans, § 1.

Chapter XIII.
How Marcus Antoninus succeeded to the empire of the Romans, with his brother Aurelius, § 1—3.

Chapter XIV.
How Lucius succeeded to the empire of the Romans, § 1.

Chapter XV.
How Severus succeeded to the empire of the Romans, § 1, 2.

Chapter XVI.
How his son Antoninus succeeded to the government, § 1.

Chapter XVII.
How Marcus succeeded to the empire of the Romans, § 1.

Chapter XVIII.
How Aurelius succeeded to the empire of the Romans, § 1.

Chapter XIX.
How Maximinus succeeded to the empire of the Romans, § 1.

Chapter XX.
How Gordianus succeeded to the empire of the Romans, § 1.

Chapter XXI.
How Philip succeeded to the sovereignty of the Romans, § 1.

Chapter XXII.
How Decius succeeded to the sovereignty of the Romans, § 1.

Chapter XXIII.
How Gallus succeeded to the sovereignty of the Romans, § 1, 2.

Chapter XXIV.
How the Romans appointed two emperors, § 1, 2.

Chapter XXV.
How Claudius succeeded to the sovereignty of the Romans, § 1.

Chapter XXVI.
How Aurelius sncceeded to the sovereignty of the Romans, § 1.

Chapter XXVII.
How Tacitus succeeded to the sovereignty of the Romans, § 1.

Chapter XXVIII.
How Probus succeeded to the sovereignty of the Romans, § 1.

Chapter XXIX.
How Carus succeeded to the sovereignty of the Romans, § 1.

Chapter XXX.
How Diocletian succeeded to the sovereignty of the Romans, § 1—9.

Chapter XXXI.
How Constantine succeeded to the sovereignty of the Romans, with his two brothers, § 1—3.

Chapter XXXII.
How Jovinianus succeeded to the empire of the Romans. § 1, 2.

Chapter XXXIII.
How Valentinianus succeeded to the sovereignty of the Romans, § 1—3.

Chapter XXXIV.
How Valens succeeded to the sovereignty of the Romans, § 1—4.

Chapter XXXV.

How Gratianus succeeded to the sovereignty of the Romans, § 1.—And how the Britons took Maximianus for their emperor against his will, § 2.

Chapter XXXVI.

How Theodosius succeeded to the empire of the Romans, § 1. —And how Valentinian afterwards succeeded to the sovereignty, 2.

Chapter XXXVII.

How Arcadius succeeded to the sovereignty of the Romans [in the East,] and Honorius to the sovereignty of the West, § 1—3.

Chapter XXXVIII.

How God exercised his mercy on the Romans, § 1, 2.

AN ENGLISH TRANSLATION

OF

KING ALFRED'S

ANGLO-SAXON VERSION OF OROSIUS

Book I, Chapter I.[1]

1. Our elders, said Orosius, divided into three parts, all the globe of this mid-earth, as it is surrounded by the ocean, which we call Garsecg[2]; and they named the three parts by three names,—Asia, and Europe, and Africa: though some said there were but two parts, one Asia and the other Europe.

2. Asia is encompassed by the ocean—the garsecg—on the south, north and east; and so, on the east part, contains one half of this mid-earth. Then on the north part of Asia, on the right hand[3], in the river Don, there the boundaries of Asia and Europe

---

[1] Alfred omits the dedication of Orosius to S. Augustine, and the first chapter, on the origin of history and of misery from Adam [initium miseriæ hominum. Haver. p. 6—10.] The royal translator commences with, l. I, c. 2, of Orosius;—Majores nostri orbem totius terræ, oceani limbo circumseptum, triquadrum statuere. Havercamp's edition, Leyden 4to 1767; p. 10: v. Introduction, p. 10, note 1.

[2] Grimm, Kemble, etc. write gár-secg, literally a spear-man, the ocean; homo jaculo armatus, oceanus.—Mr Kemble adds, " it is a name for the ocean, which is probably derived from some ancient myth, and is now quite unintelligible."—Ettmüller gives the word, thus :—Gársecg, es ; m. Carex jaculorum ; vel, vir hastatus, i. e. oceanus.

Mr Hampson suggests, that the myth of an armed man,—a spear-man,—being employed by the Anglo-Saxons, as a term to denote the Ocean, has some analogy to the personification of Neptune holding his trident. He then adds : " Spears were placed in the hands of the images of heathen gods, as mentioned by Justin.—Per ea adhuc tempora reges hastas pro diademate habebant, quas Græci sceptra dixere. Nam et ab origine rerum, pro diis immortalibus veteres hastas coluere ; ob cujus religionis memoriam adhuc deorum simulacris hastæ adduntur. l. XLIII ; c. III.

[3] In tracing the frontier of Asia from north to south, the Don is on the right hand.

lie together; and, from the same river Don, south along the Mediterranean Sea, towards the west of the city Alexandria, Asia and Africa lie together.

3. EUROPE begins, as I said before, at the river Don,⁴ which runs from the north part of the Rhipæan ⁵ mountains, which are near the ocean, called Sarmatian. ⁵ The river Don runs thence right south, on the west side of Alexander's altars to the nation of the Roxolani. ⁶ It forms the fen which is called Mæotis, [Sea of Azov]; and then runs forth, with a great flood, near the city called Theodosia [Kaffa], flowing eastward into the Black Sea; and then, in a long strait, south easterly, where the Greek city Constantinople lies, and thence out into the Mediterranean Sea.— The south-west boundary of Europe is the ocean, on the west of Spain, and chiefly at the island Cadiz, where the Mediterranean Sea shoots up from the ocean; where also, the pillars of Hercules stand. On the west end of the same Mediterranean Sea is Scotland [Ireland]. ⁷

4 Oros. l. I : c. 1, p. 11.—The river TANAIS or DON, which Alfred calls Danai, was supposed by ancient geographers, as stated by Orosius, and repeated by Alfred, to have its source in the northern parts of the Rhipæan mountains. [τὰ ῾Ριπαῖα ὄρη, and ῾Ρίπαι.] It is difficult to ascertain the precise locality of these mountains, as ancient writers give a diversity of opinions: Arrowsmith places them in Lat. 52 degrees 45 minutes, E. Long. 37 degrees. It is now known, that the Don has its source in the small lake Ivanofskoe, in the government of Toula, Russia, about 54 degrees N. Lat. and 37 degrees E. Long.

5 Sarmatico oceano, in Orosius; Alfred calls it, Sarmondisc garsecg.—FORSTER says —" It is pretty clear, that the Sarmondi must be the Sauromatæ or Sarmatæ." They dwelt in the northern part of Europe, and were supposed to extend to the northern ocean. Alfred follows Orosius, who gives the vulgar and erroneous opinion of his time. The Sermende are mentioned in Book I, CH. I, § 12, note 25.

6 Roxolani, a people of European Sarmatia. They dwelt north of the sea of Azov, in a part of the country now inhabited by the Don Cossacks.

7 This last sentence is an addition by Alfred. In early times, Ireland was called Scotland. In paragraph 28, Alfred says, " Ireland, we call Scotland."—Ireland was exclusively called Scotia or Scotland, from the fifth to the tenth or eleventh century. The first we hear of the Scoti or Scots, is as a people inhabiting Ireland. In the fifth century, they contended with the Hiberni, the earlier inhabitants, and soon gained supreme power, and gave their name to the country. About A. D. 503, a colony of these Scoti, having given their name to Ireland, emigrated to North Britain, gained influence there, and also imposed their name on that country. Skene's Highlands of Scotland, 2 vol. 8vo, 1837. But Ireland is north of Spain. Ancient geographers placed Ireland much more to the south, and Alfred, being guided by them, speaks of it, as being on the west of Spain. Orosius erroneously says—Hibernia insula, inter Britanniam et Hispaniam sita. Haver. p. 28.—Correct information was not supplied, till after the time of Alfred. Though, in most cases, he was in advance of his age, yet in regard to the position of Ireland, he appears to have fallen into the error of the time.

4. The division between AFRICA and Asia begins at Alexandria, a city of Egypt; and the boundary lies thence south, by the river Nile, and so over the desert of Ethiopia to the southern ocean. The north west limit of Africa is the Mediterranean Sea, which shoots from the ocean, where the pillars of Hercules stand; and its end, right west, is the mountain, which is named Atlas, and the island called Canary.⁸

5. I have already spoken shortly about the three parts of this mid-earth; but I will now, as I promised before, tell the boundaries of these three regions, how they are separated by water.

6. Over against the middle of Asia, at the east end, there the mouth of the river, called Ganges, opens into the ocean, which they call the Indian ocean. South from the river's mouth, by the ocean, is the port they call Calymere.⁹ To the south-east of the port is the island of Ceylon; and then to the north of the mouth of the Ganges, where mount Caucasus ends, near the ocean, there is the port Samera.¹⁰ To the north of the port is the mouth of the river, named Ottorogorre.¹¹ They call the ocean Chinese.

7. These are the boundaries of India, where mount Caucasus is on the north, and the river Indus on the west, and the Red Sea¹² on the south, and the ocean on the east. In the district

---

8 Orosius says, Insulæ quas Fortunatas vocant; Haver. p. 12. But Alfred only names one island.

9 Orosius has Caligardamna; and Alfred Caligardamana, [about N. Lat. 10 degrees, 15 minutes, E. Long. 79 degrees, 50 minutes]. Asia ad mediam frontem orientis habet in oceano Eoo ostia fluminis Gangis, a sinistra promontorium Caligardamna, cui subjacet ad Eurum insula Taprobane: e qua oceanus Indicus vocari incipit, a dextra habet Imai montes, ubi Caucasus deficit, promontorium SAMARAM [See § 10, note 17]: cui ad aquilonem subjacent ostia fluminis OCTOROGORRÆ: ex quo oceanus SERICUS [pro Sericus vulgari errore SYRICUS quidam edidit. HAVER. p. 13, note 33] appellatur. L. I: c. II. Haver. p. 12, 13: 21.

10 The modern names of places are given in the translation, except where the old name is almost as familiar as the modern designation. When the position, or present name cannot be discovered, there is no alternative, but to retain the word used in the Anglo-Saxon text, and to add the various readings in the notes. Thus Alfred has Samera, and Orosius, Samara, Somora, Samaræ and Samarata. See § 6 note 9; also § 10 note 17.—Sometimes, however, the modern names are put in brackets immediately after the ancient name, as in § 3, Mæotis [Sea of Azov].

11 The Ottorocorræ were in the N. E. of Tibet, about N. Lat. 34 degrees 20 minutes—E. Long. 99 degrees; and, according to Arrowsmith and Cluverius, the river Ottorocorre was in the same locality. See § 6 note 9, also, § 10, note 17.

12 The Red Sea, in ancient geography, comprehended not only the present Red Sea, but what we now call the Persian gulph, and the Arabian Sea: thus, the Tigris, as well as the Indus, are said to run into the Red Sea, and the whole country between the Indus and the Tigris, is described as having the Red Sea for its southern boundary.

of India are forty four nations; and, besides many other inhabited islands, the island of Ceylon, which has in it ten towns. The river Indus lies to the west of the district: between the river Indus, and that which lies to the west of it, called Tigris, both of which flow south into the Red Sea,—between these two rivers,—are these countries, Arachosia, [Candahor,] and Parthia and Assyria, and Persia, and Media;[13] though writers often name all these countries Media or Assyria; and they are very mountainous, and there are very sharp and stony ways. The northern boundaries of these countries are the Caucasian mountains; and on the south side, the Red Sea. In these countries are two great rivers, Hydaspes [Jhylum], and Arabis [Pooralee]. In this dictrict are thirty two nations: now it is all called Parthia.

8. Then west from the river Tigris to the river Euphrates,— between the rivers,—are these countries, Babylonia and Chaldea, and Mesopotamia. Within these countries are twenty eight nations. Their northern boundaries are the mountains Taurus, and Caucasus, and their southern boundaries lie to the Red Sea. Along the Red Sea,—the part that shoots to the north,—lies the country of Arabia and Saba [Saade], and Eudomane.[14] From the river Euphrates, west to the Mediterranean and north almost to the mountains, which are called Taurus, to the country which they call Armenia, and again south to Egypt,—there are many nations in these districts; that is, Comagena, and Phœnicia, and Damascus, and Coelle, and Moab, and Ammon, and Idumea, and Judea, and Palestine, and Saracene; though it is all called Syria. Then to the north of Syria are the mountains, called Taurus; and to the north of the mountains, are the countries of Cappadocia, and Armenia. Armenia is to the east of Cappadocia. To the west of Cappadocia is the country called Asia the Less. To the north of Cappadocia, is the plain of Themiscyra.[15] Then, between Cappadocia and Asia the Less, is the country of Cilicia and Isauria.

13 This involved sentence is very much shorter and clearer in Orosius.—" A flumine Indo, quod est ab oriente, usque ad flumen Tigrim, quod est ad occasum, regiones sunt istæ.—Aracosia, Parthia, Assyria, Persis, et Media. Haver. p. 14.—Arachosia is, S. E of Cabul, about N. Lat. 30 degrees 45 minutes, E. Long. 65 degrees 30 minutes. Arrowsmith.— Arachosiæ, nunc Candahor, populi Margyetæ qui ante Arimaspi, postea Euergetæ dicti, Sydri, Roplutæ, Eortæ. Urbes Arachotus, Alexandria, quæ ad Arachotum ponitur fluvium. CLUVERII Introduct. Geog. Amstel. 4to 1729. l. V : c. XIII : § IV, p. 550.

14 Orosius has " Arabia Eudæmon." HAVER. p. 14.

15 Themiscyra, in the north west of Pontus [Roum] in Asia Minor : about N. Lat. 41 degrees : E. Long. 36 degrees 56 minutes. Arrowsmith.

This Asia is, on every side, surrounded with salt water, except on the east. On the north side is the Black Sea; and, on the west, the Sea of Marmora, and the Dardanelles; and the Mediterranean Sea, on the south. In the same Asia, the highest mountain is Olympus.

9. To the north of the nearer Egypt is the country of Palestine, and to the east of it, the district of the Saracens, and to the west the country of Libya, and to the south the mountain called Climax.—The spring of the river Nile is near the cliff of the Red Sea; though some say that its spring is in the west end of Africa, near the mountain Atlas; and then soon running on sand to the east, it sinks into the sand. Nigh there, it flows up again, from the sand, and there forms a great sea. Where it first springs up, the men of the country call it Nuchul, and some Dara. Then, from the sea, where it shoots up from the sand, it runs easterly through the desert of Ethiopia, and there it is called Ion, as far as the east part; and there it becomes a great sea. It then sinks again into the earth; and, north of that, afterwards springs up, near the cliff by the Red Sea, which I formerly mentioned. Then, from this source, the water is called the river Nile. Running thence onward to the west it separates into two, about an island which is called Meroe; and thence bending northward, flows out into the Mediterranean Sea. In the winter time, the river at the mouth is so driven back by the northern winds, that it flows over all the land of Egypt; and by this flooding very thick crops are produced in the land of Egypt.—The farther Egypt lies east along the Red Sea, on the south side. On the east and south parts of the country, lies the ocean; and, on its west side, is the nearer Egypt. In the two Egypts are twenty four nations.

10. We have already written about the south part of Asia: now we will take the north part of it; that is from the mountains called Caucasus, of which we have before spoken, and which are to the north of India. They begin first on the east from the ocean, and then lie right west to the mountains of Armenia, which the people of the country call Parachoathras[16]. There, from the south of these mountains, springs the river Euphrates; and, from the

---

16 Parachoathras, Arrowsmith. Alfred writes it Parcoadras. Orosius describes it as, "mons Armeniæ inter Taurum et Caucasum." Haver. p. 19.

mountains called Parachoathras, extend the mountains of Taurus right west, to the country of the Cilicians. Then [17] to the north of the mountains, along the ocean to the north-east of this mid-earth, there the river Bore shoots out into the ocean ; and thence westerly along the ocean to the Caspian Sea, which there shoots up to the mountains of Caucasus. That district they call Old Scythia, and Hyrcania. In this district are forty three nations widely settled, because of the barrenness of the country. Then, from the west of the Caspian Sea unto the river Don, and to the fen called Mæotis, [Sea of Azov] ; and then south to the Mediterranean Sea, and to Mount Taurus ; and north to the ocean is all the country of Scythia within ; though it is separated into thirty two nations. But the countries, that are near, on the east side of the Don, are named Albani in Latin ; and we now call them Liobene.—We have thus spoken shortly about the boundaries of Asia.

11. Now we will speak, as much as we know, about the boundaries of EUROPE.—*From the river Don, westward to the river Rhine,* (which springs from the Alps, and then runs right north into the arm of the ocean, that lies around the country called Britain ;)—*and again south to the river Danube,* (whose spring is near the river Rhine, and which afterwards runs east, by the country north of Greece, into the Mediterranean [1] Sea ;)— *and*

[17] This is a description of the north and east of Asia, or rather, as Orosius states, " ab oriente ad septentrionem." Alfred has so much abridged this description, and included so large a space, in few words, that it is not easy, from the A. S. text alone, to ascertain the locality of the places, which he mentions. The original Latin of Orosius [from p. 19 to 22 of Haver.] is more full and satisfactory : from the text and the following extract, it will be seen, that the river Bore was supposed to be near the promontory of the same name, on the north or north-east coast of Asia. Its name alone would indicate this position, it being in Latin Boreus, and in Greek βόρειος northern. A short extract from Orosius will make all plain.—A fonte fluminis Gangis usque ad fontes fluminis OTTOROGORRÆ [see § 6, note 11] qui sunt a Septentrione, ubi sunt montani Paropamisadæ, mons TAURUS: a fontibus OTTOROGORRÆ usque ad civitatem OTTOROGORRAM, inter Hunnos et Scythas et Gandaridas, mons Caucasus. Ultimus autem inter Eoas et Pasiadras, mons Imaus, ubi flumen CHRYSORRHOAS, et promontorium SAMARA orientali excipiuntur oceano. Igitur a monte Imao, hoc est, ab imo Caucaso, et dextra orientis parte, qua oceanus Sericus tenditur, usque ad promontorium Boreum, et flumen Boreum, inde tenus Scythico mari, quod est a septentrione, usque ad mare Caspium, quod est ab occasu, et usque ad extentum Caucasi jugum, quod est ad meridiem, Hyrcanorum et Scytharum gentes sunt quadraginta duæ, propter terrarum infœcundam diffusionem late oberrantes. l. I; c. II. Haver. p. 21, 22.

[1] Into what is now called the Black Sea, which Alfred considered a part of the Mediterranean. Snorre calls it a gulf of the Mediterranean, in the first chapter of his Heimskringla. In other places, Alfred mentions the Black Sea, under the name Euxinus. RASK's Afhandlinger, Köbenhavn, 1834. vol. I. p. 332, note c.

*north*² *to the ocean, which is called the White Sea*³ : within these are many nations; but they call it all, Germania.⁴

12. Then to the north, from the spring of the Danube, and to the east of the Rhine are the East Franks⁵; and to the south of them are the Suabians, on the other side of the river Danube. To the south and to the east are the Bavarians,⁶ that part which is called Ratisbon.⁷ Right to the east of them are the Bohemians; and north-east are the Thuringians. To the north of them are the Old Saxons,⁸ and to the north-west of them are the Friesians. To the west of the Old Saxons is the mouth of the river Elbe and Friesland. From thence, north-west is the country called Anglen,⁹ and Zealand¹⁰ and some part of Denmark. To the north are the

---

2 From this place to the end of § 23, Alfred leaves Orosius, and gives the best information that he could collect. It is the king's own account of Europe in his time. It is not only interesting, as the composition of Alfred, but invaluable, as an historical document, being the only authentic record of the Germanic nations, written by a contemporary, so early as the ninth century.

3 The Cwen-sæ' of Alfred. The plain detail, which Ohthere gave to king Alfred, [§ 13] can scarcely be read by any unprejudiced person, without coming to the conclusion, that Ohthere sailed from Halgoland, on the coast of Norway, into the White Sea. See § 13, and note 39. The Germania of Alfred, therefore, extended from the Don on the east, to the Rhine and the German ocean on the west; and from the Danube on the south, to the White Sea on the north.

4 Alfred's Germania embraced nearly the whole of Europe north of the Rhine and the Danube. Its great extent will be seen by the countries mentioned, in the notes from 5 to 39, and in the text. See also the end of note 3, and CLUVERII Introductionis in universam Geographiam, Libri VI, Amstelædami 4to 1729. Lib. III, Cap. 1. DE VETERI GERMANIA, p. 183—186, and the map of Europe, p. 72.—Also the very learned work—Cluverii Germania antiqua. Lugd. Batavorum. Elzevir. Fol. 1616: Lib. I: cap. XI. DE MAGNITUDINE GERMANIÆ ANTIQUÆ, p. 94—98, and the map, p. 3.—Also CELLARII Geographia Antiqua. Cantab. 4to 1703. p. 309—313.—Warnefried's Hist. Longob. l. I: c. 1.

5 The locality of the East-Franks is not given with great precision: it probably varied at different periods. Alfred speaks here indefinitely of their dwelling east of the Rhine, and north the source of the Danube. They were called East-Franks to distinguish them from the Franks in the west, inhabiting Gaul.

6 A. S. Bægðware the Bavarians.

7 Regnesburh the district as well as the city of Ratisbon, on the Danube—Beme the Bohemians.

8 A. S. Eald-Seaxe, and Eald-Seaxan THE OLD SAXONS, inhabiting the country between the Eyder and the Weser, the parent stock of the Anglo or English-Saxons, and therefore of great importance in the mind of Alfred; for he speaks of other countries, as they are located in regard to the Old Saxons. They were a very warlike and powerful people, who once occupied the whole north-west corner of Germany.

9 Anglen, the country between Flensburg and the Schley, whence the Angles came to Britain. Thorpe's An.

10 In A. S. Sillende ZEALAND, or SEELAND, in Danish Sjalland, the largest island in the Danish monarchy, on the eastern shores of which Copenhagen is built.

Afdrede,¹¹ and north-east the Wylte,¹² who are called Hæfeldan. To the east of them is the country of the Wends ¹³, who are called Sysyle ; ¹⁴ and south-east, at some distance, the Moravians.¹⁵ These Moravians have, to the west of them, the Thuringians, and Bohemians, and part of the Bavarians. To the south of them, on the other side of the river Danube, is the country, Carinthia, ¹⁶ [lying] south to the mountains, called the Alps. To the same mountains extend the boundaries of the Bavarians, and of the Suabians ; and then, to the east of the country Carinthia, beyond the desert, is the country of the Bulgarians ; ¹⁷ and, to the east of them, the

11 The Laud MS. always has Afdrede [p. 12, l. 23 l : 13, 11e, 14g] Cotton has Afdrede in fol. 9a, l. 21g : Afdræde, fol. 9a, 25d ; and Apdrede, in fol. 8b. 24g. Alfred's Afdrede, were the Obotriti or Obotritæ, a Slavonic tribe, who, in the 9th century, dwelt north of the Old-Saxons, and occupied the western, and the greater part of what is now the Duchy of Mecklenburg. HAMPSON, NOTES AND QRS. No. 17, p. 257. Thorpe's An. Glos.

12 The Wylte, or Wilte, were a Slavonic race, that occupied the eastern part of Mecklenburg, and the Mark of Brandenburg. Eiginhard says, " They are Slavonians who, in our manner, are called Wilsi, but in their own language, Welatibi." [VIT. KAR. MAGN. and ANNAL. FRANCOR. ANN. 822.] The name, as Eiginhard has noticed, is Slavonic, and is an adoption of welot or weolot A GIANT, to denote the strength and fierceness which made them formidable neighbours. HAMPSON.—Why the Wilti were sometimes called Heveldi [Alfred's Hæfeldan, LAUD. p. 12, l. 24g : æ'feldan C. C. fol. 8b, 25c] will appear from their location, as pointed out by Ubbo Emmius : " WILSOS, Henetorum gentem, ad HAVELAM trans Albim sedes habentem." [RER. FRIS. HIST. l. IV, p. 67] Schaffarik remarks ; " Die Stoderaner und HAVOLANER waren ein und deselbe, nur durch zwei namen unterscheidener zweig des WELETEN stammes." Albinus says : " Es sein aber die richten WILZEN Wender sonderlich an der HAVEL wonhaft." They were frequently designated by the name of LUTICI, as appears from Adam of Bremen, Helmold, and others. The Slavonic word LIUTI signified WILD, FIERCE. ETC. Being a WILD and contentious people, they figure in some of the old Russian sagas, much as the Jutes do in those of Scandinavia. It is remarkable that the names of both should have signified giants or monsters. Notker, in his Teutonic paraphrase of Martianus Capella, speaking of other Anthropophagi, relates that the WILTI were not ashamed to say, that they had more right to eat their parents than the worms. S. W. SINGER. NOTES AND QRS. No 20, p. 313.

13 In. A. S. Wineda land, Weonod-land, Winod-land, c. Wineda lond, L. The country of the VENEDI or WENDS, which at one time comprehended the whole of the south coast of the Baltic, from the mouth of the Vistula to the Schley.—The Greeks called the Slavonians $\cdot Everoi$; the Romans, Venetæ, Veneti, Vineti, Venedi : and the Germans, Wenden, Winden. R. T. HAMPSON.

14 Sysyle, v. note 23.

15 A. S. Maroaro, the Slavi Maharenses or MORAVIANS, from the river Marus or Maharus, which runs through their country, and into the Danube a little below Vienna.

16 A. S. þæt land Carendre. The present Duchy of CARINTHIA, perhaps formerly inhabited by Slavi Carenthani, or Carentani. FORSTER.

17 In A. S. Pulgara land, the country of the Bulgarians, comprehended the present Moldavia, and Bulgaria, on both sides the Danube. Bulgaria was south of Dacia. Eiginhard says an embassy came in A. D. 824 to Charlemagne from the Abotritæ, " qui vulgo Prædenecenti vocantur, et contermini Bulgaris Daciam Danubio adjacentem incolunt. In Bk III, ch. 7, § 2, Alfred adds Iliricos, þe we Pulgare hatað, Illyrians whom we call Bulgarians.

country of the Greeks." To the east of the country Moravia, is the country of the" Wisle, and to the east of them are the Dacians, who were formerly Goths. To the north-east of the Moravians are the Dalamensan,²⁰ and to the east of the Dalamensan are the Horithi,²¹ and to the east of the Dalamensan are the Surpe,²² and to the west of them are the Sysele.²³ To the north of the Horiti is Mægtha-land,²⁴ and north of Mægtha-land are the Sermende²⁵ even to the Rhipæan mountains.—To²⁶ the west of the South-Danes

18 Creca land, the Byzantine empire and not ancient Greece, which is mentioned in a subsequent paragraph.
19 Wisle is the river Vistula. Wisleland is the country about the source of the Vistula, a part of Poland called Little Poland.
20 Dalamensan, Dalamensæ, a Slavonic race, who dwelt in Misnia, on both sides of the Elbe.
21 Horithi, Horiti, C.—Horigti, L. A Slavonic race, placed by Alfred to the east of the Slavi Dalamenti, who occupied the district north-east of Moravia with the Surpe, Serbi, or Servi, on their north, and the Sysele, Siculi, another Slavonic race, on the west. See note 23. R. T. Hampson, Notes and Qrs, No 17, p. 258.—S. W. Singer says,—The Horiti of Alfred are undoubtedly the Croati, or Crowati of Pomerania, who still pronounce their name Horuati, the h supplying the place of ch. Nor does it seem unreasonable to presume that the Harudes of Cæsar (De Bel. Gall. I, 31, 37, 51) were also Croats; for they must have been a numerous and widely spread race. They are also called Charudes, Ἀροῦδες. The following passage from the Annales Fuldenses, A. 852, will strengthen this supposition;—
"Inde transiens per Angros, Harudos, Suabos, et Hosingos . . . Thuringiam ingreditur." Notes and Qrs, No 20, p. 314.
22 Surpe, Surfe, Sorabi, or Soravi, Sorbi, or Servi, Serbi, or Servi, a Slavonic race inhabiting Lusatia, Misnia, part of Brandenburg, and Silesia. Forster.
23 Are the Sysele, Sysyle, the Szeklers, or Siculi? A part of the Hungarians is called Szekler, pronounced Sekler. In the work, known as that of the Notary of king Bela, we have :—"Siculi, qui primo erant populi Attilæ regis," Not. c. 50. Also—"Tria millia virorum, eadem de natione (Hunnorum) . . . metuentes ad Erdewelwe confinia videlicet Pannonicæ regionis se transtulere, et non Hunos sive Hungaros, sed ne illorum agnoscerentur esse residui, Siculos, ipsorum autem vocabulo Zekel, se denominasse perhibentur. Hi Siculi Hunorum prima fronte in Pannoniam intrantium. etiam hac nostra tempestate residui esse dubitantur per neminem, quum in ipsorum generatione, extraneo nondum permixta sanguine et in moribus severiores et in divisione agri cæteris Hungaris multum differre videantur." Thwrocz, ap. Schwandtn. p. 78. Dr Latham's Germ. of Tacitus, Epileg. ciii.—Porthan says, the Sysyle dwelt in the South-eastern part of Newmark. See Porthan's Swedish Trans. and notes. Also, Rask's Danish Trans. p. 344, note a.
24 Mægtha-land is north of the Horithi, and perhaps a part of Great Poland, and East Prussia, or the Polish province of Mazovia. An.
25 Sermende a people to the north of Mægtha-land, and to the east of the Burgundians, inhabiting the modern Livonia, Esthonia and part of Lithuania.
26 Alfred, having described the continent north of the Danube, goes to the islands and countries of the East-Sea or Baltic, including the Cattegat, first coming to Denmark. Porthan remarks, that the king seems to turn the north a little to the east, and to speak of North and South Denmark, as separated by the East-Sea or Baltic, for Alfred expressly says, the North-Danes are "on the continent and on the islands," that is in the province of Halland, and of Skaney or Schonen, on the continent, the present South west of Sweden, and on the islands Zealand, Moen, Falster, and Laland. To the South-Danes he assigns

is the arm of the ocean, which lies around the country of Britain; and to the north of them is the arm of the sea called the Baltic[27]; and to the east and to the north of them are the North-Danes,[26] both on the continent and on the islands: to the east of them are the Afdrede[28]; and to the south of them is the mouth of the river Elbe, with some part of the Old Saxons.[29] The North-Danes have to the north of them the same arm of the sea called the Baltic[27]: to the east of them are the Esthonian population; and the Afdræde to the south. The Esthonians[30] have, to the north of them, the same arm of the sea, and also the Wends[31] and Burgundians[32]; and to the south are the Hæfeldan.[33] The Burgundians have the same arm of the sea to the west of them, and the Swedes[34] to the north : to the east of them are the Sermende,[14] and to the south the Surfe.[35] The Swedes have, to the south of them, the Esthonian arm of the sea; and to the east of them the Sermende[25] : to the north, over the wastes, is Cwén-land,[36] and to

the islands Langland, Funen, Arroe, Alsen, as well as the provinces of Jutland, Schleswig and part of Holstein. Rask, p. 348, note c.—Mr Thorpe thinks that the South-Danes inhabited the south of Jutland; and the North-Danes, North-Jutland, the Danish islands and probably Scania.

27 In A. S. Ost-sæ´ or East-Sea, included the Cattegat as well as the Baltic. It was called Ost-sæ´ in opposition to the sea, on the west of Denmark and Norway.

28 v. note 11.   29 A. S. Eald-Seaxan, v. note 8.

30 Esthonians, Æstii, Osti, Esti, a Finnish race—the Estas of Wulfstan [note 72] and Osterlings of the present day. They dwelt on the shores of the Baltic, to the east of the Vistula. An.—See also Dr Latham's Germ. of Tacitus, p. 166—171, and Prol. p. liii.

31 Note 13.

32 Burgendas, Burgendan, Burgundiones, the Burgundians, who occupied the north part of Germany, east of the Upper Vistula, or the district between the Vistula and the river Bug.—Pliny [H. N. IV, 14] writes, " Germanorum genera quinque: Vindili, quorum pars Burgundiones, etc." Dr Latham's Germ. of Tacitus, Epileg. p. lvi.

33. Hæfeldan, Æ´feldan, v. note 12.

34. Sweon, Sweoan, Suiones, Sueones, the Swedes.

35. Surfe, Surpe, &c. v. note 22.

36. Cwén-land. The country east and west of the Gulf of Bothnia, from Norway to the Cwén or White Sea, including Finmark on the north. Malte-Brun says that the inhabitants of Cwén-land were a Fiunish race. They were called Quaines, and by Latin writers Cayani. Gerchau maintains, in his history of Finland, 1810, that the Laplanders only were called Finns, and that they were driven from the country by the Quaines. " They settled in Lapland, and on the shores of the White Sea, which derived from them the name of Quen Sea or Quen-vik." . . . Adamus Bremensis happened to be present at a conversation, in which king Sweon spoke of Quen-land or Quena-land, the country of the Quaines, but as the stranger's knowledge of Danish was very imperfect, he supposed the king had said Quinna-land, the country of women or Amazons; hence the absurd origin of his Terra Feminarum, mistaking the name of the country, for quinna a woman. Malte-Brun's Universal Geog. Edin. 1827, vol. VI, p. 495.—Dr Latham's Germania of Tacitus, 174, 179.

the north-west are the Scride-Finns,"⁷ and to the west the Northmen."¹

13. Ohthere³⁹ told his lord, king Alfred, that he dwelt northmost

37 The Scride-Finnas of Alfred,—Crefennæ of Jornandes, for Screde-Fennæ,—Scritifinni of Procopius, seem to have inhabited the present Russian Lapland, and the country around; and to have extended into the modern Swedish Finland. In short, they appear to have occupied the country to the north and west of the White Sea. They were called Scríde, Skríðe Finnas, Striding Finns, from their swiftness in passing over frozen snow, on their skates.—Skríða kann eg á skíðum, I can stride on skates. Dahlmann's Forschungen auf dem Gebiete der Geschichte, Erster Band, p. 452. Altona, 12mo. 1822. Rask, note i, p. 352.—The Scride-Finns were a branch of the Ugrians or Finns, who were a distinct race occupying Lapland, Finland, Esthonia, and Hungary. In Hungary, the Finn population is of recent introduction, the present Ugrian indigenæ being the Lapps, Finlanders and Esthonians. Dr Latham's Germ. of Tacitus, Proleg. XXXVII, and 178, 179.

38 These Northmen were Norwegians. The Northmanna land generally comprehended the present Norway, the chief locality of Northmen. But by Northmen, as the name implies, may be understood, men that dwelt in the north. [See more in Note 40.] They spoke the Old Norse language [norræna] which was common to Denmark, Norway and Sweden. In A.D. 874 it was conveyed to Iceland by Ingolf, and his followers, the first Norwegian settlers in Iceland. Norse was also the language of the Faroe Isles, Greenland, &c. The nearest representative of this old Scandinavian or Norse language, once pervading the north-west of Europe, is the present Icelandic, which, from its northern locality, has undergone so little change, that the oldest documents are easily read by the present Icelanders. See Origin of the English, Germanic, and Scandinavian languages, p. 145.

39 This name has been written Octher, Othere, Ottar, and Ohthere. The last is the only correct mode of writing it; for the Laud. MS. has Ohthere, and the Cotton MS. has the same orthography, but the word is divided into Oht here, indicating its derivation from OHT fear, dread, and HERE an army. Rask observes, that the A. S. ht answers to the Icl. tt, and ere to the Icl. ari and ar, and thus is formed the well known old Norse name, O'ttar the dreadful, timendus, metuendus, from Icl. ótti timor, metus.—Ohthere was a Norwegian nobleman of great wealth and influence, anxious to state nothing, but that to which he could bear personal testimony. It appears impossible for any one to read this simple narrative, without being convinced, that this daring Northman is giving a detail of his voyage, on the west and on the north coast of Norway into the White sea. Iceland had already been discovered by Gardar, the Dane, in A.D. 860, and it was colonized by Ingolf, a Norwegian, in 874. Greenland was discovered in 877 and inhabited by Northmen soon after. Accustomed as these Northmen were, to the most daring enterprises, it was not likely that Ohthere one of the most powerful, adventurous, bold and inquiring of them, should come to the renowned king of England, to relate the events of a common voyage. Ohthere had made discoveries, which he communicated to the king, and Alfred thought them of such importance, that he wrote and inserted this detail of them in his Geographical and Historical view of Europe. It has always been considered an extraordinary voyage. On its first publication by Hakluyt, in 1598, it was acknowledged, as every unprejudiced reader must now allow, that Ohthere doubled the north cape, and entered the White Sea. "The voiage of Octher made to the north-east parts beyond Norway, reported by himselfe vnto Alfred, the famous king of England, about the yere 890." Hakluyt's Principal Navigations, Voiages, Traffiques, and Discoueries of the English Nation, &c. page 5, Fol. 2nd Edn. London, 1598. Again, a little below, Hakluyt says:—" Wil it not, in all posteritie, be as great renowne vnto our English Nation to haue bene the first discoverers of a sea beyond the North cape [neuer certainly knowen before] and of a conuenient passage into

of all Northmen."⁰ He said that he dwelt northward, on the land by the west sea."¹ He said, however, that the land is very long thence to the north; but it is all waste [desert], save that in a few places, here and there, Finns reside,—for hunting in winter, and in summer for fishing in the sea. He said, that, at a certain time, he wished to find out how far the land lay right north; or whether any man dwelt to the north of the waste. Then he went right north near the land: he left, all the way, the waste land on the right,"¹ and the wide sea on the left, for three days. Then was he as far north as Whale-hunters ever go. He then went yet right north, as far as he could sail in the next three days. Then the land bent there right east, or the sea in on the land, he knew not whether; but he knew that he there waited for a western wind, or a little to the north, and sailed thence east near the land, as far as he could sail in four days. Then he must wait there for

the huge Empire of Russia by the bay S. Nicolas and the riuer of Duina? &c." Id. p. 5.— The subsequent editors and translators of Ohthere's voyage are of the same opinion as Hakluyt.—Sir John Spelman and Oxonienses Alumni, in 1678:—Bussæus, in 1733:— Langebek in 1773:—Daines Barrington, and J. R. Forster, in 1773: Forster again in 1786 in his Hist. of voyages and discoveries in the north.—Ingram, in 1807.—Rask, in his notes to his Danish translation, published in 1815, expressly says—" Ohthere was the first who undertook a voyage to Beormia [Permia] or sailed round the North-cape, and all Lapland," &c. note k. p. 352—355.—Dahlmann, in 1822, states that Ohthere sailed into the White Sea.—Mr Thorpe comes to the same conclusion, in 1846.—Malte-Brun, before Rask, Dahlmann, and Thorpe, speaks, in 1812, of Ohthere's northern voyage from Halgoland in Norway [see note 52 and text] to the White Sea; and south to Schleswig; and also of Wulfstan's voyage from Schleswig to Truso in Prussia. [Note 63.] Through the liberality and kindness of S. W. Singer Esq. the reader is presented with an extract from Précis de la Géographie Universelle, of the celebrated Malte-Brun:—" Othere retraçait ses voyages depuis le Halogaland en Norwége, jusqu' à la Biarmie à l'est de la mer Blanche; et, d'un autre côté, le long des côtes Norwégiennes et Danoises par le sund, jusqu' à la ville de Hæthum ou Schleswig. L'autre relation était celle d'un voyage du Danois Wulfstan, depuis Schleswig jusqu'à Truso, ville de commerce dans le pays d' Estum ou la Prusse. Tom. I, Liv. XVII, p. 382. Paris, 8vo, 1812.

40 Norðmen dwelt on Norðmanna land which extended, on the west coast of Norway, from the district [scír,] of Halgoland [Note 52] to the south of Sciringes heal, [Note 53] probably as far south as the river Gotha-Elf, both the branches of which enter the Cattegat not far from Gottenburg. The Norðmanna land is also called by Ohthere [Norðwege] Norway, which was on his left when sailing from Halgoland to Sciringes heal. These particulars are all drawn from Ohthere's simple narrative. Malte-Brun, in his Précis de la Géog. Univers., speaking of the country of Northmen, says, in p. 383, " La Norwége ou Northmannaland consistait dans la côte occidentale de la Scandinavie depuis la rivière Gotha jusqu'à Halogaland. Les côtes méridionales se nommaient Viken, c'est à dire le golfe; c'est là qu'il faut chercher la ville de Kiningsheal, le Koughille moderne, nommé Scyringes-heal par une faute de copiste." S. W. Singer.

41 A. S. West-sæ´, the sea to the West of Norway, in opposition to the Ost-sæ´, or the Baltic. See Note 27.—A. S. Steor-bord, star-board, the right hand. Bæc-bord, the left hand.

a right north wind, because the land bent there right south, or the sea in on the land, he knew not whether. Then sailed he thence right south, near the land, as far as he could sail in five days. There lay then a great river up into the land : they turned up into the river, because they durst not sail beyond it, on account of hostility, for the land was all inhabited, on the other side of the river. He had not before met with any inhabited land, since he came from his own home, but the land was uninhabited all the way on his right, save by fishermen, fowlers and hunters, and they were all Finns; and there was always a wide sea on his left. The Biarmians[42] had very well peopled their land, but they durst not come upon it : the land of the Terfinns[43] was all waste, save where hunters, fishers or fowlers encamped.

14. The Biarmians told him many stories both about their own country and about the countries which were around them; but, he knew not what was true, because he did not see it himself. The Finns and the Biarmians, as it seemed to him, spoke nearly the same language. He chiefly went thither, in addition to the seeing of the country, on account of the horse-whales, [walruses],[44]

---

[42] The Biarmians inhabited the country on the shores of the White Sea, east of the river Dwina. Alfred calls them Beormas. They were called Biarmians by Icelandic Historians, and Permiaki by the Russians, and now Permians. In the middle ages, the Scandinavian pirates gave the name of Permia to the whole country between the White Sea, and the Ural. Malte-Brun's Univer. Geog. Vol. VI, p. 419. In an Icelandic MS. on Geography, written in the 14th century, Beormia and two Cwenlands are located together. Kvenlönd II, ok ero þau norðr frá Bjarmalandi. Duæ Quenlandiæ, quæ ulterius quam Bjarmia boream versus extenduntur. Antiquitates Americanæ, p. 290.—Haldorsen's Lexicon Islandico-Latino-Danicum, edited by Rask, has—" Biarmaland, Biarmia, quæ ob perpetuas nives albicatur, Bjarmeland, Permien. Biarmia ortum versus ad mare album vel gandvikam sita est."

[43] Terfinna land, the country between the northern point of the Bothnian Gulf and the North Cape. An.

[44] One particular reason for Ohthere's sailing northward was to capture the Walrus, which was, and still is to be found in abundance in the White Sea about Archangel, and the coast of the country of the Biarmians. This is additional evidence to what was advanced in Note 39, to prove that Ohthere doubled the north cape and entered the White Sea,—that his first voyage was not into the Baltic, where the Walrus is scarcely ever found, but into the White Sea. [Forster's notes in Barrington's Orosius, p. 243.] We have Forster's opinion confirmed by the best Zoologists of the present day. Mr Broderip assures me in a letter, " I do not think it likely that Ohthere, a Norwegian, would go into the Baltic to take the Walrus.—I do not believe that Walruses or Whales were ever so numerous in that sea, within the time of authentic history, as to attract the attention of fishers."

Ohthere seems to have been a plain practical man, and to have described every thing just as he saw it. Alfred exercised his usual talent and judgment, in implicitly following the simple detail of the narrator; for, he was as fully aware as the most scientific of the present day, that he who most closely observes and describes nature, cannot wander far

because they have very good bone in their teeth : of these teeth they brought some to the king ; and their hides are very good for ship-ropes.   This whale is much less than other whales : it is not

from scientific truth. They were, therefore, upon the whole, correct in associating the monstrous Whale, and the smaller Horse-Whale, Sea-horse or Walrus, in the same class of animals; for both the Whale and the Walrus suckle their young, have warm blood, and are viviparous, and aquatic. The great Linnæus was the first to place the Whale in the class of Mammalia, in allusion to which a gentleman, who has written much and well on Zoology, Mr Broderip, has properly remarked—" Here then we find the decisive step taken, with the unflinching firmness of a master mind, relying upon the philosophical principles that demanded the separation, and no longer yielding to popular prejudice by calling that a fish, which Linnæus knew to be a mammiferous animal." May not this remark be applied to our glorious Alfred, and to this intrepid and close observing Northman, Ohthere, who first placed the Whale and Walrus in the same class of animals? I have the authority of Linnæus, as well as of Mr Bell, one of the Secretaries of the Royal Society, whose zoological works are known over the whole of Europe, for saying, that the Walrus belongs to the same class as the Whale, that is to the Mammalia, but to a very different order. The Horse-whale or Walrus belongs to the Carnivora, and to the family Phocadæ or Seals, although the structure and arrangement of the teeth remove it far from the more typical forms of this order. The bulky proportions of the body, the aquatic habits, and the modification of the limbs into paddles give a general resemblance to the cetacea, which might well lead observers, unacquainted with the details of their structure, to consider them as more nearly allied than they really are.

Mr Broderip, in writing to me, says :—You are, in my opinion, right in giving Ohthere's "hors-hwæl" as the Walrus, Morse, or Sea-horse.—Bell (British Quadrupeds p. 288) writes—"The knowledge of this chase," (that of the Walrus) " says Pennant, is of great antiquity : Octher the Norwegian, about the year 890, made a report to King Alfred, having, as he says, made the voyage beyond Norway for the more commoditie of fishing of Horse Whales; which have in their teeth bones of great price and excellence, whereof he brought some on his return to the king." Hakluyt's Coll. Voy. I, 5.—Bell, then, thus continues.—" The above quotation leads to some observations upon the Etymology of the different names which have been given to this animal.—Horse-Whale is a literal translation of Whal-ros, in Norwegian Hwal-ros. Rosmar, another Norwegian name, appears to be a compound of the Teutonic Ros horse, and the Latin mare, the sea. Morse is from the Russian Morss ; the Lapponic name being Morsk."—Charleton, physician to Charles 2nd, in his Onomasticon Zoicon, small 4to London, 1668, thus writes of the Walrus.—VII. Walrus, aliis Mors, Danis et Islandis Rosmarus (quod in Septentrionali oceano saltem reperiatur, ut credit Ol. Wormius, in Musæo) non nullis Vacca marina, nobis the Mors or Sea-cow, (quia monstrosum animal est et amphibium, bobus nostratibus, ubi adolevit, interdum majus.) Cute tegitur pilosa, nec a vitulo marino multum abhorrente. Dentes duos habet, e superiori maxilla propendentes, et ante recurvos ; cubiti nonnunquam longitudine, quorum usus ac pretium ebori comparatur. Ex iis enim varia conficiunt, annulos contra Spasmum [Cramp-Rings], manubria gladiorum, framearum et cultorum ; &c.

Mr Broderip has given the following precise information. The length of the Walrus is from 10 to 15 feet, girth 8 or 10 feet, and upwards. Length of the tusks, when cut out of the skull, generally from 15 to 20 inches, sometimes 30, and their weight from 5 to 10 lbs. Other facts have been communicated by the Rev. W. Scoresby D. D. The tusks of the Walrus, which are hard, white and compact ivory, are employed by dentists in the fabrication of teeth. The skin is used for defending the yards and rigging of ships from being chafed by friction against each other. When cut into shreds and plaited into cordage, it answers admirably for wheel ropes, being stronger and wearing much longer than hemp. In ancient times, most of the ropes of ships, in northern countries, appear to have been made

longer than seven ells;" but, in his own country, is the best whale-hunting : they are eight and forty ells long, and the largest fifty ells long; of these, he said, that he [was] one of six, [who] killed sixty in two days."

of this substance. Arctic Regions and Whale Fishery, 2 vols 8vo : and a neat little vol. with the same title, published by the Tract Society at the moderate price of 10 pence, p. 164.

Dr Scoresby speaking of the common Greenland Whale, Mysticetus, observes that the size has been much overrated. Authors of the first respectability give a length of 80 to 100 feet to the Mysticetus, and that some specimens were found of 150 to 200 feet in length, or still longer. Even Linnæus has given 100 feet. Some ancient naturalists have gone so far, as to assert, that whales have been seen of above 900 feet in length. Dr Scoresby, like Ohthere, speaking from what he had known and seen, makes this statement—" Of three hundred and twenty two individuals, in the capture of which I have been personally concerned, no one, I believe, exceeded 60 feet in length, and the largest I ever measured was 58 feet, from one extremity to the other, being one of the largest in appearance, that I ever saw.—The greatest circumference of these Whales is from 30 to 40 feet." Id. p. 140, 141.

" The largest sort of Whale is, however, not the Mysticetus, but the Physalus. This is probably the most powerful and bulky of created beings. In comparison with the Mysticetus, the Physalus has a form less cylindrical, a body longer and more slender. . . . . Its length is about 100 feet, and its greatest circumference 30 or 35 feet. . . . A whale, probably of this kind, 101 feet in length, was stranded on the banks of the Humber about the middle of September 1750." Id. p. 152—154.

45 In giving the size of the Horse-whale, or Walrus, and of the Whale, Ohthere would most probably calculate by the measure of Scandinavia, the Ell of Norway, Sweden and Denmark. Molbeck, in his Dansk Ordbog, thus defines it : — " Alen, et vist længdemaal, som deles i 24 tommer . . . Tomme een 12te fod, og een 24de alen," . . That is, Ell, a certain measure of length, which is divided into 24 inches . . . An inch one 12th of a foot, and one 24th of an ell. Alfred followed the calculation of Ohthere, who says that the Horse-whale or Walrus is 7 ells long, that is 14 feet, and the Whales 48 ells, and the largest 50, that is, 96 feet, and the largest 100 feet long. These calculations approach very nearly to those given by Mr Broderip and Dr Scoresby, in Note 44.

46 Every translator has found a difficulty in this passage, as it appeared impossible for 6 men to kill 60 whales in two days. The earliest translators understood it in its plain and obvious meaning. —" Hakluyt gave it in 1598. He affirmed that he himself was one of the six, which, in the space of three days, killed threescore." The Oxford Alumni in 1678—" Dixit se sextum fuisse, qui sexaginta bidui spatio interfecerit."—Porthan adhered to the literal sense, in his Swedish translation, in 1800. Af dessa sade han, at han sjelf sjette dödat sextio paa tvaa dagar.—For six men to kill 60 whales, of the larger sort, in two days, appears most extraordinary, though in the time of Alfred, whales seem to have been more plentiful in the northern than they now are in the southern ocean; yet, in the latter, eleven have been killed one morning, as will appear by the following extract from " The Log-book containing the proceedings on board the Barque Gipsy, commanded by John Gibson, owners Almon and James Hill, Esqrs, 13 Austin Friars, London. " Cruising from Sooloo Archipelago towards Japan—Tuesday May 31st, 1836. All these 24 hours moderate breezes and fine weather. Ship's head N. E. at 6 a. m. saw whales at 7 a. m. Lowered the boats at 9 a. m; struck and killed ELEVEN. At noon the boats employed collecting the whales to the ship."

I have so great an objection to conjectural criticism, that I have retained the text of the Cotton MS. though it is the only MS. known to exist, that contains this clause. At the same time I ought not to omit the emendation of the A. S. text suggested by my friend, the

15. He [Ohthere] was a very wealthy man in those possessions in which their wealth consists, that is in the wilder [animals]. He had, moreover, when he came to the king, six hundred tame deer of his own breeding."⁴⁷ They call these rein-deer: of these, six were decoy-deer, which are very valuable among Finns, because with them they take the wild-deer. He was amongst the first men in the land, though he had not more than twenty horned cattle, twenty sheep and twenty swine; and the little that he ploughed, he ploughed with horses. But their revenue is chiefly in the tribute, that the Finns pay them, which tribute is in skins of animals, feathers of birds, in whale-bone, and ship-ropes, which are made from the whale's hide, and from the

late Professor Rask—Instead of the Cotton reading syxa sum, he proposes syx asum, or ascum; and translates it in Danish, 1815,—" At han med 6 harpuner (eller 6 skibe) dræbte 60 paa 2 dage," i. e. that he with 6 harpoons (or 6 ships) killed 60 in two days.—Asum d. pl. of æs, or as, Lat. æs; and ascum of æsc a ship.—Dahlmann, in 1822, supposes Ohthere to mean 6 large ships; and, therefore, gives it in his German translation, " Dass er mit sechs grossen schiffen ihrer sechzig in zwei tagen tödtete."

Feeling it difficult to come to a satisfactory conclusion; and being anxious to obtain the best information on the subject, I wrote to the Rev. W. Scoresby, D.D. F.R.S. &c. an old college friend,—a man of great scientific acquirements, who published a most interesting work, on the Arctic Regions, and the Whale-fishery in 1820, and in early life had been engaged in capturing no less than 322 whales. See note 44.—To the following queries; 1st, Is it possible that 6 men could kill 60 whales in 2 days? 2dly, Could 60 be killed in 2 days with 6 harpoons, as Rask suggests? 3dly, Could 6 ships be so employed, as to kill 60 in 2 days? He replied—1. I do not conceive it at all possible, that 6 men could kill 60 Whales of the large size [Balæna Mysticetus] in two days. I know of no instance of even one whale having ever been killed, of the largest size, by a single boat's crew of 6 or 7 men. Ordinarily 3 or 4 boats, with 18 to 25 men, are deemed necessary for the capture of a single whale—2. It might be possible, if the whales were sunning in vast numbers, in any of the bays of the Arctic regions, that 60 might be killed by 6 harpoons, and men in proportion, say 36 to 40 men. But, I may add, though whales have been met with occasionally, in great numbers together, no such feat as this, I am persuaded, had ever been performed by the crew of one ship containing 6 or 7 boats and 50 men. A single whale may, on an average, cost about 3 hours for its capture, with 4 to 6 boats. If two, therefore, or three, were constantly under attack, at the same time, and neither accident nor failure happening, it would be a wonderful feat for 50 men with half a dozen or eight harpoons, to capture half the number specified!—3. Six ships, with their ordinary complement of men and boats, might, no doubt, be so employed, if the Whales were very numerous and the circumstances, as to ice or position, favourable, as to kill 10 large Whales a piece in two days. In Whales of a small size, this proportion has often been reached; but never, that I am aware of, where the kind was of the largest. The pleasing process, indeed, so interferes with the enterprize of slaughter, that more than half a dozen, of any size, is seldom killed at once. I have known 10 or 12 within one period of unceasing exertion." Upon the whole, then, it appears that the proposed emendation of the text does not remove the difficulty, and it is, therefore, best to retain the Cotton reading, as represented in the present translation.

47 Tamra deora, unbebuhtra, syx hund.—Literally, Of tame deer, unbought [non emptus, Ettmüller] untrafficked or traded in, six hundred.

seal's. Every one pays according to his means: the richest must pay fifteen skins of the marten, and five of the rein-deer, and one bear's skin, aud forty bushels of feathers, and a bear or otter-skin kirtle, and two ship-ropes, each sixty ells long, one made from the whale's hide, and the other from the seal's.

16. He said that the country of Northmen was very long and very narrow. All that can be either pastured or ploughed lies by the sea, and that, however, is in some places, very rocky; and, on the east, lie wild mountains[48] along the inhabited land. In these mountains [wastes] Finns dwell; and the inhabited land is broadest eastward, and always narrower more northerly. Eastward it may be sixty miles[49] broad, or a little broader, and midway thirty or broader; and northward, he said, where it was narrowest, that it might be three miles broad to the waste, and moreover, the waste, in some places, [is] so broad that a man may travel over it, in two weeks; and in other places, so broad that a man may travel over [it,] in six days.

17. Then, over against this land southward, on the other side of the waste, is Sweden,[50] extending to the north; and over against the land northward, is Cwena land.[51] The Cwenas sometimes make war on the Northmen over the waste; sometimes the Northmen on them. There are very large fresh water meers beyond the wastes; and the Cwenas carry their boats over land into the meers, and thence make war on the Northmen. They have very little boats, and very light.

18. Ohthere said that the district in which he dwelt was called

---

48 Rask translates it:—Der ligger vilde Fjælde östen for og oven for langs med det beboede Land. Afhandlinger, p. 313, 315.—Dahlmann:—Im Osten liegen wilde Gebirge, hoch über und längs dem angebauten Lande; p. 425.—Môr denotes waste land generally, a moor, heath: waste land from rocks, hence a hill, mountain: &c.

49 Rask observes, when Norway is reckoned 60 miles wide, in the broadest part and 3 miles in the narrowest, it is evident that the king used the exact phrase of Ohthere, and did not alter it, as on another occasion, to agree with the Anglo-Saxon measure. See note 74. One mile of the Northman, Ohthere, contained about 5 Anglo-Saxon miles,—hence the broadest part would be about 300 miles and the narrowest 15. Rask's Afhandlinger, 8vo, Köbenhavn, 1834: vol. I, p. 379, note r.—A Danish mile is 4.68 English, and a Swedish mile is 6.64 English miles.

50 A. S. Sweoland. The country of the Sweons, the Suiones of Tacitus. The names Suedia or Suecia, and Svidiodar, or Svithiodar, as applied to the Swedes, occur in their earliest annals. Wheaten, and Crichton's Scandinavia, vol. I, p. 24.

51 See note 26.

Halgoland." He said that no man abode north of him. Then there is a port, on the south of the land [Norway], which is called Sciringesheal." Thither he said, that a man could not sail in a month, if he anchored at night, and every day had a fair wind. All the while he must sail near the land.—On his right hand, is first" Iceland, and then the islands which are between

52 Halgoland, a division [scír] of the northern part of ancient Norway. Ohthere dwelt in the most northerly part of it : to the north of his residence, the country was uninhabited. Even at the present day, this district is called Helgeland. It is in Nordland, or Northland, in the province of Trondhiem, or Drontheim, pronounced Tronyem. Drontheim is now the most northerly province of Norway, extending from 62 deg. to 71 deg. 10 min. N. Lat. It is divided into Trondhiem Proper, Nordland, and Finmark. Nord or Northland was the most northerly part inhabited in Ohthere's days. Helgeland is now the southern district of Nordland, and lies on the coast between the island Leköe, N. Lat. 65 deg. 10 min., and Cape Kunnen near the arctic circle. The Kiölen range of mountains, separating Helgeland from Sweden, is about 60 miles from the sea; and, in some places, not so far. Helgeland has a rocky coast of considerable elevation. The interior is filled by mountains rising from 1000, to 1500 feet. A considerable portion of the land might be cultivated, but agriculture is often neglected, because fishing offers greater advantages. This is more particularly the case in the islands, on the coast of Helgeland, which rise to an elevation of 2000 and to 4260 feet. Such is Helgeland in the present day.—In this wild district, Ohthere first saw the light. He was brought up amid stupendous mountains, and exposed to the severity of the climate in the care of herds of deer, and in superintending the rude culture of the land. From a child he was not only accustomed to the exertions and perils of the chase in the Norwegian Alps, but to brave the dangers of the vast waves of the Northern Ocean, raging amongst the exposed and elevated islands, and the high, rocky shore of Norway. Thus educated amid the magnificent scenery of Halgoland, and inured to danger, Ohthere was well prepared for a daring enterprise, such as his exploring voyage to the most northerly regions. It was a voyage worthy of Ohthere, and deserving the permanent record which Alfred—the first man of that age—has here given of it.

53 This is a minute description of Ohthere's second voyage. His first was to the remote north: this voyage is to the south. The first place he mentions is a port " on the south of this land [Norway], called Sciringesheal." Judging from Ohthere's narrative, Sciringesheal seems to be in the Skager Rack, near the Fiord or Bay of Christiana. Snorre Sturleson, an Icelander, born in 1178, in his Ynglinga Saga, ch. 49, places Sciringesheal in Westfold, on the west side of the bay of Christiana. The note, appended to Professor Rask's Afhandlinger, published by his son, in 1834, concludes,—" Thus, it cannot be doubted, that Skiringssal really existed at that time, [the age of Snorre,] and that it is the same that Ohthere and king Alfred call Sciringesheal." vol. I, p. 384.—Ohthere says to the south of Sciringesheal is a very great sea, apparently the Cattegat, opposite to which was Jutland, and then Zealand. Sailing from Sciringesheal to Haddeby near Schleswig, Ohthere said he had Denmark on his left, that is Halland and Skaane [Scania], the early seat of the Danes. Then, two days before his arrival at Schleswig, taking a westerly course, he had Jutland on his right. As he mentions islands on his left, it appears that he sailed between Moen and Zealand. An.

54 The Cotton MS., the only one that contains this part of Ohthere's voyage, has Iralnnd. Though I have the greatest objection to conjecturale mendatious of a text, in this case, after reading the context, and all that commentators have written upon it, I prefer substituting Isaland for Iraland. To what Dr Ingram and Rask have advanced to justify the insertion of Isaland in the text, it may be added that Ireland was generally called Scotland from the fifth to the eleventh century [v. note 89]. If any other name was used, it was

Iceland and this land [Britain]. Then this land continues till he comes to Sciringesheal; and all the way, on the left, [is] Norway." To the south of Sciringesheal, a very great sea runs up into the land: it is broader than any man can see over; and Jutland" is opposite, on the other side, and then Zealand. This sea lies many hundred miles up into the land.

19. He said that he sailed in five days, from Sciringesheal to the port which they call" Haddeby [near Schleswig], which stands

Ibernia or Igbernia; thus, when Alfred is speaking of Britain, he adds, " Ibernia þæt igland,"—and, " Igbernia, þæt we Scotland hatað." In Alfred's translation of Bede, Hibernia is used, as Ybernia is, in the earliest part of the Saxon Chronicle. In the year 891, Dr Ingram inserts Hibernia in the text, and gives Yrlande in the notes, as the reading of the Cot. MS. But this is taken from a collation by Junius of one of the latest MSS. and which Dr Ingram says is of the least authority, because the writer has taken great liberties in using "his own Normanized dialect." Yrlande occurs again in the year 918, and in 1051, and 2, but these two instances do not invalidate the assertion of Alfred, just cited, that in his days Igbernia was called Scotland. Alfred confirms this, by adding to his translation of Orosius in § 3—" On the west end of the Mediterranean Sea is Scotland." Though wrong, as to geographical position, this is an additional proof that our Ireland was called Scotland in the time of Alfred.—Upon the whole then, I prefer inserting Isaland in the text.

Langebek and Porthan retained Iraland in the text and Forster sanctioned this reading, but they all thought erroneously, that Scotland was intended. Dr Ingram, in his Inaugural Lecture, published in 1807, preferred reading Isaland, and gives his reasons thus; " I suspect that the true reading in the original, instead of Ira-land, [i. e. Scotland] should be Isaland, Iseland, (or, as it is sometimes improperly written, Iceland.) How frequently the Saxon letters ʀ and r have been confounded and interchanged, is well known to every person conversant in the language. As Ohthere sailed from Halgoland, Iseland was the first land to his right, and then the islands of Faroe, Shetland, and Orkney, between Iseland and this land [i. e. England]; then this land continued on his right hand, till he entered the Baltic, which he soon afterwards describes very accurately, as running up many hundred miles into the land, and so wide that no man could see over it." p. 79, note q.—Rask in 1815, reprinted in 1834, gives Isaland in his A. S. text, and a long note to the same effect, in p. 319, note 2, of his Afhandlinger.

Professor Dahlmann in his Forschungen 1822, thinks that Ireland was intended, and that Ohthere spoke of Ireland indefinitely, placing it more to the north, and on his right hand. He has a long and interesting article in No 4 of his Erläuterungen, " Iraland, oder Isaland?" He gives a very fair statement of the opinions of Langebek, Porthan, and Rask, p. 443—449.—After all, I prefer Isaland, notwithstanding what Dahlmann and others have written.

55. A. S. Norðweg, in Saxon Chronicle 1028, Norðweg and Norweg; in 1045 and 7 Norweg, so in 1058, &c. In 1066 Norweg and Norwéi; and in 1070 Norwæg. Literally, the north way or way to the north. Pliny, l. IV, c. 16, calls it, Nerigon, and Malte-Brun suggests Nor-Rige, kingdom of the north, or rather, assuming Nor to be a gulf, kingdom of gulfs. Geog. vol. VIII, 517.

56. A. S. Gótland, the country of the Hreth Goths: Jótland, Jutland. An.—Zealand, A. S. Sillende—v. note 10. The old name of Zealand was in Danish Sia-Lund, a forest near the water, from sia sea, and lund a forest. Now sia, sea, or Zea-land, Sea land, land surrounded by the sea: like the Dutch Zee-land, Sea-land, from zee the sea.

57. A. S. þe mon hæt æt Hæðum, which Porthan translates, som kallas Hæthum, which

in the midst of the Winedi," Saxons, and Angles, and belongs to the Danes. When he sailed thitherward from Sciringesheal, then Denmark " was on his left; and, on his right, a wide sea for three

is called Hæthum. Rask more properly translates it—" som man kalder Hedeby," p. 321 and 323, and Dahlmann,—" den man zu Hädum [at Hædum, Hedaby] nennt." p. 427. Rask observes, that it is customary, especially in Icelandic, to put a preposition before the name of a place, which is then to be in the dative case; as in Icl. í Rípum, and occasionally in A. S. as, æt Hæ'ðum. These dat. sret. plur. may be read, as in the singular. The sing. Hæ'ð, is the Icl. heiðr, now heiði a heath; hence its Icl. and old Danish name Heiðuby'r, or Heiðabær, present Hedeby, from modern Danish, hede a heath, and by a town. Langebek has rightly explained, þe mon hæt æt Hæ'ðum, quem vocant Hæthe. Rask, p. 374, note n.

Hæ'ðe is mentioned, in connection with Schleswig, by Ethelweard about two centuries after Alfred; and, in the subsequent half century by William of Malmsbury as in the following extracts.—Ethelweard or Elward, is known only by his Chronicle or History of the Anglo-Saxons. He says he was descended from Ethelred, the brother of king Alfred. We are not informed when his book was compiled, but he was still alive in 1090 [Wright's Biographia Britannica Literaria, Vol. 1, p. 522]. This Ethelweard says that, " Anglia vetus sita est inter Saxones et Giotos, habens oppidum capitale, quod sermone Saxonico Sleswic nuncupatur, secundum vero Danos Haithaby." Chronicorum Ethelwerdi Libri Quatuor: v. Rerum Anglicarum Scriptores post Bedam præcipui [edited by Saville]. Fol. Francof 1601, pp. 831—850. What Ethelweard has stated, is confirmed by that " great lover of truth," William of Malmsbury, who died about 1143. He says—" In oppido quod tunc Slaswick, nunc vero Eitheisi [al. Hurtheby] appellatur, est autem regio illa Anglia vetus dicta, unde Angli venerunt in Brittanniam, inter Saxones et Giothos constituta."

Alfred says " Se [Hæ'ðe] stent betuh Winedum, and Seaxum, and Angle, and hyrð in on Dene." This agrees with the locality of Schleswig. The A. S. Hæðe and the subsequent Eitheisi, Haithaby, and Hurtheby are in the preceding extracts associated with Schleswig. The termination -by is Danish, and signifies a town. There is a place on the south of the river Schley, opposite Schleswig, engraved in the map of Mercator in 1623, Haddebuy, and called by Rask Hedeby, by Dahlmann Hedaby and by others Haddeby. This is concluded to be the Hæ'ðe of Ohthere, Wulfstan and Alfred—Dr Ingram adds, " At Hæthum, a port by the heaths, afterwards changed into Haithaby, and called to this day Haddeby, is situated on the south side of the river Schley, opposite to Schleswig, which having since become of greater importance, has eclipsed the fame of its ancient rival. Hence Sir J. Spelman, Somner, Lye, and others, following the authority of Ethelweard, a Saxon writer, have considered At-Hæthum, or Haddeby, to be the same with Schleswig." Inaugural Lecture, p. 109, note k.

58 Winede, the Venedi or Wends, who, at one time, occupied the whole coast from the Schley in Schleswig, South Jutland, to the Vistula in Prussia. An. v. Note 13, and 64.

59 A. S. Denmearc, [see note 65] That is, the provinces of Halland, Scania or Schonen, the early seat of the Danes. Halland and Schonen are in South Gothland, in Sweden, having the Cattegat, the Sound, and the Baltic for its maritime boundaries. v. note 53.

60 A. S. Engle ær hí hider on land comon, the Engles before they came hither on land, i. e. into Britain. Alfred expressly states here, that the Engles before they came to Britain dwelt not only in Jutland, but in Zealand and many islands. Hence we conclude that the Engles or Angles came hither not only from Anglen, in South Jutland, between Schleswig and Flensburg, but from the Danish islands. The majority of settlers in Britain were the Engles, and from them we derive not only our being, but our name, for England is literally, Englaland, the land or country of the Engles. The Engles were the most powerful and energetic of the tribes, that constituted the great Saxon confederacy, which, in the third and two following centuries, had the greatest extent of territory in the north west of Germany. The Saxon confederacy increased, till it possessed the vast extent of country

days; and, the two days before he came to Haddeby, he had on his right, Jutland, Zealand, and many islands. The Angles dwelt in these lands, before they came into this country.⁵⁰ And, these

embraced by the Elbe, the Sala, and the Rhine, in addition to their ancient territory between the Elbe, and the Oder. Bosworth's Origin of the Eng. and Germ. lang. and nations, p. 14—17.—It will be evident, from the following authorities, as well as from the testimony of Alfred given in the text, that in the seventh century, and in the time of Alfred, Schleswig was considered the locality from which England received its chief population. It will be interesting to see what Bede says, on the population of England, confirmed by the A. S. version of Alfred, and by the A. S. Chronicle. " Advenerant autem de tribus Germaniæ populis fortioribus, id est, Saxonibus, Anglis, Jutis. De Jutarum origine sunt Cantuarii et Victuarii, hoc est, ea gens quæ Vectam tenet insulam, et ea quæ usque hodie in provincia Occidentalium Saxonum Jutarum natio nominatur, posita contra ipsam insulam Vectam. De Saxonibus, id est, ea regione quæ nunc antiquorum Saxonum cognominatur, venere Orientales Saxones, Meridiani Saxones, Occidui Saxones. Porro de Anglis, hoc est, de illa patria quæ Angulus dicitur et ab eo tempore usque hodie manere desertus inter provincias Jutarum et Saxonum perhibetur, Orientales Angli, Mediterranei Angli, Mercii, tota Nordanhymbrorum progenies, id est, illarum gentium quæ ad Boream Humbri fluminis inhabitant cæteriquo Anglorum populi sunt orti. Duces fuisse perhibentur eorum primi duo fratres Hengist et Horsa; e quibus Horsa postea occisus in bello a Brittonibus, hactenus in Orientalibus Cantiæ partibus monumentum habet suo nomine insigne." Smith's Bede, Fol. Cambridge 1722, lib. i, ch. 15, p. 52.—Alfred's Saxon translation of which is: " Comon hi of þrim folcum þam strangestan Germanie, þæt of Seaxum, and of Angle, and of Geatum. Of Geata fruman syndon Cantware, and Wihtsætan, þæt is seo þeod þe Wiht þæt Ealond onearda'ð. Of Seaxum þæt is of þam lande þe mon hateð Eald-Seaxan, coman East-Seaxan, and Suð-Seaxan, and West-Seaxan. And of Engle coman East-Engle and Middel-Engle, and Myrce, and eall Norðhembra cynn, is þæt land þe Angulus is nemned betwyh Geatum and Seaxum. Is sæd of þære tide þe hi þanon gewiton oð to dæge þæt hit weste wunige. Wæron þa ærest heora latteowas and heretogan twegen gebroðra, Hengest and Horsa." Id. p. 483.

The Saxon Chronicle gives the following account: " An. ccccxlix. Her Martianus and Valentinianus onfengon rice, and ricsodon vii winter. On heora dagum Hengest and Horsa, from Wyrtgeorne gelaðode Brytta cyninge to fultume, gesohton Brytene on þam staeðe, þe is genemned Ypwines-fleot, ærest Bryttum to fultume, ac hy eft on hy fuhton. Se cing het hi feohtan agien Pihtas, and hi swa dydan, and sige hæfdon swa hwar swa hi comon. Hi þa sende to Angle, and heton heom sendan mare fultum, and heom seggan Brytwalana nahtnesse, and þæs landes cysta. Hi þa sendon heom mare fultum, þa comon þa menn of þrim mægðum Germanie, of Eald-Seaxum, of Anglum, of Iotum.

" Of Iotum comon Cantware and Wihtware [þæt is seo mæið þe nu earðað on Wiht,] and þæs cynn on West-Sexum, þe man nu gyt het Iutna-cynn. Of Eald-Seaxum comon East-Seaxan, and Suð-Seaxan, and West-Seaxan. Of Angle comon, se ǽ siððan stod westig betwix Iutum and Seaxum, East-Engle, and Middel-Angle, and Mearce and ealle Norðymbra. Heora here-togan wæron twegen gebroðra, Hengest and Horsa."

Though the Friesians are not named by Bede, as forming part of this migration to Britain, it is probable, from their locality in the north west of Germany, that many of them may have accompanied the Angles, Saxons, and other tribes to this Island. But we are not left in doubt, on this subject, for Procopius, who lived two hundred years nearer the Saxon expedition to Britain than Bede, expressly states, in his fourth book on the Gothic war, that Britain was peopled by three nations, the Britons, the Angles, and the Friesians [Ἀγγίλοι καὶ Φρίσσονες]. This is the opinion still prevalent among the Friesians and Dutch. They even claim Hengist as their country-man; and the old Chroniclers are at a loss whether to make Hengist a Friesian or a Saxon. Maerlant, the father of Dutch,

two days, the islands,⁶¹ which belong to Denmark, were on his left.

20. Wulfstan⁶² said that he went from Haddeby,—that he was in Truso⁶³ in seven days and nights,—that the ship was running all the way under sail. He had Weonodland,⁶⁴ [Mecklenburg and Pomerania] on the right [star-board,] and Langland, Laaland, Falster and Sconey, on his left, and all these lands belong to Denmark.⁶⁵ And then we had,⁶⁶ on our left, the land of the Burgundians⁶⁷ [Bornholmians], who have their own king.⁶⁸ After

or rather Flemish Poets, for he was born in Flanders about 1235, speaks of him, thus:—

> Een hiet Engistus een Vriese, een Sas,
> Die uten lande verdreven was;
> One, a Saxon or Friesian, Hengist by name.
> From his country was banished in sorrow and shame.
> SPIEGEL HISTORIAL, C. XV, p. 16.

Thus again:—

> Engistus wart dus onteert,
> Ende is in Vrieseland gekeert.
> Hengist was thus so much disgraced,
> That he, to Friesland, his steps retraced. Tom. III, p. 29.

The Chronicle of Maerlant is founded upon the Speculum Historiale of the Monk Vicentius, who wrote about the year 1245. Bosworth's Origin of the Eng. and Germ. Lang. and Nations, p. 15, § 4, note †: p. 52, § 50, note ‡: p. 53, § 52.—Latham's Germania of Tacitus, Epileg. p. CXXII, and 117.—Also, Latham's English Language, 3rd Edn, for Friesians and Jutes.

61 These are the islands Moen, Falster, Laaland, &c.: he, therefore, sailed between Zealand, Moen, &c.

62 Forster says—" Wulfstan appears to have been a Dane, who, perhaps, had become acquainted with Ohthere in the course of his expedition, and had gone with him to England." Northern Voyages, p. 69, note 73.

63 Truso, a town on the shore of the mere or lake Drausen, or Truso, from which the river Ilfing [Elbing] flows in its course towards the town of Elbing [v. note 75]. Forster says:—" There is at this time, a lake between Elbing and Prussian Holland, called Truso, or Drausen, from which, probably, the town Truso . . . took its name." Forster's Northern Voyages, 4to, 1786, p. 69, note 74.

64 Weonodland the country of the Wends on the coast of Mecklenburg, Pomerania, &c. in Prussia [see notes 13 and 58.].—A. S. Langa-land, the long island.—A. S. Scóneg, the beautiful island.

65 Denmark from daim low, mark ground, land, country. Malte-Brun's Geog. Vol. VIII, p. 577.—A. S. Dene-mearc—Dene The Danes,—Dene from denu a plain, vale, valley; and mearc a boundary. The Saxon Chronicle in 1005, 1023, 1035, has Denemearc; Denmearc, in 1019, 1075; Dænmarc, in 1070; Denmarc, in 1070 and 1119. In Danish, mark signifies a country; hence Denmark the low country of the Danes.—Finmark the country of the Finns. Forster says;—" Wulfstan [Alfred] is the most early writer hitherto known, who mentions this name. Notes to Barrington's Orosius, p. 257, note 36.

66 Wæron us, literally erant nobis. The pronoun of the first person plural, we and us, proves that Wulfstan is relating to the king his own account of their voyage.

67 Burgenda land is the Icl. Burgundarhólmr of which the present Dan. and Swed. name Bornholm is a contraction. Rask's Afhandlinger, p. 374, note o.

68 And þá habbað himsylf cyning, literally, and who have to themselves a king.

the land of the Burgundians, we had,⁶⁸ on our left, those lands that were called first Blekingey,⁶⁹ and Meore, and Oeland and Gothland; and these lands belong to Sweden. And we had Weonodland, on the right, all the way to the mouth of the Vistula. The Vistula⁷⁰ is a very large river, and near it lie Witland⁷¹ and Weonodland; and Witland belongs to the Esthonians.⁷² The Vistula flows out of Weonodland and runs into the Frische Haff ⁷³ [Est-

69 A. S. Blecingaæg, the province of Bleking, on the southwest of Sweden.—Meore, the Upper and Lower Moehre, in the province of Smoeland or Smaland, also in Sweden.—Eowland and Gotland, the two islands on the coast of Sweden, Oeland and Gothland.

70 A. S. Wisle, in Polish Wisla. German Weichsel: by other nations, and by Latin writers, it is called Vistula. Before reaching the Baltic, the Vistula first divides into two branches, the smaller and eastern branch of which, called the Neugat or Nogat, runs north easterly, and discharges itself into the Frische Haff [see note 73]. The larger or western branch, after flowing 35 or 40 miles farther, again divides, about 9 miles from Danzig, into two branches, the smaller of which runs easterly into the Frische Haff, the main stream of the Vistula taking an opposite direction, discharges itself into the Baltic at Weichselmünde, north of Danzig. So there are, at least, three great branches of the Vistula, the Nogat at the commencement of the great Werder; the second, above Danzig: this second branch and the Nogat run into the Frische Haff, and the third passes by Danzig into the Baltic. Jornandes, de reb. Get. c. 3, correctly describes this river. He speaks of Scancia thus:—" Hæc a fronte posita est Vistulæ fluvii; qui Sarmaticis montibus ortus, in conspectu Scanziæ septentrionali oceano trisulcus illabitur: for, besides the smaller streams of the Nogat, this river has three great branches. The most westerly is near Danzig; the easterly branches just described, enter the Frische Haff, with the Elbing. v. note 76.

71 Porthan says that Witland is a part of Samland in Prussia. In old times it extended to the eastern bank of the Vistula. The monk Alberik, who lived a century and a half after Alfred, is the first that mentions Witland.—" In Prutia [Prucia], quæ est ultra Pomeraniam, Episcopus Mutinensis, missus a Papa legatus, ingenio et sapientia sua, non fortitudine, multos paganos ad fidem attraxit. ... Erant autem hoc anno, in illis partibus, quinque tantummodo provinciæ paganorum acquirendæ: ista videlicet, de qua agitur, Prutia [Prucia], Curlandia, Lethonia, Vithlandia, et Sambria. Rask's Afhandlinger, p. 375, note q.—Witland was celebrated for its amber at the time of the Crusades, it was still called Witland. Forster's North. Voyages, p. 70.—Professor Voigt, in his Geschichte Preussens von den ältesten Zeiten, Königsberg, 1827—39, advances many arguments to prove, that part of Witland has been absorbed by the Frische Haff,—that Witland, not only occupied the north-eastern part of the Frische Haff, from the old castle of Balga or Honeda, but extended far into the sea on the west and north of Samland. The space is marked in his map. See note 76.

72 A. S. Estum dat. pl. of Este, or Estas of Alfred, mentioned in note 30 and its text. These Esthonians or Osterlings dwelt on the shores of the Baltic to the east of the Vistula. An.

73 A. S. Estmere, [est east, mere a lake] the present Frische Haff or fresh water lake is on the north of east Prussia. Hav or Haff signifies a sea, in Danish and Swedish. It is written Haff in German and it is now used to denote all the lakes connected with the rivers, on the coast of Prussia and Pomerania. The Frische Haff is about 60 miles long, and from 6 to 15 broad. It is separated by a chain of sand banks from the Baltic sea, with which, at the present time, it communicates by one strait called the Gat. This strait is on the north east of the Haff, near the fortress of Pillau. Malte Brun's Univ. Geog. Vol. VII, p. 14. This Gat, as Dr Bell informs me, " seems to have been formed, and to be kept open by the superior force of the Pregel stream." This gentleman has a perfect

mere]. The Frische Haff is, at least, fifteen miles"[74] broad. Then"[75] the Elbing"[76] comes from the east into the Frische Haff, out of the lake [Drausen] on the shore of which Truso stands; and [they] come out together into the Frische Haff, the Elbing from the east, out of Esthonia; and the Vistula from the south out of Weonodland. Then the Vistula takes away the name of the Elbing, and runs out of the lake into the sea, by a western [opening] on the north [of the Frische Haff]; therefore, they call it the mouth of the Vistula.[77] Esthonia [Eastland] is very large, and

knowledge of the Frische Haff, and the neighbourhood, as he received his early education in the vicinity, and matriculated at the University of Königsberg, near the west end of the Haff. I am indebted to Dr Bell for the map of the celebrated German Historian, Professor Voigt, adapted to his " Geschichte Preussens von den ältesten Zeiten, 9 vols 8vo, Königsberg, 1827—39." In this map, there are four openings from the Frische Haff to the Baltic. " It is certain," says Malte-Brun, that in 1394 the mouth of one strait was situated at Lochsett, 6 or 8 miles north of the fortress of Pillau." Voigt's map gives the year, 1311. Id. vol. VII, p. 15. The next is the Gat of Pillau, at present the only opening to the Baltic, with the date 1510. The third Gat, marked in the map with the date 1456, is about 10 or 12 miles south west of Pillau; and the fourth, without any date, is much nearer the west end of the Frische Haff.

74 It is evident, that Alfred has here altered the measure of Ohthere, the Northman, and has made it to agree with the Anglo-Saxon miles. Hence, the dimensions of Estmere, given by Alfred, perfectly accord with those of the Frische Haff of the present day, as mentioned in the preceding note. See also note 49.

75 Literally, Then comes the Elbing from the east into Estmere [the Frische Haff] from [out of] the mere, on the bank of which Truso stands [or, which Truso stands upon the bank of [i. e. the lake of Drausen]. Truso, therefore, was on the border of the lake Drausen, and not of the Estmere or Frische Haff. The river Elbing [Ilfing] flows from the lake Drausen towards the town of Elbing. Rask's Afhandlinger, p. 379 and 380, note a.—V. note 63.— Hence Rask has translated this passage into Danish—Ilfing löber östen fra ind i det friske Hav, og kommer fra den Sö, paa hvis Bræd Truso staar." Id. p. 325.—Dahlmann translates it—" Der Ilfing [Elbing] läuft von Osten in das Esthenmeer von der See her, an dessen Gestade Truso steht." p. 428.

76 A. S. Ilfing, the river Elbing in Western Prussia, to the east of the Vistula. The Elbing flows from the small lake Drausen to the town of Elbing called also Elbinga, in Polish Elbiag or Elblag, and urbs Drusinia. Malte Brun says:—" The flourishing and commercial town of Elbing, is built on a low and fruitful valley: its name is derived from the small river Elbach, which issues from the lake of Drausen." Univer. Geog. Vol. VII, p. 23.—V. note 75.

77 Wisle múɮa, the mouth of the Vistula. The most westerly stream of the Vistula, which flows into the Baltic, a little to the north of Danzig, is still called in German, Weichselmünde [v. note 70]. Forster observes, every thing that Alfred here mentions, incontestably shews, that Wulfstan had an intimate and personal knowledge of what he was stating. The Elbing came out of Esthonia and from the east, so far as regards that arm of the Elbing, which ran from east to west, into the Nogat the eastern branch of the Vistula; but the Vistula comes [súðan of Winodlande] out of Weonodland from the south. The two rivers, the eastern branch of the Vistula, and the Elbing, flow together under the former name, and enter the Frische Haff. This Haff or lake extends from west to north, that is in a north-easterly direction and flows into the Baltic at Pillau. Forster then adds:—" It is

there are many towns, and in every town there is a king. There is also very much honey and fishing. The king and the richest

possible, that this, as well as the western arm, may have formerly borne the name of Weichselmünde or the mouth of the Vistula." Northern Voyages, p. 71, note 83.

Barrington translates it:—"The Ilfing, having joined the Wesel, takes its name, and runs to the west of Estmere, and northward, into the sea, when it is called the Wesel's mouth." p. 17.

Dr Ingram's translation is,—"Then the Weissel deprives the Ilfing of its name; and, flowing from the west part of the lake, at length empties itself northward into the sea; whence this point is called the Weissel-mouth." Lect. p. 81.

Rask gives the whole passage thus: Ilfing löber östen fra ind i det friske Hav, og kommer fra den Sö, paa hvis Bræd Truso staar, de löbe begge tilsammen ud i det friske Hav, Ilfing östen fra ud af Estland og Vejksel sönden fra ud af Venden, da betager Vejkselen Ilfing dens Navn, og löber fra bemældte friske Hav nordvest paa ud i Söen, derfor kalder man dette [Udlöb] Vejkselmundingen. Afhandlinger, p. 325.

Dahlmann translates the same passage:—" Der Ilfing [Elbing] läuft von Osten in das Esthenmeer von der See her, an dessen Gestade Truso steht; sie strömen beide gemeinsam ins Esthenmeer aus, Ilfing aus Osten von Esthland, und die Weichsel aus Süden von Wendenland; und hier benimmt die Weichsel dem Ilfing seinen Namen, und strömt aus dem [Esthen-] Meere nordwestlich in die See; davon nennt man das Weichselmünde." Forshungen, p. 428.

The literal translation of the last sentence of the A. S. text is,—Then the Vistula deprives the Elbing of its name, and flows out of [of þæm mere, from or out of the mere or lake: v. note 75] the Lake or Haff, west and north into the sea; therefore, they call it the mouth of the Vistula.

This would seem to imply, that there were then two openings from the Frische Haff, one on the west, and the other on the north. This supposition is not impossible; for, in different ages, there have been four openings from the Frische Haff to the Baltic, one of which was near the western extremity of the Haff. [v. note 73.] But these two openings do not accord with the conclusion, where the singular is used, " therefore, they call it, the mouth of the Vistula."

Rask and Dahlmann, seeing this difficulty, have given a different translation of "west and norð"; Rask gives "nordvest," and Dahlmann "nordwestlich."—They appear to admit of only one gat or opening, and that on the north-west, towards the present Weichselmünde, on the west of the Haff, but without authority from the A. S. text, and without a reference to history to prove there was such a gat on the west.

Though the translation I have given in the text, does not accord with the present locality of Weichselmünde, and it is not translated verbally; yet, I think, it gives the plain meaning. I allude to the latter part of the sentence: and flows out of the Lake [the Frische Haff] west and north into the sea; that is, flows out of the gat or opening at Pillau, on the west side of the most northerly part of the Frische Haff, which is west of Koningsberg.

The great difficulty here is to ascertain whether there is any truth, in what Forster suggests, that the gat of Pillau was called Weichselmünde, as well as the western branch of the Vistula, which flows into the Baltic to the north of Danzig. This uncertainty, with some other difficulties, has led to several suggestions, one of which is by W. Bell Esqr, Dr Phil. who thinks that the Truso of Wulfstan is the present Dirschau about 30 miles south of Danzig, and 4 west of the Vistula. He supposes, that the Baltic may have extended so far up the valley of the Vistula, that Dirschau may have been on the shore of the Baltic, in the

men drink mare's milk,"⁸ but the poor and the slaves drink mead."⁹ There is very much war among them; and there is no ale brewed by the Esthonians, but there is mead enough.

21. There is also a custom with the Esthonians,⁸⁰ that when a man is dead, he lies, in his house, unburnt with his kindred and friends a month,—sometimes two; and the king and other men of high rank, so much longer according to their wealth, remain unburnt sometimes half a year; and lie above ground in their houses. All the while the body is within, there must be drinking and sports to the day, on which he is burned.

22. Then, the same day, when they wish to bear him to the pile, they divide his property, which is left after the drinking and sports, into five or six parts, sometimes into more, as the amount of his property may be. Then, they lay the largest part of it within one mile from the town, then another, then the third, till it is all laid, within the one mile; and the least part shall be nearest the town in which the dead man lies. All the men, who have the swiftest horses in the land, shall then be assembled, about five or six miles from the property. Then they all run towards the property; and the man, who has the swiftest⁸¹ horse, comes to the first and the largest part, and so each after the other, till it is all taken: and he takes the least part, who runs to the property nearest the town. Then each rides away with

time of Alfred. See his Ein versuch, den Ort Schiringsheal, &c. p. 8. This supposition seems to be surrounded with very great difficulties.

78 Forster observes:—This mare's milk was not merely milk, but milk which had undergone a kind of fermentation, and was changed into a species of brandy, such as the inhabitants of the desert plains of Asia Media drink in great quantities, calling it kumyss. . . . Adam of Bremen [§ 138] says, that the ancient Prussians ate horse-flesh, and drank the milk of their mares to intoxication; and Peter of Duisburg [§ 80] relates of these people, that at their feasts, they drank water, mead, and mare's milk. Northern Voyages, p, 71, note 85.

79 Mead, even so early as in the ninth century, had the name of Medo, medu and meodo in Anglo-Saxon; in the Lithuanian tongue it is called Middus; in Polish, Miod; in Russian, Med; in German, Meth. Hence it appears probable that mead is a beverage of great antiquity, as the name, by which it is known, is exactly the same in languages of so different an origin. With these it is perhaps worth while to compare the Greek verb μεθύω I intoxicate, from μέθυ wine. Id. p. 72, note 86.

80 The following particulars, relating to the manners of the Esthonians in the ninth century, the preservation of which we owe to the diligent pen of King Alfred, form a valuable supplement to the short sketches of aboriginal manners delineated by Cæsar and Tacitus. Ingram's Lect. p. 82, note e.

81 In A. S. þæt swifte hors, for þæt swiftoste, the swiftest.

the property, and may keep it all; and, therefore, swift horses are there uncommonly dear. When his property is thus all spent, then they carry him out, and burn him with his weapons and clothes." Most commonly they spend all his wealth, with the long lying of the dead within, and what they lay in the way, which the strangers run for and take away.

23. It is also a custom with the Esthonians, that there men of every tribe must be burned; and, if any one find a single bone unburnt, they shall make a great atonement."—There is also among the Esthonians, a power of producing cold; and, therefore, the dead lie there so long, and decay not," because they bring the cold upon them. And if a man set two vats full

---

82 That the ancient Prussians burnt their dead, and buried them together with their horses, weapons, clothes, and valuable possessions, appears from a treaty concluded through the mediation of the Archdeacon of Liege, in quality of the Pope's Legate, between the German Knights and the newly converted Prussians, wherein the Prussians expressly promise never in future to burn their dead, nor bury them with their horses, arms, clothes and valuables. Forster's Northern voyages, p. 72, note 88.

A similar custom is mentioned, in Cæsar's Commentaries, as prevailing in Gaul :—" Funera sunt pro cultu Gallorum magnifica, et sumptuosa; omniaque, quæ vivis cordi fuisse arbitrantur, in ignem inferunt, etiam animalia; ac, paulo supra hanc memoriam, servi, et clientes, quos ab iis dilectos esse constabat, justis funeribus confectis, una cremabantur." De Bello Gallico, l. VI, c. 19.—The custom of burning the dead, $\nu\epsilon\kappa\rho o\kappa\alpha\upsilon\sigma\tau\iota\alpha$, or cremation, was almost universal, among rude nations, from the age of Homer to that of Alfred. Ingram's Lect. p. 83, note h.

83 The A. S. gebétan to atone for, or to make atonement, is similar to the Icl. bœta, Swed. bode, to reconcile: miclum dat. pl. multo, used adverbially. The atonement, sacrifice or offering, did not apply merely to the individual, but to his whole race, as is evident by the pl. hi sceólan they shall. The meaning, as Rask says, is this :—" Saa skulle de udsone det med et stort offer." Thus shall they atone for, or expiate this, with a great offering, sacrifice, or atonement. Afhandlinger, p. 381, note œ.

Atonement is at-one-ment, an expressive English compound, from atone, to set at one, to reconcile, make peace. Thus the Greek of St Paul, in the Acts—$\kappa\alpha\iota$ $\sigma\upsilon\nu\eta\lambda\alpha\sigma\epsilon\nu$ $\alpha\upsilon\tau o\upsilon\varsigma$ $\epsilon\iota\varsigma$ $\epsilon\iota\rho\eta\nu\eta\nu$, Ch. VII, 26, is in our version, "and would have set them at one again": this follows Tyndale's translation of 1534—and wolde have set them at one agayne.—He made the Jewes and the Gentiles at one betwene themselues, even so he made them both at one with God, that there should be nothing to breake the atonement. Udal. Ephesians, C. 2.

84 Phineas Fletcher, who was ambassador from Queen Elizabeth to Russia, gives an account of the same practice continuing in some parts of Moscovy. " In winter time, " when all is covered with snow, so many as die are piled up in a hovel in the suburbs like " billets on a wood stack; they are as hard with the frost as a very stone, till the spring- " tide come and resolve the frost, what time every man taketh his dead friend, and com- " mitteth him to the ground." See a note to one of Fletcher's Eclogues, p. 10, printed at Edinburgh, in 1771, 12mo. See also a poem written at Moscow, by G. Tuberville, in the first volume of Hakluyt, p. 386, where the same circumstance is dwelt upon, and the reason given, that the ground cannot be dug. Bodies, however, are now [1773?] buried at

of ale or of water, they cause that either shall be frozen over, whether it be summer or winter."⁸⁵]

24. Now will we speak about GREECE, on the south of the river Danube.* The sea, Propontis, lies on the east of Constantinople, a city of the Greeks. On the north of Constantinople, the arm of the sea shoots up right west from the Euxine; and, on the north-west of the city, the mouth of the river Danube shoots out south-east into the Euxine sea; and, on the south and on the west side of the mouth, are the Moesians, a tribe of Greeks; and, on the west of the city, are the Thracians; and on the west⁸⁶ of these, the Macedonians. On the south of the city, and on the south side of the arm of the sea which is called Archipelago [Ægæum], is the country of the Athenians and of Corinth. To the south-west of Corinth is the country of Achaia, by the Mediterranean Sea. These countries are peopled by Greeks. On the west of Achaia, along the Mediterranean, is the country Dalmatia, on the north side of the sea; and on the north of Dalmatia are the Bulgarians, and Istria. On the south of Istria is that part of the Mediterranean Sea, which is called Adriatic; and on the west, the Alpine mountains; and on the north, that waste, which is between Carinthia and the Bulgarians.

15. Then the country of ITALY,† extends a long way north-west, and south-east;—and all around it lies the Mediterranean Sea, save on the north-west. At that end, it is bounded by the

Moscow during the winter. D. B. — As the poem of G. Tuberville, to which Mr Barrington refers, in Hakluyt, is addressed to so great a poet as Spenser, the reader may perhaps be amused with the following specimen, relating to the subject.

> Perhaps thou musest much, how this may stand with reason,
> That bodies dead can uncorrupt abide, so long a season !
> Take this for certain trothe ; as soon as heate is gone,
> The force of colde the body binds as hard as any stone,
> Without offence at all, to any living thing ;
> And so they lye in perfect state, till next returne of springe."
>
> INGRAM's LECT. p. 84, note m.

85 This power, so much admired by King Alfred, of producing cold either in summer or in winter, by which the putrefaction of dead bodies was prevented, and ale and water were frozen, must have been effected by some sort of ice-house, and this, every Prussian of any consequence had in, or near his house. Forster's Northern Voyages, p. 73.

86 A. S. and be eastan þære byrig, and on the east of the city, note 89.

* Partly from Oros. l. I, c. 2, Haver. p. 23, 24 : see note 88.

† Partly from Oros. l. I, c. 2, Haver. p. 24.

mountains called the Alps: these begin on the west, from the Mediterranean Sea, in the country Narbonensis, and end again on the east in the country of Dalmatia by the [Adriatic] Sea.

26. The countries called GALLIA BELGICA *:—on the east of these is the river Rhine, and on the south the mountains called the Alps, and on the south-west the ocean which is called Britannic; and on the north, on the other side of the arm of the ocean, is the country Britain. On the west of the Loire is the country Aquitania; and, on the south of Aquitania, is some part of the country Narbonensis; and on the south-west the country of Spain; and, on the west, the ocean. On the south of Narbonensis is the Mediterranean Sea, where the river Rhone empties itself; and, on the east of it, Provence; and on the west of it, over the wastes, the nearer Spain [Hispania Citerior], and on the west and north, Aquitania; and Gascony on the north. Provence has, on the north of it, the Alps; and on the south of it is the Mediterranean Sea; and, on the north and east of it, are the Burgundians, and on the west the Gasconians.

17. The country of SPAIN † is three-cornered, and all encompassed with water by the Atlantic " ocean without, and by the Mediterranean Sea within, more than the countries named before. One of the corners lies south-west, opposite to the island, called Cadiz, and another east, opposite the country Narbonensis, and the third north-west, towards Betanzos; a city of Galicia, and opposite Scotland [Ireland], over the arm of the sea, right against the mouth of the river called the Shannon. As to that part of Spain," more distant from us, on the west of it, and on the north is the ocean, on the south the Mediterranean Sea, and on the east the nearer Spain; on the north of which are the

---

* Oros. L. I, c. 2. Haver. p. 25. † Oros. l. I, c. 2. Haver. p. 25, 26.

87 Literally:—and all encompassed with water without, and also encompassed within, more than [ofer over, above, more than] those lands [þa land those lands, or countries Provence, Aquitania, and Gallia Belgica] both by the ocean and by the Mediterranean Sea.

88 It must be recollected, that Orosius is supposed to speak, and not Alfred.—The royal Geographer, indeed, appears to have deserted Orosius entirely, as an insufficient guide, till he came to those territories, which are situated to the south of the Danube. This, therefore, is the only part of his description which can be strictly considered as a translation. The division also of all Europe into the countries lying north and south of the Danube, so clear and simple, which is completely original, shews how much we owe to King Alfred. Ingram's Lect. p. 86, note q.

Aquitani, and on the north-east the forest of the Pyrenees,‡ and on the east Narbonensis; and on the south the Mediterranean Sea.

28. The island BRITAIN.—It extends || a long way north-east; it is eight hundred miles long, and two hundred miles broad. On the south of it, and on the other side of the arm of the sea, is Gallia Belgica; and on the west part, on the other side of the sea, is the island Hibernia"; and on the north part, the Orkney islands §. Ireland, which we call Scotland, is on every side surrounded by the ocean; and because it is nearer the setting of the sun than other lands, the weather is milder there, than in Britain. Then on the north-west of Ireland, is that outmost land called Thule; and it is known to few because of its great distance.—Thus, have we spoken about the boundaries of all Europe, as they lie.

29. Now, we will [speak] of AFRICA,* and how the boundaries lie around it.—Our elders said, that it was the third part of this mid-earth, not because there was so much of the land, but because the Mediterranean Sea has so divided it : because it breaks more into the south part than it does into the north; and the heat has taken more hold on the south part, than the cold has on the north; and because every creature can better withstand cold, than heat; for these reasons, Africa is less than Europe; both in land and in men.

‡ Pyrenæi saltus a parte septentrionis. Oros. l. I; c. II. Haver. p. 26, 8.—A. S. Be norðan eastan is se weald Pireni.

|| Britannia oceani insula, per longum in boream extenditur. Oros. l. I, c. II. Haver. p. 27, 4.

89 Ibernia, Hibernia, Igbernia, now Ireland, was denominated Scotland from about the fifth to the eleventh century. The Scoti were first heard of, as inhabiting Ireland. As they imposed their name on Hibernia, so in settling in North Britain they gave it the name of Scotland, which it still retains. [See note 54 : Also Alfred's Orosius § 3 note 7] Bede says, " Hæc [Hibernia] proprie patria Scottorum est." l. I, c. 1; p. 42. So in Alfred's translation. This [Hibernia] is agendlice Scotta eþel. id. p. 474.—Diodorus Siculus calls Ibernia, Ἴρις, Strabo Ἰέρνη, Ἰερνὶς νῆσος, Ptolemy Ἰουερνἱα, Pomponius Mela Juverna, Claudian Ierna. In the names Iris, Ierna, Juverna, Hibernia, the native Irish, Eri or Ir is discoverable. The Irish, to indicate a country, prefix Hy, or Hua denoting " the [dwelling of the] sons, or family of." In prefixing Hy to a name beginning with a vowel, a consonant is often inserted, thus; Hy-v-Each, the country or descendants of Each or Æacus. This prefix requires a genitive, which in Eri is Erin; and thus, all the variations in the name seem to be accounted for,—as Eri, or Ire-land; Hy-b-ernia, Hibernia; —Hy-ernis, Iernis.

§ Orcadas insulas habet. Oros. l. I: c. II. Haver. p. 27, 10.—A. S. Orcadus þæt igland.

* Oros. l. I: c. II. Haver. p. 28, 29.

30. On the east, Africa begins, as we said before, westward of Egypt, at the river Nile. Then the most easterly country is called LIBYA † CYRENAICA; on the east of it is the nearer Egypt, and on the north the Mediterranean Sea, [and on the south the country] that is called Libya Æthiopum; and on the west the Syrtis Major.

31. On the west of Libya Æthiopum is the farther EGYPT ‡; and on the south the sea which is called Æthiopic; and, on the west the Troglodytæ. The country Tripolitana, which is also called Arzuges:—It has, on the east of it, the Syrtis Major, and the country of the Troglodytæ; and on the north the [part of the] Mediterranean Sea, which is called Adriatic, and the country which is called Syrtis Minor; and, on the west, to the salt lake, Byzacium; and, on the south of it to the ocean, the Natobres, and Getuli, and Garamantes.

32. The country BYZACIUM,‖ in which is the city Adrumetus, and Seuges, and the great city Carthage, and the region of Numidia. They have, on the east of them, the country Syrtis Minor, and the salt lake; and, on the north of them, is the Mediterranean Sea; and, on the west of them, Mauretania: and, on the south of them, the mountains Uzera; and, on the south of the mountains to the ocean, the ever-wandering Æthiopians.—Mauretania: —On the east of it is Numidia; and, on the north, the Mediterranean Sea; and, on the west, the river Malva; and on the south, Astria, about the mountains, which separate § the fruit-bearing land, and the barren whirling-sand, which then lies south all the way to the ocean.—Mauretania is called also Tingitana. On the east of it, is the river Malva; and, on the north, the mountains, Albenas, and Calpe another mountain, where the end shoots up from the ocean, between the mountains eastward, where the pillars of Hercules stand; and, on the west of them to the ocean is the mountain Atlas; and, on the south, the mountain called Hesperium; and, on the south of them to the ocean, the country Aulolum.—Thus have we spoken about the landmarks of Africa.

† Oros. l. I: c. II. Haver. p. 29.   ‡ Oros. l. I: c. II. Haver. p. 30.

‖ Bisacium, Byzacena Regio, βυζάκιον, βυζακὶς χώρα the south part of Tunis. Oros. l. I: c. II. Haver. p. 30.

§ Qui dividit inter vivam terram et arenas jacentes usque ad Oceanum.—Tingitana Mauritania ultima est Africæ. Oros. l. I: c. II. Haver. p. 31.

33. Now, we will speak about the islands,† which are in the Mediterranean Sea.—The island CYPRUS lies opposite Cilicia and Isauria, on the arm of the sea which is called Issicus.‡ It is a hundred and seventy five miles long, and a hundred and twenty two miles broad.—The island, CRETE :—On the east of it, is the sea which is called Carpathian ; and westerly, and on the north, the Cretan Sea; and, on the west, the Sicilian, which is also called the Adriatic. It is a hundred and seventy miles long, and fifty miles broad.

34. Of the islands, called CYCLADES ¶, there are fifty three. On the east of them, is the Icarian sea; and, on the south, the Cretan; and, on the north, the Ægæan; and, on the west, the Adriatic.

35. The island SICILY ‖ is three-cornered. At each corner there are hills[90] : the north corner is called Pelorus, near to which is the city Messina : the south corner is called Pachynum, near which is the city Syracuse ; and the west corner is called Lilybæum, near which is the city Lilybæum. On the north and south,[91] it is a hundred and fifty-seven miles long; and the third side, along the [east][92] is a hundred and seventy seven. On the east of the land is [that part of] the Mediterranean Sea, which is called Adriatic ; and, on the south, that which is called African ; and, on the west, what is called Tyrrhenian ; and, on the north, is the sea, which is both narrow and rough, towards Italy.

36. The islands, Sardinia § and Corsica are separated by a little arm of the sea, which is twenty two miles broad.—SARDINIA is

---

† Oros. l. I : c. II, Haver. p. 32.

‡ 'Ο 'Ισσικὸς κόλπος Issicus sinus : Issieum sinum vocant. Oros. l. I : c. II, Haver. p. 32.

¶ Insulæ Cyclades sunt numero quinquaginta tres. Oros. l. I : c. II. Haver. p. 32.— They were called κυκλάδες, because they lay ἐν κύκλῳ in a circle.

‖ Oros. l. I : c. II. Haver. p. 33.

90 A. S. beorgas. Oros. promontoria, from promontorium. i. e. mons in mare prominens.

91 There is not in the text, the usual accuracy observed in giving the dimensions of this island. Dr Smith gives them thus :—" The north and south sides are about 175 miles each in length, not including the windings of the coast; and the length of the east side is about 115 miles." Classical Dict. of Geog. &c. 8vo. 1850.

92. A. S. west-lang. Here seems to be some mistake ; for, the north and south-west sides having been named, there only remains the east to be mentioned. The scribe seems to have erroneously written west-lang instead of east-lang.

§ Oros. l. I, c. II. Haver. p. 33, 34.

thirty three miles long, and twenty two miles broad. On the east of it, is [that part of] the Mediterranean Sea, which is called Tyrrhenian, into which the river Tiber flows. On the south is the sea which lies towards the country of Numidia; and, on the west, the two islands which are called Baleares; and, on the north, the island Corsica.

37. CORSICA:—On the east of it is the city of Rome; and, on the south, Sardinia; and, on the west, the Balearic islands; and, on the north, the country of Tuscany. It is sixteen miles long, and nine miles broad.

38. The two islands, BALEARES: *—On the [south][93] of them, is Africa; and Cadiz on the west, and Spain on the north.—We have now spoken shortly about the inhabited islands, that are in the Mediterranean Sea.

BOOK I: CHAPTER II.†

1. One thousand three hundred years before the building of Rome, [1] [B. C. 2053: Clinton, B. C. 2182.] Ninus, king of Assyria, first began to reign in this mid-earth; and, from an immeasurable longing for power, he harassed and fought for fifty years, until he had brought all Asia under his sway, from the Red Sea on the south, to the Euxine on the north. He, moreover, often went with great armies into the north country of the Scythians, who are said to be the hardiest of men; though, in worldly goods, they are the poorest. Whilst he was fighting with them, they became skilful in the arts of war, [2] though before they lived a peaceable life. They afterwards bitterly repaid him for the art of war, [3] which they had learned from him; and, in their

---

* Oros. l. I: c. 2. Haver. p. 34.
93 A. S. be norðan.
† Oros. l. I: c. 4. Haver. p. 37—39. The 3rd chapter of Orosius, "De diluvio sub Noë," Alfred has entirely omitted.
1 Before the building of Rome 1300 years, add 753 years, from the foundation of Rome to the birth of Christ, make 2053 years, B. C., according to Orosius.—Blair says, the kingdom of Assyria began under Ninus, B. C. 2059; but Clinton states, that the Assyrian Chronology of Ctesias, according to Diodorus, gives B. C. 2182, for the beginning of the Assyrian empire. Then, B. C. 2182, take 50 years, the reign of Ninus, make 2132 years B. C. for the death of Ninus, and the beginning of Semiramis's reign. She reigned 42 years; and, therefore, [from 2132 take 42, make 2090] she died B. C. 2090. As these dates appear to be the most correct, they are given in the text, and at the head of the page. Clinton's dates are generally adopted for the Chronology of Greece and Rome. See An epitome of the civil and literary chronology of Greece, etc. by Henry Fynes Clinton Esqr. M. A. late Student of Christ's Church. 8vo. Oxford, 1851. pp. 101—114.
2 A. S. wig-cræfta, war-crafts. 3 A. S. wig-cræft, war-craft.

minds, it was as agreeable to see the shedding of man's blood, as it was to see the milk of their cattle, upon which they mostly lived. Ninus overcame and slew Zoroaster, king of the Bactrians, who was the first man, that knew the arts of the wizzard.[4] At last, when he was in a city fighting against the Scythians, he was there shot dead with an arrow.

2. After his death Semiramis, his queen, succeeded, both to the war and to the kingdom. For forty two years, she carried on the same war, which she brought upon herself by her manifold wicked desires. Still, the power, which the king had gained, seemed too little for her; and, therefore, with womanly zeal, she fought against the harmless people of Ethiopia; and against the Indians, with whom no man but Alexander, either before or since, went to war. She wished to overcome them in war, though she could not accomplish it. Such desires and wars were then more fearful than they now are, because they before knew no example of them, as men now do; for they lived a harmless life.

3. The same queen Semiramis, after the kingdom was in her power, was not only always thirsting for man's blood; but also, with unbounded profligacy, formed plans for such manifold lewdness, that she enticed to her bed every one of those, that she knew to be of the king's family, and afterwards, with guile, put them all to death. Then, at last, she took her own son to her bed; and, because she could not fulfil her wicked desire without the infamy of mankind, she published, over all her kingdom, that there should be no bar to marriage between any kindred.

Book I: Chapter III.[*]

1. One thousand one hundred and sixty years before the building of Rome, [B. C. 1913 : Blair, B. C. 1897] the fruitful land, on which were the cities of Sodom and Gomorrah, was burnt up by fire from heaven. That [land] was between Arabia and Palestine. There was an abundance of fruit, chiefly because the river

---

[4] A. S. dry-cræftas, wizzard-crafts.

[*] Oros. l. I: c. 5. Haver. p. 40—43.—Alfred omits the first part of this chapter, which relates to Pentapolis [$Πεντάπολις$] the five "cities of the plain" [Gen. XIII, 12] of southern Jordan, Sodom, Gomorrah, Adama, Zeboim and Zoar, all of which, except Zoar, were destroyed, and the valley in which they stood was buried beneath the waters of the Dead Sea. Pentapolis is mentioned in the Book of Wisdom, X, 6, where Lot is said to have escaped $καταβάσιον\ πῦρ\ Πενταπόλεως$. The other parts of this chapter, Alfred has much abridged.

Jordan, every year, overflowed the mid-land with water a foot deep; and thus manured it.

2. Then the people immoderately enjoyed this great wealth, till great sensuality waxed within them; and, for this sensuality, God's wrath so came upon them, that he burnt up all the land with sulphurous fire. Afterwards there was standing-water over the land, through which the river formerly flowed. The part of the dale, which the flood did not reach, is to this day fertile in fruits of every kind;¹ and they are very fair, and pleasant to look

---

1 This is not in the original Latin of Orosius, as edited by Havercamp, but the edition of 1471 by Schuszler [see Introduction p. 10 note 2] contains the whole sentence. This would lead to the conclusion, that Alfred translated from a MS. connected with that from which Schuszler printed [See ch. XIV, § 3, note 1]. The edition of 1471 inserts—"Spectes illic poma virentia et formatos uvarum racemos, ut edentibus gignant cupiditatem, si carpas, fatiscunt in cinerem, fumumque excitant, quasi ardeant."—Hegesippus, and S. Ambrose make the same statement, in almost the very same words: see Hegesippus, or Egesippus, De bello Judaico et urbis Hierosolymorum excidio, Paris, 1511. Book IV, ch. 18.

Though POMUM is employed to denote any kind of fruit, as an apple, pear, plum, peach, cherry, grape, olive, nut, etc. [Valpy's Etym. Dict.] like the Spanish and Italian pómo, yet pómo, in these languages, is particularly used, as the French pomme, only for the fruit of the apple tree. Hence perhaps, the Latin poma has been taken in its restricted sense, to signify apples. Hence also, the expression poma Sodomitica has been translated the Apples of Sodom, and the prevalent impression that the f uit of Sodom here alluded to, as well as that by which Eve was tempted, was an apple.

It is pretty clear, that the poma Sodomitica gave rise to the strange story, that all the fruits, growing near the Dead sea, though beautiful to the sight, dissolved into smoke and ashes, when they were gathered. This exaggerated story, though alluded to by Strabo, seems to have been first generally propagated by Josephus, who, however, affirms, that he had it from eye-witnesses. His words are these—Ἔστι δὲ κἂν τοῖς καρποῖς σποδιὰν ἀναγεννωμένην, [ἰδεῖν] οἳ χρόαν μὲν ἔχουσι τοῖς ἐδωδίμοις ὁμοίαν, δρεψαμένων δὲ χερσὶν εἰς καπνὸν ἀναλύονται καὶ τέφραν· τὰ μὲν δὴ περὶ τὴν Σοδομῖτιν μυθευόμενα τοιαύτην ἔχει πίστιν ἀπὸ τῆς ὄψεως. Insuper et in fructibus cineres renascentes, qui specie quidem et colore edulibus similes sunt, manibus autem decerpti in favillam et cinerem resolvuntur. Atque his quidem, de terra Sodomitica narratis, ejusmodi fides habetur ex testibus oculatis. Flavii Josephi de bello Jud. Lib. IV, cap. VIII, § 4. Hudson, p. 1195, line 40.

The fruit is mentioned by Pliny, l. V, c. 17: Solinus c. 36 and others have given the same story as Josephus, with some alterations and additions. Tacitus says.—"Terramque ipsam specie torridam vim frugiferam perdidisse. Nam cuncta spontè edita, aut manu sata, sive herbæ tenues aut flores, ut solitam in speciem adolevêre, atra et inania velut in cinerem vanescunt." Hist. l. V, c. 6.—Syr John de Maundeville, in his "Voiage and Travailes" written about 1322, gives the story thus.—And there groweth trees, that beareth fruit of fair colour, seemeth ripe, and when men breaketh it, they findeth them nought but ashes, in tokening that, through vengeance of God, those cities were burnt with fire of hell.—

This diversity of description seems to have arisen from the indefinite expressions of the promulgators of the story—the καρπὸς of Josephus, and the pomum of others. It has been previously stated, that pomum was used to denote an apple, a plum, grape, etc. Though there is much exaggeration on the subject, there must have been some truth in it, for Moses speaks of the fruit of Sodom, in the ears of all the congregation of Israel, and surely he would not have mentioned this extraordinary fruit, if his hearers had not known of its

upon; but, when they are taken into the hand, they turn to ashes.

existence. Moses only mentions the "vine of Sodom," and that metaphorically, in the following manner,—"But their vine, [is] of the vine of Sodom, and of the field of Gomorrah; their grapes [are] the grapes of רוֹשׁ poison, their clusters are bitter: their wine is the poison of dragons." Deut. XXXII, 32.

Michaelis, in his Recueil, Quest. 64: and suppl. ad Lex. Heb. p. 345, says, that the vine of Sodom is the Solanum or night-shade, which bears a considerable resemblance to the vitis or white vine, in its leaves and fruit, which is vinous but poisonous, and which the Arabs call עֵנַב אל הַעְלָב Fox-grapes. See Parkhurst's Hebrew Lex. under נפן.

In the Solanum, night-shade, or fox-grape, though resembling the vine, there is nothing like explosion, nothing like smoke and ashes, as Hasselquist remarks, "except when the fruit is punctured by an insect [Tenthredo], which converts the whole inside into dust, leaving nothing but the rind entire without any loss of colour." Therefore, Dr Robertson objects to the Solanum, and thinks that the Asclepias gigantia vel procera of Botanists [Sprengel Hist. Rei Herbar. I. p. 252] is more in accordance with the ancient story, especially as, in Palestine, it is peculiar to the shores of the Dead Sea, while the Solanum is found in other parts of the country. The Asclepias, called by the Arabs العشر el-ösher, was seen by Dr Robertson about the middle of the western shore of the Dead Sea. He thus describes the fruit of the Asclepias or ösher. "Externally it greatly resembles a large smooth apple or orange, hanging in clusters of three or four together; and, when ripe, it is of a yellow colour. It was now fair and delicious to the eye, and soft to the touch; but, on being pressed or struck, it exploded with a puff, like a bladder or puff-ball, leaving in the hand only the shreds of the thin rind, and a few fibres."—"It must be plucked and handled with great care to preserve it from bursting." Josephus states in the preceding Greek quotation that "there are still to be seen ashes reproduced in the fruits, which indeed resemble edible fruit in colour; but, on being plucked with the hands, are dissolved into smoke and ashes." Dr Robertson then observes, "In this account, after a due allowance for the marvellous, in all popular reports, I find nothing which does not apply almost literally to the fruit of the ösher, as we saw it."

We noticed several ösher trees, the trunks of which were six or eight inches in diameter, and the whole height from ten to fifteen feet. They had a grayish cork-like bark, and long oval leaves. See Dr Robertson's Biblical Researches in Palestine, &c. 3 vols. 8vo. London vol. II, p. 235—238.

Dr Robertson seems to have been influenced by the popular opinion that this fruit of Sodom was an apple—the Hebrew תפוח an apple, or rather the citron, lemon or orange.

The Honourable Mr Curzon, in his recent and most interesting work—"Visits to the Monasteries of the Levant," thinks he has discovered this fruit of Sodom in what had the appearance of a plum. His account of the discovery is so graphic, that it must be given in his own words. "We made a somewhat singular discovery, when travelling among the mountains to the east of the Dead Sea, where the ruins of Ammon, Jerash, and Adjeloun well repay the labour and fatigue encountered by visiting them. It was a remarkably hot and sultry day: we were scrambling up the mountains through a thick jungle of bushes and low trees, which rises above the east shore of the Dead Sea, when I saw before me a fine plum-tree, loaded with fresh blooming plums. I cried out to my fellow traveller, 'Now, then, who will arrive first at the plumtree?' And, as he caught a glimpse of so refreshing an object, we both pressed our horses into a gallop, to see which would get the first plum from the branches. We both arrived at the same moment, and each snatching a fine ripe plum, put it at once into our mouths; when, on biting it, instead of the cool, delicious, juicy fruit which we expected, our mouths were filled with a dry, bitter dust, and we sat under the tree upon our horses, sputtering, and hemming, and doing all we could to be relieved of the nauseous taste of this strange fruit. We then perceived, and to my great delight, that we had discovered the famous apple of the Dead Sea, the existence of

Book I : Chapter IV.*

1. One thousand and seventy years before the building of Rome [Orosius B. C. 1823], the people of Candia [Telchines] and Scarpanto [Carpathus] began a war, and carried it on, till they were all slain, save very few. However, those Candians, that were left there, gave up their land and went to the island of Rhodes, hoping that they had fled from all war, but there the Greeks found them and utterly put an end to them.

Book I : Chapter V.†

1. Eight hundred years before the building of Rome [Orosius B. C. 1761 : Blair, B. C. 1715], the Egyptians had very great fertility in their land, for seven years ; and afterwards, they were in the greatest famine for the next seven years. Then Joseph, a righteous man, helped them by divine aid. Of this Joseph, Pompeius, the heathen bard, and his follower Justin,[1] thus said :—Joseph was the youngest of his brethren, and also the wisest of them all ; so that the brethren, being afraid, took Joseph and sold him to chapmen, and they sold him into the land of Egypt. Pompeius also said, that he there learnt the arts of magic, and that by these

---

which has been doubted and canvassed since the days of Strabo and Pliny, who first described it ; but, up to this time, no one had met with the thing itself, either upon the spot mentioned by the ancient authors, or elsewhere. I brought several of them to England."

This deceitful apple is a kind of gall-apple, about 2 inches long, produced by a small insect. "A kind of oak-gall, formed by an insect upon the branches of a species of ilex, and is the only fruit or apple hitherto met with by travellers, which answers the description of the ancient writers, though the gourds of the colchicum, solanum melongena called abeschaez, the ösher plant—have been by some thought to be the one in question."

After taking into consideration, what travellers have written, on this subject, it is difficult to determine, which is correct, and what particular fruit is meant when we speak of the apple or rather the fruit of Sodom. There seems to be some ground for the statement of Josephus, that the fruit "dissolved into smoke and ashes," if his informant had seen the gall-apple, mentioned by Mr Curzon as like "fresh blooming plums." But even the fruit itself, as well as the sort of fruit, is doubtful. Neither Maundrell nor Carne could see or hear any thing of the Apple of Sodom, and neither they nor Lord Bacon believed that it had any existence. The scriptural statement, as to the " vine of Sodom," cannot be doubted, and it seems to be followed by Orosius in his "formatos uvarum racemos." In this case, the Solanum would appear to be the fruit [not the apple] of Sodom alluded to, and mentioned by Michaelis and Hasselquist, especially if what the latter has said be considered, that when the fruit of the Solanum is punctured by an insect, the whole inside is converted into dust, without any loss of fulness or colour.

* Alfred has omitted the sixth chapter of Orosius, Comparatio cladis Sodomiticæ et Romanæ, Haver. p. 43, 44: and, in this IV chapter, he comprises the VII Chap. of Orosius, Haver. p. 45—47.

† Oros. l. I : c. 8, Haver. p. 48—51.

[1] Justin, l. XXXVI, c. 2.

arts he used to work many wonders,—that he could thus well explain dreams; and that, therefore, by this art he became very dear to Pharaoh, the king. He [Pompeius] said that he [Joseph] by the art of magic had so learned divine wisdom, that he had foretold the fruitfulness of the land for those seven years, and the want of the next seven years, that came after; and how, by his wisdom, he stored up in the former seven years, so that during the following seven years, he supported all the people in the great famine. He said that Moses was Joseph's son,[2] and that the arts of magic were naturally from him, because he wrought many wonders among the Egyptians. For the plague, which came upon the land, the bard said that the Egyptians drove out Moses with his people; because, Pompeius and the Egyptian priests said that the godlike wonders, which were wrought in their land, were ascribed not to the true God, but to their own gods, which are idols, because their gods are teachers of the arts of magic. The people still keep up this token of Joseph's law, because, every year, they give up, as tribute to the king, the fifth part of all the fruits of the earth.

2. The famine in Egypt was in the days of the king, who is called Amasis, though it was their custom to call all their kings, Pharaoh. At the same time, Belus reigned in Assyria, where Ninus was before. Among the people, called Argives, Apis reigned as king. At that time, there were not any kings, except in these three kingdoms, but afterwards their example was followed over all the world. It is a wonder, that the Egyptians felt so little thanks to Joseph for his having rid them of the famine, that they soon dishonoured his kindred, and made them all their slaves. So also it is still, in all the world: if God, for a very long time, grant a y one his will, and he then takes it away for a less time, he soon forgets the good, which he had before, and thinks upon the evil which he then hath.[3]

Book I: Chapter VI.[*]

1. Eight hundred winters and ten years before the building of

---

[2] Orosius has:—Filius Joseph Moyses fuit [non secundum carnem, sed secundum naturam, quia filius Mambre fuit Moses;] quem præter paternæ scientiæ hæreditatem etiam formæ pulchritudo commendabat. l. I: c. 8. Haver. p. 48, 49, and note 10.

[3] This is one of those beautiful moral conclusions of Alfred, which he so frequently adds to his version of Boethius.

[*] Oros. l. I: c. 9. Haver. p. 51, 52.

Rome [Orosius, B. C. 1563], Amphictyon, the king reigned in Athens, a city of the Greeks. He was the third king that reigned after Cecrops, who was the first king of that city. In the time of this Amphictyon, there was so great a flood over all the world,—though most in Thessaly, a Grecian city, about the mountains, called Parnassus, where king Deucalion reigned,— that almost all the people perished. King Deucalion received all those, that fled to him in ships to the mountains, and fed them there. Of this Deucalion, it was said, as a proverb, that he was the parent of mankind, as Noah was.

2. In those days, there was the greatest pestilence among the Ethiopians, a people of Africa; so that few of them were left.— It was also, in those days, that Liber Pater overcame the harmless people of India, and almost brought them to an end, either by drunkenness, by lusts, or by manslaughter: nevertheless, after his days, they had him for a god; and they said that he was lord of all war.

Book I: Chapter VII.*

1. Eight hundred and five years, before the building of Rome [B. C. 1558 : Blair, B. C. 1491], Moses led the people of Israel out of Egypt, after the many wonders, that he had done there.— The first was, that their waters became blood.—Then, the second was, that frogs came over all the land of the Egyptians, so many that no work could be done, nor any meat cooked, that there was not nearly as much of the vermin, as of the meat, ere it was cooked.—After that, a third evil was, that gnats came over all the land, both within and without, with fire-smarting bites, and gave endless pain to man and beast.—Then, the fourth was, what was most disgraceful of all, that dog-flies[1] came over all mankind; and they crept upon men, between the thighs, and over all the limbs, as it was well fitting that God should bring low the greatest pride, with the most vile and disgraceful punishment.—The fifth was the death of their cattle.—The sixth was, that all the people had blisters, which painfully burst, and then

---

* Oros. l. I. c. 10. Haver. p. 52—57.

1. A. S. Hûndes fleogan, literally hound's or dog's flies. Orosius wrote :—Post muscas caninas, etiam per interiora membrorum horridis motibus cursitantes, acerbeque inferentes tam graviora tormenta quam turpia. Haver. p. 55,—In Exod. VIII, 21. it is translated,—Ic send eall fleogena cynn.

putrid matter oozed out.—The seventh was, that there came hail, which was mingled with fire, so that it slew both the men and the cattle, as well as all that was waxing and growing in the land.—The eighth was, that locusts came and ate all the blades of grass, that were above the earth ; and also gnawed the germs, and roots.—The ninth was, that there came hail, and so great a darkness, both by day and night, and so thick that it might be felt.—The tenth was, that all the young men and all the maidens, who were the first-born in the land, were killed in one night ; and, though the people would not before bow down to God, they now unwillingly yielded to him. As they before hindered Moses and his people, from going away, so now they were much more eager that they should go from them. But their repentance very soon turned to a worse resolve. The king then, with his people, quickly followed after them, and wished to turn them back to Egypt. Pharaoh the king had six hundred war-chariots, and so great was his other army, that we may know why those were afraid, that were with Moses : there were six hundred thousand men ! However, God lessoned Pharaoh's great multitude, and brought low their overweening pride,—and dried up the Red Sea into twelve ways, before Moses and his people, so that they went over the sea with dry feet. When the Egyptians saw that, then their magicians, Geames, and Mambres,[1] encouraged them ; and they trusted, that, through their arts of magic, they might go the same way. When they were within the passage of the sea, then were they all overwhelmed and drowned. The mark, where the wheels of the war-chariots went, is still to be seen on the sea-shore. God gives this as a sign to all mankind : though the wind, or sea-flood, cover it over with sand, yet it is seen again, as it was before !

2. At that time, there was such excessive heat in all the world,

---

[1]. These names are the addition of Alfred. He evidently refers to the 2nd of Timothy, III, 8, which the Vulgate gives, " Iannes et Mambres restiterunt Moysi." Our authorized version has, " Jannes and Jambres withstood Moses." The names are not given in Exodus VII, 11, but St Paul quotes them from the old records of the Jews. The Targum of Jonathan ben Uzziel writes them " Janis and Jambris ": the Babylonian Talmud, " Joanne and Mambre."—Wiclif's version of A. D. 1380 has, Iammes and Manbres agenstoden Moises— Tyndale in 1534, Cranmer in 1539, and the Geneva in 1557, have, " Iannes and Jambres :" the Rheims in 1582 has, " Iannes and Mambres"—and our authorized version of 1611 has, " Iannes and Iambres." The Iammes or Jammes and Mambres of Wiclif, and of the Vulgate, in Anglo-Saxon times, would be Alfred's " Geames and Mambres."

that men not only suffered much, but nearly all the cattle died. The most southern Ethiopians had burning instead of heat; and the most northern Scythians unknown heat. Then many unwise men used this saying and leasing-speech, that the heat was not for their sins; but said, that it was for the fault of Phaëton,[1] who was only a man.

Book I: Chapter VIII.[*]

1. Six hundred and five years before the building of Rome, [Alfred, B. C. 1358, Orosius B. C. 1528] fifty men, in Egypt, were all slain in one night, by their own sons;[2] and all these men were the offspring of two brothers. When this was done, the brothers were still living. The elder, with whom this evil began, was called Danaüs. He was driven from his kingdom, and fled into the country of Argos, and Sthenelas the king welcomed him there; though he afterwards repaid him with evil, when he [Danaüs] drove him from his kingdom.

2. In those days, it was the custom of Busiris, king of Egypt, to sacrifice all the strangers that visited him, and to offer them to his gods.—Orosius said, I wish now that they would answer me, who say that this world is worse, at present, under Christianity, than it was before in heathenism, when they made such sacrifices, and were guilty of such murder, as I have just said. Where is it now, in any Christian country, that, among themselves, a man needs dread such a thing, as to be sacrificed to any gods! or where are our gods, that desire such crimes as theirs!

3. In those days, Perseus the king went from Greece into Asia with an army, and made war on those people, till they yielded to

---

[1] An allusion is here made to the fabulous account, given by the poets, of Phaëton, who drove the chariot of his father Phœbus or the sun, so near the Ethiopians, that their blood was dried up, and their skin became black, and that therefore this colour is prevalent among the inhabitants of the torrid zone.—The A. S. of the last part of the sentence is very brief:— for Feotontis foracápunge, ánes mannes, for the misconduct or fault of Phaëton, one man,— or for the fault of one man, Phaëton.

[*] Oros. l. I: c. XI. Haver. p. 59, 60. This VIII chap. of Alfred contains the XI and XIIth of Orosius, v. § 4.

[2] This is an error, from taking the Latin of Orosius in too literal a sense: —Inter Danaï atque Ægypti fratrum filios quinquaginta parricidia una nocte commissa sunt. Here, parricidium [quasi patri- vel parenti-cidium, a cædendo] is taken too literally as the murder of a father only, while it denotes the murder of any relation, and, in the present case, the murder of husbands by their wives. Reference is here made to the 50 sons of Danaüs and the 50 daughters of his twin-brother Ægyptus. The daughters of Ægyptus were given in marriage to their cousins, and they all, except Hypermnestra, murdered their husbands in the bridal night. Apollodorus, II, 1, § 5.

him. He gave his own name to the people, so they were afterwards called Persians.

4. Orosius † said, I know well that I must here pass over much, and must shorten the story which I tell,—because the Assyrians bore rule one thousand one hundred and sixty years, under fifty kings,—that it never was without war until Sardanapalus was slain,—and, afterwards, power was given to the Medes. Who is there that can count or relate all the evils, which they did!—Moreover, I will be silent about the most shameful stories of Tantalus and Pelops;—how many scandalous wars Tantalus waged, after he was king;—about the boy Ganymedes, whom he took by force;—and how he killed his own son for an offering to his gods, and he himself dressed him as meat for them.—I shall also weary if I speak about Pelops, and about Dardanus, and about the wars of the Trojans, because their wars are known in history, and in poetry. I must also pass over all things that are said of Perseus and of Cadmus; and also those which are said of the Thebans, and of the Spartans. I will, likewise, pass over in silence the wicked deeds of the Lemniades, and of king Pandion, how cruelly he was driven away by the Athenians, his own people. How Atreus and Thyestres slew their own fathers, I pass over, and all about their hateful adulteries. I also pass over, how Œdipus slew his own father, and his step-father, and his step-son. In those days, were such unbounded evils, that men of themselves said,—the very stars of heaven fled from their wickedness.

Book I : Chapter IX.*

1. Six hundred and sixty years before the building of Rome Orosius B. C. 1313.—Alfred B. C. 1413] there was that very great battle between the Cretans and the Athenians. The Cretans gained the bloody battle, and took all the most noble children of the Athenians and gave them for food to the Minotaur, which was half man and half lion.

2. It was in those days, that the Lapithæ and Thessalians were at war with each other. When the Lapithæ saw the people of Thessaly, on their horses, fighting against them, they called them Centaurs, which are half horse and half man, because they never before saw them fight on a horse.

† Oros. l. I : c. XII. Haver. p. 60—62
* Oros. l. I : c. XIII ; Haver. p. 62, 63.

Book I : Chapter X.*

1. Four † hundred and eighty years before the building of Rome, [Orosius B. C. 1233] Vesoges, king of the Egyptians, waged war in the south of Asia, until the greatest part yielded to him. Vesoges afterwards went with an army unto the Scythians, in the northern parts, and sent his message bearers before to the people, and told them to say without wavering, that they must either pay him for the freedom of the land, or he would harass and bring them to an end by war. They then wisely answered him and said,—" That it was greedy and unjust, that so wealthy a king should go to war with so poor a people, as they were." They, however, told them to say, in answer,—" That they would rather fight against him, than pay taxes." They so followed it up, that they soon put to flight the king with his people, and pursued him, and laid waste all Egypt, save only the fen-lands. They then turned towards home by the west of the river Euphrates. They forced all Asia to pay them taxes, and were there fifteen years, harassing and wasting the land, till their wives sent messengers after them, and told them,—" That they should make their choice : either they should come home, or they would choose other husbands." They then left the country, and went homeward.

2. At the same time,‡ two noble men, called Plynos and Scolopythus,[1] were driven from Scythia. They left the country, and abode between Capadocia and Pontus, near Asia the Less : there they fought till they took the land. After a short time, they were slain, through treachery, by the people of the country. Then their wives, not only the wives of the princes, but of the other men slain with them,—were so sore in their minds and so much grieved, that they took up arms with the view of revenging their husbands. Soon after, they slew all the men, that were in their neighbourbood. They did so, because they wished the other wives to be as full of grief as themselves, that they might afterwards have their help, and be more able to revenge their husbands. Then, all the women came together and waged war

---

* This chapter contains c. XIV, XV, and XVI of Orosius; Haver. p. 63—69.
† Oros. l. I : c. XIV. p. 63, 64.
‡ Oros. l. I : c. XV. Haver. p. 64—67.
[1] Oros. has Scolpythus, Scolopitus, Scolopesius and Scolopetius. Haver. p. 64, note 2.

on the people, and slew all the males, taking much of the land into their hands. In the midst of the war, they made peace with the men. It was afterwards their custom, that, each year, about twelve months, they went together, and then bore children. Whenever the women had children, they reared the females, and slew the males. They seared the right breast of the female children to stop its growth, that they might have a stronger bow; they were, therefore, called in Greek Amazons, that is in English, seared.[1]

3. Two of them, called Marpesia and Lampeto, were their queens. They divided their army into two parts;—one to be at home to hold their land,—the other to go out to war. They afterwards overran the greatest part of Europe and Asia, and built the city of Ephesus, and many others in Asia the Less. Then they sent the greatest part of their army home with their booty, and left the other part there to hold the country. Marpesia, the queen was slain there, and a great part of the army, that was with her. There also, her daughter Sinope became queen. Sinope, the same queen, besides her courage and her manifold virtues, ended her life in maidenhood.

4. In those days there was so great a dread of these women, that neither Europe, nor Asia, nor any of the neighbouring countries could think or plan, how to withstand them, till they had chosen Hercules the giant to overcome them, by all the arts of the Greeks. Yet he durst not venture to attack them with an army, before he began with Grecian ships, called Dulmunus,[2] of which, it is said, that one ship would hold a thousand men. Then he stole upon them unawares by night, and grievously slew and destroyed them; and yet he could not take away their land. In those days, two of their queens, Antiope and Orithyia, were sisters; and Orithyia was taken. After her Penthesileia took the sovereignty, who, in the Trojan war, became very great.

---

1 Orosius has.—Inustis infantium dexterioribus mamillis, ne sagittarum jactus inpedirentur, unde Amazones dictæ. Haver. p. 65.—Diodorus says, it was their custom [τὸν δεξιὸν μαζὸν ἐπικαίειν] to burn the right breast, and it was for this reason that [τὸ ἔθνος τῶν Ἀμαζόνων] the nation of the Amazons received their name [lib. II.]; that is, ἀ without, μαζός a breast. Amongst the various opinions, as to the derivation of this word, one is, that it is composed of ἀ or ἀμ intensive, and ἄζω to dry, parch, or sear. If this be correct, Alfred has given the right explanation—"On Greacisc Amazanas, þæt is on Englisc, fortende."

2 Oros. Longas naves præparârit. Haver. p. 67.

5. It is shameful, * said Orosius, to speak about what then happened, when such poor and such strange women had overcome the most powerful part, and the bravest men of all the world, in Europe and Asia. Then they almost entirely wasted and destroyed the old cities and old towns. After they had done that, they both settled kingdoms, and built new cities ; and, for nearly a hundred years, they ruled the whole world as they wished. Men were then so familiar with every trouble, that they held it as little or no disgrace, and as no evil, that the poor women [the Amazons] so tormented them.

6. Now the Goths came from the bravest men of Germany, whom both Pyrrhus, the fierce king of the Greeks, and Alexander, as well as Julius, the powerful emperor, all feared to meet in battle. —How immoderately, O Romans! do ye murmur and complain, that it is worse with you now, under Christianity, than it then was with the people, because the Goths harassed you a little, and broke into your city, and slew some of you! From their knowledge, and their bravery, they might have had power over you against your will ; but they now quietly ask a peaceable agreement with you, and some part of the land, that they may be able to help you. Ere this, it lay barren and waste enough, and you made no use of it. How blindly many people speak about Christianity, that it is worse now, than it was formerly. They will not think nor know, that, before Christianity, no country, of its own will, asked peace of another, unless it were in need ; nor where any country could obtain peace from another by gold, or by silver, or by any fee, without being enslaved. But since Christ was born, who is the peace and freedom of the whole world, men may not only free themselves from slavery by money, but countries also are peaceable without enslaving each other. How can you think that men had peace before Christianity, when even their women [the Amazons] did such manifold evils in this world!

Book I : Chapter XI.†

1. Four hundred and thirty years before the building of Rome, [Orosius B. C. 1183 : Clinton, B. C. 1192] it happened, that Alexander, [1] the son of Priam, king of the Trojans, took Helen the wife

---

* Oros. l. I : c. XVI. Haver. p. 68, 69.
† Orosius, l. I : c. 17. Haver. p. 70, 71.
1 This second son of Priam was generally called Paris, but he was also known by the

of king Menelaus, from Lacedæmon, a city of the Greeks. About her, there arose that celebrated war, and the great battles of the Greeks and Trojans. The Greeks had a thousand ships of the great Dulmunus²; and they took an oath among themselves that they would never return, till they had wreaked their vengeance. For ten years, they surrounded the city and fought. Who is there that can reckon how many men were slain, on both sides, of which the poet Homer has most clearly spoken! Orosius, therefore, said, I have no need to relate it, because it is tiresome, and also known to many. Nevertheless, whoever wishes to know it, may read in his books, what evils, and what victims there were, by man-slaughter, and by hunger, and by shipwreck, and by various misdeeds, as we are told in histories.

2. War was waged between these people for full ten years. Think then of those times, and of these, which are the better!

3 Then * that war was soon after followed by another. Æneas with his army went from the Trojan war into Italy. In books we may also see in how many labours, and in how many battles he was there engaged.

Book I: Chapter XII.†

1 Sixty four years before the building of Rome, [Orosius B. C. 817: Clinton B. C. 630] Sardanapalus, the king reigned in Assyria, where Ninus was the first king, and Sardanapalus was the last that reigned in that land. He was a very luxurious man, and effeminate, and very lascivious, so that he loved the company of women more than of men. When that was found out by Arbaces, his chief officer, who was set over the country of the Medes, he began to plot with the people over whom he was, to deceive the king, and to withdraw from him all those who, it was feared, would support him. When Sardanapalus found, that he had been deceived, he burnt himself to death; and then the Medes became rulers over the Assyrians. It is hard to say, after this, how many wars there were between the Medes, Chaldeans and

---

name of Alexander ['Αλέξανδρος, ἀλέξω to defend, ἀνήρ, ἀνδρὸς a man] because he valiantly defended the shepherds on mount Ida.

2 This is Alfred's translation of the "mille navium" of Orosius, Haver. p. 70. In page 67 he calls them "longas naves," for which the king puts Dulmunus. v. b. I: ch. X, § 4, note 2.

* Orosius, l. I: c. 18. Haver. p. 72.
† Orosius, l. I: c. XIX. Haver. p. 73—77.

Scythians; but this we may know, that, while such mighty kingdoms were at war, there must have been dreadful slaughter in their battles.

2 After this, king Phraortes reigned in Media. Next to Phraortes, Deïoces reigned, who greatly enlarged the empire of the Medes. After Deïoces, Astyages, who had no son, succeeded to the sovereignty; but he took Cyrus, his nephew, from the country of Persia, as his son. Then, as soon as Cyrus was grown up, being unwilling, as well as the Persians, to be under the power of his uncle and of the Medes, they went to war. Then Astyages, the king, especially turned his thoughts to Harpalus, his chief officer,—trusting that he, with his skill, might withstand his nephew in battle; for the king did not call to mind the many wrongs, that each had done the other in former days, nor how the king ordered his son to be slain, and afterwards to be dressed as meat for the father.[1] However, their quarrel was made up. Then the chief officer went with an army against the Persians; and soon fleeing, he wholly misled the great part of the people, and with treachery put them into the power of the Persian king. In that battle fell the power and dignity of the Medes.

3. When the king had found out the deceit, which the chief officer had practiced against him, he gathered what forces he could, and led them against his nephew. Cyrus, king of the Persians, kept a third part of his army behind him, for this reason, that, if any one in the battle should flee farther than the people that were behind, they should slay him, as they would their enemies. However, it happened that they turned a little to flee, when their wives, running towards them, were very angry, and asked, if they durst not fight, whither they would flee :—that they had no refuge, unless they went into the womb of their wives.[2] Then after the wives had so indignantly reproached them, they turned again, and put his whole army to flight, and took the king. Cyrus then gave his uncle all the honour, which he formerly had, save being king; and ʽhe gave up all that, because Harpalus the chief officer, for-

---

1 This refers to the well known account of Astyages, who, by a shocking artifice, compelled Harpagus to eat the flesh of his only son, because he had not put to death the infant Cyrus. This most horrid fact was made known to the wretched father before he left the table, by exposing to Harpagus the head and hands of his beloved and only son. Herodotus, Clio, § 119. A minute account is given, from § 107 to 129.

2 Num in uteros matrum vel uxorum vellent refugere. Oros. l. I : c. XIX. Haver. p. 77.

merly betrayed him to his own people. But Cyrus, his nephew, gave him the country of Hyrcania to govern. Thus the empire of the Medes ended, of which Cyrus with the Persians, took the government. But the towns, in many countries, which formerly paid tribute to the Medes, caused Cyrus many battles.

4. In * those days, a certain prince called Phalaris, wished to rule in the country of Agrigentum. He was of the island of Sicily; and he tortured the people with immeasurable pain, that they might submit to him.—There was there a certain brass-founder, who could make various images. Then the founder, thinking to please the prince, offered to assist him in torturing the people. He did so, and made an image of a bull in brass, so that, when it was hot, and they put wretched men into it, the noise would be greatest when they were suffering the torment; and also, that the prince should have both his pleasure and his wish, when he heard the torture of these men. When it was heated, and every thing done as the founder formerly promised the prince, he then viewed it, and said:—"That it became no man better to prove the work, than the workman, who had made it."—Then he ordered them to take him, and put him into it.

5. Why do men speak against these Christian times, and say that they are now worse, than they were, when if any one did wrong, even by the desire of kings, they could thereby find no mercy from them? Now, kings and emperors, if any one become guilty, in opposition to them, grant forgiveness for the love of God, according to the measure of the guilt.

Book I: Chapter XIII.†

1. Thirty years before the building of Rome [Orosius B. C. 783.—Clinton, B. C. 432] it was, that the Peloponnesians and Athenians, people of Greece, with all their forces, fought with each other; and the slaughter was so great on both sides, that few of them were left. In those days, the women [Amazons] who were formerly in Scythia, waged war a second time in Asia, and very much wasted and harassed it.

Book I: Chapter XIV.‡

1. Twenty years before [Clinton 30 after] the building of

---

* Orosius, l. I: c. 20, Haver. p. 77. 78.
† Oros. l. I: c. XXI, Haver. p. 79.
‡ Oros. l. I: c. XXI, Haver. p. 79—84.

Rome [Orosius B. C. 773 : Clinton B. C. 723] the Lacedæmonians and Messenians, people of Greece, had been at war with each other for twenty years, because the Messenians were unwilling that the Lacedæmonian maidens should offer with theirs, and sacrifice to their gods. At last, when they had drawn all the people of Greece to the war, the Lacedæmonians surrounded the city of Messene for ten years ; and took oaths that they would never come home till they had avenged themselves. They then reasoned among themselves, and said that they should very soon be without help from their posterity, since they thought they should be there so long, and had confirmed that by their pledges; and that they did more good than evil to their enemies. With that, they resolved that those, who were not at the taking of the oaths, should go home and have children by all their wives. The others surrounded the town, till they had taken it. They were, however, but a little while obedient to them.

2. But they chose an Athenian poet † for their king, and went again with an army against the Messenians. When they came near, then they doubted whether they were able to withstand them. Their king then began to sing and play ; and by his poetry so greatly strengthened their courage, that they said, they were able to withstand the army of the Messenians. However, there were few left on either side, and the people of Greece suffered many years, as well from the Lacedæmonians, the Messenians, and the Bœotians, as from the Athenians ; and they drew many other nations into the same war.

3. Thus, it is shortly stated what formerly happened before Rome was built, which, from the beginning of the world, was four thousand, four hundred, and eighty two years [Blair 3251] ; and, after it was built, our Lord's birth was about seven hundred and ten [1] years [Blair and Clinton 753].

4. Here the first book ends, and the second begins.

† The famous lyric poet Tyrtæus.

1 The dates are not given in the Latin text of Havercamp [see p. 10, note 1] ; but, in the first German edition by Schuszler, 1471 [v. p. 10, note 2], the following gloss has found its way into the text, and Alfred may have translated from a MS. like that, from which Schuszler printed, [see ch. III, § 2, note 1. p. 63] but differing as to the precise dates—Ab orbe condito usque ad urbem conditam anni IIII mille, CCCCLXXXVII. Ab urbe condita usque ad nativitatem Christi, DCCXV colliguntur. Ergo ab origine mundi in adventum Domini nostri anni V mille XCVIIII [5192]. Finit liber primus feliciter."

Alfred's calculation, though differing in particulars, exactly agrees in result with the MS.

Book II : Chapter I.*

1. I ween, said Orosius, that there is no wise man, who knows not well enough, that God created the first man just and good; and all mankind with him. And because he forsook the good, which was given to him, and chose the worse, then God at length avenged it; first on [man] himself, and afterwards on his children, with manifold miseries and wars throughout all the world : yea, he also lessened all the earth's fruitfulness, by which all moving creatures live. Now, we know that our Lord made us : we know also that he is our governor, and loves us with a more just love than any man. Now, we know that all empires are from him : we know also, that all kingdoms are from him ; because all empires are from kingdoms. Now, as he is governor of the less, how much more, think we, that he is over the greater kingdoms, which had such unbounded powers.

2. The first [empire] was the Babylonian, where Ninus reigned :—The second was the Grecian,[1] where Alexander reigned :—The third was the African, where the Ptolemies reigned :—The fourth is [that]of the Romans, who are yet reigning [2] [A.D. 412 ?]. These four chief empires are, by the unspeakable providence of God, in the four parts of this mid-earth. The Babylonian was the first, on the east :—the second was the Grecian, on the north :—the third was the African, on the south :—the fourth is the Roman, on the west. The Babylonian the first, and the Roman the last, were as father and son, as they could easily rule as they wished. The Grecian and African were as if they obeyed,

---

from which Schuszler printed.—Alfred gives 4482 years, from the beginning of the world to the foundation of Rome, and from thence to the birth of Christ 710 years, making a total of 5192 years, from the Creation to Christ.—Schuszler's MS. gives, for the same periods, 4487, to which add 715, making the total of 5192 years, the same as Alfred. They both follow the calculation of Eusebius, who adopted the longer generations of the Septuagint [See Book VI, Ch. 38 § 23 note,]—The shorter generations of the Hebrew Bible are generally followed, as is seen from what is given between brackets in the text, from Dr Blair : thus to 3251 add 753, make 4004 years from the creation to the birth of Christ.

* Oros. l. II. c. I, II, and III, Haver. p. 85—91 : this first chap. of Alfred, therefore, contains the first three chapters of Orosius.

1. Oros. has Macedonicum, the Macedonian empire. Haver. p. 86, 7. Alfred calls it, the Grecian empire, considering Macedonia as part of Greece.

2 Orosius lived in the time of the emperor, Arcadius, who reigned in the east, twelve years, from A. D. 396 to 408; and he wrote this work, in the time of Honorius, the emperor of the west, from A. D. 410 to 416. See Book VI, Chapter 37, § 1. Also, Introduction, p. 14, and 15.

and were subject to them. But I will tell this more fully, that it may be better understood.

3. † The first king was called Ninus, as we said before ;³ and, when he was slain, then Semiramis his queen seized the government, and built the city of Babylon, so that it should be the capital of all the Assyrians; and it stood as such for many years afterwards, until Arbaces, a chief officer of the Medes, slew Sardanapalus, king of Babylon. Then the empire of the Babylonians and Assyrians was brought to an end, and turned to the Medes. In the same year, in which this happened, Procas, Numitor's father, began to reign in the country of Italy, where Rome was afterwards built. This Procas was the father of Numitor and Amulius, and [grandfather⁴] of Silvia. This Silvia was the mother of Remus and Romulus, who built Rome.—This will I say, that the kingdoms were not strengthened by the powers of man, nor by any fate, but by the providence of God.

4. All historians say, that the kingdom of the Assyrians began with Ninus, and the kingdom of the Romans began with Procas. From the first year of Ninus's reign, till the city of Babylon was built, were sixty-four years; also, from the first year, in which Procas reigned in Italy, were sixty four years, ere the city of Rome was built. In the same year, that the kingdom of the Romans began to grow and enlarge, in the days of king Procas, in the same year Babylon fell, and all the kingdom and the power of the Assyrians. After their king, Sardanapalus, was slain, the Chaldeans had free possession of the lands, which were nearest to the city, though the Medes had the government over them, until Cyrus king of the Persians began to reign, and laid waste all Babylonia, and all Assyria, and brought all the Medes under the power of the Persians. It so happened, that, at the same time, in which Babylon fell under the power of Cyrus the king, Rome was freed from the thraldom of the most unrighteous, and the proudest kings, called Tarquins. When the eastern power fell in Assyria, the western power arose in Rome.

5. I shall now, said Orosius, speak much more fully against those who say, that empires have arisen from the power of the fates, [and] not from the providence of God. How justly it hap-

† Oros. l. II. c. 2. Haver. p. 87—89.
3 Book I, c. 2, § 1. p. 61.
4 A. S. eam, uncle.

pened to these two chief empires, the Assyrian and the Roman, [is clear] from what we have lately ‡ said, that Ninus reigned in the eastern empire fifty two years; and, after him, his queen Semiramis, forty two years; and, about the middle of her reign, she built the city of Babylon. From the year in which it was built, the empire lasted one thousand one hundred and nearly sixty four years, before it was deceived, and its power taken away by its own chief officer, Arbaces, and by the king of the Medes; though, as we lately said, there was afterwards, for a little while, about the city, the freedom of the Chaldeans without dominion. So likewise it happened with the city of Rome, about one thousand one hundred and nearly sixty-four years, that Alaric, her governor, and king of the Goths, wished to take away her empire. She, however, after that kept her full power. Yet each of these cities, through the hidden power of God, thus became an example:—First Babylon, through her own chief officer, when he deceived her king; so also Rome, when her own governor, and king of the Goths, wished to take away her empire, God did not suffer it, because of their Christianity—neither because of their emperor's, nor of their own; but they are even yet reigning [A. D. 412?] as well in their Christianity, and in their empire, as by their emperors.

§ 6. This ‖ I say now, because I wish that they understood, who speak evil against the times of our Christianity, what mercy there has been since Christianity came; and, before that, how manifold was the misery of the world;—and also that they may know how seasonably our God, in former times, settled the empires and the kingdoms,—the same, who is now settling, and changing all empires and every kingdom, as he wishes. How like was the beginning, that the two cities had, and how like their days were, both in good and in evil! But the ends of their empires were very unlike; for the Babylonians and their king lived in manifold wickedness and sensuality, without any remorse, [so] that they would not amend, till God humbled them with the greatest disgrace; when he took away both their king and their dominion. But the Romans, with their Christian king, served God, wherefore he gave them both their king and their empire. They, therefore, may mo-

‡ Oros. l. II : c. 3. Haver. p. 89, 90.
‖ Oros. l. II : c. 3. Haver. p. 90, 91.

derate their speech, who withstand Christianity, if they will remember the uncleanness of their elders, and their deadly battles, and their manifold enmity, and their want of kindness, which they had to God, and also among themselves; [so] that they could not obtain any mercy, until the remedy came to them from that Christianity, which they now most strongly blame.

Book II: Chapter II.*

1. The city Rome was built by two brothers REMUS and ROMULUS, about four hundred and forty years [Clinton B. C. 753] after Troy, a city of [Mysia],¹ was laid waste. Soon after that, Romulus sullied their beginning by killing his brother, and afterwards also by his own marriage, and [that] of his companions. Such examples he there set, when they prayed, that the Sabines would give them their daughters for wives, and they refused their prayers. Nevertheless, without their consent, they obtained them by stratagem, in as much as they prayed they would assist them, that they might the more easily sacrifice to their gods. When they granted this, then they seized their daughters for wives, and would not give them back to their fathers. There was the greatest strife about this, for many years, until they were almost entirely slain and brought to naught on both sides. They could, by no means, be made to agree until the wives of the Romans, with their children, ran into the battle, and fell at the feet of their fathers, and prayed that, for the love of their children, they would make an end of the war. So worthily, and so mildly, was the city of Rome hallowed in the beginning, with the blood of a brother, and of fathers-in-law, and with that of [Amulius]² the uncle of Romulus, whom he also slew, when he was king, and afterwards took the kingdom to himself! Thus, in the beginning, did Romulus bless the kingdom of the Romans,—the wall with his brother's blood, and the temples with the blood of their fathers-in-law, and the kingdom with his uncle's blood!

---

* Oros. l. II : c. 2. Haver. p. 92—95.

1 In A. S. Creaca burh, a city of the Greeks. An error—for the city of Priam king of the Trojans, who dwelt in Mysia, in Asia Minor. According to Alfred, the fall of Troy was B. C. 1193; for, 440 years, from the fall of Troy to the building of Rome, added to 753 years from the building of Rome to the birth of Christ, make 1193, B. C. Clinton gives the dates more accurately, thus; 430 years after the fall of Troy, added to 753, make 1183 years B. C. See Book I, 11, § 1.

2 A. S. Numetores—Numitor was grand-father to Romulus. See II, 1. § 3, p. 79.

And he afterwards betrayed his own father-in-law to death, when he enticed him to him, and promised that he would divide the kingdom with him, and then slew him.

2. Then Romulus himself, after this, undertook a war against the Cæninenses,[3] because he had, as yet, little power over the country, but only in the city. Romulus and all the Romans were thought to be mean by other states; because, in their youth, they had been servants to others. When they had surrounded the city of the Cæninenses, and were suffering great famine, they said that they would rather lose their lives by hunger, than leave the war or make peace. They, therefore, fought till they stormed the city; and, after that, they were always at war with the people of the country, on all sides, until they had taken many towns in the neighbourhood.

3. But those kings, that reigned after Romulus, were more wicked and vile than he was, and more hateful and troublesome to the people; but Tarquin, of whom we have spoken before, was the worst of them all,—the most vile, the most lustful and the proudest. He forced to adultery the wives of all the Romans that he could, and suffered his son to lie with Lucretia, the wife of Collatinus, the sister of Brutus, when they were with the army, though by the king they were the most esteemed of the Romans. For that reason, Lucretia then killed herself. As soon as Collatinus her husband, and Brutus her brother, were told of it, they left the army, which they should have commanded; and, when they came home, they drove both the king and his son, and all, who were there, of the king's family, altogether from the kingdom. After that, the Romans set over themselves leaders, whom they called consuls,—that one man should hold the government one year.

Book II : Chapter III.*

1. Two hundred and four years, after the building of Rome [B. C. 509], Brutus became the first consul. Romulus their first king, and Brutus their first consul, were equally cruel.

---

3 The people of Cænina, one of the petty cities of Latium bordering on the Sabines. They were the first to rise up in arms against the Romans to avenge the seizing of their daughters. They were routed by Romulus, and their city probably destroyed, as its name does not occur in history after this time. The victory of Romulus is recorded by Livy 1, 10; Dionys.: II, 32, 33. Eutropius says, Romulus " Cæninenses vicit, Antemnates, Crustuminos, Sabinos . . . ; hæc omnia oppida urbem [Romam] cingunt." l. I, 2.

* Oros. l. II c. 5. Haver. 96, 97.

Tarquinius þa. þæra Romana cyninga, pars. æfter Tyrcea cyninge him onfulcum foryenna þær hæten. þ he þe eað mihte Rinman. þis bruture. ⁊ þis eallum Romanum. heþa bruc sepeþ ampis-þis þæne cyning. embe heora reonotripe; ac him Tarquinius oðegune þegn on gean rande. aþnunfes runu. þær oþer moþigan. ⁊ heora þæn æðþeþ. oðegne of rloh.

Tarcuinius
Se Tarquinius Romana cyning pæf. æfþon Tyrcea cyninge hi onfulcum foryenna þorh hæth. pæche ðe reð meliæ Rinnan þe brutuþe ⁊ þið eallu Romani; heðabrucay gebræð an þis þið þone cyning. smb heþu þond scipe. Ac him Tarquinius oðegne ðegn ongean rande aþpunypr runu ðæf oþþumoðgan. ⁊ heþu þeh æðþh. oðgne of rloz;

2. Romulus slew his brother, and his uncle and his father-in-law. Brutus slew his five sons, and his wife's two brothers; because they said, it would be better, that the Romans should take back the royal family, which they had before; he, therefore, gave orders to bind them, and scourge them with rods, before all the people, and afterwards to cut off their heads with axes.

3. Then Tarquin, who was formerly king of the Romans, drew Porsenna, the king of the Tuscans, to his aid, that he might more easily overcome Brutus and all the Romans. Then, on account of this enmity, Brutus himself proposed a single combat; but Tarquin sent against him another officer, the son of Aruns,[1] the proud; and there each of them slew the other.

4. After that, king Porsenna and Tarquin surrounded Rome, and would have taken it, had it not been for Mucius, a man of the city, who frightened them with his sayings. When they had taken him prisoner, they tortured him in such a manner, that they burnt off his hand, one finger after another, and commanded him to say how many men there were, who had especially conspired against king Tarquin. When he would not tell them, then they asked him, how many men there were, such as he was. He told them, that there were many of those men, and they had also sworn, that they would either lose their own life, or [take] king Porsenna's. When Porsenna heard that, he altogether gave up the siege and the war, which he had already been carrying on for three years.

Book II : Chapter IV.

1. Afterwards [*] there was the Sabine war, which the Romans very much dreaded, and they set over themselves a higher leader than their consul, whom they called Dictator, [B. C. 501] and with the dictator they gained a great victory. After this, the Romans stirred up a great strife between the rich and the poor, and that would have ended in a lasting evil, had they not been quickly reconciled. In those days, the greatest troubles happened to the Romans both by famine and by plague, under the two consuls, Titus and Publius. Then, for a while, they put an end to their contests, though they could not to the famine and the

---

[1] It was Aruns the son of Tarquin the proud and Brutus, who killed each other in single combat. Livy, I, 56 : II, 6 : Eut. I, 10.

[*] Oros. l. II : c. 5, Haver. p. 97—99.

plague, for manifold miseries greatly afflicted the weary city. Before the plague was ended, the Veientes and Etruscans waged war against the Romans, and against the two consuls, Marcus Fabius and Cneius Manlius [B. C. 480]. The Romans marched against them, and took an oath that none of them would return home, unless they had the victory. Though they had the victory, the Romans were so very much slaughtered, that their only consul, who was left, [Fabius] would not have the triumph, which they offered him, on his way home; and he said, that they would have done better to have come to meet him with weeping than with triumph.

2. What they called a triumph † was, when they had overcome any people in battle, it was their custom for all the senators to meet their consuls, after the battle, six miles from the city, with a chariot adorned with gold and precious stones; and to bring two white horses. As they went homeward, the senators rode in chariots after the consuls, and the men, who had been taken, they drove before them bound, that their great actions might be seen in a more lordly state. But, if they brought any people under their power without a battle, when they came homeward, they were to meet them, from the city, with a chariot, mounted with silver, and one of each kind of four-footed beasts, in honour of their consuls. That was then a triumph.

3. Romulus was the first to form a senate; that was a hundred men; though, after a time, there were three hundred of them. These always dwelt within the city of Rome, in order—that they might be their counsellors, and appoint consuls,—that all the Romans should obey them,—and, that they should keep, under one roof, all the wealth which they had gained, either by tribute or by pillage,—that they might afterwards apply it, in common, to the use of all, who were free from bondage.

4. ‡ The consuls, who, in those days, undertook the Sabine war, were of the Fabian family, which was the highest in rank and the most powerful of all the Romans. Now, to this very day, it is sung in verse, what a loss their fall was to the Romans. Moreover many rivers had their names from that battle; and

---

† This account of a Roman Triumph, and the appointment of a senate in § 3, are not mentioned by Orosius: they are added by Alfred.

‡ Oros. l. II : c. 5, Haver. p. 99.

also the gates, through which they marched from Rome to the battle, took, from the family, the names, which they still keep. Afterwards, the Romans chose three hundred and six champions, that they should go alone to fight against as many of the Sabines* ; and trusted that they, by their bravery, would gain the victory ; but the Sabines, by their stratagems, slew them all but one, who made known the sad story at home.—It was not among the Romans only, but it was thus sung in poetic lays over the whole world, that there was care, and labour, and great fear.

5 || While the Sabines and Romans were waging war in the west, Cyrus, king of the Persians, of whom we have before spoken, at the same time, waged war both in Scythia and in India, till he had laid waste almost all the east. He afterwards led an army to Babylon, which was then more wealthy than any other city. But the river Gyndes,—the greatest of all fresh waters, save the Euphrates,—long hindered him from going over, because there were not any boats there. Then one of his officers proposed to go over the river by swimming with two tyncenum,¹ but the stream drove him down. Cyrus, being so vexed in his mind, and so angry with the river, threatened that he would so avenge his officer, that women should wade over it only up to the knees, where it was formerly nine miles broad, when it was flooded. He followed that up by deeds, for he divided it into four hundred and sixty streams, and then went over there with his army; and after that [he passed over] the river Euphrates, which is the largest of all fresh waters, and runs through the middle of the city of Babylon. By digging he divided it into many streams, and afterwards marched with all his people in the water-course and reached the city. How hard it is to be believed, when one states either how any man could build such a city as that was, or afterwards how it was taken!

6.‡ Nimrod, the giant, first began to build BABYLON; and, after him, king Ninus, and then Semiramis his queen finished it, in the middle of her reign. The city was built on open and very level land: it was very fair to look upon, and it was quite a true square. The greatness and firmness of the wall, when stated, is hardly to be believed. It is fifty ells broad, and two hundred ells high,

---

* See Ch. VI, § 1. || Oros. l. II : c. 6, Haver. p. 100, 101.   ‡ Id. p. 102, 103.

1 Mr Thomson suggests—tunchens [tonnikens] barrels, now puncheons—Tyncen, dim. of tunne, a tun; so Ger. tonne gives tönnchen (u : y : : o : ö).

and it is seventy miles and the seventh part of a mile, round. It is built with bricks and earth-tar; and round the wall is a very great dike, in which runs the deepest stream. Outside the dike, a wall is built two ells high. Above, and all round the greater wall, stone towers are built. This very city, Babylon, which was the greatest and first of all cities, is now the least and most desolate. Now the city, which was formerly the strongest, most wonderful and greatest of all works, is as if it were set for a sign to all the world; and as if it spoke to all mankind, and said:—
" Now I am thus fallen and gone away : lo! in me ye may learn and know, that ye have nothing with you so fast and strong, that it can abide for ever!"

7. * At the time, when Cyrus, king of the Persians, stormed Babylon, Croesus, king of the Lydians, came with an army to help the Babylonians; but, when he knew that he could not help them, and that the city was stormed, he went homeward to his own kingdom. Cyrus followed after him, till he took and slew[1] him.—Now, our Christians speak against Rome, because her walls decay with age,—not because she has been disgraced by pillage, as Babylon was: but Rome, for her Christianity, is even yet so shielded, that both she and her empire are fallen more from age, than by the violence of any king.

8. ‡ Cyrus, after that, led an army into Scythia, and there a young king, and his mother Tomyris, marched against him with an army. When Cyrus went over the boundary,—the river Araxes,—there the young king might have stopped his going over; but he would not, because he and his people trusted that they should be able to entrap him, after he was within the boundary, and had taken a place for his camp. When Cyrus understood that the young king would attack him there, and also that the drinking of wine was almost unknown to that people, he went away from the camp, into a hiding place, and left behind him every thing that was good and sweet; the young king, therefore, thought it much more likely, that they had fled, than that they durst practice a stratagem. When they found the camp so

---

* Oros. l. II : c. 4, Haver. p. 103, 104.

1 This is a mistake of the translator. Orosius says,—Croesum cepit, captumque et vita et patrimonio donavit. Herodotus gives all the particulars of Croesus being taken, devoted to the flames and saved by Cyrus, for uttering the name of Solon. Croesus was then taken as the friend and counsellor of Cyrus, and of his son Cambyses.

‡ Oros. l. II : c. 7, Haver. p. 104, 105.

forsaken, they, with great joy, drank so much wine, that they had little power over themselves. Then Cyrus there ensnared and slew them altogether. Afterwards he marched where the king's mother was waiting with two parts of the people, he having entrapped the third part with the king. Then, she—the queen Tomyris,—in great grief, was thinking about the slaughter of the king, her son, and how she might wreak her vengeance. She carried out her wish, by dividing her people into two parts, both women and men; for there, women fight the same as men. She, with one half, went before the king, as if she were fleeing, till she led him into a great plain, and the other half followed after Cyrus. There Cyrus was slain, and two thousand men with him. The queen then commanded the king's head to be cut off, and to be thrown into a vessel, which was filled with man's blood; and thus said :—" Thou, who for thirty years hast thirsted for man's blood, drink now thy fill."

Book II : Chapter V.

1. * Two hundred and six years after the building of Rome [Clinton B. C. 529 : Orosius B. C. 508 : Alfred B. C. 547] Cambyses, son of Cyrus, succeeded to the kingdom of the Persians. When he overcame Egypt, he did what no heathen king durst do before, which was, that he cast off all their worship of idols, and then overthrew them altogether.

2. † After him reigned Darius, who brought back to the Persians all the Assyrians, and Chaldeans, that had formerly gone from them. He then waged war on the Scythians, both because of their slaughter of Cyrus, his kinsman, and also because they would not give him a wife. His army was seven hundred thousand, when he went against the Scythians. The Scythians, however, would not attack him, in a pitched battle; but, when they were scattered over the land, they slew them in parties. This made the Persians have very great fear and dread, lest the bridge, which was at the boundary, should be broken down; for then, they knew not how they could come from thence. Then the king, after a great many of his people were slain, left eighty thousand behind him to carry on the war still longer. He himself went thence into Asia the Less, and laid it waste; and afterwards

---

* Oros. l. II : c. 8. Haver. p. 106.
† Oros. l. II : c. 8. Haver p. 106—109.

against the Macedonians, and against the Ionians, a tribe of the Greeks, and overcame them both. And further, he went against the Greeks, and waged war against the Athenians, because they had helped the Macedonians. As soon as the Athenians knew, that Darius would attack them in battle, they chose eleven thousand men and marched against him. They met the king on the plain, called Marathon. Their leader was named [Miltiades], who did more by bravery, than by great forces: he gained great glory in that battle. Two hundred thousand of the Persians were then slain, and the others put to flight. When Darius had again gathered an army among the Persians, and thought to wreak his vengeance, then he died.

3. ‡ After Darius, his son XERXES succeeded to the empire of the Persians. For five years, he secretly built ships, and gathered forces for the war, which his father had undertaken. There was then with him, from Lacedæmon, a city of the Greeks, a stranger named Demaratus, who told the plot to his country, by writing it on a board, and afterwards covering it with wax. When Xerxes went against the Greeks, he had eight hundred thousand of his own people, and he had asked four hundred thousand from other nations. He had one thousand two hundred of the large ships, Dulmunus; and there were three thousand ships, which carried their food. His whole army was so very large, that it might well be said, it was a wonder where they could find land, on which to encamp, or water to quench their thirst. However, it was then easier to overcome this very great multitude of people, than for us now to reckon or think.

4. * LEONIDAS, king of Lacedæmon, a city of the Greeks, had four thousand men, when he marched against Xerxes, in a narrow land-fastness, and withstood him there in battle. Xerxes scorned the other people so much, that he asked, why there should be any more help against so small an army, save from those only whose anger was before roused, in the former battle, on the plain of Marathon. He formed, into one band, those men, whose kinsmen were slain in that country, for he knew they would be more eager for revenge, than others, and so they were, as they were almost all slain there. Xerxes, being very angry that so many of his people were killed, then marched thither himself, with all the

---

‡ Oros. l. II: c. 9, Haver. p. 109, 110.
* Oros. l. II: c. 9, Haver. p. 110—112.

force that he could bring together, and there they fought for three days till there was a very great slaughter of the Persians. He then gave orders to surround that fastness [fast-land] that they might be attacked on more sides than one. When Leonidas understood that they would thus surround him, he went away and led his army into another faster land, and waited till night. He gave orders that all the citizens, whom he had asked to help him, from other countries, should go away that they might be safe; for he could not bear that any more should die, for his sake, than himself and those of his own country. But he thus spoke and lamented :—" Now we undoubtedly know, that we shall lose our own lives, because of the very great hatred there is in those who are coming after us. Let us, however, plan how we can, in this night, most weaken them, and earn by our deaths the best and most lasting praise." How wonderful it is to say, that Leonidas, with six hundred men, so brought to shame six hundred thousand, by slaying some, and putting the others to flight!

5. Xerxes,[1] with his very great multitude, had twice been so put to shame, on the land, that he wished to try a third time, what he could do in the war with a fleet, and he induced the Ionians, a tribe of the Greeks, to give him their help. They formerly turned to him of their own mind, and promised him that they would first finish the war by themselves. They were afterwards unfaithful to him, when they were fighting on the sea.

6. The leader of the Athenians was called Themistocles. They were to have come to help Leonidas at the former battle, but they could not reach him. Themistocles reminded the Ionians of the old hatred, that Xerxes had shewn towards them: how he had brought them under his power by pillage and by the slaughter of their kinsmen. He begged them also to remember the old faith, and the very great friendship, which, in olden times, they had both with the Athenians, and the Lacedæmonians; and besought them, that, by some stratagem, they would, ere long, turn from Xerxes, the king; that they and the Lacedæmonians might make an end of the war with the Persians. They granted his prayer.

7. When the Persians saw, that those were leaving them, on whom they most trusted to gain the victory, they themselves fled;

---

[1] Oros. l. II: c. 10, Haver. p. 112—114.

and there, many of them were slain, and drowned, and taken. The general of Xerxes was called Mardonius, who earnestly advised, that he should rather go homewards, than abide there longer, lest any strife should arise in his own kingdom. He said, it was better that the further carrying on of the war, with the forces that were still left there, should be intrusted to him, and that the king would have less blame, if the people still went on badly without him, as they did formerly. Xerxes, the king, in great faith, listened to his general, and went thence with some part of his forces. On his way home, he came to the river, over which, when going to the west, he ordered a very large bridge to be built with stone, in token of his victory which he thought to gain in that warfare. The river was then so much flooded that he could not come to the bridge. The king was greatly troubled in his mind, that he was not with his army, and that he could not go over the river. Besides, he was very much afraid, that his enemies were following him. Then a fisherman came to him, and with much trouble brought him over alone. God so humbled the greatest pride, and the greatest undertaking in so worthless a trust in self, that he, who formerly thought that no sea could keep him from covering it with his ships and with his army, afterwards begged for a poor man's little boat that he might save his life.

8. Mardonius,[2] general of Xerxes, left the ships, in which he sailed, and marched to a city in Boeotia a country of the Greeks, and stormed it. After that, they were speedily repaid, when they were put to flight, and to very great slaughter. This victory, and the plunder of the Persian wealth became the great ruin of the Athenians; for, when they were more wealthy, they also became more luxurious. Afterwards Xerxes was thought unworthy of trust by his own people, and his chief officer Artabanus plotted against him, and slew him.—" Oh!" said Orosius, " what joyous times there were, in those days! as they say, who are wranglers against Christianity, that we should now long after such times, as those were, when so many people, in so short a time, were slain in three pitched battles;—that is nineteen hundred thousand from the kingdom of the Persians alone, besides their enemies, whether Scythians or Grecians. Leonidas shewed, in the last battle between him and the Persians, what

[2] Oros. l. II: c. 11, Haver. p. 115—118.

slaughter there was in the country of the Greeks, with manifold deaths, when, at his dinner, he thus spoke to his comrades, before he went to the fight.—" Let us now enjoy this dinner, as those ought, who must take their supper in another world."³ Though he said so then, he afterwards used another saying:— " Though I said before, that we must [go] to another world, yet I trust to God, that he may keep us to better times, than those in which we now are." Leonidas said, that the times were then evil, and he wished that they might afterwards be better. Yet some men say, that they were better then, than they are now. Hence they thus disagree, when both the former were good, as some men now say, and also the latter, as they formerly said, who were not of that mind. If they then spoke not true, then they were not good,—neither then nor now.

9 " Now,⁴ " said Orosius, " we must again turn nearer Rome, where we formerly left off; for, at last, I cannot take notice of all the manifold evils, as I know not the greater part of the world, but what happened in two empires,—in the first, and in the last: these are, the Assyrian and the Roman.

---

3 Oros. has:—Prandete, tamquam apud inferos coenaturi, Haver. p. 188, 4. Inferi often denotes the dead, as distinguished from those living upon the earth; apud inferos must therefore imply, in the lower world, in Hades or the place of departed spirits. Hades denotes the state of the dead, the place of departed souls whether good or bad. It was the general term of Greek writers by which they expressed that state; and this Hades was Tartarus to the wicked, and Elysium to the good. Ἅδης Hades, is from ἀ not, and ἰδεῖν to see,—the invisible receptacle or mansion of the dead, the state of separate souls or the unseen world of spirits, answering to the Hebrew שאול, which Gesenius says " Pro certo habeo, esse pro שעל cavitas, locus cavus et subterraneus, plane ut Germ. Hölle ejusdem originis est atque Höhle, et Lat. coelum est a Gr. κοῖλος hohl, cavus."

Alfred has translated the apud inferos of Orosius, by the Anglo-Saxon on helle, that is, in a concealed place. The A. S. on helle seems to have an analogy with the Hebrew לשאול, and the Greek εἰς ᾅδου, as given in Psalm XVI, 10, לא תעזב נפשי לשאול, which is translated into Greek, οὐκ ἐγκαταλείψεις τὴν ψυχήν μου εἰς ᾅδου, Acts II, 27, and also with the expression in the creeds, descendit ad inferos, descended into hell, and the A. S. he nyðer astah to helle. In the Anglo-Saxon paraphrase of the Psalms, published by Mr Thorpe, Oxon. 1835, the Latin, Non derelinques animam meam in inferno, is thus enlarged in A. S. þu ne forlætst mine sawle, ne min mod to helle. Psalm XV, 10, page 30. Our present English word Hell, in the Anglo-Saxon, denoted a concealed place, from the verb helan or helian to cover, conceal, hele, hill. Even to this very day, they say in Derbyshire, hill or hell it up, for cover it up; and in Cornwall the covering or tiling of a house is called the helling. At the present time, the word Hell, is used only for " the place of the devil and wicked spirits," that word could not, therefore, be employed in the translation, as it would not give the meaning of the A. S. text.

4 Oros. l. II: c. 12, Haver. p. 118.

Book II: Chapter VI.[1]

1. Two hundred and eighty years after the building of Rome [Alfred B. C. 473 ? Orosius 463 ? Clinton 477]—the same year, in which the Sabines led the Romans into a snare,[2] when three hundred and six men from each side went to fight alone, a great wonder was seen in the heavens, as if all heaven were burning. That token was made very clear among the Romans by the great raging[3] of the plague, which soon after came upon them, so that half of them died, and their two consuls, who were then over them. Yea, at last, those, that were left, were so wearied, that they could not put the dead into the earth.

2. Soon afterwards, all their slaves fought against their masters, and took from them their head-place, which they called Capitolium. They had much fighting about it, till they had slain the only consul, whom they had lately chosen. The masters, however, in the end, had a poor victory.—Soon after that, in the following year, the Romans fought with the Æqui Volsci, and there was very great slaughter. The part, that was left, was driven into a fastness, and there they would have died of hunger, if those, who were at home, had not helped them. They, at that time, [B. C. 458] gathered all the men, that were left there, and took a poor man [Cincinnatus] for their consul, when he was in his field and had his plough in his hand. They then marched into the country of the Volsci and let the Romans free.

3. After[4] that, for a full year, the earth was quaking and opening over all the Roman empire. Every day, men came to the Senate times without number, and told them of cities, and of towns, sunk into the earth; and they themselves were, every day, in dread lest they also should sink into the earth. Afterwards there came so great a heat upon the Romans, that all the fruits of

---

1 Oros. l. II: c. 12, Haver. p. 119, 120.
2 See, Book II: chap. 4, § 4.
3 A. S. Wol-bryne, the pest-fire, the burning or rage of a pest.
4 Abridged from Oros. l. II: c. 13; but Alfred adds to the following statement of Orosius: Per totum fere annum tam crebri tamque etiam graves in Italia terræmotus fuerunt, ut de innumeris quassationibus ac ruinis villarum oppidorumque, assiduis Roma nuntiis fatigaretur. Deinde ita jugis et torrida siccitas fuit, ut præsentis tunc futurique anni spem gignendis terræ fructibus abnegârit. Haver. p. 122, 4—9.

the earth, yea also they themselves nearly died away. Then, there was the greatest famine there.

4. After [5] that, the Romans chose ten consuls where they formerly had two, that they might overlook their laws. One of them was named Claudius, who wished to take to himself the power of the others, though they would not grant it, but strove against him, till some of them turned to him, and others would not. But being divided into two parties, they strove so among themselves, that they forgot the foreign wars, which they had on their hands, till all the other consuls agreed together, and beat the one named Claudius to death with clubs. Afterwards they guarded their own land.

5. "Lightly [6] and shortly," said Orosius, "I have spoken of their wars at home, though to them they were almost the greatest and the most fearful, which also the sulphurous fire of Etna betokened, when it sprang up from the gate of hell in the land of Sicily, and slew many of the Sicilians, with fire and with stench. What hardships were then, to what they are now! But, after it became Christian, the fire of hell was thenceforth so calmed (as all evils were) that it is now without such marks of mischief as it formerly had; though each year it is broader and broader.

Book II: Chapter VII.

1. Three [7] hundred and one years after the building of Rome, [Alfred B. C. 452] the Sicilians quarrelled among themselves. Half of them drew over the Lacedæmonians to help them, and the other half the Athenians a people of Greece, who formerly fought together against the Persians. But, after they had fought

---

5 Abridged from Oros. l. II; c. 13, Haver. p. 120, 121. Potestas consulum decemviris tradita. Haver. p. 121, 1.—The Decemviri or the Ten men, were appointed about 451 B. C. and existed only for two years, till B. C. 449. They drew up a body of Laws divided into ten tables: the Decemviri of the following year added two new tables. These were engraved on tables of metal and they constituted the Twelve Tables, the foundation of the Roman laws. This was the first Roman code, which was not superseded for more than a thousand years, till the completion of the Emperor Justinian's Corpus Juris Civilis, in A. D. 564.

6 Much abridged from Oros. l. II: c. 14, Haver. 123—127; though Alfred has given the impression of his age, respecting volcanos, for Orosius only speaks thus of Etna.— "Aetna ipsa, quæ tunc cum excidio urbium atque agrorum crebris eruptionibus æstuabat, nunc tantum innoxia specie ad præteritorum fidem fumat. Haver. 124, 2—4.

7 Oros. l. II: c. 15, Haver. p. 128, 129.—Chapters XVI and XVII of Oros. are omitted by Alfred.

against the Sicilians, they then also fought among themselves, until Darius, king of the Persians, because of the wars of his forefathers, came to the help of the Lacedæmonians against the Athenians. Was it a great wonder, that all the power of the Persians, and of the Lacedæmonians could more easily lay waste the city of Athens, than make that people yield to their wills?

2. Soon [8] after that, in the same year, Darius, king of the Persians died; and his two sons Artaxerxes and Cyrus fought about the kingdom, till one of them drew most of the people against the other, and they carried on the quarrel with battles, until Cyrus, the younger of them, was slain.—In those days,[9] there was a city in Africa, which was near the sea, until a sea-flood came and laid it waste, and drowned the people.

Book II : Chapter VIII.

1. Three[1] hundred and fifty-five years after the building of Rome, [B. C. 398] the Romans beset the city Veii, ten years. The siege did more harm to them, than to those who were within both in hunger and in cold; moreover, they themselves were often pillaged, as well as their land at home. They would then have soon perished before their enemies, if they had not broken into the city by a device, which was most shameful, though it was afterwards thought most worthy of them; that was to dig under the earth, from their camp until they came up within the city, and stole upon them by night, in the first sleep, and altogether laid the city waste. This useful device, though it was not honourable, was found out by their Dictator, Camillus.

2. Soon afterwards there was the war of the Romans, and of the Gauls,[2] who were from the city Sena, which at first arose, because the Gauls had besieged the city, Tuscia. The Romans then sent ambassadors to the Gauls, and asked them to make peace with them. After they had thus spoken, on the same day, the Gauls attacked the city. When they saw the Roman ambassadors fighting against them with the town's-people, they were so

---

8 Abridged from Oros. l. II : c. 18, Haver. p. 138, 139.

9 Oros. is more precise,—Tunc etiam Atalante civitas, Locris adhærens, terræ contigua, repentino maris inpetu abscissa, atque in insulam desolata est. Haver. p. 139, 14.

1 Oros. l. II : c. 19, Haver. p. 143—143.

2 Galli Senones, urbem Clusini, quæ nunc Tuscia dicitur, obsederunt. Oros. l. II : c. 19, Haver. p. 140, 12. 13.

angry at it, that they left the city; and, with all their forces, marched against the Romans. Fabius [3] the consul, came against them in battle, and he was soon after chased into the city of Rome, and the Gauls followed him, till they were all within it. Just as if one were mowing a meadow, they were slaying without any regard, and pillaging the city. The remembrance of the slaying of the consul, Fabius, is still kept up in the name of the river.

3. "I ween," said Orosius, "that not any man can tell the harm, which was done to the Romans, at that time, even if they had not burnt the city, as they then did. The few, that were left there, gave a thousand pounds of gold for their lives; and they did that chiefly, because they thought that they should afterwards be their subjects. Some fled into that fastness, which they called Capitolium. They beset these, till some of them died of hunger, others fell into their hands, and they afterwards sold them to other people for money."

4. "How," said Orosius, "does it now seem to you, who slander the times of Christianity? After the Gauls went out of the city, then what joyful times the Romans had! when the wretches, who were left there, crept out of the holes in which they lurked, and so wailed, as if they had come from the other world, when they looked around upon the burnt and wasted city; so that they then had a peculiar dread, where they formerly had the greatest joy. Besides this evil, they had neither food within, nor friend without."

5. "These were the times, after which the Romans now sigh, and say that the Goths have made worse times, than they had before, although they plundered them only for three days; and the Gauls were formerly plundering within the city, and burning it, for six months; and still, they thought that they had not done them harm enough, unless they also took away their name, that they should be no more a people. Moreover, the Goths, for the honour of Christianity, and through the fear of God, plundered there a less time, and neither burnt the city, nor had the wish to take from them their name, nor would they harm any of those, who had fled to the house of God, though they were heathens;

---

3 Oros. has Fabius, but Haver. says, "Nullus Fabius hoc tempore consul fuit"; sed eo anno, quo Roma capta est, tres Fabii Tribuni militum consulari potestate fuerunt. Haver. p. 141, note 9.

but had much rather that they would settle among them in peace. In former times, scarcely any could flee away, or hide themselves from the Gauls. When the Goths plundered them, for a little while, one could only hear of few being slain. There was seen God's anger, when their brazen beams and their statues could not be destroyed by the fire of the Gauls; but, at the same time, fire from heaven consumed them."

6. " Now," said Orosius, " as I have a long story to tell, I think I cannot end it in this book, I shall therefore begin another."

Book III: Chapter I.[4]

1. Three hundred and fifty-seven years after the building of Rome [Orosius, B. C. 389: Alfred, B. C. 396], in the days, in which the Gauls had laid Rome waste, the chief and most shameful peace was made between the Persians and the Lacedæmonians, in the country of Greece. After the Lacedæmonians had often overcome the Persians, then the Persians proposed, that they should have peace with them, for three years, and with all who wished, and whoever would not, that they would wage war against them. The Lacedæmonians gladly agreed to that peace, for they had little fear from such an agreement. Hence it may be clearly understood, how great a wish they had for the war, as their bards sang in their lays, and in their false stories. " Does not such a war seem pleasant to thee," said Orosius, " and the times more so, that one's enemy may so easily be restrained by words?" After the Lacedæmonians had overcome the city of the Athenians —their own people,—they raised themselves up, and began to wage war on every side, both against their own countrymen and against the Persians, and against Asia the Less, and against the city of Athens, which they had formerly laid waste: for, the few that had fled out of it, had entered into the city again, and had drawn over the Thebans, a people of Greece, to help them. The Lacedæmonians were so lifted up, that they themselves, and all the neighbouring nations thought, that they could have power over them all. But the Athenians, with the help of the Thebans, withstood them, and beat them in battle.

2. After that, the Lacedæmonians chose, for their leader, Der-

---

[4] Alfred omits the preface of Orosius to this third book. Chapter I, paragraphs 1—4, are abridged from Oros. l. III: c. 1, Haver. p. 146—152.

cyllidas, [B. C. 397] and sent him into Persia with forces to fight against them. The Persians then came against him with their two officers: one was called Pharnabazus, the other Tissaphernes. As soon as the leader of the Lacedæmonians knew, that he must fight against two armies, it seemed to him more reasonable to make peace with one, that he might, the more easily, overcome the other. He did so, and sent his messenger to the one, and told him to say, that he wished more earnestly for peace, than for war. The officer then, in good faith, received the messenger with peace; and the Lacedæmonians, the while, routed the other officer.

3. Afterwards the king of the Persians took his power from the officer, who had before made peace with the Lacedæmonians, and gave it to a man, banished from Athens, a city of Greece, who was named Conon, and sent him with a fleet from the Persians against the Lacedæmonians. The Lacedæmonians sent to the Egyptians, and asked help from them; and they gave them one hundred large boats with three rows of oars. The Lacedæmonians had, for their leader, a wise, though a lame man, who was called Agesilaus; and they had a by-word "that they would rather have a lame king, than a lame kingdom." They afterwards engaged on the sea, and there fought so very fiercely, that they were nearly all killed, and neither could gain the victory. There the power and the glory of the Lacedæmonians were laid low. "I ween," said Orosius, "that not any two leaders fought more equally."

4. After that, Conon again led an army upon the Lacedæmonians; and in all things he utterly laid waste the land outside the city; so that they, who formerly yearned for power over other nations abroad, then thought it well if they could keep themselves from slavery at home. One of the Lacedæmonian leaders was called Lysander: he attacked Conon with ships, when he went from the Lacedæmonians, and there was much slaughter of the people on both sides. So many of the Lacedæmonians were slain there, that, afterwards, they neither kept their name, nor their power. But their fall was the rise of the Athenians, so that they were able to revenge the old wrongs which, in former days, they often bore. They and the Thebans gathered themselves together, and attacked the Lacedæmonians in battle, and routed them, and drove them into their city, and afterwards besieged them. Then the citizens sent to Agesilaus, who was with their army in Asia, and begged that

he would quickly come home and help them. He did so, and came suddenly upon the Athenians and routed them. The Athenians were then in great dread, lest the Lacedæmonians, because of the little advantage which they had gained, should reign over them, as they did formerly. They, therefore, sent into Persia after Conon and prayed that he would help them. He granted their prayer, and came to them with a great fleet and destroyed almost all the Lacedæmonians, and made them feel that they were both poor and weak. After that, Conon came to Athens, his old birth-place; and he was welcomed there with great joy by the citizens. He there caused a lasting remembrance of himself, by forcing both the Persians and the Lacedæmonians to repair the city, which they had formerly sacked,—and also by bringing the Lacedæmonians, who before had long been their enemies, to be thenceforth under the city of Athens. It was after these wars, that the Persians offered peace to all the people of Greece. It was not because they wished to do them any good; but because, being at war with the Egyptians, they thought to bring that war the more easily to an end.

5. But [5] the Lacedæmonians, in the mean time, had a greater wish for war, than the power, and rather made war on the Thebans, than sought their help; and stole up on them with small bands, until they overcame the city of the Arcadians. After that, the Thebans marched against them with an army, and the Lacedæmonians brought another against them. When they had fought for a long time, then the general [6] of the Lacedæmonians called to the Arcadians, and besought them to stop the fight, that they might bury the dead, which were slain. It is a custom with the Greeks, that by this saying it is shewn which side has the victory.

6. Thus I wished to tell, said Orosius, how the war of the Greeks was first raised from the city of the Lacedæmonians,—and, in the language of history, to describe it,—first against the city of the Athenians, and then against the Thebans,—the Boeotians,—and the Macedonians : these were all people of Greece : then against

---

[5] Abridged from Oros. l. III : c. 3, Haver. p. 152—155.
[6] Orosius is more explicit :—In eo prælio Archidamus, dux Lacedæmoniorum, vulneratus, quum jam cædi suos ut victos videret, occisorum corpora per præconem ad sepulturam poscit : quod signum victoriæ traditæ inter Græcos haberi solet. Thebani autem ha confessione contenti, dato parcendi signo finem dedere certamini. Haver. p. 153, 3—8.

Asia the Less, and against the greater; and then against the Persians, and the Egyptians. I shall also hereafter tell the history of the Romans, which I had begun.

Book III : Chapter II.[7]

1. Three hundred and seventy-six years after the building of Rome [B. C. 377.], there was an earth-quake in Achaia; and two cities, Bura and Helice, sank into the earth. I may also speak of a like beginning, in our own times, though it had not the same end,—that Constantinople, a city of the Greeks, had the same quaking, and it was foretold by soothsayers that it should sink into the earth; but it was shielded by the Christian emperor Arcadius, and by the Christian people, who were in the city. This shewed Christ to be the help of the lowly, and the fall of the high-minded. I remember more of this, than I have spoken, even altogether : if any one wish to know more of it, he must seek it for himself.

2. It was in those days, that the Volsci and Falisci, who formerly fought seventy years against the Romans, then overcame them and pillaged their land. Soon after that, the Sutrini waged war on the Romans, even to the gates of the city. The Romans afterwards quickly repaid them with war and with pillage, and put them to flight.

Book III : Chapter III.[8]

1. Three hundred and eighty-three years after the building of Rome, [Orosius, B. C. 369 : Alfred, B. C. 370] when Lucius, whose other name was Genucius, and Quintus, whose other name was Servilius, were consuls in Rome, the great pestilence was in the land,—not as it is wont from unseasonable weather, that is from wet summers, and from dry winters, and from parching spring-heats, and very heavy harvest-rains, and after-heats; but a wind came off the wold of Calabria, and the plague with the wind. This pestilence was upon the Romans full two years, over all men alike : though some died, others, grievously afflicted, got over it. Then their priests said, that their gods ordered them to build an amphitheatre, that they might then have heathen games therein, and their devil worship, which were plainly all uncleanness.

---

[7] Oros. l. III : c. 3, Haver. p 155, 156.
[8] Oros. l. III : c. IV, V, Haver. p. 157—159.

2. Here,[9] said Orosius, may those, who withstand Christianity, now answer me, how, by their sacrificing and by their devil-worship, their gods gave help in the pestilence; but they did not understand by what magic and by what craft the devils did it, (it was not the true God,)—that they troubled the men with that evil, to the end that they might trust to their offerings, and their idolatries, and that they might thence come to their souls, and harass them with the greatest blasphemy. But their amphitheatres were then without number, and [too] manifold for me now to speak of; for, "Thou, father Augustine, hast plainly told them, in thy books[1]; and I will teach every one to look there, who wishes to know more of it."

3. Afterwards,[2] in the same year, the earth opened within the city of Rome. Then their priests said again, that their gods told them to give a living man, as it seemed to them, that they had too few of their dead. The earth so kept yawning till Marcus, whose other name was Curtius, with horse and with weapons, leaped into it: and the earth then closed together.

Book III : Chapter IV.[3]

1. Three hundred and eighty-eight years after the building of Rome, [B. C. 365.] the Gauls ravaged the Roman lands to within three miles of the city, and might easily have taken it, if they had not stopped there: for, the Romans were so frightened, and so out of heart, that they thought they could not guard the city. But, in the morning, Titus, their leader, whose other name was Quinctius, attacked them with an army. There Manlius, whose other name was Torquatus, fought a single combat with a man of Gaul, and slew him; and Titus Quinctius partly routed and partly slew the others. By this we may understand how many must have been slain there, when so many thousands of them were taken.

Book III : Chapter V.

1. Four[4] hundred and two years, after the building of Rome, [B. C. 351] the ambassadors of Carthage came to Rome, and pro-

---

9 This paragraph is amplified by Alfred.
1 Augustine's "City of God," l. III : c. 17. See Introduction to this translation, p. 14, for a short account of this work of S. Augustine.
2 Oros. l. III : c. 5, Haver. p. 158, 159.
3 Oros. l. III : c. 6, Haver. p. 159, 160.
4 Oros. l. III : c. 7, Haver. 161, 162.

posed that there should be peace between them, because they were then making war on a country,—that was on Beneventum. When the ambassadors came to Rome, then came also with them very great misfortune and misery of many nations, which increased for a long time afterwards. So the stars of heaven made it known in those times,[5] for it was night till mid-day; and, in summer time, it hailed stones over all the Romans.

2. In those days,[6] Alexander was born among the Greeks, as if a great storm had come over all the mid-earth; and Ochus, king of the Persians, whom by another name they called Artaxerxes, after he had plundered Egypt, then went into the land of the Jews, and plundered many of them. Afterwards he settled many of them in the land of Hyrcania, near the Caspian sea; and they are settled there even until this day, with extensive nations, in the hope, that God will some time bring them thence to their own land.[7]—Then Artaxerxes sacked Sidon, which, in those days, was the most wealthy city of the Phœnicians.[8]

3. Then[9] the Romans began the Samnite war about the land of the Campanians. They fought about it, long and often with alternate victories. Then the Samnites drew over to their side, Pyrrhus, king of Epirus, the greatest enemy of the Romans.[1] That war, however, was stilled for a while, because the Carthaginians began to wage war against the Romans.

4. "Since that war began, if there be any one," said Orosius, "who can find in historians, that the doors of Janus were shut, (save in one year, and that was because the Romans lay, all that year, under a pestilence,) it was first in the time of Octavianus Cæsar.[2]" The Romans had formed that building with this one design, that, on whatever side they should be at war,—whether south, or north, or east, or west, then they undid the door, which

---

5 Orosius says:—Tunc etiam nox usque ad plurimam diei partem tendi visa est: et saxea de nubibus grando descendens, veris terram lapidibus verberavit. l. III, c. 7, Haver. p. 161, 11—13.

6 Quibus diebus etiam Alexander Magnus, vere ille gurges miseriarum, atque atrocissimus turbo totius Orientis est natus. Haver. p. 161, 13—15.

7 Quos ibi usque in hodiernum diem amplissimis generis sui incrementis consistere, atque exinde quandoque erupturos, opinio est. Haver. p. 162, 3—5.

8 Sidonem opulentissimam Phœnicisprovinciæ urbem delevit. Haver. p. 162, 6.

9 Oros. l. III : c. 8, Haver. p. 162, 163.

1 Bellum ancipiti statu gestum, Pyrrhus, vel maximus Romani nominis hostis, excepit. Haver.. 162, 28, 29.

2 This account of the temple of Janu is one of the numerous additions made by Alfred.

opened on that side, they thus knew whither they should march. As soon as they saw any of the doors open, then they drew their clothing above the knee, and made themselves ready for war. Thus they knew that they had not peace with some people. When they had peace, then all the doors were shut, and they let their clothing [3] down to their feet. But when Octavianus Cæsar took the empire, then the doors of Janus were shut, and there was peace and quietness over all the mid-earth.

5. Afterwards [4] the Persians made peace with the Romans: then all nations wished to be under the Romans, and to be ruled by their laws. They loved peace so much, that they would rather have Roman kings, than those of their own race. Thus it was plainly shewn, that no earthly man could cause such love and such peace, as there was then over all the world [5]. But it was because, in those days, Christ was born, who is the peace of the dwellers in heaven and earth. This was also plainly shewn by Octavianus, when the Romans wished to offer sacrifice to him, as was their custom, and said that the peace was from his power. But he eschewed both the sacrifice and the saying; and moreover said himself that the peace was not his;—nay also, it could not be any earthly man, that could bring such peace to all the world, as no two nations could formerly have; and, what was less, no two families.

Book III: Chapter VI.

1. Four [6] hundred and eight years after the building of Rome [Orosius B. C. 344, Alfred B. C. 345], it happened that the Romans and the Latins were at war. In the first battle, the consul of the Romans, Manlius, whose other name was Torquatus, was slain; and their other consul, called Decius, and by his other name, Mus, killed his own son, because he broke their fixed order, which was that they should press upon the Latins all together. But one broke out there from the army of the Latins, and challenged to single combat; and the consul's son came against him,

---

3 They put on the Roman Toga or long robe, instead of the short military dress.

4 Oros. l. III : c. 8, Haver. p. 163, 164.

5 Cognoscere faterique coguntur, pacem istam totius mundi et tranquillissimam serenitatem, non magnitudine Cæsaris, sed potestate filii Dei, qui in diebus Cæsaris adparuit, exstitisse, nec unius Urbis imperatori, sed creatori Orbis universi, Orbem ipsum generali cognitione paruisse. Oros. l. III : c. 8, Haver. p. 164, 6—10.

6 Oros. l. III. c. 9. Haver. p. 164, 165.

and slew him there. For that fault, his father then ordered him to be put to death : because of that death, the Romans would not, as was their custom, offer the triumph to the consul, though he had gained the victory.

2. In the year following, there was a woman, named Minucia, who, in their manner, should have been a nun [7] [vestal virgin]. She had vowed to the goddess Diana, that she would ever live a life of virginity. Then she soon forlay herself. Because of that sin, by which she belied her vow, the Romans buried her alive. And now, in remembrance of the sin, the ground, where she was buried, is yet, to this day, called Sinfield.[8]

3 Soon[9] afterwards, in the time of the two consuls, Claudius, whose other name was Marcellus, and Valerius, whose other name was Flaccus, it then happened,—" though to me, said Orosius, it is scandalous—that some Roman women were under such phantasy,[1] and such mad fervour, that, as far as they could, they wished to kill every person, both female and male, with poison, and to give it them to take in meat or in drink. And they did it for a long time, before the people knew whence the evil came,—but that they said; it came from above out of the air,—till it was laid open by a male-slave.[2] Then all the women were called before the Roman senators, of whom there were three hundred and eighty ; and were there forced to take the same, which they had formerly given to others; and they died there forthwith before all the men.

Book III : Chapter VII.

1. Four[3] hundred and twenty two years after the building of Rome, [Orosius and Alfred, B. C. 331] Alexander, king of the

---

7 Orosius calls her Virgo vestalis, Haver. p. 165, 9 ; but Alfred styles her, Nunne, a nun. The Vestal virgin made a vow of perpetual chastity. This custom of the Roman priesteses led king Alfred, not unreasonably, to identify the Vestal virgin with a nun.

8 Vivaque obruta in campo, qui nunc Sceleratus vocatur. Haver. p. 165, 10.

9 Oros. l. III : c. 10. Haver. p. 165, 166.

1 Incredibili rabie et amore scelerum Romanæ matronæ exarserunt. Oros. l. III : c. 10, Haver. p. 165, 25. 26.

2 This differs from Oros. who says :—Cum existente quadam ancilla indice et convincente primum multæ matronæ ut biberent, quæ coxerant, venena, compulsæ : deinde simul atque hausêre, consumptæ sunt. Tanta autem multitudo fuit matronarum in his facinoribus consciarum, ut trecentæ septuaginta damnatæ ex illis simul fuisse referantur. Haver. p. 166, 2—6.

3 Oros. l. III : c. 11, Haver. p. 166, 167.

Epirotæ, uncle of the great Alexander, began to wage war against the Romans with all his power, and settled at the boundary of the Samnites and the Romans, and drew over the neighbouring country-people on both sides to help them, until the Samnites fought with them, and slew the king.—" Now being reminded here of this Alexander," said Orosius, " I will also then call to mind the great Alexander, the other's nephew, when, in the course of time, I have told about the wars of the Romans."

2. I must,[4] however, turn back, that I may tell some small part of Alexander's deeds; and how Philip, his father, four hundred years after the building of Rome, [Orosius and Alfred, B. C. 353 : Clinton, B. C. 359] took Macedonia in Greece, and held it twenty-five years ; and, within these years, he over-ran all the kingdoms that were in Greece. One was the Athenians :—another was the Thebans :—a third was the Thessalians :—a fourth the Lacedæmonians :—a fifth the Phocians :—a sixth the Messenians :—a seventh the Macedonians, which he had first. Philip, when he was a boy, was given by his own brother, Alexander, who then held the kingdom of Macedonia, as a hostage to the Thebans,—to Epaminondas, the brave prince, and the most learned philosopher, and was taught by him, for the three years, when he was there. Then his brother Alexander was slain by his own mother,[5] though she formerly slew her other son also, because of her lewdness. She was Philip's step-mother. Then Philip succeeded to the kingdom of Macedonia, and held it all the while in great danger and in great trouble, because both strangers from other lands fought against him, and also his own people plotted against his life, so that, at last, he would rather fight abroad, than be at home. His first battle was against the Athenians, and he overcame them : after that against the Illyrians, whom we call Bulgarians; and he slew many thousands of them, and took their chief city, Larissa. Afterwards he turned the war upon the Thessalians, chiefly with the wish of drawing them over to help him, because of their skill in war, and because they were known to be the best of all people in horsemanship. They turned to him at first, both for their fear and for his flattery. With their force and with his own, he then

---

4 Oros. l. III : c. 12. Haver. p. 167.

5 So says Orosius, who follows Justin ; but Haver. adds, " Eurydices innocentiam ex testimonio scriptorum, qui eodem tempore vixerunt, demonstravimus. p. 168, note 4.

made up an army both of horse and foot, such as could not be overcome.

3. After[6] Philip had brought the Athenians and Thessalians under his power, he took for his wife the daughter of Aruba, king of the Molossi : she was called Olympias. Aruba thought that he should enlarge his kingdom, when he gave his daughter to Philip; but he deceived him in that hope, and took all that Aruba had, and afterwards banished him till the end of his life. Then Philip fought against the city of Methone, in the kingdom of the Thebans[7]; and there, one of his eyes was shot out with an arrow. He, nevertheless, took the city, and killed every one, that he found therein. By his wiles, he afterwards overcame all the people of Greece, because it was their custom that every city should have its own government, and none would be under another, but they were often at war among themselves. Then they asked Philip first from one city, then from another, to help them against those with whom they were at war. When he had overpowered those, against whom he was then at war, and also the people, who before asked him for help, he then brought both under his sway. Thus he beguiled all the Greeks into his power.[8]

4. When[9] the Greeks understood that, and also being very angry, that one king should so easily, almost without any struggle, bring them under his power, just as if they were enslaved to him; he, indeed, often sold them into slavery to other nations, whom formerly none could take in war,—they then all rose in war against him; and he humbled himself to the people, whom he there most sorely dreaded. These were the Thessalians, whom he prevailed upon to join him in war against the Athenians. When they came to the boundary with their army, they had closed their passes.[1] As Philip could not get within to wreak his

---

6 Oros. l. III: c. 12, Haver. p. 168—170.
7 Methone, where Philip lost his eye, was in Macedonia, on the Thermaic gulf.
8 Græciam prope totam, consiliis præventam, viribus domuit. Quippe Græciæ civitates dum imperare singulæ cupiunt, imperium omnes perdiderunt: et dum in mutuum exitium sine modo ruunt omnibus perire, quod singulæ amitterent, oppressæ demum servientesque senserunt : quarum dum insanas concertationes Philippus, veluti è specula observat, auxiliumque semper inferioribus suggerendo, contentiones, bellorum fomites, callidus doli artifex fovet, victos sibi pariter victoresque subjecit. Haver. p. 169, 5—10, and p. 170, 1—3.
9 Oros. l. III: c. 12, Haver. p. 170—172.
1 Igitur Philippus ubi exclusum se ab ingressu Græciæ, præstructis Thermopylis videt, paratum in hostes bellum, vertit in socios: nam civitates, quarum paulo ante dux fuerat ad gratulandum ac suscipiendum patentes hostiliter invadit, crudeliter diripit : omnique societatis conscientia penitus abolita, conjuges liberosque omnium sub corona vendidit, templa

vengeance, he then turned upon those, who alone were faithful to him, sacked their city, killed all the people, and overthrew their places of worship, as he did all that he found everywhere, yea also his own; until the priests told him, that all the gods were angry with him, and withstood him. Although they were all angry with him, for the twenty-five years in which he was at war, he was not overcome. Then he marched into the land of Cappadocia, and there by treachery slew all the kings.[2] Afterwards all the Cappadocians gave way to him. He then turned against his three brothers, and one he slew, and two fled into the city of Olynthus, which was the strongest and most wealthy[3] in the kingdom of Macedonia. Philip marched after them, and stormed the city, and slew the brothers and all that were therein. The three were not the brothers of Philip by his mother, but by his father.

5. At that time,[4] in the country of the Thracians, two kings, who were brothers, were quarrelling about the kingdom. They sent to Philip, and asked him to settle the kingdom, and to be witness that it was equally divided. Philip came to their meeting with a great army and slew both the kings, and all the counsellors, and seized both the kingdoms.—Afterwards the Athenians asked Philip to be their leader against the Phocians, though they formerly closed their passes against him; and that he would do one of two things, either make peace for them, or help them to overcome the Phocians. He promised that he would help to overcome them. At the same time also, the Phocians begged his help against the Athenians. He promised them, that he would make peace for them. After he had both the passes in his power, he also brought the kingdoms under his sway; and scattered his army throughout the cities, and told them, that they were to pillage the land, till they had laid it waste, so that the people were sorry, both that they must bear the greatest evil, and that they durst not free themselves from it. But he told them to slay all the most powerful; and the others,— some he sent into banishment,—some he settled in other marches. Thus

---

quoque universa subvertit spoliavitque, nec tamen unquam per viginti quinque annos quasi iratis diis victus est. Haver. p. 171, 4—10.
2 Per dolum, finitimos reges interfecit. Id. p. 171, 11.
3 Urbem antiquissimam et florentissimam. Id. p. 172, 3.
4 Oros. l. III : c 12, Haver. p. 172—174.

Philip humbled the great kingdoms: though each of them formerly thought that it might have power over many others, they at last found themselves brought to nought.

6. Afterwards [5] it seemed to Philip, that, on land, he had not power to satisfy the people with rewards, who were always fighting together with him; but he gathered ships, and they became pirates, and forthwith took, at one time, a hundred and eighty trading ships. He then chose a city near the sea called Byzantium, because he thought that there they might best have peace within; and also that there they should be most handy for waging war upon every land. But the citizens withstood him. Philip surrounded them with his army, and fought against them. The same Byzantium was first built by Pausanias, a leader of the Lacedæmonians, and afterwards enlarged by the Christian emperor Constantine, and from his name, it was called Constantinople, and is now the highest royal seat, and head of all the eastern empire. After Philip had long surrounded the city, he was grieved that he had not so much money to give his army, as they were accustomed to receive. He then divided his army into two parts: some he set round the city, and with other bands he went and plundered many cities of the Chersonesians, a people of Greece. Afterwards [about 339 B. C.] he marched with his son Alexander into Scythia, where king Atheas [6] had the sovereignty, who was formerly his companion in the war against the Istrians; and he would then march into that country. But the people of the land guarded themselves against him, and marched towards him with an army. When Philip heard of it, he sent to those, who had surrounded the city, for more help, and marched against them with all his force. Though the Scythians had a great many more men, and were themselves more brave, yet Philip entrapped them by his wiles, in as much as he hid the third part of his army, and himself with it, and ordered the two parts, that, as soon as they began to fight, they should flee towards him, that then, he might entrap them with the third part, when they had

---

5 Oros. l. III: c. 13. Haver. p. 174—176.

6 Ad Scythiam quoque cum Alexandro filio prædandi intentione pertransiit. Scythis tunc Atheas regnabat: qui quum Istrianorum bello premeretur, auxilium a Philippo per Apolloniensces petiit: sed continuo Istrianorum rege mortuo, et belli metu, et auxiliorum necessitate liberatus, pactionem fœderis cum Philippo habitam dissolvit. Oros. l. III: c. 13. Haver. p. 175, 6—11. Atheas first asked Philip to assist him against the Istrians, and then laughed at him for sending an army. Hence this expedition. Justin. l. ix: c. 2.

passed by. Twenty thousand Scythians, women and men, were there slain and taken; and twenty thousand horses were taken: however, they met with no store of riches, as they had before when they gained the mastery of the battle-field. The poverty of the Scythians was first found out in that battle. After Philip turned from thence, other Scythians, called Triballi,[7] went after him with a small force. Philip thought their warfare unworthy of him, until a Cwene[8] shot him through the thigh, and killed the horse on which he sat. When his army saw that he fell with his horse, they all fled and left all the booty, that they had formerly taken.[9] It was a great wonder, that, on the fall of the king, so great an army fled, which before would not flee, although many thousands were slain. When Philip was wounded, he craftily gave leave to all the Greeks, that their governments might stand among them, as they formerly did in olden times. But as soon as he was healed, he pillaged Athens.[1] Then they sent to the Lacedæmonians, and prayed that they would be friends, though they had formerly long been foes; and prayed also that they all would so strive together as to be able to drive their common enemy from them. Some of them agreed, and gathered a greater force of men than Philip: others, for fear of him, durst not.[2] Philip then thought that he could no longer withstand them in a pitched battle; but he often harassed them

7 The Triballi were a powerful Scythian race. They were, like all the Scythians, warlike and brave, as is evident by their attack upon Philip and by their victory. Justin, whom Orosius chiefly follows, is in this instance more precise than Orosius, stating why the Triballi opposed Philip:—Revertenti ab Scythia Triballi Philippo occurrunt; negant se transitum daturos, ni portionem accipiant prædæ. Hinc jurgium et mox prœlium; in quo ita in femore vulneratus est Philippus, ut per corpus ejus equus interficeretur. Justin. l. IX: c. 3.—Alfred distinctly states, that these Triballi were Scythians,—offór hine [Philippum] oþere Sciþþie, . . . Tribaballe wæron hatene. Though the Triballi were victorious in the present attack, and took immense spoil from Philip, they were afterwards completely routed by his son, Alexander the Great. B. C. 335.

8 Cwéne, one from Cwén-land [See p. 38, note 36]. It seems that some of the Cwénes migrated with the Triballi and other Scythian tribes from the north to the Danube, for they were now [B. C. 339] amongst the Triballi, as is evident from one of them wounding Philip.

9 Quum omnes occisum putarent, in fugam versi, prædam amiserunt. Haver. p. 175, 19, 20.

1 Aliquantula deinde mora dum convalescit a vulnere, in pace conquievit. Statim vero ut convaluit, Atheniensibus bellum intulit. Haver. p. 175, 20—23.

2 Totius Græciæ civitates legationibus fatigant, ut communem hostem, communibus viribus petant. Itaque aliquantæ urbes Atheniensibus sese coniunxêre, quasdam vero ad Philippum belli metus traxit. Haver. p. 176, 1—4

by foragers, scouting about, till they were separated, and he then suddenly marched with his army upon Athens. At that time the Athenians were so dreadfully slaughtered, and beaten down, that afterwards they had neither any power, nor any freedom.³

7. After⁴ that, Philip led an army against the Lacedæmonians and against the Thebans, and greatly troubled and disgraced them until they were utterly routed, and kept under. After Philip had brought all the Greeks under his power, he gave his daughter to Alexander, the king, his own kinsman, to whom he had formerly given the kingdom of Epirus. On that day, they tilted⁵ on horse-back, both Philip and Alexander, to whom he gave his daughter, and Alexander his own son, and also many others with them, as was their custom at such times. When it happened that Philip rode out from the crowd to the sport, then one of his old foes met him and stabbed him to death.⁶

8. "I wot not,"⁷ said Orosius, "why those former wars are so much liked by you Romans, and are so pleasant to hear in songs; and why you praise so highly the times of such sorrows. Now, though only a little of such sorrows comes upon you, yet you bemoan these as the worst times, and can as bitterly weep over them, as you can joyfully laugh over the other. If you be such heroes, as you think you are, then should you as willingly bear your own sorrows, since they are less, than what you hear of theirs. Then would these times seem to you better than those, for your sorrows now are less, than theirs then were. Philip harassed the people of Greece for twenty-five years, both burning their cities and slaying their people, and banishing some into foreign countries,⁸—while the sorrows of you Romans, of which you always speak, were only for three days. The mischief of Philip

3 Pugnam longe omnibus anterioribus bellis atrociorem fuisse, ipse rerum exitus docuit. Nam hic dies apud universam Græciam adquisitæ dominationis gloriam, et vetustissimæ libertatis statum finivit. Haver. p. 176, 6—9.
4 Oros. l. III: c. 14, Haver. p. 176—177, 17.
5 In A. S. Plegedon hy of horsum, they played on horse-back.
6 Die nuptiarum, quum ad ludos magnifice adparatos inter duos Alexandros, filium generumque, contenderet, a Pausania, nobili Macedonum adolescente, in angustiis sine custodibus, circumventus, occisus est. Haver. p. 177, 14—17.
7 Much enlarged by Alfred, from Oros. l. III: c. 14, Haver. p. 177, 17—22, and p. 178, 1—3.
8 Per viginti quinque annos incendia civitatum, excidia bellorum, subjectiones provinciarum, cædes hominum, opum rapinas, prædas pecorum, mortuorum venditiones captivitatesque vivorum unius regis fraus, ferocia, et dominatus agitavit. Haver. p. 178, 2—5.

might, however, still seem in some measure within bounds, before the devourer, Alexander, his son, took to the kingdom.—— However, I shall now, for awhile, be silent about his deeds, until I tell those of the Romans, which were done in those times.

Book III: Chapter VIII.

1. Four[9] hundred and twenty-six years after the building of Rome [Blair B. C. 321 : Alfred B. C. 327] : the place Furculæ Caudinæ[1] became well known for the disgrace of the Romans, and is so to this day. It came to pass after the battle, which the Romans and the Samnites had, when, as we said before, twenty thousand Samnites were slain, under Fabius the consul. But the Samnites, in another battle, came to meet the Romans with a greater force, and with greater wariness than formerly, at the place called Furculæ Caudinæ. There the Romans were ensnared, chiefly because the land was less known to them than it was to the Samnites; and they marched unwittingly into a narrow pass, till the Samnites surrounded them on the outside; and then they must do one of two things,—either lose their lives for want of food, or fall into the hands of the Samnites. In their power, the Samnites were so bold, that the prince called Pontius, who was their leader, told them to ask the king, his father, who was at home, whether he would rather that he should kill them all, or order them while living to be put to shame. The prince then tortured them with the shame, which was the greatest in those days,—he stripped them of their clothes, and their weapons; and took six hundred hostages into his power, with the view, that afterwards, they should always be his slaves. The prince told some of his people to bring the consuls of the Romans, and their elders into their own country, and drive them before them as slaves, that their shame might be the greater.

2. "We would," said Orosius, "more willingly be silent about the shame of you Romans, than to speak of it, if we could for your own murmuring, which ye have against Christianity. Lo! ye know, that to this day ye would have been slaves to the Samnites, if ye had not belied your pledge and your oaths, that ye

---

9 Oros. l. III: c. 15. Haver. p. 178—180.
1 Caudine Forks, or narrow passes in the mountains, between Capua and Beneventum, in Samnium, where the Romans submitted to the Samnites, and passed under the yoke B. C. 321. It is at present called the valley of Arpaia.

gave them ; and ye now murmur, because many of the people over whom ye had power would not fulfil what they promised. Will ye not think, how hateful it was to yourselves to keep your oaths to those, who had the power over you!"

3. Soon afterwards, in the following year, the Romans broke their oaths, which they had taken to the Samnites; and, with Papirius, their consul, followed them, and gained a deadly victory; because the people on both sides were eager for the fight,—the Samnites for the power which they had on each side, and the Romans for the shame, which they had formerly put upon them. The Romans took the king of the Samnites, and forced their fortress, and made them tributaries. This same Papirius, after the battle, was held in such esteem by the Romans, that they had chosen him to withstand the great Alexander in war ; if, as he had said, he should come from the east, out of Asia into Italy.

Book III : Chapter IX.[1]

1. Four hundred and twenty six years after the building of Rome, [Oros. B. C. 327 : Clinton, B. C. 336], Alexander took the kingdom of the Macedonians after his father, Philip, and at that time shewed his first generalship,[2] when by his skill he brought all the Greeks under his power,—all those who raised war against him.

2. It now first happened, that the Persians gave Demosthenes, the philosopher, ready money, with which he seduced all the Greeks to strive against Alexander. The Athenians offered battle to Alexander, but he so quickly slew, and routed them, that, ever after, they had very great dread of him. The citadel of the Thebans, which was formerly the chief seat of all the Greeks, he stormed and quite overthrew. Afterwards he sold all the people into banishment for money, and he made all the other nations, which were in Greece, tributaries, save the Macedonians, who first turned to him. He marched thence against the Illyrians and against the Thracians, and brought them all under him. He then gathered an army against the Persians, and while he was gathering it, he slew all his kinsmen, whom he could reach. In his army were thirty-two thousand foot, and four thousand five

---

1. Oros. l. III : c. 16, Haver. p. 180—184.

2. (Alexander) primam experientiam animi et virtutis suæ, compressis celeriter Græcorum motibus, dedit. Haver. p. 180, 17—18.

hundred ⁵ horse, and one hundred and eighty ships ⁶ —" I wot not," said Orosius, " which was the greater wonder,—that with so small a force he could over-run the greatest part of this mid-earth, or that, with so small an army, he durst begin so much."

3. In the first battle, which Alexander fought against Darius in Persia, Darius had six hundred thousand in his army. He was, however, overcome more by Alexander's skill, than by his fighting. There was a very great slaughter made of the Persians; and of Alexander's no more than an hundred and twenty of the cavalry, and nine of the foot.⁵ Then Alexander marched thence into Phrygia a country of Asia, and stormed and overthrew their city, called Sardis. It was told him there, that Darius had again gathered an army in Persia. Alexander had a dread of the narrow place in which he was; and because of that fear he quickly went thence over mount Taurus, and marched a surprizingly great way in the day,⁶ till he came to the city Tarsus, in the country of the Cilicians.

4. On that day, he found a river called Cydnus, which had intensely cold water. When he began to bathe himself therein, while sweating, then all his veins shrunk because of the cold, that they had no hope of his life.⁷

5. Shortly after Darius came with an army against Alexander: he had three hundred thousand foot, and a hundred thousand horse. Alexander was much afraid because of the great multitude, and because of the few that he himself had; though he with the same, had formerly overcome the greater one of Darius. That battle was fought with great earnestness by both the armies, and there both the kings were wounded. Of the Persians, there

---

3. In A. S. fifte healf M. when healf is placed after an ordinal it diminishes it by half, as fifte healf four and a half, or fifte healf M. four thousand and a half, i. e. four thousand five hundred. See Bosworth's A. S. Dict. under healf.

4. In exercitu ejus fuêre peditum triginta et duo millia, equitum quatuor mille ducenti, et naves centum et octoginta. Oros. Haver. p. 181, 5—7.—Arrian says, of foot οὐ πολλῷ πλείους τρισμυρίων, of horse ὑπὲρ τοὺς πεντακισχιλίους.—Diodor. gives of foot XXX. M. of horse IV. M. D. The first Paris and Venice editions give the same numbers as Alfred in his A. S. text, i. e. " Peditum XXXII millia; equitum IV millia D; naves CLXXX. Haver. p. 181, note 8.

5. In exercitu autem Alexandri, centum et viginti equites, et novem tantum pedites defuêre. Oros. Haver. p. 181. 12, 13.

6. Quingentis stadiis sub una die cursu transmissis, Tarsum venit. Haver. c. 182, 4, 5.

7. Ibique quum sudans in Cydnum præfrigidum amnem descendisset, obriguit, contractuque nervorum proximus morti fuit. Oros. Haver. p. 182, 5—7.

were slain ten thousand horse, and eighty thousand foot, and eighty thousand taken prisoners, and very much wealth was found in their camps. The mother of Darius was taken, and his wife, who was his sister, and his two daughters. Then Darius offered Alexander half his kingdom for the women; but Alexander would not give them up.—Darius, yet for the third time, then gathered an army from the Persians, and also the help, that he could draw over from other countries, and marched against Alexander. While Darius gathered an army, Alexander sent Parmenio his admiral, to disperse the fleet of Darius, and he himself marched against the Syrians: they came to meet him, and received him with kindness; nevertheless he ravaged their country; and the people,—some he allowed to abide there,—some he drove away,—others he sold abroad for money.

6. The ancient and the wealthy city of Tyre he beset, sacked, and utterly overthrew, because they would not receive him gladly. Afterwards he marched into Cilicia, and pressed the people under him: then into the island of Rhodes, and pressed the people under him. After that, he went against the Egyptians, and pressed them under him. There he ordered the city to be built, which they afterwards called after him Alexandria. He then went to the temple, which the Egyptians said was that of their god, Ammon, who was the son of Jupiter, their other god, to the end that he might clear his mother from Nectanebus, the wizzard, by whom, they said, she was forlain, and that he was Alexander's father. Then Alexander told the heathen priest to creep into the statue of Ammon, which was within the temple, before he and the people assembled themselves there, and told him how he wished him to answer before the people, what he asked him. Now has Alexander let us know, clearly enough, what it is to worship the heathen gods, that what they say is more from the plots of their priests, and from their own destiny, than from the power of their gods.

7. From [a] that place, Alexander marched a third time against Darius, and they met at the city of Tarsus. In that battle, so many of the Persians were slain, that henceforth they found their great and lasting power as nothing against Alexander. When Darius saw that he must be overcome, he wished himself to be

8 Oros. l. III: c. 17. Haver. p. 184—186, 3.

killed in the battle, but his officers took him away against his will, so that he afterwards fled with the army. Alexander was thirty-three days in the place, ere he could spoil the camps and the slain. He then marched into Persia, and overcame the city Persepolis, their capital, which is yet the wealthiest of all cities. It was told Alexander, that Darius had been bound by his own kinsmen [9] with a golden chain. Then he marched towards him with six thousand men, and found him lying alone by the way, hardly alive, thrust through with spears. Alexander shewed a little kind-heartedness to him alone, when dead, for he ordered him to be buried in the tomb of his elders, which he would, by no means, afterwards grant to his kindred, neither to his wife, nor to his mother, nor to his children, nor, what was least of all, would he take his youngest daughter, but in bondage: she was a little child.

8. They [1] can hardly be believed, who speak of such manifold evils as happened in those three years, in three pitched battles between the two kings: there were fifteen hundred thousand men slain in them; and, as is before said, there were slain of the same people, a little before, nineteen hundred thousand men, besides great pillage, which took place within the three years, in many a nation. All the nation of Assyria was laid waste by Alexander, and many cities in Asia, and the great city Tyre all overthrown, and the country of Cilicia all laid waste, and the country of Cappadocia, and all the Egyptians brought into slavery, and the island of Rhodes entirely laid waste, and many other countries about the mountains of Taurus.

9. There [2] were then, not only the wars of these two, in the east part of this mid-earth; but, at the same time with them, Agis, king of the Spartans, and Antipater, another king of the Greeks, were at war with each other; and Alexander, king of Epirus, the great Alexander's uncle, who wished for the west part, as the other did for the east part, and led an army into Italy, and was there very soon slain. At the same time, Zopyrion, king of Pontus, set out with an army, and he and his people utterly perished there. After the death of Darius, Alexander

---

9 Darium vero, quum a propinquis suis vinctum compedibus aureis teneri comperisset, persequi statuit. Oros. Haver. p. 185, 10—12.
1 Oros. l. III: c. 17, Haver. p. 186, 3—13.
2 Oros. l. III: c. 18, Haver. 186, 30—187, 14.

overcame all the Mardi, and all the Hyrcanians; and, while he was fighting there, Minothæa,³ the Scythian queen, with three hundred women, boldly sought him out, that they might have children by Alexander and by his greatest warriors.

10. After⁴ that, Alexander fought against the Parthians, and he nearly slew them all, and brought them to nought, ere he could overcome them. Afterwards he overcame the Drangæ,⁵ and Evergetæ, and Parapammeni, and Adaspii, and many other nations, which are settled about the mountains of Caucasus, and there ordered a city to be built, which they afterwards called Alexandria.⁶

11. His⁷ frenzy and his ravaging were not only upon strangers,⁸ but he also killed and harassed those, who were marching and fighting together with him. First he killed Amyntas, his aunt's son, and afterwards his brother, and then Parmenio, his general, and then Philotas, and then Attalus, then Eurylochus, then Pausanias, and many others, who were most powerful in Macedonia; and Clitus, who was both his own general, and also formerly of Philip, his father. At a certain time, when they sat at their feast drunk, they began to debate whether Philip or Alexander had done the greatest deeds. Then Clitus, from old friendship, said that Philip had done more than he. For that saying, Alexander then leaped up, and slew him. Alexander, besides pressing down both his own people, and those of other kings, was always thirsting for man's blood.

12. Soon⁹ after this, he marched with an army against the Chorasmi, and against the Dacians, and forced them to pay him tribute. He killed Callisthenes, the philosopher, his fellow scholar (taught together by their master Aristotle), and many men with him, because they would not pray to him as to their god.

---

3 Thalestris sive Minothæa regina, excitata suscipiendæ ab eo subolis gratia, cum trecentis mulieribus procax Amazon invenit. Haver. p. 187, 12—14.

4 Oros. l. III : c. 18, Haver. p. 187, 14—188, 2.

5 Inde Drangas, Euergetas, Parimas Parapamenos, Adaspios . . . . subegit. Oros. l. III : c. 18. Haver. p. 187, 16—188, 1.—Justin. XII, 5, 9.

6 Populos qui in radice Caucasi morabantur, subegit, urbe ibi Alexandria super amnem Tanaim constituta. Haver. p. 188, 1, 2.

7 Oros. l. III : c. 18, Haver. p. 188, 2—12.

8 Sed nec minor ejus in suos crudelitas, quam in hostem rabies fuit, Haver. p. 188, 2, 3.

9 Oros. l. III : c. 18, Haver. p. 188, 12—189, 3.

13. After[1] that, he marched into India, that he might enlarge his kingdom to the eastern ocean. On the way, he over-ran Nysa, the capital of the Indians, and all the Dædalian mountains, and all the kingdom of queen Cleophis, and forced her to concubinage, for which he gave her the kingdom again. After Alexander had brought all India under his power, save one city, which was very strong with surrounding rocks, he was told, that Hercules, the giant, had come there, in former days, as he thought to storm it; but he did not begin, as there was an earthquake there at that time. Alexander undertook it, chiefly because he wished that his great deeds should be more than those of Hercules; though he took it with great loss of the people.

14. Afterwards[2] Alexander had a battle with Porus, the strongest king of the Indians. In that battle there was very much blood shed on each side: Porus and Alexander fought hand to hand on their horses. Porus killed Alexander's horse, called Bucephalus, and might [have slain] him there, had not his thanes come to help him. He[3] stabbed Porus with many wounds, and also made him yield, after his thanes came to him. [Alexander] let him have his kingdom again for the heroism, with which he so bravely fought against him. Alexander ordered him afterwards to build two cities: one was called Bucephalus, after his horse; the other Nicæa.

15. He[4] afterwards went against the Adrestæ, the Cathæi, the Præsidæ, and the Gangaridæ, and fought with them all, and overcame them. When he went into the eastern boundaries of the Indians, there came against him two hundred thousand cavalry, and Alexander could hardly overcome them, because of the summer heat, and of their frequent battles. He would afterwards have larger camps than he had formerly; because, after that battle, he thenceforth encamped more than he did before.

16. He[5] then went out on the ocean, from the firth of which the river is called Acesines, to an island peopled by the Sibi and the Gessonæ, whom Hercules formerly brought and settled there;

---

1 Oros. l. III: c. 19, Haver. p. 189, 5—13.
2 Oros. l. III: c. 19, Haver. p. 189, 14—190, 6.
3 Alexander cum ipso Poro singulariter congressus, occisoque dejectus equo, concursu satellitum præsentiam mortis evasit. Porus multis vulneribus confossus, et captus est; quo ob testimonium virtutis in regnum restituto. Oros. l. III: c. XIX, Haver. p. 190, 1—4.
4 Oros. l. III: c. 19, Haver. p. 190, 6—11.
5 Oros. l. III: c. 19, Haver. p. 190, 11—191, 4.

and he made them subject to him. Afterwards he went to the island, the people of which are called Malli, and Oxydracæ, and they brought against him eight hundred thousand foot, and sixty thousand cavalry. They were long engaged before either could overcome the other, till at last Alexander gained an unworthy victory.

17. He [6] then marched to a fastness: when he came to it, he could see no man in the fastness, from without. Alexander wondered why it was so without men; and he himself at once climbed over the wall, and he was there drawn in by the towns-people. They then pursued him so closely, both with arrows, and with the throwing of stones, and with all their weapons of war, that it is hardly to be believed when it is said,—all the towns-people could not force him alone to give himself up into their hands. But when the people pressed most upon him; he stepped to a corner of a wall and there defended himself. All the people were so taken up with him alone, that they gave no heed to the wall, till Alexander's thanes broke through it and came in, over against him. There Alexander was shot through with an arrow, underneath one breast.—Now we do not know, which is more to be wondered at, how he alone defended himself against all the towns-people,—or again, when help came to him, how he so pressed through the people, that he killed the same man, who before shot him through; or again, the undertaking of the thanes, when they undoubtedly thought that their lord was in the power of their enemies either alive or dead, that they, nevertheless, did not refrain from breaking the wall, that they might revenge their lord, whom they found weary, and resting on his knees.

18. He [7] then brought the city under his power, and marched to another city, in which Ambira the king dwelt. Many of Alexander's army died there from poisoned arrows. But, in the same night an herb was shewn to Alexander in a dream: he took it in the morning, and gave it to the wounded to drink, and they were healed by it: they then overcame the city.

19. He [8] afterwards turned homeward to Babylon. Ambassadors were waiting there from all the world; that was from Spain, and from Africa, and from France, and from all Italy. Alexander was

6 Oros. l. III: c. 19, Haver. p. 191, 4—192, 1.
7 Oros. l. III: c. 19, Haver. p. 192, 2, 6
8 Oros. l. III: 20, Haver. p. 192, 19—194, 12.

so dreaded, when he was in India in the east of this mid-earth, that they who were on the west, were afraid of him. Moreover, ambassadors came to him, even from many nations, to whom, none of Alexander's company thought that his name was known, and wished for peace with him. Even yet, when Alexander came home to Babylon, there was still in him the greatest thirst for man's blood. When his servants understood that he would not leave off war, but said he would march into Africa, then his cup-bearers planned among themselves how they might take away his life, and gave him poison to drink : then he died.

20. Orosius said [9]—" Oh ! how great is the folly of men, in these Christian days ! Though they have but little uneasiness, how woefully they bemoan it ! It is one of these two,—either they do not know, or they will not know, in what wretchedness they were, who lived before them. Now let them think, how it was with them, who were in Alexander's power, when they, who were in the west of this mid-earth, so much dreaded him, that they, for the sake of peace, sought him out in the east, at great risk and in great uncertainty, both in dread of the sea, and of wild beasts in deserts, and of many kinds of serpents, and in the languages of nations. But we very well know, that now, for very cowardice, they neither dare seek peace from far, nor even defend themselves at home in their own houses, when they are attacked there : yet they can slander these times."

BOOK III : CHAPTER X.

1. Four[1] hundred and fifty years after the building of Rome, [Alfred 303 : Clinton B. C. 295]—under two consuls,—one Fabius, called also Maximus ; the other Quintus, called also Decius,—in their fourth consulship, four of the strongest nations in Italy, which were the Umbrians, Etruscans, Samnites and Gauls, agreed among themselves to go to war with the Romans. They very much feared that they could not withstand them all at the same time, and anxiously devised means to separate them, and sent a regular army against the Etruscans, and against the Umbrians to pillage and to destroy the people. When they heard of it, they turned homeward, that they might defend their own

9 Oros. l. III : c. 20, Haver. p. 194, 12—195, 11.
1 Oros. l. III : c. 21, Haver. p. 196—197, 4.

lands. At the same time the Romans marched against the Samnites, and against the Gauls, with their greater army, that they had at home. Quintus the consul was slain in the battle; and, after his fall, Fabius, the other consul, gained the victory. Forty thousand Samnites and Gauls were slain, and seven thousand Romans, in the division in which Decius was killed. Livy said that one hundred and fifty thousand foot and seven thousand cavalry of the Samnites and Gauls were slain.

2. Orosius [2] said, "I have, moreover, of a truth heard say, that the Romans, in those days, had war not only with other nations, but among themselves, with manifold plagues and pestilence: so it then was."

3. When [3] Fabius, the consul, came homeward from the battle, they went before him in triumph, which was their custom when they gained a victory. But the joy was very soon turned to grief in their hearts, when they saw the dead, who were before at home, so thickly borne to the earth; for, at that time, the great pestilence was there.

4. About [4] a year afterwards, the Samnites fought with the Romans, and routed them, and drove them into the city of Rome. Soon after,[5] the Samnites changed their clothing to another fashion, and covered all their weapons over with silver, in token that they would do one or the other,—either conquer or all die.[6] In those days, the Romans chose Papirius for their consul, and soon led an army against the Samnites, though their priests said that their gods were against their going to battle. But Papirius upbraided the priests very much for that saying, and nevertheless he went to the warfare; and he gained as honourable a victory, as if he had not before dishonoured the priests of their gods. Twelve thousand Samnites were slain there, and four thousand taken. Soon after that glorious victory, they were again afflicted with pestilence, which was so raging and lasting, that they willingly tried, at last, whether they could

---

2 Oros. l. III : c. 21, Haver. p. 197, 4—8

3 Oros. p. 197, 8—11.

4 Oros. l. III : c. 22, Haver. p. 197, 31—199, 2.

5 Postea vero Samnites novum habitum animumque sumentes, hoc est, deargentatis armis ac vestibus, paratoque animo, ni vincant, mori, bello se obferunt. Oros. l. III : c. 22, Haver. p. 197, 32—198, 2.

6 A. S. oððe ealle libban, oððe ealle licgean, either all live, or all die. Oros. has—ni vincant, mori. v. note 5.

stop it by enchantments, and fetched Æsculapius the magician with the immense snake, which was called Epidaurus'; and acted just as if such an evil had never come upon them before, nor would ever come again.

5. In* the following year, Fabius, their consul, whose other name was Curius, fought with the Samnites, and basely fled homeward. The senate wished to degrade him, because he had led the people to flight ; but his father, who was also called Fabius, begged that the senate would forgive this fault, and that they would grant, that he might go with his son, the next time, against the Samnites with all their forces; and they granted it. The father then told the consul to march forward with his army, and he stopped behind with some of the forces. When he saw that Pontius, king of the Samnites, had ensnared the consul, his son, and surrounded him with his people, he then came to his help, and greatly raised his spirits; and they took Pontius, king of the Samnites. There were twenty thousand Samnites slain, and four thousand taken with the king. There the war of the Romans and Samnites, which they formerly carried on for fifty nine years, was ended, because they had taken their king.

6. In* the next year after this, Curius the consul with the Romans fought against the Sabines, and gained the victory, making an immense slaughter of them, which might be known by this, as he and the consuls could not count the slain.

Book III : Chapter XI.

1. Four ' hundred and sixty-three years after the building of Rome, [Alfred B. C. 290 : Clinton B. C. 283] when Dolabella and Domitius were consuls in Rome, then the Lucani, Bruttii, Samnites, and the Senonian Gauls began to war against the Romans. Then the Romans sent ambassadors to the Gauls about peace :, they killed the ambassadors. They next sent Cæcilius their

---

7 Ut libros Sibyllinos consulendos putârint, horrendumque illum Epidaurium colubrum cum ipso Æsculapii lapide advexerint : quasi vero pestilentia aut ante sedata non sit, aut post orta non fuerit. Oros. l. III : c. 22, Haver. p. 198, 10—199, 2.

8 Oros. l. III: c. 22, Haver. p. 199, 2—15.

9 Anno subsequente cum Sabinis Curio consule bellum gestum est, ubi quot millia hominum interfecta, quot capta sint, ipse consul ostendit : qui quum in senatu magnitudinem adquisiti agri Sabini, et multitudinem capti populi referre vellet, numerum explicare non potuit. Oros. l. III : c. 22, Haver. p. 199, 15—19.

1 Oros. l. III: c. 22, Haver. p. 199, 19—200, 9.

Prætor with an army, where the Gauls and Bruttii were together, and he was slain there, and the people with him, namely eighteen thousand. As often as the Gauls fought against the Romans, the Romans were overcome. "Therefore, ye Romans," said Orosius, "while you always murmur about the only battle that the Goths had with you, why will you not think of the many former, which the Gauls often waged insultingly against you!"

2. I will[2] also bring to mind, in part, what those, that came after Alexander, did, in the times, when this happened in Rome: how they killed one another in many battles.—"It is," said he [Orosius,] "when I think of it, just as if I sat on a high hill, and saw, on a smooth field, many fires burning; so over all the kingdom of the Macedonians, that is over all the greater Asia, and over the greatest part of Europe, and all Libya, there was nothing but hatred and wars. Those, who were the first under Alexander, laid waste by war the very places, where they ruled after him, and where they did not, they brought the greatest gloom, as the bitterest smoke rises up, and then widely spreads."

3. Alexander,[3] for twelve years, filled with fear and crushed under him this mid-earth; and his followers, for fourteen years after, pulled and tore it asunder, just as when the lioness brings to hungry whelps something to eat: they then shew in the food, which of them can embowel the most.

4. Thus[4] then did Ptolemy, one of Alexander's generals, when he swept together all Egypt and Arabia; and Laomedon, his other general, who seized upon all Assyria,—and Philotas Cilicia,—and Philo Illyricum,— and Atropates the greater Media,—and Stromen? Media the less,—and Perdiccas Asia the less.—The people of Susiana [came to Coenus],—the greater Phrygia [to] Antigonus,— Lycia and Pamphilia [to] Nearchus.—[Cassander took] Caria,—and

---

2 Oros. l. III: c. 23. Haver. p. 200—201, 8.
3 Oros. l. III: c. 23, Haver. p. 201, 8—12.
4 Oros. l. III: c: 23, Haver. p. 201, 12—203, 3.

4 The Anglo-Saxon of Alfred, both in the Lauderdale and the Cotton MSS, has so many mistakes in the names, that it is necessary to refer to the Latin of Orosius, who follows Justin almost verbatim [See l. XIII: c. 4, p. 302—306, and the notes, in the accurate edition of Grævius, 8vo. Lugd. Bat. 1683].—Orosius says—Prima Ptolemæo Ægyptus et Africæ Arabiæque pars sorte provenit. Confinem huic provinciæ Syriam Laomedon Mitylinæus, Ciliciam Philotas, Philo Illyrios accipiunt. Mediæ majori Atropatus, minori socer Perdiccæ præponitur. Susiana gens Scyno, Phrygia major Antigono Philippi filio adsignatur. Lyciam et Pamphyliam Nearchus, Cariam Cassander, Lydiam Menander sortiuntur, Leonnatus minorem Phrygiam accipit. Thracia et regiones Pontici maris Lysimacho.

Leonnatus Phrygia the less,—and Lysimachus Thrace,—and Eumenes Cappadocia and Paphlagonia.—Seleucus had all the most eminent men of Alexander's army; and with them, he at length gained all the country of the east. Cassander had the warriors with the Chaldeans. In Bactria and in India were the Prefects, whom Alexander appointed; and Taxiles had the land between the two rivers, the Indus and Hydaspes. Pithon had the people, the colonies' in India. Oxyartes had the Paropamisii [in Afghanistan and the Punjab west of the Indus], at the end of the Caucasian mountains. Sibyrtius had the Arachosii [part of Afghanistan and Beloochistan]. Stasanor had the nations of Drangiana [part of Iran], and Ariana. Amyntas had the [Bactrians]. Scythæus had the people of Sogdiana [part of Turkestan and Bokhara]. Nicanor had the Parthians, and Philip the Hyrcani. Phrataphernes had the Armenians. Tlepolemus had the Medes. Peucestas had the Babylonians. Peleusus had the Archi, and Archelaus Mesopotamia.

5. All⁶ their wars first arose from Alexander's letter, because he therein ordered that all the exiles, who were in the countries which he himself had formerly over-run, should be allowed to go home. Then the Greeks would not listen to the order, because they dreaded that, when they gathered themselves together, they would avenge the wrongs, which they had formally borne from them. Moreover they denied that they would any longer serve with the Lacedæmonians, amongst whom was their chief city. Soon after that, the Athenians led thirty thousand people, and two hundred ships against Antigonus, the king, who was to have all the realm of the Greeks, because he was the bearer of the message from Alexander. They fixed upon Demosthenes, the philosopher, as their leader; and drew over the towns people of

---

Cappadocia cum Paphlagonia Eumeni data: summa castrorum Seleuco Antiochi filio cessit; stipatoribus regis satellitibusque Cassander filius Antipatri præficitur. In Bactriana ulteriore et Indiæ regionibus præfecti priores, qui sub Alexandro esse coeperant, permanserunt. Seras, inter duos amnes Hydaspem et Indum constitutos, Taxiles habuit. In colonias in Indis conditas Pithon Agenoris filius mittitur. Parapamenos fines Caucasi montis Oxyartes accepit. Arachosii Gedrosiique Sibyrtio decernuntur. Drangas et Areos Stasanor, Bactrianos Amyntas sortitur, Sogdianos Scythæus, Nicanor Parthos, Philippus Hyrcanios, Phrataphernes Armenios, Tlepolemus Persas, Peucestes Babylonios, Archon Pelasgos, Archelaus Mesopotamiam adepti sunt. Haver. 201, 12—203, 3.

5 The A. S. is Ithona hæfde calonie þa þeode on Indeum, Ithona had the people Coloni in India. The A. S. translator has mistaken colonias colonies of Oros. for the name of a people. See note 4.

6 Oros. l. III: c. 23, Haver. p. 203, 3—16.

Corinth, and of Sicyon and of Argos to help them; and besieged king Antipater in a fastness, because he gave help to Antigonus. There Leosthenes, one of their leaders, was shot dead with an arrow. When they were returning homeward from the city, they met Leonatus, who should have come to help Antipater, and he was there slain. Afterwards Perdiccas, who had Asia the less, began to wage war against Ariarathes, king of the Cappadocians, and drove him into a fastness. The towns-people themselves set fire to it, on four sides; and there every thing perished, that was within.

6. After[7] that, Antigonus and Perdiccas vowed to fight with each other; and they were long contriving where they should meet. They laid waste many islands in the strife which of them could gain the most help. With that hope, Perdiccas marched with an army into Egypt, where Ptolemy was the king, because it was told him that he would assist Antigonus. Then Ptolemy gathered a great army against him. While they strove to come together, two kings Neoptolemus and Eumenes fought: Eumenes routed Neoptolemus, who came to king Antigonus, and persuaded him to march with an army suddenly upon Eumenes. Then Antigonus sent [Neoptolemus] himself, and one of his generals Polyperchon with a great force, that they might defeat him. When Eumenes was told of it, he waylaid them, where they had thought of waylaying him, and slew them both, and put the others to flight. Afterwards Perdiccas and Ptolemy fought, and there Perdiccas was slain. It then became known to the Macedonians, that Eumenes and Pithon and Illyrius, and Alcetas brother of Perdiccas, would wage war against them, and contrived that Antigonus should come against them with an army. In the battle, Antigonus routed Eumenes, and drove him into a fastness and besieged him while there. Eumenes then sent to king Antipater, and begged for his help. When Antigonus understood that, he left the siege: but Eumenes thought there was great treachery in Antigonus thus going home, and drew over to his side those, who were formerly Alexander's warriors, who were called Argyraspides, because all their weapons were silvered over. When in doubt whether they would so rashly fulfil his wish, Antigonus came upon them with an army, and took from

---

[7] Oros. L. III: c. 23, Haver. p. 203, 16—205, 10.

them their wives, and their children, and their land and all their hoarded riches, that they had gained under Alexander; and they themselves with difficulty fled to Eumenes. They then sent to Antigonus in their greatest disgrace, and begged that he would give up what he had before taken from them. He told them he would do that if they brought to him their lord, king Eumenes, bound; and they did so. But he treated them again with reproach, and set them in the most disgraceful land, which was at the utmost end of his people; and, moreover, he would not give them any thing, for which they had asked.

7. Then Eurydice, queen of Arrhidæus, king of the Macedonians, did much evil to the people, through Cassander, her lord's general, with whom she had secret adultery; and therefore she taught the king to raise him up so high, that he was above all who were in the realm next to the king. She so acted by her intrigues as to raise up all the Macedonians against the king, till they determined to send for Olympias, Alexander's mother, that she might assist them to bring both the king and the queen into their power. Olympias then came to them with the force of Epirus, her own kingdom, and asked Æacides, king of the Molossi, to help her. They slew both the king and the queen, and Cassander fled away. Olympias took the sovereignty, and did much evil to the people, while she had the government. When Cassander heard that she was loathsome to the people, he gathered an army. As she heard that so many of the people had turned to him, she did not believe that the other part would be faithful to her; but she took her daughter-in-law, Roxana, Alexander's widow, and Alexander's son, Hercules, and fled to the fastness, which was called Pydna. Cassander marched after her, and stormed the fastness, and slew Olympias. The townspeople, when they understood that the fastness was to be stormed, carried off the daughter-in-law with her son, and sent them into another and stronger fastness. Cassander gave orders to besiege them there; and he ruled in full power over the kingdom of Macedonia.

8. It was then thought, that the war among Alexander's followers was ended, when they were fallen, who fought the most:— they were Perdiccas, and Eumenes, and Alcetas, and Polyperchon,

8 Oros. l. III: c. 23, Haver. p. 205, 10—206, 2.
9 Oros. l. III: c. 23. Haver. p. 206, 2—208, 8.

and Olympias, and Antipater, and many others. But Antigonus, who had unbounded yearning for power over others, marched to the fastness, where Alexander's widow and his son were, and took them; because he thought that the people would more easily bow to him, who had their old lord's son in his power. After Cassander heard of it, he agreed with Ptolemy, and with Lysimachus, and with Seleucus, the eastern king, and they all waged war against Antigonus, and against Demetrius his son,—some on land, others on water. In that war, though some were with Antigonus, and others with Cassander, the greatest part of the Macedonian nobility fell on both sides. There Antigonus and his son were routed. Afterwards Demetrius, son of Antigonus, fought with ships against Ptolemy, and drove him into his own land. Antigonus then ordered, that they should call both him and his son, king; though the followers of Alexander were before only called generals. In the midst of these quarrels, Antigonus feared that the people would choose Hercules, Alexander's son, for their lord, because he was of the true, kingly race. Then he ordered both him and his mother to be slain. When the other three heard that he had the thought of over-reaching them all, they gathered themselves together again, and waged war against him. Cassander durst not go himself in the expedition, because he was closely surrounded with enemies, but he sent help to Lysimachus, his ally, and had entrusted his affairs chiefly to Seleucus; because he had overcome in battles many powers in the east:—First, Babylon and Bactriana. Afterwards, he marched into India where no man before or since durst go with an army, save Alexander. Seleucus brought under his power all the generals; and they all went to Antigonus and his son Demetrius with an army. In that war Antigonus was slain, and his son was driven from the kingdom.—" I ween not," said Orosius, " that there is any man, who can tell, how many fell in that battle."

9. At [1] that time [B. C. 297] Cassander died, and his son Philip succeeded to the kingdom. Then it was thought again the second time, that the wars of Alexander's followers were ended. But

---

1 Cassandro defuncto, filius Philippus succedit. Sic quasi ex integro nova Macedoniæ bella nascuntur, Antipater Thessalonicen matrem suam, Cassandri uxorem, quamvis miserabiliter pro vita precantem, manu sua transverberavit. Alexander frater ejus, dum bellum adversus fratrem ob ultionem matris instruit, a Demetrio, cujus auxilium petierat, circumventus occiditur. Oros. l. III: c. 23, Haver. p. 208, 8—13.

they soon after had war among them. Seleucus, and Demetrius son of Antigonus, joined together, and waged war against the three,—Philip, son of Cassander, and against Ptolemy, and Lysimachus. They began the war just as if they had never begun it before. In the strife Antipater killed his mother, widow of Cassander, though she pitifully prayed to him for her life. Then her son Alexander begged Demetrius to assist him, that he might revenge his mother's death on his brother; and they soon after slew him.

10. After[2] this Demetrius and Lysimachus went to war; but Lysimachus could not withstand Demetrius, because Dromichætes king of the Thracians fought against him. In the meanwhile, Demetrius was very much encouraged, and led an army against Ptolemy. When he heard of it, he gained over Seleucus and Pyrrhus king of Epirus to help him. Pyrrhus assisted him chiefly because he wished to get the government of Macedonia for himself. They drove Demetrius from it, and Pyrrhus succeeded. Afterwards Lysimachus slew his own son Agathocles, and his son-in-law Antipater. In those days, the city Lysimachia[3] sank into the earth with the people altogether. After Lysimachus had done so to his son, and to his son-in-law, his own people hated him, and many turned from him, and drew over Seleucus, that he might overcome Lysimachus. Moreover, the strife between the two could not be appeased, though they were the only two of Alexander's followers then alive. But old as they then were, they fought. Seleucus had lived seventy-seven winters; and Lysimachus seventy-three winters. There Lysimachus was slain; and, about three nights afterwards, Ptolemy, whose sister Lysimachus married, came and, as he was going homeward, stealthily followed after Seleucus, till his army was dispersed, and there slew him.

11. The peace[4] and kindheartedness, which they had learned from Alexander, were then brought to an end. These two, who lived the longest, had slain thirty kings,—their own old comrades,—and afterwards they took to themselves the whole of the governments, which they all formerly held. Amid the struggles,

---

2 Oros. l. III : c. 23. Haver. p. 208, 13—209, 15.
3 Lysimachia civitas formidolosissimo terræmotu eversa, oppressoque populo suo, crudele sepulchrum fuit. Oros. l. III: c. 23. Haver. p. 209, 8, 9.
4 Oros. l. III: c. 23, Haver. p. 209, 15—210, 7.

Lysimachus lost his fifteen sons: some he himself slew, others were slain in battle before himself.

12. "Such brotherhood!" said Orosius, "they had among them, who were fed and educated in one family! It is very disgraceful to us, that we speak about what we now call war, when strangers and foreigners come upon us, and rob us of a little, and soon leave us again; and we will not think what it was, when no man could redeem his life from another; nor would even those be friends, who were brothers by father and by mother!"—And here the third book ends, and the fourth begins.

BOOK IV: CHAPTER I.

1. Four hundred and sixty four years after the building of Rome [Clinton B. C. 280: Alfred B. C. 289], the Tarentines were playing in their theatre, which was built within their city Tarentum, when they saw Roman ships sail on the sea. Then the Tarentines hastily went to their own ships, and followed after the others, and took them all but five. Those, who were taken, they treated with the greatest cruelty; some they slew, some they scourged to death, others they sold into bondage. When the Romans heard of it, they sent ambassadors to them, and demanded that they should atone for the wrong, which they had done them. Again, they treated the ambassadors with the greatest disgrace, as they before did the others, and then let them go home.

2. Then the Romans marched against the Tarentines; and so fully did they levy their forces, that even the proletarii were not allowed to stay at home. Those were they, whom they left that their wives might have children, when they went to war. They said, it seemed to them wiser, that they should not lose those who could go out, whoever might have children. The Romans then went against the Tarentines, and laid all waste where they came, and stormed many towns.

3. Then the Tarentines sent everywhere for help, where they could hope for any. Pyrrhus, king of Epirus, came to them with

---

5 Oros. l. III: c. 23. Haver. p. 210, 7—20.

1 Oros. l. IV: c. 1, Haver. p. 214—218. Alfred omits the preface of Orosius, Haver. p. 211—214.

2 Proletarii, persons of little or no property. Being of the lowest rank, they were not called to serve in war, and deemed of little use but to increase (prolem) the population.

the greatest force, as well in infantry, and in cavalry, as with a fleet. In those days, he was famous above all other kings, as well for his great forces, and for his forethought, as for his knowledge of war. Pyrrhus assisted the Tarentines, because the city Tarentum was built by the Lacedæmonians, who then belonged to his kingdom. He had the Thessalians and Macedonians to help him, and in that battle, he had with him twenty elephants,—[animals] which the Romans never saw before. He was the man, that first brought them into Italy. He was also, in those days, most skilful in warfare and in contest; but in this only, his gods and his idolatry, which he followed, deceived him. When he inquired of his gods, which should have victory over the other,—he over the Romans, or the Romans over him, they answered him ambiguously and said;— " Thou shalt have [it], or shalt not."[3]—The first battle, that he had with the Romans, was in [Lucania], near the river which is called [Siris]. After there had been great slaughter on both sides, Pyrrhus ordered the elephants to be brought into the battle. When the Romans saw that such a stratagem was employed against them, as they had never before seen, nor heard speak of, they all fled but one man, called Minutius: he went boldly under an elephant, that he might stab it in the navel. After it was wounded and angry, it killed many of the people: not only did they perish who were upon it, but it so gored and enraged the other elephants, that they also, who were upon them, almost all perished. Though the Romans were routed, still they were encouraged, because they knew what they could do to the elephants. In that battle [4] fourteen thousand of the Roman infantry were slain, and eight hundred and eighty taken; and one thousand three hundred of their cavalry were slain; and there were seven hundred banners taken. It was not said how many of the army of Pyrrhus fell, because it was not the custom, in those times, that they should tell any of the slaughter on that side, which was the more powerful, save where very few were slain, as it was with Alexander, in the first battle

---

3 Neither the Anglo-Saxon nor the English admits of the ambiguity, so evident in the sentence recorded by Ennius—" Aio te, Æacida, Romanos vincere posse." An allusion is evidently made to this answer of the oracle, though Orosius does not quote the sentence.

4 Orosius gives the following account,—Victos fuisse Romanos turpis fuga prodidit, quorum tunc cecidisse referuntur peditum quatuordecim millia octingenti et octingenta: capti mille trecenti et decem: equites autem cæsi ducenti quadraginta duo, capti octingenti et duo, signa amissa vigiuti duo. Haver. p. 216, 9—13.

that he fought with Darius, where no more than nine of his people were slain.⁵ But Pyrrhus afterwards shewed, what he thought of the victory that he had over the Romans, when he said, at the door of his god, and so wrote upon it :—" Accept thou [my] thanks, O Jupiter, that I have been able to overcome those, who before were never overcome ; and I am also overcome by them."⁶ Then his generals asked him, why he spoke such lowering words of himself—" that he was overcome." He answered them and said,—" If I gain such a victory again from the Romans, then I must afterwards go back to the land of the Greeks without any soldier."⁷ Before the battle, it was shewn to the Romans as a bad token, that, in this warfare, the people would meet with great destruction; when thunder killed twenty-four of their foragers, and the others came away afflicted.⁸

4. Afterwards Pyrrhus and the Romans fought in the country of Apulia. There Pyrrhus was wounded in one arm, and the Romans gained the victory, and had learned more contrivances for overcoming the elephants, inasmuch as they took stakes, and struck many sharp iron nails into one end, and wound them round with flax, and set it on fire, and then thrust them into the elephants behind, that they became raging both from the burning of the flax and the goading of the nails : thus, those, who were upon them, were first destroyed by each, then many of the other people, who should have been shielded, were killed. In that battle, eight thousand of the Romans were slain and eleven banners taken. Twenty thousand were slain of the army of Pyrrhus, and his standard taken.—It was then made known to Pyrrhus, that Agathocles king of the Syracusans was dead in the country of Sicily. Then he went thither, and forced that kingdom to submit to him.

5. As soon ⁹ as the war with the Romans was ended, there was the most manifold calamity by pestilence,—yea, no bearing

---

5 See Book III : ch. 9, § 3.
6 Sed Pyrrhus atrocitatem cladis, quam hoc bello exceperat, diis suis hominibusque. testatus est, adfigens titulum in templo Tarentini Jovis, in quo hæc scripsit :—
    Qui ante hac invicti fuvêre viri, pater optime Olympi,
    Hos ego in pugna vici, victusque sum ab iisdem.
These verses are from Ennius. Oros. l. IV : c. 1. Haver. p. 217, 3—7, note 22.
    7 Ne ego, si iterum eodem modo vicero, sine ullo milite Epirum revertar. Haver. p. 217, 9, 10.
    8 Semineces relicti. Haver. p. 217, 15.
    9 Oros. l. IV : c. 2. Haver. p. 218, 219.

creature, neither women nor cattle, could bring forth any thing alive,—that, at last, they doubted whether any human being would ever be added to them.¹ Then Pyrrhus returned again from Sicily against the Romans, and Curius the consul came against him. Their third battle was in Lucania on the plain of Arusium.² Though the Romans had, at one time, thought more of flight than of battle, ere they saw that the elephants were brought into the fight; but, after they had seen them, they so irritated them, that they killed many, whom they should have protected: the army of Pyrrhus, was, for that reason, mostly put to flight. In that battle Pyrrhus had eighty thousand foot, and five thousand horse; and there thirty-six thousand were slain, and four hundred taken. Then Pyrrhus went out of Italy, about five years after he first came into it. Soon after he came home, he wished to storm the city Argos; and he was there struck dead with a stone.

6. When³ the Tarentines heard that Pyrrhus was dead, they sent into Africa to the Carthaginians for help, and went again to war with the Romans: soon after they came together, the Romans had a victory. There the Carthaginians found that they could be overpowered, though no people before could overcome them in battle.—While Pyrrhus was at war with the Romans, they had eight legions. They had then appointed the eighth to help the Rhegians. When the eighth part of the legions believed, that the Romans could not withstand Pyrrhus, they began to pillage and oppress those, whom they ought to have protected. When the Romans heard of it, they sent thither Genucius, their consul, with an army, to punish them, because they had slain and oppressed those, whom all the Romans wished to protect; and he did so. Some he put to death, others he bound and sent home; and there they were afterwards scourged, and then their heads cut off with broad axes.

1 The A. S. is so brief and indefinite, that the more full and clear account of Orosius is cited:—Pestilentia gravis urbem ac fines ejus invasit, quæ quum omnes, tum præcipue mulieres pecudesque corripiens, necatis in utero foetibus, futura prole vacuabat, et inmaturis partubus cum periculo matrum extorti abortus projiciebantur: adeo ut defectura successio, et defuturum animantium genus, adempto vitalis partus legitimo ordine crederetur. Haver. p. 218, 22—219, 1.
2 Tertium bellum, . . . apud Lucaniam in Arusinis campis, gestum est. Haver. p. 219, 2, 3.
3 Oros. l. IV: c. 3, Haver. p. 220, 221, 5.

Book IV: Chapter II.

1. Four[4] hundred and seventy-seven years after the building of Rome [Clinton B. C. 269 : Alfred B. C. 276], there were these evil wonders in Rome. The first was that thunder shattered the house of their highest god, Jupiter, and also threw down to the earth much of the city wall :—And that also three wolves, in one night, brought the body of a dead man into the city, and afterwards tore it there piece-meal, till the men awoke and ran out : then they fled away. In those days it happened, that, in a plain near Rome, the earth opened and burning fire came up from the earth ;—that, on every side of the fire, the earth for five acres broad was burnt to ashes.

2. Soon after, in the following year, Sempronius the consul marched with an army against the Picentes, a people of Italy. When they had set themselves in array and wished to engage, there was an earthquake, and each of the armies thought assuredly, that they should sink into the earth. They were thus kept in dread, till the cause of fear passed away ; and afterwards they fought most fiercely. There was the greatest blood-shed in the armies on both sides : though the Romans had the victory, there were few left alive. It was there seen that the earthquake betokened the great drenching of blood, which they shed upon the earth, at that time.

Book IV: Chapter III.

1. Four[5] hundred and eighty years after the building of Rome [Orosius, and Alfred B. C. 272], among the many other wonders, which happened in those days,—blood was seen to spring out of the earth, and milk to rain from heaven. In those days the Carthaginians sent help to the Tarentines, that they might more easily withstand the Romans. When the Romans sent ambassadors to them, and asked why they did that ; then they swore to the ambassadors with the most disgraceful oaths, that they never gave them help ; although the oaths were more wicked than true.

2. In those days, the Volscians and the Etruscans nearly all perished through their own folly ; because they freed some of

---

4 Oros. l. IV : c. 4. Haver. p. 221, 222, 9.
5 Oros. l. IV : c. 5. Haver. p. 222—223, 13.

their slaves, and were also too mild and too forgiving to all of them. Those who were partly free ⁶ took it amiss, that they freed the slaves and would not free them. They then rose up against their masters, and the slaves with them, and thus had power over them. They afterwards drove them entirely from the country; and took their masters' wives for their own. Afterwards the masters applied to the Romans, and they enabled them to regain their own.

Book IV: Chapter IV.

1. Four ⁷ hundred and eighty one years after the building of Rome [Orosius and Alfred B. C. 272], so great a pestilence came upon the Romans, that, at last, they did not ask, how many were dead, but how many were then left alive. And the devils which they always worshipped, in addition to the other manifold abominations which they taught, so bewildered them, that they could not understand that it arose from the wrath of God; but directed their priests to tell the people that their gods were angry with them, in order that they should still make more offerings, and sacrifices, than they had done before.

2. In those same times, there was a priestess (nun) ⁸ of their gods named Capparonia. It then happened that she forlay herself. For that offence the Romans hanged her, and him also who was guilty with her, together with all those who knew of her guilt, and concealed it.—How can we now think, that the Romans themselves composed and wrote such things for their own glory and praise; and yet, amidst the praise, spoke of such reproaches among themselves? Can we think how many greater reproaches they concealed, as well for the love of themselves, as of their country, and also for the fear of their senate.

6 Orosius, [Haver. p. 223, 3.] calls them Libertini, which Alfred properly translates by Ceorlas, who were freemen of the lowest rank. These Ceorlas were subject to many restrictions, one of which was that they were compelled to have a person of superior rank to be responsible for them.—Among the Romans, the manumitted slave was called Libertus, because he was liberatus or freed from slavery. The Libertus, being freed from legal servitude, belonged to the class Libertinus; but the Libertini, like the Greek ἀπελεύθεροι, had not all the liberties and privileges of citizens, any more than the Ceorlas among the Anglo-Saxons.

7 Oros. l. IV: c. 5. Haver. p. 223, 13—224, 14.

8 Eodem tempore Capparonia, virgo Vestalis incesti rea, suspendio periit: corruptor ejus consciique servi, supplicio adfecti sunt. Haver. p. 224, 2—4. The Nunne, or Nun of Alfred, and virgo Vestalis of Oros. denote a Priestess. See Minucia, III, 6, § 2, n. 7.

OF THE WAR OF THE CARTHAGINIANS.

3. "Now,"[9] said Orosius, "we shall take up the war of the Carthaginians, that is of the people of Carthage, which city was built by the woman Elissa [Dido] seventy two years before Rome. Likewise the evil of their citizens, and a little of their disgrace, have been spoken and written of, as recorded, by Trogus [Pompeius] and Justin, their historians: for their affairs on no occasion went on well either at home or abroad. Besides these evils, they ordained, when a great pestilence came upon them, that they should sacrifice men to their gods. The devils also, in which they trusted, taught them to offer the healthy, for those who were unhealthy. The men were so foolish, that they thought they might thus check the evil; but the devils were so deceitful, that they thereby increased it; for, as they were so very foolish, the wrath of God came upon them in wars besides other evils, which mostly happened in the islands of Sicily and Sardinia, in which they were most frequently at war. When they so often suffered, they began to blame their generals and soldiers for their troubles, and sent them into banishment and into foreign lands. They soon afterwards prayed, that they might return to their own country, and try whether they could overcome their misfortunes. This being refused, they marched against them with an army. In the warfare, the chief general, Mazeus, met his own son, clothed in purple as a priest. He was angry with him, on account of his dress, and ordered him to be seized and crucified,[a] as he thought that he wore such a robe out of contempt for him, because it was not a custom with them, that any should wear purple, but kings. They soon afterwards took Carthage, and slew all the best men that were in it, and forced the others under them. At last, he was himself overcome and slain. This happened in the days of Cyrus king of the Persians.

BOOK IV: CHAPTER V.

1. After that,[1] Himilco, king of the Carthaginians, went with an army into Sicily, and there so sudden a plague[2] came upon them, that the men were dead as soon as it seized them, so that

---

9 Oros. l. IV : c. 6. Haver. p. 224—226, 10.   [a] In crucem .. suspendit. Id. p. 226, 6.
1 Oros. l. IV : c. 6. Haver. p. 226, 10—232, 5.
2 The A. S. is færlic yfel, a sudden evil or calamity. Oros. has—repente horribili peste exercitum amisit. Haver. p. 226, 11.

at last, they could not bury them ; and, for fear, he turned from thence against his will, and went home with those who were left. As soon as the first ship came to land and told the fearful tidings, all the citizens of Carthage were moved with violent groaning and weeping,—every one asking and inquiring after his friends ; and they surely thought there was no hope for them, but that they must have altogether perished. While the citizens were thus sorrowful, the king himself came with his ship to land, clad in miserable apparel[3] ; and both he himself went homeward weeping, and the people that came to meet him, all followed him weeping. The king stretched his hands up towards heaven, and with excess of feeling bewailed both his own misfortunes, and those of all the people. He then did to himself what was worst of all : when he came to his house, he shut the people out, and locking himself alone within, he slew himself.

2. There was afterwards a wealthy man in Carthage, called Hanno, who had an immoderate longing for the kingdom ; but it appeared to him, that he could not come to it by the will of the senators, and he fixed upon the plan of asking them all to a feast at his house, that he might then kill them by poison. But it was made known by those, that, he thought, would assist him in the plot. When he knew that it was found out, he gathered together all the slaves and bad men, that he could, thinking to come upon the citizens unawares ; but it was known to them beforehand. When he was unsuccessful in that city, he went to another with twenty four thousand men, and thought that he could take it. As the citizens had the Mauretani to help them, they came out of the fortress against them, and took Hanno, and put the others to flight. He was afterwards tortured there. First, he was scourged, then his eyes were plucked out ; and afterwards his hands were cut off, then his head. All his kindred were slain lest his death should be avenged in after times, or any other should dare to begin the same again. This happened in the time of king Philip.

3. Then, the Carthaginians heard that the great Alexander had stormed the city Tyre, which, in former days, was the birth-place of their elders ; and they feared that he would also come to them. They, therefore, sent thither Hamilcar, their most pru-

---

3 Sordida servilique tunica discinctus. Oros. Haver. p. 227, 5.

dent man, to watch Alexander's conduct; so he forwarded to them at home an account of it, written upon a board; and, after it was written, he covered it over with wax. After Alexander was dead, and Hamilcar came home, the elders of the city accused him of treacherously plotting with Alexander against them; and, on that charge, put him to death.

4. The Carthaginians afterwards made war upon Sicily, where they seldom had success, and beset their chief city Syracuse. It did not then seem possible to Agathocles their king, that he could fight against them out of the fortress, nor that they could all abide within it, for want of food; they, therefore, left such a part of their forces within the fortress, as could keep it; and, at the same time, have food enough. With the other part, the king went to Carthage in ships; and, as soon as he came to land, he ordered the ships to be burned, because he was unwilling that his enemies should afterwards get possession of them. There he soon built a fortress, and from it slew and harassed the people, till Hanno, their other king, attacked him in the fortress with twenty thousand men. But Agathocles routed him, and slew two thousand of his people, and followed him till he was within five miles [4] of Carthage, and there he built another fortress. He harassed and burnt all around, so that the Carthaginians, when on a march from the city, could see the fire and the havoc.

5. It was about this time, that the brother of Agathocles, named Antander, who was left behind at home in the city, came unawares by night upon the forces which were besieging them, and nearly slew them all; and the others fled to their ships. As soon as they came home, and the tidings became known to the Carthaginians, they were so much disheartened, that not only many cities became tributary to Agathocles, but they themselves in crowds, also yielded to him; so likewise king Ophellas, with his people the Cyrenians, sought to him. But Agathocles dealt so unfaithfully with him, that he took him unawares, and put him to death : so also, it afterwards befel himself. If it had not been for that one act of treachery, he from that day might, without trouble, have gained the sovereignty of all the Carthaginians.

---

4 Castra deinde ad quintum lapidem a Carthagine statuit, ut damna rerum opulentissimarum vastationemque agrorum et incendia villarum de muris ipsius urbis specularentur Haver. p. 229, 11—13.

At the time that he acted so deceitfully, Hamilcar,[5] king of the Carthaginians was coming in peace towards him with all his people. But a disagreement arose between Agathocles and his people, and he himself was slain. After his death the Carthaginians went again with ships to Sicily. When they heard of it, they sent to Pyrrhus, king of Epirus, and for a while, he assisted them.

Book IV: Chapter VI.

1. Four[6] hundred and eighty-three years after the building of Rome, [Orosius and Alfred B. C. 270: Clinton 264], the Mamertini,[7] a people of Sicily, sent to the Romans for help, that they might withstand the army of the Carthaginians. The Romans then sent to them Appius Claudius their consul with an army. Then, after they had marched together with their people, the Carthaginians fled; and they wondered, as they themselves afterwards said, that they fled before they came near together. Because of this flight, Hanno, king of the Carthaginians, with all his people, became tributaries to the Romans, and every year paid them two hundred talents of silver: each talent weighed eighty pounds.

2. Then the Romans besieged the elder Hannibal, king of the Carthaginians, in Agrigentum, a city of Sicily, till he almost died with hunger. Then the other king of the Carthaginians, named Hanno, came to his assistance with a fleet, and was there routed. The Romans afterwards stormed the fortress, and Hannibal the king fled out by night with a few men, and gathered eighty ships, and pillaged the coasts of the Romans. In revenge the Romans first determined to build ships, which Duilius, their consul, so speedily carried out, that in sixty days, after the timber was cut, a hundred and thirty were ready, both with mast and sail. The other consul, called Cornelius Asina, went with sixteen ships to the island Lipara to a private conference with Hannibal, when he slew him. When Duilius, the other consul, heard of it, he went to the island with thirty ships and slew three

---

5 Oros. has—Bomilcar, dux Poenorum. Haver. p. 230, 8.
6 Orus. l. IV: c. 7. Haver. p. 232—234.
7 The Mamertini were an Oscan people from Campania, who migrated to Messana or Messena, on the N. E. coast of Sicily, under the protection of the god Mamers, or Mars, about B. C. 312. They were conquered by the Carthaginians; and to procure their freedom they applied to the Romans for help. Thus, the Mamertini of Sicily were the cause of the first Punic war, B. C. 264—242.

hundred of Hannibal's people, and took thirty of his ships, and sank thirteen in the sea, and put [Hannibal] himself to flight.

3. Afterwards the Poeni, who are the Carthaginians, set Hanno over their ships, as Hannibal had been before, that he might guard the islands of Sardinia and Corsica against the Romans. He soon after fought against them with a fleet and was slain.

4. In the year* after this, Calatinus the consul went with an army to Camarina a city of Sicily; but the Carthaginians had blockaded the way, where he should pass over the mountain. Then Calatinus took three hundred men with him and went over the mountain at a secret place, and the men feared that they were all fighting against him, and left the way without defence, so that the army afterwards went through there. All the three hundred men were slain there, save the consul alone: he came away wounded.

5. After that, the Carthaginians again agreed that the old Hannibal should wage war on the Romans with ships; but again, when he would pillage there, he was soon put to flight, and in his flight his own companions stoned him to death.

6. Then the consul Atilius laid waste Lipara and Malta, islands of Sicily. Afterwards, the Romans went to Africa with three hundred* and thirty ships. Then they sent their two kings Hanno and Hamilcar against them with ships, and there they were both routed, and the Romans took from them eighty-four ships. Afterwards they stormed their city Clupea, aud pillaged even to their chief city Carthage.

7. Then the consul Regulus undertook the Carthaginian war. When he first marched thither with an army, he encamped near a river, which was called Bagrada. Then, there came out of the river a serpent which was immensely large, and killed all the men who came near the water.

OF THE SERPENT. Then Regulus gathered all the bowmen that were in the company, that they might overcome it with arrows; but, when they struck or shot it, the arrows glided on its scales,

---

8 Oros. l. IV: c. 8. Haver. p. 235—237.

9 Oros. says, Cum trecentis triginta navibus, Haver. p. 236, 2.—Both the Cotton and the Lauderdale MSS. in the table of contents give þrim, three: here, by some mistake, the A. S. is feower, four.

as if they were smooth iron. He then ordered the balistas, with which they broke walls when they fought against a fortress,—that with these, they should throw at it cross-ways. Then, at the first throw, one of its ribs was broken, so that afterwards it had not power to defend itself, but was soon after killed; because it is the nature of serpents, that their power and their motion are in their ribs, as that of other [1] reptiles is in their feet. After it was killed, he told them to flay it, and to take the hide to Rome, and there to stretch it out as a wonder, because it was a hundred and twenty feet long.

8. Afterwards [B. C. 255], Regulus fought against three Carthaginian kings in one battle,—against the two Hasdrubals, and the third, called Hamilcar, who was in Sicily, [and] fetched to help them. In that battle seventeen thousand Carthaginians were slain, and five thousand [2] made prisoners, and eleven elephants taken, and eighty two towns yielded to him.

9. When [3] the Carthaginians had been put to flight, they wished for peace from Regulus; but, after they understood that he would have unreasonable tribute for the peace, they said that they would rather, that death should take them away in this kind of strife, than that they should have peace on such hard terms. They, therefore, sent for help both to Gaul and Spain, and also to Lacedæmon, to Xantippus the king. When they were all gathered together, they put all their military forces under Xantippus; and he then led the troops, whither they had before agreed, and placed two troops secretly, one on each side of him, and the third behind him, and told the two troops, when he himself with the first part should flee towards the hindermost, that they on each side, should then come across upon the army of Regulus. There thirty thousand of the Romans were slain, and Regulus was taken with five hundred men. This victory of the Carthaginians happened in the tenth year of their war with the Romans. Soon afterwards, Xantippus went back to his own kingdom, and the Romans were afraid, because by his skill they had been overreached in their engagement.

10. Then, Æmilius Paulus the consul went into Africa with

---

1 A. S. oðera creopendra wyrma, other creeping worms.
2 Oros. has—Capta autem quinque millia. The Lauderdale MS. has VX, that is V from X.
3 Oros. l. IV: c. 9. Haver. p. 238—241.

three hundred ships to the island of Clupea, and there the Carthaginians came against him with as many ships, and were there routed, and five thousand of their people slain, and thirty of their ships taken, and a hundred and four sunk. Of the Romans one thousand one hundred were slain, and nine of their ships sunk. They built a fortress on the island; and there the Carthaginians sought them again, with their two kings, who were both named Hanno. There, nine thousand of them were slain, and the others put to flight. The Romans, when they were going home, so overloaded their ships with the booty, that two hundred and thirty of them sank, and seventy were left, and with difficulty saved by casting out almost all that was in them.

11. Afterwards, Hamilcar, king of the Carthaginians, went into Numidia and Mauritania, and pillaged them, and made them tributaries, because they formerly yielded to Regulus. About three years [4] after this [B. C. 253], Servilius Cæpio and Sempronius Blæsus, the consuls, went with three hundred and sixty ships into Africa and stormed many towns of the Carthaginians, and afterwards went homewards with great booty, and so overloaded their ships again, that one hundred and fifty of them sank.

12. Then Cotta the consul went into Sicily and pillaged it all. There was so great a slaughter on both sides, that, at last, they could not bury them.

13. In the days of the consul Lucius Cæcilius Metellus, and of Caius Furius Pacilus [B. C. 251], Hasdrubal, the new king of the Carthaginians, came to the island Lilybæum with thirty thousand horse, and one hundred and thirty elephants, and soon after fought with Metellus the consul. But, after Metellus had overcome the elephants, he then also easily put the other forces to flight. After the flight Hasdrubal was slain by his own troops.

14 The [5] Carthaginians were then so overcome, and so troubled among themselves, that they found they had no power; but they agreed that they would seek peace from the Romans. Then they sent Regulus, the consul, whom they had with them in bondage for five years, and he swore to them, in the name of his gods, that he would both deliver the message they had given him, and also again tell them the answer. He did so, and announced

---

4 Tertio anno. Oros. IV, 6 § 12, Haver. p. 240, 1.
5 Oros. l. IV : c. 10. Haver. p. 241,—243.

that each nation should give up to the other, all the men whom they had taken in war, and afterwards keep peace between them. After he had announced it, he besought them, not to agree to aught of the message, and said that it would be a great disgrace to them to exchange on such even terms; and also that it was not becoming, that they should think of themselves so meanly, as if they were like them. Then, after these words, they prayed that he would stay at home with them, and take the government. Then he answered them, and said that it must not be that he should be a ruler of nations, who had before been a slave to a people. When he came back to the Carthaginians, his companions said how he had delivered their message, then they cut the two nerves on the two sides of his eyes, so that afterwards he could not sleep, till pining away he lost his life.

15. Afterwards [B. C. 250], Atilius Regulus and Manlius Vulso, the consuls, went against the Carthaginians to the island Lilybæum with two hundred ships, and there besieged a fortress. Then the young king, Hannibal, son of Hamilcar, came upon them unawares, as they were set round the fortress; and there, all were slain save a few. Then the consul Claudius went against the Carthaginians again, and Hannibal came out against them on the sea, and slew all but those on board thirty ships, which fled to the island Lilybæum : there were slain nine thousand, and twenty thousand taken.

16. Afterwards, the consul Caius Junius set out for Africa, and perished at sea with his whole fleet. In the following year, Hannibal sent a fleet against Rome, and there they ravaged to excess.

17. Then the consul Lutatius, went against Africa with three hundred ships to Sicily, where the Carthaginians fought against him. Lutatius was there wounded through one knee. On the morrow, Hanno came with Hannibal's army, and there Lutatius, although he was wounded, fought against him, and put Hanno to flight, and followed after him, till he came to the city Erycina. Soon afterwards the Carthaginians came to him again with an army, and were put to flight, and two thousand slain.

18. Then,[6] the Carthaginians a second time sued for peace to the Romans; and they gave it to them on the ground that they

---

6 Oros. l. IV : c. 11. Haver. p. 243,—244, 8.

should not hold Sicily or Sardinia; and should, moreover, pay them three thousand talents each year.

Book IV: Chapter VII.

1. Five[7] hundred and seven years after the building of Rome [Orosius and Alfred B. C. 246], there happened an immense fire among the Romans, and no man knew whence it came. When the fire left them, the river Tiber was so flooded as it never was before, nor [has been] since; so that it swept away all the people's food, that was in the city, yea, even in their houses. At the time, when Titus Sempronius and Caius Gracchus were consuls in Rome, they fought against the people Falisci, and slew twelve thousand of them.

2. In[8] that year, the Gauls,[9] who are now called Longobards, were at enmity with the Romans; and, soon afterwards, led their armies together. Three thousand of the Romans were slain, in their first battle; and, in the following year, four thousand of the Gauls were slain, and two thousand taken. When the Romans went homewards, they would not have a triumph before their consuls, as was their custom, when they gained a victory; because they fled at the former battle; and they afterwards for many years did that in various victories.

3. When Titus Manlius Torquatus, and Caius Atilius Bulbus were consuls in Rome [B. C. 235], the Sardinians, as the Carthaginians advised them, began to make war on the Romans, and were soon overpowered. Afterwards the Romans waged war on the Carthaginians, because they had broken the peace. They then sent their ambassadors twice to Rome for peace; and could not obtain it. Then, for the third time, they sent ten of their oldest senators, and they could not obtain it. For the fourth time, they sent Hanno their most unworthy officer and he obtained it.

4. "Truly," said Orosius, " now we are come to the good times with which the Romans taunt us; and to the plenty of which they are always boasting before us, that ours are not like those. But then, let any one ask them, after how many years the peace was made, from the time they first had war with many nations?

---

7 Oros. l. IV: c. 11. Haver. p. 244, 8—245, 5.
8 Oros. l. IV: c. 12, Haver. p. 245—247.
9 Oros. has Galli Cisalpini. Haver. p. 245, 19.

It is after four hundred and fifty years. Let him then ask again, how long the peace lasted? It was one year.

5. Soon after, in the following year, the Gauls waged war on the Romans; and, on the other side, the Carthaginians. "What think you now, Romans, how the peace was made sure, whether it be very like one taking a drop of oil, and dropping it on a large fire, and thinking to quench it, when it is much more likely, that, when he thinks he quenches it, he nourishes it still more. It was so then with the Romans, when they had peace for one year, that, under that peace, they came to the greatest strife."

6. In their first war [1] Hamilcar, king of the Carthaginians, when he wished to march against the Romans with an army, was then surrounded by the Spaniards and slain. In that year, the Illyrians slew the ambassadors of the Romans. Then Fulvius Postumius, the consul, on that account, led an army against them, and though he had the victory, many were slain on both sides.

7. Soon afterwards, in the following year, the Roman priests taught such new opinions, as they had very often done before, when people were warring against them on three sides,—not only the Gauls on the south of the mountains, but the Gauls on the north of the mountains, and also the Carthaginians,—that they should sacrifice human beings to their gods, and that should be a Gaulish man and a Gaulish woman. Then the Romans, by the direction of their priests, buried them alive. But God wreaked vengeance on them, as he always did before, when they sacrificed men: they paid with their living for the murder of the guiltless. That was first seen, in the battle which they had with the Gauls,—though there were eight hundred thousand of their own force, besides other nations which they had drawn over to them,—when they soon fled, because their consul was slain, and three thousand of their own people. That seemed to them as the greatest slaughter, which they often before held as nothing. At their second battle, nine thousand of the Gauls were slain.

8. In the third year after this, Manlius Torquatus and Fulvius Flaccus were consuls in Rome. They fought against the Gauls and slew three thousand of them,[2] and took six thousand.

---

[1] Oros. l. IV: c. 13. Haver. p. 248—251.
[2] Oros. Viginti tria millia. Haver. p. 250, 10.

9. In the following year, many wonders were seen. One was, that in the wood, Picenum, a spring welled with blood; and in the country of Thrace, they saw, as if the heaven were burning; and in the city, Ariminum, it was night till mid-day; and there was so great an earth-quake that, in the islands of Caria and Rhodes, there were great ruins, and the Colossus fell down.

10. This year, the consul Flaminius disregarded the saying, which the soothsayers had falsely told him, that he ought not to go to war with the Gauls; but he carried it through, and ended it with honour. There seven thousand of the Gauls were slain, and seventeen thousand taken. Afterwards, Claudius the consul fought against the Gauls, and slew thirty thousand of them; and he himself fought with the king single-handed, and slew him, and took the city, Milan. After that, the Istrians waged war on the Romans; then they sent their consuls, Cornelius and Minucius, against them. There a great slaughter was made on both sides, though the Istrians were brought under the Romans.

Book IV: Chapter VIII.

1. Five[3] hundred and thirty-three years after the building of Rome [Alfred B. C. 220: Orosius and Clinton 219], Hannibal, king of the Carthaginians, beset Saguntum, a city of Spain, because they had always kept at peace with the Romans; and settled there for eight months, till he had killed them all by hunger and overthrown the city, though the Romans sent their ambassadors to him, and begged that he would leave off the siege; but he so contemptuously slighted them, that he would not bear the sight of them in that war, and also in many others. After that, Hannibal shewed the malice and the hatred, that he swore before his father, when he was a boy of nine years old, that he would never become a friend of the Romans.

2. When Publius Cornelius Scipio, and Titus Sempronius Longus were consuls [B. C. 218], Hannibal rushed in war over the mountains called the Pyrenees, which are between France and Spain. Afterwards he went over many nations, till he came to the mountains [named] the Alps, and there also rushed over, though he was often withstood in battles, and made the way over mount Jove. So, when he came to the separate rock, he ordered

---
3 Oros. l. IV: c. 14. Haver. p. 252—253.

it to be heated with fire, and then to be hewed with mattocks; and with the utmost toil went over the mountains. Of his army there were one [hundred]⁴ thousand foot, and twenty thousand horse.

3. When he had marched on the level ground till he came to the river Ticinus, then Scipio, the consul, came against him there, and was dangerously wounded, and would also have been slain, if his son had not saved him, by standing before him till he took to flight. There a great slaughter of the Romans was made. Their next battle was at the river Trebia; and again the Romans were beaten and routed. When Sempronius, their other consul who was gone into Sicily with an army, heard of it, he went thence, and both the consuls came with an army against Hannibal; and their meeting was again at the river Trebia, and the Romans were also put to flight, and very much slaughtered, and Hannibal wounded. Afterwards Hannibal went over the mountain Barda [one of the Apennines⁵], although there was about that time, so great a snow storm, that many of the horses perished, and all the elephants but one; and the men themselves could hardly bear the cold. But he went boldly over the mountain, chiefly because he knew, that Flaminius, the consul, thought that he might without fear abide in the winter-quarters in which he was then, with the army that he had gathered, and undoubtedly thought that there was no one, who durst or could begin the journey about that time for the unwonted cold. As soon as Hannibal came to that land, he halted in a secret place, near the other army, and sent some of his army throughout the land to burn and to pillage; so that the consul thought that all the troops were spread throughout the land, and were marching thitherward, and thought that he should surprise them in the plundering; and led the army without order, as he knew the other was, till Hannibal came upon him crossways with the force that he had together, and slew the consul and twenty-five thousand of the other people, and took six thousand; and two thousand of Hannibal's people were slain. Then, the consul Scipio, brother of the other Scipio, was fighting many battles in Spain and took Mago, a general of the Carthaginians.

4 Centum millium peditum. Haver. p. 252, 17.
5 In summo Apennino. Haver. p. 253, 10.

4. Many [6] wonders happened at this time. The first was, that the sun was as if it were all lessened. The second was, that they saw, as if the sun and the moon were fighting. These wonders happened in the land of Arpi. In Sardinia they saw two shields sweat blood. The people of the Falisci saw the heaven, as if it were opened. And to the people of Antium it seemed, when they had reaped their corn, and filled their baskets, that all the ears were bloody.

Book IV: Chapter IX.

1. Five [7] hundred and forty years after the building of Rome [Orosius and Alfred B. C. 213: Clinton B. C. 216], when Lucius Æmilius Paullus and Caius Terentius Varro were consuls, they marched with an army against Hannibal; but he misled them by the same stratagem, as he did at their former meeting, and also by the new one that they knew not before, which was, that he left some of his people in a strong place, and with some he went against the consuls; and, as soon as they came together, he fled towards those who were behind, and the consuls followed after him, and slew his people, and thought that, on that day, they should have the greatest victory. But, as soon as Hannibal came to his forces, he routed all the consuls, and made so great a slaughter of the Romans as never had been made, in one battle, neither before nor since,—that was forty-four thousand, and slew two of their consuls, and took the third; and, on that day, he might have come to power over all the Romans, if he had gone forward to the city. Afterwards, Hannibal sent three measures of golden rings [8] home to Carthage, in token of his victory. By the rings, they might know, what Roman nobility had fallen; because it was a custom with them, in those days, that no one might wear a golden ring, unless he was of noble race.

2. After that battle, the Romans were so much cast down, that Cæcilius Metellus, who was then their consul, also all their senate, had thought that they should leave Rome, yea, even all Italy. And they would have done so, if Scipio, who was the eldest of the warriors, had not withheld them, for he drew his

---

6 Oros. l. IV: c. 15. Haver. p. 254, 255.
7 Oros. l. IV: c. 16. Haver. p. 256—259.
8 Tres modios annulorum aureorum misit. Haver. p. 256, 18. A modius contained 1 gallon, 7.8576 pints: the three modii would, therefore, be a little less than 3 English pecks.

sword, and swore that he would rather kill himself than leave his father-land; and said also, that he would follow after every one of them as his enemy, who would speak a word, that he thought of leaving Rome. With that, he forced them all to take oaths, that they would altogether either fall in their own land, or live in it. They then chose a Dictator, who was called Decimus Junius, that he should be ruler over the consuls. He [raised recruits from those who were] but seventeen years old.[9] They chose Scipio as consul, and they freed all the men, that they had in bondage, on condition, that they took oaths, that they would serve them in the wars. Some of them who would not free theirs,—or who did not think it fit, that they should,— the consuls paid for with their public money, and then set them free; and all those, who before were condemned, or had forfeited their freedom, they forgave it all, on condition that they should give their full service in the wars. There were six thousand of these men, when they were gathered together. All Italy forsook the Romans, and turned to Hannibal, because they had no hope that the Romans would ever regain their power. Then Hannibal went to Beneventum, and they came to meet him, and turned to him.

3. Afterwards, the Romans collected four legions of their people, and sent Lucius Posthumius, their consul, against the Gauls, whom they now call Longobards, and he was there slain and many of the people with him. Then the Romans chose Claudius Marcellus as consul, who was before the colleague of Scipio. He went secretly with a powerful force, on that end of Hannibal's army, in which he himself was, and slew many of his people, and put Hannibal himself to flight. Then had Marcellus made it known to the Romans, that they could put Hannibal to flight, though they before questioned, whether they could rout him by any human force.

4. During these wars, the two Scipios, who were then consuls, and also brothers, were in Spain with an army, and fought against Hasdrubal, uncle of Hannibal, and slew him; and of his army they partly slew and partly took thirty thousand. He was also another king of the Carthaginians.

5. Afterwards Centenius Penula, the consul, begged that the

---

[9] Qui, delectu habito ab annis decem et septem. Haver. p. 257, 5, 6.

senate would give him troops, that he might attack Hannibal in battle; and he was there slain and eight thousand of his people. Then Sempronius Gracchus, the consul, went again with an army against Hannibal, and was put to flight; and a great slaughter was made of his army.

6. "How can the Romans now," said Orosius, "in truth say, that they had then better times, than they have now, when they had undertaken, at the same time, so many wars?—One was in Spain; another in Macedonia; a third in Cappadocia; a fourth at home against Hannibal; and they were also very often put to flight and disgraced. But it was very evident, that they were then better warriors, than they are now; that they, however, would never shrink from the war, though they often stood on a small and hopeless foundation, so that, at last, they had the mastery over all those, who, before, nearly had it over them.

Book IV : Chapter X.

1. It was[1] five hundred and forty-three years after the building of Rome [Orosius, Alfred, Clinton B. C. 210], that Claudius Marcellus, the consul, went with a fleet to Sicily, and took Syracuse, their wealthiest city, though he could not take it in the former expedition, when he besieged it, because of the skill of Archimedes, an officer of the Sicilians.

2. In the tenth year, after Hannibal waged war in Italy, he went from the country of Campania till within three miles of Rome, and encamped by the river, called Anio, to the greatest fear of all the Romans, as from the behaviour of the men, it might be understood, how frightened and astonished they were, when the women ran with stones towards the walls, and said that they would defend the city, if the men durst not. On the next morning, Hannibal marched to the city, and drew up his army before the gate, called Collina. But the consuls did not think themselves so cowardly, as the women had before spoken of them, that they durst not defend themselves within the city; but they set themselves in array against Hannibal without the gate. But when they wished to engage, then there came such overwhelming rain that not one of them could wield any weapon; and, therefore, they separated. When the rain ceased, they went together again, and

---

[1] Oros. l. IV : c. 17. Haver. p. 259—262.

again there was another such rain, and they again separated. Then Hannibal understood, and said within himself, though he was wishing and hoping for power over the Romans, that God did not grant it.

3. " Tell me now, O Romans ! " said Orosius, " when or where it came to pass that, before Christianity, either you or others could have rain by praying to any gods, as they could afterwards, since Christianity came, and may now have much good from our Saviour, Christ, when they have need. It was however very evident that the same Christ, who afterwards turned them to Christianity, sent them that rain as a guard, though they were not worthy of it, to the end that they themselves, and many others through them, might come to Christianity and to the true belief."

4. In the days when this happened, two consuls were slain in Spain : they were brothers, and were both named Scipio. They were deceived by Hasdrubal, king of the Carthaginians.—At that time Quintus Fulvius, the consul, so frightened all the leading men, that were in Campania, that they killed themselves with poison. He slew all the leading men that were in Capua because he thought they would be a help to Hannibal, though the senate had strictly forbidden that deed.

5. When the Romans were told, that the consuls were slain in Spain, the senate could not find a consul among them, who durst march into Spain with an army, but the son of one of the consuls, named Scipio, who was a youth. He earnestly begged that they would give him troops, that he might lead an army into Spain ; and he chiefly undertook that expedition, because he thought that he could revenge his father and his uncle, though he strictly hid it from the senate. But the Romans were so earnest for the expedition, although they were much straitened in their treasure which they had for public use, because of the wars which they had on four sides, that they gave him all that they had in aid of the expedition, but that each woman kept one ounce of gold, and one pound of silver, and each man one ring and one collar.'

6. When[2] Scipio had marched to the new city, Carthage, which they now call Cordova, he besieged Hannibal's brother;

---

[2] Bullasque sibi ac filiis, Oros. Haver p. 262, 10. The bulla was an ornament worn round the neck, chiefly by children and young men.

[3] Oros. l. IV : c. 18. Haver. p. 263—267.

and because he came upon the townspeople unawares, he, in a little time, brought them under his power by hunger, so that the king himself fell into his hands, and of all the others, some he slew,—some he bound, and sent the king bound to Rome, and many of the chief senators with him. Within the city much treasure was found: some of it Scipio sent to Rome,—some he ordered to be dealt out to the army.

7. At that time, Lævinus, the consul, went from Macedonia to Sicily with a fleet; and there overcame the city, Agrigentum, and took Hanno, their leader. Afterwards forty towns fell into his hands; and twenty-six he overcame by fighting. At that time, Hannibal slew Cneius Fulvius the consul in Italy, and eight thousand with him. Afterwards, Hannibal fought with the consul Marcellus, for three days: on the first day the people fell on both sides alike; the next day, Hannibal had the victory; the third day, the consul had [it]. Then Fabius Maximus, the consul, went with a fleet to the city, Tarentum, unknown to Hannibal, and stormed the city by night, so that they, who were therein, knew it not; and slew Hannibal's general, Carthalo, and thirty thousand with him.

8. In the year afterwards, Hannibal stole on Claudius Marcellus, the consul, where he was placed with the army, and slew him and his people with him. In those days Scipio routed Hasdrubal, Hannibal's other brother, in Spain; and eighty towns of this people fell into his hands. So hateful were the Carthaginian people to Scipio, that when he had routed them, though he sold some of them for money, he would not keep the money, which was given for them, but gave it to other people. In the same year Hannibal again over-reached two consuls, Marcellus and Crispinus, and slew them.

9. When Claudius Nero, and Marcus Livius Salinator were consuls, Hasdrubal, Hannibal's brother, went with an army from Spain into Italy to help Hannibal. Then the consuls heard of that before Hannibal, and came against him, when he had passed over the mountains, and there they had a long fight ere either of the armies fled. That Hasdrubal was so long in fleeing, was rather owing to this reason, because he had elephants with him; and the Romans had the victory. Hasdrubal was slain there, and fifty three thousand of his army, and five thousand taken.

Then the consuls gave orders to cut off the head of Hasdrubal, and to throw it before Hannibal's camp. When it was known to Hannibal, that his brother was slain, and so many of the people with him, then he first had a fear of the Romans, and he went into the land of the Brutii. Then Hannibal and the Romans had one year of stillness between them, because very many of both the armies died of fever. In that stillness, Scipio over-ran all Spain, and afterwards came to Rome, and gave advice to the Romans, that they should go in ships into the country of Hannibal,. Then the Romans sent him to be the leader of the expedition; and, as soon as he came upon Carthage, Hanno, the king, came against him unwarily, and was slain there. At that time, Hannibal fought with Sempronius, the consul, in Italy, and drove him into Rome.

10. After that, the Carthaginians marched against Scipio with all their force, and encamped in two places near the city, which is called Utica: in one were the Carthaginians,—in the other the Numidians, who were to help them, and had thought, that they should there have winter-quarters. But when Scipio learned that the forewarders were set far from the fastness, and also that no others were nearer, he secretly led his army between the warders, and sent a few men to one of their fastnesses, with the view of setting fire to one end of it, that then almost all, who were within it, might run towards the fire with the thought of quenching it. Then Scipio, in the mean time, almost slew them all. When the others, who were in the other fastness, found that out, they ran thitherward in crowds to help the others; and Scipio was, all that night, until day, slaying them as they came; and afterwards, throughout all the day, he slew them fleeing. Their two kings Hasdrubal and Syphax fled to the city Carthage, and gathered the troops, which they had there, and came against Scipio, and were again chased into Carthage. Some fled to the island, Cirta; and Scipio sent a fleet after them, so that some they slew,—some they took. Syphax, their other king, was taken, and was afterwards sent to Rome in chains.

11. In [4] these battles, the Carthaginians were so cast down, that afterwards they reckoned themselves as nothing against the Romans; and sent into Italy for Hannibal, and prayed that he

---

4 Oros. l. IV: c. 19. Haver. p. 267—269.

would come and help them. He granted that prayer weeping, because he must leave Italy, in the thirteenth year after he first came into it; and he slew all his men, who were of those countries, and would not [go] over the sea with him.

12. When he sailed homeward, he told a man to climb up the mast, and to look whether he knew the land, towards which they were [sailing]. Then he said, that he saw a broken tomb such as it was their custom to build of stones above ground for rich men. Then, after their heathenish custom, that answer was very unpleasant to Hannibal; and he told him his dislike to the answer, and ordered all the army with their ships to turn from the place, which he had before thought of, and came to the town, Leptis, and quickly went to Carthage, and begged that he might speak with Scipio, and wished that he might be able to make peace between the nations. But their private conference, which they held together between the armies, brought on a quarrel, and they prepared for battle. Soon after they came together, Hannibal's army was put to flight, and twenty thousand slain, and five hundred and eighty elephants, and Hannibal fled with three others to the fortress, Adrumetum. The citizens then sent to Hannibal from Carthage, and said that it would be best for them to seek for peace from the Romans. When Cneius Cornelius Lentulus, and Publius Ælius Pætus were consuls, [B. C. 201], peace was granted to the Carthaginians by Scipio with the Senate's consent, on the ground that the islands of Sicily and Sardinia should belong to the Romans, and that every year they should pay them as many talents of silver as they then gave them; and Scipio ordered five hundred of their ships to be drawn up and burnt, and afterwards went homeward to Rome.— When they brought the triumph towards him, there came with it Terentius, the great Carthaginian poet, who bore a hat on his head, because the Romans had lately enacted, that, when they had overcome any people, those who might wear a hat, might then have both life and freedom.

Book IV: Chapter XI.

1. Five[5] hundred and fifty years after the building of Rome [Orosius B. C. 207: Alfred 203: Clinton 201], the second war of the Carthaginians and the Romans was ended, which they

---

5 Oros. l. IV: c. 20, Haver. p. 269—276.

were carrying on for fourteen years. But the Romans soon after began another against the Macedonians. The consuls then cast lots, which of them should first undertake that war. It was then allotted to Quintius Flamininus, and he in that war fought many battles, and very often had the victory, until Philip, their king, asked for peace, and the Romans granted it; and he then went to the Lacedæmonians, and Quintius Flamininus forced both the kings to give their sons for hostages. Philip, king of the Macedonians, gave his son Demetrius, and Nabis, king of the Lacedæmonians, gave his son Armenes. The consul gave orders to all the Roman men, whom Hannibal had sold into Greece, that they should all shave their heads, as a token that he loosed them from slavery.

2. At that time, the people of the Isubres, the Boii, and the Cænomani gathered themselves together by the advice of Hamilcar, brother of Hannibal, whom he had formerly left behind him in Italy; and they afterwards marched into the lands of Placentia, and Cremona, and laid them altogether waste. Then the Romans sent thither Claudius Fulvius, the consul, and he with difficulty overcame them. Afterwards Flamininus, the consul, fought against Philip, king of the Macedonians, and against the Thracians, and against the Illyrians, and against many other nations, in one battle, and put them all to flight. There eight thousand of the Macedonians were slain, and six thousand taken. After that, Sempronius, the consul, was slain in Spain with all his army. At that time Marcellus, the consul was put to flight in the land of Etruria, when Furius, the other consul, came to help him, and gained the victory; and they afterwards laid waste all that land.

3. When Lucius Valerius Flaccus, and Marcus Porcius Cato were consuls [B. C. 195], Antiochus, king of the Syrians, began to wage war against the Romans, and went with an army out of Asia into Europe. At that time, the Romans ordered, that they should take Hannibal, king of the Carthaginians, and afterwards bring him to Rome. When he heard of it, he fled to Antiochus, king of the Syrians, whilst he was abiding in doubt, whether he should dare to wage war against the Romans, as he had begun. But Hannibal led him to carry on the war longer. The Romans then sent Scipio Africanus their ambassader to Antiochus, when he told Hannibal to speak with the ambassadors, and answer them. When they did not agree to any peace, afterwards Scipio,

the consul came with Glabrio, the other consul, and slew forty thousand of the army of Antiochus. In the year following this, Scipio fought against Hannibal out at sea, and had the victory. When Antiochus heard of it, he asked Scipio for peace and sent home to him his son, who was in his power, though he knew not how he came to him, unless, as some men said, he had been taken in pillaging or on guard.

4. In the farther Spain, Æmilius, the consul, was cut off with all his army by the Lusitanian nation. In those days, Lucius Bæbius, the consul, was cut off with all his army, by the Etruscan people; so that there was no one left to tell it at Rome.

5. Afterwards Fulvius, the consul, went with an army into Greece, to the mountains which they call Olympus, where many of the people had fled to a fastness. Then, in the battle, in which they wished to break into the fastness, many of the Romans were shot dead with arrows, and struck off with stones. When the consul understood, that they could not break into the fastness, he then gave orders to some of the soldiers, that they should go away from the fastness, and the rest he told that they should flee towards the others, when the battle was hottest, that they might thus entice those out, who were within it. In the flight, which the townspeople afterwards made towards the fastness, forty thousand of them were slain, and those that were left there, came into his hands. In those days, Marcius, the consul, marched with an army into the land of Liguria, and was put to flight, and four thousand of his army slain.

6. When Marcus Claudius Marcellus, and Quintus Fabius Labeo were consuls [B. C. 183], Philip, king of Macedon, killed the Roman ambassadors, and sent Demetrius, his son, to the senate, that he might appease their anger; and, though he did so, when he came home, Philip ordered his other son to kill him with poison, because he accused him of speaking of him unbecomingly to the senate. At the same time, Hannibal by his own will killed himself with poison. At that time appeared the island Volcano, near Sicily, which was not seen before then. At that time [B. C. 179] Quintus Fulvius Flaccus, the consul, fought against the farther Spaniards, and had a victory.

7. When Lepidus and Mucius were consuls, the most powerful nation, which was then called Basternæ and is now called

Hungarian, would wage war on the Romans: they wished to come to the help of Perseus, king of the Macedonians. The river Danube was then so much frozen over, that they believed they might march over the ice; but there they almost all perished.

8. When Publius Licinius Crassus, and Caius Cassius Longinus were consuls [B. C. 171], the Macedonian war arose, which may well be reckoned among the greatest wars; because, in those days, all the Italians were helping the Romans, and also Ptolemy, king of Egypt,—and Ariarathes, king of Cappadocia,—and Eumenes, king of Asia,—and Masinissa, king of Numidia. And Perseus, king of Macedonia, had all the Thracians, and Illyrians to help him. Soon after they came together, the Romans were put to flight; and soon after that, in a second battle, they were also put to flight. After these battles Perseus, all that year, sorely harassed the Romans, and afterwards he marched upon the Illyrians, and stormed their city Sulcanum, which belonged to the Romans; and many of the people,—some he killed,—some he led into Macedonia. Afterwards, Lucius Æmilius, the consul, fought with Perseus and overcame him, and slew twenty thousand of his people; and he himself fled at that time, and was soon afterwards taken, and brought to Rome, and there slain. There were many battles in those days in many lands, of all which it is now too tiresome to speak.

Book IV: Chapter XII.

1. Six[6] hundred years after the building of Rome [Orosius and Alfred B. C. 153: Clinton 151], when Licinius Lucullus, and Aulus Posthumius Albinus were consuls, the Romans had the greatest fear of the Celtiberians, a people of Spain: and they had not any man that durst go thither with an army, but Scipio the consul, who was called Africanus after that expedition, because he then went a second time thither, when no other durst; although the Romans had agreed, a little before, that he should go into Asia; but he had many battles in Spain with various victories. In those days, Servius Galba, a colleague of Scipio, fought against the Lusitanians, a people of Spain, and was routed.

2. In those days, the gods of the Romans gave orders to the

---

6 Oros. L. IV: c. 21. Haver. p. 276—278.

senate to build them a theatre for plays; but Scipio often sent orders home that they should not begin it; and also, when he came home from Spain, he himself said, that it would be the greatest folly, and the greatest mistake. Then the Romans, by his chiding and by his teaching, would not listen to the gods; and all the money, that they had there gathered together, which they would have given for the pillars and for the work, they gave for other things.—Now may those Christians be ashamed, who love and follow such idolatry, when he so much scorned it, who was not a Christian, and should have furthered it, according to their own custom.

3. Afterwards, Servius Galba marched again upon the Lusitanians, and made peace with them, and under that peace deceived them. That deed did wellnigh the greatest harm to the Romans, so that no people, that were under them, could trust to them.

Book IV: Chapter XIII.

1. Six' hundred and two years after the building of Rome [Orosius and Alfred B. C. 151: Clinton 149], when Lucius Marcius Censorinus, and Marcus Manilius were consuls, then happened the third war of the Romans and Carthaginians; and the senate agreed among themselves, that, if they overcame them a third time, they would overthrow all Carthage. Again they sent Scipio thither, and he routed them in their first battle, and drove them into Carthage. They then begged for peace from the Romans, but Scipio would not grant it to them on any other ground, than that they all gave up their weapons to him, and left the city, and that no one should settle within ten miles of it. After that was done, they said they would rather perish together with the city, than that it should be overthrown without them. Those who had iron, again made themselves weapons; and those who had not, made them,—some of silver,—some of wood, and set the two Hasdrubals over them, as their kings.

2. " Now," said Orosius, " I will tell, what sort [of a city] it was:—Its circumference was thirty miles; and it was all surrounded by sea, but three miles. The wall was twenty feet thick and forty ells high; and there was within another less fastness, on a cliff of the sea,' which was two miles [in extent].' The

---

7 Oros. l. IV: c. 22. Haver. p. 279, 280.   8 Imminens mari. Haver. p. 280, 5.   9 The

Carthaginians at that time guarded the city, although Scipio had before broken down much of the wall, and afterwards he went homeward.

3. When Cneus Cornelius Lentulus and Lucius Mummius were consuls [B. C. 146], Scipio went a third time into Africa, because he wished to overthrow Carthage. When he came thither, he was fighting against the city for six days, till the citizens begged that they might be their servants, since they could not defend themselves. Then Scipio ordered all the women first to go out, of whom there were twenty-six thousand; and then the men, of whom there were thirty thousand. Hasdrubal, the king, killed himself, and his wife with her two sons burnt themselves because of the king's death. Scipio ordered all the city to be overthrown, and every hewn stone to be broken to pieces, that they might not afterwards [be used] for any wall. The city was burning within for sixteen days, about seven hundred years after it was first built.

4. Then the third war of the Carthaginians and the Romans was ended, in the fourth year after it was first begun; although the Romans had before a long consultation about it, whether it was more reasonable for them utterly to destroy the city, that they ever after might have peace on that side, or they should let it stand, to the end that war might again arise from thence, because they dreaded, if they did not sometimes wage war, that they would too soon become drowsy and slothful.

5. "So that, to you, Romans, it is now again made known, since Christianity came," said Orosius, "that ye have lost the whetstone of your elders, of your wars, and of your bravery; for ye are now fat without and lean within; but your elders were lean without and fat within, of a strong and firm mind. I also know not," said he, "how useful I may be at the time that I speak these words, but that I may lose my pains. It is also desirable that a man briskly rub the softest malmstone,† if he think of making it

---

A. S. has—twegra mila heah, two miles high! But Orosius only speaks of its superficial extent. " Arx ... paulo amplius quam duo millia passuum tenebat. Haver. p. 280, 3.

* Oros. l. IV: c. 23. Haver. p. 281—283.

† The late Dr Ingram, President of Trinity College Oxford, in his notes, written in his copy of Orosius, and left with his other books, to his College, states—" There is a kind of stone, which is still called in Wiltshire, *Malmstone*, of which there is great abundance in that county,—a county well known to king Alfred,—the theatre of his most glorious battles, etc." The Wiltshire and Oxfordshire *Malm-stone* is chalk and other friable stone [*Plot*. Nat. Hist.

the best whetstone. So then, it is now very difficult for me to whet their mind, since it will be neither sharp nor hard.

Book V: Chapter I.

1. "I know," said Orosius, "what the boast of the Romans chiefly is,—because they have overcome many nations, and have often driven many kings before their triumphs. Those are the good times of which they always boast; just as if they now said, that those times were given to them only, and not to all people; but, if they could rightly understand it, then they might know, that they were common to all nations. If they say that those times were good, because they made that one city wealthy, then may they more truly say that they were the most unhappy, because, through the riches of that one city, all the others were made poor.

2. If they do not believe this, let them then ask the Italians, their own countrymen, how they liked those times, when they were slain, and kept down, and sold into other lands for one hundred and twenty years.

3. If they do not believe them, then let them ask the Spaniards, who were bearing the same for two hundred years, and many other nations; and also many kings, how they liked it, when they drove them in yokes, and in chains before their triumphs towards Rome for their own glory; and afterwards they lay in prison until they died. And they harassed many kings, to the end that they should give all that they then had

---

Oxon. p. 69]. In A. S. mealm signifies, sand or grit. So, in cognate languages, we find the same word. The Goth. malma *sand*. Old Ger. " malm *arena*; malmen, *in pulverem redigere*." Wachteri Glos. Dutch " Molm *caries, et pulvis ligni cariosi*. Kilian." The modern Ger. has zermalmen, *to crush to pieces*. Mr Thomson observes: " In the north of England maum, and in Scotland maumie, signify *mellow or soft*; but the old Ger, malu, I grind, may shew the reason of the name,—a stone that may be ground down, or pulverized." Wacher says malm *pulvis*. Old Ger. malen *molere*. My friend would have the latter clause rendered thus: " After which, that he think to obtain the best whetstone."—" It is desirable that after he has rubbed off the rust with the malmstone—whatever that was—he should look out for a good whetstone to finish with. The mind of the Romans is figured by a rusty blade—the rebukes of Orosius, like the hard or brisk rubbing, are not enough to give it an edge; he must think of something more effacious as a whetstone, or else his labour will be lost." Such is Mr. T's view,—mine is given above.

1 This Vth book of Alfred contains the Vth and VIth of the original Latin of Orosius. Alfred entirely omits the last four chapters of book V, namely;—21, 22, 23 and 24, For the omissions in Book VI, see book V chapter 11 § 3, 4; note 2, 3.

2 Oros. l. V: c. 1. Haver. p. 284—287. This is the first introductory chapter of Orosius, that Alfred has translated; but he has greatly abridged it.

for their wretched life. But it is, therefore, unknown to us and not to be believed, because we are born in that peace, which they could hardly buy with their life. It was after Christ was born, that we were loosed from all slavery, and from all fear, if we will fully follow him.

Book V : Chapter II.

1. Six [3] hundred and six years after the building of Rome [Orosius and Alfred B. C. 147 : Clinton 146],—that was in the same year, in which Carthage was overthrown—after its fall—Cneus Cornelius Lentulus and Lucius Mummius overthrew Corinth, the chief city of all the Greeks. In its burning, all the statues, which were in it, of gold, and of silver, and of brass, and of copper, were melted together, and sunk into pits. Even to this day, they call all the vessels Corinthian, that were made of it, because they are handsomer and dearer than any other.

2. OF THE SHEPHERD VIRIATHUS.[4] In those days, there was a shepherd in Spain, who was called Viriathus, and was a great thief ; and in the stealing he became a robber; and, in the robbing, he drew to himself a great force of men, and pillaged many villages. Afterwards his band waxed so strong, that he ravaged many lands, and the Romans had a great dread of him, and sent Vetilius, the consul, against him with an army, and he was routed there, and the greatest part of his people slain. At another time, Caius Plautius, the consul, went thither, and was also routed. A third time, Claudius, the consul, went thither, and thought that he should take away the shame of the Romans, but he rather added to it in that expedition, and he hardly escaped.

3. Afterwards, Viriathus, with three hundred men, met one thousand Romans in a wood, where seventy of the people of Viriathus were slain, and three hundred of the Romans, and the others were put to flight. In the flight, a soldier of Viriathus was following the others too long, till they shot his horse under him. When all the others would slay or bind him by himself, he then so struck a man's horse with his sword, that its head flew off. Afterwards, all the others had so much fear of him, that they durst no longer go against him.

4 Afterwards Appius Claudius, the consul, fought against the

---
3 Oros. l. V : c. 3. Haver. p. 289—291. Chapter 2 is omitted by Alfred.
4 Oros. L V : c. 4. Haver. p. 291—296.

Gauls, and was put to flight; and soon after, again led an army against them and had a victory, and slew six thousand of them. When he was [coming] homeward, he begged that they would meet him with a triumph; but the Romans unfaithfully denied it, and excused it, on the ground, that he formerly, on another occasion, had not the victory.

5. OF THE PESTILENCE. There was afterwards so great a pestilence in Rome, that no stranger durst come thither, and many lands within the city were without any heir. They, however, knew that that evil went over without sacrifice, as many did before, which they thought that they had checked by their idolatries. Doubtless, if they could have then sacrificed, they would have said that their gods helped them. But it was by the grace of God, that all those, who would have done it, lay [sick], till it went over of itself.

6. Then Fabius, the consul, went with an army against Viriathus, and was put to flight. The consul did what was most disgraceful to all the Romans, when he enticed to him from Scythia six hundred men of his comrades; and, when they came to him, he ordered all their hands to be cut off. Afterwards Pompeius, the consul marched upon the Numantines, a people of Spain, and was put to flight. About fourteen years after Viriathus began to war against the Romans, he was slain by his own men; and as often as the Romans attacked him in battle, he always put them to flight. There, however, the Romans did themselves a little honour, that those, who had betrayed their lord, although at the time they hoped for rewards, were hated and despised by them.

7. I must needs be silent also about the many wars, which happened in the east lands: I shall be tired of the wars of the Romans. At that time, Mithridates, king of Pontus, overcame Babylonia, and all the lands, that were between the two rivers, the Indus and Hydaspes, which had before been in the power of the Romans. He afterwards enlarged his kingdom eastward to the boundaries of India; and Demetrius, king of Asia, attacked him twice with an army. At the first time, he was put to flight; at the second, taken. He was under the power of the Romans, because they had placed him there.

8. Then Mancinus, the consul, marched upon the Numantines, a people of Spain, and was fighting there, till he made peace with

that people; and afterwards he stole away. When he came home, the Romans gave orders to bind and bring him before the gate of the fortress of Numantia. Then, neither those, who led him thither, durst lead him back home, nor would they receive him to whom he was brought; but he was very cruelly left so bound in one place, before the gate, until he yielded up his life.

9. In [5] those days, Brutus, the consul, slew sixty thousand of the people of Spain, who had been helping the Lusitanians; and soon afterwards he marched again upon the Lusitanians, and slew fifty thousand of them, and took six thousand. In those days, Lepidus, the consul, went into the nearer Spain, and was put to flight, and six thousand of his people were slain; and those that came away, fled with the greatest shame. But, can the Romans now blame any man for saying how many of their people perished in Spain, in a few years, when they boast of happy times, while they were the most unhappy to themselves?

10. When [6] Servius Fulvius Flaccus, and Quintus Calpurnius Piso were consuls [B. C. 135], a child was born in Rome, that had four feet, and four hands, and four eyes, and four ears.—In that year, the fire of Etna sprang up, in Sicily, and burnt up more of that land, than it ever did before.

Book V: Chapter III.

1. Six [7] hundred and twenty years after the building of Rome [Orosius and Alfred B. C. 133: Clinton 137], when Mancinus made the bad peace with the Numantines, as the Romans themselves said, that a deed more shameful had not been done, under their rule, save at the battle of Caudinæ Furculæ, then the Romans sent Scipio to the Numantines with an army. They are in the north-west of Spain, and they had before defended themselves, for fourteen years, with four thousand, against forty thousand of the Romans, and mostly had victory.

2. Then Scipio besieged them for half a year in their fastness, and distressed them so much, that they would rather hazard themselves, than bear those miseries any longer. When Scipio understood that they were in such a mood, he ordered some of his people to make an assault on the fastness, that they might thereby

---

5 Oros. l. V: c. 5. Haver. p. 298, 299.
6 Oros. l. V: c. 6. Haver. p. 299, 300.
7 Oros. l. V: c. 7. Haver. p. 300—303.

entice the people out. The citizens were then so glad, and so joyful, that they must fight, that, in the midst of their joy, they drank too much ale, and ran out at two gates. In that city ale-brewing [8] first began, because they had not wine. By that stratagem, the chief of the Numantians fell, and the part that was left there burnt the whole city, because they would not give up their old treasures to their enemies, and they then destroyed themselves in the fire.

3. When [9] Scipio turned homeward from that country, there came to him an old man, who was a Numantian. Then Scipio asked him to what it was owing, that the Numantines so soon became weak, so brave as they long had been. He then told him, that they were brave while they had agreement and simplicity among themselves, and as soon as they had disagreement they all perished. That answer was then very fearful to Scipio and to all the Roman senators: when he came home, they were put into great fear by that answer and by those words, because they then had disagreement among themselves.

4. At that time,[1] one of their consuls was called Gracchus, and he began to wage war against all the others, till they killed him.

5. And also at that time, the slaves fought against their masters, and were not easily overcome, and seven thousand were slain ere they could be brought under. Only in one city, Minturnæ, four hundred and fifty were hanged.

Book V: Chapter IV.

1. Six [2] hundred and twenty one years after the building of Rome [Alfred B. C. 132: Orosius and Clinton 131] Publius Licinius Crassus Mucianus, the consul, who was also the chief priest of the Romans, went with an army against Aristonicus, the king who wished to take to himself Asia the Less, though Attalus, his own brother, had before given it by will [3] to the Romans. Many kings from many lands came to help Crassus;—one [4] was from Nicomedia?—a second from Bithynia,—a third

---
8 A. S. ealo-geweorc *ale-work*.
9 Oros. l. V : c. 8. Haver. p. 304, 305.
1 Oros. l. V : c. 9. Haver. p. 306, 307.
2 Oros. l. V : c. 10. Haver. p. 308—311.
3 Per testamentum. Haver. p. 308, 6.
4 The A. S. text of the Lauderdale and Cotton MSS. are both so incorrect, the translator having taken the names of kings for the names of countries, that it is necessary to cite the

from Pontus,—a fourth from Armenia,—a fifth from Argenta?—a sixth from Cappadocia,—a seventh from Pylemene?—an eighth from Paphlagonia. Nevertheless, soon after they came together, the consul, though he had a great army, was put to flight. When Perperna, the other consul, heard of it, he speedily gathered an army, and came suddenly upon the king, when his army was all abroad, and drove him into a fortress; and besieged him till the townspeople gave him up to the consul, and he afterwards ordered him to be brought to Rome, and thrust into prison, and he lay there till he yielded up his life.

2. At that time, Antiochus, king of Assyria, thought that he had not power enough; and, wishing to gain Parthia, he marched thither with many thousands. There the Parthians easily overcame him, and slew the king, and took the kingdom to themselves; because Antiochus cared not what number of men he had, and took no heed of what sort they were; therefore, more of them were bad than good.

3. At that time Scipio, the best and most successful of the Roman senators and warriors, complained of his hardships to the Roman senators, when they were at their meeting, and asked them why they treated him so unworthily in his old age,—why they would not remember all the pains and toils he had borne for their sake and from necessity, at countless times, for many years;—and how he had kept them from the slavery of Hannibal and of many other people;—and how he had brought all Spain and all Africa under their power. In the night of the same day, on which he spoke these words, the Romans thanked him for all his labour, with a worse reward than he had deserved from them, when they smothered and stifled him in his bed, so that he lost his life.—O Romans! who can now trust you, when you gave such a reward to your most faithful senator!

4. When M. Æmilius Lepidus and L. Aurelius Orestes were consuls [B. C. 126], the fire of Etna flew up so broad and so great, that few of the men, who were in the island Lipari, which was next to it, could abide in their dwellings, for the heat and for the stench. Also, all the cliffs, that were near the sea, were burnt to ashes, and all the ships, that were sailing near that sea,

---

original Latin of Orosius. Hoc est—Nicomede Bithyniæ, Mithridate Ponti et Armeniæ, Ariarathe Cappadociæ, Pylemene Paphlagoniæ, eorumque maximis copiis adjutus,—conserto tamen bello, victus est. Haver. p. 308, 7—10 v. also Eutropius l. IV: c. 20.

were consumed. Also, all the fishes, that were in the sea, died from the heat.

5. When [5] Marcus Fulvius Flaccus was consul [B. C. 125], locusts came into Africa, and ate off every thing, that was waxing and growing in the land. There then came a wind, and blew them out into the sea. When they were drowned, the sea cast them up; and afterwards almost every thing perished that was in the land, both men, and cattle, and wild beasts, because of the stench.

Book V: Chapter V.

1. Six [6] hundred and twenty-seven years after the building of Rome [Orosius and Alfred B. C. 126: Clinton 123], when Quintus Cæcilius Metellus, and Titus Quinctius Flamininus were consuls, the senate agreed that Carthage should be rebuilt. But in the night of the same day, in which they had marked out the city with stakes, as they wished to build it, wolves pulled up the stakes, and the men therefore left the work and had a long meeting about it, whether it betokened peace or war; they, however, rebuilt it.

2. At that time, Metellus [7] the consul went to the Balearic islands; and, though many of the islanders also perished, he overcame the pirates, that ravaged these islands.

Book V: Chapter VI.

1. Six [8] hundred and twenty-eight years after the building of Rome [Orosius and Alfred B. C. 125: Clinton 121], Fabius the consul met Bituitus, king of the Gauls, and overcame him with a small force.

Book V: Chapter VII.

1. Six [9] hundred and thirty-five years after the building of Rome [Orosius B. C. 114: Alfred 118: Clinton 111], when Scipio Nasica and Lucius Calpurnius Bestia were consuls, the Romans waged war against Jugurtha, king of the Numidians. The same Jugurtha was a kinsman of Micipsa, king of the

---

5 Oros. l. V: c. 11. Haver. p. 311, 312.
6 Oros. l. V: c. 12. Haver. p. 315—318.
7 Oros. l. V: c. 13. Haver. p. 318.
8 Much abridged, from Oros. l. V. c. 14. Haver. p. 319, 320, as all these chapters are. This will be evident by observing the quantity of Latin text referred to in the preceding and following notes.
9 Oros. l. V: c. 15. Haver. p. 321—326.

Numidians, and he took him, in his youth, and ordered him to be fed and taught with his two sons. When the king died, he commanded his two sons to give a third part of the kingdom to Jugurtha. But, when the third part was in his power, he beguiled both the sons: one he slew, the other he drove away, who afterwards went to the Romans for shelter, and they sent with him Calpurnius, the consul, with an army. But Jugurtha bribed the consul with his money, so that he did little in the warfare. Afterwards Jugurtha came to Rome, and covertly bribed the senators, one by one, so that they all were wavering about him. When he returned homeward from the city, he blamed the Romans, and greatly reviled them with his words, and said, that no city could be more easily bought with money, if any one would buy it.

2. In the year afterwards, the Romans sent Aulus Posthumius the consul with sixty thousand [men] against Jugurtha. Their meeting was at the city Calama, and there the Romans were overcome; and, after a little while, they made peace between them, and then almost all Africa turned to Jugurtha. Afterwards the Romans sent Metellus again with an army against Jugurtha; and he twice gained a victory. At the third time, he drove Jugurtha into Numidia, his own country, and forced him to give three hundred hostages to the Romans; and nevertheless, he afterwards plundered the Romans. Then, after that, they sent Marius the consul, against Jugurtha, as he was always so cunning, and so crafty; and he went to a city, just as if he thought of storming it. But as soon as Jugurtha had led his forces to the city against Marius, then Marius left the fortress, and marched to another, where he heard, that Jugurtha's treasure was, and forced the citizens to come into his hands, and they gave up to him all the treasure that was in it. Then Jugurtha, after that, did not trust his own people, but joined himself to Bocchus, king of the Mauritanians, and he came to him with a great body of men, and they often stole upon the Romans, till they determined upon a general battle between them. For that battle, Bocchus had brought sixty thousand horse, besides foot, to help Jugurtha. Neither before nor since, had the Romans ever so hard a fight, as they had there, because they were surrounded on every side; and also most of them perished, because their meeting was on a sandy down, so that they could not see for dust, how they should

defend themselves. In addition to which, they were weakened both by thirst and heat, and all that day, they bore it, until nigh*. Then, on the morrow, they did the same, and were again surrounded on every side, as they were before. When they had much fear, whether they could escape, they settled, that some should guard them behind, and some, if they could, should fight [their way] out, through all the troops. When they had done so, there came so heavy a rain, that the Mauritanians were wearied by it, because their shields were covered with the hides of elephants, so that few of them could lift them for the wet: because an elephant's hide will drink wet like a sponge; and, therefore, they were put to flight. There were slain of the Mauritanians, sixty thousand and one hundred men. Then Bocchus made peace with the Romans, and gave up Jugurtha to them, bound; and he was afterwards put into prison, and his two sons, until they all died there.

Book V: Chapter VIII.

1. Six [1] hundred and forty-two years after the building of Rome [Orosius and Alfred B. C. 111 : Clinton 105], when Caius Manlius was consul, and Quintus Cæpio proconsul, the Romans fought with the Cimbri, and with the Tutones, and with the Ambrones—these nations were among the Gauls—and all but ten men, were slain there, that was forty thousand. Of the Romans, there were slain eighty thousand, and their consul and his two sons. Afterwards, the same nations besieged Marius the consul in a fortress, and it was a long time before he could march out to battle, till it was told him, that they would go into Italy, the country of the Romans. But afterwards, he marched out of the fortress to them. When they met them on a down, the army of the consul complained to him of the thirst, which was pressing upon them. He then answered them and said,—" We can easily see, on the other side of our enemies, where the water is lying, which is nearest to us; but, because they are nearer to us, we cannot come to it without a battle." There the Romans had victory; and two hundred thousand of the Gauls, and their leader, were slain, and eighty thousand taken

Book V: Chapter IX.

1. Six [2] hundred and forty-five years after the building of Rome

1 Oros. l. V : c. 16. Haver. p. 327—331.   2 Oros. l. V : c. 17. Haver. p. 332—334.

[Orosius and Alfred B. C. 107 : Clinton 101], in the fifth year that Marius was consul, and also when the Romans had peace from all other nations, the Romans then began to stir up the greatest strife among themselves. I shall, however, said Orosius, now shortly say, who were the beginners of it.

2. First, it was Marius, the consul, and Lucius Appuleius Saturninus, because they drove into banishment the consul Metellus, who was consul before Marius. It was then very displeasing to the other consuls, Pompey and Cato, although by the resentment they could be of no use to the banished; they however contrived to kill Lucius Saturninus, and then prayed that Metellus might [return] to Rome; but Marius and Furius still withstood them. Afterwards the enmity between them increased, though they durst not shew it openly, for fear of the senate.

BOOK V : CHAPTER X.

1. Six* hundred and sixty-one years after the building of Rome [Orosius B. C. 94 : Alfred 92 : Clinton 91],—in the sixth year that Julius Cæsar was consul, and Lucius Marcius,—there was, over all Italy, deliberate and well-known hostility between Julius and Pompey; although they had formerly quite hidden it with themselves. Also, in that year, there happened many wonders in many lands.—One was, that they saw as if a fiery ring came from the north with a great noise.—Another was at a feast in the city Tarentum,⁴ when they cut the loaves for eating, then blood ran out.—The third was, that it hailed for a week, day and night, over all the Romans:—and, in the country of the Samnites, the earth burst asunder, and fire flamed up thence towards the heavens, and people saw, as it were, a golden ring in the heavens, broader than the sun, and reaching from the heavens down to the earth, and again going towards the heavens.

2. At that time, these nations,—the Picentes, and Vestini, and Marsi, and Peligni, and Marrucini, and Samnites, and the Lucanians, all agreed among themselves, that they would turn from the Romans, and killed Caius Servilius, a Roman nobleman, who was sent to them with messages. In those days, the cattle and the dogs, which were among the Samnites, went mad.

3 Oros. l. V : c. 18. Haver p. 335—340.
4 Apud Arretinos quum panes per convivia frangerentur, cruor e mediis panibus, quasi e vulneribus corporum, fluxit. Oros. l. V : c. 18. Haver. p. 335, 10—13.—Oros. refers to Arretium in Etruria; but Alfred to Tarentum on the west coast of Calabria.

3. Afterwards, Pompey, the consul, fought against all these nations, and was routed. Julius Cæsar fought against the Marsi, and was routed. Soon afterwards Julius fought against the Samnites and against the Lucanians, and routed them. After that, he was called Cæsar. He then asked, that they should bring the triumph to meet him, when they sent a black cloak[5] to meet him, in mockery, instead of a triumph. Afterwards they sent to meet him a garment, which they then called a toga,[6] that he might not come to Rome altogether without honour.

4. Afterwards [B. C. 88], Sulla, the consul, colleague of Pompey, fought against the people of Æsernia, and routed them. After that, Pompey fought against the nation of the Picentes, and routed them. Then the Romans brought the triumph to meet Pompey with great honour, for the little victory which he then had, and would not give any honour to Julius, but a toga,[7] though he had done a greater deed; and thus their quarrel was much strengthened. Afterwards, Julius and Pompey stormed Asculum a town of the Marsi, and there slew eighteen thousand. Then Sulla, the consul, fought against the Samnites, and slew eighteen thousand of them.

Book V: Chapter XI.

1. Six[8] hundred and sixty-two years after the building of Rome [Orosius and Alfred B. C. 91 : Clinton 88], the Romans sent Sulla, the consul, against Mithridates, king of [Pontus]. Then the consul Marius, uncle of Julius, was displeased that they would not intrust that war to him, and asked that the seventh consulship and also that war, should be given to him; because it was a custom with them, that, after a twelvemonth, they made every consul's seat one cushion higher, than it was before. When Sulla was told, on what ground Marius came to Rome, he speedily marched towards Rome with all his force, and drove Marius into Rome with all his army; and the citizens afterwards seized and bound him, and then thought of giving him up to Sulla. But he escaped the same night from the bonds, with which they had

---

5 Sagum, hoc est, vestem moeroris. Oros. Haver. p. 337, 8.
6 Antiquum togæ decorem recuperavit. Oros. Haver. p. 337, 9, 10. v. note 7.
7 Oros. Haver. p. 337, 16: but Alfred uses ' tunice ' *a tunic*, or common garment of the Romans.
8 Oros. l. V : c. 19. Haver. p. 241—346.

bound him in the day ; and afterwards fled south, over the sea into Africa, where most of his force was ; and soon turned again towards Rome. He was assisted by two consuls, Cinna and Sertorius, who were always the beginners of every evil.

2. As [9] soon as the senate heard that Marius was coming near Rome, they all fled into the country of Greece to Sulla and Pompey, whither they were gone with an army. Sulla then marched with great earnestness from Greece towards Rome, and bravely fought a battle with Marius, and routed him, and slew all within the city, Rome, who had helped Marius. All the consuls but two, died soon after. Marius and Sulla died a natural death ; [1] and Cinna was slain in Smyrna, a city of Asia ; and Sertorius was slain in Spain.

3. Then [2] Pompey undertook the Parthian war, because Mithridates, their king, seized for himself Asia the Less, and all the country of the Greeks; but Pompey chased him out of all that country, and drove him into Armenia, and followed after him till other men slew him, and forced the general Archelaus, to be his servant.—" It is now not to be believed," said Orosius, " to tell what perished in that war, which, ere it could be ended, they carried on forty years, both in pillaging nations, and in murders of kings, and in hunger."

4. When [3] Pompey was [returning] homeward, the people of the land would not give up the fortress at Jerusalem. They had the help of twenty-two kings. Then Pompey ordered that the fortress should be stormed, and even attacked it day and night, one party after another unweariedly, and thus so tired the people, that they came into his hands about three months after they had first begun. There thirteen thousand of the Jews were slain, and the wall was thrown down to the ground ; and Aristobulus was led to Rome bound : he was both their king and their priest.

Book V: Chapter XII.

1. Six [4] hundred and sixty-seven years after the building of

---

9 Oros. l. V : c. 20. Haver. p. 346—349.
1 A. S. him sylf *by themselves.*
2 Oros. l. VI : c. 4. Haver. p. 377—380.—The Chapters 21, 22, 23, and 24 of book V, and the Chapters 1, 2 and 3 of book VI, Haver. p. 349—377, Alfred has omitted.
3 Oros. l. VI : c. 6. Haver. p. 383—385. Chap. 5 is omitted by Alfred.
4 Much abridged from Oros. l. VI : c. 7. Haver. p 385—391. Alfred on its Chapter 8.

Rome [Orosius B. C. 60 : Alfred 86 : Clinton 55], the Romans gave Caius Julius [Cæsar] seven legions, to the end that he might wage war five years on the Gauls.

2. When [5] he had overcome them, he went into the island Britain, and fought against the Britons, and was routed in the land, which is called Kentland. Soon afterwards he fought again with the Britons in Kentland, and they were routed. Their third battle was near the river, which is called Thames, near the ford called Wallingford. After that battle, the king came into his hands, and the townspeople that were in Cirencester, and afterwards all that were in the island.

3. Then [6] Julius [Cæsar] went to Rome, and asked that the triumph should be brought to meet him. They then ordered that he should come to Rome with few men, and should leave all his forces behind him. But when he went homeward, the three senators, who were his supporters, came to meet him, and told him that for his sake they were driven away ; and also, that all the legions, that were in the power of the Romans, were given to help Pompey that he might have the safer contest with him. Julius then returned to his own army ; and, weeping, bemoaned the dishonour that they had so unworthily done him, and chiefly for those men who were ruined for his sake. He afterwards drew over to him the seven legions that were in the land of Sulmo.

4. When Pompey and Cato, and all the senate heard of it, they went among the Greeks, and gathered a great army on the down of Thrace. Julius then marched to Rome and broke open their treasure-house, and divided all that was in it. Orosius said—" It is hardly to be believed in saying, what there was of it all." He then went to the land of Marseilles, and left there three legions behind him, to the end that they might force the people under him ; and he himself, with the other part, went into Spain, where the legions of Pompey were, with his three generals; and he forced them all under him. He afterwards went into the country of the Greeks, where, on a down, Pompey waited for

---

5 Oros. L VI : c. 9. Haver. p. 395, 396.—Bede has taken the substance of this chapter of the original Latin of Orosius, for l. I : c. 2 of his Eccl. Hist. Smith says in his note to this c. 2 of Bede, p. 42, Totum hoc caput ex Orosio, l. VI : c. 9—Alfred omits chapters 10, 11, 12, 13, and 14.

6 Oros. l. VI : c. 15. Haver. p. 415—422.

him with thirty kings, besides his own force. Pompey then went where Marcellus, the general of Julius, was, and slew him with all his army. Afterwards Julius besieged Torquatus, the general of Pompey, in a fortress, and Pompey marched after him. Julius was there put to flight, and many of his army slain, because they fought against him on both sides: on one side Pompey,—on the other the general. Afterwards Julius marched into Thessaly, and there gathered again his army.

5. When Pompey heard of it, he marched after him with an immense army. He had eighty-eight cohorts, which we now call truman, each of which was, in those days, one thousand five hundred men. All these he had, besides his own army, and besides that of Cato, his colleague, and that of the senate. And Julius had eighty cohorts. Each of them had his army in three parts, and they themselves were in the middle, and the others on each side of them. When Julius had routed one of the parts, Pompey called to him about the old Roman agreement, though he himself did not think of keeping it,—" Comrade, comrade, mind that thou do not too long break our agreement and fellowship." He then answered him and said: "At one time, thou wast my comrade; and, because thou art not now, all is most loved by me, that is most loathsome to thee." The agreement, which the Romans had made, was this, that none of them should strike another in the face, wherever they met each other in battle.

6. After these words Pompey was routed with all his army; and he himself afterwards fled into Asia, with his wife and with his children; and he then went into Egypt, and asked help from Ptolemy the king. Soon after he came to him, he commanded his head to be cut off, and afterwards ordered it to be sent to Julius, and his ring with it. But, when they brought it to him, he bemoaned the deed with much weeping, for he was, of all men in those days, the most kindhearted. Afterwards, Ptolemy led an army against Julius, and all his army were put to flight, and he himself taken; and Julius ordered all the men to be put to death, who gave advice for putting Pompey to death; and, nevertheless, he let Ptolemy go back to his kingdom. Afterwards, Julius fought against Ptolemy thrice, and each time had victory.

7. After[7] that warfare, all the Egyptians became subjects of

[7] Oros. l. VI: c. 16. Haver. p. 423—425.

Julius, and he then returned to Rome, and replaced the senate; and they set him higher than consul, what they called a Dictator. He afterwards went into Africa after Cato, the consul. When Cato heard of it, he instructed his son that he should go to meet him, and seek peace of him; "Because," said he, "I know that in this life, no man so good as he is, lives, though he is the most loathsome to me; and, therefore, I cannot myself decide, that I should ever see him." After these words, he went to the walls of the city, and threw himself over, so that he burst all asunder. But, when Julius came into the city, he greatly bewailed that he came not to him alive, and that he died such a death.

8. Julius afterwards fought against the nephew of Pompey, and against many of his kinsmen, and he slew them all, and then went to Rome; and he was so venerated there, that, when he came home, they granted him a triumph four times. He then marched into Spain, and fought against the two sons of Pompey, and his army was so much slaughtered there, that, for a while, he thought that he should be taken; and for fear of that, he rushed the more into the army, because he would rather that they should slay him, than bind him.

9. He [9] afterwards came to Rome, and all the laws which were too harsh and too hard, he made lighter and milder. Then the consuls, and all the senate, taking it amiss that he would change their old laws, all jumped up, and stabbed him with their daggers in their senate house. There were twenty-three wounds.

BOOK V: CHAPTER XIII.

1. Seven [1] hundred and ten years after the building of Rome [Orosius and Alfred B. C. 43 : Clinton 44], Octavianus, after the murder of Julius his kinsmen, seized upon the empire of the Romans, against their wish, because Julius had before made it fast to him, by writings, that after him he should take to all his riches; because, being a kinsman, he had taught him and brought him up. He afterwards full royally fought and gained four battles, as Julius, his kinsman, had done before:—one against Pompey,—another against Anthony the consul,—a third against Cassius and Brutus,—a fourth against Lepidus, though he soon after became his friend; and he also made Anthony his friend,

---

8 Much abridged from Oros. l. VI : c. 17. Haver. p. 425—428.
9 Much abridged from Oros. l. VI : c. 18. Haver. p. 428—435.

so that he gave his daughter to be the wife of Octavianus, and Octavianus also gave his sister to Anthony.

2. Afterwards [1] Anthony brought all Asia under his power. He then forsook the sister of Octavianus, and declared war and open hostility against [Octavianus] himself. He ordered Cleopatra, the queen, to be brought to him for a wife, whom Julius had before, and therefore he had given her all Egypt. Soon afterwards Octavianus led an army against Anthony; and when they came together quickly routed him. About three days after, they fought out at sea. Octavianus had two hundred and thirty large ships with three ranks of rowers, in which sailed eight legions. Anthony had eighty ships, in which sailed ten legions; but just as many as he had less, by so much they were better and larger; for they were so built, that they could not be overladen with men, though they were not ten feet high above the water. That battle was very famous; however, Octavianus had the victory. There were slain twelve thousand of [Anthony's] people, and Cleopatra, his queen, was put to flight, when they came to her army. Then Octavianus fought against Anthony, and against Cleopatra, and put them to flight. That was at the time of the first of August, and on the day which we call Lammas. Octavianus was afterwards called Augustus, because at that time he gained the victory.

3. Afterwards Anthony and Cleopatra gathered a fleet on the Red Sea; but, when it was told them that Octavianus was coming thither, all the people turned to Octavianus, and they themselves fled to a town, with a small army. Cleopatra then ordered her burying place to be dug, and went into it. When she had lain down there, she ordered the serpent Ipnalis [*] to be taken and put to her arm, that it might bite her, because she thought that it would be least painful on that limb, for it is the nature of that serpent, that every creature, that it bites, must end its life in sleep. She did that, because she was unwilling to be driven before the triumph towards Rome. When Anthony saw that she prepared herself for death, he stabbed himself, and ordered that they should lay him, thus half dead, in the same burying place with her. When Octavianus came thither, he ordered another kind of serpent [2] to be taken, called Psyllus, which can

---

1 Oros. l. VI : c. 19. Haver. p. 436—440.   * For hypnalis, from ὕπνος *sleep*.
2 The translator has misunderstood Orosius, who says:—Frustra Caesare etiam Psyllos

draw poison of every sort out of man, if it be brought in time; but she was dead before he came thither. Afterwards Octavianus took Alexandria the chief city of Egypt, and with its wealth greatly enriched Rome, so that every thing on sale could be bought two-fold cheaper, than it could before.

Book V: Chapter XIV.

1. Seven[3] hundred and thirty-five years after the building of Rome [Orosius B. C. 28: Alfred 18: Clinton 29], it came to pass that Octavianus Cæsar, in his fifth consulship, shut the doors of Janus; and it came to pass that he had the rule of all the world, as was plainly foreshown, when he was a youth, and they took him towards Rome after the murder of Julius. On the same day, in which he was made consul, it came to pass, that they saw, as it were, a golden ring around the sun; and, within the city Rome, a spring welled up oil for a whole day. By the ring it was betokened, that, in his days, he should be born, who is more bright and shining than the sun; and the oil betokened mercy to all mankind. So also Octavianus himself gave many tokens, which afterwards came to pass, though he did them unwittingly by God's working.

2. First,—one was, that he gave orders over all the world, for every tribe to come together in the course of a year, that every man might more easily know where he belonged.[4] That betokened,—that, in his days, he should be born, who has bidden us all to one meeting of kindred, which shall be in the life to come.

3. Another was,—he gave orders, that all mankind should have one kindred, and pay one tax. That betokened,—that we all should have one faith, and one mind for good works.

4. A third was,—he gave orders, that every one of those who were abroad, both bond and free, should come to his own land, and to his father's home; and whosoever would not, he

---

admovente, qui venena serpentum e vulneribus hominum haustu revocare atque exsugere solent. Haver. p. 439, 21—23.—The Psylli were the poison-suckers of the Lybian desert. A Psyllus was, therefore, not a serpent but one of the Psylli, in Greek Ψύλλοι. Martinius says,—" A Ψύλλος pulex.—Cæterum hoc nomen Psylli Africanum esse puto. Possit referri ad Arab. שׁוה separare, distinguere; quod proprietate quadam adversus serpentes ab aliis distinguerentur.

3 Oros. l. VI: c. 20. Haver. p. 440—143.

4 A. S. Hwær he gesibbe hæfde *where he had kindred.*

gave orders that they should all be slain. There were six thousand of these, when they were gathered. That betokened,—that we are all commanded to come out of this world to our father's home, that is, to the kingdom of heaven; and whosoever will not, he shall be cast out, and slain.

Book V: Chapter XV.

1. Seven[*] hundred and thirty-six years after the building of Rome [Orosius B. C. 28: Alfred 17: Clinton 27], some of the people of Spain became hostile to Augustus. Then he undid again the doors of Janus, and led an army against them, and put them to flight, and afterwards besieged them in a fortress, so that then some killed themselves,—some died by poison—some by hunger.

2. Afterwards many nations waged war against Augustus,—both Illyrians, and Pannonians, and Sarmatians, and many other nations. The generals of Augustus had many great battles against them, without Augustus himself, ere they could overcome them.

3. Augustus then sent Quintilius [Varus] the consul into Germany with three legions; but every one of them was slain, save the consul alone. At that loss, Augustus was so grieved that he oft unwittingly struck his head against the wall, when he sat on his seat; and he ordered the consul to be put to death. The Germans afterwards, of their own mind, sought to Augustus for peace; and he forgave them the hatred, which he knew [they had] to him.

4. Then [*] all this world wished for peace and friendship with Augustus; and nothing seemed so good to all men, as to gain his good will, and to become his subjects. Therefore, no nation wished to keep its own law, but in such wise as Augustus ordered it. Then the doors of Janus were again shut, and his locks rusty, as they never were before. In the same year that all this came to pass, which was in the forty-second year of the reign of Augustus, he was born, who brought peace to all the world; that is, our Lord Jesus Christ.

5. "Now," said Orosius, "I have told how, from the beginning of this world, all mankind paid for the first man's sins with great

---

5 Oros. l. VI: c. 21. Haver. p. 444—447.
6 Oros. l. VI: c. 22. Haver p. 448,—449.

pains and torments. I will also now further tell what mercy and gentleness there has been since Christianity came,—just as if the hearts of men were changed, because the former things had been atoned for.—Here the fifth book ends and the sixth begins.

Book VI[1]: Chapter I.[3]

1. " I[3] will now," said Orosius, " in an introduction to this sixth book, shew—how equally the four powers of the four chief empires of this world stood,—that, although it was stern, it still was the command of God."

2. The first was in Assyria, in the most easterly empire, in the city Babylon; which stood twice seven hundred years in its power, ere it fell,—from Ninus, their first king, to Sardanapalus, their last,—that is one thousand four hundred years.

3. When Cyrus took away the Babylonian power, then the Roman first began to grow.—Also, in those days, the most northerly was enlarging in Macedonia, which stood a little longer than seven hundred years,— from Caranus, their first king, to Perseus, their last.

4. So also in Africa, the most southerly city, Carthage, also fell after seven hundred years and a little time after the woman Dido first built it, till Scipio the consul afterwards overthrew it.

5. So also that of the Romans, which is the greatest and most westerly,—about seven hundred years and a little more, there came a kind of great fire, and a great burning in Rome, which burnt fifteen wards; yet no one knew whence the fire came, and there almost all that was in it perished, so that hardly any atom of foundation was left. It was so much wasted by that burning, that it never afterwards was such [as it had been], till Augustus, in the year when Christ was born, rebuilt it so much better, than it ever was before, that some men said, it was adorned with precious stones. That help and that work Augustus paid for with many thousand talents.

6. It was also clearly seen, that it was God's providence, ruling the powers of those kingdoms, when the coming of Christ was promised to Abraham, in the forty-second year after Ninus

---

1 This is the VIIth book of the original Latin of Orosius: the Vth and VIth of the Latin being included in the Vth book of King Alfred's Anglo-Saxon Version.
2 Alfred has greatly abridged most of the chapters of this book; and he has entirely omitted the following chapters, namely, 1, 26, 27, 41, 42 and 43.
3 Oros. 1. VII: c. 2. Haver. p. 453—456.

began to reign in Babylon. So also,[4] in the last and most westerly empire, that is of Rome, the same was born who was formerly promised to Abraham, in the forty-second year after Augustus began to reign; that was seven hundred and fifty-two[5] years after the building of Rome.

7. Afterwards Rome stood twelve years, in great wealth, while Augustus kept that lowliness towards God, with which he had begun: that was, that he shunned and forbade, that he should be called a god, as no king would, that was before him, but wished that people should worship them, and make offerings to them. But, in the twelfth year afterwards, Caius, his nephew, went from Egypt into Syria,—Augustus had given it to him to govern—then he would not worship the Almighty God, when he came to Jerusalem. When Augustus was told of it, he praised that pride and blamed it not a whit. Soon afterwards, the Romans paid for this word with so great a famine, that Augustus drove from Rome half that were within it. Then the door of Janus was opened again, because the leaders in many countries disagreed with Augustus, although no battle took place.

BOOK VI: CHAPTER II.

1. Seven [6] hundred and sixty-seven years after the building of Rome [Orosius, Alfred and Clinton A. D. 14], Tiberius, the emperor, succeeded to the government after Augustus. He was so forgiving and so mild to the Romans, as no ruler had ever been to them before, until Pilate sent him word from Jerusalem about the miracles of Christ, and about his martyrdom, and also that many took him for a god. But when he told it to the senate, they all very much withstood him, because they had not been told of it sooner, as it was a custom with them, that they might afterwards make it known to all the Romans; and said, that they would not have him for a god. Then Tiberius was as wroth and as hard with the Romans, as he before had been mild and easy to them, so that he hardly left alive one of the senators, nor of the twenty-two

---

4 Oros. l. VII: c. 3. Haver. p. 457—459.
5 The Fasti Consulares and Cato, followed by Dionysius of Halicarnassus, Solinus and Eusebius, fix the era of the foundation of Rome to B. C. 752. Terentius Varro, however, more correctly refers it to B. C. 753, which date was adopted by the Roman Emperors, and by Plutarch, Tacitus, Dion, Aulus Gellius, Censorinus, Onuphrius, Baronius, bishop Beveridge, Strauchius, Dr Playfair, Dr Hales, Mr Clinton and by most modern chronologists: It is followed in this work.
6 Oros. l. VI: c. 4. Haver. p. 459—463.

men, whom he had chosen to help him, that they should be his advisers, whom they called patricians. All these, but two, he ordered to be put to death; yea, his own two sons. How God then avenged that very great pride upon the people, and how dearly they bought it from their own emperor! although it was not so greatly avenged upon all the people in other countries, as it often had been before.

2. In the twelfth year of the reign of Tiberius, God's wrath was again upon the Romans, while they were in their theatre at their plays, when it all fell down, and killed twenty thousand of them. "They then perished by a deserved wrath," said Orosius, "when they should have rued their sins, and amended their deeds, rather than go to their plays, as their custom was before Christianity."

3. In the eighteenth year of his reign, when Christ was crucified, there was great darkness over all the world, and so great an earthquake, that massy stones fell from mountains; and what was the greatest wonder, when the moon was full, and farthest from the sun, that it was then eclipsed. The Romans afterwards killed Tiberius with poison. He held the empire twenty-three years.

Book VI: Chapter III.

1. Seven [7] hundred and ninety years after the building of Rome [Orosius, Alfred and Clinton A. D. 37], Caius Caligula was emperor for four years. He was very full of vices, and of sinful lusts, and he was altogether such as the Romans then deserved, because they scoffed at the commandment of Christ, and passed over it. But he was so very wroth with them, and they were so hateful to him, that he often wished that all the Romans had one neck, that he might most readily cut it off; and very much lamented, that there was not then such strife, as there often was before; and he himself often went into other countries, and wished to find war; but he could only find peace.

2. "The times," said Orosius, "were unlike, after Christ was born, when men could not find war; and, before that, they could by no means keep from it."

3. In those days, the wrath of God came also upon the Jews,

---

7 Oros. l. VII: c. 5. Haver. p. 463—466.

so that they had disagreement both among themselves, and with all nations; although it was chiefly in the city of Alexandria, and Caius ordered them to be driven out. They then sent Philo, their most learned man, to the end that he might ask the mercy of Caius for them. But he sadly ill treated them for that wish, and commanded that they should be oppressed on every side where they could, and ordered that they should fill the temple at Jerusalem with idols,—that they should set his own idol there in the midst, which was his own image. He held Pilate in threatening, till he stabbed himself.—He had doomed our Lord to death.

4. Soon afterwards the Romans put Caius to death while sleeping. Then were found in his treasury two chests, which were full of poison; and in one was a letter, in which were written, lest he should forget, the names of all the richest men, whom he thought of killing. Then they poured the poison out into the sea, and soon after there came up a woeful quantity of dead fishes. God's wrath was clearly seen, that he let the people be tried, and also his mercy, when he would not let them perish as Caius had intended.

Book VI : Chapter IV.

1. Seven [8] hundred and ninety-five years after the building of Rome [Orosius, Alfred and Clinton A. D. 42], Tiberius Claudius succeeded to the government of the Romans. In the first year of his reign, Peter, the Apostle, came to Rome, and men first became Christians there through his teaching. The Romans then wished to put Claudius to death, for the deeds of his kinsman, Caius, the former emperor, and all that were of that family. But when they embraced Christianity, they were so mild and so peaceable, that they all forgave the emperor the mischief that he had formerly done them; and he forgave all of them the wrong and injury, that they thought of doing to him.

2. At that time, when Christianity had come to them, there was also, in the government of the Romans, another token, which was, that the Dalmatians wished to give their kingdom to Scribonianus their general, and then to wage war against the Romans. But, when they were gathered together, and wished to make him king, they could not raise the standard, as was their custom, when

---

8 Oros. l. VII : c. 6, Haver. p. 465—470. This chapter is adopted by Bede; l. I : c. 3. In a note to Bede, Smith says, Hoc etiam caput Orosio debetur. p. 43.

they settled governments; but were angry with themselves that they had ever begun it, and put Scribonianus to death.—" Now," said Orosius, " let him deny who will or who dares, that that undertaking was not stopped for the good of Christianity; and say where, before Christianity, any war, if it were begun, took such a turn."

3. Another wonder happened also in the fourth year of the government of Claudius, that he himself searched for war, and could find none.—In that year there was a great famine in Syria and in Palestine, but that Helena, queen of the Adiabeni, gave corn enough to the monks, who were in Jerusalem, because she had lately become a Christian.

4. In the fifth year of the government of Claudius, an island appeared between Thera and Therasia, five miles broad and five miles long.—In the seventh year of his government, there was so great a disagreement in Jerusalem, between those who were not Christians, that thirty thousand were there slain, and trodden to death at the gate; yet no man knew whence the strife came.—In the ninth year of his government, there was a great famine in Rome, and Claudius ordered all the Jews, that were within, to be driven out. Then the Romans blamed Claudius for the famine, which was afflicting them, and he became so angry with them, that he ordered thirty-five of the senators to be put to death, and three hundred of the others, who were the highest among them. The Romans afterwards killed him with poison.

Book VI: Chapter V.

1. Eight[9] hundred and nine years after the building of Rome [Orosius A. D. 55: Alfred 56: Clinton 54], Nero succeeded to the government of the Romans, and held it fourteen years. He had still more vices than his uncle Caius had before. Besides the manifold evils that he did, he ordered, on one occasion, the city Rome to be burnt, and commanded his own men, always to seize as much as they could of the treasure, and to bring it to him, when it was snatched out [of the fire]. He himself stood on the highest tower, that was within it, and began to make a song about the fire, which was burning six days and seven nights. But he unwittingly wreaked his vengeance, first on the city for their misdeeds, because they martyred Peter and Paul; and then upon himself,

---

9 Oros. l. VII : c. 7. Haver. p. 470—473.

when he stabbed himself. He was the first man that persecuted Christians. After his death the family of the Cæsars fell away.

BOOK VI: CHAPTER VI.

1. Eight [1] hundred and twenty-four years after the building of Rome [Orosius and Alfred A. D. 71 : Clinton 68], Galba succeeded to the government of the Romans. In the seventh month after, a man [called] Otho, slew him and seized the government.

2. When the Romans first persecuted Christians, as Nero began it, all the nations, that were on the east of Syria became their adversaries; yea, they themselves had also disagreement among them. Vitellius, king of the Germans, fought thrice against Otho, and slew him in the third month after they began to wage war.

BOOK VI: CHAPTER VII.

1 Eight [2] hundred and twenty-five years after the building of Rome [Orosius and Alfred A. D. 72 : Clinton 69], Vespasian succeeded to the government of the Romans. Then, there was again peace over all the Roman Empire. He gave orders to his son Titus, that he should overthrow the temple in Jerusalem, and all the city, and forbade that either should be rebuilt; because God would not that they should any longer be a hindrance to Christianity. He destroyed eleven hundred thousand Jews,— some he slew,—some he sold into other countries,—some he killed by hunger. Afterwards they made a triumph for them both, Vespasian and Titus. The sight was a great wonder to the Romans, because they had never before seen two men sitting together in a triumph. They shut the doors of Janus. Afterwards, Vespasian, in the ninth year of his reign, died of dysentery, in a dwelling on the outside of Rome.

BOOK VI: CHAPTER VIII.

1. Eight [3] hundred and twenty-nine years after the building of Rome [Orosius A. D. 75 : Alfred 76 : Clinton 79], Titus succeeded to the government of the Romans, and held it two years. He was of so good a disposition, that he said, he lost the day, on

---

1 Abridged from Oros. l. VII : c. 8. Haver. p. 474—478.
2 Very much abridged from Oros. l. VII : c. 9. Haver. p. 478—482, 9.
3 Oros. l. VII : c. 9. Haver. p. 482, 10—19.

which he did not do any good. He died also in the same dwelling as his father did, and of the same disease.

Book VI : Chapter IX.

1. Eight [4] hundred and thirty years after the building of Rome [Orosius and Alfred A. D. 87 : Clinton 81], Domitian, brother of Titus, succeeded to the government of the Romans, and held it fifteen years. He again was a persecutor of Christians; and was lifted up with such great pride, that he commanded the people to bow down to him, as to a god. He gave orders that the Apostle John, should be taken from other Christian men into banishment to the island Patmos. And he also ordered that all of David's race should be put to death, to the end that, if Christ were not then born, he might not afterwards be born; because soothsayers said, that he should come of that race. After that order he was himself disgracefully put to death.

Book VI : Chapter X.

1. Eight [5] hundred and forty-six years after the building of Rome [Orosius and Alfred A. D. 93 : Clinton 96,] Nerva succeeded to the government of the Romans; and, because he was old, he chose the man, [called] Trajan, to help him. They then agreed between themselves, that they would change all the laws and all the orders, which Domitian had before settled, because he was formerly hateful to them both; and they ordered John to be brought back to his minster in Ephesus, from the worldly sorrows which he for awhile had borne.

2. Then Nerva died; and Trajan [6] held the government nineteen years after him. He brought back to the Romans all the nations which had lately gone from them; and he gave orders, that all his prefects should persecute Christians. Then one of them, named Pliny, told him, that he ordered what was wrong, and sinned much in it. He then readily forbade it.

3. At that time, the Jews were in great strife and in great hostility against the people of the land, where they then were, till many thousands of them perished on both sides. At that time, Trajan died of a dysentery in the city Seleucia.

---

4 Oros. l. VII : c. 10. Haver. p. 483, 484.
5 Oros. l. VII : c. 11. Haver. p. 484, 485.
6 Oros. l. VII : c. 12. Haver. p. 486—488.

Book VI: Chapter XI.

1. Eight[7] hundred and sixty-seven years after the building of Rome [Orosius and Alfred A. D. 114 : Clinton 117], Hadrian, Trajan's nephew, succeeded to the government of the Romans, and held it twenty-one years. Soon afterwards Christian books were known to him, through one of the followers of the apostles, named Quadratus; he [then] forbade, over all his empire, that they should annoy any Christian man. If any Christian were guilty, he was then to be taken before him, and he himself would at once judge him as he thought right.

2. He then became so dear to the Romans, and so honoured, that they never called him any thing but father; and, in honour of him, they called his wife, Empress. He ordered all the Jews to be put to death, because they tortured the Christians, that were in Palestine, which is called the land of Judea. He commanded that they should build on the place of the city Jerusalem, and that they should afterwards call it by the name of Ælia.

Book VI: Chapter XII.

1. Eight[8] hundred and eighty eight years after the building of Rome [Orosius and Alfred A. D. 135 : Clinton 133], Antoninus, whose other name was Pius, succeeded to the government of the Romans. Justin, the philosopher, out of friendship, gave him a Christian book. When he had read it, he became dear and very friendly to Christians, to the end of his life.

Book VI: Chapter XIII.

1. Nine[9] hundred and three years after the building of Rome [Orosius A. D. 158 : Alfred 150 : Clinton 161], Marcus Antoninus[*] succeeded to the government of the Romans, with his brother Aurelius. They were the first that divided the Roman empire into two parts; and they held it fourteen years [M. Antoni-

---

7 Oros. l. VII: c. 13. Haver. p. 488—490.
8 Oros. l. VII; c. 14. Haver p 490, 491.
9 Oros. l. VII: c. 15. Haver. p. 492—495.
* Marcus Aurelius Antoninus, who reigned 19 years, from A. D. 161 to 180, was adopted by Antoninus Pius, at the same time with Lucius Aurelius Verus, who reigned conjointly with Aurelius for 8 years, from A. D. 161 to 169. M. Aurelius was commonly called the philosopher. We still possess his noble view of philosophical heathenism in his work entitled Τὰ εἰς ἑαυτὸν or *Meditations*, which give his thoughts and feelings on moral and religious subjects. It has been translated into English. Though devoted to philosophy and literature, he shewed his bigotry by the martyrdom of two eminent fathers of the Christian church.—Polycarp in A. D. 166, and Irenæus in 177.

nus 19 years, and Aurelius only 8.] They gave orders that every Christian should be put to death. They had afterwards a great war with the Parthians, because they had laid waste all Cappadocia and Armenia, and all Syria. They then made peace with the Parthians, and afterwards there came upon them so great a famine, and so great a plestilence, that few of them were left.

2. There then came upon them the Danish war, with all the Germans. On the very day, on which they would fight, there came so great a heat and so great a thirst upon them, that they had no hope of their lives. They then understood that it was from God's wrath, and asked the Christians, that they would in some way help them. Then they prayed to Almighty God, and it rained so much, that they had water enough upon the plain; and there came such heavy thunder, that it killed many thousand men in the midst of the battle.

3. Afterwards all the Romans became so kind to Christians, that they wrote in many temples, that every Christian should have freedom and peace; and also, that every one of them, who wished, might embrace Christianity. Antoninus forgave all the tribute, that they should have paid to Rome, and ordered the deed to be burned, in which it was written, what they should pay in a year; and he died in the year following.

Book VI: Chapter XIV.

1. Nine ' hundred and thirty years after the building of Rome [Orosius, Alfred and Clinton A. D. 177], Lucius Antoninus succeeded to the empire, and held it thirteen ' years. He was a very bad man as to all morals, but he was brave, and often fought single combats. Many of the senators, who were the best there, he ordered to be put to death. Afterwards a thunderbolt shattered their Capitol, the house, in which their gods and their idols were; and their library was set on fire by the lightning, and all their old books in it were burnt. There was even as great a loss by the fire, as was in the city Alexandria, where, in their library, four hundred thousand books were burnt.

---

1 Oros. l. VII: c. 16. Haver. p. 495—498. Lu. Antoninus Commodus reigned only 12 years and nearly 10 months; then Pertinax and Julianus each reigned about two months, making altogether, from the death of Commodus to the accession of Severus, a little more than 13 years. *Fasti Romani, p.* 267.

Book VI: Chapter XV.

1. Nine [2] hundred and forty-three years after the building of Rome [Orosius A. D. 191 : Alfred 190 : Clinton 194], Severus succeeded to the government of the Romans, and held it seventeen years. He besieged Pescennius in a fastness, till he fell into his hands; and he afterwards ordered him to be put to death, because he would reign in Syria and in Egypt. He then put Albinus to death in Gaul, because he also would wage war against him.

2. He afterwards went into Britain, and often fought there against the Picts and Scots, before he could defend the Britons against them; and ordered a wall to be built quite across all that country from sea to sea. Soon afterwards, he died in the city of York.

Book VI: Chapter XVI.

1. Nine [3] hundred and sixty-two years after the building of Rome [Orosius and Alfred A. D. 209 : Clinton 211], his son, Antoninus, succeeded to the empire, and held it [not full] seven years. He had two sisters for his wives. He had gathered an army, and wished to fight against the Parthians; but, in the march, he was put to death by his own men.

Book VI: Chapter XVII.

1. Nine [4] hundred and seventy years after the building of Rome [Orosius, Alfred and Clinton A. D. 217], Marcus Aurelius succeeded to the government of the Romans, and held it four years. His own men slew him, and also his mother.

Book VI: Chapter XVIII.

1. Nine [5] hundred and seventy four years after the building of Rome [Orosius and Alfred A. D. 221 : Clinton 222], Aurelius Alexander succeeded to the government of the Romans, and held it [thirteen] [6] years. Mammæa, his good mother, sent for Origen, the most learned mass-priest, and afterwards she became a well-

---

2 Oros. l. VII : c. 17. Haver. p. 498— 503.
3 Oros. l. VII : c. 18. Haver. p. 504—506, 3.
4 Oros. l. VII : c. 18. Haver. p. 506, 3—507, 1.
5 Oros. l. VII : c. 18. Haver. p. 507 1—508, 5.
6 Both the Anglo-Saxon MSS. have XVI, but Oros. has—tredecim annis, Haver. p. 507, 4; and Clinton gives 13 years. *Fasti Romani*, p. 267.

taught Christian through him; and she made her son very friendly to Christians. He marched with an army into Persia, and slew Xerxes, their king. He afterwards lost his life in the city, Mayence.

Book VI: Chapter XIX.

1. Nine[7] hundred and eighty-seven years after the building of Rome [Orosius and Alfred A. D. 235 : Clinton 236], Maximinus succeeded to the government of the Romans. He gave orders that Christians should be again persecuted, and that the good Mammæa should be martyred, and all the priests who followed her, save Origen : he fled into Egypt. Maximinus, in the third year of his reign, was put to death by his own prefect in the city Aquileia.

Book VI: Chapter XX.

1. Nine[8] hundred and ninety years after the building of Rome [Alfred A. D. 237 : Orosius and Clinton 238], Gordianus succeeded to the empire, and he held it six years. He put to death the two brothers, who had formerly put Maximinus to death; and he himself died soon after.

Book VI: Chapter XXI.

1. Nine[9] hundred and ninety-seven years after the building of Rome [Orosius, Alfred and Clinton A. D. 244], Philip succeeded to the government of the Romans, and held it seven years. He was secretly a Christian because he durst not [be so] openly. In the third year of his reign, which was about one thousand years after the building of Rome, it came to pass, as God had ordained it, that not only was the emperor a Christian, but that, at the emperor's palace, they also, in thankfulness to Christ, partook of the great feast, which, every year before, they kept to their idols. It was in honour of devils, that all the Romans would, after a twelve-month, bring together the best part of their goods, gathered for their sacrifice, and afterwards enjoy them together for many weeks.—Then Decius, a rich man, ensnared the emperor, and afterwards seized the government.

---

7 Oros. l. VII: c. 19. p. 509,9.
8 Oros. l. VII : c. 19. Haver. p. 509, 10—511.
9 Oros. l. VII : c. 20. Haver. p. 512—515.

Book VI: Chapter XXII.

1. One[1] thousand and four years after the building of Rome [Orosius, Alfred, and Clinton A. D. 249], Decius succeeded to the government of the Romans, and held it three[2] years; and soon gave a plain token, that he had before plotted against Philip, as he ordered Christians to be persecuted, and many were thus made holy martyrs. He settled his son in the government with him, and soon afterwards, they were both slain together.

Book VI: Chapter XXIII.

1. One[3] thousand and eight years after the building of Rome [Orosius A. D. 254: Alfred 255: Clinton 251], Gallus Hostilianus succeeded to the empire, and held it two years. Then God's wrath was again upon Rome: as long as there was the persecution of Christians, so long was there a very great plague pressing upon them, so that there was not a house in the city, which had not suffered by the wrath. Then Æmilianus put Gallus to death, and had the government to himself. In the third month afterwards, he also was put to death.

Book VI: Chapter XXIV.

1. One[4] thousand and ten years after the building of Rome [Orosius and Alfred A. D. 257: Clinton 254], the Romans appointed two emperors: one was within the city Rome, and was called Gallienus; the other was with the people of Æmilianus,[5] and was called Valerian. These were ever to be waging war, where it was needful. Then they both commanded Christians to be persecuted, but the wrath of God quickly came upon them both. Valerian marched with an army, against Sapor, king of the Persians, and was there taken; and afterwards, to the end of his life, he was appointed to stoop, when Sapor, the king, would mount his horse, that the king might have his back as a stirrup.

---

1 Oros. l. VII: c. 21. Haver. p. 515—516, 11.
2 Orosius and Alfred say 3 years, but Clinton, 2 years and two months.
3 Oros. l. VII: c. 21. Haver. p. 516, 1—11.
4 Very much abridged from Oros. l. VII: c. 22. Haver. p. 516—519.
5 Oros. says—Valerianus in Rhetia ab exercitu Augustus est adpellatus. Haver. p. 516, 22, 23. Æmilianus, after being in power 3 months, was slain by his soldiers in A. D. 254, and Valerian and Gallienus were chosen emperors.

2. Many nations waged war upon the other [emperor], Gallienus, so that he held his power with great disgrace, and great difficulty. First the Germans, who were on the Danube, overran Italy, to the city Ravenna; and the Suevi overran all Gaul, and the Goths all the country of Greece, and Asia the Less; and the Sarmatians forced all Dacia from the government of the Romans; and the Huns overran Pannonia; and the Parthians overran Mesopotamia, and all Syria. Besides which, the Romans had war among themselves. Gallienus was afterwards put to death by his own men, in the city Milan.

Book VI: Chapter XXV.

1. One [6] thousand and twenty-five years after the building of Rome [Orosius and Alfred A. D. 272: Clinton 268], Claudius succeeded to the government of the Romans. In the same year, he overcame the Goths and drove them out of Greece. The Romans made him a golden shield, as a worthy tribute for that deed, and a golden likeness, and hung them up in their Capitol. In the following year he died, and his brother Quintillus succeeded to the government; and, on the seventeenth day after, he was put to death.

Book VI: Chapter XXVI.

1. One [7] thousand and twenty-seven years after the building of Rome [Orosius and Alfred A. D. 274: Clinton 270], Aurelian succeeded to the government of the Romans, and held it five years and six months. He drove the Goths to the north of the Danube, and marched thence upon the Syrians, and forced them again under the government of the Romans. He then marched upon the Gauls, and slew Tetricus, because he had drawn them under his government. He then gave orders for a persecution of Christians, and was slain shortly afterwards.

Book VI: Chapter XXVII.

1. One [8] thousand and thirty-two years after the building of Rome [Orosius and Alfred A. D. 279: Clinton 275], Tacitus succeeded to the government of the Romans; and, in the sixth

---

6 Oros. l. VII: c. 23. Haver. p. 520, 521, 7.
7 Oros. l. VII: c. 23. Haver. p. 521, 8—522.
8 Oros. l. VII: c. 24. Haver. p. 523, 1—3.

month after, he was slain in the country of Pontus.—Then Florianus succeeded to the government, and was slain in the third month after, in the country of Tarsus.

Book VI : Chapter XXVIII.

1. One thousand and thirty-three years after the building of Rome [Orosius and Alfred A. D. 280 : Clinton 276], Probus succeeded to the government of the Romans, and kept it six years, and four months. He drove the Huns out of Gaul, and slew Saturninus, who was striving for the government. He afterwards slew Proculus and Bonosus, who yearned for the government. Then he himself was slain on the down of Sirmium.

Book VI : Chapter XXIX.

1. One thousand and thirty nine years after the building of Rome [Orosius and Alfred A. D. 286 : Clinton 282], Carus succeeded to the government of the Romans, and held it two years. He fought twice against the Parthians, and took two of their cities, which were on the bank of the river Tigris. He was killed soon afterwards by a thunder bolt, and his son Numerianus succeeded to the government, and shortly after he was put to death by his own father-in-law.

Book VI : Chapter XXX.

1. One thousand and forty-one years after the building of Rome [Orosius and Alfred A. D. 288 : Clinton 284], Diocletian succeeded to the government of the Romans, and held it twenty years. He placed a younger emperor under him, called Maximian, and sent him into Gaul, because they had lately stirred up a war, but he easily overcame them. At that time, three kings were waging war upon Diocletian :—Carausius in Britain,—Achilleus in Egypt,—and Narses from Persia. He then placed three Cæsars under him :—One was Maximian,—the second Constantius,—the third Galerius. He sent Maximian into Africa, who overcame their opponents. He sent Constantius into Gaul, who overcame the Alamannic nation, and he then overran the island Britain.—And Diocletian himself went into

9 Id. Haver. p. 523, 4—11.
1 Oros. l. VII : c. 24. Haver. p. 523, 12—524.
2 Oros. l. VII : c. 25. Haver. p. 525—529. Alfred omits Chaps 26 and 27.

Egypt, and besieged Achilleus, the king, eight months, in the city Alexandria, till the citizens gave him up to Diocletian, who afterwards overran all Egypt.—He sent Galerius into Persia, who fought twice against Narses, the king, but neither of them had the victory. In their third battle, Galerius was routed, and came to Diocletian in great fear; but he received him with great dishonour, and ordered him to run, in his own purple robe, many miles before his chariot. After his courage had been whetted by that disgrace, he marched again upon the Persians, and routed them, and took Narses, and his wife and his children. Diocletian then received Galerius honourably.

2. Diocletian and Maximian ordered Christians to be persecuted,—Diocletian in the east, and Maximian in the west; and, because of this order, there were many martyrs in the space of ten years.

3. They then agreed between themselves, that they would give up their governments, and lay aside the purple robes, which they wore, and would end their days in peace; and they did so. Diocletian settled in the city Nicomedia, and Maximian settled in the city Milan. They left their governments to Galerius and to Constantius, and they divided it afterwards into two.—Galerius took Illyricum, and beyond that, the east, and the chief part of this world.—Constantius took all Italy, and Africa, and Spain, and Gaul, and Britain; but he had little wish for these worldly things and for great power; and, therefore, of his own will, he gave up Italy and Africa to Galerius. Then Galerius placed two kings under him:—One was named Severus, to whom he gave Italy and Africa; and he placed Maximinus in the eastern countries.

4. In those days, Constantius, the most merciful man, went into Britain, and died there; and gave the empire to Constantine, his son, whom he had by Helena his concubine.

5. Then [3] Maxentius, son of Maximian, wished to have the government of Italy. Galerius, therefore, sent against him Severus with an army, to whom the government had before been given, and he was betrayed there by his own men, and slain near the city Ravenna. When Maximian heard that his son had seized the government, he quickly left the city, in which he was settled, and thought to overcome his son, and afterwards to take

[3] Oros. l. VII: c. 28. Haver. p. 537, 17—541.

the government; but, when the son found it out, he drove away the father, who fled into Gaul and wished to overcome Constantine, his son-in-law, and to have the government to himself; but his daughter found it out, and told it to Constantine, and he then banished him to Marseilles, and he was there slain.

6. Galerius then gave Italy and Africa to Licinius, and he ordered all the best Christians, that were there, to be banished. Galerius was then brought into great weakness, and ordered many physicians, and none of them could do him any good, but one of them told him, that it was from the wrath of God. He, therefore, gave orders that the Christians should be brought into their own country again, each where he was before; yet he died of that sickness, and Licinius succeeded to the government.

7. There was afterwards war between Constantine and Maxentius; and soon after [A. D. 312] Constantine slew Maxentius at the Mulvian bridge in Rome.—In those days Maximinus ordered Christians to be persecuted, and soon afterwards died in the city Tarsus.—At that time, Licinius gave orders that no Christian should come into his household nor into his train; and soon afterwards there was war between him and Constantine, and frequent battles, until Constantine took Licinius, and ordered him to be beheaded, and then succeeded to all the government of the Romans.

8. In those days [A. D. 318—325], Arius, the mass-priest, fell into a mistake about the right belief. About this time [A. D. 325], three hundred and eighteen bishops were gathered together to refute and to excommunicate him.

9. In those days, Constantine put to death Crispus his son, and Licinius his sister's son; and no one knew what their guilt was, but him alone. He then brought under him many nations, which before were not under the Romans; and ordered a city to be built in Greece, and to be called after him Constantinople [A. D. 330]. He was the first man, that ordered churches to be built, and every idol-temple to be closed. He died about thirty-one years after he gained the empire, in a dwelling near the city Nicomedia.

Book VI : Chapter XXXI.

1. One [4] thousand and ninety-one years after the building of

---

[4] Oros. l. VII: c. 29, Haver. p. 541—544. A tabular arrangement of the emperors, mentioned in this chapter, will make it more clear.

Rome [Orosius A. D. 339 : Alfred 338 : Clinton 337], Constantius, with his two brothers, Constantine and Constans, succeeded to the empire; and Constantius held it twenty-four years. All the brothers were in the Arian heresy. Constantine and Constans waged war upon each other, till Constantine was slain. Then Magnentius slew Constans, and seized upon the government, that is of Gaul and Italy. In those days, the Illyrians appointed Vetranio to their government, that they might then wage war against Magnentius; and they forced him to learning, though he was aged; but Constantius took from him both the government and the purple that he wore, and also the school in which he learned. He then fought against Magnentius and routed him, and drove him into the city Lyons, and he afterwards stabbed himself. Then Constantius appointed Julian to be Cæsar under him, who had before been ordained a deacon, and sent him into Gaul with an army; and he quickly overcame all those, who were waging war in Gaul; and, after that deed, he was so lifted up, that he wished to take to himself all the government of the Romans, and marched with an army, [to the place] where Constantius was with another army against the Parthians. When Constantius heard of it, and was going against him, he died on the march.

2 Julian[5] succeeded to the government [A. D. 361], and held it one year and eight months. He soon wished secretly to overturn Christianity, and openly forbade that a man should learn any fast-book, and also said, that a Christian should not hold any of his offices, and thought thus to entrap them. " But they were all of that mind, as we have often heard it reported," said Orosius, "that they would rather follow Christianity, than hold his offices."

3 Then he gathered an army, and would go into Persia, and ordered, that, when he should come homeward again from the east, they should have an amphitheatre built at Jerusalem into which he might put God's servants, that wild beasts might there tear them to pieces. But, in that undertaking, God very justly

	Years	From A. D.
Constantine II reigned	3	337 to 340
Constantius II	24	337 — 361
Constans I	13	337 — 350
Julian	2	361 — 363

5 Oros. L VII : c. 30. Haver. p. 545, 546.

avenged the wicked thought of this wicked man, when a man met him, as he came from the city Ctesiphon, just as if he were a deserter, and told him he could lead him through the desert, that he might come upon the Persians unawares. But, when he had led him into the midst of the desert, he beguiled him, so that no man of the expedition knew where he was; but they went wandering about the desert, and knew not where he could get out, until many of the people perished both from thirst and from heat. Then an unknown man came towards them and stabbed Julian.

Book VI: Chapter XXXII.

1. One [6] thousand one hundred and seventeen years after the building of Rome [Orosius and Alfred A. D. 364: Clinton 363], Jovian succeeded to the government of the Romans. He was chosen in the desert, on the same day that Julian was stabbed. He gave the Persians the city, Nisibis, and half the country of Mesopotamia, with the view that they might go out of the country without harm.

2. In the eighth month after he succeeded to the government, he would go into Illyricum. One night, when he was in a newly-plastered house, he ordered a large fire to be made in it, because it was cold weather. The plaster then began to fume excessively, and Jovian was smothered by the vapour.

Book VI: Chapter XXXIII.

1. One [7] thousand one hundred and eighteen years after the building of Rome [Orosius and Alfred A. D. 365: Clinton 364], Valentinian succeeded to the government of the Romans, and he held it eleven years. He was before a chief officer of Julian's soldiers. Julian ordered him either to leave Christianity or his office, when he chose rather to leave his office, than Christianity. But God afterwards brought him to greater honour, since he had forsaken the less for the love of him, so that he had the government of the very empire, that his adversary before held.

2. Soon afterwards he gave half his empire [8] to his brother Valens; and he ordered Procopius, who then wished to reign, to

---

6 Oros. l. VII: c. 31. Haver. p. 547.
7 Oros. l. VII: c. 32. Haver. p. 548—550.
8 The army unanimously elected Vale ntinian emperor Feb. 26th 364, and he declared

be, put to death, and many others with him. Valens had been taught by an Arian bishop, named Eudoxius; but he hid it very closely from his brother, because he knew that he would avenge it, if he found out that he was in one belief, and himself in another; for he knew how steadfast he was before in his belief, when he had less power.

3. In the same year [A. D. 364], Athanaric, king of the Goths, made many martyrs of the Christians among his people. In those days Valentinian forced the Saxons back to their own country, when they would wage war against the Romans: they were settled near the ocean. He also with-held the Burgundians from waging war upon the Gauls. What mostly with-held them was, that baptism was promised them. In the eleventh year of his reign, the Sarmatians pillaged Pannonia: when he was going thither with an army, he died of a rushing of blood [apoplexy].

Book VI : Chapter XXXIV.

1. One* thousand one hundred and twenty-nine years after the building of Rome [Orosius A. D. 375. Alfred 376: Clinton 364], Valens, brother of Valentinian, succeeded to the government of the Romans ; and Gratian, son of Valentinian, succeeded to the government of Italy, and of Gaul and of Spain, under Valens. What he had before closely hidden, he shewed openly when he ordered that monks—who ought to forsake worldly things, and weapons of war—should take arms and fight with them, and do evil with other men. He sent into Egypt, and ordered to put down all the monkish customs, which his brother had before settled ; and some of the monks he ordered to be put to death,—some driven into banishment.

2. In those days there was in Africa, a man, called Firmus, who wished for the government. Then Valens sent thither his officer,

his brother Valens Augustus, and gave him half the empire on the 28th of March following. *Clinton, p.* 127. The empire was thus divided into the

Western empire,		and		The Eastern empire.		
	years reigned		From A. D.		years reigned	From A. D.
Valentinian I	11	. .	364 to 375.	Valens	14. . .	364 to 378
Gratian	⎡16	. .	367 — 383.			
	⎣ 6	. .	378 — 384.	Theodosius I.	16. . .	379 — 395
Valentinian II.	17	. .	375 — 392.	Arcadius	13. . .	395 — 408
Theodosius I.	3	. .	392 — 395.			
		[Emperor of the West as well as the East]				
Honorius	28	. .	395 — 423.			

9 Oros. l. VII : c. 33. Haver. p. 550—554.

Theodosius, with an army,—father of the good Theodosius, who was afterwards emperor. Firmus was taken in that expedition, and led forth to be put to death; then he himself begged that he might first be baptized. When he was baptized, he had, by the teaching of the mass-priest, who baptized him, such full belief of the kingdom of heaven, that he said to the people—" Do now as you will"; and leaned forward to them, that they might cut off his head; and he became a martyr of Christ.

3. In those days, Gratian fought in Gaul against the Alamanni, and slew many thousands of them. In the third year of his reign, when he did the greatest wrong to the servants of God, the Goths drove him out of their country; and they afterwards went over the river Danube into the dominion of Valens, and asked that they might settle peaceably in his dominion. Then he scorned either to forbid or grant it; but let them settle where they would. But his procurators and officers pressed them for tribute, and they had great strife about it, until the Goths routed them in battle.

4. When Valens heard of it, in the city Antioch, he was very sorry and thought of his misdeeds, how they had prayed for a right belief and font of baptism; and, for teachers, he sent to them Arian bishops, and heretics, as he himself was; and what he had often done to the injury of God's servants. However, where he knew any one to be living, he gave orders to send for him, and then, though it was late, he commanded him to be honoured.—In the fourth year of his reign he fought against the Goths, and was routed and driven into a village, and was burnt to death in a house. Thus it was ended by a very just judgment, when they burnt him in this world, who thought to burn them for everlasting.

Book VI: Chapter XXXV.

1. One [1] thousand one hundred and thirty-three years after the building of Rome [Orosius A. D. 379: Alfred 380: Clinton 378], Gratian [2] succeeded to the government of the Romans, and held it six years. He chose Theodosius to help him, because he thought that the nations, that were their enemies, were become

---

1 Oros. l. VII: c. 34. Haver. p. 554—556.
2 Gratian was raised to the rank of Augustus by his father Valentinian in A. D. 367 at the age of eight years. He succeeded to the Eastern Empire in 378 on the death of his uncle Valens; but, as the Goths were troublesome, he appointed Theodosius to be the Emperor of the east in 379. See chap. 33, § 2, note 8.

too strong to be any longer overcome by war. Theodosius, therefore, made peace with them; and, in that peace, he took with him to Constantinople Athanaric, their king, who, shortly afterwards, died there. As soon as the Goths heard how good Theodosius was, both they, and all the people that were in Scythia, wished for peace with him.

2. In those days, the Britons chose Maximus for their emperor, against his will, who was worthy of the government of all the Romans, for his manifold virtues, save that he then fought against his lord by the advice of other men. Soon afterwards, he went into Gaul, and slew Gratian, and drove Valentinian, his brother, out of Italy, and he fled to Theodosius.

Book VI : Chapter XXXVI.

1. One [3] thousand one hundred and thirty-eight years after the building of Rome [Orosius and Alfred A. D. 385 : Clinton 378], Theodosius succeeded to the government of the Romans, and held it eleven years. Six years before, he had the government of the eastern parts. Theodosius then thought how he could avenge Gratian his lord, and also bring his brother to the government, and led an army into Italy, where Maximus was encamped with a force at the city Aquileia, and had ordered his general Andragathius to keep the pass; but the general intrusted the keeping of it to sluggish men, and thought of going round by the east in ships, and then stealing upon Theodosius behind. But as soon as he was gone from the pass towards the ships, Theodosius came to it and found few men there, who were bad and sluggish; and he soon drove them away, and broke through the pass, and then went over the mountains till he came to Aquileia, and slew Maximus. When the general heard that, he drowned himself. By the fall of these two, how easily God ended the great war, which Maximus and his general had stirred up with many nations!

2. After that, Valentinian again succeeded to the empire. About two years afterwards, when he came into Gaul, Arbogastes his general smothered him, and then hung him up with ropes by the neck, just as if he had put himself to death, without knowing what he was doing. He placed Eugenius as emperor, with the name of the sovereignty and took to himself the power; for he

---

3 Oros. l. VII : c. 35. Haver. p. 557—562.

could not have the name of emperor, because he was not a Roman; but he taught the other to enter fully into idolatry. Then Theodosius again led an army against them both, to the same pass, which he formerly took from Maximus. Theodosius then sent before him an army of the Goths to break through the pass; but they were surrounded from the mountains, and all slain: they were ten thousand. Theodosius, therefore, marched thitherward, and knew that they would surround him by the same stratagem. When they were before each other, Eugenius and Arbogastes thought that they could first drive them from the mountains by the shots of their arrows; but God sent such a wind against them, that they could not shoot an arrow from them, without every one of them coming either upon themselves or upon the earth. Theodosius had the wind with him, so that his army could fasten almost every one of their arrows in their enemies. Eugenius was slain there, and Arbogastes stabbed himself. Then Theodosius went into Italy; and, when he came to the city Milan, he died, and gave up the government to his two sons.

Book VI : Chapter XXXVII.

1. " One [4] thousand one hundred and forty-nine years after the building of Rome [Orosius and Alfred A. D. 396 : Clinton 395], Arcadius succeeded to the government of the eastern part, and held it twelve years [5]; and Honorius to the western part, and even yet holds it," [6] said Orosius.

2. And, because they were young, [7] Theodosius placed them under the care of his two generals: Arcadius was placed under Rufinus, and Honorius was placed under Stilico. But they soon afterwards made known what lordly faithfulness they thought of shewing to their old master's children, if they could have done it. Rufinus wished to have the government of the east for himself; and Stilico wished to give this of the west

---

4 Very much abridged from Oros. l. VII : c. 36. Haver. p. 563—566.
5 Clinton says 13 years, from A. D. 395 to 408. See l. VI : c. 33 § 2 note 8.
6 This chapter must, therefore, have been written after A. D. 408, in which year Arcadius died. Augustine, writing to Jerome in A. D. 415, calls Orosius a young man. See p. 11. Orosius, therefore, wrote this history early in life, probably between A. D. 410 and 416. See l. II : c. 1 § 2 note 2, p. 78; and Introduction p. 14 and 15 note 24.
7 Oros. l. VII : c. 37 and 38. Haver. p. 567—572.

to his son. And because of this fiendish feeling, he left the Goths in Italy, with their two kings, Alaric and Rhadagaisus, and thought, when the people were overcome, that they would afterwards do all that he wished; and hoped also that he could soon keep back the Goths from the war, because he was born in their land. Shortly afterwards, Alaric became a Christian, and Rhadagaisus remained a heathen, and daily sacrificed to idols by slaying men, and he was always most pleased, if they were Romans.

3. "Even now, it may shame you Romans," said Orosius, "that ye should have had so mean a thought, for fear of one man, and for one man's sacrificing, as when ye said, that the heathen times were better than the Christian, and also, that it were better for yourselves to forsake Christianity, and take to the heathen customs, which your elders formerly followed. Ye may also think how worthless he afterwards was, in his sacrifices, and his idolatry, in which he lived, when ye had him bound and then treated him as ye would, and all his army, which, as ye yourselves said, was two hundred thousand, yet not one of you was wounded."

Book VI : Chapter XXXVIII.

1. One[8] thousand one hundred and sixty-four years after the building of Rome [Orosius and Alfred A. D. 411 : Clinton 410], God shewed his mercy to the Romans, when he allowed their misdeeds to be avenged, and yet it was done by Alaric, the most Christian and the mildest of kings. He sacked Rome with so little violence, that he ordered no one should be slain,—and that nothing should be taken away, or injured, that was in the churches. Soon after that, on the third day, they went out of the city of their own accord; so there was not a single house burnt by their order.

2. There[9] Ataulf, Alaric's kinsman, took the sister of Honorius,

---

8 Oros. l. VII : c. 39. Haver. p. 573—575.
9 Oros. l. VII : c. 40. Haver. p. 576—578. Alfred has omitted chap. 41, 42 and 43 of the original Latin of Orosius. In this 43rd chapter, which Alfred has omitted, Orosius, addressing his aged friend, Augustine, thus speaks of the space of time embraced by his history. Explicui, adjuvante Christo, secundum tuum præceptum, beatissime pater Augustine, ab initio mundi usque in præsentem diem, hoc est, *per annos quinquies mille sexcentos et septemdecim*, cupiditates et punitiones hominum peccatorum, conflictationes seculi, et judicia Dei. Haver. p. 587, 8. Mr Clinton, in writing to me on the subject, says, "That the numbers 5617, quoted by you from Oros. l. VII : c. 43, are the genuine numbers of Oros. appears from l. I : c. 1. Haver. p. 7, 1," where he says—Sunt ab Adam,

the king, and afterwards agreed with him, and took her for his wife [A. D. 414]. Then the Goths settled there in the country,—some by the wish of the emperor,—some against his wish: some of them went into Spain, and there settled,—some into Africa.

primo homine, usque ad Ninum, quando natus est Abraam, *anni ter mille centum octoginta et quatuor*. 3184
A Nino autem vel Abraam, usque ad nativitatem Christi, colliguntur *anni bis mille quindecim*. 2015
    Add the date of the work of Orosius 416

    These numbers make together the sum of . . . . . . 5615.
Orosius follows Eusebius who gives these numbers,—
From Adam to the Flood 2242
From the Flood to Abraham 942

Making together from Adam to Abraham . . . . 3184.
From Abraham to Christ 2015
Add the 416 years 416

The sum of these dates from Eusebius is the same as those above from Orosius   5615.
Eusebius obtained these periods by following the longer generations of the LXX. The shorter generations of the Hebrew Bible would be from Adam to Christ 4004, to which add 416 will give 4420 years, over which the history of Orosius extends. See before, p. 77, note 1: and p. 61, note 1.

KING ALFRED'S VERSION

OF

VENERABLE BEDE'S ECCLESIASTICAL HISTORY

OF THE ENGLISH NATION;

LITERALLY TRANSLATED FROM THE ORIGINAL ANGLO-SAXON

BY

𝕰. 𝕮𝖍𝖔𝖒𝖘𝖔𝖓 𝖊𝖘𝖖.

NOTE BY THE TRANSLATOR.

In proceeding with this edition of Alfred's Works, it has been judged most proper to let the General History of the World by Orosius be immediately followed by Bede's Ecclesiastical History of the English Nation. In his treatment of this subject, King Alfred has adopted the same plan of selection and condensation as in the other treatise. The number of Books is the same as in the Original; but many chapters are left unnoticed; of some the titles or rubrics only are given; of others the historical portion is translated or paraphrased more strictly or more liberally, as seemed best, with the omission of Letters, Official Documents, &c. which seem to have been left, for the researches of the learned, in the Original Latin. The Translation here given may seem to need a few words of apology. It was undertaken at a very short notice by one, who, though he had read a good deal of Anglo-Saxon, had not included Alfred's Bede in his course of study, and who entertains a strong prejudice against the mixed mode of forming a language. While he feels it a pleasure to read Homer or Herodotus in Greek, Livy or Virgil in Latin, Göthe or Schiller in German, Cædmon or Alfred in Anglo-Saxon, he can also relish the writings—in prose or rhyme —of the great authors of our own more composite and heterogeneous form of speech during the last five centuries. But in attempting to render the pure English of the ninth century into the language of the present day, it has been thought worthy of attention to give a decided and universal preference to words of native English growth, though some of these might be deemed a little antiquated; care being taken at the same time to render faithfully the sense and spirit of Alfred's original English. Scarcely any reader, moderately acquainted with our current literature, would require a glossary for such words as 'lore' doctrine or advice, 'shed' separated, 'main' power, from 'mayen' to be able—'felled' suppressed, 'mood' mind, 'wilsomeness' resolution or devotedness, 'fordoom' condemn, 'go (or come) on hand (into hand)' to surrender, 'after-follower' successor, 'hallowed' consecrated, and a few others. The authorised version of holy writ has preserved many a phrase, as well as single words, in their ancient sense and structure, as woe 'worth' (be or happen), 'do to wit' make to know, 'all tobrake' or (tobroke) completely broke asunder, &c.

The text of Smith's edition (Cantab. 1722,) has been followed except in a very few cases, where a marginal reading, especially of the MS. which he has marked with the letter *B*, appeared worthy of preference.—The marks by which the MSS. are distinguished are *B*. Bennet, *C*. Cotton, *Ca*. Cambridge,—basis of Smith's, as it was of Whelock's text, *O*. Oxford, *T*. Tanner's—*Alf.* is used in the notes for Alfred, *Bd*. Bede, *Ch*. Chaucer, *Eng.* English, *Sc.* Scottish, *Sm.* Smith.

E. T.

King Alfred's Version

OF

BEDE'S ECCLESIASTICAL HISTORY.

To KING KEOLWULF.[1]

I Bede, Christ's servant and mass-priest, send to greet the most beloved king Keolwulf[2]: And I send thee the history which I lately wrote of the English people and Saxons; for thyself to read, and at leisure to study, and also in more places to write, and to teach. And I trust in thy earnestness, for thou art very careful and studious of old men's words and deeds; and most of all, of the great men of our nation. For this writing either says good of good men, and he who hears it, imitates that [good]; or it says evil of evil men, and he who hears it, flees that [evil] and shuns [it]: for it is good to praise a good man, and to blame an evil [one,] that he may thrive who will hear it,—if the other will not, how else will he be taught? For thy profit and for thy people's I wrote this: because God chose thee king, it behoves thee to teach thy people. And that thou may the less doubt whether this be true, I will shew whence these spells[3] came to me.

2. My first helper and teacher was the reverend abbot Albinus, who was far travelled and learned, and was best skilled in the English nation. Chiefly he told me—from the memory of Theodore, who was bishop in Canterbury, and abbot Adrian, for he was chiefly taught by them—all in the province of Kent and also in the countries which were adjoining thereto—all that he understood either in writings or in old men's sayings, or by the disciples of the blessed pope saint Gregory,—all those [things] which were worthy of memory he sent to me through Nothhelm the

---

(1) King of Northumberland in the time of Bede.
(2) Cyning and halettan—Smith, who takes haletta for a different form of hæleða, from hæleð, vir, a hero. But there is no authority for either hæleða or haletta :(—)" & halettan," for ' vel halettan,' not in MS. B, is a misplaced gloss to gretan—or say " to greet and hail."
(3) Spell, a speech, story, message, set form of words, *carmen*, a charm or incantation.

pious mass-priest in London—either sent him to me, or wrote in letters ⁴ and sent to me. From the beginning of these books to the time when the English race received Christ's belief, until this present time, by old men's sayings, we chiefly learnt what we here write; and under what king that was done, by the disciples of the blessed pope saint Gregory, through Albinus the abbot's remembering, through Nothhelm's errands and sayings. Very many things they told me—from what sundry bishops, and in what king's times, East-Saxons, and West-Saxons, and East-Anglians, and North-Humbrians, received the grace of the Christian faith. Through Albinus chiefly I grew so bold that I durst begin this work; and also with [the help] of Daniel the reverend bishop of the West-Saxons, and also about the Isle of Wight chiefly he sent me in writings; and through Kedde the reverend bishop of the Mercians, and Keadda, about the people of the Mercians, and of the East-Saxons; and also about the life and death of the bishops, we asked of the brethren of the monastery which they themselves founded, named Lestingeu. The things that were done in East-Anglia, we partly found from the writings or sayings of old men, partly learnt by the conversation of the reverend Abbot Isi. And what was done in Lindsey about the Christian belief, we learnt through the conversation of the reverend bishop Kynebright, and through his epistles, and [those] of other, very truthful, living men. And [what we learnt in Northumbria about the Christian faith until this present day, not by one man's advice, but by the saying of innumerable faithful witnesses, who knew and remembered those things; and then what I myself understood, that I left not unwritten. And what I wrote of the holy father Cuthbright, either in this book, or in another book of his deeds, some I first took out of the writings which I found written by the brethren of the Church at Lindesfarn, some, which I might understand through the telling of very true men, I added. And I now humbly beg and entreat the learner, if he meet or hear any thing about this in another wise, that he blame not me for that.

3. Moreover I humbly beg of all to whom this history [may] come to be read or heard, that they for my weaknesses both of mind and of body often and earnestly intercede with the supreme mercy of almighty God; and in every one of their provinces give me this meed of their recompence, as I have earnestly toiled to write to thee

---

(4) '*Stafas*,' *staves*, in Anglo-Saxon—still applied to songs and ballads.

concerning sundry provinces, or the higher places, which I believed mind-worthy, and to the inhabitants thank-worthy, that I with all [may] find the fruit of pious intercession.

BOOK I. CHAPTER I.

Of the situation of Britain, and of Ireland the isle of the Scots and of their earlier inhabitants.

1. Britain is an island of the ocean which was of yore named Albion, and is set betwixt North-deal and West-deal, at a great distance over against Germany and Gaul and Spain, the largest divisions of Europe; that is North eight hundred miles long, and [West] two hundred miles broad. It has from the South-deal the province over against it which is called Gallia Belgica. This island is wealthy in fruits and in trees of various kinds; and it is meet for the feeding of sheep and neat [cattle]; and in some places vineyards grow. This country is also productive of various fowls and sea-animals, and fish-breeding waters and well-springs: and here are often caught seals, and whales, and sea-swine; and here are often taken, of various kinds, wilkshells and muscles; and in these are often found the best pearls of every hue; and here in great plenty are the wilks, from which is made the wilk-red *(or crimson)* colour, which neither sun may bleach nor rain impair; and the older it is, the fairer it is. This land has also salt-pits; and it has hot water, and hot baths meet for every age and sex by means of separate places. It is also productive in metallic ores of copper and iron, lead and silver. Here is also coloured agate: this stone is a black gem; if one puts it into the fire then the adders there flee away. This island was also formerly adorned with the noblest cities, thirty wanting one; which were built with walls, and towers, and gates, and the strongest locks; besides other less towns innumerable. And because this island lies next under the very North-deal of the earth, it has light nights in summer, so that oft at mid-night strife comes to the beholders, whether it be the evening twilight or the morning dawn. In this it is evident that this island has much longer days in summer and also nights in winter, than the southern parts of the earth.

2. This island, now, answerably to the number of the five books of Moses, in which the divine law is written, studies and confesses one wisdom of the high truth and the true highness in five

peoples' speeches; that is, in the speech of the English race, and of the Britons, and Scots, and Picts, and Latins; only the Latin, in the study of the Scriptures, is common to all the others. In the beginning, the Britons alone were at first the inhabitants of this island, from whom it received [its] name: it is said that they came from the province Armorica into Britain, and seated themselves in the southern parts of this island, and made them their own.

3. Then it happened afterwards that the nation of the Picts came from the land of the Scythians in ships, and then ran round all the coasts of Britain, till they came up into Scotland *(Ireland)*, and there found the Scots people, and begged of them a seat and dwelling-place in their land among them. The Scots answered them, that their land was not so much that they might have two nations, but they said, "We may give you wholesome advice, what ye may do: we know, not far hence, another island right east, which we may oft on light days see; if ye will seek that, then may ye there have a dwelling-place; or if any one shall withstand you, then will we help you." Then went the Picts into Britain, and began to inhabit the north parts of this island, and the Britons, as we ere said, the south parts. As the Picts had not wives, they asked them from the Scots; then agreed they to the condition, and gave them wives, " that if the matter should come into doubt, then they should choose a king to themselves of the female kin rather than of the male kin"; which yet to-day is held by the Picts.

4. Then in forthgoing time, after the Britons and Picts, Britain received a third race—[that] of the Scots in the Picts' portion. They were come out of Ireland, the island of the Scots, with their leader named Reada, [and] either by friendship or by fighting, gained to themselves a settlement and a dwelling place among them, which they now yet have: that race until to-day were called Dalreadings.

5. Ireland, the isle of the Scots, both in the breadth of its state and healthiness and mildness of the air, is much better than the land of Britain, so that there snow seldom lies longer than three days; and there no man mows hay in summer for winter's cold, nor builds stalls for his cattle, nor is any sneaking or venemous worm seen there, nor may any adder live there: for adders were brought from Britain in ships; as soon as they smelt the air of

the land, they died; besides, nearly all things that come thence are good against every poison. It is a token [of this] that some men saw those who were bitten by adders—that one shaved the leaves of the books which came out of Ireland, and put the shavings into water, and gave it to the men to drink, and soon was the poison overtaken, and they were healed. The island is rich in milk and in honey, and vineyards wax in some places, and it is fish-breeding and fowl-breeding, and famous in the hunting of harts and roes. This is properly the country of the Scots; hence came the third race of the Scots into Britain, as we said before, as well as concerning the Britons and Picts.

CHAPTER II.
That the first emperor of the Romans Caius Julius sought Britain.

The Island Britain was unknown to the Romans until Caius Cesar, by surname Julius, sought it with an army, and subdued it, sixty winters ere Christ's coming.

CHAPTER III.
That the second emperor of the Romans, named Claudius, sought the same island and added the Orkney Isles to the empire of the Romans. Yea, also, Vespasian was sent by him, and he subjected the isle of Wight to the Roman empire.

Then after that Claudius the emperor, who was the fourth from Augustus, again led an army into Britain; and there, without heavy fighting and bloodshed, received a great deal of the land into his dominion. He likewise added the Orkney isles, which were out in the ocean beyond Britain, to the Roman empire; and in the sixth month after he came hither, he returned to Rome. This expedition was led in the fourth year of his reign: that year was from Christ's coming hither the forty-sixth. By the same emperor Claudius was Vespasian sent into Britain, who reigned after Nero. He overran the Isle of Wight, and subjected it to the dominion of the Romans: it is thirty miles long east and west, and twelve miles broad south and north. Then Nero took to the empire after Claudius Cesar, who began nothing profitable in the state; but among other innumerable damages of the Roman empire he lost the rule of Britain.

CHAPTER IV.
That Lucius king of the Britons sent a letter to Eleutherius the pope, prayed that he might be a Christian, and also obtained his request.

Then it was from Christ's hithercoming a hundred and fifty-six years, that Marcus by surname Antoninus, who was the fourteenth from Augustus Cesar, received the empire of the Romans with Aurelius his brother. In the times of these kings the holy man Eleuther was bishop and pope of the Roman church. Lucius king of Britain sent a letter to him, prayed and entreated him, that by his command he might be made a Christian. Aud quickly the performance of the pious prayer followed : and then the Britons received baptism and Christ's faith, and held that [faith] in mild peace until Diocletian's time—the evil emperor.

CHAPTER V.
That Severus the emperor took a great deal of Britain, and separated it with a dike from other untamed races.

Then it was about a hundred and eighty-nine winters from [our] Lord's incarnation, that Severus Cesar, who was of African kin, from the city called Leptis, [and] who was the seventeenth from Augustus, received the empire, and had it seventeen years. This emperor firmly ruled the state. But yet he came in war to Britain with an army, and there with great and heavy battles received a great deal of the island into his dominion, and begirt and fastened it from other barbarous races with a dike and an earth-wall, from sea to sea, and he there died of sickness in the city York, and Basianus, his son, received the government of Britain.

CHAPTER VI.
Of Diocletian's reign and how he was persecuting Christian men.

Then it came to pass about two hundred and eighty-six winters after the Lord's incarnation, that Diocletian the emperor, who was the thirty-third from Augustus, had the empire twenty years ; he chose Maximianus to the help of his reign, and gave him the west-deal of the earth ; and he took the royal weeds, and came into Britain. Then among the many evils which they did—Diocletian in the east-deal of the earth, and Maximianus in the west-deal—they oppressed and harried God's church, and harmed and slew Christian men. They took the tenth place in the persecution of God's churches after the emperor Nero. The persecution of wicked kings was more immoderate and more lasting than all that were done before on the earth. For through ten years fully the burnings of God's churches, and the for-doomings of guiltless [men], and the slaughter of holy martyrs, were incessantly done.

Britain too was then raised very high in much belief and confession of God.

CHAPTER VII.

The suffering of Alban and his companions, who at the same time shed their blood for the Lord.

1. Likewise at that time in Britain suffered saint Alban, of whom Fortunatus the priest, in the 'Praise of Virgins,' when he mentioned the blessed martyrs who came to the Lord out of all the earth, thus said :—" The fruit-bearing Britain brings forth the noble Albanus." Alban was yet a heathen, when the commands of the truthless kings raged against Christian men; then it fell out that he received in hospitality some man of God, in priesthood, who was fleeing from the fierce persecutors. And when he saw him then to be busied in constant prayers and in watchings, day and night, then was he suddenly sown with the divine grace and obtained mercy; and he soon began [to shew] examples of his faith and piety; as also piece-meal he was taught by his wholesome exhortations, [so] that he forsook the darkness of devil-worship, and from his inward heart became a Christian. With that when the foresaid man of God was many days with him as a guest, then came it to the ear of the wicked alderman, that Alban had Christ's confessor secretly with him. Then quickly ordered he his officers to seek and ask for him. Then as soon as they came to the martyr's house, saint Alban arrayed himself for the stranger whom he entertained, [who was] also his master, in his monkish garb, and went on hand to them, and they led him bound to the [alderman].

2. Then it fell out at the same time that Alban was led to him, that the judge stood at his altars, and offered sacrifice to devils. When he looked at saint Alban, then he soon became angry, because he by his own will had been so bold that he gave himself into the power of such danger for the stranger whom he entertained as a guest; then he ordered [them] to drag and lead him to the idol-altar at which he was standing.—He thus spoke to him : " Because thou wouldest hide from me the offender, and the adversary, and the despiser of our gods, rather than tell my officers, know thou then, that thou shalt undergo the same punishment which he deserved, if thou thinkest to go off from the observance of our religion." And saint Alban then of his own will showed

and opened to the persecutors of God's belief, that he was a Christian, and that he did not dread the threatening of the alderman. But he was begirt with the weapons of the ghostly warfare, and he openly said that he would not obey his commands. Then said he *(the alderman and judge)* to him; Tell me of what family and of what kin thou art. And then answered him saint Alban; What concerns it thee from what root I be sprung? But if thou wish to hear the truth of my religion, then wit thou that I am a Christian, and will serve Christian offices. Then said the judge to him: Tell me thy name, what thou art called. Then said he; I am called Alban from my parents; and I always worship the true and living God, who made heaven and earth and all creatures, and to him I pray.

3. Then the judge became wroth and said to him; If thou wish to brook the happiness of this life with us, delay not to sacrifice to the great gods with us. Then answered St Alban; The sacrifices which have been yielded to devils by you, cannot help the devotees, nor fulfil their desires nor their wills. But yet truer it is that whosoever offers sacrifice to these likenesses and idols, he shall receive for his meed the everlasting torments of hell's pain. When the judge heard these words, then was he with much heat and anger stirred up. Then he ordered and commanded them quickly to scourge and torture the acknowledger of God: he thought and weened that by scourging he should soften the boldness [1] and steadfastness of his heart, which by words he could not [do]. When he then was weakened [2] with severe scourging and tortures, and bore and sustained all the pains that were inflicted upon him patiently and joyfully for the Lord, and when the judge then knew that, and then understood that he could not overcome him by tortures and by scourging, nor could turn him from the observance of the Christian religion, then he ordered [them] to cut off his head.

4. While he then was led to death, then came he to a very rapid river, which flows nigh the city-walls, and he saw there a great multitude of people of either sex, and there were men of various ages and conditions. The multitude of people, without doubt, was called by divine instigation to attendance upon the blessed martyr, and they were so busied on the bridge of the stream, that they could scarcely go over before evening; and, nearly all going

---

(1) Byldo *B.*—bedu *Smith.* (2) Or affected, treated; But MS. *B* reads—not weakened.

out, the judge abode in the city without attendance. But St Alban, in whom was a burning wilsomeness of mood, that he might most quickly come to suffering, went to the foresaid stream, and hove his eyes up to heaven; then the stream soon dried up, and bent before his feet, so that he might go over dry. When, among others [who] saw this wonder, [was] the executioner himself who was to slay him; then was he by a divine impulse inwardly admonished, so that he threw away the sword which he had in his hand, and fell at his feet, and earnestly prayed that he might suffer with the martyr, or for him, whom he formerly was to slay. Then was this man, through God's grace, of a persecutor, become a friend of truth and of the Christian belief. Then the most venerable acknowledger of God ascended with the multitude up into the hill, which was then timely green and fair, and with various blossoms of herbs adorned and apparelled everywhere about.

5. It was worthy of it, that the place were so beautiful and so fair, which was afterwards to be honoured and hallowed with the blessed martyr's blood. On the top of this hill St Alban begged of God that water might be given him for some of his service, and then immediately a well sprang up before his feet, that all men might understand that the water was sent for his service, as he had before wished to God. And now the wilsomeness and the service of the blessed martyr being fulfilled, the well and the water left off the witnessing of the service, and returned to kind.[1] The place was about half a mile from the city-wall, and from the stream, which he formerly went over with dry feet. There was beheaded the strongest martyr St Alban, and there he got the crown of everlasting life which God has promised to all them that will love him.

6. But the executioner who stretched his wicked hands over the godly neck of the martyr, and struck off his head—he was not left to rejoice over him dead; but the eyes shot out of his head, and together with the martyr's head fell on the earth. Then was likewise beheaded and martyred the man who was formerly chid by the heavenly might, so that he gainsaid that he should slay the acknowledger of God. Of whom then it is certain, that though he was not washed with the water of the baptismal bath, he was however cleansed by the bath of his blood, and became worthy of the heavenly kingdom.

(1) Nature—their natural state.

7. Then was the judge, after these things, greatly troubled and affrighted with the newness of so many heavenly wonders. Then he soon ordered [them] to stop from the persecution of Christian men, and began to reverence the suffering of holy martyrs, through which he formerly weened that he might turn them from the religion of the Christian belief. The blessed Alban suffered the tenth day of the kalends of July *(22 of June)*, nigh the city which the Romans called Verolamium, which now is by the English nation named Werlamecaster, or Weclingacaster. Then was it soon after that, that calmness of Christian times came, and there a church was made and built of wonderful workmanship, and worthy of his suffering and martyrdom. In that place now indeed to this present day, the healing of sick men and the working of heavenly mights are often much spoken of and manifold wonders happen.

8. At that time likewise suffered Aaron and Julius, who were burghers of Leicester, and also many others of either sex in various places; who were wrested with various torments, and wounded with unheard of tearing asunder of the limbs: well ended warfare sent their souls to the joy of the lofty city of the heavenly kingdom's glory.

CHAPTER VIII.
The persecution stopped, the church in Britain for some time had peace, till the time of the Arian heresy.

1. And after the trial of the persecution was stilled, then went forth the Christian men and the faithful, they who formerly in the perilous time of the persecution hid and darkened themselves in woods, and in wastes, and in dens; and they then renewed God's churches which were formerly cast down, and also built churches, and hallowed them to holy martyrs, and broadened their places, and honoured them as a victorious token, and celebrated feast-days, and with clean mouth and clean heart, hallowed and performed the divine mysteries.

2. This peace lasted in the churches of Christ which were in Britain until the time in which the Arian heresy arose. In these times Constantius, who in the lifetime of Diocletian held and ruled the kingdom of Gaul and of Spain, and who was a mild man and good for the age, died in Britain, and left his kingdom to his son Constantine, the good emperor who was born of the woman Elena. Eutropius writes that Constantine was born in Britain,

and took to the empire after his father. In this king's times the Arian heresy came up, and not only spread the deathbearing venom of its truthlessness in all the churches of the earth, but likewise came into this island. This error was, in the Nicene Synod, put down and felled in Constantine's days.

CHAPTER IX.[1]
That, in the reign of Gratian, Maximus, being chosen[2] emperor in Britain, returned with a great host into the kingdom of Gaul.

CHAPTER X.
That, in the reign of Archadius, Pelagius the Briton took upon [him] unright lore[3] against the belief of God's grace.

CHAPTER XI.
That, in the reign of Honorius, Gratian and Constantius were chosen emperors in Britain; and the former was slain among the Britons, and the other in the kingdom of Gaul.

1. When it was about four hundred and seven years after [our] Lord's incarnation, Honorius the emperor, who was also the forty fourth from Augustus Cesar, succeeded to the sovereignty, two years ere the city Rome was broken into and forharried. The harrying was done through Alaric king of the Goths.

2. The city Rome was broken into by the Goths about a thousand one hundred and sixty four years after it was built: from that time the Romans ceased to reign in Britain. They had the sovereignty of Britain four hundred years and seventy of the fifth [hundred] after Caius, by second name Julius, the emperor, sought the same island; and cities, and towers, and streets, and bridges, were wrought in their reign, which we to-day may see. The Britons dwelt to the south-deal, within the dike which we mentioned that Severus ordered to be trenched overthwart the island.

CHAPTER XII.
That the Britons were forharried by the Scots and Picts, and they begged help from Rome.

1. Then began two peoples, the Picts by north, and the Scots by south, to war on them, and to take and harry their goods, and afflicted and oppressed them many years. Then in that unstill-

(1) Alfred gives the headings only of many chapters.
(2) Creatus "chosen," mistaken by Alfred for "born" both here and in p. 210, last line.
(3) Or "wrong doctrine," heterodoxy.

ness they sent ambassadors to Rome with a letter, and with a weeping prayer begged help of them, and promised them humble obedience and perpetual subjection, if they helped them, that they might overcome their foes. Then sent they a great army to their help, and as soon as they came into this island they fought against their foes, and made a great slaughter among them, and drove and banished them out of their territories, and strengthened them and taught them to build fastnesses for their protection against their foes; and so with much triumph went home.

2. When the former enemies understood that the Roman army was gone away, then came they soon with a ship-army into their boundaries, and slew and killed all that they met; and, as a ripe harvest, fortrod, and plundered and harassed them all. And they then again sent ambassadors to Rome, and with weeping voice begged help of them, that their poor country might not be altogether blotted out, nor the name of the Roman people, which had shone so long and so bright with them, should be taken away and blotted out by the wickedness of foreign nations. Then was an army again sent hither, which came at an unexpected time, in harvest; and they soon fought against their foes, and had victory, and all those who could escape death, they chased over the sea [to the] north,—those who every year robbed and harried over the sea. Then said the Romans anon to the Britons, that they could no more be troubled with so warlike expeditions for their protection; but they encouraged and advised them to make weapons, and to take strength of mind, that they might strive and withstand their foes. And they then also, for their counsel and comfort, resolved that they should in common make a fastness for their protection—a stone wall in a straight course from the east sea to the west sea, where Severus the emperor anciently ordered to trench and build an earth-wall, which one may still see to-day eight feet broad, and twelve feet high. Likewise on the sea-shore to the south, whence the ship-army came upon them, they built towers to guard the sea. Then as soon as this fastness was wrought, they gave them strong exhortations and many patterns how they should make weapons for themselves, and withstand their foes; and then greeted [them] and shewed them that they never more would visit them; and they departed over the sea, victorious.

3. When the Picts and Scots learnt that they were gone home,

and also that they would not come hither to them again, then they became bolder, and soon seized and settled all the north-deal of this island as far as the wall. Against these the sluggish infantry of the Britons stood on the top of the fastness, and with frightened heart remained there day and night. Then their enemies sought them engines, and made them hooks, with which they dragged them wretchedly down off the wall, and they were dead as soon as they reached the ground. They then left the wall and their city, and fled away, and their enemies pursued them, and smote them, and felled them to death. This fight was bloodier and sterner than all that were done before, for, as sheep are devoured by wolves and [other] wild beasts, so the wretched townsmen were torn and destroyed by their foes, and bereft of their goods, and abandoned to hunger.

CHAPTER XIII.
That, in the reign of Theodosius, in whose times Palladius the bishop was sent to the Scots who believed in Christ, the Britons were begging help to themselves from Ætius the king (consul), at Rome, and got none.

1. When [it] was about four hundred and twenty-three years after our Lord's incarnation, Theodosius the emperor undertook the government after Honorius, and had it six and twenty winters: he was the forty-fifth from the emperor Augustus. In the eighth year of this emperor's reign, bishop Palladius was first sent to the Scots who believed in Christ, by the bishop of the Roman church [who] was called Celestinus. Likewise in the twenty third year of his reign, there was one called Ætius, a famous man, who was long before a high alderman *(a patrician)*, and then was the third time consul and king in Rome. To this [man] the needy remains of the Britons then sent a letter,—[of which] the beginning was thus written :—" To Ætius thrice king, the sighing and groaning of the Britons." And in the forthgoing of the letter they thus unfolded their hardships :—" The barbarians drive us to the sea; the sea shoves us back to the barbarians; between them two we thus suffer a two-fold death—are either stabbed, or drenched in the sea." Though they said these things, they could get no help from him, for at the same time he was busied with heavy fights against Blædla and Atila, kings of the Huns. Likewise in those times came a great hunger in Constantinople the head city of the Greeks, and a pestilence followed

soon after, yea also many walls with seven and fifty towers rushed and fell; and likewise many other cities were overthrown; and the hunger and the plague-bearing air cut off and destroyed many thousands of men and beasts.

CHAPTER XIV.
That the Britons [being] pressed by the famous hunger drove the barbarians off their boundaries; and soon after that, great crops, and lechery, and pestilence, and ailings, and uprooting of the nation followed.

1. The foresaid hunger came likewise hither to the Britons, and so greatly weakened them, that many of them went into the hands of their foes, and yet there were more who would not do that. But when every human help ceased, that they might trust more to divine help, they then first began to fight against their foes, who for many years before harried and plundered on them, and they then made a great slaughter among them, and bedrove them home, and had a victory. After this came a good year, and also much abundance of fruits in the land of Britain, so as no after age since can remember, wherewith then lechery began to wax, and soon a pest of all sins[1] together hastened on—that was cruelty, and hatred of truth, and the love of a lie, and leasing. And not only men of the world did those things, but likewise the Lord's flock and its keepers; and they put their neck under drunkenness, and pride, and chiding, and strife, and envy, having cast away the light and sweet yoke of Christ. Among these things then came suddenly a great and grim pestilence upon those men of perverse mind, which swiftly seized and killed a great multitude of them, [so] that the quick were not enough to bury the dead; but yet those who were living would [do] naught the better for the fear of death, nor could be called back from the death of their souls.

2. Therefore, not a great while after, a grimmer vengeance of that grim wickedness was following after the sinful people. Then they gathered a meeting, and consulted and advised what they were to do, and where they were to seek help to check and to shove back so fierce and so frequent harrying of the northern nations; and it then liked them all with their king named Vortigern, that they should call and invite the nation of the

---

1. For *monna*, *I read* mana scelerum. *Bd.*

Saxons from the parts beyond sea for their help. It is certain that that was ordained by the Lord's might, that evil vengeance should come upon the reprobate, as in the end of the matters is manifestly shewn.

CHAPTER XV.
That the English nation was invited by the Britons into Britain; and they soon at first drove their enemies far [off]. But not a long time after they covenanted with them, and turned their weapons against the Britons their allies.

1. Then it was about four hundred and forty-nine years from [our] Lord's incarnation that Marcianus the emperor undertook the government, and held it seven years; he was the forty sixth from Augustus the emperor. Then the nation of the English and Saxons was invited by the foresaid king, and came into Britain in three great ships, and received a dwelling place in the eastern part of this island, by command of the same king who invited them hither, that they should war and fight for their country. And they soon made war against their enemies, who had oft before harried on them from the north; and the Saxons then got the victory. Then they sent home messengers, and bade them tell of the fruitfulness of this land, and the sloth of the Britons; and they soon sent hither a greater ship-force of stronger warriors, and there was an invincible host, when they were joined together. And the Britons gave them a dwelling-place among them, that they should war and strive against their foes for the peace and safety of their country, and they should give them a livelihood and honour for their labour.

2. They came from the three strongest nations of Germany, that [is] from the Saxons, the Angles, and the Geats (*Jutes*). From the Jutes' origin came the Kentish men and the Wight-setters, that is, the nation which inhabits the isle of Wight. From the Saxons, that is, from the land which is called Old Saxony, came the East Saxons and South Saxons and West Saxons. And from the Angles (*or English*) came the East Anglians, and Middle Anglians, and Mercians, and all the Northumbrian kin; the country which is named Angulus is betwixt the Jutes and the Saxons. It is said that from the time when they went thence until to day, it lies waste. Their leaders and generals then at

---

1 Hyrdas, herds, &c.—*hence* goat-herd, neat-herd, &c.

first were two brothers Hengist and Horsa. They were the sons of Wightgilse, whose father was called Witta, and his father was called Wihta, whose father was named Woden, from whose stock the kingly kin of many tribes drew its beginning.

3. There was then no delay, so that greater hosts came heap-meal from the nations which we mentioned before; and the folk which came hither began to wax and spread so much that they were a great terror to the same inhabitants of the land who had formerly invited and called them hither.

4. After these things they made a truce for some time with the Picts, whom they had formerly driven far away by fighting; and then the Saxons sought causes and opportunities of their separation from the Britons, and shewed openly and told them, unless they gave them a greater livelihood, that they would themselves take and harry where they could find it; and they soon fulfilled the threat with deeds,—burnt and harried and slew from the east sea on to the west sea, and none withstood them. The vengeance was not unlike that by which the Chaldeans long ago burnt the walls of Jerusalem, and destroyed the kingly buildings with fire for the sins of God's people. So then here by that wicked nation, yet by the righteous judgement of God, nearly every city and land were forharried. Royal buildings and private rushed and fell, and every where priests and mass-priests together were struck and killed among the altars; bishops with the people, without any respect of dignity, were consumed with steel and flame, nor was there any who might give burial to those who were so cruelly killed; and many of the miserable remnant were seized in waste places and stabbed heap-meal; some for hunger went into the hands of their foes, and promised perpetual servitude on condition that food should be given to them; and some went sorrowing over sea: some abode in their country fearing, and, in wretched life, always dwelt in woods, and wastes, and on high cliffs, with sorrowing mind.

CHAPTER XVI.
That the Britons at first got a victory over the English nation. Their general was one Ambrosius a Roman.

1. And then after the army returned home, and had driven out and scattered the inhabitants of this island, then began they

piece-meal to take mind and main, and went forth of the dark places in which they formerly were be-hid, and all with one-minded consent prayed for heavenly-help, that they might not be everywhere blotted out even to utter destruction. Their general and leader at that time was Ambrosius, by surname Aurelianus. He was a good man, and a moderate man of Roman kin. In this man's time the Britons took mind and main, and he called them forth to the fight, and promised them victory, and they also in the fight through God's help got the victory; and then from that time, sometimes the Britons, sometimes the Saxons obtained the victory, until the year of the besetting of Baddesdown [hill], when they made a great slaughter among the English kin, about four and forty years after the English kin's coming into Britain.

CHAPTER XVII.
That Germanus the bishop, coming to Britain in a ship with Lupus, by divine might stilled first the rage of the sea, afterwards [that] of the Pelagians.

CHAPTER XVIII.
That the same [prelate] enlightened the alderman's blind daughter, and after that, coming to the holy Alban, there first received his reliques, and also set thereto the reliques of the holy Apostles and of other martyrs.

CHAPTER XIX.
That the same bishop by reason of infirmity was detained there [1,] and by prayer quenched the burnings of the houses, and was himself healed of his illness by a vision.

CHAPTER XX.
That the same bishops gave the Britons divine help in a fight, and so returned home.

CHAPTER XXI.
That, the twigs of the Pelagian pestilence sprouting again, Germanus, coming back to Britain with Severus, first renewed the steps of a halt youth, and after that, having condemned and reformed the heretics, he renewed the steps of right belief to God's people.

CHAPTER XXII.
That the Britons rested from foreign wars, vexed themselves with intestine broils, and sunk themselves in many sins.

CHAPTER XXIII.
That the holy pope Gregory sent Augustine with monks to preach God's word and belief to the English nation; and likewise with a confirmatory epistle strengthened them, that they should not leave off the labour.

1. When according to forthrunning time [it] was about five hundred and ninety-two years from Christ's hithercoming, Mauricius the emperor took to the government, and had it two and twenty years; he was the fifty-fourth from Augustus. In the tenth year of that emperor's reign, Gregory the holy man, who

---

1. Thær was gebæfd, *B.* feria g. *Sm.* kept holiday.

was in lore and deed the highest, took to the bishophood of the Roman Church, and of the apostolic seat, and held and governed it thirteen years, and six months, and ten days. In the fourteenth year of the same emperor, about a hundred and fifty years from the English nation's hither coming into Britain, he was admonished by a divine impulse, that he should send God's servant Augustine, and many other monks with him, fearing the Lord, to preach God's word to the English nation.

2. When they obeyed the bishop's commands, and began to go to the mentioned work, and had gone some deal of the way; then began they to fear and dread the journey, and thought that it was wiser and safer for them that they should rather return home, than seek the barbarous people, and the fierce, and the unbelieving, even whose speech they knew not; and in common chose this advice to themselves: and then straightway sent Augustine (whom they had chosen for their bishop if their doctrines should be received) to the pope; that he might humbly intercede for them, that they might not need to go upon a journey so perilous and so toilsome, and a pilgrimage so unknown.

3. Then St Gregory sent a letter to them, and exhorted and advised them in that letter: that they should humbly go into the work of God's word, and trust in God's help; and that they should not fear the toil of the journey, nor dread the tongues of evil-speaking men. But that, with all earnestness, and with the love of God, they should perform the good things, which they by God's help had begun to do; and that they should know that the great toil would be followed by the greater glory of everlasting life; and he prayed Almighty God that he would shield them by his grace; and that he would grant to himself that he might see the fruit of their labour in the heavenly kingdom's glory, because he was ready to be in the same labour with them, if leave had been given him.

CHAPTER XXV.
That Augustine came into Britain—first in the Isle of Thanet, and preached Christ's belief to the king of the Kent-men; and so with his leave preached God's word in Kent.

1. Then Augustine was strengthened by the exhortation of the blessed father Gregory, and with Christ's servants who were with him, returned to the work of God's word, and came into Britain. Then was at that time Ethelbert king in Kent, and a mighty one who had rule as far as the boundary of the river Humber, which

Chapter 25.] ETHELBERT'S INTERVIEW WITH AUGUSTINE.

sheds asunder the south folk of the English nation and the north folk. Then [there] is on the eastward of Kent a great island, [Thanet by name,] which is six hundred hides large, after the English nation's reckoning. The isle is shed away from the continuous land by the stream Wantsum, which is three furlongs broad, and in two places is fordable, and either end lies in the sea. On this isle came up Christ's servant Augustine and his fellows— he was one of forty. They likewise took with them interpreters from Frankland (France), as St Gregory bade them; and he sent messengers to Ethelbert, and let him know, that he came from Rome, and brought the best errand, and whosoever would be obedient to him, he promised him everlasting gladness in heaven, and a kingdom hereafter without end, with the true and living God.

2. When [he then] the king heard these words, then ordered he them to abide in the isle on which they had come up; and their necessaries to be there given them until he should see what he would do to them. Likewise before that, a report of the Christian religion had come to him, for he had a Christian wife, who was given to him from the royal kin of the Franks—Bertha was her name; which woman he received from her parents on condition, that she should have his leave that she might hold the manner of the Christian belief, and of her religion, unspotted, with the bishop whom they gave her for the help of that faith; whose name was Luidhard.

3. Then [it] was after many days that the king came to the isle, and ordered to make a seat for him out [of doors], and ordered Augustine with his fellows to come to his speech (*a conference*). He guarded himself lest they should go into any house to him; he used the old greeting, in case they had any magic whereby they should overcome and deceive him. But they came endowed—not with devil-craft, but with divine might. They bore Christ's rood-token—a silvern cross of Christ, and a likeness of the Lord Jesus coloured and delineated on a board; and were crying the names of holy men; and singing prayers together, made supplication to the Lord for the everlasting health of themselves, and of those to whom they come.

4. Then the king bade them sit, and they did so; and they soon preached and taught the word of life to him, together with all his peers who were there present. Then answered the king,

and thus said: Fair words and promises are these which ye have brought and say to us; but because they are new and unknown, we cannot yet agree that we should forsake the things which we for a long time, with all the English nation, have held.

But because ye have come hither as pilgrims from afar, and since it seems and is evident to me, that ye wished to communicate to us also the things which ye believed true and best, we will not therefore be heavy to you; but will kindly receive you in hospitality, and give you a livelihood, and supply your needs: Nor will we hinder you from joining and adding to the religion of your belief all whom you can through your lore.

5. Then the king gave them a dwelling and a place in Canterbury, which was the chief city of all his kingdom, and as he had promised to give them a livelihood and their worldly needs, he likewise gave them leave that they might preach and teach the Christian faith. It is said that when they went and drew nigh to the city, as their custom was, with Christ's holy cross, and with the likeness of the great King our Lord Jesus Christ, they sung with a harmonious voice this Litany and Antiphony :—Deprecamur te, &c. "We beseech thee, Lord, in all thy mercy, that thy fury and thy wrath be taken off from this city and [from] thy holy house, because we have sinned. Alleluia."

CHAPTER XXVI.

That Augustine in Kent imitated the life and lore of the early Church, and received a bishop-seat in the king's city.

1. Then it was soon after they had entered into the dwelling place which had been granted to them in the royal city, when they began to imitate the apostolic life of the primitive church— that is, served the Lord in constant prayers, and waking, and fasting, and preached and taught God's word to whom they might, and slighted all things of this world as foreign; but those things only which were seen [to be] needful for their livelihood they received from those whom they taught: according to that which they taught, they [themselves] through every thing lived; and they had a ready mind to suffer adversity, yea likewise death [it-]self, for the truth which they preached and taught. Then was no delay that many believed and were baptised. They also wondered at the simplicity of [their] harmless life, and the sweetness of their heavenly lore.

2. There was by east wellnigh the city a church built in honour of St Martin long ago, whilst the Romans yet dwelt in Britain, [in which church the queen [was] wont to pray, of whom we said before that she was a Christian.] In this church at first the holy teachers began to meet, and sing, and pray, and do mass-song, and teach men, and baptize, until the king was converted to the faith, and they obtained more leave to teach everywhere, and to build and repair churches.

3. Then came it about through the grace of God, that the king likewise among others began to delight in the cleanest life of holy [men] and their sweetest promises, and they also gave confirmation that those were true by the shewing of many wonders; and he then, being glad, was baptized. Then began many daily to hasten and flock together to hear God's word, and to forsake the manner of heathenism; and joined themselves, through belief, to the oneness of Christ's holy church. Of their belief and conversion [it] is said that the king was so evenly glad, that he however forced none to the Christian manner [of worship], but that those who turned to belief and to baptism he more inwardly loved, as they were fellow-citizens of the heavenly kingdom. For he had learnt from his teachers and from the authors of his health, that Christ's service should be of good will, not of compulsion. And he then, the king, gave and granted to his teachers a place and settlement suitable to their condition, in his chief city, and thereto gave their needful supplies in various possessions.

CHAPTER XXVII.

That the same being made bishop sent word to pope Gregory of the things that had been done in Britain, and at the same time asked and received his answers about the needful things.

1. During these things the holy man Augustine fared over sea, and came to the city Arles, and by Ætherius archbishop of the said city, according to the behest and commandment of the blessed father St Gregory, was hallowed archbishop of the English people; and returned and fared into Britain; and soon sent messengers to Rome, that was Laurence a mass-priest and Peter a monk, that they should say and make known to the blessed St Gregory that the English nation had received Christ's belief, and that he had been consecrated as bishop. He likewise requested

his advice about many causes and questions which were seen by him [to be] needful; and he soon sent suitable answers of them.

2. Asked by St Augustine, bishop of the Church of Canterbury: First, of bishops, how they shall behave and live with their fellows. Next, on the gifts of the faithful which they bring to holy tables and to God's churches—how many doles of them shall be.

Answered by Pope St Gregory:—Holy writ makes it known, quoth he, which I have no doubt thou knowest, and sunderly the blessed Paul's epistle which he wrote to Timothy, in which he earnestly trained and taught him, how he should behave and do in God's house. For it is the manner of the apostolic seat, when they hallow bishops, that they give them commandments, and that of all the livelihood which comes in to them there shall be four doles. One in the first place to the bishop and his family for food, and entertainment of guests and comers; a second dole to God's servants; a third to the needy; the fourth to renewing and repair of God's church. But because thy brotherliness has been trained and taught in monastic rules, thou shalt not however be asunder from thy fellows in the English church, which now yet is newly come and led to the faith of God. This behaviour and this life thou shalt set up, which our fathers had in the beginning of the new-born church, when none of them said that aught of that which they owned was his in sunder; but they all had all things common. If then any priests or God's servants are settled without holy orders, let those who cannot withhold themselves from women, take them wives, and receive their livelihood outside. For of the same fathers, of whom we spoke before, [it] is written, that they dealt their worldly goods to sundry men as every [one] had need.

3. Likewise concerning their livelihood it is to be thought and foreseen, (i. e. *provided,*) that they live in good manners under ecclesiastical rules, and sing psalms, and keep wakes, and hold their hearts and tongues and bodies clean from all forbidden [things] to Almighty God. But as to those living in common life, what have we to say how they deal their alms, or exercise hospitality, and fulfil mercy?—since all that is left over in their worldly substance is to be reached and given to the pious and good, as the master of all, our Lord Christ, taught and said:

Quod superest, &c. "What is over and left, give alms, and to you are all [things] clean."

4. Asked by St Augustine:—Since there is one faith, and are various customs of churches; there is one custom of mass-song in the holy Roman church, and another is had in the kingdom of Gaul.

Answered by Pope St Gregory:—Thou thyself knowest the manner and custom of the Roman church, in which thou wert reared; but now it seems good, and is more agreeable to me, that whatsoever thou hast found either in the Roman church, or in Gaul, or in any other [church], that was more pleasing to Almighty God, thou should carefully choose that, and set it to be held fast in the church of the English nation, which now yet is new in the faith. For the things are not to be loved for places; but the places, for good things. Therefore what things thou choosest as pious, good, and right from each of sundry churches, these gather thou together, and settle into a custom in the mind of the English nation.

5. Asked by Augustine:—I pray thee, what punishment shall he suffer—whosoever takes away any thing by stealth from a church?

Answered by Gregory:—This may thy brotherliness determine from the thief's condition, how he may be corrected. For there are some who have worldly wealth, and yet commit theft; there are some who are in this wise guilty through poverty. Therefore need is that some be corrected by waning of their worldly goods, some by stripes; some more sternly, some more mildly. And though the punishment be inflicted a little harder or sterner, yet it is to be done of love, not of wrath nor of fury; because through the throes of this is procured to the man, that he be not given to the everlasting fires of hell-torments. For in this manner we ought to punish men, as the good fathers are wont [to do] their fleshly children, whom they chide and swinge for their sins, and yet those same whom they chide and chastise by these pains, they also love, and wish to have for their heirs, and for them hold their worldly goods which they possess, whom they seem in anger to persecute and torment. For love is ever to be held in the mind, and it dictates and determines the measure of the chastisement, so that the mind does nothing at all beside the right rule. Thou likewise addest in thy inquiry,—How those things should be compensated which have been taken away from a church by theft : But oh! far be it, that God's church should receive with increase what she seems to let alone of earthly things, and seek worldly gain by vain things.

6. Asked by Augustine :—Whether two lawful brothers may receive in marriage two sisters who are procreated of a race far distant from them.

Answered by St Gregory :—This may so be : and by all means it is permitted ; for no where is it found in holy books, that this question seems [to be] gainsaid.

7. Asked by Bishop St Augustine :—At what generation shall Christian people be joined among themselves in marriage with their kinsfolk ? And is it permitted to stepmothers and brother's wives that they be joined in marriage ?

Answered by St Gregory :—Some earthly law, quoth he, in the Roman State permits, that the son and daughter [1] either of a brother and a sister, or of two brothers, or of two sisters, may be joined in marriage. But we certainly know and understand, that offspring could not grow nor wax from such marriage; and the holy law [beweareth and] forbids to uncover the shame of kinsfolk ; therefore need is that Christian people wive among themselves in the third generation, or in the fourth, because the second generation, of which we spoke before, is by all means to be forborne and forletten (*avoided*). Heavy is the sin and the divine vengeance, that a man should "meddle him" with his stepmother; for it is written in God's law,—Uncover thou not the shame of thy father. But because it is written, *Erunt duo in una carne :* Male and female : they two shall be in one body. And whoever dares to uncover the shame of his stepmother, who was one body with his father, lo ! he truly uncovers his father's shame. Likewise [it] is forbidden that a man join himself with his brother's wife ; for through the former connexion she became his brother's body. For that thing likewise John the Baptist was beheaded [2], and ended his life by holy martyrdom, when he had said to the king, that it was not permitted him that he should brook and have his brother's wife.[3]

1. That is the son of one, and daughter of the other, of the parties mentioned.
2. Literally " head-becorven." 3. Not in point,—Herod's was a case of adultery more than of incest—his brother being still alive,—To " brook and have "—i. e. use and possess.

8. But because there are many in the English nation, [who], while they were then yet in unbelief, are said to have been joined together in this sinful marriage, now, they are to be admonished, since they have come to the faith, that they hold themselves off from such iniquities, and understand that it is a heavy sin, and dread the awful doom of God, lest they for fleshly love receive the torments of everlasting death. They are not however for this cause to be deprived of the communion of Christ's body and blood, lest this thing may seem to be revenged on them, in which they through unwittingness sinned before the bath of baptism. For at this time the holy church corrects some things through zeal, bears with some through mildness, overlooks some through consideration; and so bears and overlooks, that often by bearing and overlooking she checks the opposing evil. All those who come to the faith of Christ are to be reminded, that they may not dare to commit any such thing. But if any shall commit them, then are they to be deprived of Christ's body and blood; for as some little is to be borne with in regard to those men who through unwittingness commit sin, so on the other hand it is to be strongly pursued in those who dread not to sin wittingly.

9. Asked by bishop St Augustine :—If a great distance of journey lies between, so that bishops may not easily come, whether may a bishop be hallowed without the presence of other bishops?

Answered by Gregory :—In the English church indeed, in which thou alone as yet art found a bishop, thou canst not hallow a bishop otherwise than without other bishops; but bishops must come to thee out of the kingdom of Gaul, that they may stand as witness at the bishop's hallowing; for the hallowing of bishops must not be otherwise than in the assembling and witnessing of three or four bishops, that they may send [up] and pour [forth] their petitions and prayers to the Almighty God for his favour.

10. Asked by Augustine :—How must we do with the bishops of Gaul and Britain?

Answered by Pope Gregory :—Over the bishops of Gaul we give thee no authority; because from the earlier times of my predecessors, the bishop of the city Arles received the pallium, whom we ought not to degrade nor to deprive of the received authority. But if thou happen to go into the province of Gaul, have thou a conference and consultation with the said bishop, what is to be done, or if any vices are found in bishops, how they shall be corrected and reformed; and if there be a supposition that he is too lukewarm in the vigour of his discipline and chastisement, then is he to be inflamed and abetted by thy brotherliness's love;[1] that he may ward off those things which are contrary to the behest and commands of our Maker, from the manners of the bishops. Thou mayest not judge the bishops of Gaul without their own authority; but thou shalt mildly admonish them, and shew them the imitation of thy good works. All the bishops of Britain we commend to thy brotherliness, in order that the unlearned may be taught, the weak strengthened by thy exhortation, and the perverse corrected by thy authority.[2]

CHAPTER XXIX.
That the same Pope Gregory sent Augustine a pallium and more help to teach God's word.

1. Augustine likewise bade [his messengers] acquaint him, that a great harvest was here present and few workmen. And he then sent with the foresaid messengers more help to him for divine learning, among whom the first and greatest were Mellitus and Justus, and Paulinus, and Rufinianus, and by them generally all those things which were needful for the worship and service of the church,—communion vessels, altar-cloth, and church-ornaments, and bishops' robes, and deacons' robes; as also reliques of the apostles and holy martyrs, and many books. He likewise sent to Augustine the bishop a pallium, and a letter in which he intimated how he should hallow other bishops, and in what places [he should] set them in Britain.

Chapters XXX and XXXI are omitted by Alfred.

CHAPTER XXXII.
That the pope sent a letter and gifts to Ethelbert the king: that Augustine renewed Christ's Church, and built St Peter's monastery.

The blessed Pope Gregory likewise at the same time sent a letter to king Ethelbert, and along with it many worldly gifts of

---

1. A brother is here styled "his brotherliness," as a pope "his holiness."
2. The remainder of this is not translated here for a reason which any one may understand from the original Latin, or the English of Dr Giles's translation.

diverse sorts: he wished likewise by these temporal honours to glorify the king, to whom he had, by his labour, and by his diligence in teaching, opened and made known the glory of the heavenly kingdom.

CHAPTER XXXIII.
That Augustine with the help of king Ethelbert renewed and wrought Christ's Church. That Augustine built the monastery of the apostles Peter and Paul; and concerning its first abbot, Peter.

1. And then St Augustine, as soon as he received the bishop-seat in the royal city, renewed and wrought, with the king's help, the church which he had learnt was wrought long before by old Roman work, and hallowed it in the name of our Lord Jesus Christ, and he there set a dwelling-place for himself and all his afterfollowers. He likewise built a monastery by east of the city, in which Ethelbert the king, by his exhortation and advice, ordered to build a church worthy of the blessed apostles Peter and Paul, and he enriched it with various gifts; in which church the body of Augustine, and of all the Canterbury bishops together, and of their kings, might be laid. The Church however, not Augustine, but bishop Laurentius, his afterfollower, hallowed.

2. The first abbot at the same monastery was a mass-priest named Peter, who was sent back as a messenger into the kingdom of Gaul, and then was drowned in a bay of the sea, which was called Amfleet, and was laid in an unbecoming grave by the inhabitants of the place. But the Almighty God would shew of what merit the holy man was, and every night a heavenly light was made to shine over his grave; until the neighbours, who saw it, understood that it was a great and holy man, who was buried there; and they then asked who and whence he was: they then took his body and laid and buried it in a church in the city Boulogne, with the honour befitting so great and so holy a man.

CHAPTER XXXIV.
That Ethelfrith king of the Northumbrians overcame the nation of the Scots in fight, and drove them out of the boundaries of the English people.

1. In these times, over the kingdom of the Northumbrians was a very powerful king, and very desirous of glory, Ethelfrith by name; who more than all the English kings and governors wasted and harried the nation of the Britons, even so that he

might be compared to Saul, long ago king of the nation of the Israelites, but that he was unwitting of the divine religion. Never was there any king or governor that more deprived them of their lands, and subjected them to his power; for he made them tributary to the English nation, or drove them from their lands. Very well might be applied to him the saying which Jacob the high-father[1] spoke in the person of Saul the king, when he blessed his son: "Benjamin is a ravening wolf; in the early morning he shall eat the prey, and in the evening he shall deal the spoil." Then for his stoutness was stirred up Aedon, king of the Scots who dwell in Britain. He then led an army on him, and came with an immense and strong host to fight against him; but nevertheless he was overcome and fled away with few [of his men]. This battle was fought in the famous place which is called Degsa-stone, where almost all his host was slain. In that battle likewise Theodbald, Ethelfrith's brother, was slain with all the host which he led. This fight Ethelfrith accomplished in the eleventh year of his reign, which he had four and twenty winters. That was the first year of Phocas the Emperor, who had the sovereignty of the Romans. Since that time no king of the Scots durst come to a fight against the English nation until this present day.

Here endeth the first book, and beginneth the second.

BOOK II—CHAPTER I.

1. In these times, that is six hundred and five years after our Lord's incarnation, the blessed Pope Gregory, after he had gloriously held and ruled the seat of the Roman and Apostolic church thirteen years and six months and ten days, died and was led to the everlasting seat of the heavenly kingdom.

2. He held and ruled the church in the times of the emperors Mauricius and Phocas; and in the second year of the same Phocas he went forth of this life, and went to the true life, which is in heaven, and his body was buried in St Peter's church, before the housel-porch, the fourth day before the Ides *(the* 12th *day)* of March, and some time hereafter he shall, in the same [body], rise in glory, with other pastors of the holy church.

1. Patriarch.

And on his burying [place] is written an epitaph of this import :—

> Receive, thou earth ! a body from thy body taken,
> That thou may give it back when him God makes alive.
> The spirit sought high heaven, no power of death shall scathe it,
> To which, of other life death's self is more the way.
> The limbs of the high bishop are within this barrow tined,[2]
> Who always liveth everywhere in numberless good deeds.
> The poor men's hunger he o'ercame with food, their cold with clothing,
> And by his holy monishings their souls from foes[3] he shielded.
> And he with deed fulfil'd whate'er with word he taught,
> The mystic words he spake, that he life's pattern were of saints :
> To Christ the English he brought round by piety of lore,
> And in that nation gained new hosts to the belief of God.
> This toil, this zeal, this care thou hadst, thus thou our pastor didst,
> That to the Lord thou mightest bring much gain of holy souls.
> In these (and such-like) triumphs thou, God's bishop, may'st rejoice,
> For of thy works eternal meed thou hast in endless glory.[4]

3. We must not omit to mention the opinion, which has come to us by the tradition of old men, concerning the blessed Gregory : by what cause he was induced to take such an earnest care about the salvation of our nation. They say that one day chapmen had newly come thither from Britain, and brought many market-things to market; and also many came to buy the things. Then it happened that Gregory among others came thither also, and then saw among other things boys for sale set there, [who] were persons of a white body, fair countenance, and fine hair. When he saw and beheld them, he asked from what land, or from what nation they were brought. It was said to him that they were brought from the island Britain, and that the inhabitants of that island were men of such complexion. Again, he asked whether the same land's folk were Christians, or yet lived in the errors of heathenism. It was said and told to him, that they yet were heathens. And he then from his inward heart sighed heavily, and thus said : "Alas ! it is a woful thing, that the prince of darkness should own and possess so fair a soul, and persons of so bright a countenance." Again, he asked what

---

2. A. S. "betyned" enclosed. 3. L. hoste, A. S. feondum; foe (i. e. satan) were better.

4. These uncouth rhymes, blank as they are, present a literal translation, very nearly in the exact order of the A. S. words, of Alfred's prose version of the Elegiac stanzas preserved by Bede. The last line rather cloaks the seeming tautology of "ece mede butan ende," eternal reward without end.

the nation was named which they came from. Then it was answered him, that they were named Angli. " Well may it be so," quoth he, " for they have angelic looks ; and it is likewise fit that they be fellow-heirs with the angels in heaven." He yet further asked and said, " What was the name of the province, from which those youths were brought hither ?" Then answered him one and said, that they were named Deiri.[1] "That," quoth he, " is well said,—Deiri, that is *de ira eruti, (rescued from wrath)* they must be rescued from the wrath of God, and called to the mercy of Christ." Then yet he asked what their king was called : and one answered him and said, that he was called Ella. Then played [2] he with his words to the name, and said, " Alleluia, it is meet that the praise of God our maker be sung in those parts."

4. And he then soon went to the bishop and (to the) pope of the Apostolic seat, for he himself was not yet made bishop, and prayed him that he would send some teachers into Britain to the English nation, that through them they might be converted to Christ, and said that he himself was ready with God's help to perform that work, if it liked [3] the apostolic pope, and it were his will and his leave. Then the pope would not grant that, nor the citizens the more, that so noble, so venerable, and so learned a man should go so far from them. But he, as soon as ever he was made bishop, accomplished the work which he had long wished; and sent the holy teachers hither, of whom we spoke before: and St Gregory, by his exhortations and by his prayers was helping, that their lore might be fruitful of God's will, and the good of the English kin.

CHAPTER II.

That Augustine taught and advised the bishops of the Britons for the peace of the right-believing *(orthodox)*, a heavenly wonder also being done before them. And also what wreak followed after those despising it.

1. Then it was that Augustine, with the help of king Ethelbert, invited to his speech the bishops and teachers of the Britons, in the place which is yet named Augustine's Oak, on the borders of the Hwiccii and West-Saxons. And he then began, with brotherly love, to advise and teach them, that they should have right love and peace between them, and undertake, for the Lord,

---

1. The name of the people.   2. Played to the name, *alludens ad nomen, Bd.*
3. Pleased.

the common labour of teaching divine lore in the English nation. And they would not hear him, nor keep Easter at its right tide [*]; and also had many other things unlike and contrary to ecclesiastical unity. When they had held a long conference and strife about those things, and they would not yield any things to Augustine's instructions, nor to his prayers, nor to his threats, and [those] of his companions, but thought[1] their own customs and institutions better than [that] they should agree with all Christ's churches throughout the world; then the holy father Augustine put an end to this troublesome strife, and thus spoke.

2. " Let us pray Almighty God,[2] who makes the one-minded to dwell in his Father's house, that he vouchsafe to signify to us by heavenly wonders, which institution we ought to follow, by what ways to hasten to the entrance of his kingdom. Let an infirm man be brought hither to us, and through whose prayer soever he be healed, let his belief and practice be believed acceptable to God, and to be followed by all."

When his adversaries had hardly granted that, a blind man of English kin was led forth: he was first led to the bishops of the Britons, and he received no health nor comfort through their ministry. Then at last Augustine was constrained by righteous need, arose[3] and bowed his knees, [and] prayed God the Almighty Father, that he would give sight to the blind man, that he through one man's bodily enlightening might kindle the gift of ghostly light in the hearts of many faithful. Then soon, without delay, the blind man was enlightened, and received sight; and the true preacher of the heavenly light, Augustine, was proclaimed and praised by all. Then the Britons also acknowledged with shame, that they understood that it was the way of truth which Augustine preached: they said however that they could not, without consent and leave of their people, shun and forsake their old customs. They begged that again another synod should be [assembled], and they then would attend it with more counsellors.

3. When that accordingly was set, seven bishops of the Britons

---

[*] Literally 'nor hold right Easters at their tide, or time'—we still use noontide, eventide, and *tides* of the sea, the *times* of its rising or sinking.

1. A. S. "letton" *Ca*, instead of [dydon] *Sm*.
2. A common designation of our Saviour in Anglo-Saxon authors.
3. Arcs *Sm.* is rejected here for "aras" *B.* the indispensable reading. It has also appeared suitable to read ðegnunge for Bede's *ministerio*, rather than segnunge *blessing*, as the last word of the preceding sentence.

came, and all the most learned men who were chiefly from the city Bangor: at that time the abbot of that monastery was named Dinoth. When they then were going to the meeting, they first came to a [certain] hermit, who was with them holy and wise. They interrogated and asked him, whether they should for Augustine's lore forsake their own institutions and customs. Then answered he them; "If he be a man of God, follow him." Quoth they to him; "How may we know whether he be so?" Quoth he, "[Our] Lord himself hath said in his gospel, Take ye my yoke upon you, and learn from me that I am mild and of lowly heart. And now if Augustine is mild and of lowly heart, then it is [to be] believed that he bears Christ's yoke and teaches you to bear it. If he then is unmild and haughty, then it is known that he is not from God, nor [should] ye mind his words." Quoth they again, "How may we know that distinctly?" Quoth he, "See ye that he come first to the synod with his fellows, and sit; and if he rises towards you when ye come, then wit ye that he is Christ's servant; and ye shall humbly hear his words and his lore. But if he despise you and will not rise towards you since there are more of you, be he then despised by you." Well, they did so as he said.

4. When they had came to the Synod-place, the archbishop Augustine was sitting on his seat. When they saw that he rose not for them, they quickly became angry, and upbraided him [as being] haughty, and gainsaid and withstood all his words. The archbishop said to them; "In many things ye are contrary to our customs and so to [those] of all God's churches, and yet if ye will be obedient to me in these three things: That first ye celebrate Easter at the right tide, That ye fulfil the ministry of baptism, through which we are born as God's children, after the manner of the holy Roman and apostolic church, And that thirdly ye preach the word of the Lord to the English people together with us: we will patiently bear with all other things which ye do that are contrary to our customs." They said that they would do none of these things, nor would have him for an archbishop: they said among themselves, "If he would not now rise for us, much more if we shall be subjected to him, will he contemn us for naught." It is said that the man of God St augustine, in a threatening manner foretold, "If they would not receive peace with men of God, that they should receive unpeace

and war from their foes; and if they would not preach among the English race the word of life, they should through their hands suffer the vengeance of death."

5. And through every thing, as the man of God had foretold, by the righteous doom of God it came to pass; and very soon after this Ethelfrith king of the English, of whom we spoke before, collected a great army, and led it to Legcaster, and there fought against the Britons. And made the greatest slaughter of the faithless[1] people. Whilst he was beginning the battle, king Ethelfrith saw their priests and bishops and monks standing aloof in a safer place, that they should pray and make intercession to God for their warriors: he inquired and asked what that host was, and what they were doing there. When he understood the cause of their coming, then said he, "So! I wot if they cry to their God against us, though they bear not a weapon, they fight against us, for they pursue us with their hostile prayers and curses. He then straightway ordered to turn upon them first, and slay them. Men say that there were twelve hundred of this host, and fifty of them escaped[2] by flight; and he so then destroyed and blotted out the other host of the sinful nation, not without great waning of his [own] host; and so was fulfilled the prophecy of the holy bishop Augustine, that they should for their trowlessness[3] suffer the vengeance of temporal perdition, because they despised the skilful counsel of their eternal salvation.

CHAPTER III.
That Augustine hallowed Mellitus and Justus to Bishops, and of his decease.

1. After these things Augustine bishop [of Britain] hallowed two bishops: the one was named Mellitus, the other Justus. Mellitus he sent to preach divine lore to the East-Saxons, who are shed off from Kentland by the river Thames, and joined to the east sea. Their chief city is called Lundencaster *(now London)*, standing on the bank of the foresaid river, and it is the market place[4] of land and sea-comers. The king in the nation at that time was Seabright *(or Sabert)* Ethelbert's sister-son, and his vassal. Then he and the nation of the East-Saxons received

---

1. *Lit.* trowless.   2. *Lit.* loosed away.   3. Ger. treulosigkeit, perfidy. The 'less' of the Eng.—less of A. S. treowleas,—loos-, & -los-, are the same element—loose, free, void, quite different from less, læsse *minor;* The adj. does not mean having less truth, but altogether void of truth or fidelity.   4. *Lit.* Cheapstow.

the word of truth and the faith of Christ through Mellitus the bishop's lore. Then king Ethelbert ordered to build a church in London, and to hallow it to St Paul the apostle, that he and his afterfollowers might have their bishopseat in that place. Justus he hallowed as bishop in Kent itself at Rochester, which is four and twenty miles right west from Canterbury: In which city likewise king Ethelbert ordered to build a church, and to hallow it to St Andrew the apostle; and to each of these bishops the king gave his gifts and bookland and possessions for them to brook with their fellows.

2. After these things then father Augustine beloved of God departed [this life], and his body was buried without [doors], nigh the church of the blessed apostles Peter and Paul, which we mentioned before, because it was not then yet fully built nor hallowed. As soon as it was hallowed, then his body was put into it, and becomingly buried in the north porch of the church, in which likewise the bodies of all the afterfollowing archbishops are buried but two, that is, Theodorus and Berhtwald, whose bodies are laid in the church itself, because no more might [be so] in the foresaid porch. Wellnigh in the middle of the church is an altar[1] set and hallowed in name of St Gregory, on which every Saturday their memory and decease are celebrated with mass-song by the mass-priest of that place. On St Augustine's tomb is written an inscription of this sort:—Here resteth Sir[2] Augustine, the first archbishop of Canterbury, who was formerly sent hither by the blessed Gregory, bishop of the Roman city: and was upheld by God with working of wonders. King Ethelbert and his people he led from the worship of Idols to the faith of Christ, and having fulfilled the days of his ministry in peace, departed[3] on the 26th day of May in the same king's reign.

CHAPTER IV.
That Laurentius with his fellow-bishops [4] admonished the Scots on the oneness [5] of the holy church, and most of all [6] about the holding of Easter; and that Mellitus came to Rome.

1. After Augustine followed in the bishophood Laurentius,

---

1. *Lit.* holy table, wigbed A. S.   2. "Sir" in Eng. ('Schir' Scot.) equal to *Dominus*, L. was five or six centuries ago prefixed to the name of every ordained priest.
3. *Lit.* forthfared—went out.
4. *Lit.* evenbishops. So emn (r. euin) cristen Ch. fellow-christian.
5. Confounding (as some yet do) "oneness" or unity with uniformity.
6. Eallea mæst—how different from our 'almost'!

whom he in his lifetime had hallowed for this reason, lest after his decease the state of so new a church, any while without a herdsman, should begin to totter. And in that he followed the example of the first herdsman of God's church, St Peter the apostle: When he at Rome first established Christ's church, it is said that he hallowed Clement for the help of divine lore, and for his afterfollower. When he then—Laurentius—had received the archbishophood, he began strongly to eke the foundations of the church, which he had seen nobly laid, and by the frequent voice of his holy exhortation and lore, and by continual examples of pious working, he began to heighten and enlarge [the church] to a due height of prosperity. Not that only, that he took care of the new church, which was gathered from English kin, but likewise of the old inhabitants, the Britons and Scots. For he understood that in many things they disagreed with God's church; and most of all that they did not celebrate the solemnity of the holy Easter, and the day of [our] Lord's againrising at the right tide; he [therefore] wrote and sent a letter to them, prayed and besought them, that in oneness of peace, and in the holding of right Easters, they would agree with the church of Christ, which is spread abroad through all the earth. But though he did these things, how much he sped—now yet these present times shew the same customs.

2. In these times came Mellitus, bishop of London, to Rome about the needful occasions of the English church, and he then was treating with the apostolic pope Bonifacius, who was the fourth bishop of the Roman church from St Gregory. And he then this same pope assembled a synod of Italian bishops, and set in order about the life of monks and their stillness. This synod was in the eighth year of Phocas the emperor's reign. And Mellitus sat among them at the synod, and the things which were there regularly deemed, he, by his authority, and the token of Christ's rood, wrote and fastened, and returned to Britain, and brought them with him in writing, to be held by the English church, together with the epistle which the same pope sent to the God-beloved archbishop Laurentius, and all his fellows, and to king Ethelbert, and all the English nation, for their comfort and for confirmation of right life.

CHAPTER V.

The Kings Ethelbert and Sabert being dead, their afterfollowers were following idolatry, therefore Mellitus and Justus went from Britain.

1. Then about six hundred and sixteen winters from our Lord's incarnation, that was about one and twenty years after Augustine, with his fellows, was sent to teach in the English nation, Ethelbert, king of the Kentmen, after the temporal kingdom which he wonderfully held six and fifty years, [died][1] and then with gladness ascended to the heavenly kingdom. He was the third king among the kings in the English nation that wielded all the southern provinces, and had rule to the river Humber. The first who had rule of this sort was Elle, king of the South-Saxons. The second was Keawlin, king of the West-Saxons. The third was, as we said before, Ethelbert, king of the Kenters.[2] The fourth was Rædwald, king of the East English. The fifth was Edwin, king of the Northumbrians, who had rule over all the Britons but[3] the Kenters alone. He likewise subjected to the rule of the English kin the Menavian[4] isles of the Britons, which are situate betwixt Hibernia, the island of the Scots, and Britain. The sixth was Oswald, the best and most Christian king of the Northumbrians, who had rule in these same territories. The seventh was Oswy, his brother, who likewise overcame and rendered tributary, in a great deal, the nations of the Picts and Scots.

2. Then died king Ethelbert, twenty-one years after he had received baptism and the faith of Christ, and was buried in the church of the blessed apostles Peter and Paul, in St Martin's porch: and there also Berhta his queen was buried. This king, among other good things which he performed for his people by his counsel, also appointed institutes of right dooms after the example of the Romans, by the advice of prudent men; and ordered to write them in English; which even now until this [day] are had and holden by them *(the English)*. In these he first set [down]

---

1. Either this word must be supplied, or "and" is superfluous.
2. Cant-wara is Cant-er in "Canterbury," and Kenters (or Kentmen) both looks and sounds better than Canters. They are all kings of the people—not of the country only; sometimes *in* the country—"on Kent-lande."
3. "All but the wakeful nightingale." P. L.
4. Monige Brytta ealond—*Alf.* Menauias Britonum insulas, Bede, by a very common, error in confounding *u* (*v*) with *n*, printed Mevanias. For Menavia, the Mona of Cesar, now Man, see Orosius, I, xi. In the next line, for Smith's Scotlande, I read, with MS. *B*, Scotta iglande. Ireland (Hibernia) and Scotland for North Britain, were names unknown to Bede or Alfred.

how one should make amends who took away the goods of a church, or of a bishop, or of other orders, by theft,—he would afford protection to those whose lore he had received. This same Ethelbert was the son of Irminric, whose father was named Octa; and his father, Oeric, whose surname was Oesc, from whom the kings of Kent were named Oesk-ings. Oesc's father was Hengist, who was the first leader and general of the English kin in Britain, as we said before.

3. After Ethelbert's decease Eadbald his son succeeded to the government; and he soon wrought much waning and damage to the tender growth of the church: for he not only would not receive the faith of Christ, but was besmitten [1] with unlawful and shocking fornication, so that he went to his father's wife. By both of these sins he gave occasion of returning to their former uncleanness, to those who under his father's reign, either with his kingly help, or for fear of him, had received the law of cleanness and the faith of Christ. Nor were the whips of heaven's threatenings wanting to the trowless king, that through them he should be cleansed and set right. For he was frequently troubled with madness [2] of mood, and invasion of the unclean ghost.

4. The death of Sabert, king of the East-Saxons, likewise increased the storm of this confusion, for when he sought the everlasting kingdom, he left as heirs of the temporal kingdom his three sons. They soon began to serve idols, which they had seemed to forsake a little in their father's lifetime; and they gave free leave to the people who were subject to them to worship idols. When they saw the bishop celebrate the solemnity of the mass in God's church, and give the housel to the people, they were inblown with barbarous folly, and said to him: "Why dost thou not reach us the white loaf which thou gavest to our father Saba (they named him so), and even now givest to people in church?" The bishop answered them: "If ye will be washen in the healing well of baptism's bath, as your father was washen, then may ye likewise be partakers of the holy bread, as he was a partaker. But if ye despise life's bath, ye may not for any sake receive life's bread." They said; "We will not go into the bath,

---

1. Defiled or infected. In Scotland "smit" is infect, "smittable" infectious,—hence E. smut, smutty.

2. Wedenheortnesse (*Alf.*) wodheartness, "There saw I wodnesse laughing in his mood,"—Ch. Why should the pure English "ghost" be given up for the shortened Latin "spirit"—or unclean ghost, for impure spirit?

because we know that we have no need of it, but nevertheless we will be fed with the bread." When they were oft and earnestly admonished by him, that it might by no means be, that without the holy cleansing of baptism's bath, they should have communion of the holy bread, then at last they were stirred up with fury,[1] [and] said to him ; " If thou wilt not indulge us in so easy a thing which we ask, thou canst not dwell in our province nor in our community," and drove him away, and ordered him, with his fellows, to go out of their kingdom.. When he was driven away, he came to Kent, sought and consulted with Mellitus and Justus, his fellow-bishops, what he ought to do concerning these things. And then they resolved with common counsel, that it was better and safer for them to return to their country, and there with a free mind serve the Lord, than to sit longer without fruit among the barbarians, and those fighting against the faith of Christ. Then first the bishops, Mellitus and Justus, went over sea, and came into the realm of Gaul, and determined that they would there abide an end of the affair. But the wicked kings, not a great while after they had driven the preacher of truth from them, that they might freely minister the worship of devils, came against the West-Saxons to battle, and all fell together, and were slain with their war-host; and though their princes were slain, the folk could not even then be set right, that had before been led to sins, nor be called back to the faith of Christ, nor to the love of God.

CHAPTER VI.

That Laurentius the archbishop being reproved by the apostle St Peter converted king Eadbald to Christ ; and the bishops Mellitus and Justus returned hither to preach.

1. When Laurentius the archbishop then would have followed the other bishops his fellows, and have left Britain, then ordered he, in the same night when he would set out in the morning, a bed to be made ready for him in the church of the blessed apostles Peter and Paul, of which we have often spoken, that he might rest him ; and then first, for a long while of the night, was [engaged] in holy prayers, and [shed] his tears, and sent his prayers to God for the state of the church ; and being worn out and weary, set his limbs then to rest, and for a little fell asleep.

2. Then soon appeared to him the most blessed prince of the

---

1. *Literally* hot-heartness, *furore Bd.*

apostles, St Peter, and during much time of the dark night, with grim scourgings swinged and rebuked him, and asked him with apostolic sharpness, why he would forlet [2] God's flock, which he had bidden him keep, or to what herdsman he was in his flight leaving Christ's sheep, that were set in the midst of wolves? He also said to him, "Hast thou forgotten my example, how, for the sake of Christ's children, whom, in tokening of his love, he commended to me, I suffered and sustained bonds, and scourgings, and prison, and many afflictions, and at last death itself, yea the death of the cross, from unbelievers and foes of Christ, that I might be crowned with Christ?" Then was Christ's servant, Laurentius, greatly emboldened by the apostle's scourging and admonitions, [and] came early in the morning to the king, and opened his garment, and shewed him with how much scourging he had been corrected and punished. Then wondered he very much, and asked who had been so daring, that he had done such harm to so great a man. When he then, the king, heard and knew that he, the bishop, had suffered so great torments and pains from Christ's apostle, for the sake of his salvation, then he became very much affrighted, and in great dread for himself; and soon cast away all the service of idols, which he formerly served, and forlet [2] the unright wiving, and received Christ's belief, and the bishop baptized him; and he soon protected and helped the possessions and goods of the church, in all things, to the utmost of his power.

3. And he likewise sent messengers into the kingdom of Gaul, and bade them call home the bishops Mellitus and Justus, and ordered them to return freely home to their bishop ships. And they returned home about a year after they formerly went from Britain. Justus returned to Rochester, where he formerly was bishop; bishop Mellitus the Londoners would not receive; but loved more to serve the bishops of their idols; and they heeded not the words of king Eadbald, for his rule was not over them as his father had. However he with his people, with those of Kent, after he was converted to the Lord, served and obeyed the divine commandments. Lastly, as a token of that, he ordered to build a church in St Peter's monastery in honour of the blessed virgin St Mary, which Mellitus afterwards hallowed in her name, when he was archbishop.

2. Forsake, leave; we still say 'let alone' for leave alone.

CHAPTER VII.

That Mellitus was archbishop after Laurentius, he quenched by prayer the flames of his burning city.

1. In this king's reign the blessed archbishop St Laurentius died, and ascended the heavenly kingdom, and was buried in the church of the monastery of the blessed apostle St Peter, beside his foregoer St Augustine, the fourth day of the nones *(2d day)* of February. After that Mellitus, who was formerly bishop of London, took to the bishop-seat of Canterbury church—third bishop from St Augustine. Bishop Justus was still living, and ruled the assembly at Rochester: and they both with great care and toil held and ruled the English church. Mellitus was sorely weighed down by infirmity of body—by foot-ill or gout; but yet, with hale steps of his mind, he gladly overleaped all earthly things, and ever with his mind was flying to love, to ask, and to seek the heavenly. He was by bodily birth noble, but by height of mind much nobler.

2. We must tell some witnessing of his might, that we may the more easily understand his other virtue. It befel at one time that the city Canterbury was through sinful carelessness inburnt with fire, and the fire and the flame greatly waxed and spread; and nobody by oncasting of water might withstand them; and a great deal of the city was laid waste. Then went the raging flame and spread itself to the bishop; then trusted he in divine help, where the human was wanting; he ordered his attendants to bear himself towards the fire, and to set him where the flame and the danger were greatest, and infirm [as he was] began through his prayer to drive away the danger of the fire, which formerly the firm hand of stronger men, through much toil, might not do; and straightway the wind, which formerly blew from the south, and strewed the fire into the city, shifted itself from the north, and drove the fire out from it, and soon through his prayer the fire was altogether quenched and staunched. And because the man of God strongly burnt within with the fire of divine love, he often by his frequent prayers and exhortations shielded and shoved off the storms and fierceness of cursed ghosts from scathing of himself and his fellows: It was worthy of this, that he should be able to prevail against the earthly winds and flames, lest they should scathe him or his friends. And this holy bishop, after he had held and ruled the church five winters,

in Eadbald's reign departed to heaven, and was buried in the oftnamed monastery, in St Peter's church, the eighth day of the kalends of May (*24th day of April*).

CHAPTER VIII.

1. His immediate afterfollower in the bishophood was Justus, who was formerly bishop at Rochester, and hallowed in his stead another bishop of that church, [who] was called Romanus: for he had received authority from Pope Boniface, that he might ordain bishops.

CHAPTER IX.

Of the reign of Edwin, and that Paulinus coming preached the gospel to him, and first taught his daughter, with other persons, by the holy mysteries of the Christian belief.

1. At that time likewise the Northumbrian nation, with their king Edwin, received Christ's belief, which Paulinus the holy bishop preached and taught to them. To the king the reception of Christ's belief and of the heavenly kingdom, was likewise a token of [2] the waxing might of his earthly kingdom, so that none of the English kings ere him got into his dominion all the British territories where either their provinces of the English kin, or those of the Britons are dwelt in,—all which he got into his dominion, and likewise subjected the Menavian isles of the Britons to the sovereignty of the English kin, as we ere before [3] said.

2. The first occasion to this nation, that is, the Northumbrians, to receive Christ's belief, was that their foresaid king, Edwin, was by affinity joined to the kings of Kent. He received thence to wife Ethelburga the daughter of king Ethelbert; (she by another name was called Tate). When he first sent ambassadors to her brother Eadbald, who was then king of Kent, and begged and desired the marriage of this maiden, then answered he, " That it was not permitted that a Christian maiden should be given to wife to a heathen man, lest the faith and the mysteries of the heavenly king should be profaned by the marriage of a king who

---

2. Or rather " was betokened by "—The structure of this sentence is very hard to unravel, and argues a misconception of the Latin. Bede says—" as a presage of his receiving the faith and the heavenly kingdom, the power of his earthly empire had likewise increased." Alfred makes both " onfengnes" (reception), and " meaht " (power), nominatives (apparently) to goweox.   3. Sic A. S.

knew not the worship of the true king." When the ambassadors told these words again to Edwin, then promised he straightway, that he would do naught against the Christian belief which the maiden held, but that she might [hold] the belief and the worship of her religion [along] with all her companions who came with her,—[might] live in the Christian manner, and well hold it. Nor did he withsay¹ that he himself likewise might undertake the same religion, if wise counsellors determined that it might be deemed holier, and more loved of God. Then was the maiden betrothed and after a space sent to Edwin, and according to that which they had formerly determined, the God-beloved man St Paulinus was hallowed as a bishop, who was to go with her, in order that he might, both by the celebration of the holy mysteries, and by his daily lore, confirm the maiden and her fellows, that she might not be besmitten or infected in the intercourse of the heathen.

3. Paulinus was hallowed for bishop by Justus the archbishop the twelfth day of the kalends of August (21st of July). Then came he with the forespoken-of maiden to Edwin the king, as if he were the companion of a bodily gathering; but he rather with all his mind intended, that through his lore he might call the nation which he was seeking, to a knowledge of the true God, and to the belief of Christ. When he came into the province with the maiden, then toiled² he much that he might both, through the Lord's grace, hold his fellows who had come with him, that they sprung not away from their belief, and, if he were able, that he might convert some of the heathen to the belief of Christ. But, as the apostle says, though he so long time toiled in his lore, that "God has blinded the mind of the unbelieving, lest to them shine the enlightening of Christ's gospel and of his glory."

4. Then in the following year, came into the province of the Northumbrians a man whose name was Eomer; he was sent by the king of the West-Saxons, whose name was Quickhelm, that he should bereave king Edwin at the same time both of kingdom and of life. He had and bore with him a two-edged hand-seax or dagger, which was poisoned, that, if the wound were not enough for³ the king's death, the poison might help. He came

---

1. Gainsay, deny, refuse.   2. So *Bd.*—*A. S.* wende seems an error.
   3. *Lit.* too little sufficed to.

to the king on the first Easter day by the river Derwent, where was then the king's chief abode. Then went he in as if he should say his lord's errand; and while he then with crafty mouth was telling the lying errand and falsely glozing[2] it, he suddenly stood up, and, having drawn the dagger under his garment, rushed on the king. When Lilla, the king's thane the most faithful to him, saw that, (he had not a shield at hand that he might shield the king with,) [but] set his body between, before the sting or thrust, and he (*the assassin*) through-stang[3] the king's thane, and wounded the king. Then was he soon hemmed in with weapons on every side; lo! he then too in the tumult, killed with the hateful[4] weapon another king's thane, who was named Forthhere.

5. On that same night of the holy Easter, it was that the queen bore to the king a daughter, who was called Eanfled. When the same king, in the bishop's presence, was thanking his gods for the daughter that was born to him, the bishop, on the other hand, began to give thanks to the Lord Christ, and let the king know, that he by his prayers had obtained from Him, that the queen, sound, and without heavy sore, should bring forth the child. When the king heard this, then began he to shew gladness at the bishop's words, and promised that he himself would forsake idols, and that he would choose Christ's service, if he gave him life and victory in the war which he had resolved on, against the king, by whom the murtherer was formerly sent, who had wounded him; and his same daughter he gave the bishop to hallow to Christ, as a pledge that he would fulfil that promise. She was baptized on the holy day of Pentecost, the first person[5] of the Northumbrian nation, with eleven other maidens of the queen's household; she was the twelfth.

6. At that time also was the king healed of his wound, which was formerly given him; then assembled he his army against the West-Saxons, and came thither; and soon after he fought on them, all his foes were made known to him, who had formerly plotted against his life; and some of them he slew, some he

---

2. Fleswede *Sm*—not to be found in Dict.—supposed an error for gleswede,—glesan, to gloze, *Somn.*
3. So *Ch.* "throughgirt with many a wound"—thrust through—pierced.
4. Manfullan, *Alf.* sinful—wicked.
5. Ærest manna, first of men—the first human being.

received into his dominion. And he thus went home again victorious; not that he soon would rashly and inconsiderately receive the mysteries of the Christian belief, though it was so that he no further served idols, after he had promised himself to Christ's service: but he first earnestly aye [1] from that time, both from the venerable man, St Paulinus, learned the reason of the Christian faith, and with his aldermen whom he wist [to be] wisest and most prudent—with them he frequently consulted and sought, what was to be done concerning these things. Yea he also himself, since he was by nature a most sagacious man, oft sat alone with his silent mouth, but with inward heart speaking many [things] with himself, [and] studied what was best for him to do, and what religion was to be holden by him.

CHAPTER X.

That the pope Boniface, having sent a letter, exhorted the same king to right belief.

At that tide likewise the bishop of the apostolic seat, pope Boniface, sent Edwin greeting and a letter, whereby he exhorted him to receive Christ's belief.[2]

CHAPTER XII.

1. There was likewise a Godspeech [3] and a heavenly revelation, which the Divine Mercy unfolded to him long before, when he was an exile with Redwald king of the East-English, which greatly helped his understanding to receive and to understand the admonitions of the wholesome lore. When bishop Paulinus then saw that he could not easily turn the highness of the royal mind to humility, so that he would receive his eternal salvation, and the mystery of the life-giving cross of Christ, he, at the same time, for the salvation of the king and of the nation over which he was, both strove with men by word of exhortation, and also pleaded for them with the Divine Mercy, by word of his prayers. Then at last he learnt in ghost, and it was unfolded to him, what heavenly revelation long before appeared to the king, when he was an exile. He delayed then no longer, but went immediately

---

1. A. S. á or aa, ever, always.—Hence "ever and o" or "oo." *Old Eng.*
2. The letter to Edwin, and ch. xi, containing another addressed to his queen, are omitted by Alfred, as also the title of Ch. XII.
3. Godæpræse, *Alf.* Oraculum, *Bd.*—compare Godspell, gospel.

to the king, and admonished him, that he should fulfil his promise, which he had promised in the revelation or vision which appeared to him, if he should escape the hardships of that tide, and come to the highness of the kingdom.'

2. This [God-speech and this] vision was of this sort:—When Ethelfrith, who was king before him, persecuted him, and he was a fugitive through diverse places many years' tide, then sought he at last and came to Redwald, king of the East-English, and begged that he would shield his life against the snares of his great persecutor, and be his life-herd. And he gladly received him, and promised that he would do as he prayed him. Afterwards when king Ethelfrith learnt that he was with king Redwald, then soon sent he messengers to him and much fee, to the end that he should slay him, or give him to be killed: in that, however, he sped not a whit. He sent messengers again a second time; he sent a third [time and much greater gifts and fee, than he formerly sent him, for his murther, and ordered also to inform him, that he would seek him in battle with an army, if he slighted his word and his gifts. Then was his mind both frightened by the threatenings, and corrupted by the gifts, that he agreed to the king's prayers, and promised that he would slay Edwin, or give him to his foes to kill.

3. Then was there a king's thane, his truest friend, who heard and understood these things; then went he to his inn where he would rest him, and it was the fore part of the night, and called him out, and told him how they would do about him. He further said to him, "If thou wilt, in this same hour, I will lead thee out of this province, and bring thee into the place where neither Redwald nor Ethelfrith may ever find thee." Quoth he to him, "In thank' to me are thy words and thy love. Yet I cannot do that which thou advisest me, that I should break the covenant, which I took to so great a king, when he has done me naught of evil, nor shewn aught of hate. But if I must suffer death, I would rather that he, than a less noble man, put me to death,—Or oh! whither can I now longer flee? many years' tide have I been a fugitive over all Britain, that I might save and secure myself from his hate." Then went his friend

---

4. Regni, *Bd.* Reign, realm—here Royalty.
5. Acceptable to me. So Oros. 11. 5 § 8, p. 91, l. 13, Eng. "Of that mind" should perhaps be read "to their mind" or "they were not thankful for them."

away from him, and Edwin remained alone there without, sat very sorrowful on a stone before the hall, or palace, and began to be afflicted with many heats of his thoughts, and wist not whither he should go, nor what were best for him to do.

4. When he then for a long while, by the silent anxieties of his mind, and the blind [or hidden] fire, was scorched, then suddenly, in the middle of the night, he saw a man go towards him, of strange[1] countenance and uncouth[1] apparel: when he was come to him, he became frightened. Then he went to him, greeted him, and asked, why he, at that tide, when other men slept and rested, was sitting alone, so sorrowful, on a stone, waking. Then asked he him, what of that concerned him, whether he slept or waked, or whether he were out or in. Then answered he and said to him: "Think not thou that I know not the cause of thy sorrow, and thy waking, and the singularity of thy outsitting; but I certainly wot both who thou art, and why thou grievest, and what future evil thou fearest [to be] at hand. but tell me what meed thou wilt give to that man, if any such be, who will free thee from these anxieties,[2] and persuade Redwald in his mind, that he neither do thee aught of harm, nor give thee up to thy foes, to death." Then answered he, and said that he would give all the goods that he could, as a reward of such kindness. Then eked he yet further his speech, and said, "And if he shall promise thee in truth a future kingdom, thy foes being cut off, so that thou shalt far overstep not only thy elders, but also all the kings that have been in Britain before thee, in might and in dominion." Then was Edwin become bolder on that inquiry, and quickly promised, that whosoever would bestow so great kindness upon him, he would do him worthy thanking for it. He that was speaking to him said to him the third time, "And now, if he who foretells to thee such gifts, and others so much more true to be hereafter to thee, and likewise can shew thee counsels of thy salvation, and of a better and more profitable life, than any of thy kinsmen or elders ever heard,—say, wilt thou receive his wholesome admonitions, and be obedient to him?" Then Edwin lingered not a whit, but quickly promised that he would in all things be obedient to him, and gladly receive his lore, who should save him from so many hardships and griefs,

---

1. Uncuþes, *Alf.* uncouth, i. e. unknown, strange.
2. *Lit.* narrownesses, or straits.

and lead him forth to the height of kingly power. When he then had received this answer—he who was speaking with him—then he instantly set his right hand on his head, and thus said: "When such a token as this shall come to thee, then remember thou this time and our speaking together, and linger thou not to fulfil the things which thou hast now promised to me." When he had spoken these words, then wist he not whither he suddenly went [3],—he would that he should understand that it was not a man that appeared to him, but that it was a ghost.

5. And whilst he then, the young prince, was yet sitting there alone, and greatly rejoicing at the comfort which was promised him, but nevertheless with anxious mood earnestly thought who he was, or whence he came, who had spoken these things to him; then came again to him his foresaid friend, and with a blithe countenance hailed and greeted him, and thus spoke, "Arise and go in; rest thy body and thy mind without care; ' for the king's heart is turned; he will not do thee aught of harm, but he will rather hold his truth and his promise to thee, and by thy life-herd. He told him afterwards, "that the king had privately disclosed to the queen his thoughts about that which I formerly told thee, then she wound him from the evil thought of his mind, taught and advised him that it nothing became so noble and so honourable a king, that he should sell his best friend, in needy circumstances, for gold; and, for the greed and love of money, lose his truth, which was dear-worther [5] and more than all treasures.

6. What shall we say more of this? the king did as it was said before, not that only that he gave not to death the exile who had sought him, but he likewise helped him [so] that he came to the kingdom. For soon after the messengers returned home who had treated for his death, Redwold called out his forces, and gathered a great host to make war against Ethelfrith. Then went he to meet him with an unlike host, for he would not leave him time that he might assemble all his host. Then went they together, and fought on the borders of the Mercian nation, at the east-deal of the river which is named Idle; and there Ethelfrith

---

3. *Lit.* suddenly where he came.
4. *Lit.* Sorrow,—compare Ger. Sorge.
5. Thanks to the queen of Kent for this opportunity of restoring a word which ought never to have fallen in abeyance, for the Latin *pretiosus*,—mid deorwurthum blode alysdest, *pretioso sanguine redemisti—Te Deum.*

was slain. Likewise in the same fight Redwald's son was slain, who was named Regenhere; and so Edwin, according to the God-speech, which he formerly received, not only then escaped the snares of the unfaithful king, but likewise, after his slaughter, succeeded him in the honour of the kingdom.[6]

7. Whilst he then—bishop Paulinus—preached and taught God's word, and the king then yet delayed to believe; and through some time, as we said before, accidentally sat alone, and earnestly studied and thought with himself, what were best for him to do, and which religion were to be holden by him; then one day the man of God went in to him, where he sat alone, and set his right hand on his head, and asked him whether he could understand that token. Then knew he it soon clearly, and became much frightened, and fell at his feet; and the man of God raised him up, and spoke familiarly to him, and thus said: "Lo! now you have through God's gift escaped the hands of your foes, whom you dreaded; and by his grant and gift have received the kingdom, which you desired: but remember now that you make good the third thing which you promised, that you receive his belief, and keep his commandments, who has saved you from temporal calamities, and also raised you to the honour of temporal sovereignty; and if you will be obedient to his will, which he now through me preaches and teaches, then he will also save you from the torments of everlasting evils, and make you partaker with himself of the everlasting sovereignty in heaven."

CHAPTER XIII.
What counsel the same king held with his aldermen about the reception of Christ's belief.

1. When the king then heard these words, then answered he him and said, that he both would and should receive the belief which he taught. He said however, that he would have a conference and consultation with his friends, and with his aldermen, and with his *witan*[1] or privy council; and if they would agree with him, they all together should in life's well be hallowed to Christ. Then did the king so as he said, and the bishop agreed to it. Then held he a conference and consultation with his counsellors

---

6. Sovereignty, rank and dignity of a king.
1. Alfred is probably right in making three parties —*amicis* freondum, *principibus* ealdormannum, and *consiliariis* witum.

and asked sundrily from them all, what [to] them seemed and appeared this new lore, and the divine worship which therein was taught.

2. Then his elder bishop (or chief priest,) who was named Coifi, answered him : " See thou, king, what this lore is, which is preached to us. I truly own to you, that I have certainly learnt, that this religion, which we until this have held and practised, has naught of power nor usefulness. For none of your thanes has more strictly or more willingly subjected himself to the worship of our gods, than I ; and naught the less there are many who have received more gifts and favours from you, than I, and in all things have had more prosperity. Lo! I wot, if our gods had any might, then would they help me more, for I have more carefully served and obeyed them. Therefore methinks it [1] wise, if you see the things which are newly preached to us [to be] better and stronger, that we should receive them."

3. To these words another counsellor and alderman of the king gave assent, and took up the discourse, and thus spoke : " Such appears to me, O king, this present life of men on earth in comparison of the time that is unknown to us,—so like as [if] you were sitting at a banquet with your aldermen and thanes, in winter tide, and a fire were kindled, and your palace warmed, and it rained and snew, [2] and stormed without ; then came a sparrow and quickly flew through the house ; and came in through one door, and went out through another. Lo! in the time that he is within he is not touched by the storm of the winter ; but that is [only] an eye-blink, and the least space ; and he soon comes from winter to winter again. So this life of men appears for a short space : what goes before it, or what follows after it, we know not. Therefore if this new lore brings aught more certain and more suitable, it is worthy of this, that we follow it." With such like words other eldermen and the king's counsellors spoke.

4. Then yet Coifi added and said ; that he would more willingly hear bishop Paulinus speaking about the God whom he preached. Then the king bade [him] do so. When he then heard his words [3], then cried he and thus said, " Readily I under-

1. *Lit.* It thinks (i. e. seems) to me.
2. Vulg. " snowed," good as *blowed, throwed, knowed,* &.
3. When Coifi had heard Paulinus speak, the former cried out, &c.

stand, that it was naught which we worshipped; for the more earnestly I in that worship sought the truth itself, the less I found it. But now I openly acknowledge, that in this lore the truth itself shines, which may [1] give us the gifts of everlasting blessedness, and the health of everlasting life. Therefore I now advise, O king, that the temple and the altars, which without fruits of any usefulness we hallowed—that we straightway destroy and burn them with fire." Well! the king then openly declared to the priest and to them all, that he would firmly "withsake" and renounce idolatry, and receive the faith of Christ.

5. When the king then sought and asked from the foresaid "bishop" or high priest, who should first profane and overthrow the sanctuary which they formerly venerated, the altar and the temples of the idols, with the hedges wherewith they were surrounded; then the priest answered, "Lo! I have long with folly worshiped those gods; who therefore may more becomingly overthrow them as an example to other men, than I myself, through the wisdom which I have received from the true God?" And he then soon threw from him the idle folly which he had practised, and prayed the king to give him a weapon and a studhorse, that he might mount [him], and overthrow the idols; for the high priest of their sanctuary had not leave to bear arms, nor to ride otherwise than on a mare. Then the king gave him a sword, that he might begird himself with [it], and he took a spear in his hand, and leapt on the king's steed, and went to the idols. When the folk saw him so accoutered, then weened they that he wist not good, but that he was mad. As soon as he alighted at the temple, then shot he with his spear, and sticked [2] it fast in the temple; and he was vehemently rejoicing in the knowledge of the worship of the true God; and then he ordered his fellows to throw down and to burn all the temple and the buildings. This place of the idols in old times, is yet shewn—not far from York city, beyond the river Derwent, and yet to-day is named Godmundingham, where the priest overthrew and fordid [3] the altar which he himself had formerly hallowed.

1. Is able.
2. Active form,—*stuck* is the neuter pret. in the sense of remaining fixed.
3. Why wilt thou thus thyself alas fordo? *Ch.*—Compare Lat. *per* in *perdo, perimo, pereo*, &c.—*for* and *fore* differ as much as *per* and *præ*.

CHAPTER XIV.
That the same Edwin with his nation became faithful, and was baptized.

1. Then king Edwin with all the princes of his nation, and with much people, received Christ's belief and the bath of baptism, the eleventh year of his reign. He was baptized by bishop Paulinus, his teacher, on the holiest Easter-day, in York city, in the church of St Peter the apostle, when he had there built a church of wood, with hasty work, after he was christened. He likewise gave his teacher and bishop, Paulinus, a bishop-seat in that city; and soon after he was baptized, he began by the bishop's advice to build a larger and higher church of stone, and to construct it about the church which he had formerly wrought. But before the height of the wall was complete and ended, the king was by wicked murder slain, and the same work was left for his afterfollower, Oswald, to finish. From that time full six years, that is till the end of the king's reign, bishop Paulinus with his help preached and taught God's word in that province, and men believed and were baptized—as many as were predestined to everlasting life; among whom were Osfrith and Eadfrith king Edwin's sons, who were both born to him when he was an exile, of Quenburga, who was daughter of Kearl king of the Mercians. In afterfollowing time were also baptized his other children, born of Queen Ethelburga, [namely] Ethelhun, and Etheldrith his daughter, and his other son, named Wuscfrea; but the former twain died under the Chrism [1] and were buried in a church in York city. Osfrith's son Yffi was likewise baptized, and many princes of the kingly kin. It is said that there was so much ardour and desire for the faith of Christ and the bath of baptism, in the nation of the Northumbrians, that Paulinus the bishop at one time came with the king and the queen into the royal country-house, which was named Atgefrin, and there abode six and thirty days, that he might there christen and baptize the people; and that he did naught else on all the days, from early morn until even, than with divine lore edify the people of Christ, coming thither from all the country-houses and places [around],[2] and wash them in the bath of the forgiveness of sins, in the stream which is named Gleni. This country-house was forsaken in the times of the succeeding kings, and another was therefore built in

---

1. Chrism-cloth, a white garment worn by persons newly baptized.
2. Lit. "towns" and "stows"—Topographical names, in whole or in part, throughout all England.

the place which is called Melmen. These places are in the province of the Bernicians: but likewise in the province of the Deiri, where the bishop oft was with the king, he baptized the folk in the stream Swale, which lies by the town Cataract: because there were not yet churches built, nor baptismal places, in the beginning of the new-born church. And yet in Donafield where the king's dwelling was, Edwin ordered to build a church, which after a space the heathens, by whom the king was afterwards slain, burnt with all the dwelling. Therefore the succeeding kings afterwards built them a country-house in the land which is called Loidis.

CHAPTER XV.
That the province of the East-English received the Christian belief.

1. Edwin the king had so much wilsomeness of the worship of Christ's belief that he likewise drew Eorpwald king of the East-English, Redwald's son, to that [mind], that he forsook the emptiness [1] of idol-worship, and received the mysteries of the Christian faith, with his province of the East-English. His father Redwald had long before in Kent been instructed into the mysteries of Christ's belief, but in vain; for when he came home again, he was overreached by his wife and some unright teachers, so that he forsook the purity of the faith of Christ, and his latter times were worse than the former; so that, in the way that the old Samaritans of yore did, he was seen to serve Christ and also idols, and he had in the same temple an altar for Christ's sacrifice, and another for devils' sacrifice. The temple stood there till the time of Aldwulf king of the same province, who said that he saw it when he was a boy. The foresaid king Redwald was of noble birth, though he was ignoble in deeds: he was the son of Titel, whose father was called Wuffa, from whom the kings of the East-English were named Wuffings.

2. Moreover [2], after not much time king Eorpwald was slain by a heathen man, [who] was called Ricbert; thenceforth the province was full three years living in error; until Sighebert, Eorpwald's brother, got the kingdom, who was through every thing most Christian and most learned. In his brother's life-time

---

1. Idlenesses, *Alf.* Vanis superstitionibus—vain, idle, (i. e. void or empty) superstitions. 2. Hwæt ða, *Alf.* What then? Lo! or Well then!

he was an exile in the land of Gaul, and there was well taught in the mysteries of Christ's belief. Of this belief he would make his people partakers, as soon as he got the kingdom. And his good will was well helped by bishop Felix, who came with him from the parts of the kingdom of the Burgundians, where he was born and hallowed. He came first hither over sea to archbishop Honorius, and told him his will and his desire. Then sent he him to teach divine lore among the East-English; and he soon, the godly husbandman of the ghostly land, found a great crop of faithful folk in that nation, and after the mystery of his name,[1] set all that nation free from long wickedness and unblessedness; and led it to Christ's belief, and to works of righteousness, and to gifts of everlasting blessedness. He also received a bishop-seat in Dommoc city, and when he had held bishoply rule[2] fourteen winters, he there ended his life in peace.

CHAPTER XVI.
That Paulinus in Lindsey province was preaching Christ's belief. Of the peace and stillness of king Edwin's reign.

1. St Paulinus the bishop likewise taught God's word in the province of Lindsey, which is next on this half the river Humber, and lies out into the sea, and [he] then first turned to our Lord's belief the reeve of Lincoln city whose name was Blecca, with his household. He likewise built in that city, a stone church of noble workmanship; of which òne may yet to-day see the walls standing; and where yet every year are shewn many wonders of healing of the sick, who seek the place with belief. In the same church St Paulinus the bishop, when bishop Justus went to Christ, hallowed Honorius as bishop for him, as we shall again hereafter mention. Concerning the belief of this province, quoth Bede, a reverend mass-priest and abbot of Peartanea the "ham," who was called Deda, said to me, that an old wita, or counsellor, told him that he was baptized at mid-day by bishop Paulinus, in king Edwin's presence, and a great multitude of the folk, in the river Trent, near Tealfingcaster. The same man told what the hue or personal appearance of the bishop St Paulinus was: [he] said that the man was long in body, and a little bent forward, had black hair, and a pale countenance, and a small

---
1. Felix, happy, prosperous.
2. *Lit.* was before in episcopal government, "on bisceoplicum gerece."

thin nose, and was both venerable and awful to look upon. He had for a help to him in the divine ministry James the deacon ; who was well learned and famous both in Christ and in the church : he lived until our time.

2. [It] is said that at that time there was so great peace in Britain, everywhere around, where Edwin's reign was, that though a woman would [go] with her newborn child, she might go without any scathe, from sea to sea, over all this island. Likewise the same king contrived for the use of his people, that in many places where clear wells ran (or sprung up) by the folk-known streets, where the greatest faring of men was, he there ordered, for the refreshment of the way-faring, to set up staples, and thereon to hang brazen jugs ; and yet for fear of him, and for love of him, none either durst or would touch them, but to his own needful service. He likewise had so great highness and stateliness in the kingdom, that they not only carried his banner before him in fight, but likewise in the time of peace, where he rode between his " hams" and towns with his thanes, yea though he walked, that token was always borne before him.

CHAPTER XVII.

1. At that time Honorius had the bishop-hood of the apostolic seat, as Boniface's afterfollower. When he then, the pope, learnt it, that the nation of the Northumbrians, with Edwin their king, was converted to Christ's belief through Paulinus's divine lore, then sent he hither to the same bishop a pallium, and likewise to king Edwin he sent an encouraging letter, and was firing him with fatherly love ; that they should always stand fast and abide in the belief of soothfastness which they had received.

CHAPTER XVIII.
Of Justus the archbishop's decease, and that Honorius was chosen for him, and was hallowed by Paulinus in Lincoln ; and that he received a letter and pallium from pope Honorius.

1. Amidst these things Justus the archbishop was led to the heavenly kingdom, the fourth day of the Ides of November (10th *of the month*), and Honorius [as he] was called, who was chosen bishop for him, came to St Paulinus, that he should hallow him ; and he went towards him to Lincoln, and in the church of which we spoke before, he then hallowed him as bishop :—he

was the fifth archbishop of Canterbury from St Augustine. The same pope Honorius likewise sent the bishop a pallium, and a letter in which he appointed and advised, that so oft as the bishop of Canterbury or of York fared out of this life, he that was living of the order, should have power to hallow another bishop to his place, where the other had died, lest need should be that they were always troubled, over so long a way by sea and land to Rome, for the hallowing of an archbishop.[1]

CHAPTER XX.
That, Edwin being slain by Penda, king of the Mercians, bishop Paulinus came back to Kent, and received a bishop-seat in Rochester.

1. Moreover, after Edwin had wonderfully held the kingdom seventeen winters over the English nation and Britons together, of which winters he [for] six winters fought for Christ's kingdom, then Cadwalla king of the Britons strove against him, and was helped by Penda, the stoutest[2] man of the kingly kin of the Mercians; and he, Penda, from that time was over the same nation of the Mercian kingdom two and twenty winters with various lot. Then was joined a heavy and great fight, in Heathfield; and there Edwin the king was slain, the fourth day of the ides of October (12th *of the month*). [He] had then seven and forty winters, and all his host was either slain or put to flight. Likewise in the same fight Osfrith one of his sons a very keen warrior, fell ere him. And Eadfrith the other, for need, stooped to king Penda, and after a space was by him, when Oswald was king, unrighteously slain, against oaths and covenants.

2. At that time was the greatest slaughter made in the nation and church of the Northumbrians. Nor was that without cause; for one of the army-leaders was a heathen, who made the fight; the other was wrother and grimmer than the heathen, for he was a barbarian. Penda, with all the nation of the Mercians, was given to idolatry, and was unwitting of the Christian name. But Cadwalla, though he owned the Christian name, was nevertheless in his mood and in his thews so barbarous, that he spared not

---

1. The papal epistles mentioned in these two chapters, and the whole xixth ch. containing letters of the popes Honorius and John to the Scots, upon the observance of Easter, and the Pelagian heresy, are omitted by Alfred.
2. Fromest, *Alf*. How the good old English "stout" is abused by modern mouths may be known from the description of the *cowardly* Falstaff as a "stout" man. 3. So in A. S.

even womanhood¹ or the unscathing age of children; but with wild-beastly cruelty gave [them] all to death through torture; and for a long time he went throughout all their province like a mad-man; and, in his mind, thought and threatened, that he would drive all the English kin by flight out of the bounds of Britain. And though he should have been² a Christian, he would not show³ any favour to the Christian religion, which had come up with them; as yet to-day the way and thew of the Britons is, that they have for naught the belief and religion of the English kin, nor will for any sake communicate with them more than with heathen men.

3. Then was brought Edwin's head, the king's,⁴ to York city, and after that again was put into the church of Peter the apostle⁵ which he began to build, but Oswald his afterfollower ended it, as we said before: It was set (or laid) in the porch of St Gregory the pope, from whose disciples he had received the word of life and the faith of Christ.

4. Then after Edwin's slaughter, and for the perilousness of these times, St Paulinus the bishop took with him queen Ethelburga, whom he formerly brought, and in his shipfaring returned to Kent: their leader was Bassa, the stoutest of king Edwin's warriors; and they were very honourably received by Honorius the archbishop, and Eadbald the king. They likewise had with them Eaufleda Edwin's daughter, and Wuscfrea his son; likewise Uffa, his son Osfrith's son. The mother afterwards sent them, for fear of Eadbald and Oswald the kings, into the kingdom of Gaul, to king Dagbert, who was her friend, to be brought up by him; and they both died there in childhood; and with honour suitable to their high birth and innocence, were buried in church. The queen brought with her many dearworth vats of king Edwin, among which was a great golden Christ's cross, and a golden cup hallowed to the holy table's service; which now yet until this may be seen in Canter[bury] church.

5. At that tide the church at Rochester was herdless, because Romanus, bishop of that church, was sent by Justus the archbishop as ambassador to Honorius the pope, and then was

---

1. "Wifely-hood," *Alf.* 'female sex' in shortened Latin.
2. *Lit.* should be, i. e. as in Ger. was said to be.
3. Witan, *Alf.* to wit or know; compare Fr. savoir gré.
4. Is not Alfred's collocation, here shewn, more effective than any now approved arrangement could be? 5. Peter's church the apostle's, *Alf.*

drowned in the waves of the sea; and through that the foresaid bishop St Paulinus took on him the care of the church at the call of the archbishop and king Eadbald, and had it until he in his tide went up to the heavenly kingdom, with fruit of his wonderful toil: in the church he left his pallium, and his body rests in peace. He left also in his church, in York city, James the deacon; and that was a churchly and holy man in all things; and he abode a long time after in that church, and carried off much booty from the old foe through his lore and baptism; and the town in which he oftest dwelt, well nigh Cataract, is yet to-day called by his name. And because he was most learned in church-song, and, after a space, times of peace came on the province of the Northumbrians, and the number of the faithful waxed, he was many people's master of church-song after the manner of the Romans and Cantuarians: and he then, old and full of days, according to what the holy writings speak, followed the way of his fathers.

Here endeth the second book.

BOOK III. CHAPTER I.
That the first afterfollowers of king Edwin befouled the faith of their own nation; [and lost the kingdom] [1] and Oswald the most Christian king renewed both of them.

1. When Edwin was slain in the fight, his uncle Elfric's son, who was called Osric got the kingdom of the Deiri, for from that province Edwin had the beginning of his kindred and kingdom. Osric had been taught the mysteries of Christ's belief by St Paulinus the bishop. Then Ethelfrith's son, whose name was Eanfrith, got the kingdom of the Bernicians, for he was of the kingly kin of that province. Into these two provinces the nation of the Northumbrians was of yore todealt.[2] And all the time that Edwin was king, this Eanfrith, Ethelfrith's son, with many young princes, lived in exile, both with the Scots and with the Picts, and there, through lore of the Scots, [they] received Christ's belief, and were baptized. And as soon as Edwin their foe was slain, they returned home to their country, and Eanfrith took to the kingdom of the Bernicians. But both of the kings,

---

1. This clause is omitted in A. S. though necessary to the sense of the next. For "their own," the A. S. has "his agenre," by a common error in the rendering *suæ*, or *suus* in any case.
2. 'Todæled, *A. S.* parted asunder.

after they had the kingdom, forsook the mysteries of the heavenly kingdom, with which they were hallowed, and returned to the old uncleanness of idolatry, and through that forlost [1] themselves.

2. And soon, without elding or delay, Cadwalla, king of the Britons, with wicked hand, but with righteous vengeance, killed them both; and first, the next summer, he came upon Osric unawares with his army in a municipal city,[2] and cut him off with all his host. After that, all the year, he had the whole [3] of the Northumbrian provinces—not as a victorious king, but as a folk-hater; and, raging, destroyed and wounded them in the likeness of tragic slaughter. Then at last Eanfrith came to him, twelve in company, without the advice of his counsellors, because he would ask peace and protection from him; whom by a like lot he put down and slew. This unhappy and godless year yet to day remains loathsome, both for the flight of those kings from Christ's belief, and turning back to idolatry, and for the madness of the folk-hating king of the Britons. For that then liked and pleased all generally which they reckoned to the times of the kings, that they might do away the memory of the faithless kings; and they reckoned that same year to the reign of the afterfollowing king; that is of the God-beloved man Oswald. Then it befel, after the slaughter of his brother Eanfrith, that Oswald came with a small host, but strengthened by Christ's belief; and the wicked king of the Britons with his immense hosts, which he boasted that naught might withstand, he slew and killed, in the place which the English name Denisses burn.[4]

CHAPTER II. (Ch. 1, continued, MSS.)

1. The place is yet to day shown, and is had in much veneration, where Oswald came to this fight, and where he reared the holy token of Christ's rood, and bowed his knees, and prayed God that he would, in so great needfulness, help his worshippers with heavenly aid. [It] is said that he wrought the Christ's-cross with hasty work, and "dolve" [5] a pit in which it should stand; and

---

1. Or "forlore," whence "forlorn," i. e. lost, as "forlorn hope."
2. Or in the city Municep municipio oppido, *Bd.*
3. Onwealh, *Sm.*—anweald, *C.* andweald, *B.* power.
4. Brook,—"burn" still used in North of Eng. and in S. "Denisses."—Can Denis's be pronounced, otherwise than Alfred's orthography shews?
5. Or dalfe nearer to "adulfe" than *delved* would be.

the king himself was burning in his faith, and took the Christ's-cross, and set it in the pit, and held it with both his hands, and held it, till his thanes with mould bestrewed and fastened it; and when it was reared, he uphove his voice and called to all the host, "Let us all bow our knees to the Almighty God, the living, and the true, that he with his mercy shield us from the haughty and cruel foe, for he knows that we strive righteously for the welfare of our nation." Then did they all as he bade; and soon on the morrow, as it began to dawn, he marched on the army which had been gathered against him, and according to the earning of his belief, they overcame their foes, and had victory. In the praying-place, after that, many virtues and tokens of healing were exhibited, in tokening and remembrance of the king's faith; and many yet to-day take chips and shavings off the tree of the holy Christ's-cross, and put them in water, and sprinkle the water on sick men or beasts; or give it them to drink, and soon they receive health. The place is in English named Heavenfield; it was of yore so named for tokening of the wonders to come, for there the heavenly beacon of triumph should be reared, and there heavenly triumph was given to the king, and there yet to day heavenly wonders are celebrated.

2. It is not therefore unbecoming that we mention one virtue, and one wonder out of many, which was done at this holy Christ's-cross. There was a servant of God, [one] of the brethren of the church at Hagostaldsea, whose name was Bothelm. He went one night on ice unwarily; then fell he suddenly upon his arm and severely bruised and broke it, and he was very much distressed with the heaviness of the broken arm, so that for the soreness he could not even put his hand to his mouth. Then he heard one of the brethren say, that he would go to Christ's holy cross; then he begged that he would bring him some deal of the worshipful tree when he came home again; [and] said that he believed that he might through that receive healing by the Lord's gift. Then the brother did as he bade him, and came back in the evening, home, when the brethren were sitting at board; then brought he him some deal of old moss which had waxen on the holy tree. He was then sitting at board, and had not then at hand where he should hold the offered gift; he then put it in his bosom. When he went to rest, then forgot he that he should hold it in [some] other place, but let it still remain in

his bosom. Then at midnight when he awoke, he wist not what he felt lying cold at his side, he tried then with his hand, and sought what it was. Then found he his arm and his hand so hale and so sound, as [if] never breach nor hurt had been done them.

CHAPTER III.
That the same king obtained by request from the nation of the Scots a bishop called by name Aidan, and gave him a bishop-seat in the island Lindesfarne.

1. And then the same king Oswald, as soon as he received the kingdom, loved and wished that all the nation over which he was, should be taught with the gift of the Christian belief, which belief and witnessing he had most received in his victories over barbarous races. Then sent he ambassadors to the aldermen of the Scots, among whom he had for a long time been an exile, and from whom he had received the mysteries of baptism with his thanes who were with him, he prayed them that they would send him a bishop; by whose lore and ministry the English nation, which he governed, might learn the gift of our Lord's belief, and receive the bath of baptism. And they gladly granted it him, and sent him a bishop called Aidan, a man of much mildness, and piety, and moderation; and he had much zeal and love of God.

2. When he then, the bishop, came to the king, then gave he him a place and a bishop-seat in Lindesfarne isle, where he himself asked and wished, and the king meekly and gladly listened to his admonitions in all things, and he willingly built and reared Christ's church in his kingdom; and oft a fair sight happened, that when the bishop who did not fully know English, was teaching divine lore, the king himself, who had fully learnt Scottish, became interpreter of the heavenly lore to his aldermen and thanes. From that tide many came daily from the land of the Scots into Britain, and, in the provinces of the English nation over which Oswald was king, with much wilsomeness preached and taught Christ's belief; and those who were of the priesthood ministered baptism to them. Then were also churches built in many places, and thither came folk of English kin, fain to hear God's word, which they preached and taught; and the king gave and granted them possessions and land to build a monastery; and the Scots instructed young and old in regular discipline, because monks were they who came hither to teach. A monk was also the same bishop Aidan: he was sent from the isle (and from the monastery)

that is named Hii; which monastery [1] for a long time held authority and preeminence [2] among all the northern Scots, and all the monasteries of the Picts: but however the Picts granted and gave it to the Scottish monks, because they formerly, through their lore, received Christ's belief.

CHAPTER V. (Ch. IV omitted in A. S.)
Of bishop Aidan's life.

1. And from this isle, and by the friendship of these monks, to teach Christ's belief to the English nation, was bishop Aidan sent. And he then—the bishop—among other lore to men [how] to live, left the fairest example to his disciples, that he was of great self-denial and self-command; [3] and it most powerfully helped his lore and teaching, that he lived not otherwise but as he taught; for not a whit sought he or loved the things that were of this world. But all the worldly goods that were given him by kings and wealthy men of this world, soon he gladly reached and gave to the needy who came towards him. He went through all places, both of the monastery and of the [country] folk; nor would he ever come on horse-back, [4] unless some need were more pressing, but he went [it] all on his feet; and wheresoever he came, or whomsoever he met, whether rich or poor, then turned he to them: If they were unbelievers, then he called them to receive the mysteries of Christ's belief; or if they were believers, he strengthened and trimmed them, that they might abide stedfastly in their belief, and to alms [giving] and following of good deeds he awakened them both by words and by deeds.

2. And so far did his life shy off [5] from the slothfulness of our times, that all those who went with him, both cleric and laic, [6] in what place soever they came, they should either learn psalms or other holy writings, or thirdly, stand on holy prayers. This was his daily work, and all theirs who were with him; and if it [so] was, which however seldom happened, that he were invited to the king's banquet, he went in with one or with two of his priests; and as soon as they were a little refreshed, he quickly arose and

1. From the isle which is called Hii, whose monastery *Bd*.
2. *Lit.* elderdom and highness.
3. Or abstinence and precaution of life.
4. *Lit.* horse's ridge (—riggin *Sc.*).
5. Differ—toscegde, *Alf.* (—skeigh in *Sc.* shy, distant.)
6. *Lit.* beshorn and lewd, priests and laymen.

went out to his praying, or to learn with his fellows. By this holy man's example all religious men and women were at that time encouraged, [so] that they adopted as their custom, that all the year, except fifty nights over Easter, they fasted till noon (*the third hour after midday*) on the fourth week-day and on the sixth. And he—this bishop—never, for honour or for fear, kept silence to rich men, if they had any way a guilted[1] but with hard rebuke spoke against and corrected them, and to no powerful man would he ever give fee[2] but only meat and entertainment to those who visited him; but rather the gifts and the fee which rich men gave him, he either dealt to the needy for use, or gave it for the releasing of those men who had been unrighteously sold; and he took many of those, whom he loosed with [their] worth, as his disciples; and after a space, through his instructions, trained and taught them for the priesthood.

3. Men say [that] when king Oswald asked from the isle of the Scots a bishop, who might minister and hold Christ's belief and baptism to him and his nation, then was first sent another bishop, a man of harsh mood. When he then had for a while preached and taught to the English nation, and he sped naught in his lore, nor would the folk willingly hear him, then he returned into his native land among the Scots, and in a meeting of their elders said, that he could not speed a whit in his teaching to the nation which he had been sent to, for the men were untamed and of a hard and barbarous mood. And they then, as men said, had in the meeting much musing and consultation what they were to do; and said that it was agreeable to them, and they wished that they might be to the nation for salvation, for which they were asked, and sorrowed much on that [account], that they would not receive the teacher whom they had sent to them. Then sat Aidan among other elders, and said to the bishop after he had heard his words:—" Me thinketh, brother, (quoth he) that thou wert harder to the unlearned men, than it was right, in thy lore; and thou gavest them not first, according to the apostolic discipline, milk of the soft lore to drink, until thou stick-meal[3] fed them with the word of God, that they might receive God's per-

---

1. Or " guilted"—*Ch.* offended, or done amiss.
2. Money, or property, of any sort.
3. By degrees,—stick, a piece of any thing; so piece-meal, a piece at a time; A. S. mæl time.

fect and higher commandments." When they then—the elders—
heard these words, then they all turned their eyes and their faces
to him, and earnestly considered what he said ; and by all their
doom it was deemed, that he was worthy of the bishophood, and
that he should be sent to the English kin [as] teacher, who by
God's grace had found such discretion in their council. And they
so did, hallowed him as bishop, and sent him to king Oswald,
their friend, as a teacher. When he then had received the bishophood, as he had formerly found [good counsel?] by the moderat-
ing of discretion,⁴ so after a space he appeared adorned with
other ghostly virtues.

CHAPTER VI.
Of king Oswald's religion and wonderful piety.

1. And by this bishop's lore Oswald, with the English nation,
over which he was king, being taught, not only learnt from him
that he should hope to receive the high kingdom of heaven, but
likewise received an earthly kingdom, more than any of his
elders, from the same God who shoop⁵ and formed heaven and
earth. For he received into [his] dominion all Britain-kin,⁶ and
the tribes which are to-dealt into four tongues, that is, Britons,
and Picts, and Scots, and English; and though he was [a hoven
and] exalted with the highness of the earthly kingdom, naught-
the-less, it is a wonder to say, he was always lowly and kind, and
openhearted to the needy and outlandish.⁸

2. Men say that it befel, at one tide, on the holy Easter-day,
that he sat with the foresaid bishop at his dinner,⁹ and a table
was set for¹ him, and thereon stood a great silvern dish, and it
was filled with kingly meats, and the bishop took loaf and blessed, and gave to the king; then went suddenly one of his thanes
in, whom he had bidden tell the errands of needy and wretched
men, and said to the king, that from every side came a great
crowd of needy folk, that the street sat full [of them], begging
alms of him. Then straightway the king bade [them] take the

4. It is difficult to make out Alfred's meaning here and Bede is not very perspicuous.
5. Now ' shaped,' made, created.   6. Or British race—the Welsh and Cornish.
7. Room-mood *Alf.*—of a roomy or large mind.
8. Men of other speech *literally* ; peregrinis *Bd.* pilgrims.
9. *Lit.* undern-meal,—time between 9 o'clock and midday.
1. A board was raised—*lit.*

meat and [other] victuals which had been set before him, and bear to the needy; and also ordered that they should break the dish to sticks and deal [it] to the needy. When the bishop, who sat by him, saw that, then the king's godly deed liked him [so that he] took him by the right hand, and kissed it, and thus said: "Let not this hand ever be forelded."² Which also befel after the wish of his blessing; for when he was afterwards slain in fight, then it happened that the hand was hewn off with the arm, from the body, and now yet remains uncorrupted. It was brought into the kingly borough, which is named Bamborough³, and there in St Peter's church they⁴ are worshipfully holden in a silvern chest. Likewise by his care and earnestness this king drew and blended the two Northumbrian provinces of the Deiri and the Bernicians into one peace and one people,—those who, until that, had been disagreeing and unpeaceable among themselves. This Oswald was nephew of Edwin the noble king,—his sister-son. It was worthy of it, that so noble a foregoer should have such an heir of his piety and kingdom, of his own kindred.

CHAPTER VII.
That the province of the West-Saxons, by the preaching of bishop Birinus, received God's word; and of his afterfollowers Aghilbert and Eleutherius.

1. At the time when the nation of the West-Saxons with Kyneghils their king received Christ's belief, bishop Birinus, who, by the advice of pope Honorius, came into Britain, preached to them and taught God's word. He promised him (*i. e. to Honorius*), that he would, in the farthest deals of the English kin, where no teacher had before come, sow the seed of the holy belief: then the pope bade hallow him, and sent him into Britain. Then came he first up⁵ among the West-Saxons, and there found them heathens; then it seemed to him better and more useful that he should preach and teach God's word there, than that he should go farther into Britain; and he then so did,—taught there divine lore, and turned the king to Christ's belief, and christened him, and after a space washed him in the bath of

2. Decayed for age.   3. In Alfred's day, Bebbanburg, from a queen Bebba.
4. The hand and arm—"It" (foregoing)—the hand. Has not *silvern* as good a liferent in our language as *golden, brazen*, &c.?
5. Came up [from the sea]—landed.

baptism, with his people of the West-Saxons. It befel at the same tide that the king was baptized, that there the holy and victorious [2] king of the Northumbrians, Oswald, was present,—he had bewedded him [3] his daughter to wife; he received and took him from the bath of baptism at the bishop's hand, as his godson by the divine office. Then both the kings gave and granted to the bishop a dwelling-place and a bishop-seat in Dorchester; and there the bishop lived to God, and built and hallowed a church; and by his pious toil turned many folk to the Lord: and he there ended his days and went to the Lord, and was buried in the same city; and many years afterwards bishop Hedde bade take up his body and bring to Winchester; and it was worshipfully laid in the church of the blessed apostles Peter and Paul.

2. After this then died king Kyneghils, and his son Kenwalch succeeded to his kingdom, who refused to receive the faith and the mystery of the heavenly king, and soon, after a short space, lost the might of the earthly kingdom. He also forlet Penda's sister, whom he had formerly taken to wife, and took him another wife. Then Penda led an expedition and an army on him, and bereft him of his kingdom. Then went he to the king of the East-English, who was called Anna, with whom he was three years an exile, and he there learnt and received the belief of the truth, and was baptized. For the king, with whom he was an exile, was a good man, and blessed with good and holy offspring, as we may again hereafter observe.

3. When he then Kenwalch was set in his kingdom again, then came to the West-Saxons a bishop from the Ireland, isle of the Scots, whose name was Aghilbert. He was of Gaulish kin, but for learning of the holy writings he was much tide 'wonning' in Ireland [4], the isle of the Scots; and he then wilsomely attached himself to the king, and taught him divine lore. When the king saw his 'learnedness' and his earnestness, then prayed he him that he would abide in his nation, and be their bishop, and he would look out for an honourable bishop-seat for him, and he yielded to his prayers, and was many years over that same nation

2. Holiest and most victorious *Alf.*—like many other superlatives in *A. S.* used as intensely high positives.
3. Affianced to him.—Wedding i. e. pledging preceded marriage,—as we have seen above, christening preceded baptism.
4. Won *to dwell* is scarcely old.—Ireland is here again Hibernia.

in bishoply authority. At last the king, who knew the speech of the Saxons only, was weary of his outlandish speech, and drew to West-Saxony another bishop, who knew his speech, who was called Wini, and he had been hallowed in the kingdom of the Gauls; and he then todealt the province of the West-Saxons into two bishopshires, and gave Wini a bishop-seat in Winton-caster.[1] Then was Aghilbert very wroth because the king had done so without his advice,—went then out of Britain, and returned to his own people in Gaul, and he there received a bishop-shire in his own city which is called [2] Parisiaca, and there, old and full of good deeds, he died. Then it came to pass not many years after his awaygoing from Britain, that Wini was driven by the same king from his bishop-seat; then went he to Wulfhere, king of the Mercians, and bought from him with fee the bishop-seat in London city, and was its bishop until the end of his days; and so the church of the West-Saxons was a long time without a bishop.

4. At the same time then likewise the foresaid king of that nation was often harassed by his foes with the heaviest wanings of his kingdom. Then at last it came to his mind, that his unfaithfulness formerly drove him from his kingdom, and again, when he learnt Christ's belief, he got back his kingdom; and then also understood that he had done wrong that the province was without a bishop, and that it was at the same time forsaken by divine help. Therefore he then sent into the kingdom of Gaul to bishop Aghilbert, and with humble supplication and entreaty prayed him, that he would return to the bishop-seat of his nation. Then he excused himself, and said, that he could not come hither, for as much as he had undertaken the bishop-shire of his own city, and yet for his earnest prayers, by which he sought his help, he sent to him Eleutherius,[3] his nephew, and said he could, if he wished it, ordain him as bishop to him, and he wist him worthy of it, in the merits of his life. And soon he was worshipfully received by the king and all the people; and they prayed Theodore, who then was archbishop of Canterbury church, that he would hallow him as bishop; and he then did so,

---

1. Winchester.—On the contrary we now have Lancaster, where 5 centuries ago was Lanchestre.
2. 'Urbs' understood, the city of the Parisii, i. e. Paris.
3. A mass-priest.

hallowed him in the same city, and he alone, after the doom of the whole synod, [during] many years, held and wielded the bishop-hood of the West-Saxon nation with much authority.

CHAPTER VIII.
That Erconbert king of Kent ordered idolatry to be overthrown; and of his daughter Ercongota and her kinswoman Ethelberga, maidens hallowed to God.

1. Then it was *(or befel)* about six hundred and forty winters from our Lord's incarnation, that Eadbald king of the Cantuarians departed from this life, and Erconbert his son took his kingdom to [himself], and nobly held and steered [1] it twenty-four years and one month. This king, first of English kings, ordered in all his kingdom to overthrow and [sted]-fastly forlet idolatry; and likewise by his royal authority [2] commanded the forty days' fast to be holden ere Easter " by wite," or under a penalty. The king's daughter, Ercongota, was a maiden of much virtue, as it became so noble a birth,—this maiden was serving the Lord in the monastery which was built in France by the noble abbess Fara, in the place which is called " In Brie." For at that time there were not yet many monasteries built in the English nation; and therefore many from Britain for the sake of monk-life were wont to seek the monasteries of the Franks, and of Gaul.[3] Likewise kings and great men sent their daughters thither to be taught, and to be wedded to the heavenly Bridegroom: and mostly in these monasteries, in Brie, and in Chelle, and in Andelys: among whom was Sethrith, wife's daughter of Anna, king of the East-English, and this same king's natural daughter Ethelburga, each of whom was outlandish there, and nevertheless for their life's earning (and meritorious conduct) were raised to that dignity, that they both were abbesses in the monastery in Brie. The same king's elder daughter Sexburga was the wife of Erconbert king of Kent, she had a daughter called Ercongota, of whom we are now speaking.

2. Of this maiden hallowed to God many works of ghostly virtues, and many a token of heavenly wonders, are wont to be told by the indwellers of that place. But we shall now hastily

---

1. Styrde—as a steer's (or helm's) man would a ship.—One month is the exact sense of sumne monath—though Bede says *aliquot menses*, several months.
2. Elderliness, *Alf*,—" elder," a ruler, chief or prince.
3. *Galliarum*, Gauls, i. e. provinces of Gaul, which is now called France, not so in the times of Bede or Alfred.

say a little about her death—how she sought the heavenly kingdom.—On the day on which her call[1] from this life drew nigh, then began she to go round the mynster-houses of the sick handmaids of Christ, and mostly of those who were of ripe[2] age, or were more and better in choiceness of their thews and way of life; and of them all humbly begged their prayers, and said and made known to them, that she had learnt in a vision that her end-day and forthfare was *(were)* very nigh. She told them that the vision or revelation was this like :—said that she saw a great troop of men *(people)* white and fair go into that same monastery, and that she then asked them what they sought, or what they would there. Then answered they and said, that they were sent thither to the [end] that they should take with them the golden medal which came thither out of Kent. Then was it in the utmost deal of the same night, that is when it began to dawn, that she overstept the darkness of this present world, and went to the upper light of heaven's kingdom; and many of the brethren of the same monastery, who were in other houses, said that they clearly heard a song of angels, and also heard the sound of a great multitude go into the church, and they soon arose and went out, [they] would know what it was: then saw they a great heavenly light coming there; the light loosed the holy soul from the bonds of the body, and led [it] to the everlasting joy of the heavenly country. And they added also, and told other wonders which were divinely shown in the same monastery, which now are too long to say. Then was buried the body of the worshipful maiden and Christ's bride in the church of St Stephen, the first and blessed martyr. Then it seemed [good] to the brethren on the third day after she was buried, that they would lay the stone, with which the grave was covered, higher and more becoming, in the same spot. When they did it away, then, came from the inside of the grave so much smell of sweetness, that it seemed to all the household, who there stood by, as if they had opened a storehouse of balm, and of the costliest[3] and sweetest spices that were in the world.

3. Likewise her aunt Ethelburga the beloved of God, of whom we spoke before, kept the glory of her perpetual purity and

---

1. Summons—*lit.* calledness —'gekighednes.'
2. Or, advanced—*provectæ*.
3. Lit. Dearworthest.

maidhood in great constraint of her body: what her virtue was, appeared after her death. When she was abbess, she began to build in her monastery a church in honour of all the holy apostles, in which she wished her body to be buried. But when the work of the church was nearly half wrought, then was she snatched away [1] by death, ere she might end it, and was buried in the same place of the church where she wished. Then after her death, the brethren took more care of other works, and forlet the building of the church seven years. When the seven years were fulfilled, then they settled firmly, that, on account of the immensity of the labour, they should altogether forlet the building of this church, and take up the bones of the Abbess, and lay them in another church, which was fully built and hallowed. And they then untined her grave, and found her body as unspotted and as sound as she was clean and unspotted from the corruption of bodily desire: and they washed the body again, and arrayed it in other clothes, and laid it in the church of the blessed martyr St Stephen. The reminding-day of the Abbess is celebrated till this time in that place with much honour, on the day which is named Nones (that is the 7th day) of July.

CHAPTER IX.

That in the place where king Oswald was slain, frequent wonder-works were done, and that there first a wayfaring man's beast was healed, and after that, a maiden that was formerly lame.

1. The most Christian king Oswald had the kingdom of the Northumbrians nine years, the year being reckoned to [them] in which the wildbeastly [2] wickedness of the king of the Britons, and the abominable apostasy of the English kings, came on, as we said before. When the run of these years was fulfilled, then was Oswald slain. A heavy and great battle was fought by the same heathen king, and the heathen nation of the Mercians, by whom also his foregoer Edwin was slain, in the place which is called Maserfield. And Oswald had of bodily age thirty-seven winters when he was slain, on the fifth day of the month [of] August.

2. What this king's faith and wilsomeness of mood towards God was, was shown after his death by wonders of virtues.[3] For

---

1. Foregrippen *lit.* i. e previously seized.
2. Wildeorlic—q ? wilderly, as wil-deor-ness, wilderness not wild-er-ness as some dream, but " will" now *wild*, " deor" *a beast*, ' with ness',—a state or condition fit for wild beasts.
3. Mægena wundrum, *Alf. miracles.*

in the place where he fought for his country with his men, and was slain by the heathens, there, until the present day, healings of sick men and beasts are celebrated. Thence it befel, that many men took that same mould where his body fell, and put it in water, and gave it to their sick men and beasts to drink, and soon it was well with them; and men did that so often stickmeal, that they took the mould, till there a deep pit was dolven, that a man might stand in up to the neck. Nor is it much to be wondered that sick men received health at the place of his death, since he always, while he lived, was kind to the sick and needy, and gave alms, and was their helper in their sores. And many wonders of virtues were told, which befel in that place, yea of moulds¹ which were taken in that place; but it will be enough for us now, that we hear two or three.

3. It befel not much time after his slaughter that a man was riding by the spot, when his horse began suddenly to weary and stand still, leaned its head on the earth, and the foam went out of the mouth, and the unmeted sore waxed and grew great until it (*the horse*) fell on the earth; then the horseman lighted, and drew the bridle off, and abode there a while until his horse should be better, or he should leave it there dead. Then was it long with heavy sore much tossed, and wound and twisted itself in various directions, when suddenly it came upon the spot where the memorable king was slain, nor was there elding [*delay*] then, till the sore was stilled, and it stayed from the unhealthy stirring of the limbs, and, in the wonted way of horses after weariness, began to wallow, and often warp itself over on either side, and soon arose thoroughly hale and sound, and began greedily to eat the grass.²

4. When the man saw that, then understood he by sharp wisdom, that something of wonderful holiness was in the spot where his horse was so quickly healed, and he there set a token and marked the spot, and leapt on his horse and rode whither he ere had meant. When he then came to the man whom he would seek [*call upon*,] then found he there a maiden, who was niece of the householder whom he sought; and she was sorely borne down by

---

1. Particles of earth—in Scotland still called *mools*.
2. Without much straining of either text or translation, the whole paragraph is modernized in Saxon, except three words, " various directions—memorable." Meted (see Matt. vii. 2,) is English for measured, therefore "unmeted" corresponds to *immensus*—and "warp" is the same as *throw*, as *warp* or *throw* on a web, *silk-thrower*, &c.

a long ailing of lame-sickness.² Then the inmates began to sigh before him for the bitter unhealthiness of the maiden, then he began to tell of the spot where his horse was healed. Well! they soon made a wain ready, and set the maiden in, and led to the spot, and there set her [down]. When she then was set on the spot, then was she weary and slept there a little. As soon as she awoke, then felt she that she was healed of her bodily unsoundness, and asked for water, and washed her, and rid her hair, clothed herself with a sheet, and, with the men who led her thither, walked home on her feet hale and sound.

CHAPTER X.
That the dust of the same spot was good against fire.

1. Likewise at the same time another man, said to have been from the nation of the Britons, was going by the same spot on which the foresaid fight was done. Then he saw part of one spot greener and fairer than the others; then he began with a wise mind to think and muse, that [for] no other sake was the greenness and fairness of that spot, unless that there some man a little holier than the other host had been slain. Then he took some deal of the mould on the spot, bound it in his sheet,— thought that the same mould might be for the leechdom and healing of unhealthy men; and he again went forth on his way. Then came he to a house at even-tide, and went into the house where the housefolk was all gathered to a banquet; and he was taken in by the lord of the house, and they gave him a seat; and he sat with them at the banquet. He hanged the sheet with the mould which he brought on a stud (or peg) in the wall; and there was a great fire kindled in the middle of the house. Whilst they banqueted there long, and were drunken; and the sparks flew up to the house's roof which was wound with twigs and covered with thatch, then it befel that the house was all fired within and began to burn. When the banqueters saw that, then flew they out frightened, and could make no help to the burning house, but it clean forburnt, all but the stud on which the mould hung, which stood and abode sound and untouched by the fire. Then they wondered greatly, and thoughtfully sought what that was owing to; then it was made known to

2. Or lame lair,—Alfred's definition of palsy. For "elding or *delay*" we might say "loss of time."

them that thereon hung the mould which was taken on the spot where king Oswald's blood was shed. Then were these wonders far and wide much talked of and made known; and many men afterwards daily sought the spot, and there began to take the gift of health to themselves and their friends.

CHAPTER XI.
That over his remains the heavenly light was all night overstanding and shining, and that devil-sick [men] were healed at his remains.

1. Among these things it is not to be left untold, what a heavenly wonder and virtue was shown when his bones were found [and met with], and brought to the church where they are now holden [and preserved]. This was brought about through the care of Osthrida queen of the Mercians, who was the daughter of his brother Oswy, who after him got the kingdom of the Northumbrians.

2. [There] is a noble monastery in Lindsey named Beardanea, which monastery the same queen, with her husband Ethelred, mightily loved, reverenced and worshipped, in which she wished to hold the worshipful bones of her uncle. When the wain in which the bones were brought came into the foresaid monastery, then the inmates who were in the monastery would not willingly take them in. For though they wist him holy, yet because he was of another province, and got the kingdom over them, they pursued him, even when dead, with old feuds. Then it happened the same night, that the bones brought [thither] stayed without, and only a tilt[1] was spread over them. But the appearance of a heavenly wonder shewed how worshipfully they were to be received by all the faithful. For all the night there stood as it were a bright sun-beam high up to heaven, which one might clearly see from almost all places of Lindsey. On the morrow when it was day, then the brethren of the monastery who had formerly gainsaid [it], began earnestly to beg that the holy and God-beloved reliques might be holden by them. And they then washed the bones and did them into a chest, and so set them in the church with becoming honour. And that the kingly rank of the holy man might have everlasting remembrance, his banner

---

1. An awning,—from teld, teild, tild. The martial pastime of *tilting* was so named, because the combatants took to the *tented* field.

which was adorned with gold and purple was set over his tomb,[1] and the same water that they washed the bones with, they poured into a corner of the church. From that time it happened that the same earth which received the worshipful bath was good for the healing of fiendsick men and of other unsoundnesses.

3. It befel in afterfollowing tide, when the foresaid queen was dwelling in the same monastery, then came a worshipful Abbess to her, who was called Ethilhild, [and] was sister of the holy men Ethelwin and Aldwin; the one of whom was bishop in Lindsey, the other was abbot in the monastery which is called Portanea[2], not far from which was the monastery of the abbess. When she then had come to the queen, and they had spoken, and then among other things spoke about Oswald,—quoth the abbess that she saw that night the light over his bones high up to heaven; quoth the queen that from the mould of the floor, on which the water of the bones' washing was poured, many sick men had been healed. And she then begged that they would give her some deal of the healing mould, and they did so; and she wound it in a cloth and put it in a chest, and fared her[3] home. Then in afterfollowing time, when she was in her monastery, thither came a guest who was often in the night time on a sudden heavily afflicted by an unclean ghost. When he had been kindly taken in and after his evening meal would rest him; then was he suddenly grippen by a devil, and began to cry and shout, and "gristbite" with his teeth; and the foam went out of his mouth: and he began to twist his limbs by diverse stirrings. When no man then could hold nor bind him, then one of the attendants ran and knocked[4] at the gate, and told the abbess, and she quickly untined the gate of the monastery, and went with one of her handmaids to the men's place, and called the mass-priest to her, that he might go with her to the unsound man. When they came thither, they saw there many men with him, who were carefully trying to still his madness, but they could not. The mass-priest sang and read prayers, which were written for that illness, and did those things which he knew to be best against it; and he however did no good by that. When none of

---

1. Tumbam, Bd.—byrigenne, *Alf.* q! shrine.
2. Peartaneu, Bd. which is the reading of some editions in § 2 where Smith gives Beardanea, Lat. *Beardaneu*.
3. That is, conveyed herself, *or* went her way.
4. *Lit.* slew a token—struck a sign or signal.

them could find any help for him, then suddenly the foresaid mould came into the abbess's mind. Then she quickly bade her handmaid go and fetch her the chest in which the mould was; when she then with the chest went into the court of the house in which the fiend-sick man was writhing, then he suddenly became silent, and leaned his head as if he would sleep, and set his limbs in stillness. Then they all became silent and were still, and anxiously waited [to see] what the thing would come to. Then after a little while he sat up, and heavily sighed, and said, "Now I think soundly; now I recover the wits of my mind." Then they earnestly asked him how that befel. He said, "As soon as the maiden with the chest which she bore came nigh the court of this house, then all the accursed ghosts which afflicted and oppressed me went away and left me, and nowhere afterwards appeared." Then the abbess gave him a dole of the mould, and the mass-priest read prayers, and they prayed for him; and he rested him all night hale and sound; and then from that time the accursed ghosts durst not greet or assail him with any awe nor with any vexation.

CHAPTER XII.
That at his tomb a little boy was healed of a Lent-illness or Spring-fever.

1. In time following after these things, a boy in the monastery at Beardanea was heavily afflicted with a lingering Lent-illness (*or ague.*) Then it was *so* one day that he was sorrowfully waiting when the illness would come to him. Then one of the brethren went in to him and said, "Wilt thou, my child, that I teach thee how thou mayest be healed from the heaviness of this illness? arise and go to church, to the body of the holy Oswald, and sit there and remain quiet, and see thou go not out thence ere the illness be gone from thee, then will I come to thee and lead thee thence home." Then he did as he taught him, went to sit at the holy man's body, then the sickness did not come to him that day, but it went from him so dreading, that neither on the second day nor on the third, nor over that since, durst it touch him a whit. One of the brethren came thence, quoth Bede, and told me that thus it was done; and said also that the same brother was yet living in the monastery in which, when he was a boy, this wonder of healing was done. Nor was it then to be wondered

though this king's prayers, when he was reigning with the Lord, had power with him and were effectual, since he formerly, whilst he held this temporary kingdom, was more wont always to strive and to beseech God for the everlasting kingdom.

2. Men said it who knew it, that from the time of the early laud-song until bright day he stood and continued in prayers, and for the frequent custom of his prayers, wheresoever he sat, his wont was that he held his hands upreared over his knees, and always said the Lord God thank for his goodness. It was likewise celebrated and turned into the custom of a song (*or proverb* [1]) that he also amidst the words of a prayer ended his life; for when he was thronged about with weapons and with foes, and he himself understood that he must be slain, then prayed he for the souls of his host; of which they have thus said in song:—

"Lord God, have mercy on the souls of our men,"
Quoth the holy Oswald, when he sank to the earth [again].[2]

3. His bones were also brought, and holden in the monastery which we formerly spoke of at Beardanea. Moreover the king who slew him, bade set his head upon a stake; and he bade hang to it his hand with the arm that was struck off his body. Then after a year's space, the afterfollower of his reign, his kinsman Oswy, came with an army, and took them there, and brought his head to Lindesfarne and there buried it in a church, and his head with the arm are holden in the kingly city of Bamborough.

CHAPTER XIII.

That in Ireland [3] a man was recovered from the article [4] of death by his (Oswald's) reliques.

1. The fame of this noble man not only shone throughout all the bounds of Britain, but likewise the fame of his wonders came by south the sea, into Germany, and also the parts of Ireland, [3] the isle of the Scots. For the venerable bishop Acca was wont often to say, that when he was going to Rome, and was staying with Wilbrord the holy bishop of the Friesians, he frequently

---

1. Proverbii Bd.—gyddes, *Alf.* The old English or Saxon proverbs were all metrical, as also their historians were all Bards or Scopas. See Orosius *A. S.* l. v. 1. where Pompeius (Trogus) and Justin are introduced "singing."—A stumbling-block to the hon. Daines Barrington.
2. Probably thus:—Miltsa, Drihten God, Minra leoda saulum, Cwæð se halga Oswald, a he on eorðan sah.
3. Hiberniâ, *Alf.*
4. Articulo, *Bd.*—liþe, *Alf.* a joint.

heard him, in that province, speak of the wonders which were done at the bones of the worshipful king.

2. The bishop likewise said, "that when he then yet was a mass-priest in Ireland, and there lived in pilgrimage for the love of the kingdom of heaven, he there in that island heard the report of his holiness often spoken of, far and wide; then may we now tell one wonder which he told among many others. He said, that, in the time of the great pestilence and mortality which wasted and for-harrowed the isles of Britain and Ireland with much havock; then was struck by the calamity of the same pestilence, among many others, a learning-man in the school of the Scottish kin. This man was well skilled in the scriptures, but, about the care of his eternal salvation, he was too slothful and too reckless. When he then saw that he was nigh death, then began he to fear and dread (him),[1] that, as soon as he were dead, he should, for earnings of his sins, be dragged to the locks (and bars) of hell. He cried and called me, as I was in his neighbourhood, and, amid sickly sobbings, with a frightened and weeping voice, was speaking and sighing, and thus to me quoth, "Lo! you see that this illness, and this heaviness of my body greatly waxes, so that I must needs quickly undergo death. I doubt not then aught that after the death of the body I shall quickly be dragged to the everlasting death of my soul, and be subject to the torments of hell, because, for a long time, amid the study of divine learning, I gave myself to sins and vices, more than to God's commandments. I have it now fast in my mind, if the Mercy above us will give me any space to live, that I will forsake my wicked ways, and stedfastly turn my mind and life to the precepts of the Divine Will. I wot for sooth[2] that it is not of my earning, that I may obtain longer time to live, or may hope to obtain it, unless God will shew mercy to me wretched and unworthy, through help of those who have faithfully served him. We have heard, and the report is most widely spread, that there was in your province a king, of wonderful holiness, called Oswald, the highness of whose faith[3] and virtue shone and brightened after his death likewise, in the working of frequent wonders. I pray thee, oh, if thou have any of his reliques with

1. Him, i. e. to or for himself.
2. English as good and clear as "I know for true."
3. Of which king's belief. *Alf*.

thee, that thou give [it] me, it may easily be that the Lord will have mercy on me through his merits." "Then I answered him," quoth he, "I have a dole of the tree on which his head was set when he was slain, and if thou with a steadfast heart believest, then may the divine mercy, through the earning of so great a man, both give thee a longer space of this life, and also make thee worthy of an ingoing to the everlasting life." He was not then lingering, but soon answered and said, that he had fast and sound belief in these things. Then I hallowed water, and put in [it] scrapings of the foresaid tree, and gave the sick man to drink. And soon it was better with him, and he was strengthened, and recovered from the sickness, and he lived a long time after that, and with all his heart and deeds turned steadfastly to God; and wheresoever he came, he told and published to all men the mercy of the gracious Creator, and the honour of his faithful servant.

CHAPTER XIV.

That bishop Paulinus being dead, Ithamar received the bishop-seat at Rochester, for him; and of the wonderful humility of king Oswin, who was cruelly slain by Oswy.

1. When Oswald was led to the heavenly kingdom, then his brother Oswy received the seat of the earthly kingdom after him. He had thirty winters when he got the kingdom, and toilsomely held and had it eight and twenty winters. [There] fought and strove against him Penda, the king, and the heathen nation of the Mercians, as also his own son Elfrith, and his brother, the son of Ethelwald, who had the kingdom before him. Then (was) in the second year of his reign (that) the venerable father Paulinus, who long before was bishop in York city, and then was in Rochester, died and went to the Lord, the sixth day of the Ides [2d day] of October, nineteen winters and two months and one and twenty days after he received bishophood; and he was buried in the church of St Andrew the apostle, which king Ethelbert ordered to be built in the same Rochester. In that place Honorius, the archbishop, hallowed Ithamar, who was of the Kentish people, but in his life and in his learning he was like his foregoers.

2. King Oswy had in the earliest times of his reign an even-sharer [1] of the kingly dignity, whose name was Oswin of king

---

1. *Lit.* " even-lotter," or say " lot-fellow," *consors*, Bd.

Edwin's kin,—he was the son of Osrie, of whom we have spoken before. Oswin was seven winters king of the Deiri in the greatest abundance of all things, and was an upright and pious man, and therefore beloved by all his people; but, notwithstanding that, he could not have peace with the king who had the other share of the Northumbrian kingdom, that is of the Bernicians; but so great dissension and strife arose between them, that they gathered their hosts and their troops together. When Oswin saw that he could not war against him, because he had more help and more might, then he thought of more useful things, and deemed that he should waive the fight, and hold himself to better times. He then dismissed his host, and commanded that every man should go home—from the place which is named Wilfaresdun (or -hill), which is ten miles right west from the village Cataract. Then he turned with one attendant whom he reckoned most trusty, whose name was Tondhere, to the house of Earl Hunwald (whom he formerly believed to be most friendly to him), because he would hide himself there. But it was far otherwise; for the same earl betrayed him there with his foresaid attendant; and he was there hatefully killed through Ethelwin the reeve or steward [of king Oswy].[1] This was done the thirteenth day of the Kalends of September, (12*th of August*,) the ninth year of Oswy's reign, in the place which is called Ongetlingum, where after a space, for the sake of cleansing this wickedness, a monastery was built, in which, for the loosing of either king's soul, both of the slain, and his who bade slay him, prayers and supplications should be daily offered to the Lord.

3. King Oswin was both fair in countenance, and tall in body, and winsome[2] in speech, and mild in manners, and munificent to all—both noble and ignoble. Thence it befel, that for his kingliness both of mind and countenance, and for the worth of his merit, he was loved by all men, and on every side almost, out of all these provinces, the noblest men always came to his retinue and to his service.

4. Amidst the other virtue and moderation of this king, the glory of a singular blessing is likewise told,—that he was [a man] of the greatest humility, as we may by one example clearly know. He gave and granted the best horse and of the fairest

---

1. So Bede, but Alfred makes Ethelwin the earl's steward.
2. Pleasant—(a fine old word—see Hamilton of Bangor's " Braes o' Yarrow.'

hue to bishop Aidan, though he was more wont to go [on foot] than to ride, that he might, however, on it override the fords when he came to any river, or if any need befel that he should go more hastily. Then [was] after a little time when he was sitting on the horse, [that] a needy man came towards him, and asked alms of him; then he soon alighted, and bade give the needy man the horse, with the kingly trappings which stood on it; for he was very merciful, and attentive to the needy, and as it were a father of the wretched. When this was told to the king, as they were going to their dinner, he said to the bishop, "Why wouldest thou, sir bishop, give the needy man the kingly horse, which it became thee to have as thy own. But had not we many another uncomelier horse, and of another kind, which we might bestow as a gift to the needy, though thou gave them not the horse which I chose especially for thy possession?" Then the bishop quickly answered him and said, "What sayest thou, king? Is the son of a mare[1] dearer to thee than the child of God?"[2] When they had thus spoken, they then went in to dinner, and the bishop went [and] sat in his place on his seat.

5. The king then, because he had come from hunting, stood at the fire and warmed him with his attendants; and then suddenly, amid the warming, he remembered the word which the bishop had [just] before said to him, he ungirt then his sword and gave it to his attendant, and then stept hastily before the bishop, and fell at his feet, and prayed that he would be blithe to him, and said, "Never over this will I speak a whit more, or deem what thou give or how much of our fee thou give to God's children." When the bishop saw the king's humility so great, then dreaded he greatly, and hastily arose towards him, and raised him up, and promised that he would be very blithe to him, and earnestly besought him that he would go to his seat, and sit to his dinner, and lay sorrow aside from his heart. When the king then by the bishop's command and request had recovered [his] cheerfulness, then began the bishop on the other hand to be sorrowful, and so sorrowful was, that he began to weep with bright tears. Then his mass-priest inquired and asked him in his own tongue, which the king knew not, nor his courtiers,—why he wept. Quoth he, "I wot that this king will not live long after this; for I never ere this saw so humble a king: therefore I understand that he must

1. Myran sunu.   2. Thæt Godes bearn.

soon go from this life; and this people is not worthy that they [should] have such a ruler and king." Nor was it a long space after, that the bishop's dire foretelling was fulfilled, when the king was killed by a hateful murder, as we said before. Yea also the same bishop Aidan, not more than the twelfth day after the slaying of the king whom he loved, that is the day before the kalends of September, (31*st of August,*) was led from this world, and received an everlasting meed of his labours from the Lord.

CHAPTER XV.
That bishop Aidan foretold the coming storm to the shipfaring [men], and also gave them hallowed oil, with which they might still the storm.

1. And of what merit this bishop was, the inward Judge, Almighty God, likewise made known to men by tokens of wonders; but it is now enough for us, that we tell three out of many, for the sake of keeping him in mind. There was a venerable mass-priest, whose name was Utta—he was a man of great steadiness and truth; and therefore was loved and honoured by all, yea by the great men of this world; he was also at one time sent to Kent, that he might fetch, as wife to king Oswy, Eanfleda, the daughter of king Edwin, who had been led thither formerly, when her father was slain. Then he determined and planned that he would take his way thither by land, and return home with the maiden by ship-voyage.[2] Then went the mass-priest to bishop Aidan, and asked him that he should pray for him, and make supplication to God for his companions, and for their health and safety, when they should go so great a journey. Then he did so—prayed for them and blessed them, and commended [them] to God;[3] he likewise gave the mass-priest hallowed oil, and said to him, " I wot that as soon as ye go on ship-board, over you will come a great storm and roughness, and a contrary wind will rise; but mind thou that thou send this oil, which I now give thee, into the sea, and instantly the winds will be still, and calmness of the sea will follow after, and will let you come blithe on your desired voyage home.

2. And all these things befel and were fulfilled in order, as the

1. Se inlica, who is within.
2. *Lit.* shiplode—leading or course of a ship.
3. *Lit.* bade to God—bade them a-Dieu!

bishop had foretold. And first, as soon as they went into the ship and passed out, contrary winds arose, and the waves of the sea boiled and maddened. Then began the thralls[1] and the shipmen to draw up the anchors, and to send them into the sea, they would fasten the ship with [them]; although they did this, they sped naught by it; but the waves boiled and swept about, and filled the ship on every side, [so] that they had no hope of safety, but all saw death itself present to them. Then at last the mass-priest called to mind the bishop's words, took then his phial, and sent some deal of the oil into the sea, and instantly, as it had been foretold, the sea stilled itself from the boiling. And thus it was brought about that the man of God, by the spirit of prophecy, foresaw the storm to-come, and through virtue of the same spirit, when the storm came up, he allayed and stilled it, though he was bodily absent there. The order of this miracle no doubting man told, but the most truthful mass-priest of our church, called Kynemund, said this to me; he said that he heard it from the same mass-priest Utta, in whom and through whom this wonder was fulfilled.

CHAPTER XVI.
That the same bishop by his prayers turned away the fire [that was] set to the kingly city.

1. Moreover many who knew it well, tell another memorable wonder of the same father, which befel in the time of his bishophood, that Penda, king of the Mercians, led an army into Northumberland, and robbed and harried it far and wide with cruel havock. Then came he at last to the kingly city which is named Bamborough. When he then saw that the city was so fast that he could not break into it nor take it, either by fight or by blockade, then would he burn it up with fire; he then tore asunder all the villages about the city, which he found in its neighbourhood, and bore to the city, and gathered a great pile of beams, and rafters, and walls, and wattles, and thatch, and with all these surrounded the city to a great height, on the quarter at which it is joined to the land. When the wind blew right on the city, then he kindled the pile and would burn up the city.

2. Then at that time the venerable bishop Aidan was in the island which is named Farne, that is two miles from the foresaid

---

1. Galley-slaves? Needlings, *Alf.* from *need* compulsion.

city, where the man of God was wont very oft to go into the island, because he desired there in secret to go about ¹ his prayers and to serve God. Likewise in the same island, always to the present day, a servant of God dwelt in a lonely seat. ² When he then, the bishop—saw that the pile was kindled, and the wind drove the fire and the smoke into the city over the walls, it is said that he then hove his eyes and his hands up to heaven, and with tears called and said, "Lord see how much evil Penda worketh!" These words thus spoken, the wind soon warped itself from the borough, and drove the fire on those who before were kindling it, so that some of them were hurt by the fire, and all so much frightened that they durst not any further fight against the borough, for they knew that God shielded it.

CHAPTER XVII.

1. When death drove this holy bishop to the utmost day of his life, that he must go from the body, he was in a dwelling-house of the king's not far from the foresaid borough, for he there had a church and a rest-house (or bed-chamber,) and it was his custom that he often dwelt there, and thence then went on every side thereabout, to teach right belief, and to exhort: which it was likewise his custom to do at other dwelling-seats of the king, as it might more easily be ; for he had naught of his own but his church, and thereto four acres. ³ The men who then waited on him, pitched a tilt on the west half of the church, fast on the church, that he might rest him therein. And then it befel that the holy bishop leaned him to one of the studs which were set to the church, to prop it up, and there then gave [up] his ghost. He died in the seventeenth year of his bishop-hood, on the kalends *(or first day)* of September, and his body was brought to the island which is named Lindesfarne, and buried in the lyke-town ⁴ of the brethren. And then after a space of years, when a greater church was built there, and hallowed in name of the blessed apostle St Peter, then were the foresaid bishop's bones brought thither, [and] were worthily holden on the right half of

1. This literal rendering of "begangan" is still in use in *Sc.* "To go about worship" (in the family) is in *Eng.* "to say (or read) prayers."
2. *Lit.* anchorite-settle.
3. The text is most erroneously pointed here in the printed copy.
4. That is a corpse-yard or body-enclosure. Lyke-wake is still in use for corpse-watching.

the altar, as it well became so venerable a bishop. And Finan afterfollowed him in the bishop-hood, who came from Hii, an isle of the Scots (*Irish*), and abode in the bishop-hood many years. And then it befel after many years that Penda king of the Mercians sought the same place with all his army; and when he destroyed with weapons and with fire every thing that he could reach, then was also the country-seat in which the foresaid bishop died, and the church, burnt up; but in a most wonderful manner the prop-stud alone, upon which the holy bishop [was] leaning [when he] died, stood untouched by the fire, when all the church and the other building were forburnt. This wonder being known a church was soon reared there again, and the foresaid prop-stud was set as a prop to the wall, as it was before. And it then again befel after a space through heedlessness, that the same country-seat was burnt, and the church, and yet the flame could not touch the stud, but most wonderfully the fire went along the nails with which the stud was fastened to the wall, through the holes, and touched not the stud. And the third time a church was built there, and they did not set the stud without, as they did before, as a prop to the wall, but they set it in the church. In mind of this wonder it is also known that at the same time many men fetched healing of their bodies in the place; many men also carved splints from the same stud, and then for whatsoever sick men had need, scraped them into water, and thence many men were healed through it.

3. Truly I have written this about the works of the foresaid man, but nevertheless it liked me not in him, that he held not nor wist aright the observance of Easter, but I greatly loathed it, as I have most clearly shown in the book which I made *de Temporibus*.[1] But I, as a truth-telling historian, have written the things which were done concerning him or through him; and the things that herein were worthy I have praised. He had very great care of peace, and sooth-love (*or charity*), and continence, and humility: he had in him neither anger nor pride; neither avarice nor vain glory reigned in him; but he had the wisdom to keep and to teach God's commandments, and he had the carefulness to read the holy writings and to go about wakes; and he had priest-becoming authority to rebuke the proud and the

---

1. Of Times.—The treatise is published in the original Latin among Bede's other works.

wealthy; and he had mildheartness[1] to comfort the sick and the needy. Thus I now say in few words about that which they said who knew him, that of every thing that is commanded in holy books to be holden, he left naught [undone] through carelessness, but he fulfilled it all as far as he could. These things in the foresaid bishop I greatly love, for I doubt not they please God; that he did not hold Easter at its right tide, because he either wist not its set times; or, though he wist it, for the authority of his own nation, cared not for it. I praise him not in the celebration of Easter, although he nether believed nor worshipped nor preached aught other, but the same that we; that is, the loosing (and redemption) of mankind, through the suffering,[2] and resurrection, and ascension into the heavens, of the Mediator of God and men, the man Jesus Christ. Nor held he Easter, as some men ween, with Jews, on the fourteenth night of the moon, whatever day of the week, but aye always on Sunday, from fourteen nights of the moon to twenty nights, for the belief of our Lord's resurrection; which resurrection he believed to have been on one of the restdays; and also for the hope of our future resurrection, which he, with the holy and right-believing assembly,[3] truly believed to be to-come on one of the rest-days, which now is named Sunday.

CHAPTER XVIII. (MS. B.)

At this time, after Earpwald, Redwald's son, Sighebert, his brother, a very good and pious man, held the kingdom of the East-English. This Sighebert, when he was an exile in Gaul, fleeing Redwald's fiendship, there then received baptism, and returned to his birth-land, and got the kingdom. And soon he wished to imitate the things which he saw gone about in Gaul, that is, the right belief; he set up a school, and in it he let boys be taught, with the help of bishop Felix, whom he had brought from Kent, and he set them teachers after the way of the Kentish men. So much the king loved the heavenly kingdom, that he at last left the earthly kingdom, and entrusted it to Ecgric his kinsman, who

---

1. Better late than never—Alfred's *misericordia*, (for which we have *mercy*,) or his *clementia*.
2. "Throing, againrising, and upstighing." Old Eng.—From *stig*, or *stigh*, we have *stile, stairs, stirrup*, &c.—while birth and death alike remind us of *throes*.
3. "Orthodox church" of other phraseology.

also had some share of the kingdom; and then went into the monastery which he had built for himself, and received the tonsure, and in the monastery fought for the heavenly kingdom.

2. When he had long done this, it befel, that the nation of the Mercians, through leading of Penda their king, would fight against the East-English. When the East-English saw that they had less help than their foes, then prayed they Sighebert, that he would go with them to the fight, and encourage and embolden their forces. When he refused, and said that he would not [do] that, then took they him from the monastery, and led him by force with them to the fight, that they might be the bolder and more fearless, and have the less thought of flight, as they had so good and so noble a man with them. But he was most mindful of the vow which he had vowed to God; and even then when he was ringed about by his foes, he would take nothing in his hand but his own rod only, and he then was there slain with king Ecgric, and of their army much was there slain by the heathen; and the whole dispersed.

3. And Anna, the son of Eni, then took to the kingdom after them: he was also of the kingly kin, and was a very noble man, and begat very noble children, of whom we will again speak further in this book; and this Anna, king of the East-English, was also slain by Penda, king of the Mercians.

CHAPTER XIX.

1. Whilst Sighebert then yet held the kingdom, [there] came from Hibernia the isle of the Scots a holy man whose name was Furseus, who was in words and in deeds bright and shining; likewise he was in noble virtues become famous; he wished, wheresoever he could find a suitable place, to live in pilgrimage for the love of God. Then he came into the nation and province of the East-English, and he was by the foresaid king honourably received; and he soon followed the work which was his wonted care, that he taught gospel lore, and by the example of his virtue, and the encouragement of his word, he persuaded many unbelievers to the faith of Christ.

2. Then he was there afflicted with some infirmity of his body, in which he earned that he brooked an angelic vision, in which he was admonished that he should earnestly insist upon the

begun ministry of the divine word, and carefully observe his wonted wakes and prayers; because certain death awaited him, and uncertain the time of the same death, of which the Lord hath said, "Watch ye, for ye know not the day nor the hour." Then was the man of God encouraged by the vision,—began then hastily to build the places of the monastery, which he had received from the foresaid king, and held it with regular discipline. Then was a fair monastery built in a wood nigh the sea, in a city [1] which was named in English Knoversborough. [2] Afterwards Anna, the king of the province, and many noble men, adorned and honoured the borough [3] with high buildings and gifts. This man Furseus was of the noblest kin of the Scots, but far much [4] nobler he was in his mind than in worldly birth; and from the very time of his boyhood he had great care of holy learning and likewise of monastic discipline; and, what most becomes holy men, all that he learned to do, he heedfully toiled to hold.

3. Then it was in forthgoing time, that he built him a sunderly dwelling,[5] that he might in it freely serve God. There he was seized with an infirmity of body, as the book saith which was written about his life, and clearly shews that he was led out of the body, and, from evening until cockcrowing, was unclothed of his body, and saw a host of angels and their countenances; and he earned that he also heard the holy praisings, how they lauded and praised God. He was wont to say that he openly heard them, among many other songs, shout and sing: *Ibunt sancti de virtute in virtutem, videbitur Deus deorum in Sion:* The holy [ones] shall go from strength into strength, the God of saints shall be seen in the beauty-view.[6] Then was he led back into the body, and on the third day was again led out of the body, and saw not only the greater joy of the blessed ghosts, but also the greatest stripes and war of the accursed ghosts. Then those accursed ghosts strove against him, and by frequent accusations

---

1. Ceastre, *Alf.* castro, BD.—"area of a castle," *Giles.*
2. Cneoferisburh, *Alf.* Cnobherisburg, BD. The *f* of Wessex, and the *bh* of the Scoto-Irish, here adopted by BD, had the sound of our *v*. Thus heaven, A. S. heofon, is heben in an early specimen of Northumbrian English. See Cædmon in the Ely MS. and BD, IV, 24, 3.
3. Bede says the monastery.
4. Sic *Alf.*   5. For Alfred's sunderly wic, (monasterium, BD,) we might say a "several house," as in 2 Chr. xxvi, 21.
6. Wlite sceawung, Alf. seeing of beauty, *or* of majesty—his version of "Sion." See Ps. lxxxiv, 17.

endeavoured to forset and shut up the heavenly way to him; however they sped naught in that, but the angels shielded him.

4. Whilst he was then uphoven on high, then was he bidden by the angels that led him, that he should look on this earth; and he then bowed his eyes, and looked hither on these netherly things: then saw he as [it were] a dark den only set beneath him. He saw also four fires kindled in the 'lift' or air, at no great distance apart among themselves. Then asked he the angels what those fires were. Quoth they, These are the fires which are burning and wasting the earth. One is, in the first place, the fire of a lie, that is, that we fulfill not that which we promise at baptism, that we renounce the devil and all his works. The second is the fire of unright wishing, that is when we foreset and prefer the wealth of this world, and think it more to be loved than the love of the heavenly blessedness. The third is the fire of unpeace or strife, that is when we fear not lest we anger the mind of neighbours for idle things. The fourth is the fire of wickedness, that is when we think it nothing to us, that we rob and plunder the wretched of their possessions and their goods. Then waxed the fires mightily, and joined and gathered themselves together, till they were united and collected into one immense flame. When the fire then drew near him, then was he greatly dreading him, and affrighted, and said to the angel, "My lord, behold the fire comes mighty near me." And he then answered him and said, "What thou hast not kindled before, that will not burn thee; for though this fire is seen great and awful, yet it deemeth and burneth every one after the earning of his works, for every one's unright wishing shall burn in this fire. For if any man burns strongly in the body through unlicensed pleasure, so he again, loosed from the body, shall burn by due punishment."

5. Then saw he one of the three angels, who were his leaders in each vision,[1] going before into the flame to deal the fire, and the twain flew on two sides of him, and shielded him from the peril of the fire. He saw likewise the accursed ghosts flying through the fire, and they raised the burning of wars against the righteous, and they also were against them, and uttered accusations and evil speeches against [him]. But there was a greater

---

1. The text is much corrupted here; "wæron" and wæs have changed places and "leader" stands instead of "leaders."

sight of good ghosts and of the heavenly hosts, who shielded him. Likewise he there met and knew holy men of his kin, who formerly were nobly endowed with priesthood, and had a report that they diligently obeyed God, from whom he heard many things, which, to himself and also to all who would hear them, were very wholesome to know. When they then had ended their words and speech, and likewise returned with the angelic ghosts to heaven, then tarried with the blessed Furseus the three angels of whom we spoke before. When they then again came nigh the foresaid great fire, then the angel again todealt the flame of the fire before him, as he did before; but as soon as the man of God came to the open door betwixt the flames, then the unclean ghosts caught one of the men whom they were burning and torturing in the fire, and hurled him, thus burning, on him, and he touched his shoulders and his cheek, and they burnt him so. Then he knew the man; and it came to his mind that he received his clothing when he died. Then the angel quickly took the man, [and] hurled him into the fire. Then said the accursed fiend, "Why shove ye back the man whom ye formerly received? For as ye formerly received his sinful goods, so ye ought to be partakers of his punishment." Then the angel gainsaid him, "Nay," quoth he, "he did not receive his goods for greediness; but because he would save his soul." And then the fire ceased from him. Then the angel turned to him and said, "What thou kindledst, that burneth against thee, for if thou hadst not received this man's goods who died in his sins, his fire would not burn against thee." And the angel spoke many things to him, and with wholesome words taught him, what was to be done about the salvation of those who at the death repented of their sins.

6. And then after a little space [he] was sent back into the body, and all his life's tide, bore on his shoulder and on his cheek the token of the burning which he underwent in his soul; as might be seen by all men, and, in a wonderful way, found that the body openly shewed forth what the soul had suffered in secret. Then the man of God took care, as he was wont to do before, always earnestly, both to shew by examples, and to preach by words, to all men the works of virtue. And the order of his visions he would make known to those men only who questioned and asked him, for the lust of contrition, and the love of heaven's

kingdom. [There] is now yet an old brother living, of our monastery, who said and quoth to me, who wrote this book, that a very pious and respectable man told him, that he saw (the) Furseus in the province of the East-English·(kingdom), and then heard his sights from his *own* (self's) mouth, and then yet eked to, that it was winter's tide and the winter was grim and cold and frosty, and with ice ybound; quoth he, that the holy man sat in thin clothing, and [yet] that among these his sayings, for greatness of the remembered awe, yea sweetness, of his sights, he swet as strongly as if he had been in the sultry heat[1] of midsummer.

7. He then, the man of God, [for] many years, first among all the Scots boded[2] and taught God's word. When he could not easily bear the unstillness of the onrushing crowds, then he forlet all the things that he had in the world for God's name, and also went from his birth-land, and with a few brethren came through the [land of the] Britons into the province of the East-English; and there boded and taught God's word, as we ere have said; and built a noble monastery. When he then had set it in monastic and customary order[3], then wished he to withdraw himself from all the business of this world, gave up the charge of the monastery to his brother Fullan and two mass-priests, Gobba and Dicul, and, free from all things of earth, he settled to end his life in leading the life of an anchorite. He had also another brother who was called Utta, who from daily trial of the monastery was come to anchorite-life, and he lived a whole year with him in much continence and in prayers, and in hand-works.

8. After this he saw the province troubled by heathen harrowing, and he foresaw much peril awaiting God's churches and monasteries. Then left he the province, and sailed over sea into the kingdom of Gaul, and he was there honourably received by Lothewic (Louis or Clovis[4]), king of the Franks, and Erkenwald his alderman; and he there built a monastery in the place which is named Latiniac. Then it was after no great space that he was

---

1. In the "swelth,"—Swoloth *Alf.* etymon of *sultry,*—*swelth* ought to be English, as well as *sultry*, i. e. *sweltry*.
2. BODE, to proclaim, has been confounded with its compound, *forebode*, to proclaim beforehand.
3. "Set it minsterly and thewly," *Alf.*
4. Clovis—*C* for *H* of Hlothowic.—Though ruled by the Franks, the country was not yet known by the name of France; this name therefore would involve some anachronism.

attacked by sickness in which he ended his days; and the same alderman Erkenwald took his body and kept it in a porch of a church of his, which he was building in his town, of which the name is Perrone, till the church was hallowed.

9. Then it was brought about, that after seven and twenty days they took his body up from the porch, and would bring it into the church nigh the altar; then was he found as unscathed as if at the same time he had been led from this light. Then it was, after four winters again, that another church was built, and it seemed to them all more becoming, that his body should be laid on the east deal of the altar: then yet he was found without spot of corruption, and they laid him there with worthier honour. And there his earnings (and merits) often shine and brighten through divine working with great virtues.

CHAPTER XX.

1. Among these things Felix, bishop of the East-English, dying seventeen years after he had received the bishop-hood, archbishop Honorius hallowed Thomas his deacon, as bishop, in his stead, who was from the province of the Girvii, and after five years of his bishophood he was led out of this light. Then was Bertgils, by another name called Bonifatius, of the province of Kent, set in his place as bishop. And he then likewise, Honorius, the archbishop, went away from this light [on] the day before the kalends of October (*30th Sept.*) about six hundred winters and three and fifty from our Lord's incarnation; and the bishop-hood stopped a whole year and six months of the next; then was chosen, [as] sixth archbishop, to the seat of Canterbury, Deusdedit, who was of the nation of the West-Saxons. Hither came to hallow him Ithamar, the bishop at Rochester; then was he hallowed the seventh day of the kalends of April (*26th of March*); and he held and ruled the church nine years and four months and two days; and him dying,' Ithamar hallowed for him Damian, who was of the South-Saxons' kin.

CHAPTER XXI.
That the province of the Middle-English, under Peada Penda's son, became Christian.

1. In these times the Middle-English with Peada, the son of

5. The A. S. text is here so incorrectly pointed as to make Ithamar him that died.

Penda, the king, received Christ's belief and the mysteries of soothfastness. Peada was a young prince, and good, and well worth¹ the name and rank of king; and his father therefore gave him the kingdom. Then came he to Oswy, king of the Northumbrians, and begged that he would give him Elfleda his daughter to wife, but they would not grant his prayer any otherwise, unless he received Christ's belief, with the nation over which he was king. When he then heard the preaching and lore of soothfastness, and the promise of the heavenly kingdom, and the hope of again-rising and the future undeadliness, then he acknowledged that he would gladly be a Christian, though he should not for that receive the maiden. And he was most [of all] drawn on to receive Christ's belief by king Oswy's son, whose name was Elfrith, who was his near relative and friend, and had his sister to wife, who was named Kyneburga, the daughter of king Penda.

2. Then he was baptized by bishop Fillan, with all his feres² who came with him, and the king's thanes, and all their servants, in the king's famous town which is named "At the Wall." And the king took him up,³ and gave him four mass-priests, who should teach and baptize his nation; they were both in their learning and in their life great and good; and he with much gladness so returned home. The mass-priests were thus named: Kedd, and Adda, and Beté, and Deoma: the last was of Scottish kin, and the others were English. Adda was the brother of Utta, the famous mass-priest, and Abbot of the monastery which is named "At Gate'shead,"⁴ whom we mentioned before. When the said priests were come into the province with king Peada, and there boded and taught God's word, they were there gladly heard, and many, both noble and ignoble, daily renounced the uncleanness of idolatry, and by the bath of baptism were washen from their sins. Nor had king Penda the more forbidden, if any man would teach God's word among the Mercian kin, that they might not. But yet more he despised and hated those men who, he understood, had been taught Christ's belief, and would not have the works of that belief; and he said that they were worthless

1. Sic A. S.
2. Companions—the word was good English to the earl of Surry in the days of Henry the eighth, as it had been to the King of the Scots a hundred years before.
3. Stood sponsor for him.   4. That is Goat's head,—*gait* Sc. a goat; See *Ed.*

and wretched, that they would not obey their God, who made them, and in whom they lived.

3. These things were begun two years ere the death of king Penda. But when he was slain, and the Christian king Oswy got his kingdom, as we shall hereafter say, then Deoma, one of the four priests aforesaid was made bishop of the Middle-English, and also at the same time of the Mercians: for the fewness of the priests made it needful that one bishop should be over two folks. And he then in little time won and begat much folk to the Lord through his lore; and he died among the Middle-English in the folkland which is named "In Feppingum." Then after him came to the bishophood Keollach; who was also of Scottish kin. He after a little time left his bishopshire, and went back into his birth-land, to the isle of Hii, which the Scots held [as] the top and head of many monasteries. Then took after him to the bishophood Frumhere, a godly man, who had been taught in monk-life; and he was of English kin, but he was hallowed a bishop by the Scots. This was done in the times of king Wulfhere, of whom we shall hereafter say.

CHAPTER XXII.
That the East-Saxons, by the carefulness of king Oswy, and by Kedd preaching to them, received again the right faith of God, which they had formerly cast off under Sibert their king.

At that time likewise the East-Saxons again received, by the earnestness of king Oswy, the belief which they had a while before cast off, when they shoved out bishop Mellitus. For the king of the same nation, Sighebert, who, after the other Sighebert, received the kingdom, was king Oswy's friend, and often came to him, and sought him in the province of Northumberland. Then king Oswy was wont to exhort and teach him, that he might understand that they could not be Gods which were wrought by men's hands of earthly stuff either of wood or of stone, that the offcuttings and leavings of the wood were either burnt in the fire, or made into some vats of human uses, or at least were cast out, and thought worthless, and trodden with feet, and turned into earth. But God was rather to be understood in incomprensible majesty, invisible to human eye, almighty, eternal, who made heaven, and earth, and mankind, and all creatures; and that he was to come to judge the world in righteousness;

whose dwelling was to be believed eternal in the heavens, and not in earthly, corruptible, transitory adorning; and that it was rightly to be understood, that all who learnt and wrought the will of Him by whom they were created, were then to receive eternal rewards from Him. While king Oswy oft and many a time spoke these words and also many such to king Sighebert, by way of friendly and brotherly advice; then at last, with the help and consent of his friends, he believed; and then had advice with his counsellors and friends, and by their exhortation, and help, and consent, received the faith of Christ, and, with his companions, was baptized by bishop Finan in the kingly town which we mentioned before, which is named " At the wall," and is nigh the wall with which the Romans of old begirt the isle Britain, twelve miles from the east sea.

2. And when king Sighebert was made a citizen of the eternal kingdom, and would again seek the seat of his temporary kingdom, then he prayed king Oswy, that he would give him some teachers, who might bring his nation to Christ's belief, and wash them with the healing well of baptism. And he then, the king, sent errand-bearers to the Middle-English, and called to him Kedd, the holy man of God, and gave him as a companion another mass-priest for his help; and sent them to preach God's word to the nation of the East-Saxons. When they had gone through all those lands, and begotten and won great churches and assemblies [1] to the Lord, then it befel on a time that Kedd went home, and came to his church at Lindesfarne for a conference with Finan the bishop. When the bishop understood that he earnestly stuck to the gospel-lore, and had turned the nation to Christ's belief, then he ordained him bishop to the East-Saxons, and called to him two other bishops to the ministry of his hallowing. When he then had received the bishophood, then returned he to the province of the East-Saxons, and with greater authority fulfilled the begun works, built churches in many places, and hallowed mass-priests and deacons, who should help him in divine lore, and in the ministry of the bath of baptism, chiefly in the place which is named Ithancaster, and in another place which is named Tilbury; the one place is on the bank of the river Pante, the other is on the bank of the Thames. In

---

1. So " general *assembly* and *church* of the *firstborn*." Heb. c. xii.

these he gathered a great host of Christ's servants, and taught them to hold the discipline of regular life, as far as the new Christians then yet could take it.

3. Whilst then for a good while, to the gladdening of the king and the evengladdening of all the folk, in the foresaid province, the institution of heavenly life was taking a daily increase, it befel, by the instigation of the foe of all good [men], that the king was slain by his own kinsmen. [They] were two brothers who perpetrated this wickedness: when they were afterwards asked why they did this, they could answer naught else, but that they were angry and foes to the king for that [reason], because he was wont to spare his foes too much, and when injuries had been committed by them, as soon as they besought him and begged forgiveness, he with mild and blithe mood forgave them every thing. Thislike was the sin for which the king was slain, for that he held and fulfilled the gospel laws with wilsomeness of heart, yet in this his innocent death his true sin was punished, as had been foretold by the man of God, the holy bishop.

4. For one of those earls who slew the king, had [made] an unlawful marriage, and when the bishop could not hinder that nor set it right, then he excommunicated him, and bade all those who would hear him, not to go into his house nor to take meat of his banquets. Then the king slighted his bidding, and the earl invited him to his home, and he visited him, and went into his house, and took his food. When he then was going away thence, the bishop met him. When the king then saw him, he was afraid, and lighted off his horse, and fell at his feet, and begged forgiveness of his guilt. Then lighted the bishop also at the same time, and being angry he touched the king as he lay, with the rod which he had in his hand, and with bishoply authority bore witness and thus said: "I tell thee," quoth he, "inasmuch as thou wouldest not withhold thee from the house of the lost and condemned man, thou shalt, in the same house, swelt [1] and suffer death." But it is to be believed, that such a death of the godly man, not only blotted out such sins, but also increased his merit, for it so befel him for the sake of his piety, and for his holding of Christ's commandments. Then came after Sighebert

---

1. To "swelt," in the 15th century, sometimes meant to die, sometimes to faint—neither could be adopted in the text—so let the original word speak for itself:—qu.? "swelt in the throes of death;" v. *Alf*.

to the kingdom of the East-Saxons Swithhelm, son of Sexbald, who was baptized by the same Kedd in the province of the East-English, in the kingly dwelling which is named Rendelsham; and Ethelwald, king of the East-English, brother of their king Anna, took him up from the bath of baptism as his godson.

CHAPTER XXIII.

That the same bishop Kedd having received from king Ethelwald a place to build a monastery on, then with holy prayers and fastings hallowed it to the Lord; and of his death.

1. This same man of God, when he was brooking the office of a bishop among the East-Saxons, was wont frequently to seek and visit his own people of the province of the Northumbrians for the sake of divine lore. When Ethelwald son of king Oswald, who had the kingdom of the Deiri, saw and understood him [to be] a holy and wise man, and good in his manners, then he begged him to receive from him a portion of land, that he might build a monastery on it, and assemble God's servants; in which the king might frequently say his prayers, and hear divine lore; and also when he died should be there buried. And he said that he truly believed that he might be much helped by the daily prayers of those who in that place served the Lord. The same king had with him the bishop's brother, who was named Kelin, a mass-priest, and evenly a man of God, who taught divine lore to him and his household, and administered the mysteries of the holy belief; and through his acquaintance it chiefly happened that the king loved and knew the bishop. Then the bishop helped the king's will, and chose himself a place to build a monastery, up among high mountains, where were rather seen the hiding-places of robbers and the ravenings of wild beasts, than the dwellings of men; according to the prophecy of Isaiah, In the cliffs in which dragons formerly dwelt, was uprunning a growth of reeds and rushes: that is to be understood, that there were brought forth fruits of good deeds, where formerly either wild beasts dwelt, or men were wont to live like wild beasts.

2. Then toiled he soon, the man of God, first by prayers and fastings to cleanse the received place of the monastery from the impurities of the former misdeeds and abominations, and then to lay the foundation of the monastery. He then asked the king to give him means and leave, that he might dwell there for the sake of his prayers, all the time of the forty-day fast before Easter,

which was to come. And all the days but Sundays he fasted till evening, as his custom was; and then he took only a little dole of bread, and a hen's egg with a little milk mingled with water. Moreover he said that it was the custom of those from whom he learnt regular discipline, that the new places received to build a monastery or a church, they should first hallow to the Lord with prayers and fasts. When yet ten days of the forty-day fast were left, an errand-bearer came, who called him to go to the king; and he then bade Kynebill his mass-priest, who was also his own brother, fulfil and end his godly undertaking, since he might not, lest the pious work should be left undone for the sake of the king's business; and he then willingly complied with him, and earnestly fulfilled the fastings and prayers, built there a monastery which is now called Lestingau, and set and established it with religious customs, after the customs of Lindesfarne, where he was brought up.

3. When he then during many years had administered the bishophood in the foresaid province, and likewise taken charge of this monastery, and there set a provost and aldermen, then befel it that he came to the same monastery in the time of the great deadliness and pestilence which was come upon mankind. Then was he there overtaken by bodily unhealthiness and died; and his body was first buried without. Then was, after forthgoing time, in the same monastery a stone church built, in honour of the blessed maiden [1] saint Mary, and then his body was laid in it by south the altar.

4. The bishop gave the monastery to his brother Keadda to rule after him, who afterwards became bishop, and a holy man of God, as we shall hereafter say. They were four brothers, Kedd, and Kynebill, and Kelin, and Keadda, all priests of God, which is seldom found, famous and good; twain were bishops, and twain mass-priests, all the best. When the brethren then, who were in his monastery in the province of the East-Saxons, heard that their bishop was dead and buried in the [land of the] Northumbrians, then went thirty of them from the monastery, and came thither; they willed and wished, at their father's body, either to live to God, if that pleased God, or dying, there to be buried;

1. This in early English almost uniformly, and in A. S. equally with fæmne, represented the Latin *Virgo*,—hence the expressive alliteration—Mother and maiden, blessed Mary!

and they were gladly received by the brethren of the monastery, and they all very soon died there by the stroke of the foresaid pestilence, and were buried,—[all] but one boy, of whom it standeth known, that he was shielded from death by the prayers of the holy bishop. For when he lived much time after, and carefully learned and studied the holy writings, then at last he understood and learnt in ghost, that he had not been born a child of God, with the water of the bath of baptism, and he soon was washen from his sins with the well of the wholesome bath, and after a while throve [and did so well], that he was hallowed to mass-priest, and was profitable and useful to many in God's churches. About this man it is not to be doubted, but is to be believed, as we said before, that he was shielded from the time of death by the intercession of his father, to whose body he had come for the sake of his love, that he might both escape the everlasting death, and likewise by his teaching and by the example of his life, might furnish to other brethren the ministry of life and of eternal salvation.

CHAPTER XXIV.
That the province of the Mercians, after their king Penda was slain, received Christ's belief; and king Oswy, for the victory given him, granted many possessions and twelve booklands to build a monastery to God on.

1. In these times king Oswy, while he suffered the cruel and intolerable harrowings of the oftnamed Penda, king of the Mercians, who also slew his brother, then at last was driven by need that he besought him for his peace, and promised innumerable treasures and kingly gifts, more than many men can believe, on the [condition] that he should return home with his army, and not harrow his land and his kingdom to destruction. When he then, the faithless king, would for no sake grant his prayers,—he who had meditated and resolved in his mind, that he would fordo and blot out all his nation from the younger to the elder, then looked he to the Divine Mercy for help, since he could find no peace from the merciless king. And then he bound himself with a vow, and thus said, "Since that heathen knows not to receive our gifts, let us give and bring them to Him who knows to receive them—our Lord Jesus Christ." And he then promised, if the Lord would give him victory, that he would give up his daughter to the Lord, and hallow her in clean

maidhood, and also that he would give to God possessions of twelve booklands, to build a monastery on. And so with a small host he went to the fight.

2. It is said, that the heathens had thirty times more men; then king Oswy, with his son Elfrith, trusting in Christ's help, with a small host came against them; for Ecgferth his other son was at that time in the land of the Mercians with queen Kynwise, being given as a hostage. But Ethelwald, king Oswald's son, who should have been a help to them, was on the side of their adversaries, fighting and striving against his country, and against his uncle. Then as soon as they began the fight, the heathens were smitten and put to flight; and thirty aldermen and captains, who had come to help the king, were almost all slain: among whom was Ethelhere, brother of Anna, king of the East-English, who got the kingdom after him, who was the beginner of the war, who also was slain, with all the fighting men whom he had brought with him. And forasmuch as this fight was fought nigh the stream Winwed, the stream was then very fierce from a great fall of rain, and much heaven-flood sat on [it]; then it befel that when they were fleeing, many more of mankind were there drowned, than were slain with the sword.

3. Then king Oswy did according to that which he had vowed to the Lord, and for the victory given him said thank to God, and gave up his daughter Elfleda to God, and hallowed her to everlasting cleanness; and likewise the twelve booklands he freed of earthly warfare and of earthly obedience, to carry on the heavenly warfare; and set it for monks' places, and gave them worldly wealth and possessions, that they should pray for him, and for the peace of his nation. Of all this land there were a hundred and twenty hides, sixty in the province of the Deiri, and sixty in [that of] the Bernicians. Then went king Oswy's foresaid daughter, hallowed to God, into the monastery which is named Heorutea, *(or Hart's isle,)* in which at that time Hilda was abbess; who two years after bought ten hides of land into her possession, in the place which is called Streones-halch, where she built a monastery, in which the king's said daughter was first a disciple and a learner of regular life, and then after that a school mistress and teacher of the monastery, until the number

---

1. " Gode þanc " transposed, and stript of the dative case vowel, is still preserved in the pious ejaculation " thank God !" i. e. Deo gratia.

of the days was fulfilled, that is sixty winters wanting one, when as a blessed maiden she entered to the embrace and marriage of the heavenly Bridegroom. In which monastery, she and Oswy her father, and her mother Eanfleda, and her mother's father Edwin, and many other noble persons were buried, in the church of St Peter the Apostle.

4. King Oswy ended this war [1] in the thirteenth year of his reign, in the land that is called Loidis, on the seventeenth day of the kalends of December (*15th of November*), with great advantage of each folk; for he delivered and saved his [own] nation from the fiendlike [2] harrowing of the heathens, and likewise, having hewn off the faithless head, Penda, converted the nation of the Mercians and of the neighbouring provinces to the grace of Christ's belief. Diuma was first made bishop of the Mercians, and of Lindesfarne, and of the Middle-English, as we said before; who died and was buried in [the country of] the Middle-English. The next was Kellach, who left his bishop-ministry among the English, and, living, returned to the Scots; each of them was of Scottish kin. The third bishop was Frumhere, who was of English kin, but he was taught and hallowed by the Scots. He was Abbot in the monastery, which is called Ongetlingum, which is the place where king Oswine was slain, as we mentioned before; and therefore queen Eanfleda, his kinswoman, for the cleansing of his unrighteous slaughter, asked king Oswy, that he would give land to build a monastery on, to the foresaid servant of God, Trumhere, because he likewise was a kinsman of the slain king; and in the monastery there should be continual prayers for the eternal salvation of each king, both of the slain, and of him who bade slay him.—And lo! the same king Oswy, after the slaughter of Penda, during three full years, was in authority over the nation of the Mercians, and likewise the other folks of the southern provinces; and moreover he subjected the nation of the Picts, for the most deal, to the dominion of the English kin, and drew them into obedience to him.

5. At that time also king Oswy gave and granted to Peada, the son of king Penda, because he was his relation, the kingdom of the South-Mercians, who are those that men say to be five thou-

---

1. Or fought this battle.
2 Feond, fiend, a foe,—" fiendly harrowing," hostile ravaging.

sand folks, or families;[1] and who are toshedden and parted by the river Trent from the North-Mercians, of whose lands there are seven thousand. But he then, the same Peada, the next spring, was most wickedly killed through the treachery, as men say, of his own wife, at the festival of Easter-tide.

6. When the three winters were ended after the slaughter of king Penda, then warred and fought against Oswy the captains and aldermen of the Mercians, Immen, and Eafa, and Eadbert; and raised Wulfhere, son of Penda, to king of the Mercians, a youth whom they had secretly held and kept; they cast off the aldermen of the strange king, and got back their land and their boundaries, and recovered their freedom. And they, thus free, with their king, joyfully served the Lord Christ, the true King, for the everlasting kingdom in heaven. Wulfhere was king of the Mercians fourteen winters, and he had first bishop Trumhere as his teacher, of whom we spoke before: the next was Gearumon; the third was Keadda; the fourth Winfred. All these in their order, in his day, brooked the bishophood in the nation of the Mercians.

CHAPTER XXVII. [Ch. 25 and 26 are omitted.]
That the holy man Egbert, born of English kingly kin, was leading monk-life in Ireland.

1. Then happened, about six hundred winters and four and sixty after our Lord's incarnation, a solar eclipse, that is, a waning of the sun, that it had not brightness, and was dismal to behold: it was on the third of the month [of] May, nearly about the tenth tide of the day. After that, also the same year, a pestilence and sickness suddenly ravaged and wasted first the south-deals of Britain, and likewise harassed the province of the Northumbrians, and, with grim slaughter, long raging far and wide, felled and carried off a great multitude of men. By which stroke also Tuda, Christ's servant, who was, after Coleman, bishop of the Northumbrians, was taken out of the world, and was honorably buried in the monastery which is named Pegnalech. This same plague also smote and tormented Ireland, the isle of the Scots, with like mortality. There at that time were many from the English nation, both noblemen and others, who in the time of bishops Finan and Coleman left their birth-turf, and went thither, some for divine

---

1. Folces, *Alf.* familiarum, Bo. for which in the next clause we find landa, lands.—May Alfred's "folkes" mean folk-lands?

learning, some for the sake of a stricter life ; and some soon faithfully served the Lord in minsterly conversation in regular life ; some went throughout the monastery, and sought divine teachers to themselves. And the Scots (*or Irish*) received them all gladly, and gave them daily food without purchase, and likewise gave and granted them books to learn on, and teachers, without payment or reward.

2. Among these were two young princes, men of great ability, of the English nation, Ethelhun and Egbert ; the former was brother to Ethelwin, a man beloved of God, who [him] self likewise in the following age visited Ireland for the sake of divine learning, and when he was well taught, he returned to his native land ; and was made bishop in the land of Lindsey, and for a long time nobly and well held and governed the church of God. They were in the monastery which is named in the Irish tongue Rathmelsigi, and all his fellows were either taken out of the world in the deadliness of the plague, or were dispersed through other places. Then were they both greatly pained and heavily afflicted by the infection of the same deadliness, and were not expected to live. Then arose Egbert, as an old venerable mass-priest told me that he heard from his own mouth, when he reckoned and weened that he should swelt and suffer death ; then went he out in the dawn from the house in which the sick men rested, and sat alone in a secret place, and began earnestly to think of his deeds, and was goaded by the remembrance of his sins, and wept, and washed his face with tears, and from his inward heart prayed God, that he might not then yet die, before he had from that time more perfectly cleansed his by-gone carelessness, of which he had been guilty in childhood or in youth, and also more abundantly exercised himself in good works. He likewise vowed a vow, that he aye would live his life in pilgrimage for God, and never return to the isle of Britain, where he was born, and that besides the psalm-singing of regular time, if unhealthiness of body withstood him not, he would every day sing the whole psalter, in memory of the divine praise, and that in every week he would fast a day together with the night. When he had ended this vow, and his prayers, and his tears, then went he back to his house, and then found he his companion sleeping ; he then likewise went up into his bed, and wished to rest him a while ; and when he had rested a little space, then his companion awoke, and looked at him and

thus spoke, "O brother Egbert, O (quoth he) what hast thou done? I hoped and weened that we now should quickly go into the everlasting life together, but know thou, however, that thou shalt get what thou hast asked." For he through a vision had learnt what he had asked of God, and had desired from him, and that his prayers were heard. Why shall we speak more of this? Well! Ethelhun died the next night, and Egbert recovered of the sickness, and lived a long time afterwards, and received bishophood, and adorned the office with even-worthy deeds, and after many goods of ghostly virtues, as he had wished, when he was ninety winters old, he went to the heavenly kingdom. He lived his life in much humility, and meekness, and continence, and simplicity, and soothfastness,[1] and perfection. And thereby he improved both his own nation, and also the kindreds of the Scots and Picts among whom he lived in pilgrimage, both by the example of his life, and by his teaching, and by his authority; and also enriched them by the munificence of his gifts, out of the goods which he received from rich men. He added also to his vows which we told before, that in the forty-day fast before Easter he ate only once a-day, and took nothing else but a little bread with thin milk: the manner of which same abstinence he likewise held [during] the forty days ere Christ's birth-tide, and the forty days after Pentecost (or *Whitsuntide*).

CHAPTER XXVIII.

That Tuda being dead, Wilfrith was sent into Gaul, and there was ordained by bishop Aghil-bert [2], and Keadda among the West-Saxons by bishop Wine, and they both were hallowed bishops to the Northumbrians.

1. Among these things king Elfrith, Oswy's son, sent Wilfrith, his mass-priest, that he should be hallowed bishop to him and his folks. He sent him over sea to be ordained—to bishop Aghilbert, of whom we told before, who formerly left Britain, and was made bishop of the city Paris, and he was hallowed by him with much honour, many bishops coming together to the hallowing, in the kingly town which is called "In Compendia," in after times Compiegne. When he then yet after his hallowing was tarrying in the parts beyond sea, then king Oswy imitated the earnest care of his son, and sent into Kent a holy man, and moderate in his

---

[1]. Or righteousness—justitiæ perfectione Bn. i. e. perfection of humility, &c.
[2]. Æthelbyrht *here*,—Ægelbyrht *elsewhere*,—to guard the pronunciation *h* has been added after *g*. So Gearumon p. 300, *l.* 16, Ghearumon *or* Yaraman.

manners, and well taught in the learning of the holy writings, and who carefully followed in his works the things which he learnt in writings to do, who should be hallowed as bishop of the church of York city. This was the mass-priest named Keadda, brother of Kedd, the venerable bishop, whom we have often mentioned before. The king likewise sent with him his mass-priest, called Eadeth, who afterwards in Ecferth's reign was made bishop in Ripon. When they came into Kent, then found they the archbishop Deusdedit carried out of the world; and no other bishop was then yet set in his stead.

2. Then turned they to the province of the West-Saxons, where Winé was bishop, and by him the foresaid man of God was hallowed as bishop. He took two bishops of the British (or Welsh) nation into fellowship of the hallowing. There was not at that time any bishop but this Winé in all Britain, who had been rightly [1] hallowed. Then was this Keadda hallowed a bishop by him; and he soon began to take the greatest care of the kirkly soothfastness,[2] and cleanness; and to give heed to humbleness, and continence, and learning; and to thoroughfare[3] cities, and lands, and towns, and hamlets, and houses, for gospel lore,—not riding on a horse, but, in the way of the apostles, going on his feet. He was of the disciples of Aidan, the good bishop, and strengthened and taught his hearers by his deeds and thews, after the example of his brother Kedd. Then came likewise Wilfrith into Britain, when he was hallowed a bishop, and likewise brought many regulations of the right-believed observance of the Romish church, to the churches of the English kin, by his lore. Whence it was brought about, that the right-believed lore was daily waxing, and all the Scots who dwelt among the English, and were unfriendly to the right-believed lore, both in the holding of right Easter, and in many other things, either gave their truth that they would hold right with him, or returned home to their birth-land.

---

1. Canonice, *Bd*, rihtlice (or rightliky) *Alf.*—that is, according to law.
2. Ecclesiasticæ veritatis, *Bd*. Alfred's rendering, as above, is surely as intelligible as "ecclesiastic verity."
3. To travel through—but Alfred's verb should be as good as our noun "thoroughfare."

CHAPTER XXIX.

That the mass-priest Wighard was sent from Britain to be ordained archbishop, whence they soon sent hither a letter of the apostolic pope, and shewed that he had died there.

1. In these times, the noblest English kings, Oswy king of the Northumbrians, and Egbert king of the Kent-men, held a conference between them, and a consultation, what was to be done about the state of the English kin's church; for Oswy truly understood, though he himself was brought up and taught by Scots, that the Roman and apostolic church was right-believed.[1] Then chose they and took, with consent of the holy church of the English nation, a good man and fit for bishophood, a mass-priest, whose name was Wighard, of the fellowship of bishop Deusdedit, and they sent him then to Rome, that he should there be hallowed a bishop, that he might there receive the office of archbishop, and might afterwards ordain right-believed bishops to the churches of the English kin through all Britain. When he then, Wighard, came to Rome, before he could come to the bishophood, he was forgrippen[2] by death, and there deceased.

2. Then sent pope Vitalian to Oswy, king of the Saxons, an affectionate letter,[3] when he learnt his pious will, and his hot love of God, which he had for the blessed life, and because he, by the Lord's protection, was converted to the true and apostolic belief; and said that he hoped, as he reigned temporally[4] in his nation, so he might hereafter reign eternally with Christ. And he likewise there in the letter mentioned Wighard's death, that they were much grieved that he should have died there; and promised him so soon as a fit man and worthy of the office could be found, that they would hallow him as bishop, and send him hither.

What bishop then was chosen and hallowed for Wighard,—this we shall write and say more properly and more conveniently in the afterfollowing book.

CHAPTER XXX.

That the East-Saxons in the time of the pestilence had returned to idolatry, and again through the earnestness of bishop Germanus (Jaruman) they were turned back from their error.

1. In the same time were, in the province of the East-Saxons,

---

1. Held the right belief—was orthodox.   2. Snatched away.
3. Lovesomely errand-writ, *Alf.*
4. Willendlice A. S. most probably an error for hwilendlice, temporally—in contrast with "ecelice" (next clause), eternally.

after Swithhelm, of whom we spoke before, two kings, Sighehere and Sibba, though they were subject in obedience to Wulfhere king of the Mercians. When the same province [of] the East-Saxons was whacked with the scourge of the foresaid deadliness, then this Sighehere, with the deal of his folk which he held, forsook the mysteries of the Christian belief, and was turned to heathenness. For this same king, and his aldermen, and many of his folk loved this deadly life, and sought not that which is to come, nor even believed that it ever would be. Then began they to renew the temples which they had formerly forsaken, and to worship and adore images, as if [1] by these things they could be shielded from the pestilence and the deadliness. Moreover Sibba his colleague and coheir of the same kingdom, with all his folk, held the received belief of Christ with great earnestness, and with much happiness faithfully fulfilled his life, as we shall again hereafter say.

2. When king Wulfhere then understood that, and it was made known to him, that in the province of the East-Saxons Christ's belief was partly profaned or blotted out, [2] then sent he bishop Germanus, who was Trumhere's afterfollower, into the province of the East-Saxons, to correct the error, and to call them back to the belief of the truth. And he then, the bishop, did that with much earnestness (and skill), as the mass-priest, who was his fellow and helper in the divine word, told me. The bishop was a pious and good man, and went through all the lands and dwellings [3] far and wide; and led the folk and the foresaid king back to the way of righteousness; [4] so that they forsook, and overthrew the temples and the idols, which they had formerly made, and untined God's churches, and gladly owned Christ's name, which they had formerly gainsaid; and were more willing to die with the belief of the everlasting life, and of the resurrection of glory, than to live in uncleanness and faithlessness [5] among idols. When this then was thus done, then the bishop and their teachers returned home with joy and gladness.

---

1. Swilce, *Ca.* swa swa, *Sm.*   2. Aidlad, *Sm.* adilgod *B.*   3. Or peoples.
4. Soþfæstnesse *Alf.* in both places: veritatis in the former, justitiæ in the latter, *Bd.*
5. "Impurities of perfidy," according to *Bd.*—Alfred very often resolves a word in regimen, by a similar use of the conjunction, as justitiæ perfectione, soþfæstnysse and fulfremednysse. 3, 27.

BOOK IV. CHAPTER I.

That Archbishop Deusdedit being dead, Wighard was sent to Rome to receive the bishophood, but when he died there, Theodore was hallowed Archbishop, and, with Abbot Adrian, was sent to Britain.

1. In the year mentioned—that of the foresaid solar eclipse, and soon after the ensuing pestilence and mortality, in that year Deusdedit, the sixth archbishop in Canterbury church, died the day before the Ides (14th of the month) of July. Erconbert, king of Kent, likewise died the same month and day, and left the seat of his kingdom to his son Egbert, which he had and held twenty winters wanting one. When the bishopdom had stopt a long while, then was Wighard a mass-priest sent to Rome by Egbert and by Oswy, king of the Northumbrians, as in the foregoing book we have already said in few words. This man was well instructed in Ecclesiastical discipline, [and was] of English kin. They likewise, both the kings, together, sent great gifts in many gold vessels and silver vessels to the apostolic Pope, and prayed that he would hallow Wighard archbishop to the churches of the English kin. When he then came to Rome, Pope Vitalian was at that time chief bishop of the apostolic seat. After he had shown the occasion of his journey to the apostolic pope, then after a little time Wighard and almost all his companions who had come with him were destroyed and carried off by the pestilence that came upon them.

2. When the apostolic pope had thought about these things, and carefully sought whom he should send as archbishop to the churches of the English nation, then was in the Niridan monastery, which is not far from the city Naples, in the province of Campania, Abbot Adrian. This man was well instructed in the holy scriptures, and in monastic and ecclesiastic discipline, and worthily trained both in the Latin tongue and in the Greek. Then the Pope bade call the man to him, and ordered him to receive bishophood, and go to Britain. Then answered he him, and said, that he was unworthy of so great a degree, and said that he could shew another, who was worthy of bishophood, both in learning and in the merit of his life, and in suitable age. He then shewed the Pope, in the neighbouring monastery of nuns, a fit [person, a] monk, whose name was Andrew, but then his bodily infirmity withstood him that he might not be a bishop. Again the Pope drove Abbot Adrian to receive the bishophood.

Then he begged delay and truce [to see] whether he might after a space find another, who might be ordained a bishop.

3. There was at that time in Rome a monk who was known to Abbot Adrian, whose name was Theodore, who was born in Tarsus of Cilicia. The man was well instructed both in worldly writings and in divine, and also in Greek and in Latin; and he was good in his manners, and of a venerable age, that is he had six and sixty winters. This man Abbot Adrian shewed to the Pope and said that he might be hallowed a bishop, and he granted that; and moreover they concerted this between them, that the Abbot should be his guide into Britain, because he had already twice, for various occasions, gone and visited the parts of the kingdom of Gaul; and because the way of the journey was enough known to him; and likewise that he was well manned in his own fellowship; and moreover that he should be his helper in divine lore, and that he should carefully observe that he might not, in the manner of the Greeks, introduce any thing contrary to the true belief into the church of the English kin, over which he was to be. Then he was first hallowed to sub-deacon, and then waited four months until his hair waxed, so that he might be shorn as priest; because he formerly had the shearing, in the East-people's manner, of saint Paul the Apostle. Then was he by pope Vitalian hallowed as bishop about six hundred and sixty eight winters from our Lord's incarnation, on the Lord's day, and the seventh day before the kalends of April (26th of March), and so together with Abbot Adrian, on the sixth of the kalends of June (26th of May), was sent to Britain.

4. Then went they together, first to Marseilles, and thence by land to Arles¹ and came to John, the archbishop of the city, and gave the letter of Pope Vitalian, that they should be received with honour; and he did so, had them with much honour with him, until Ebrinus the alderman gave them means and leave to go whithersoever they would. Then went Theodore the archbishop to Aghilbert, bishop of Paris, of whom we spoke before, and was kindly received by him, and was well had² by him a long time. Adrian went first to Emme of Sens, and afterwards to Fano of Meaux, bishops; and was long well had² by them. For the coming winter forced them to stay still wheresoever they

---

1. Through Arles [the] land, *Alf.*   2. Hospitably entertained, "well gehæfd." *Alf.*

might. When trusty errand-bearers told king Egbert, that the bishop was in the kingdom of the Franks, whom he and Oswy had asked from the Roman bishop, then soon sent he thither Redfrith his reeve, that he should fetch him hither, and lead [him] to him. When he then came thither, then took he bishop Theodore with leave of Ebrinus the alderman, and led him to the port which is named Quentowic, where some sickness came upon him, and he tarried there a while; and as soon as he began to get better, so went he into ships, and fared to Britain. Ebrinus the alderman took Abbot Adrian, and had him in a fastness, because he guessed that he had some errand of the emperor to the kings of Britain, against the kingdom of the Franks, of which he then had much care. But when he truly understood and found, that it was not so as he had guessed, then onleased [3] he him, and let him fare after the bishop. And as soon as he came to him, then gave he him St Peter's monastery, where the bodies of the archbishops are buried, as we said before; for the Apostolic pope had charged bishop Theodore, when he went from him, that he should foresee and give him a fit place in his bishopshire, in which he might dwell with his fellows.

CHAPTER II.
That Archbishop Theodore having gone through the churches of all the English kin, bade them be teaching with right believing soothfastness [4]; and likewise in holy writ, and in Stavecraft [or Grammar], and that Putta was hallowed bishop at Rochester instead of Damian.

1. Then came he, bishop Theodore, to his church in Canterbury, the year after his hallowing, the sixth day of the kalends of June (*27th of May*); and he lived in his bishophood twenty-one winters and three months and six and twenty days. And he soon thorough-fared all the isle of Britain, whereabout soever English nations lived and dwelt; and he was gladly received by all; and they willingly heard his words; and he shewed them the right order of life, and taught them to keep right Easters: and abbot Adrian went with him, and helped to every right. He was the first of Archbishops to whom all English kin yielded obedience; and as they were both, the bishop and the abbot, as we said before, well learned both in divine writings and in worldly, they gathered a great crowd of learners; and, among

3. H. Tooke, v. UNLESS.
4. Catholic verity—" teaching with " or instructing [the people] in orthodox verity, &c.

THEODORE VISITS THE CHURCHES.

holy books and ecclesiastical discipline, trained and taught them in metrecraft and stavecraft, and grammarcraft. [Of this] it was a clear token, that their scholars were well skilled both in the Greek language and in the Latin, and these were as familiar to them as their own, in which they had been reared. Never were here, since the English kins sought Britain, happier times nor fairer. There were strong and truly Christian kings, and [had] in much awe by all the barbarous kins without; and the wills of all leaned to hear the joys of the heavenly kingdom; and what men soever wished to be trained in holy learning, they had ready masters who should teach and train them. Likewise to sing tunes in churches, which hitherto men knew in Kent only, from that time they began to learn in all the churches of the English kin. And besides James the singer, of whom we spoke here before, there was a song-master of the church of the Northumbrians, who was named Edde, whose free-name was Stephen; he was drawn out of Kent by the venerable bishop Wilfrith, who first among the bishops who were from the English nation, told and taught the regular way of living to the churches of the English kin.

2. Then went bishop Theodore through all the province of the English kin, and hallowed [bishops in fit places, and with their help righted and bettered the things which he found imperfect. Among these when he chid bishop Keadda, because he had not been rightly hallowed, then answered he in a humble voice, "If thou knowest that I have not rightly received bishophood, I will gladly retire from the ministry, for I never deemed myself worthy of the office, but being called, I for the sake of obedience consented to undertake the office, though I was unworthy." When he then heard the humility of his answer, he said that he should not forlet the bishophood; but he afterwards completed his ordination by the law of the church. In the time when Archbishop Deusdedit was dead, a bishop of Canterbury was sought and sent to be ordained, and bishop Wilfrith also was sent from Britain to Gaul to be ordained. He then too ordained mass-priests and deacons] in Kent, until archbishop Theodore came to his seat. Soon after he came to Rochester, where, bishop Damian being dead, the bishophood was stopt a long while, then ordained he a man who was more skilled in church discipline and simplicity of life than active in worldly things—

whose name was Putta. He was most expert in church-songcraft after the Roman manner, which he had learnt from St Gregory's disciples.

CHAPTER III.

That Keadda, of whom we ere above spoke, was given as bishop to the province of the Mercians: and of his life, and of his death, and of his burial.

1. At that time Wulfhere was king in the province of the Mercians. Bishop Gearomon being dead, he requested bishop Theodore, that he would find and give a bishop to him and his people; then would he not hallow a new bishop, but asked Oswy king of the Northumbrians to give them Keadda the hallowed bishop, who then lived in his monastery that is in Lestingau, in stillness. Then bishop Wilfrith administered the bishophood in York city, and likewise among all the Northumbrians, and also among the Picts as far as the reign of king Oswy was. And whereas it was the custom of the same venerable bishop that he performed the work of the holy gospel more by going on his feet, than by riding on his horses, bishop Theodore bade him ride where the way happened to be longer for him, and thenceforth he strove mightily for earnestness and for love of the pious labour. Then the archbishop urged him strongly, that he should ride whithersoever there was need of it, and lo! at last with his own hands uphove him on [his] horse; for he found the man holy and great in his life's earnings. Then Keadda received the bishopdom of the nation of the Mercians together with Lindesfarne, and straightway, after the example of holy fathers, in much perfection of life held and administered the bishophood. King Wulfhere gave and granted him fifty hides of land in Lindsey to build a monastery on, in the place which is named Atbarwe, [*or at the grove*]; in which monastery now yet until to-day the traces remain of regular life which he established there.

2. He had a bishop-seat in the place which is called Litchfield, where he died and was buried, where yet to-day is the seat of the afterfollowing bishops of the province of the Mercians. He built also a sunderwic *(separate residence)* not far from the church in which he privately, with a few brethren, that is, seven or eight men, was wont to pray and read his books, as oft as he had

leisure[1] from the toil of the ministry of divine lore. When he then had wonderfully held and ruled the churches in that province two years and the third half,[2] then, by the ordinance of Sovereign Doom, came the time of which speaketh Ecclesiastes the book: "Tempus mittendi lapides, et tempus colligendi": That there was a time to send stones, and a time to gather. Then came much sickness and mortality divinely sent, which, through the body's death, bore the living stones from earthly seats to the heavenly building. Whilst then many of the same venerable Bishop's assembly were led away from the body, then came his time that he should go from earth to the Lord. Then it befel one day that he was dwelling in the foresaid wic with one brother, whose name was Owini; his other fellows had gone for suitable occasions to the church in the monastery. This same Owini was a monk of much merit, and with a pure regard to the heavenly recompense was forsaking the world, and he was through every thing worthy and chosen to God[3] and to him the Lord especially unfolded his secrets. He came with queen Etheldrith from the East-English; and he was her thane of her house, and over-alderman of her retinue. When God's belief[4] waxed and was hot, then thought he that he should renounce the world, and unslothfully he did so; and to that length unclothed and stript[5] himself of worldly things, that he forlet all that he had but his onefold garment, and came to Lestingau, to the monastery of the venerable bishop Keadda, bearing axe and adze in his hand; whereby he gave token that he went into the monastery, not for idleness, as some others [did], but for labour: and he himself likewise shewed that by deeds. And because he little sufficed in study and learning of holy writings, the more he toiled and wrought with his hands the things that were needful. Of this it is a token, that he was had with the bishop among the brethren, in the foresaid dwelling, for his respectability and diligence, when they were at their learning and read and studied their books, then was he without working whatsoever was seen to be needful.

1. *Lit.* was empty.   2. That is 'half of a third year.'
3. Gode gecoren, chosen, or here, approved of God.
4. The Christian faith.   5. *Lit.* nakeded,—" to nake " was formerly in use,—" Why nake ye your backs?" Ch. *Quid (stulti) terga nudatis?* Boet. For *nake* the printed reading is *make* with no meaning.

3. When he then one day was doing some such [thing] without, and his fellows had gone to the borough to church, as they often did, and the bishop was alone in the church, diligent either in reading books or in prayer, then he (*the monk*) heard suddenly, as he afterwards said, the sweetest and the fairest voice of [persons] singing and rejoicing descend from heaven to earth. The voice and the song he said that he at first heard from east-south-deal, that is, from the highness of the winterly sunrising, and thence it gradually came near to him, until it came to the thatch of the oratory, which the bishop was in, and then going in it filled and encompassed in [its] circuit all the house; and he, then carefully stretched his mind to the things which he heard. Then heard he again, as it were, in the space of a half hour, the same blissful song ascend from the roof of the same oratory, and return up to heaven with unspeakable sweetness, the same way by which it came. Then remained he there some space of time wondering and amazed, and with heedful mind thought and studied what those things should be; then the bishop opened the window of the oratory, and struck token with his hand, as his custom was, that if any man were without he should go in to him. Then he soon went in to him, and the bishop said to him, "Go quickly to the church and bid our seven brethren come hither to me, and be thou likewise with them. When they came to him, then he admonished them, first that they should carefully hold the virtue of love and peace among themselves, and among all God's men; and likewise should fulfil and follow, with unwearied earnestness, the institution of regular discipline, which they had learnt from him, and seen in him, or had found in the deeds and words of the deceased fathers. Afterwards he subjoined and said to them, that the day of his death stood very nigh, and he thus spoke: "That dear and lovely guest, who was wont to visit our brethren, has come to day also to me, and called and invited me from the world, therefore return ye now to the church, and bid our brethren commend my decease to the Lord, by their prayers and supplications; and likewise remember to forecome and anticipate their own departure, whose time is unknown, by watchings, and prayers, and good works."

4. When he had spoken these words and many of this kind to

6. "Cyricean" here stands for *oratorio*, the oratory.
7. "Eyethirl," compare *nostril*, i. e. nose thirl.

them, and they having received his blessing had gone out very sorrowful from him, then he who had heard the heavenly song returned alone to him, and humbly stretched himself on the earth before the bishop, and thus spoke, "My father, may I ask thee aught?" Quoth he, "Ask what thou wilt." Quoth he, "O I beseech and pray thee, for God's love, that thou say to me, what the song of glad [ones] was, which I heard coming from heaven over this oratory, and after a time returning to heaven." Then the bishop answered, "If thou hast heard the voice of the song and understood that the heavenly host came over us, I charge thee in the Lord's name, that thou shew or tell it to none ere my decease. I tell thee truly that they were ghosts of angels who came there, and called and invited me to the heavenly meeds, which I always loved and desired; and they promised me to return and come after seven days, and that they would then lead me with them"; which was truly fulfilled by deeds, as had been told him. Then was he soon touched with bodily sickness, which daily waxed and was heavier; and then on the seventh day, as had been promised him, after he had comforted his decease by receiving the Lord's body and blood, the holy soul was loosed from the heaviness of the body, and by the guidance and fellowship of angels, as there is a right to believe, ascended and sought the everlasting joy and the heavenly blessedness.

5. Is it any wonder, though he was glad to see the day of his death, or rather the day of the Lord, for which he had alway carefully waited until it came? For among many earnings of his virtues, in his continence, in humility, in divine love, and in prayers, and in willsome poverty, and also other virtues, he was so much subjected to the fear of the Lord, and so very mindful of his last days, in all his works, that, as one of the brethren told me, one of those who trained and taught me in writings (*the Scriptures*), and who was brought up and taught in his monastery and under his mastership, whose name was Trumbert, if he sat at learning (said he), or did any thing else, [and] if suddenly a greater blast of wind arose, he immediately called upon the Lord's mercy, and then begged compassion to mankind. But if a stronger wind arose, then he shut his books and fell forward on his face, and earnestly uttered his voice in prayer. And then yet if a stronger storm and a cloud were more threatening, and

lightning, and thunder-peals[1] awed and frightened earth and air, then went he to church, and heedfully continued with fast mood in prayers, and psalmsinging; until calmness of the air returned and came. When his fellows enquired and asked him why he did this, then answered he, "But have ye not learned [this?]— *Quia intonuit de cœlo Dominus, et Altissimus dedit vocem suam. Misit sagittas suas et dissipavit eos: fulgura multiplicavit et conturbavit eos.* "That the Lord thundereth[2] from heaven, and the Highest giveth his voice: He sendeth his bolts,[3] and scattereth them (*his enemies*); He manifoldeth his lightnings and troubleth them.' For the Lord cleaveth the air, waketh the winds, shooteth the lightnings, thundereth from heaven, that he may awake the dwellers on earth to dread him, that he may call their hearts into a minding of the coming doom, that he may cast down their pride, and trouble their boldness, by bringing to their minds the frightful time, when, heaven and earth being on fire, he shall come in the clouds of heaven in great might and majesty, to deem the quick and the dead. Therefore it behoveth us that we answer his heavenly warnings with becoming awe and love, and, as oft as he stirreth the lift,[4] and sheweth his hand, as it were, threatening to strike us, and not yet however strikes, that we forthwith call and beseech his mercy, and search the secrets of our hearts, and cleanse the filthiness of our vices, and heedfully do so that we never earn that we should be struck."

6. To the revelation and the saying of the foresaid brother concerning this bishop's decease agrees also the word of the venerable father Egbert, of whom we spoke before; who long before, with the same Keadda, in Ireland, the isle of the Scots, when they were both young, lived to God in monk-life, in prayers, and continence, and learning of holy writings, but Keadda after a space returned to his birthland, into Britain, and Egbert abode there in pilgrimage, for the name of God, until his life's end. Then after a long time came to him from Britain, for the sake of a visit, a most holy and most continent man, Hygbald, who was Abbot in Lindsey. Then spoke they of the

1. *Lit.* thunder-rods.
2. The same verb, "bleoþrian" is employed here for *intonuit*, and above for "uttered his voice."—Any connexion with *intoning* of prayers?
3. Shafts, arrows,—hence 'thunder-bolts.' 4. Air, or sky, Sc.

life of the holy fathers, as it became holy men, and also wished to imitate the same. Among these came them to mind [1] of the venerable bishop Keadda. Then quoth Egbert, " I know a man in this isle, now yet living in the body, who, when that man went out of the world, saw the soul of his brother Keadda, with a host of angels, who descended from heaven, and fetched his soul, and took it with them and returned to the heavenly kingdom." Whether he said this of himself or of some other man, is to us unknown : however, when so great a man said it, we know that it was sooth.

7. Then died Keadda on the sixth day of the nones (*2nd day of the month*) of March, and was first buried by St Mary's Church ; but after a space, a church of the blessed Prince of the apostles, St Peter, being built there, his bones were then laid in it. In each of these places, to the betokening of his virtue, and of his holiness, wonders of healing are often wont to be done. It is for a token, that lately a frantic man, when he ran and went wandering through many places, then came thither, in the evening, the keepers of the place not knowing, or not heeding, and rested there all the night: and then in the morning, with healed wits arose and went out. Then wondered all men, and were fain of it, that such a wonder of healing through God's gift was shown and done. Over his burial-place is a wood-work wrought in the likeness of a small house, provided with a coverlet, then there is in the wall a small hole made, through which the men who come thither for devotion's sake, are wont to put in their hand, and take a dole of the mould thence, [and] when they put that into water, and give it to sick men and cattle to taste, then they are soon freed from the heaviness of their disease, and recover the joy of desired health.

8. In this bishop's place, Archbishop Theodore hallowed Winfrith, a good and moderate man, who in ministry of the bishophood, like his foregoers, was over the provinces of the Mercians, and Middle-English, and Lindesfarne, over all whom Wulfhere, who was yet living, had sovereign power. This Winfrith was of the fellowship of the bishop whom he succeeded, and under him for a long time exercised the ministry of a deacon.

---

1. Fell me to mind of many divers things, Of this and that, &c. *K. Ja.* (1423).

CHAPTER IV.

That bishop Colman having left Britain, wrought two monasteries among the Scots, one for the Scots, another for the English whom he led thither with him.

1. Among these things, when bishop Colman, who came from the Scots,[1] left Britain, and took with him all the Scots whom he had gathered in Lindsey isle, as also thirty men of the English nation, both of whom were carefully and well taught in the leading of monkish life; and left some brethren[2] in the church. First he came to the isle of Hii, whence he had been sent to preach and to teach God's word to the English nation. Afterwards he went to a small isle that is far apart from Ireland to west-ward, and is named in Scottish Inhisbofinde, that is, the isle of the white heifer. When he then came into that isle, then built he there a monastery, and there settled the monks whom he had gathered from either kin, and brought with him.

2. When they were settled and set there, then they could not accord and agree among themselves; for in summer and in harvest-tide, when people gathered the crops in, the Scots left the monastery, and wandered and went through known places, and then in winter returned home, and wished to brook in common the goods which the English had procured by labour. Then Colman sought a way of healing this dissension and strife, went about many places both nigh and far; then found he a place in Ireland suitable to build a monastery on, which is in the Scottish tongue named Magheo; and he bought a small portion of the land, there to build a monastery—from some earl who was the owner of the land, the condition being added, that likewise for him who gave them the place, the monks standing there should aye cry to the Lord, and make supplication for him. And he quickly built a monastery there, and the earl, and all the people nigh, helped him; and he set and settled the English men there, and left the Scots in the foresaid isle. The monastery even until to-day is held by English men [who dwell] there in pilgrimage. It is the same monastery, which from small having now become great, is wont to be named Magheo; and, all being long ago turned to better institutions, it now yet takes and contains a noble host of monks[3], who are gathered there from English kin,

---

1. That is from Ireland.
2. Sumne brothor, *Sm.*—one of the brethren—but Bede says several brethren—*fratribus aliquot;* and " sume" *B*—right.
3. Munecas A. S. *monachorum* Bd.—read therefore " muneca."

and after the example of venerable fathers, under rule and abbot, in great continency and cleanness of life, live by their own hand-working.

CHAPTER V.
Of the death of Oswy and Egbert, the kings; and of the Synod which was held at Hertford to which Archbishop Theodore was foresitting.

1. Then, about six hundred and seventy winters from our Lord's incarnation, that is the year after bishop Theodore came into Britain, Oswy king of the Northumbrians was over-taken by sickness, in which he also died, when he had eight and fifty winters of age. This king was at that time come into so great love of the institution of the Roman and Apostolic church, that, if he were healed of the sickness, he would go to Rome, and there at the holy places end his life, and he asked bishop Wilfrith to be the guide of his journey, and offered him much fee (and unlittle) for that. Then died he on the fifteenth day of the ka-lends of March (*Feb. 15th*), and left his son Egferth heir of his kingdom.

2. In the third year of that king's reign, archbishop Theodore assembled a meeting and synod of bishops, together with many church-masters, who both loved and knew the regular institution of holy fathers. When they then were assembled together, he then began earnestly to advise them to hold, in the mood in which it became a bishop,² the things which agreed with the oneness of the peace of the church. And the writ of the Synodly deed is of this kind:

3. "In the name of our Lord God and ³ Saviour, Jesus Christ, reigning for ever, and governing his church! It has been thought right for us to come together after the manner of the worshipful laws, to deliberate about the needful occa-sions of God's church. We came together in the place which is named Hertford, the twenty-fourth day of the month September, being the first indiction,—I Theodore, though I be un-worthy, being sent by the Apostolic seat as bishop of the church of Canterbury, and the most reverend priest and our brother Bisi,

---

1. Or foresitter, i. e. President.
2. So *Alf.* instead of "to advise them, in a mood (*with a mind*) becoming a bishop, to hold the things that were agreeable to the unity of ecclesiastic peace."
3. So *Bd.*—"of the Lord God and our"—*Alf. Sm.* drihtnes hælendes Cristes *B.* of the Lord Jesus Christ.

bishop of the East-English, and likewise our brother, and priest, Wilfrith, bishop of the Northumbrians, being present by his own legates; likewise our brethren, and priests, Putta, bishop of the Kentish city which is called at Rochester, Eleutherius, bishop of the West-Saxons, and Winfrith, bishop of the Mercians, being present. When we had come together, and sat in order in the same place, quoth I. "I pray you, most beloved brethren, for the awe, and for the love of our Redeemer, that we all in common advise for our belief, that the dooms and the ordinances which have been devised and appointed by all holy and approved fathers, may be unspottedly holden by us all." When I then had spoken these and many other things, which tended to the love of God, and to the oneness of the holy church, then asked I each one of them in order whether they consented to hold the dooms, which of old had been set by holy fathers. And all the bishops answered [me][1] and said, that all those things liked and pleased them well; and that they all with blithe mood would gladly hold them. Then soon I shewed them the same book of the rules, and out of the same book ten chapters, which I had written or marked through places,[2] and knew to be most needful; and bade them all carefully hold them.

4. The first chapter, that we all in common hold the holy day of Easter on the Lord's day after the fourteenth moon of the first month.[3]

The second is, that no bishop invade another's bishopshire, but that he be thankful with the government of the folk entrusted to him.

The third is, That it be lawful for no bishop to disturb the monasteries which are hallowed to God, in any things; nor to take away aught of their goods by violence.

The fourth is, That monks remove not from [one] place to another, nor from [one] monastery to another, unless through leave of its own Abbot; but that they abide in the obedience which they promised to God at the time of their conversion.

Then the fifth is, That no servant of God, of the bishop's fellowship, forsake his own bishop, and go and run through diverse places, nor be received where he comes, without the bishop's

---

1. Him Alf.   2. Or "in their respective places."
3. The 14th day of the moon—in March, which was the first month of the ecclesiastical year.

token and writ: but if he be at one time received, and, being called, will not return home, [that] he who entertained him, and he who was entertained, be both guilty to the bishop's doom.

Then is the sixth, That outlandish bishops and servants of God be thankful[1] with their hospitality and entertainment; and to none of them it be lawful to do any priestly service without the bishop's leave, in whose shire they are entertained.

The seventh is, That twice a year a synod be assembled; but whereas diverse occasions and hindrances often befal, it seemed good to us all, in common, that on the kalends (1*st day*) of August, once a year, a synod be assembled, in the place which is named Cloveshook.

The eighth is, That no bishop be overbearing to another through unright willing (or ambition); but each understand the time and order of his hallowing.

The ninth was considered in common, That as the number of the faithful waxes, more bishops should be added.

The tenth is for marriages, That to none be leave given to have other than lawful marriage, nor any be guilty of incest or uncleanness; nor any forsake his own wife, unless, as the holy gospel teaches, for the cause of fornication. If any man put away his own wife, that was given and joined to him by lawful marriage, if he will be rightly a Christian, let him not gather himself to any other, but abide so, or agree with his own wife."

5. This synod was made *(held)* in the year about six hundred and seventy-three winters from our Lord's incarnation. In that year likewise Egbert king of Kent died, in the month of July, and Lothere his brother obtained his kingdom; which he had thirteen years and seven months.

6. Then Bisi, bishop of the East-English, who, as we have said, was in the foresaid synod, was afterfollower of bishop Boniface, whom we formerly mentioned; he was a man of much holiness and godliness; for when Boniface died, after seventeen years of his bishophood, archbishop Theodore hallowed this Bisi as bishop after him. And, while he was still living, when he was hindered from the episcopal ministry by heavy sickness, two bishops, Ecki and Beadwin, were chosen and hallowed for him; from which time until to-day that province has two bishops.

---

1. That is "content."

CHAPTER VI.

That Winfrith being set down from the bishoprick, Seaxulf got his bishoprick, and Erconwald was given as bishop to the East-Saxons.

1. After these [things] not much time having forthrun, archbishop Theodore was angered by Winfrith of the Mercians, through merit of some disobedience; then he took from him his bishopshire, and in his stead hallowed Seaxulf bishop, who was builder and abbot of the monastery which is named Medeshamstead in the land of the Girwians. Winfrith returned to his monastery, which is named Atbarwe, and there in good behaviour ended his life.

2. Then he likewise set Erconwald bishop to the East-Saxons, in London city; their kings at that time were Sebbi and Sig-here, whom we mentioned before. This bishop's life and conversation in bishophood, yea before bishophood, is said to have been most holy, as likewise was afterwards shewn by tokens of heavenly virtues. And therefore long after, his horse-bier on which he was borne when he was sick, was kept by his disciples; and many unhealthy [persons] who were wearied with lent-fever [1] or other heaviness and sickness, received health from it. And not only the sick who were set under or to the bier, were healed, but likewise the chips that were taken from it, and carried to sick men, quickly bore and brought healing [2] to them. This holy man, ere he was made a bishop, built two noble monasteries, the one for himself, the other for his sister Ethelburga, and both of them he well set with regular discipline. For himself he built in the land of Surrey by the river Thames, in the place that is named Chertsey,[3]—for his sister, in the province of the East-Saxons, in the place which is called Berkingum, in which she might stand a teacher and foster-mother of women devoted to God. When she then had received the government of the monastery, she proved herself in all things, equally worthy of the bishop her brother, in right and regular life; as likewise it was afterwards shown by heavenly wonders.

CHAPTER VII.

That in the monastery at Berkingum it was marked by a heavenly light, where the bodies of holy virgins should be laid.

1. For in this monastery that is in Berkingum many tokens of

---

1. Or ague.   2. Leechdom, if we might say so—a good word.
3. From Kerotes ea, Kerot's isle.

ghostly virtues were wrought, which were written by many who knew them, for their remembrance and the edification of their after-followers; some of which we now have taken care to insert in this our ecclesiastical history.

2. When the violence of the oft-mentioned pestilence was for-harrowing and wasting everything far and wide, then came it likewise into the part of this monastery in which the men were, and daily everywhere [some] were taken from the world to the Lord; Then the abbess and mother of the assembly was heedfully and carefully thinking, at what time the same scourge might touch the part of the monastery in which the company of those who served God in womanhood was. Then began she often in the assembly of the sisters to seek and ask, in what place of the monastery they would have their graveyard set, that they might be buried, when it should happen that they were taken from the earth, by the same destruction by which they saw others [carried off]. When she then could find no certain answer, though she carefully sought [it] from the sisters; then it fell out that she herself with all the sisters received the most certain answer of divine providence. For one night when the psalm-song of praise before the dawn was ended, then Christ's handmaids went out of the church to the burying-ground of the brethren, who had gone before them from this light, and there as was wont sang praise to the Lord. Then was there suddenly a heavenly light sent, and it came over them all, and, as a great sheet, overspread them all, and struck them all with so much fear and amazement, that in their fright they left off the song which they were singing. The brightness of the sent light was more than the light of the sun is at mid-day. Then after a little space it was uphoven from the place, and went on the south side of the monastery, that is by west the church, and there then remained a space and then discovered to them there the place about which they formerly consulted; and so, while they all were glad, it went up into heaven; and none of them had a doubt that the same light was to lead and to receive the souls of Christ's handmaids into heaven; and that it likewise had shown them the place where their bodies should rest, and abide the day of the againrising.[1] The brightness of that light was so great, as an old brother said in the morning, who at the same time was in the church with another, a

---

1. Resurrection.

younger, brother, at prayer,—quoth he that the glare of the light came in through the chinks of the door and of the window, that it overshone all the brightness of the daily light.

CHAPTER VIII.

That a little dying boy named by name the minster-maiden or nun who was to follow after him, and that another [nun], going out of the body, saw some deal of the heavenly light.

1. There was in the same monastery a boy-child[1] not older than three winters, whose name was Isica, who for his childish age was yet fed and taught in the monastery of the maidens hallowed to God. Then was he touched by the foresaid sickness; and when he came to his utmost day, then he cried out thrice and called one of the maidens hallowed to Christ, by her own name, as if he spoke to her being present, and said Eadgyth! Eadgyth! Eadgyth! and so ended his temporal life, and entered the everlasting. And then the maiden whom the dying [child] called, was soon touched by the same sickness in the place where she was, and, on the same day on which she was called, was withdrawn from this light, and followed him who called her, into the heavenly kingdom.

2. Again one of the same handmaids of God was afflicted with the foresaid sickness, and brought to her last day. Then began she suddenly at midnight to call to those who waited on her, and bade them quench the candle and the light[2] that was burning there within. And this she often asked and advised, and none of them however would do her bidding.[3] Then at last, quoth she, " I wot that ye ween that I speak with unwitting mood, but however wit ye that it is not so; for I say you sooth, that I see this house filled with so much light, that your candle and light[2] seems wholly darkness." And though she thus spoke, none of them even then answered her or would fulfil her wish. Quoth she again, " Burn now your candle and light as long as ye will, wit ye, however, that it is not mine, for my light will come to me when it begins to dawn." [She] began then to say that a holy man of God, who had died the same year, appeared to her, and told her that, when the dawn-tide came, she should go to the everlasting light. The truth of the vision was quickly shown and

---

1. Vulgarly man-child.
2. So *Alf.*—the two understood as one " candle-light."
3. *Lit.* hear her.

proved, about the uprun of day, by the maiden's death and forth-going.

CHAPTER IX.

What heavenly tokens were shown, when the mother herself of the congregation went out of the world. That Tortgith God's handmaiden, three years after the lady's death, was then yet had in life.

1. When the religious mother of God's beloved congregation, abbess Ethelburga, was to depart out of the world, then appeared a wonderful sight to a good sister, whose name was Tortgyth, who was dwelling in the same monastery many years, and who always, in all humility and sincerity and chastity, diligently served God, and was a helper of regular discipline to the mother abbess, and taught and cleansed the younger ones both by her lore and by her way of life. That the sister's strength, after the saying of the Apostle, might be perfect in weakness, she was suddenly touched with heavy sickness of body, and through nine full years, by the gracious providence of our Redeemer, was sorely afflicted, to the end that whatsoever uncleanness happened [to be] in her among the virtues, through unwittingness or carelessness, the furnace [1] of the long trial might seethe it all out. This sister, one night when it began to dawn, was going out of her cell,[2] in which she dwelt; then she saw clearly as it were the body of a human being[3] wound about with a sheet, which was brighter than the sun: borne aloft it was uphoven from the house in which the sisters rested [and slept]. When she looked more earnestly [to see] by whom drawing it, the bright and wonderful body, which she saw, was uphoven, then she saw as if it were hoven aloft by golden ropes, until, heaven opening, it was led in, and could no more be seen by her. Then she thought of the sight, and had no doubt that some one of the congregation would soon die, whose soul should be hoven and drawn up to heaven by her good and shining works, which she had done, as if by golden ropes. Which then soothly so befel; for, not many days being set between, the God-beloved mother of the congregation was led away from the heaviness of the body, and her holy soul ascended to the entrance of the heavenly country.

2. Moreover in the same monastery was a noble nun after the worthiness of this world, and in the love of the world to come,

---

1. Ofn *Alf.* oven   2. Cleofan *Alf.*   3. *Lit.* a man's body.

much nobler, who, for many years, was so left and forsaken of all service of her body, that she could not stir a limb. When she then learnt that the body of the venerable abbess was brought and laid in the church, until it should be buried, then begged she that she might be borne thither. When that then so was, then leaned she herself to the body, and in the manner of those praying spoke to her as if living, and prayed that she would try and obtain from the mercy of the gracious Creator, that she might be released from so great and so continual torments; nor were her prayers later heard than after twelve days, that she was led out of the body, and for the temporal affliction received an eternal meed and reward.

3. When the foresaid servant of Christ, Tortgyth was still had in this life, three years after the death of the lady, and was so much wasted [1] by the distemper which we mentioned before, that the bones only were left: and at last, when the time of her dissolution drew nigh, she ceased from stirring not only her other limbs, but likewise her tongue. Then were there three days and three nights that she was speechless. Then was she suddenly gladdened by a ghostly sight, and opened her mouth and her eyes, and looked up to heaven, and thus began to speak to the sight which she beheld: " Thy coming," quoth she, " is to me in much thank[2], and thou art dearly welcome." When she had thus said, she was silent a little while, as if she waited for his answer whom she saw, and to whom she spoke. Again, as if she were lightly angered, she afterwards said, " For no sake can I blithely bear this." Again she was silent a little space. Quoth she the third time, " If for no sake it might be to day, I beseech that there be not long space between." She then kept silence again for a little, as she did before, and then thus shut up and ended the word, " If it be thus decreed and this sentence may not be changed, I pray and beseech that there be not more space between than this next night only." When she had said this, then the bysitters asked her with whom she was speaking: quoth she, " With my dearest mother Ethelburga." Then understood they by that, that she had come thither to tell her the right tide of her departure. And even so it was, as she prayed, when the

---

1. *Lat.* decocta, boiled down. *A. S.* asoden, sodden.
2. Very agreeable, thanc or thonc, *gratia*, favour, in which sense " thank " was very commonly used by the early writers of English.

day and the night had gone forth, that she was loosed from the bonds of her body and of her sickness, and entered to the joy of eternal salvation.

CHAPTER X.
That at the grave-yard of the monastery a blind woman prayed, and received the light of her eyes.

1. Then after Ethelburga followed, in the office of Abbess, the devout servant of God whose name was Hildelith; and during many years, that is, until her utmost age, was over the same monastery with much ability, both in providing the things which belonged to the common works, and also in the holding of regular discipline. Then it seemed good to her, for the narrowness of the place in which the monastery was built, that she would take up the bones of Christ's servants, which were there buried, and lay them in the church of the blessed maiden, St Mary, and there keep them in one place. And there very often since, the brightness of a heavenly light has appeared, and also much sweetness of a wonderful smell has come, and many other tokens and wonders have been seen, which, whoever reads them, may find in the book, from which we gathered them.

2. Then there is a miracle of healing which we must not leave out, which the same book says was done at the grave-yard of God's dear congregation. There was an earl in the neighbourhood, whose wife had a distemper in her eyes; and then through days they grew worse and were darkened so that she could not see a particle of a ray of light. When she had been some while in this blindness, then it was one night when she was shut up, that it came into her mind, that if she were led to the monastery of God's holy maidens, and there prayed at the reliques of the saints, she might recover the lost light. Nor did she lose any time, but soon fulfilled what had come into her mind. Then she was led [1] by her servants and handmaids to the monastery which was therenigh, and she there acknowledged that she had unshaken belief of her recovery. Then was she led to the graveyard of God's servants; and when she had long prayed there with bent knees, she soon earned that her prayers were heard; and as soon as she arose from prayer, ere ever she went from

---

1. Or brought, or carried.

the place, she received the gift of the light prayed for; and she who had been brought thither by the hands of her servants, free in her feet-goings, blithely returned home; most like as if she had lost a temporal light, to the end that, by her recovery, she might shew how much light Christ's saints in heaven possessed, and what the grace of their virtue was.

CHAPTER XI.
That Sebbi, the king of the same province, ended his life in the character of a monk ("in monkhood").

1. Over the kingdom of the East-Saxons was at that time, as the same book says, the man devoted to God, whose name was Sebbi, whom we mentioned before. This man was religious in his deeds, and often in holy prayers, and very earnest in pious fruits of alms; and preferred sunder-life and monk-life to all the wealth and honours of the earthly kingdom: that life he would oft and long before have chosen, and have forsaken the earthly kingdom, if the adverse mind of his wife had not withstood him. Thence it was seen and often said by many, that a man of such mind ought rather to be hallowed a bishop than to be a king. When he then had remained thirty years in the kingdom, and had been a soldier of the heavenly kingdom, then was he sorely afflicted with great bodily sickness, and in that he died. Then (when thus afflicted) he admonished his wife, that they should then yet together serve God, when they could no more together love the world, nor serve the world. When he then, for his sickness, had with difficulty carried that through, then came he to the bishop of London, whose name was Waldhere, who was bishop Erconwald's afterfollower, and through his blessing received the order of religion which he long before desired. He likewise brought to the same bishop much fee (and unlittle) to deal to the needy, and kept nothing of it all to himself, but rather wished to remain poor in spirit for the love of heaven's kingdom.

2. When he was heavily pressed by the foresaid illness, and understood that the day of his death was coming on, then this man of a kingly mind began to dread, lest, when he were come to death, and afflicted with great pain, he should do any thing unworthy or unbecoming, with his mouth, or with the stirring of his other limbs. He then called to him the bishop of the foresaid

city, London, in which he then dwelt, prayed him that he would grant him, when he should be dying, that no more men should be there within, than the bishop and his two attendants.

3. Then the bishop promised that he would gladly do as he asked him. Then after a little space, the same man of God set his limbs in stillness, and would rest him, and fell asleep. Then saw he a comforting vision, which removed the anxiety of the mentioned care, and also shewed him on what day he should end his temporal life. He saw, as he himself afterwards said, three men come to him, clothed in bright garments, one of whom sat before his bed, and his other companions, who came with him, stood; then they asked the sitting one about his state, how it should happen to the sick man, whom they had come to visit. Quoth he that his soul, without any sore, but with much brightness, should go out of the body; and shewed him also and said, that he should die on the third day: each of which things was fulfilled, as he had learned from the vision. For on the third day after, past noon-tide, then it was as if he lightly fell asleep, [and] without any feeling of pain, gave up the ghost, and died.

4. Then they prepared to bury his body in a stone coffin. But when they began to lay the body in it, then the body was a span longer than the coffin. Then hewed they the stone as much as they could, and added to the length of the coffin a measure of two fingers,[1] but not even then could it admit the body. When much difficulty arose about his burial, then thought they and spoke, that they should either seek another coffin, or bend the body at the knees, that they might be able to put it there in. But then a wonderful and even heavenly thing happened, and forbade either of these to be done. There stood by the body the bishop and the king's two sons, Sighard and Swefred, who obtained the kingdom after him, and also a great multitude of men. Then was the coffin found of a suitable length to the measure of the body, so that on the part of the head, a pillow might be set between; and on the part of the feet, the coffin was four fingers longer than the body. Then was the man of God buried in the church of St. Paul the apostle, by whose admonitions he had been taught and had learnt that he should hope for the heavenly blessedness.

---

[1]. That is, finger breadths or inches, *digitorum*.

CHAPTER XII.

That Heddi received the bishophood of the West-Saxons for Eleutherius, and Quickhelm received that at Rochester for Putta, and for him Gifmund; ² and likewise who were then bishops of the Northumbrians. The star appeared which is called cometa, and remained three months, and always upran in the early morning. In the same year Egfrith, king of the Northumbrians, drove away the venerable bishop Wilfrith.

1. The fourth bishop of the West-Saxons was called Eleutherius; the first was Birinus, the next was Aghilbert, the third was Winé. When king Coinwalch died, in whose reign the same Eleutherius was made bishop, then aldermen got the government of the nation, and divided it among them, and held it ten winters. And in their reign bishop Eleutherius died, and archbishop Theodore hallowed for him Heddi, as bishop, in London. And in this bishop's time the aldermen were evercome and put to flight, and Cadwalla obtained the kingdom of the West-Saxons. And when he had held the kingdom and been king two years, then was he instigated by the love of the heavenly kingdom, and left the earthly kingdom in the same bishop's time, and went to Rome, and there ended his life, as hereafter is more distinctly to be told.

2. Then it was about six hundred and seventy winters after our Lord's incarnation, that Ethelred king of the Mercians led a wicked host, and ravaged Kent, and, without respect of piety, or of the fear of God, perverted and destroyed churches and monasteries; and Rochester likewise in which Putta was bishop, though he was not at that time there present, he laid waste in the general havock. When he then found that his church was bereaved and forharrowed of all its goods, then turned he to Seaxulf bishop of the Mercians, and he gave him the possession of a church and a little land, and he served God in that church, and went about wheresoever he was asked, and taught church-song, and there in peace ended his life. For him bishop Theodore hallowed Quickhelm as bishop in Rochester: but he, after a little time, for scantness of worldly goods, went from the bishopseat; then the archbishop set Gefmund as bishop for him.

2. Then about two years after Ethelred king of the Mercians had ravaged Kent-land, that is the ninth year of king Egfrith's reign, in the month [of] August, appeared a new star, which is called a comet, and remained three months, and rose at uht-tide ¹ and bore a great brightness as of a shining flame. The same year was dissension and strife arisen between king Egfrith and the

---

2. That is, Givmund, *Gebmundus* Bd.
1. One of the canonical hours, half-way between midnight and sunrise.

worshipful bishop Wilferth ; and the same bishop was shoven and driven from his bishopseat and two bishops set in his place, who were over the nation of the Northumbrians ; that was Bosa who governed the province of the Deiri, and Eata, of the Bernicians. Bosa had his bishopseat in York, and Eata in Hagustald's isle and in Lindesfarne : these were both chosen from monkhood into bishophood. With them was also Eadheth hallowed as bishop in the province of Lindsey, which king Egfrith had newly won, when he overcame Wulfhere in battle, and put him to flight ; and the same province first received this [its] own bishop. The second was Ethilwin ; the third, Eadgar; the fourth, Kynebert. Before Eadheth the province had Seaxulf as bishop, who was likewise bishop of the Mercians and of the Middle English ; but he was driven from Lindsey when Egfrith conquered it ; and he remained in the government of the other provinces. Eadheth and Bosa and Eata were hallowed in York by bishop Theodore ; and he likewise, three years after Wilfrith's away-going, added two bishops to the number of these ; Trumbert to the church of Hagustald, and Eata went to Lindesfarne, and Trumwine to the province of the Picts, which at that time was subject to the kingdom of the English nation. He set Eadheth as bishop to the church of Ripon, when he came from Lindsey, because Ethelred had recovered and gained that province.

CHAPTER XIII.
That bishop Wilfrith converted the province of the South-Saxons to Christ ; which however, when he went thence, on account of the cruel oppression of foes, could not have [its] own bishop.

1. When bishop Wilfrith was driven from his bishopshire, he wandered long through many places, visited Rome, and returned to Britain ; although, for the enmity of the mentioned king, he could not be received into his own country, nor into his bishopshire. He could not however be hindered from the ministry of preaching the gospel : but he turned to the province of the South Saxons, which, after Kent, reaches south and west to the boundary of the West-Saxons ; of this land there are seven thousand hides ; and they at that time followed heathen rites. To this nation the bishop ministered the word of Christ's belief, and the bath of baptism. Ethelwalch, the king of that nation, had not much time before been baptized in [the land of] the Mercians, by

the lore and carefulness of Wulfhere, king of the Mercians. And the king likewise, when he was washen in the bath of baptism, received him as godson, and as a token of that relationship, gave him two provinces of Meanware in the nation of the West-Saxons.

2. The king was very fain of the bishop's coming; and he first washed the aldermen and king's thanes, with the holy well of the bath of baptism. And the mass-priests, Eappa, and Padda, and Burghelm, and Eodi, both then and in afterfollowing time, baptized the other folk. The queen, moreover, whose name was Ebba, had been baptized in her own province, that is, of the Wiccii. She was the daughter of Eanfrith, the brother of Eanher, who were both Christians, with their folk; and all the province of the South-Saxons was ignorant of the divine name and belief.

3. A monk of Scottish kin was there, who was called Dicul; he had a small monastery in a place which is named Bosanham, encompassed with woods and with sea, and in which were five or six brethren serving the Lord in needy and poor life. But no man in that province would imitate their life or hear their lore.

4. When bishop Wilfrith taught divine lore in the nation, he saved them not only from the miseries of eternal damnation, but also from the horrible[1] calamity of temporal destruction. For, three years before his coming into the province, no rain had come in those places, and the grimmest hunger scourged the folk, and felled them with a cruel death. As a token of that, men say that often forty or fifty persons together, who were scourged by the hunger, wretchedly took one another by the hands, and all together outfell from the sea-shore, and would either fell or drench themselves to death. And then on the same day that the nation received Christ's belief, and baptism, a mild rain came down, great and abundant; and the lands grew and blossomed, and after [that] came a good and fruitful year.

5. And so they cast off the old foolishness, and forsook idolatry, and the hearts and bodies of them all rejoiced in the living God; and they understood that he is the true God; and that they themselves, both in the inner goods, and in the outer, were by heavenly grace enriched. For the bishop, when he came into the province, and saw so great pain of hunger there,

---

1. Manfullan A.S., nefanda L.

taught them they should seek food lor themselves by fishing; for both the sea and their river abounded in fish, but the nation knew not the craft of fishing, unless for eels only. Then the bishop's men gathered the eel-nets everywhere that they could, and cast them into the sea, and the divine favour helped them, so that they soon caught three hundred fishes of diverse kinds; and those they dealt in three, they gave a hundred to the poor, a hundred to those who owned the nets, and kept a hundred for their own use. By this kindness the bishop turned the hearts of them all to his love, and they the more heedily hoped for the heavenly goods through his lore, by whose attention they had received and enjoyed the temporal goods.

6. At that time king Ethelwalch gave and granted to the venerable bishop Wilfrith eighty-seven hides of land, of which the name is Selesea,² in which he might have his men who were in exile with him. The place is surrounded by the sea on all sides but the west, where they have an entrance of so much breadth as one can throw with a sling. When the bishop then had received the place, he there founded a monastery, and set it to regular life, chiefly of the brethren whom he had brought with him; which yet to-day his afterfollowing bishops have. The venerable bishop Wilfrith exercised the ministry of a bishop in those parts honourably five years, that is until the death of king Egbert. And because king Ethelwalch gave and granted him, with the possession of the foresaid place, all the goods that were therein, with land, and with men, he settled them all in Christ's belief, and washed them with the bath of baptism. Among these he baptized two hundred and fifty male and female slaves; and as by baptism he saved all these from the devil's service, he likewise loosed and freed them from human thraldom.

CHAPTER XV. *

Among these things Keadwalla, prince of the West-Saxons, young and valiant, being then an exile, came with a host, and slew king Ethelwalch, and wasted the province with cruel slaughter and robbery. But he was soon driven thence by the

---

2. "That is, the island of the sea-calf," adds Bn.—Seal's ey.
* Chapter xiv. and the heading of this, are not in the A. S.

king's aldermen Berthun and Andhun, who afterwards had the government of the province, of whom the former was slain by the same Keadwalla when he was king of the West-Saxons, and subdued the province with heavier thraldom. Ina likewise, who got the kingdom after Keadwalla, harmed the province with like distress many years' time. For that cause it came to pass that, during all that time, they could not have [their] own bishop. But when Wilfrith, their first bishop, was called home again, they were thenceforth subject to the bishops of the West-Saxons, who were in Winchester.

CHAPTER XVI.
That the isle of Wight received Christian inhabitants; and two kingly youths belonging to it, after receiving the bath of baptism, were immediately slain.

1. After Keadwalla had become mighty and strong in the kingdom of the West-Saxons, then he also overran and took the isle of Wight, which till that time was all given to idolatry; and he, after the likeness of the tragic slaughter, would root out all the inhabitants of the land, and plant it with men of his own people. Men say that he also bound himself with a vow, though he was not as yet born again in Christ through the bath of baptism, that, if he might win the island, he would give the fourth part of it, and of the booty, for God. And he so fulfilled it, that he gave bishop Wilfrith that part to brook for God, as he at that time had come thither from his own nation, and was there present. The measure of that island, after the reckoning of the English kin, is twelve hundred hides; and he gave the bishop three hundred hides in possession; and he also added thereto. He then committed the part which he received to one of his priests, whose name was Bertwin,[3] who was his sister's son; and gave him a mass-priest, whose name was Hiddila, who should administer the word of God and the bath of baptism to all who would be saved.

2. It is not to be passed over in silence that, among the first who from that island were saved through faith, were two kingly youths, who by the special favour of God received the crown of victory: they were brothers of Arwald the king of the island. When king Keadwalla went with the army into the island, then

---

3. Bertwine Bp.

fled the youths out of the island and were brought into the neighbouring province which is called Eot-land or the country of the Jutes,⁴ to a place which is named At Stone; they wished and weened that they might there be secret and hid from the face of the ruthless⁵ king; then were they there betrayed, and the king ordered them to be slain. When a certain abbot and mass-priest heard that, whose name was Kynebert, who had a monastery not far thence, in a place which is called Reedford; then came he to the king, who was then hiding him in the same parts, to be healed of his wounds, which had been given him when he fought and made war on the isle of Wight, and besought him, if the youths must at once be slain, that he would give him leave that he might teach them the mysteries of the Christian belief. Then the king granted him that, and gave leave; and he then instructed and taught them by the word of truth, and washed them from sins by the bath of baptism, and taught them, and did them to wit, of the in-going to everlasting life. And the executioner overstood them, and they straightway unaffrighted and blithe underwent the temporal death, through which they doubted not to be going to the eternal life of their souls.

3. In this order, after all the provinces of Britain had received Christ's belief, the isle of Wight also received it, in which, however, for the misery of foreign subjection, none received the office of a bishop's ministry ere Daniel, who then was bishop of the West-Saxons.—This island is set against the middle of the South-Saxons and the West-Saxons, and a sea is set between three miles broad, which is called Solente; in which sea are two sea-floods, which come and arise about Britain from the unended northern ocean; and, daily fighting between them, come against [each other]; and the strife being ended, they are poured back into the sea and flow thither whence they formerly came.

CHAPTER XVII.
Of the synod which was held in the field which was named Heathfield; present, the archbishop Theodore.

1. In these times bishop Thodore heard that the belief of the church at Constantinople was much troubled by the heresy of Eutyches; and he then wished that the church of the English kin,

---
4. Eot, Iot, Jut, i. e. Yut, are supposed to be corruptions of Geat, Gaut or Goth.
5. Unholdan *Alf.*—*victoris* Pp.

over which he then was, should abide clean from a plague of this kind; and having called together a band of reverend bishops and many teachers, he asked them one by one of what belief they were, and, by the one-minded acknowledging of all, found them in the right belief; and this belief he took care to commend and fasten by a synodal epistle for the instruction and remembrance of the afterfollowers. Of that epistle [1] and writ this is the beginning:—

2. "*In nomine Domini nostri Jhesu Christi Salvatoris,*—In [the] name of our Lord Jesus Christ, ruling us the religious lords, Egbert, king of the Northumbrians, the tenth year of his reign, under the fifteenth day of the kalends of November (*Oct.* 17th), and Ethelred, king of the Mercians, the sixth year of his reign, and Ealdulf, king of the East-English, the seventeenth year of his reign, and Lothair, king of the Kentishmen, the seventh year of his reign; foresitting Theodore, by the grace of God, archbishop of the isle Britain, and of the city Canterbury; sitting together with him other bishops of the isle Britain, reverend men, and the right holy gospels laid before them, in the place which is named Heathfield, we together were considering right belief and right glorifying;[2] and we have set [forth] as our Lord Jesus Christ, in man's flesh, gave to his disciples, who saw him present and heard his words; and the watch-word [3] of holy fathers, that is, the Creed, and generally, all holy and universal synods, and the whole band of approved doctors of the right-believing church, have given [or handed down]. These we follow in a pious and orthodox manner, according to the teaching of those who were divinely inspired; and we here now confessing, harmoniously believe and acknowledge, after the holy fathers, properly and truly, Father, and Son, and Holy Ghost, threeness in oneness consubstantially, and oneness in the threeness, that is, one God in three substances or persons, consubstantial, of evenly glory and honour.

3. And after many things of this kind, which belonged to the acknowledging of right belief, the holy synod likewise added these [words] to its epistle, "We have received the five holy and right-

---

1. "Of those staves" *Alf.* and above—"Synodly staves."
2. The right and orthodox faith *Bd.* Let us excuse the unsuccessful attempt of the worthy king; he knew that *ortho* meant right, and *doxa*, glory.
3. 'He gave the watch-word' seems to be sense in A. S. whereas the noun (symbolum) is in the nominative case.

believing synods of blessed fathers approved of God ; that is those which were assembled in Nice, of three hundred and eighteen bishops,—against the most impious Arius and his lore ; and in Constantinople (were assembled), of a hundred and fifty bishops, against the madness of Macedonius and Eudoxius and their lore ; and in Ephesus, of two hundred ¹ bishops, against the most wicked Nestorius and his lore. And in Chalcedon of six hundred and thirty bishops against Eutyches and Nestorius again, and their lore ; And again in Constantinople, the fifth synod was assembled in the time of Justinian the younger emperor, against Theodore and Theodoret, and Iba the heretic, and their doctrines. And we acknowledge also the synod which was held in Rome, in the blessed pope Martin's time, the ninth year of the reign of Constantine, the pious emperor. And we glorify our Lord Jesus Christ, ² as they glorified him, not adding or subtracting any thing of that by which they glorified ; and we excommunicate with heart and mouth those whom they excommunicated, and those whom they received we likewise receive, glorifying God, the Father without beginning, and his only begotten ³ Son, generated of the Father, before ages, and the holy Ghost forthgoing from the Father and from the Son unspeakably ; as they preached and taught, whom we mentioned above, the holy apostles, and prophets, and doctors : and we all have fastened with the token of Christ's rood, ⁴ and underwritten, who have set forth the universal and right belief with archbishop Theodore."

CHAPTER XVIII.

Of John, the high-singer of the apostolic seat, who for [the purpose of] teaching came to Britain.

1. In this synod was a venerable man, who at the same time confirmed the dooms of the universal belief, [namely] John the high-singer of the church of St Peter the apostle, and abbot of St Martin's monastery, who had newly come from Rome through

---

1. Instead of 200 the printed text gives 102, twa and hund, instead of tuwa hund,—but "tu hund" *T*.
2. This clause may perhaps account for the strange paraphrase of *orthodoxam*.
3. Acennedan *Sm. read* ancennedan, *unigenitum*. Bp.
4. The sign of Christ's cross; this form of confirming is not mentioned by Bede,—he has merely *subscripsimus*

command of pope Agatho; his guide was the reverend abbot who was called Benedict. When the same Benedict had built a monastery in Britain, in honour of St Peter the chief apostle, in the place which is called At Weremouth, then came he to Rome with his fellow-workman and fere in the same work, Heolfrith, who was abbot of the same monastery after him; he was also often wont formerly to be over it: and he was honourably received by pope Agatho of blessed memory; and asked and received from him, in confirmation of the freedom of the monastery which he had built, a *privilegium* confirmed by apostolic authority. After he wist that it was the will of king Egfrith and his leave, since he had given and granted him possession of the land on which he had built the monastery,[1] then he took also the foresaid abbot John and led [him] into Britain, that he should teach in his monastery, for twelve months, the song which he had learned from St Peter. Then John did as the pope's command was; taught the singers of the foresaid monastery the order and manner of the song with the quick voice; and those which the circle of the whole year required, he likewise wrote in staves, and set in a book, which is holden in the same monastery to this [day], and has, since that time, been written off by many, everywhere about.

2. John likewise received another command from the apostolic pope, that he should earnestly know and learn, of what belief the church of the English kin was, and tell him that when he returned to Rome: for that end was the synod, of which we spoke before, assembled in Britain. Then was found in all an unspotted and right belief; and a copy of the synod's decree[2] was given him in writing, that he should bear it to Rome. And he then was returning to his own country; then a little while after he had passed over sea, he was touched with sickness and died; and his body was carried by his friends, and for the love of St Martin, to Tours, and there honourably buried in the monastery over which he had been in abbotdom. And though he died on his journey, the pattern of the belief of the English church was carried to Rome, and was thankworthily received by the apostolic pope, and by all who heard or read it.

---

1. In Bede the sentence ends here, and not at " authority, after he wist"—2 lines before.
2. Or " the pattern of the synod was given."

CHAPTER XIX.

That the queen Etheldrith remained a clean maiden, whose body could not be corrupted in the tomb; and of the hymn which we made about her.[1]

1 King Egfrith took a mate and wife, whose name was Etheldrith, daughter of Anna, king of the East-English, of whom we have often made mention before, who was a good and pious man, and through all, both in mind and in deeds, noble. Another man had taken her to wife before him, an alderman of the South-Girvii, whose name was Tonbert: but in a little space after he had taken her to wife, he died. Then she was given and yielded to the foresaid king, and while she was brooking his company twelve years, nevertheless she wonderfully remained in everlasting soundness of maidhood; as to myself asking (when it came into doubt with some men, whether it were so) bishop Wilfrith of blessed memory told, and said that he was the most certain witness of her cleanness and maidhood; so that king Egfrith promised to give him both land and much fee, if he could persuade and exhort the queen that she would brook his marriage, for he well knew that she loved no man more than him.

2. It is not to be doubted that that could be in our age, which true histories shew and say happened in a past age, through the grace of our Lord, the same who promised that he would abide with us always until the world's end. It was likewise a manifest token of the divine miracle, that the buried body of the same maiden could not decay, and that she remained unharmed by man's touch. She had long besought the king that she might leave worldly care and business, and that he would let her in a monastery serve Christ, the true king: and she at last with difficulty accomplished it. Then went she into the monastery of the abbess Ebba, who was king Egfrith's aunt, which is situate in the place which is named Coludsburgh, and she there received the holy veil and God's service from the foresaid bishop Wilfrith. Then it was about one year after this, that she became abbess in the country which is called Ely, where she built a monastery; and she began to be a maiden-mother of many maidens devoted to God[2] both by a pattern of heavenly life and also by [her] instructions.

1. The hymn is contained in chapter XX, of which there is no notice in the A.S.
2. So Bede,—the A. S. order connects " Gode wilsumra fæmnena" with the building of the monastery.

3. Men say of her, that after she sought the monastery, she never would wear linen clothes, but woollen ; and seldom would bathe her in hot baths, unless on the highest festivals and times, at Easter, and Whitsuntide, and the twelfth day after yule '; and then she first by her own service and that of her maidservants washed the other servants of Christ who were there ; then would she last of all bathe and wash herself. And seldom, unless in times of great solemnity, or of great need, would she take food more than once a-day. And always, if heavier sickness hindered not, from the early morning song until broad day she stood on holy prayers in the church ': some men also said that she, by the spirit of prophecy, foretold the sickness in which she should die, and likewise that she clearly shewed to all the number of God's servants, who from her monastery were to be carried out of the world. Then she departed to the Lord in the midst of her folk, seven years after she had received the office of an abbess ; and like as she commanded, was buried, not in another place, but in the midst of her own folk, after the order in which she died, in a wooden coffin.

4. Then she was succeeded in the office of abbess by Sexburga her sister, whom Erconbert king of Kent had to wife : and when Etheldrith had been buried sixteen years, then it liked the abbess her kinswoman that she should take her bones up and lay them in a new coffin, and put them in the church. Then she bade some brethren go and seek the stone, that one might hew and work the coffin of it. Then went they into a ship, for Ely-land is on every side encompassed with waters and with fens, nor has it great stones ; then came they to a fallen city not far thence, which is in English called Grantacaster, and they soon found by the city-walls a coffin of white stone, fairly wrought, which was also suitably lidded with the like stone. Then understood they that their errand and their journey had been hastened and furthered by the Lord himself, and they said thank to God for that, and carried the coffin to the monastery.

5. When the tomb was opened, and the body of the holy maiden and Christ's bride was brought forth into light, then was it found as uncorrupted and as unblemished, as if she had died and been buried that same day ; as the foresaid bishop Wilfrith

---

3. The name by which Christmas is still known in the north.
4. Alfred uses " stod " for insisted, was instant.

and many others, who knew it, shewed and said. But yet of more certain knowledge, Kynebert, the leech, who was with her when she died, and again when they hove her body up from the tomb, was wont to say, " When she was sick, and had a great swelling on her neck, then I was ordered (quoth he) to pierce the swelling, that the hurtful wet that was in it might flow out. When I then had done that, she seemed through two days to be lighter, and was so well, that many reckoned that she might be healed from the sickness. On the third day she became heavy again with the former sores, and soon was touched, and taken out of the world, and exchanged all the sore and the death with everlasting health and life. When after so many years her body was hoven up from the tomb, they stretched and fastened a tilt over it, and all the gathering of brethren and sisters stood around on two halves, singing; and the abbess went into the tilt, and a few with her, wishing to take the bones up, and wash and cleanse them, as they were wont to do. Then suddenly heard we the abbess within cry with a loud voice, 'Glory be to the name of the Lord.' Then after a little while they cried and called me in, and unfolded the doors of the tilt, then saw I the body of God's holy maiden uphoven from the tomb, and laid on a bed; and it was liker to the sleeping than to the dead. Then unclothed they also her face, and shewed me the wound of the cut which I had long before made: then was it so fastly healed, that in a wonderful way, instead of the open and yawning wound, with which she had been buried, the thinnest and least scar was to be seen."

6. Yea also all the sheets in which the body had been wound, appeared as sound, and new, and clean, as on the same day on which they were wrapped round her clean limbs. Men say also that when she was troubled and afflicted with the swelling and sore of her neck, she greatly rejoiced at this kind of illness, and was wont often to say, " I know truly that I deservedly bear the burden of this sore, and of this distemper on my neck, on which I remember, formerly when I was young, I bore the idle burden of golden jewels; and I believed that the divine clemency would therefore have me afflicted with soreness of my neck, that so I might be loosed from the guilt of that vain looseness [of life], when now, instead of gold and gems, the redness and burning of this irksome swelling appear on my neck."

7. Lo! then it befel, that by the touch of those same clothes,

which were taken off her body, diseases of the devil-sick, and of many others, were often healed. Likewise the coffin in which she was first buried, was for healing to many men, whose eyes had become sore and dim ; then they bent their head and their eyes to it, and soon the inconvenience of the sore and of the dimness went from their eyes. And lo ! they then washed and bathed the body of the holy maiden, and clothed it with new garments, and bore it into the church, and laid it in the stone coffin, which had been brought thither ; and there, now yet to this present day, it is had in much reverence. That was also a great wonder, that the coffin was found so meet for the maiden's body, as if it had been especially prepared for her : moreover the head place seemed most skilfully wrought, and conveniently shapen to the size of her head.

8. The land of Ely in the province of the East-English, of about six hundred hides, in likeness of an island, is all, as we have said, encompassed with a fen, and with water ; and takes its name from the abundance of eels, which are caught in the same fens.

CHAPTER XXI.
That bishop Theodore made peace between Egfrith and Ethelred, the kings.

Then in the ninth year of king Egfrith's reign, a heavy strife was joined and begun, and a great fight, between him and Ethelred king of the Mercians ; then was slain in the fight, near the river Trent, Elfwin, king Egfrith's brother ; he was a young prince of eighteen winters, and was very lovely and dear to both nations ; for Ethelred, king of the Mercians, had his sister, who was called Osthrith, to wife. When matter of grimmer fight and longer fiendship, seemed to have arisen between the angry kings and folks, then bishop Theodore beloved of God, by divine grace and help, wholly quenched the begun burning of so great a danger by his wholesome exhortation and lore, so that he made peace between the kings and the folks, that no man's life was lost, nor more blood shed for the king's slain brother, but he agreed with him for money, so that peace was between them. The covenant of that peace continued a long time afterwards between the same kings and their kingdoms.

CHAPTER XXII.

That a captive's bonds were loosed when masses were sung for him.

1. In the foresaid fight, in which Elfwin the king's brother was slain, a memorable thing happend, which is not to be left untold, but will avail to the salvation of many, if it be told. A young thane belonging to king Egfrith, whose name was Imma, was struck down [1] among others in the fight. When he then had lain there among the slain, like one dead, that day and the after-following night, then at last he got breath and came to life again, and sat up, and himself bound up his wound, as [well] as he could, and afterwards rested him a little while. Then hove he himself up, and began to go away, if anywhere he could find any friend, who might take care of him, and dress his wounds. When he then was doing that, then was he found and taken by the men of the hostile army; and these led him to their lord, that was king Ethelred's earl. Then dreaded he to acknowledge that he was a king's thane, but said that he was a common man and needy and had wived, and that he had therefore come to the host, that he should carry their food and meat to the king's thanes with his [2] fellows. Then the earl received him, and took care of him, and bade [them] dress his wounds. When he began to strengthen and heal, then he bade them bind him, lest he should flee and steal away by night. Then they could not bind him: for as soon as they who had bound him went away, then the bonds slipt off, and were loosed asunder.

2. He had an own brother, a mass-priest, whose name was Tunna, who was abbot in the monastery and city, which now at this day, from his name, is named Tuncaster. When he heard that he had been slain in the fight, then came he and sought his body among the dead, if he might find it; then found he another through every thing the likest to him, and thought that it was he, bore him to his monastery, and buried him honourably, and for the release of his soul often did mass-song. By which celebration that was done which I said before, that no man could bind him, but straightway the bonds slipt asunder, and he was loosed.

3. Among these things then also, the earl who had him, began to wonder, and to ask him, why he might not be bound; and

---

1. Slain, *occisus* Bd.—ofslægen *Alf.*
2. Their *Sm.* his *A* & Bp.

asked him, whether he knew the loosing runes, and the written staves with him, about which men say and speak the leasing-spells[1]; that therefore he could not be bound. Then answered he that he knew nothing of such crafts. "But I have," quoth he, "in my province, a brother, a mass-priest, and I wot that he thinks me slain, and for me often masseth, and if I now were in the other life, then were my soul, through his intercession, there loosed from everlasting bonds and torments." When he had been held a little while by the earl, then understood they who carefully watched him, from his looks, and from his manners, and likewise from his words, that he was not from needy folk as he said, but that he was of noble lineage. Then the earl called him privately to him, and asked him then earnestly whence he was, and what he was; and promised him that he would do him naught of harm or evil, if he would tell him openly what he was. Then did he so, owned and said to him that he was a king's thane. Then answered he him and quoth, "Through thy sundry answers, I understood and knew, that thou wert not a common man as thou saidest; and I now say to thee, that thou art guilty of death towards me[2]; for all my brothers and kinsmen were slain in that fight, and yet I will not slay thee, lest I break my promise and my truth."

4. When he then was fully strengthened, then sold he him in London and gave him to a Friesian; then would he bind him; but neither by him, when he was leading him thither, could he for any sake be bound, though his foes set one kind of bonds upon him, and again another; and oftest his bonds slipt off and were loosed at undern-tide,[3] when they oftest sing mass. When he then who had bought him saw that he could not be held fast by bonds, he then gave him leave to loose himself with money, if he could. And he gave him oaths that he would either come back to him, or send him his ransom. Then came he to Kent, to king Lothaire, who was sister's son to queen Etheldrith of whom was said above, for he had formerly been that queen's thane, and asked him to give him the worth of his loosing; and he granted him [that], and [he] sent it to his lord as he had promised.

5. And he then after these things returned to his own land,

---

1. Fables, *literally* lying stories.
2. Deservest death from me.   3. The third hour of the day.

and to his brother; and told him every thing in order, both what adversity, and what comfort in that adversity, had come to him. And he knew by his sayings that mostly at those times his bonds were loosed, at which the solemnities of the mass were celebrated for him; yea, also many other advantages and benefits, which had befallen him in his perilous condition through those brotherly ministrations; and which he knew and understood were granted him from heaven, through the offering of the wholesome sacrifice. And many persons who heard say of these things from the foresaid man, were burning in faith, and in will of godliness, to pray, and to give alms, and to offer to God the sacrifice of the holy oblation, for the deliverance of their friends, who had departed out of the world. For they understood that the wholesome sacrifice availed and profited to the eternal redemption both of body and of soul. This spell [was] told me [by] some of those who heard it from the man himself, on whom it was done; therefore I clearly and undoubtedly believed it [fit] to be added and inserted into our Ecclesiastical History.

CHAPTER XXIII.
Of the life and death of Hilda, the abbess.

1. (Was) about six hundred and eighty winters from our Lord's incarnation, (that) the pious servant of Christ, Hilda abbess of the monastery, which is called Streones-halch, as we said before, after many heavenly deeds, which she did on earth, being carried away from earth to receive the meed of heavenly life, departed on the fifteenth day of the kalends of December,[1] when she had six and sixty winters. These years being todealt by evenly deal, the first three and thirty she nobly filled up in leading a worldly life: and as many afterfollowing she more nobly hallowed to the Lord in monastic life. She was also noble by worldly birth, as she was the daughter of king Edwin's nephew, whose name was Hereric. With that king, at the preaching and lore of Paulinus, of blessed memory, the first bishop of the Northumbrians, she [2] received the belief and mysteries of Christ, which she held unspotted until she earned that she [2] should come to the sight of [Christ] himself.

1. The seventeenth day of November.
2. He *Alf.*—contrary to all probability.

2. When she then (Hilda) forsook the worldly condition, and resolved to serve God only, then went she into the province of the East-English, for she was the king's kinswoman: she wished thenceforth, if she could, to leave her own land, and all that she had in the world, and would come into the kingdom of Gaul, and live in pilgrimage for the Lord, in the monastery of Calé, that she might the more easily earn the everlasting kingdom, and a country in heaven; for in the same monastery her sister Hereswith, who was mother of Aldulf, king of the East-English, underlying regular discipline, was at that time waiting for everlasting victory; whose example she was following in the purpose of pilgrimage, and for a whole year was had in the foresaid province of the East-English, until she was called and drawn home again by bishop Aidan. Then she received the land of one household on the north side of the river Wire; and there likewise for one year led a monastic life with a few companions.

3. After this she was made abbess in the monastery which is called Heoretea. This monastery was made and built not long before by the religious servant of Christ, Hegu, who first of women is said to have taken the monastic condition and the holy veil in the province of the Northumbrians, through bishop Aidan's hallowing. But she, not a long time after the monastery was built, went to the city which in English is called Calcacaster, and set herself there a dwelling, in which she lived to God. Then Hilda the servant of Christ got the ruling of the monastery; and she soon settled and ordered it with regular life, so as she could learn from learned men. For bishop Aidan and many other pious and good men who knew her, often visited her and sought her and truly loved her, for her prudence and wisdom, and for love of the divine service; and carefully trained and taught her.

4. When she then had been many years over this monastery, with great earnestness in the lore of regular life, then it happened that she undertook to build and order a monastery in the place which is called Streones-halch; and the work which was entrusted to her she unslothfully fulfilled. For she settled and trimmed this monastery with the same discipline of regular life as the former.[1] And she there likewise carefully taught the holding of

---

1. Alfred by mistake says, "She instituted and established (inset and trimmed *lit.*) the same [persons] who formerly held and ruled the monastery." It was necessary to follow Bede.

truthfulness, and godliness, and cleanness, and many other ghostly virtues, and especially peace and God's love; so that, after the example of the primitive church, none there was rich, and none poor, but to all was every thing common, and nothing seemed to be any one's own. She was of so much prudence and wisdom, that not only middling men came about their needfulnesses, but likewise kings and aldermen often sought counsel and wisdom from her, which they readily found there. And she likewise made those who were put under her care, exercise themselves so much in the learning of divine writings, and in works of righteousness, that many might there be found who were fitted for the ecclesiastical condition, that is, for the service of the altar. Of this it is a token, that we afterwards saw five bishops, who came from the same monastery, and had been taught there, and they all were men of great worth and holiness; who were thus named, Bosa, Etla, Oftfor, John, and Wilfrith. Of the first we have said above, that he was hallowed as bishop in the city York. Of the second, it is readily to be known, that he was hallowed as bishop in Dorchester. Of the last two is hereafter to be said, that the former was hallowed as bishop at Hagustaldsea, and the latter in the city York.

5 We have now to speak of the middle [one]; when he had diligently stuck and holden fast to his learning of the holy writings in each monastery of abbess Hilda, then at last he wished in his mind for perfect things—came then to Kent, to archbishop Theodore, of blessed memory: after he had there for a while betaken himself to holy learning, then would he also seek Rome; which [to do] was at that time taught and believed [to be] of great might (*virtue*). When he came back thence, then sought he Britain again, went then into the province of the Wiccii, where Osric was then king; and he there preached and taught God's word and the holy belief, and at the same time furnished a pattern of life in himself, to all who saw and heard him: and he abode there much time. In the same time the bishop of the province, who was called Bosel, was afflicted with so great weakness of his body, that he could not by himself discharge the office of bishop. Therefore, by the doom of all, the foresaid man was chosen into bishophood for him; and then by order of Ethelred, king of the Mercians, bishop Wilfrith, of blessed memory, who at that time administered the bishophood of the Middle-English, hallowed him

as bishop; for archbishop Theodore was then dead, and no other bishop was then yet hallowed for him. In the same province a little before, that is, before the foresaid man of God, Bosel, there was also chosen as bishop, a valiant and very learned man, and of sharp wit, from the monastery of the same abbess, whose name was Tatfrith; but before he could be ordained, he was snatched away by a sudden death. And the foresaid servant of Christ, abbess Hilda, whom all who knew her, in token of her piety and God's grace, were wont to call and name "mother," not only in her monastery stood a pattern of life to those who were present, but likewise to many dwelling far off, to whom the happy report of her diligence and virtue came, and furnished occasion of good conduct and salvation.

6. It was also meet, that the dream should be fulfilled, which her mother Bregoswith saw in her childhood. When her husband Hereric was in exile under Kerdic, king of the Britons, where he was killed by poison, then saw she through a dream, as if he were suddenly hoven off and carried away from her. Then sought she him with all diligence, and no trace of him appeared anywhere. When she then was heedfully and earnestly seeking him, then found she suddenly under her garment a golden jewel, very dear-worth and precious. When she then carefully viewed and beheld it, then was it seen¹ to shine with so much brightness of light that it filled all the bounds of Britain with the shine of its light; which dream was truly fulfilled in her daughter, of whom we now speak; for her life was a pattern of light, not to herself only and her subjects, but likewise to many [far and] wide, who were willing to live well to God.

7. When she then had been many years over this monastery, which is at Streoneshalch, in the office of abbess, then it pleased the merciful Author of our salvation, that her holy soul should also be tried and scorched with long sickness of her body, that, after the apostle's example, her strength might be perfect and confirmed in weakness. Then was she seized with a heavy illness, and through six long years incessantly struggled with the pain of the same heaviness, and in all that time she never ceased to give thanks to Almighty God, her Maker, yea also to warn and teach the flock entrusted to her, that they all should be mindful of her

---

1. Gesawen. This form was not so well known as 'gesewen' or 'gesegen' when "gesawen mid" was rendered 'sown with,' p. 207 l. 15, instead of 'regarded by.'

example, that, in prosperous things, and received health of body, they should diligently serve and obey the Lord; and in adverse things, or unhealthiness of body, they should always faithfully give thanks to the Lord.

8. Then in the seventh year of her illness, the sickness and the sore turned into her bowels, and she was coming to her last day, and about cock-crow [1] she received the way-food (called in Latin *viaticum*) of the holy communion of Christ's body and blood. Then she called God's servants to her, who were in the same monastery, and she then yet warned and taught them, that they should hold peace and love among them and all God's people; and amidst the words of her exhortation and advice, she blithely saw death, and yet more truly I may say in [our] Lord's words,— "from death she went to life."

9. On the same night the Almighty Lord deigned, by a manifest vision, to reveal her death in another monastery, set far off, which she had built in the same year, and is named Hacanos.

There was in the same monastery a holy nun, whose name was Begu, who was hallowed to the Lord in clean maidhood, more than thirty years, and she there served the Lord in monastic life. Then was she resting in the sleep-room of the sisters; then heard she suddenly in the air the known sound and ring of their bell, by which they wont to be called and awaked to prayers, when any of them had gone out of the world. Then having opened her eyes, she saw, as it seemed to her, from the house's roof above a great light come, which filled all the house. When she then looked heedfully on the light, and earnestly beheld it, then saw she the soul of God's servant aforesaid, the abbess Hilda, up-borne to heaven in the same light, with hosts of angels leading her.

10. When she then had shaken off sleep, then saw she the other sisters resting about her; then understood she, that, either by a dream, or by a sight of her mind, had been shown her what she saw; and she soon arose affrighted with much awe, and ran to the maiden [lady] who then was abbess of the monastery, and was Hilda's younger,[2] whose name was Freogyth, and was with weeping and tears much overflowed, and drawing a long sigh, told her, that the [3] mother of them all,[3] abbess Hilda, was gone from

---

1. Hanered utan, (uhtan.)
2. Or rather disciple
3. "Their aller mother"—mid. Eng.

the world ; and, in her sight, with much light, and with a host of angels, had ascended to the everlasting light of the glory of heaven's kingdom, and to the fellowship of the heavenly citizens. When she then heard that, she awakened all the sisters, and bade them go to church, and by prayers and by psalmsinging intercede for their mother's soul. When she then had heartily done that the remainder of the night-tide, then came, very early in the dawn, some brethren who brought word of her death, from the place where she died. Then answered they, and said that they understood and wist the same before, and when they related to the brethren, in order, how and when they had learnt those things, and they told them at what time she departed from earth, then it was found that her departure was at the same time that was shown to her by the vision. And by the fair agreement of the things it was divinely provided, that, when they saw her outgoing from this life, they then learnt her upgoing into the everlasting life of holy souls. There are between the two monasteries thirteen meted miles.

(*The concluding paragraph of the Latin is omitted by Alfred.*)

CHAPTER XXIV.
That in her monastery was a brother, to whom was divinely given the gift of singing.

1. In this abbess's monastery was a brother especially distinguished and honoured by divine favour, for he was wont to make agreeable songs which befitted religion and piety, so that whatsoever he learnt from divine writings through bookmen, that he after a little space adorned in poetical language with the greatest sweetness and feeling, and brought it forth, for the most part, in the English tongue; and by his songs the minds of many men were often fired with a contempt of the world and a desire of the heavenly life. And likewise many others after him, in the English nation, have begun to make religious songs, but none however could do it like him : for he not only was not taught by men, nor through man, that he should learn the song-craft, but he was divinely assisted, and through God's gift received the art of poetry. And therefore he never could compose anything of leasing, or of idle song, but even those only which belonged to religion, and became his pious tongue to sing.

2. This man was set in worldly condition until the time that he

was of an advanced age, and he never learned any poetry, and therefore, at entertainments, when it had been deemed [proper] for the sake of mirth, that they all in turn should sing to the harp, when he saw the harp approach him, then rose he for shame from the banquet, and went home to his house. One time when he had done that, he left the house of the entertainment, and went to a neat-stall, the care of which was committed to him that night; when he there then at the proper time had set his limbs to rest, and fallen a-sleep; then a man stood by him in a dream, and hailed and greeted [1] him, and named him by his name. "Kedmon, sing me some what": then answered he, and said, " I cannot sing any thing," and I therefore went out from the entertainment, and came hither, for I could not sing." Again he who was speaking with him said, "However thou canst sing to me." Quoth he, "What shall I sing ?" Quoth he, "Sing me Creation." When he then had received this answer, then began he at once to sing, in praise of God the Creator, the verses and the words, which he had never heard. Of which the order is this:—

3. "Now we owe to praise the Warden of heaven's kingdom, the Maker's might, and his mood-thought, the works of the glorious Father ; how of all wonders the eternal Lord installed the beginning. The holy Creator first shaped heaven for a roof to earth's children; then the Warden of mankind, Eternal Lord, Almighty Master, afterwards made the earth, a fold for men."

Nu we sceolan herigean [2]	Nu scylun hergan [3]
Heofon-rices Weard,	Hefaen ricaees Uard,
Metodes mihte,	Metudæs maecti,
And his mod-geþanc	End his mod-gidanc
Weorc wuldor-fæder ;	Uerc uuldur-fadur :
Swa he wundra gehwæs [4]	Sue he uundra gihaeus
Ece Drihten	Eci Dryctin
Ord onstealde :	Or astelidæ.
He ærest gescop	He aerist scop

1. Halette and grette. This unexpected confirmation of the view taken of "and halettan" in note 2, at the beginning of this work, decides the case of "haletta," and should have been quoted there—if it had been observed, "I Bede send to greet and hail—" is right.
2. Frumsceaft or Creation, King Alfred's text.   3. An older text from the Ely MS.
4. Line 6, wundra MS. B., and one in C. C. Col. Oxon. not mentioned by Smith ; (miraculorum, Bd.) not "wuldres" as in some MSS.

4. Then arose he from sleep, and all that he sleeping had sung he held fast in memory, and soon added to those words many words, after the manner of a song worthy of God. Then came he on the morrow to the town-reeve, who was his alderman; and told him what gift he had received; and he led him to the abbess, and shewed and told it her; then she ordered to assemble all the most learned men, and the learners, and bade him in their presence tell the dream and sing the song, that by the doom of them all it might be proved what [it was], or whence it came. Then it seemed to all, as it was, that a heavenly gift had been given him by the Lord himself. Then they related and said to him a holy speech, and words of divine lore; and then bade him, if he could, turn that into the melody of song. When he then had received the matter, then went he home to his house, and came again on the morrow, and sang and gave them what had been committed to him, composed in the best poetry.

5. Then began the abbess to cherish and love the grace of God in the man; and she then admonished and taught him, that he should forsake the wordly condition, and enter the monastic order. And he readily granted that; and she received him into the monastery with his goods, and joined him to the congregation of God's servants, and bade [them] teach him the number of the holy story and spell [that is, the whole course of sacred history]. And all that he learnt by hearing, he remembered by himself, and, as a clean beast chewing the cud, converted it into the sweetest verse, and his song and his verse were so winsome to hear, that his teachers themselves wrote and learnt them from his mouth. He sang first of the creation of the world, and of the origin of mankind, and all the history of Genesis, which is the first book of Moses; and again of the outgoing of Israel's folk

Eorþan bearnum	Ælda barnum
Heofon to rofe,	Heben til hrofe,
Halig Scyppend;	Haleg Scepen;
Ða middan-geard	Þa middun-gard
Mon-cynnes Weard,	Mon-cynnæs Uard
Ece Drihten	Eci Dryctin
Æfter teode	Æfter tiadæ
Firum foldan	Firum fold[-u],
Frea ælmihtig.	Frea allmectig.

from the land of the Egyptians, and of the ingoing of the land of promise, and of many other spells of holy writ—the book of the Canon; and of Christ's incarnation, and of his suffering, and of his ascension into [the] heavens; and of the coming of the Holy Ghost, and the lore of the Apostles; and again he made many a lay of the awe of the future doom, and of the fear of hell's torment, and of the sweetness of the heavenly kingdom; and he likewise made many others of the divine kindnesses and dooms. In all these he earnestly cared that he might draw men off from the love of sins, and from misdeeds, and awaken them to the love and carefulness of good deeds: for he was a most pious man, and humbly subject to regular discipline, and was fired with the heat of great jealousy against those who would do otherwise; and therefore he tined and ended his life by a good end.

6. For when the time of his departure and death drew nigh, then was he, fourteen days before, afflicted and oppressed with bodily sickness, yet so moderately that all that time he could both speak and go. There in the neighbourhood was a sick men's house, into which it was their custom that they should bring the sick, and those who were near death, and there wait upon them together. Then in the evening of the night in which he was going from the world, he asked his waiting-man to make ready a place for him in that house, that he might rest. Then the man wondered why he asked this, for it seemed to him that his death was not so nigh; he did, however, as he said and bade. And when he had there gone to rest, and with joyful mood was speaking some things, and joking together with those who were there before, then over midnight he asked whether they had any housel (that is consecrated bread) in the house. Then answered they and said, "What need hast thou of housel? thou art not so near death, since thou art so cheerfully and gladly speaking to us." Quoth he again, "Bring the housel to me however." When he had it in his hand, then asked he, whether they all had a kind and blithe mind, without any ill will towards him. Then answered they all, and said that they wist no ill will towards him, but were all of very blithe mood to him; and they in turn begged him to be blithe to them all. Then answered he and said, "My dear brethren, I am of very blithe mood to you, and to all God's men; and he so strengthened himself with the heavenly way-food [of the eucharist], and prepared his entrance into the other life. Then

yet he asked how nigh it was to the hour that the brethren should rise, and rear God's praise, and sing their early morning song. Then answered they, "It is not long to that." Quoth he, "Good: let us well wait that hour"; and then he prayed, and signed himself with the token of Christ's rood, and leaned his head to the bolster, and slept a little while, and so with stillness ended his life. And so it befel, that as he had served the Lord with a pure mind, and a meek and calm devotion, so he likewise left the world by a calm death, and came to the sight of him [whom he had served]. And the tongue, which set so many wholesome words to the Creator's praise, likewise concluded the last words to his praise, while the dying man was signing himself, and committing his spirit into his Creator's hands. It is also said that he was aware of his own death, from the things which we have now heard say.

CHAPTER XXV.
What sight appeared to a man of God before the monastery at Coludsburg was consumed by fire.

1. In these times the nun-minster which is named Coludsburg, which we mentioned before, was destroyed by the flame of fire through the sin of carelessness; yet all who knew it, might understand that it happened by the malice and wickedness of those who dwelt there in the borough, and chiefly of them who were aldermen there. But yet they had no want of warning from the Divine Mercy, that they might correct and amend their sins by fasting and weeping and prayer, and turn away the anger of the righteous Judge from them, in the likeness of the Ninevites.

2. There was in the same monastery a man from the nation of the Scots, who was called Adamnan. This man lived his life very devoted to God, in great continency, and in holy prayers; so that he never took meat nor tasted victuals but on the Lord's day and the fifth week-day; and often insisted and continued whole nights awake in holy prayers. The sharpness of this hard life came to him first of need, for boot of his sins; but with forthgoing time, he turned the need into a custom. It happened to him in his youth, that he was guilty of some wickedness, and when the guilt turned to his heart, then he shuddered at it heavily, and dreaded (him) that he should be sternly punished for it by the sharp Judge. He went then to a mass-priest, by whom he

weened that the way of salvation might be shown him, acknowledged to him his guilt, and begged that he would give him counsel, how he might flee from the wrath to come. When he then heard his guilt, then quoth he, "A great wound needs a great cure; and therefore, as much as thou canst, stick thou to thy fasts and psalmsongs and prayers, that thou come before [2] the Lord's face in confession, and earn that thou find him mild to thee." And he, whom the excessive sore had seized, and the knowledge of his guilt overwhelmed, wished to be quickly loosed from inward bonds of the sins with which he was loaded; quoth he to the mass-priest, "I am of a young age, and hale in my body, whatsoever thou layest on me, and biddest me do, that I may be saved in the day of the Lord, all that I will easily bear, though thou bid me stand all night watching in prayers, and though I must fast the whole week, I will lovingly do it." Quoth he, "Much it is that thou abide a whole week, without bodily food; but a two daily fast or a three daily, [3] is enough to hold. Do this (quoth he) until I, after a space of time, come again to thee, and then more fully show what thou must do, and how long thou must abide in penance." Then went the mass-priest from him. Then it befel, that for some occasion he suddenly went into Ireland, the isle of the Scots, whence he formerly came, nor returned he more to him according to their (his) word. He however was mindful of his command, and of his own promise, and served the Lord in penance, tears, and holy wakes, and much abstinence; so that he never fed nor tasted victuals ofter than on the Lord's day and the fifth week-day, as I said before; on other days he remained fasting. When he then heard that the mass-priest had gone to Ireland, and there died, he always from that time held and followed the manner of abstinence which has been mentioned. And what he, through compunction for his guilt, and because of the fear of God, had once begun, he afterwards also stedfastly followed out, for the love of God, rejoicing in the eternal rewards.

3. When he had for a long time followed and done this, then it happened one day that he was going far from the monastery for some things, and one of the brethren was his companion, and

---

1. Amends (or atonement); deed-boot, *penitentia.*—See p. 352. l. 31.
2. Forecome *Alf.* i. e. prevent, anticipate.
3. Understand a fast of 2 or 3 days.

went with him. When they had gone their journey, they returned home; and when they came near the monastery, and saw the buildings highly reared and uphoven, then darkened the man of God suddenly, and began sorely and bitterly to weep; and opened and shewed the sorrow of his heart by the tokening of his looks. When his companion saw and understood that, then asked he him, what ailed him, why he behaved so. Quoth he, "All those buildings which thou seest and beholdest, both the greater and smaller—it is nigh that the fire shall consume them all, and turn them to ashes. When the brother heard this, as soon as they went into the monastery, he shewed and told it to his mother of the congregation, the abbess, who was called Ebba. Then was she with reason greatly troubled by such a prophecy, and became frightened; then she called the man of God to her, and earnestly asked him whence he knew and learnt that thing. Quoth he, " I was lately busied at night in watches and psalms and prayers; then suddenly I saw stand by me a man of strange countenance, then I was greatly frightened at his presence; then he comforted me, and told me not to be afraid; and, as if in a familiar voice, said to me : " Thou dost well (quoth he) that thou in this time of nightly stillness hast not given thyself up to sleep, but wouldest rather stick to watching and prayer." Quoth I, " I wot that I have great need that I stick to holy watching, and earnestly beseech the Lord for my errors and sins." He that was speaking with me answered, " Sooth thou sayest (quoth he). There is need of that both to thee and to many, that they may redeem their sins by good works, and when they cease from the labours of temporal things, that they may the more freely labour for the desire of the eternal goods; but yet only few do this. Sooth I say, that I have now gone through all this monastery in order, and have seen the houses and beds of the sundry [indwellers]; and none of all, but thee, I found to be busied about his soul's health; but all, both men and women, either were sunk in heavy sleep, or waked for sin. And these houses which were built to pray and to learn in, are now turned into houses of gluttony and drunkenness, and loose speaking and other unlawful faults.[1] And also the maidens who have been hallowed to God, having slighted the

---

1. *Illecebris*, enticements, seems to have suggested the notion of *illicitis*, AS. unalyfedum unpermitted, *impermissa gaudia*. Hor. Loose speaking is "leasung-spell," *fabulationibus*.

reverence of their profession, so often as they have leisure, weave and work fine garments, with which they either may adorn themselves in likeness of brides, to the peril of their state, or purchase to themselves the friendship of men without.' Therefore a heavy wreak from heaven is deservedly prepared for this place and its inhabitants, by raging flames." Quoth she, the abbess, to him, " Why wouldest thou not sooner shew and tell me this secret?" Then answered he and said, " I dreaded for reverence of thee, that thou shouldest be too much troubled and affrighted; and yet thou hast this comfort, that this punishment shall not come upon this city in thy days."

4. When this vision spread abroad, then the inhabitants of the place, for some little space, that is, for a few days, began to be afraid, and to cleanse (and correct) themselves, and to forsake their evil deeds; but soon after the death of the abbess, they returned to their former uncleanness, and also committed greater sins; and while they were saying, " Now is peace and security," immediately, when they least weened, they were smitten with the punishment of the foresaid vengeance. All these things thus done were told me by my fellow-mass-priest, the reverend Eadgils, who dwelt and led his life in that monastery; and afterwards lived a long time in our monastery, and there died. Afterwards many of the inhabitants went thence for the destruction of the city. This spell we have therefore set in our book, that we might warn men, that they should behold the works of the Lord, how awful he is in his counsels over the children of men, lest we at any time be serving our bodily licentiousness, and less fear and dread God's doom than we ought; and his wrath suddenly oppress us, and either justly afflict and scourge us with temporal miseries, or strictly condemn us to everlasting destruction.

CHAPTER XXVI.
Of the death of the two kings, Egfrith and Lothere.

1. Then it was about six hundred and eighty four winters after our Lord's incarnation, that in that year Egfrith king of the Northumbrians sent a host and an army, of which Beort was the leader and general, into Ireland the isle of the Scots; and they wretchedly forharrowed the harmless nation, always

2. Not in the monastery—laymen.

the most friendly to the English kin; so that the warlike hand neither spared nor pitied church or monastery. And the land-folk themselves, as well as they could, warded them off, and fought against them, and called on the Divine Mercy for help, and, with continual prayers, long begged that they might be avenged from heaven. And although those who curse cannot possess God's kingdom, yet it was believed, that those who were deservedly cursed for their impiety, quickly, through the Lord's vengeance, suffered the punishment of their guilt.

2. For truly, the next year after this, when the same king had daringly led an army to forharrow the province of the Picts, and his friends warned him against that, and most of all Cuthbert, of blessed memory, who had then been newly hallowed a bishop; he, however, led an army against the Picts: then they feigned to flee[1] before him, and drew him into a narrow fastness of inaccessible mountains, and he, with the most deal of his host, was slain, in the fortieth year of his age, and the fifteenth year of his reign, the thirteenth day of the kalends of June (*20th of May*). And, as I said before, his friends warned him, that he should not begin the war: but because he would not, the year before, hear the reverend father Egbert, that he should not fight against the Scots, who were not scathing him, then was given him, through punishment of that sin, that he again should not hear those who wished to call him from his death.

3. From that time the hope and might of the English kin's kingdom began to flow asunder and to be waned. For the Picts got back their own land, which the English formerly had; and the Scots who were in Britain, and a great deal of the Britons likewise, recovered their freedom. There, among many in the English nation, who were slain with the sword, or given over to thraldom, or fled away from the land of the Picts, the reverend man of God, Trumwine likewise, who was their bishop, went away with his fellows who were in the monastery of Abercurney, which stands in the land of the English,[2] but, however, nigh the

---

1 "Then lied they flight," literally.
2. Englaland AS. now England; Æbercurnig, now Abercorn, is named from a station at the mouth of the Carron, and is here declared to be in England, a name applicable to the southern shore of the Forth, earlier than to the banks of the Thames.

sea [3] which separates the land of the English and the land of the Picts: and he then, the bishop, commended his fellows to his friends throughout the monasteries, wheresoever he could; and he chose for himself a dwelling (and wick) in the oftsaid monastery which is called Streoneshalch; and he there, with a few of his followers, lived many years' tide in hardness of monk-life, for good, not to himself only, but to very many [besides]. And he there also died, and was buried in the church of St Peter the apostle, with honour becoming his life and his order. The abbess of the same monastery at that time was the kingly maiden, Elfled, together with her mother Eanfled, whom we have mentioned before: but when the bishop came thither, the God-devoted maiden found in him a great help of her government, and comfort of her life. Then Egfrith was succeeded in the kingdom by Aldfrith, who was said to be his brother, and a son of king Oswy, and was a man most learned in [holy] Scripture. And he nobly renewed the fallen state of the kingdom, though it was within narrow bounds.

4. In that year then, that is, six hundred and eighty-five winters from our Lord's incarnation, Lothere, king of Kent, ended this deadly life, and departed: after his brother Egbert, who had reigned eight years, he obtained the kingdom and had it twelve years. He was wounded in a fight of the south-Saxons, whom Edric, Egbert's son, had gathered against him, and whilst he was under medical care, he died; and then after him the same Edric had the kingdom a year and a half. When he died, then, for a space of time, doubtful and strange kings wasted and destroyed the kingdom, until their right king, Wictred, that was, Egbert's son, was strengthened in the kingdom; and he then, both by his godliness and by his carefulness, saved and delivered his nation from outward harrowing.

CHAPTER XXVII.

That the Lord's servant, Cuthbert, was made bishop, and that he, as yet settled in monastic life, taught and preached.

1. In the same year in which king Egfrith came to the end of his life, he made the holy and venerable man Cuthbert be hallowed as bishop of the church at Lindesfarne, who before that

---

3. The firth of Forth.

in a small island which is named Farne, had led an anchorite-life through many years, in much abstinence of body and mind. This island stands out in the ocean, about nine miles distant from the same church. And this holy man of God, from the first age of boyhood, had always burnt with desire and yearning for a religious life; but when he was waxen and grown up, then he desired and obtained the condition of a monk.

2. And first he went into the monastery of Melros, which stands on the bank of the river Tweed; that monastery was then held and ruled by abbot Eata, who was a mild and simple man, and was afterwards made bishop in Hagustaldsea, and in Lindesfarne, as we mentioned before. The provost and rector of the monastery at that time was Boisil, who was a mass-priest of great virtue, and of a prophetic spirit. To this man's training Cuthbert humbly submitted, and from him took knowledge of the holy Scriptures, and example of good works.

After he departed to the Lord, then was Cuthbert made rector of the same monastery, and he, both by the authority of his mastership, and by the example of his visible deeds, set and instituted many to regular life; and he not only furnished the monastery itself with admonitions to regular life, and at the same time the example of his own life, but likewise earnestly took care to convert the surrounding folk, far and wide, from the life of foolish custom, to the love of heavenly gifts. For many profaned the belief which they had, by unright work, and likewise, many, in the time of the great pestilence and mortality, neglected the mysteries of the holy faith, in which they had been instructed, and hastened and crowded to the erring cures of idolatry, as if they could ward off the punishment sent by God their Maker, by their magic or charms, or any other secrets of devilcraft. But to correct both errors, the man of God often went out of the monastery; sometimes he sat on a horse, but ofter went on his feet; came to the towns lying around, and preached and taught to the erring the way of soothfastness; and likewise Boisil his master was wont to do the same in his time.

4. It was at that time the custom with folk of the English kin, that, when a mass-priest or any other came into a town, they all, at his bidding, came together to hear God's word, and gladly heard the things that were taught them, and likewise eagerly followed by deeds, the [words] which they could understand. Moreover

the holy man of God, Cuthbert, had so much skill and learning to speak, and so much love to the divine lore which he had begun to teach, and such a light of angelic looks shone from him, that none of those present durst hide the secrets of his heart from him; but all openly bore forth their deeds by confession; for they thought (and it seemed to them) that only the omitted were hid from him [1]: and the acknowledged sins they bettered with worthy fruits of true repentance, as he bade. He was wont chiefly to go through these places, and to preach divine lore in those hamlets, which were set far [up] on high and rugged mountains, and were frightful to others to visit, and both by the poverty and by the ignorance [of those who dwelt there] hindered the approach of the teachers; which [hindrances] he, however, by pious labour, and great diligence in heavenly lore, willingly overcame; and went out from the monastery often a whole week, sometimes two, or three; often also a whole month, that he did not return home, but abode in the moorlands,[2] and called and invited the unlearned folk to the heavenly life, both by the word of his lore, and by the work of his virtue.

5. When the venerable servant of the Lord had been many years dwelling in the monastery of Melros, and there shone and blazed with great tokens of ghostly mights, then at last the reverend abbot Eata took him to Lindesfarne, that there also he might impart to the brethren the observance of regular discipline, both by the authority of his lore, and by his own actions, might shew and make [it] known. For in the same place which this reverend father Eata held and governed with the power of abbot, there was formerly in old times a bishop with his fellows, and also an abbot dwelt with his monks; they, however, belonged to the bishopshire as a family; because the holy man of God, Aidan, who was the first bishop of the place, by being a monk, came thither with monks, and established the conversation of monastic life in the monastery.

1. This is not very clear, nor, amid the various readings of the MSS, is it easy to settle the text. Bede says "they thought that none of their actions could be hidden from him."
2. Or mountainous districts.

CHAPTER XXVIII.

That the same man, Cuthbert, being settled in anchorite life, brought a spring of water up from dry earth by prayer; and got a crop from the labour of his own hand, over the time of sowing.

1. Thereafter when the merits of his pious intention increased, he likewise came to the privacy and stillness of the divine contemplation, of anchorite-life, as we have said before. But because we have many years ago written enough about his life and virtues, both in meter-verse and in ready speech, this one now at present is enough to be mentioned, which, when he would seek the island, he made known to the brethren, and thus said: " If the divine goodness will give me to live in this place by my own hand-working, I will gladly dwell there : if it shall be ought otherwise, I will readily, with God's will, return to you." The place was destitute both of water and of earth-crops, and of trees; but in it was a host of accursed ghosts, and [their] dwelling-place; and [it was] unfit for any human habitation. But then, at the will of the man of God, it became thoroughly habitable; and for his coming the accursed ghosts soon went away thence. And then when the fiends were driven away, then wrought he himself a narrow wick and dwelling, and surrounded and fastened them with a ditch and an earthen wall, and in them, by the hands and help of the brethren, built the needful houses; that is, a church and common dwelling house; and then bade the brethren delve a pit in the floor of the same house; the earth was so hard and so stony, that nothing of a well-spring could be seen therein. When the brethren did that at the faith and entreaties of God's servant, then next day it was found full of water; [and] the same water till this present day ministers abundance of its heavenly gift to all coming thither. Then the man of God requested them to bring thither to him iron tools with wheat, to till [and sow] the land with. When the land was tilled, and he had sown it with wheat at the suitable time, then came up no growth there, nor grain, nor even blades, until summer's tide. When the brethren visited and sought him again, as their custom was, then he bade them bring him beer-seed[1] if it was thought that that was the kind of earth, or the will of the heavenly Giver, that a crop of that grain should rather be uprunning there. When the seed was brought to him, which

---

[1] " Beer " and " big " are still in use for varieties of " barley."

he sowed in the same land over all time for sowing, and over all hope of bearing grain, then an abundant crop of grain soon ran up there, and furnished the desired food to the man of God, of his own labour.

2. When he then had served the Lord there many years in anchorite life, then it befel, that a great synod was assembled near the river Alne, in the place which is called At Twyford [2] under the presence of king Egfrith, over which synod archbishop Theodore sat in authority; and there he was, by the unanimous consent of all the counsellors, chosen bishop of the church at Lindesfarne, and they sent many messengers and letters to him, and yet they could by no way draw him to them, from his wics and from his place. Then at last the foresaid king, and the holy bishop Trumwine with him, and many other religious and powerful men sailed to the island; and likewise many of the brethren from Lindesfarne came together to him; and all bowed their knees and shed tears, and besought and prayed him by the living Lord, until they drew him, likewise full of tears, from his sweet privacy, and brought him to the synod. When he came thither, though he was very reluctant, he was overpowered by the unanimous will of all, and compelled to accept the ministry of bishophood. He was most overpowered by the word which the Lord's servant, Boisil [had spoken]; when he by the spirit of prophecy opened and said to him all the things which were coming upon him, he then likewise foretold, that he should hereafter be a bishop.

3. His hallowing was not, however, soon determined, but when the winter then coming had gone forth, it was fulfilled at the same feast of Easter, in the city York, in presence of king Egfrith; and seven bishops came together to his hallowing, among whom bishop Theodore of blessed memory had presidency.[3] He then, in obedience to the blessed apostles, adorned the undertaken bishophood with works of ghostly virtues, And the folk committed [to him] which he should hold to God, he both shielded by his constant prayers, and called and invited to heavenly life by his wholesome admonitions and instructions. And, which is wont most to help holy teachers, whatsoever he taught by his word, he fulfilled beforehand by his deed. He was before all things hot and burning with the fire of divine love, and moderate in the virtue of patience, diligent and earnest in the devotion of holy

2. Two fords. 3. Elderdom.

prayers: and he was affable to all who came to him for the sake of comfort. And that itself he reckoned in the place of holy prayer, if he gave help to the weak brethren by his exhortation and advice; for he knew and remembered, that he who has said, " Love thou the Lord thy God," the same has said, " Love thou thy neighbour." He was worthy and famous by the cleansing of abstinence, and always intent upon heavenly things by the grace of compunction. That was a token that, when he offered sacrifice to God and sang mass, he hove his voice up on high, but with tears poured forth, from his inmost heart commended his wishes to the Lord.

4. When it was two years that he sat and held the bishop-seat, then was he divinely admonished to return to his island and his wic, as he desired, for the day of his death drew nigh, or rather the entrance of that life which alone is to be truly called life; as he himself at that time opened and shewed to many men with his wonted simplicity, in dark words; which, however, after a while could be clearly understood. But to some he unfolded and shewed the same openly.

CHAPTER XXIX.

That the same bishop Cuthbert foretold his death, then to come, to Herebert the anchorite.

1. There was a mass-priest, of venerable life, whose name was Herebert; who was early and long united to the man of God in a bond of ghostly friendship. He was in anchorite life, in an island of the great mere, from which the beginnings of the river Derwent spring. It was his wont that he visited and sought him every year, and heard from him advices of eternal salvation. When he heard that the bishop was come to the city Lugubalia, then came he thither to him, as his custom was, and desired that he might be more and more inburnt and excited to heavenly desires by his wholesome exhortations. When they spoke between them of the life of holy fathers, and pledged each other to the holy war¹ of the heavenly life, then quoth the bishop among [other things], " Remember, brother Herebert, that thou now ask me and speak to me whatever thou wilt and needest; for after we shall now be

---

1. Skinked between them the holy war *Alf.* apparently. But if *beado wig* be an error for *beado-weg*, war-cup,—pledged each other to the war, will be nearly the meaning. *Dum sese alterutrum coelestis vitæ poculis* debriarent, Bp,—dark enough still.

gone asunder from each other we shall not see one another over that, in this world, with bodily eyes. For I truly wot that the time of my dissolution and of my decease is very nigh." When he then heard these words, then fell he at his feet, and with much sighing, shed his tears, and sorely wept, and thus said, "I beseech thee by the living Lord, that thou leave me not, but that thou be mindful of thy faithful comrade, and pray the heavenly kindness, that as we two have served God together on earth, we may likewise together go to heaven, there to see and behold his grace. For thou knowest that I have always laboured to live at the bidding of thy mouth, and, in like manner, have laboured to amend speedily, at the doom of thy will, whatsoever I have done amiss through ignorance or frailty." Then the bishop leaned on his crook and prayed; and immediately was taught in ghost, that he had obtained from the Lord the boon which he had asked, and said, "Arise, my brother, and weep not, but rejoice and be glad, for the heavenly kindness has granted what we asked."

2. The truth of this promise and of this prophecy was verified and confirmed by the things that came after; for when they had parted from each other, they did not again see each other with their bodily eyes; and on one day, that is, the thirteenth day of the kalends of April (20th of March), they went out of the body, and their ghosts were soon united to each other by blessed vision, and by angelic ministry were brought together to the heavenly kingdom. But Herebert was before that severely afflicted by a lasting sickness. It is to be believed that this was done by the dispensation of the Divine Mercy; that whatsoever less merit he had than Cuthbert, it might be filled up and cleansed by the sore of the long sickness; that so he might be made equal to his intercessor by grace, that as he departed from the body at one and the same time with him, so he might likewise deserve to be received into a like seat of everlasting blessedness with him.

3. The venerable father Cuthbert died in the island Farne, and earnestly besought the brethren, that he might likewise be buried there, where he had a long time fought for the Lord. And yet at last he was overcome by their prayers, and granted that his body should be carried to Lindesfarne, and laid in the church. When that was done, then the venerable bishop Wilfrith held the bishophood of that church one year, until a bishop were chosen, who

would be hallowed for bishop Cuthbert. Then afterwards Eadbert was hallowed as bishop, a man who was worthy and famous for knowledge of divine scripture, and likewise for keeping the heavenly commandments, and most [of all] for works of alms-deeds; so that every year according to the law of Moses, he would give the tenth deal (or tithe) not only of four-footed cattle, but likewise of all corn, and apples and garments in alms to the poor, for God.

CHAPTER XXX.

That his body, eleven years after his burial, was found clean from all corruption, and not long after that, his afterfollower departed from this world.

1. Divine Mercy would then more openly shew in how great glory the Lord's servant Cuthbert lived after his death, whose life before death opened and shewed it by high tokens of heavenly wonders. Then about eleven years after he was buried, God put it into the mind of the brethren, that they would take and raise his bones up out of the earth; they thought and weened that the rest of his body was consumed and become dust, in the way of all dead men; and that they would put his bones in a new chest, and set and establish them in the same spot above earth with befitting honour.

2. Then they told and shewed it to Eadbert their bishop, that it liked them, and was desirable if it were his will; then he agreed to their purpose, and bade them do it on the day of his commemoration, and of his death; and they did so. They opened his tomb, and found all his body whole and sound as if he then yet lived; and he was flexible in the joints of his limbs, and was much liker a sleeping man than a dead. Likewise all the garments with which he was clothed, not only were unspotted, but likewise appeared so wonderfully white and new, as if he had been clothed with them the same day. When the brethren saw that, they became much afraid, and then hastened to shew and tell the things which they there found, to the bishop, who then dwelt alone in a place apart from the church, which was on every side begirt by the waves of the sea. In this place he was always wont to be in the time of the forty day [1] fast before Easter, and again the forty before Christ's birth-day, in much abstinence, and in much devotion of prayers, and shedding his tears. In that place likewise his venerable prede-

---

1. Quadragesimal fast—Lent, a term which merely expresses lengthening of the day.

cessor, Cuthbert, before he sought the isle of Farne, had some time fought for the Lord in secret. They brought thither also to the bishop a part of the garments, with which the holy body had been clothed, and he thankfully received the gift, and gladly heard the wonders, and kissed the same garments with wonderful love, as if they had still been wrapped about the body of the holy father, and thus spoke, " Provide the body with new garments and clothes for these which ye have taken from it, and so lay it in the chest which ye have provided, for I truly wot that the place will not long stay empty, which has been hallowed by so great a gift of heavenly glory : and most happy shall he be, to whom the Lord, who is the author and giver of all blessings, shall grant that he may rest in that place." When the bishop had ended these words, and many of this kind, with many tears, and much compunction of heart, and also with a trembling tongue, then the brethren did as he had bidden, and clothed the body with new garments, and put it in the new chest, and set it above the floor in the church.

3. Nor was it long till the God-beloved Eadbert was afflicted and attacked by a grim disease, which daily waxed, and grew worse ; so that he, not a long while after, went to the Lord ; that is, on the first day of the nones (6*th day*) of May ; whose body the brethren laid in the grave of the blessed father, Cuthbert, and set above it the chest, in which they had placed the incorruptible limbs of the same father. In that place likewise are often shown heavenly virtues, and health-tokens [1] of the sick, in witness of the merits of them both. [2] Some of which we formerly wrote for memory in the book of Cuthbert's life ; but in this history we shall (must) eke one which, it has happened to us, that we have newly heard.

CHAPTER XXXI.
That one was healed from lift-ail at his tomb.

1. There was in the same monastery a [certain] brother, whose name was Beadothen [1] who had been a long time waiting man [2] to the guests who visited the monastery, and he said [3] that he was

1. Miraculous cures.
2. Their bothis merits—14th or 15th century.

1. Bedothegn, properly, *Alf.*—þeng *Sm.* 2. Arthane, servant of honour.
3. These are not Bede's words, but Alfred's concerning Bede.

still living when he wrote this. He had knowledge and witness from all the brethren, and from all the guests who visited the monastery, that he was a man of much piety and religion, and humbly submissive to the ministry enjoined upon him, for the sake of heavenly meeds.

2. Then went this brother one day, that he would wash and clean his rug and cope (which he wore in the guest's bower) in the sea. When he then was returning home, he was suddenly, in the middle of his journey, touched and seized with a heavy illness; so that he dropt down and fell on the earth, and lay prostrate a long time; and then at last arose. When he had risen, then felt he that the half deal of his body, from the head to the feet, was struck with the illness which the Greeks name "paralysis," we name "lift-ill," [1] and with the greatest toil supporting himself with his crutch, he came home. The illness waxed piece-meal, and soon the same night, became heavier, so that when day came, he could hardly either rise or go by himself. When he then was troubled and distressed with the disease, then thought he in his mind a useful purpose, that he would, in such a way as he could, come to the church, and to the tomb of the venerable father Cuthbert, and there bow his knees, and humbly beseech the Supreme Mercy, that he either might be freed from the sickness, if that were better for him, or, if he, by the Divine Foresight, should be longer cleansed and corrected with the sickness, that he might patiently, with a calm mind, bear and sustain the sore.

3. Then did he as he had thought in his mind, and supporting his sickly limbs with his crutch, went into the church, and stretched himself in prayer at the body of the man of God, and with pious earnestness, prayed, that, through his help, the Lord would be gracious and merciful to him. And then, amid his prayers and petitions, he slept a little; then felt he, as himself afterwards said, as if a great and broad hand touched his head, in the part in which the ill or sore was; and by the same touch all that part of his body which had been oppressed with the sickness, was pervaded, whilst the pain gradually fled, and health followed in its stead. When this was done, as soon as he awoke, he arose hale and sound, and afterwards gave thanks to the Lord, and to the

---

1. Lift is air or sky; why the name was given to palsy, is a question for the medical antiquary.

holy man for the favour of his aid; and likewise shewed and told to the brethren, what had been done for him. And they all rejoiced at it, and were fain, and he, after the affliction, returned more cleansed to his service, which he had formerly well and carefully held and gone about.—Moreover the clothes and garments with which they had clothed the hallowed body of Cuthbert, either formerly living, or afterwards dead,—these addled not from grace of healing, as whosoever reads and learns will find in the book of his life and virtues.

CHAPTER XXXII.
That at his reliques a man was lately healed of the soreness of his eyes.

1. Moreover that is not to be left untold which now three years ago through his reliques was done, and was now lately made known to me by the brother on whom it was done. This was done in the monastery which was built near the river Dacore, and from that river took its name. Over the monastery, in abbot's power, was Swithbert, who was a pious man. There was in the monastery a young man, whose eye-brow was harmed and marred by an unsightly and fearful swelling, which was daily waxing, and threatened the loss of the eye; physicians treated him, and wished to soften it by salves and bathings, but they could not; some advised that it should be cut away; some forbade that for fear of a greater peril. When the foresaid brother had laboured a long time under this inconvenience, and the hand of man could not save his eye from the threatening peril, but aye daily it was worse and worse, then it befel, that he was suddenly healed by favour of the Divine Mercy, through the reliques of the holy father Cuthbert.

3. For when the brethren had many years after his burial, found his body unblemished and uncorrupted, then took they some deal of his hair as a relique, that they might give to their friends who asked it, or shew in token of the wonder. A dole of these reliques was at that time had by a mass-priest of the same monastery, whose name was Thrythred, who was afterwards abbot of the same monastery. Then he one day went into the church, and opened the chest of the reliques, that he might give a dole to his asking friends, when it happened that the same young man who was diseased in his eyes, was present in the same church. When the mass-priest then had given the dole that he would to his

friend, then gave he the others to the young man, and bade him lay and put them in their place. When he then got the hair of the holy head, he was admonished by a wholesome suggestion, that he should lay [it] to the diseased brow, and touch and soften the troublesome swelling with it. When he had done that, he laid the reliques in their chest, as he had been ordered; and believed that his eye would quickly be healed for the hair of the man of God, with which it had been touched; nor did his belief aught deceive him. It was then the second hour of the day, as himself said, when he did it, and then during the day did what he thought to do; when it was before mid-day of the same day, he suddenly touched his eye, then found he it as hale and as sound with the brow, as if no swelling or unsightliness had appeared on it.

BOOK V. CHAPTER I.

That Ethelwald, St Cuthbert's afterfollower, settled in the seat and life of an anchorite, by praying laid and stilled the storm for the brethren in danger at sea.

The man of God, Cuthbert, was succeeded in the anchorite life, which he had led in the isle of Farne, before the times of his bishophood, by the venerable man Ethelwald, who many years before, in the monastery which is called At Ripon, hallowed the undertaken ministry of priest-hood, by deeds worthy of that office; What the merit of this man of God, or [what] his life was, will be more clearly seen, if I tell one of his miracles, which one of the brethren told me, for whom and on whom it was wrought. That was Cuthfrith, the venerable servant of God, and mass-priest, who likewise afterwards was over the brethren of the church of Lindesfarne, in which he had been educated, in the office of Abbot.

2. Quoth he, I came with two brethren to the isle of Farne; I wished to speak with the venerable father, Ethelwald. When I then was well refreshed by his speech, and had asked his blessing, and we were returning home, when we were in the middle of the sea, then suddenly the calmness of the sky, in which we had formerly sailed out, was burst asunder, and so great a wind rushed on us, and so wild storms came, that neither by sailing nor by rowing could we do any good, and we thought of naught else for us but death itself. When we had long fought and striven in vain against the wind and the sea, then at last we looked behind

us whether it were likely that we could in any way even get back to the island, which we had lately left; but turned we us whithersoever we turned, we found ourselves foreset and foreclosed on every side by the like storm, and no hope of safety left for us. When after a long space we hove our sight far up, then saw we on the isle of Farne, the beloved of God, father Ethelwald, go out of his hiding place, to behold our voyage, and see what befel us, for he had heard the noise of the storm and of the boiling sea. When he then beheld and saw us beset with danger and despair, then bowed he his knees to the Father of our Lord Jesus Christ, and prayed for our safety, and for our life. And when he had ended his prayer, he then at the same time smoothed the swollen sea, and stilled the storm; so that the rage of the storm thoroughly ceased, and fair winds wafted us, over the smoothest sea, to land. When we then were come up to land, and had also borne the ship up from the waves, then immediately the same storm returned and came, which for our sake had been stilled a little while, and was all day very great and strong, that men might clearly understand, that the little space of stillness, which there came, was granted from heaven to the prayers of the man of God, for the sake of our safety. This same man of God dwelt in the isle of Farne twelve years, and there died, but was buried in Lindesfarne, beside the bodies of the foresaid bishops, in the church of St Peter the apostle. These things were done in the times of king Aldfrith, who was in kingly power over the nation of the Northumbrians, after his brother Egfrith, twenty winters all but one.

CHAPTER II.
That bishop John healed a dumb man by praying.

1. In the beginning of the foresaid king's reign died bishop Eata, and then John, the holy man, received the bishophood of the church at Hagustaldsea; of which bishop, those who knew him familiarly, are wont to tell many a miracle of ghostly virtues; and most of all the soothfast Berhtun, who was his deacon, and afterwards was abbot of the monastery which is called "In Dyrawood." It has seemed right to us, that we should mention some of the miracles in this book.

2. There are some retired dwellings surrounded by a wall and

a wood, not far from the church of Hagustaldsea, which is about the space of a mile and a half: the river Tyne flows between; the dwellings have a prayer-house and a church of St Michael the high angel, in which the man of God often remained quiet with a few of his companions to go about his learning and holy prayers, especially in the time of the forty-day fast before Easter. When he then, one time in the beginning of the Easter fast, had come thither to remain, he bade his companions seek some wretched beggar, oppressed with much sickness and poverty, that they might have him with them on those days, and do alms to him. For it was his custom always to do so. Then there was in a village not far off a young beggar, who was both dumb and leprous; and who was known to the bishop, for he had often before come before him and received his alms; who never could speak one word; but he had so much leprosy and scurf on his head, that never any hair could grow on the upper part of the head, but horrid bristles stood around. Then the bishop ordered to bring this one to him, and bade them make a small house for him in his court, that he might stay in it and receive his daily food. When one week of the fast was fulfilled, then on the first Lord's day he bade the beggar go in to him. When he was within, he bade him put forth his tongue, and shew it him; then he took him by his chin, and signed it with the token of the holy rood. When he then had signed it, he bade him draw it back into his mouth, and bade him speak, and thus said, "Say now some word, say now yea." Then instantly was the bond of his tongue loosed, and he said what he was bid. The bishop quickly added, and bade him say the names of the letters, "Say now A," he said A; "Say now B;" he said it. When he had said the sundry names of the letters through, after the bishop, then he bade [them] say syllables and words before him, and in all he answered suitably. Then he ordered longer sayings to be spoken before him; and he always repeated them properly. And over that, all the day and the afterfollowing night, he stopt not, while he could keep awake, as they said who were there present, but was aye saying something, and shewing to other men the secrets of his will and of his thoughts, which he never ere that could do.—In likeness of the man who had long been halt, and so born from his mother's womb, so that his elders had to carry him, and he could not go; when the apostles Peter and John healed him, quoth the book, he stood up, and began to leap, and went with the apostles into the temple; and aye was going, and leaping, and praising the Lord. He was fain, as it no wonder is, of the use of his feet, of which he had been so long time benumben and deprived.

Then was the bishop rejoicing with him at his healing, and ordered his physician that he should likewise heal and cure the leprosy of his head, and he so did, and was helped by the bishop's blessing and prayers, and the young man became hale in body, and fair in looks, and ready in speech, and he had crisp locks and fair, who formerly was an unsightly beggar, and leprous, and dumb. And thus he was rejoicing at the received soundness of his health, and then likewise the bishop granted him, that he might remain in his society, if it were agreeable to him; but he rather chose to return home.

CHAPTER III.

That the same bishop healed an ailing maiden by praying.

1 The same Berhtun told another wonder about the foresaid bishop. When the venerable man, bishop Wilfrith, after long exile, was restored to the bishophood of the church at Hagustaldsea, and this same John, when bishop Bosa died, who was a man of great holiness and humility, was settled for him in York city, then came he at one time to a nunnery, [1] which is named Wetadun, over which Hereburga then was in authority as abbess.

2. When we then came thither, quoth Berhtun, and were received with great joy of all, the abbess told us that a maiden of the number of the nuns, who was her bodily daughter, was labouring under a heavy illness, she said that she had lately had blood let in the arm, and that in the blood-letting she was seized with illness. And this soon waxed and became worse, to that degree, that her arm was turned into a great swelling, and so much swollen that it could not be spanned about with two hands, and she was lying in bed, and it was not thought that she would live. The abbess therefore prayed the bishop that he would condescend to go in, to her, and bless her, and said that she believed, that it would soon be well with her after his blessing. Then the bishop asked when she had first had blood-letting; and when he learnt that it was done on a four-night moon, quoth he, "Most

---

1. Nun-mynster A. S.

unwisely and unskilfully ye did, that ye should let blood on a four-night moon; for I remember that archbishop Theodore, of blessed memory, said, that at that time blood-letting was very dangerous, when there is the light of the moon and the waxing of the sea's flood.² But what can I do to the maiden if she is near death?" And she earnestly prayed and besought him, for her daughter; for she loved her much, and meant to set her as abbess for herself. Then at last the bishop agreed that he would go to the sick person.

3 When he then went in, to the maiden who lay there, he took me with him; she was drawn together with a great sore, as I said before, and the arm was so great and so swollen, that it had no bending at the elbow. Then stood the bishop beside her, and said prayers over her and blessed her, and signed her, and went out. When we, at the proper time were sitting at board at victuals, then came one of the hinds and called me, and bade me go out, and said, "Quenburh, (that was the maiden's free-name³) begs that you quickly go back to her." When I did that and was going in, I found her glad in looks, and hale, and sound; and whilst I then sat by her, quoth she, "Wilt thou that we ask [something] for us to drink?" Quoth I, "I will, and it will be agreeable to me, if thou may." Then they brought a cup forth to us, and we both drank; then she began to speak to me, and said, "Soon after the bishop had read the prayers over me, and blessed me, and signed me, and gone out, I instantly got the turn and was better⁴: and though as yet I have not my former strength, yet all the sore and the ache was taken away from my arm, where it was hotter and more burning, and from all my body, even as if the bishop had borne the sore and the ache out with him; and though the swelling of the arm is still to be seen, yet the soreness is all gone off." When we went thence the swelling was soon laid, and the maiden was hale and sound, and freed from death; and she said praise and glory for it to the Lord Jesus, together with the other servants of God, who were there.

---

2. So A. S.—but " leoht " should be "leohtes," r. the waxing of the moon's light and of the sea's flood (or of the tide).

3. Freo nama, supposed to mean surname, *nomen gentile.*

4. " Was warping," turning, changing, " and it was better to me," or with me.

CHAPTER IV.
That he cured an earl's sick wife with hallowed water.

1. The same abbot also told another wonder, not unlike this, about the foresaid bishop, and thus said : " There was not far from our monastery, that is, at the distance of nearly two miles, the country-seat of a certain earl, whose name was Puh,[5] whose wife had laboured under a severe illness about forty days ; so that for three full weeks she could not come out of the house in which she lay. Then it happened at the same time that the man of God was called thither by the same earl, to hallow a church. When the church was hallowed, and he had sung mass, then the earl asked him to go into his house, and there take meat ; the bishop refused, and said that his monastery was nigh, that he should go thither. Then the earl stuck to his entreaties, and promised that he would give alms to the poor, if he would condescend to go into his house to take food, and break his fast.[6] I also entreated together with him, and likewise promised that I would give alms to the needy, if he would comply with us, and go into the earl's house, and would bless,[7] and take food. When we then slowly and hardly brought it through that he would consent to that, then went we in to our meat.

2. Then the bishop sent to the woman who there lay sick a portion of the holy water, which he had hallowed for the church, by one of the brethren who had come with me ; and ordered him to give her the water to taste, and wherever she had most soreness and aching, that she should wash with the water. When this was so done, then immediately the woman arose hale and sound; and not only got free of the long sickness, but likewise at the same time fully recovered her formerly lost strength, and went in, and bore drink to the bishop, and ministered and skinked to us all, until the banquet was ended. She imitated the mother-in-law of St Peter the apostle, when she had been afflicted with the heat and burning of a fever, that she received at the same time health and strength at the touch of [our] Lord's hand, and arose and ministered to the Saviour and his apostles.

---

5. Puch *Bd.*—both *h* and *ch* probably sounded alike, and as *ch* in German.
6. This seems a more probable arrangement than that of the A. S.
7. " Give his blessing,"— comes last in *Bd.*

CHAPTER V.
That the same bishop called an earl's lad from death by prayer.

1. Again at another time the bishop was called to hallow the church of an earl, whose name was Addi. When he then had fulfilled the required service, the earl prayed him to go in to one of his servants, who was oppressed and afflicted with a most cruel sickness, so that he was lame and benumbed [1] and bereft of the ministry of all his limbs, and to men it seemed that he was near death. A coffin was also prepared and made for him, in which when dead he should be buried. The earl also added to his entreaties that he shed tears and wept, and earnestly prayed and besought him to go in to the sick man, and pray for him; and said that he was dear to him, and his life needful to him: and said that he believed, that if he would lay his hands on him and bless him, he would get well.

2. Then went the bishop in thither to him, and saw him near death, and all the people who were with him sorrowful; and the coffin set beside him, in which he should be laid for burial. Then sang he [2] prayers over him, and blessed and signed him. When he would go out, he spoke the wonted word of comforters, "Strengthen thee soon and well." Then was after this that they were sitting at board and at meat, then the sick man sent to his lord, and prayed him to send him a draught of wine, saying that he was thirsty. Then was he very fain that he could drink, and sent him a glass vat full of wine, which the bishop had blessed. As soon as he had drunk it, he rose immediately, and was strengthened of the old weakness, and clothed himself with his garments, and went out thence, and went to the bishop, and greeted him and those sitting round, and said that he desired to eat and drink with them. They bade him sit with them at meat, and were very glad at his soundness and health. He sat and took food, and drank and was merry with them, and lived many years after that, and continued in the same health which he had recovered. This wonder the Abbot mentioned [before] told, that it was not thus done in his presence, but that those told him who were there present.

---

1. "Benumen," deprived, hence numb, benumb, &c.
2. Or chanted.

CHAPTER VI.

That alike by praying and blessing, he rescued from death one of his priests, who had fallen from a horse and been bruised.

1. Nor is that miracle to be passed over in silence, which Herebald, the servant of Christ, said to have been wrought by him, and that too on himself. He was then living in his society; and afterwards was abbot in the monastery at the mouth of the river Tyne. Quoth he, " The bishop's life, so far as it is right for men to esteem, which I being present knew well, I found to be every way worthy of a bishop. Yea also of what merit he was held by the inner Judge, I understood from many others, although most of all from myself; for, as I may say, he called me from death's threshold and brought me to life's way, by his prayer and blessing.

2. I was in the earliest tide of my youth living in his society, and was entrusted to him, to the end that I should learn both books and song; but did not yet perfectly restrain my mind from youthful indulgences. It happened one day that we were travelling with him, and we came to a smooth and wide field, which was a convenient race-course. Then began the young men who were with him, chiefly the laymen, to ask the bishop, that he would give them leave to run, and try which of them had the swiftest horse. Then the bishop gainsaid it at first; and told them that it was idle and unprofitable which they asked and desired; but then at last he was overcome by the unanimous wish of many. Quoth he, " Do so, if ye will; however let Herebald altogether withold himself from the strife." Then I earnestly prayed and besought that leave were given me also to run and to strive with them, for I trusted my horse, which the bishop had given me, as the best; and though I earnestly prayed, I could not for any sake obtain leave. When I then frequently turned me hither and thither, and the bishop aye beheld me, then they ran some time, and returned; and I was, overcome by a frolicksome mood and could not restrain myself: the bishop for bade me, but I mixed me to the play, and began to run along with them.

3. When I did so, I heard the bishop behind me say with a sigh " O how much evil and harm thou doest me with thy running!" And I heard the words, and naught the sooner stopt from running. Nor was it long, till the horse ran most violently and was fired, and with a more powerful rush overleapt and oversprang a slough in the way, when I slid and fell off him, and im-

mediately swooned, and lost my wits and all my stirring. There was in the same place a stone even with the earth, hidden with thin turf, and no other stone could be found in all the field. Then it happened by the Divine Foresight, to punish the sin of my disobedience, that, when I fell, I came driving on the stone with my head and hands, and my thumb was broken, and the joining of my head broken and loosed asunder, and, as I said, I was like [one] dead, and could not stir a limb. Then they raised a tilt over me, in which I lay; it was about the seventh hour of the day, that is one hour over midday; from that time till evening I lay still, and as if dead; when it then was evening, then I quickened a little, and my companions bore me home, and I remained silent all that night, and spewed blood, for my inwards were torn in the fall.

4. And the bishop sorrowed heavily for the fall, and for my death; for he loved me with a sundry[1] love; nor would he that night remain with his companions, as his custom was, but, alone, continued in prayers and waked all the night; I ween that he was beseeching the mercy above [us] for my health, and soon on early morning he came in to me, and sang prayers over me, and named me by my name; then was I soon as if I were awaked from a heavy sleep. Then he asked me whether I wist who it was that was speaking to me. Then opened I my eyes, looked on him, and said, " I wot well that you are my dear bishop." Quoth he, " Seems it [to] thee that thou canst live ?" Quoth I, " I can through your prayers, if the Lord will." Then he laid his hand on my head, and signed and blessed [me], and returned to his prayers; and after a little while he came to see me again, and wished to know how I was. Then he found me sitting, and I could speak. Then began he to ask me, and to enquire whether I had been rightly baptized, without scruple : he was admonished by a divine instinct, as it soon after was shown. I answered him, that I knew without a doubt, that I had been washed with the bath of baptism for the forgiveness of sins, and named to him the name of the mass-priest, by whom I wist that I was baptized. Quoth the bishop, " If thou wert baptized by that mass-priest, then thou art not perfectly nor rightly baptized; for I knew him when he was hallowed a mass-priest; and he never, for his dullness and his unsharpness, could learn aright the office of [either]

---

[1] Singular, special.

christening or baptizing, and I therefore forbade him that ministry because he could not rightly fulfill it." When he had said this, he soon at the same time then christened me.¹ Then it came to pass, as soon as he blew on my face, I instantly felt myself getting better and turning. Then he called his medical man to him, and ordered him to set and wreath the loosened joining of my head-wound. And as soon as I had got his blessing, then I grew better, and was strengthened, so that on the morrow I leapt on my horse, and went with him to another home in another place; and a little while after I was fully healed, then I was also rightly washed and cleansed with the lively water, that is, the bath of baptism.

5. This man of God remained in bishophood thirtythree years, and so ascended to the heavenly kingdom, and was buried in St Peter's porch in his monastery that is called Inderawood. Because he for great age could not minister the bishophood, Wilfrith, his mass-priest, was ordained into bishophood in the city York, and he went to the foresaid monastery, and there ended his life in conversation worthy of God.²

CHAPTER VII.

That Keadwalla, king of the West-Saxons came to Rome to be baptized. As also his after-follower Ina afterwards sought the same thresholds of the blessed apostles.

1. In the third year of king Aldfrith's reign, Keadwalla king of the West-Saxons, when he had stoutly held the sovereignty of his nation two years, forsook his earthly kingdom for the Lord, and for the everlasting kingdom in the heavens, and came to Rome, and wished to obtain the singular glory, that he should, at the place of the blessed apostles, be washed in the well of the baptismal bath, in which alone he had learnt that the entrance of heavenly life was open to mankind; and he likewise hoped, that, as soon as he was baptized, he should be loosed from his body, and [being] clean should depart to the eternal joy of the heavenly kingdom's glory. And each of these things which he had foreset in his mind, was through the Lord's help fulfilled. For he came thither, and was baptized by pope Sergius, on the holy day of the Easter-rest-day, and under the Chrism was soon attacked by sickness, and on the twelfth day of the Kalends of

1. See Additional Notes.
2. So Bd,—Alfred less correctly gives "in God with *(by)* worthy conversation."

May (20th *of April*), he was kindly loosed, and departed, and was joined to the kingdom of the blessed. Likewise at the time of baptism, the pope [now] mentioned gave him the name [of] Peter, that to the most blessed prince of the apostles, to whose most holy body he, with pious love, had come from far, from the boundaries of the earth, he might also be joined by a partnership of his name. And he was buried in his church, and the pope ordered to write an inscription on his tomb, that both the memory of his devotion might abide fast through all ages, and also that the example of his deeds might inflame those men who read or heard the inscription, to the love of piety.

2. When Keadwalla went to Rome, then Ina, who was also of the kingly strain, took after him to the kingdom of the West-Saxons; and when he had held the kingdom of the nation seven and thirty winters, he likewise left the kingdom and entrusted it to his youngers, and went to the seat of the blessed apostles, at which time Gregory (by name) was pope. He wished to lead a pilgrim's life on earth for a time in the neighbourhood of the holy places, that he might earn to be received in a more familiar way by the holy men in heaven. Which in those times many of the English kin, noble and ignoble, both lay and clerical, both men and women, strove with each other in doing.

CHAPTER VIII.

That Theodore being dead, Bertwald got the archbishophood; and, among many others whom he ordained, likewise hallowed Tobias, a most learned man, bishop of the church at Rochester.

1. The next year after Keadwalla died at Rome, archbishop Theodore, of blessed memory, died, old and full of days, that is, when he had eight and eighty winters: which same number of years, he had often foretold to his friends, that he had learnt by the unfolding of his dream, that he should have. He abode in bishophood two and twenty winters, and was buried in St Peter's church, in which the bodies of all the bishops of Canterbury are laid. Of whom, together with his lot-fellows of the same degree, it may rightly and truly be said, that their bodies are buried in peace, and their name shall live for ever in eternity. And this I readily say, that in the time of his bishophood so much spiritual good began to be done in the churches of the English kin, as never ere that could be.

2. Then after Theodore, Bertwald, who was abbot in the monastery which is named Raculfe, took to the archbishophood. He was a man well skilled in the knowledge of the Scriptures, and also highly instructed in ecclesiastical and monastic discipline; although he be not to be compared with his predecessor. He was chosen into bishophood the first day of the month of July; Wightred and Swevherd were then kings in Kent. He was hallowed the third day of the kalends of July (29th of June), being the Lord's day, by Godwin, elder bishop of the kingdom of Gaul, and he sat on his seat in Kent the day before the kalends of September (31*st* of August), the Lord's day. When Gevmund, bishop of the church at Rochester, died, then hallowed he likewise, among many bishops, Tobias for him as bishop, who was a man much instructed and well skilled in the Latin tongue, and in Greek, and in English.'

CHAPTER IX.

That the holy man Egbert would come into Germany, to preach divine lore; but he could not, but Wightbert came thither from him, and there did no good, and then returned home to Scotland (*Ireland*), whence he came.

1. At that time the venerable servant of Christ, and priest, Egbert, the holy [man] of whom we told before that he lived in pilgrimage in Ireland the isle, for [the sake of] obtaining the everlasting home in heaven foreset and thought in his mind that he would do good to many, that is, that he would imitate the Apostolic work, teach and preach God's word and gospel to some of those nations which had not then yet heard it. Many of those races he knew to be in Germany, whence the English and Saxons had come, who now dwell in Britain. There were the Frisians, the Rugins, the Danes, the Huns, the old Saxons, the Boructers; there were also many other folks in the same parts then yet following heathen rites, to whom the foresaid champion of Christ, having sailed about Britain, would come if it were thought [likely] that he might there snatch some from the devil, and bring them to Christ; or if that might not be, [he] thought that he would seek Rome, and see the holy place of blessed apostles and martyrs of Christ, and worship there. But the heavenly revelations, and, at the same time, works, withstood him, that neither of these he performed or carried through.

3. It is worthy of remark, that Bede's *Saxonica* is Alfred's " Englisc;" though the former was, by birth, English; the latter, Saxon.

2. Then he chose him companions who, both in their deeds and in their learning, were stout and sharp to preach and teach God's word, and got all things ready which seemed needful for " travellers by sea " : then came to him one day, in the early morning, one of the brethren, who was formerly, in Britain, a disciple and attendant of Boisil the priest, beloved of God, when the same Boisil was rector of the monastery in Melros under Eata the abbot, as we said before, and told him his vision which had appeared to him the same night. Quoth he, " When we had ended our early morning song and our prayers, and I had laid my limbs in bed, and a light sleep had overrun me, then appeared to me my former master and foster-father, my dearest Boisil, and asked me whether I could know him. " Yea," quoth I, " thou art my [own] Boisil." Quoth he, " For that am I come hither, that I should bring our Lord the Saviour's errand to Egbert, which thou however must tell and shew him. Tell him for sooth that he cannot accomplish the voyage which he has meant ; for it is God's will that he rather go to Columba's monastery and teach." Columba was the first teacher of the Christian belief in the moorlands, which are to the north-deal of the kingdom of the Picts ; and he first built and founded the monastery in the isle of Hii, which was long held in veneration by many folks of the Picts and of the Scots. It was the same Columba whom the Scots have since named Columkill. When Egbert heard the words of this vision, then commanded he the brother, that he should not tell the vision to any other man ; saying that it might easily be that it was shown him through a mockery. However he considered the thing in silence, and dreaded that it was true ; nor did he aught the more stop from the preparation of his voyage, by which he would go to teach the nations. And a few days after, the foresaid brother came to him again and told him that on that same night Boisil had appeared to him, after the early morning song was ended, and said to him, " Why saidest thou to Egbert so carelessly and so listlessly the things which I bade thee say to him ?—but go now and tell him, will he, nill he, he must come to Columba's monastery ; for their plough is going unrightly, but he must lead them into the right way."

3. When he then heard these words, then ordered he the brother again, that to no man more should he open or shew it ; though he was now made certain through the appearance of the

vision, naught the less he prepared his voyage with the brethren mentioned. When they then had loaded the ship with the things which the need of so long a voyage required, and they had waited many days for wind and weather, then happened one night so grim and so wild a storm, that the things which were in the ship were of a great deal lost; and it left the ship among the waves, lying on its side. Then the man of God knew that he might not go, and said, "This storm came and was sent on my account"; and he withdrew from the voyage, and went home sorrowful.

4. Nevertheless one of his companions, who was called Wightbert, who contemned the world, and was famous in the knowledge of divine lore, and, as a pilgrim, had led an anchorite life in Ireland, many a year, in great perfection.—Then he went on board a ship and came into the land of the Friesians, and, during two full years, preached and taught the word of salvation to that nation and Redbede,[1] their king. However he could not find any fruit of so much labour with the barbarians. Then returned he to the beloved land of his pilgrimage, and in the wonted stillness lived to the Lord. And because he could not profit the foreigners for belief, he then took care to be more profitable to his companions by the examples of his virtues.

CHAPTER X.

That Wilbrord preaching in Friesland turned many to the Lord, and that two of his companions suffered high martyrdom.

1. When Egbert the man of God saw that he was not permitted to preach divine lore to the nations, but that he was held back for an other use of the holy church, of which he was forewarned by a divine revelation, and that Wightbert had not done any good, though he had come into those parts; then began he still to send twelve holy and earnest men on the work of divine lore, of whom the head man was Wilbrord, a masspriest of great merit. When they then came thither to land, then turned they first to Pepin, king of the Franks, and were thankworthily received by him. And for as much as he had newly overcome the farther Friesians,[2] and thence driven out

---

1. So *Alf.* Rathbed *Bd.* perhaps Rædbæd. A. S. ræd is Ger. rath, counsel, old Ger. raat.
2. So *Alf.*—Hither Frisia *Bd.*

king Redbed, he sent them thither that they should there preach and teach God's word; and he likewise helped them by his kingly authority, that none should dare to do them any hurt or harm, and honoured with many kindnesses those who would receive Christ's belief. Thence it came about that, through the Lord's grace and help, they quickly brought many round from idolatry to the faith of Christ.

2. This example was followed by some two mass-priests of English kin, who had lived much time in Ireland (the isle), in pilgrimage, for the love of the kingdom of heaven. They came to the province of the Old Saxons, if it were thought likely that they might there win any to Christ through their lore. They were both called by one name, as they were likewise of one wilsomeness; either of them was named Heawald. There was this distinction, however, that, from the mislike hue of their hair, the one was called the black Heawald, the other the white Heawald. Each of them was piously taught, the black Heawald, however, was more instructed in the knowledge of the holy scriptures.

3. When they then were come into [the land of] the Old-Saxons, then went they into the guest-room of one who was town-reeve or steward, and besought him that he would send them on to the alderman, who was over him; they said they had a profitable errand and a profitable cause, which they should carry to him. For these same Old Saxons had not an own king; and when the time of strife and fighting came, then they cast lots to the aldermen, and whomsoever of them the lot shewed to them, then chose they him for general and leader; and all followed him and obeyed him; when the fighting and the strife were ended, then they were again of equal power, and were all aldermen. Then the town-reeve received them, and promised to them, that he would send them on to his alderman, as they asked; and he then kept them with him some days. When they then, the barbarians, understood, that they were of another religion, for they were always singing their psalms, and serving God in holy prayers, and daily offering sacrifice to God and singing mass, (they had with them a hallowed board instead of an altar,) then were the heathens consulting and speaking among themselves, that if they should come to the alderman, and speak with him, they would draw him away from their gods, and

bring him over to the new religion of the Christian belief; and so, step by step,[1] all their province would be forced to forsake their old worship, and take up the new. They then suddenly took the men of God, and slew them: the white Heawald they slew by a ready death, with a sword; the black Heawald they long tortured, and tore, limb by limb. When they then were slain, then threw they their bodies out into the river Rhine. When the alderman then heard it, how they had done about the men who wished to see and to seek him, then was he very wroth. [He] sent then a host thither and bade slay all the town-ship, and forburn the town. The foresaid servants of Christ and mass-priests suffered on the fifth day of the nones (3rd *day*) of October. Nor were heavenly wonders wanting to their martyrhood;[2] for when they were slain, and their bodies thrown into the river by the heathens, as we said before, it befel, that the bodies were borne against the rush of the forthgushing stream, whole forty miles, to the place in which their known men and their companions were. And likewise a great brightness of heavenly light shone from above, every night, over the place where their bodies happened to come; and the heathens also, who slew them, saw and beheld them. Moreover one of the martyrs appeared in a vision of the night to one of his fellows, whose name was Tilman. (That was a famous man, and, for the world, also of noble birth: he was first a king's thane, and afterwards became a monk.) He told him, that he might find their bodies in the place where he saw the light shine from heaven to earth; which also was so fulfilled. Then soon found they their bodies, which were buried with the honour becoming martyrs; and the day of their suffering, and [that] of the finding of their bodies, are celebrated in those places with worshipful veneration. When Pepin, the famous king of the Franks, then heard and learnt these things, then sent he men, and bade [them] bring the bodies to him; and buried them with much wonder and worship, in a church of the city Cologne, by the Rhine. At the same place until this present day plentiful water forth-flows and gushes for the service of men, and for honour [of the martyrs].

---

1. Or piece-meal, though stick-meal and step-meal were before it.
2. The condition of such as have suffered martyrdom.

CHAPTER XI.

That the venerable men, Swithbert in Britain, and Wilbrord at Rome, were hallowed as bishops to the nation of the Friesians.

1. Soon in the first times after the teachers came into the land of the Friesians, and Wilbrord had got leave from the king that he might teach there, then would he hastily come to Rome. Then was pope Sergius bishop of the apostolic seat, and he wished, with his leave, and with his blessing, to begin and to fulfil the devout work of teaching the gospel to the nations; and at the same time he wished to obtain from him reliques of the blessed apostles, and of Christ's martyrs; that, when he had overthrown idolatry, and built and reared churches, in the nation which he taught, he might have reliques of saints there ready to set in them, and might becomingly, in honour of the Saints, hallow sundry places to each of the saints, wherein their reliques might be [kept]. Moreover many other needful things, he wished and sought, either there to learn, or thence to obtain. In all which his wishes being fulfilled, he returned to [teach] divine lore.

2. At that time the brethren who were among the Friesians with him, in the ministry of God's word, chose out of their number a man moderate in his habits, and meek in heart, Swithbert, that he might be hallowed as bishop to them. They sent him then to Britain, and at their request bishop Wilfrith hallowed him,—who was at that time driven from his country and lived in exile in the land of the Mercians, and because the Kenters had not a bishop; archbishop Theodore was dead, and Bertwald his afterfollower had not yet come to his seat; for he had been sent over sea to be ordained. When Swithbert had received bishophood, then went he again from Britain, and after a short space went to the nation of the Bructuarians, and by his lore, turned many of them to the way of soothfastness. But when, not a long time after, the same nation was overcome by the Old-Saxons, and the faithful men who had received God's word were widely driven asunder, then the bishop with some of his companions repaired to Pepin, king of the Franks, and Blithrid, his queen, earned from him that he gave him a dwelling place in an island by the Rhine, which is in their speech called and named In litore (on the beach); in which he built a monastery, which now yet his heirs possess, and he there lived a while in great continence, and there ended his days.

3. After they who came with him had taught divine lore some years in the kingdom of the Friesians, then Pepin, with the consent of them all, sent the venerable man Wilbrord to Rome to pope Sergius, and prayed him, that he would hallow him as archbishop to the nation of the Friesians; and he did as he prayed. He was ordained in the church of the holy maiden and martyr St Cecilia, on the day that was her commemoration-day, and the pope named him by surname Clement, and as soon as he was hallowed, that is, fourteen days after he came to Rome; he sent him back to his bishop-seat. The pope gave and granted him a seat in his famous castle, which by an old word of the nation is named Wiltaburg. The Gauls name it Ultrajectum, (Utrecht,) we say at Ættreocum; in which the venerable bishop built a church; and, far and wide about, preached and taught God's word and Christ's belief; and converted many from heathenism, and from the error of their life; and he built many monasteries and churches in the land, and, after a space, set and hallowed many bishops from the number of those who came with him, or after him, to preach divine lore; of whom many also died in the Lord. But Wilbrord, whom the pope named Clement, had a long and venerable age, that is, he lived six and thirty winters in bishophood, and, after the manifold strife of the heavenly warfare, came to the meeds of the reward that is above.

CHAPTER XII.

That one in the province of the Northumbrians, rising from death, told some things very horrible, and some desirable, which he saw.

1. In these times a memorable wonder, and like the old wonders, happened in Britain; for, to the awakening of living men from the death of the soul, a man was some time dead and rose again to the life of the body, and told many mind-worthy things, which he saw, some of which we will here hastily relate and write.

2. There was a father of a family and master of hinds in a district of the Northumbrians, which is called In Cuningum[1] —he lived a religious life, with his household. Then was he touched and seized with bodily sickness, which daily waxed until he was brought to his last day, and in the foretime of the night he died; but in the dawning he quickened again and suddenly

---

1. Supposed to be Cuningham, a district of Ayrshire.

sat up, and all they who sat weeping by his body, were struck with immoderate awe, and fled out, [all] but his wife only, who most loved him; she alone staid in, though she was greatly frightened and trembling. Then he comforted her, and said, "Dread thou not, for I have truly risen from death, and am let live with men; not, however, the life which I formerly lived, but very unlike, from this time, I must live." And then he straightway arose and went to the church of the town, and there stood (continued) in prayer until bright day; and soon after that he dealt all his goods in three: one deal he gave to his wife, another to his children, the third, which fell to himself, he immediately dealt to the needy; and after a little space left all the things of the world, and came to the monastery of Melros, which is for the most part enclosed by a bend of the river Tweed; and there took on God's ministry and was shorn,[2] and went into a hidden anchorite-seat, which the abbot had provided for him, and there, till the day of his death, hardened[3] and abode in so great contrition and restraint of mind and body, that men might understand, that he had seen many things both awful and delightful, which were hid from other men; and which, though the tongue was silent, his life spoke.

3. He told in this way what he had seen, and said, "Of a shining face and countenance, with a bright garment, was he who led me. We went silent, as it seemed and appeared to me, towards the north-east sky, where the sun's upgoing is at midsummer. As we went the while, we came to a valley which was of great breadth and deepness and unended length, lying on our left hand, one part was full of burning flames, most awful; the other was naught the less intolerable with cold, full of hail and snow. Each of them was filled with men's souls, which seemed to be warped and thrown alternately on two sides, as it were, by the violence of a great storm: when they could not bear the force of the excessive heat, then leapt they wretchedly into the middle of the excessive cold, and when they could find no rest there, they leapt back into the middle of the burning fire, and unquenchable flame. When they were tormented with this unhappy exchange far and wide as I could see, without interval of rest, by an innumerable multitude of swart ghosts, then began

---

2. Received the monastic tonsure. inured to pain and privation.　　3. Alfred's rendering of *duravit*, became

I to think and weened that this was hell, of whose intolerable torments I had often heard say. Then answered he my thoughts —the guide, who went before me, and thus said, " This is not," quoth he, " the hell which thou thinkest and weenest."

4. When I was greatly affrighted and terrified by this horrible sight, then led he me, step by step, forth into a farther land. Then saw I suddenly before us the place begin to darken, and be all filled with great darkness. When we then entered into the darkness, and it gradually became so great and so thick, that I could see nothing, unless that the face shone and the garments were bright, of him who led me; and whilst we were going forward under the shadow of the dark night, then suddenly appeared before us many heaps of swart flames, which were ascending as from a deep pit, and again were falling and going [down] into the same pit. When I then was led thither, then suddenly I wist not where my guide had gone ; and he left me in the midst of the darkness, in that horrible sight. And whilst the same heaps of the fires without stopping sometimes mounted up on high, sometimes sunk into the abyss of the pit, then I saw and beheld that all the top of the ascending flames was full of men's ghosts, which in likeness of ascending sparks were sometimes thrown up on high with the smoke; sometimes, the vapours of the fires being drawn back, they were again slidden into the abyss, and to the bottom. Moreover an intolerable foulness was boiling up with the steam of the fire, and filled all the places of the darkness. When I stood long there affrighted, and it was unknown to me what I should do, or whither I should go, or what end would come to me, then heard I suddenly behind me a great noise of excessive and wretched weeping, as also a great laughter and giggling, as of rude folk mocking their foes. When the noise was nearer me, and came to me, then saw I many of the accursed ghosts drag and lead five souls of men, wailing and sighing, into the midst of the darkness, while they themselves rejoiced and laughed. Of the men (or persons), so far as I could know, one was a shorn priest, one was a layman, one was a woman. The accursed ghosts dragged them, and went down with them into the middle of the abyss of burning flame. When they were gone farther, and I could not distinctly

---

1. Quinque animas hominum Bd. wifmonna saula *Sm*. *r*. fif monna saula.

hear the weeping of the men and the laughter of the devils, however I had the mingled sound in my ears. Amidst these things, then came up some of the dark ghosts from the abyss and the place of torment, and compassed me about. They had fiery eyes, and blew out foul fire from their mouths and noses, and had fiery tongs in their hands, and narrowed and hemmed me in, and threatened that they would snatch me with them, and send me to perdition: although they so frightened and terrified me, they durst not, however, touch me.

5. When I then was surrounded on every side by the fiends, and tined about by the blindness of the darkness, then hove I my eyes up and looked hither and yond, whether any help were to come to me, that I might be rescued; then appeared to me along the way by which I formerly came amid the darkness, as it were the brightness of a shining star, and the light was waxing more and more, and quickly hastening to me, and as soon as it came nigh me, then were scattered and away fled all the witherward ' ghosts, which formerly threatened me with their tongs: it was my guide, who formerly led me. Then turned he at once to the right hand, and began to lead me south-east, into the sky where the sun upgoes in winter. Then were we soon brought out of the darkness, and he led me into fairness of mild light. When he had led me into open light, then saw I before us the greatest wall, of whose length on two halves (*both sides*), or of its height, no end was seen. Then began I to wonder why we were going to the wall, when I could see no door nor window in it, nor stile every where on any side. When we then came to the wall, then all at once, I wot not how, we were on its height, above the wall; and then I saw there the roomiest and the fairest field, which was all full of one sweetness of growing blossoms, and the wonderful sweetness of the great smell soon drove away all the foulness of the dark oven, which formerly swayed through me. And so much light and brightness shone over all the place, that it seemed brighter than all the brightness of day, or the glare of the midday sun. In this field were innumerable gatherings of white and fair men, and many a seat of glad and blissful hosts. While he then led me through the midst of the throngs of happy hosts, then began I to think, and at least it seemed to me, that this was the kingdom of heaven, of which I oft before heard

2. Or adverse.

preach and say. Then answered he my thought, and said, "This is not the kingdom of heaven, as thou thinkest and weenest."

6. When we then were forthgoing, and had walked over the abode of the blessed ghosts, then saw I before us a much greater favour of light and brightness, than I had formerly seen, in which I also heard the sweetest voice [1] of [them who were] singing God's praise. Moreover from the place was sent so much sweetness of a wonderful smell, that the sweetness which I tasted before, and [which] methought much, seemed little and small, to be set against the light and sweetness which had come after. So likewise the light and the brightness of the blossoming field seemed small. When I hoped that we were in-going into the winsomeness of this place, then suddenly my leader stood, and without staying wended his way back, and led me back the same way that we formerly came.

7. When we then returning came to the blithe dwelling of the white and fair ghosts, quoth he to me, "Wotst thou what all these things are which thou hast looked upon and seen?" I answered him, "Nay, (quoth I) I wot them not." Quoth he, "The den, which thou sawest to be awful with burning flames and stern chills, (that) is the place in which are to be tried and chastised the souls of [those] men who delayed to acknowledge, and to atone for, their sins and the wickedness of which they were guilty; and however at last, in the same time of their death, fled to repentance, and so went out of the body; who however for as much as they had confession and repentance in death itself, shall all at doom's day come to the kingdom of heaven. And besides, the petitions and prayers, and alms, and fasting of living men, and, most of all, mass-song, help many, that they ere doom's day may be delivered. And wit thou that the fire-belching and foul pit, which thou sawest, (that) was hell's torment's mouth, into which whosoever once falls, never to eternity shall he thence be delivered. The blossom-bearing field then, in which thou sawest the fair host shine and rejoice in youth, (that) is the place in which are received the souls of the righteous, who go out of the body in good works, and yet are not of so much perfection, that they are soon led into the kingdom of heaven; they all, however, on doom's day shall enter to the sight of Christ, and to the joy of the heavenly kingdom. For whosoever are perfect in every word and

---

3. "Sweetest steven" we might have said with Chaucer and Alfred.

work and thought, as soon as they go out of the body, come to the heavenly kingdom. To the neighbourhood of this kingdom belongs the place where thou heardest the sound of sweet song, with the smell of the sweetness, and sawest the brightness of the great light. But forasmuch as thou shalt return to the body, and again live among men, if thou wilt carefully hold thy deeds and ways, and thy words, in righteousness and simplicity, then shalt thou after death receive a dwelling-place among the rejoicing host of blessed ghosts, whom thou hast now last seen and looked upon: and also wit thou, that when I went from thee a while, I did it to the end that I would ask and know what should be done about thee." When he then had told me that I should return to the body, then I abhorred it, and it was loathsome to me, for I was delighted with the sweetness of the place, and the beauty which I saw there, and at the same time to brook the fellowship and blessedness of those whom I beheld in the place, and yet I durst not ask my leader aught; but now among these things, I wot not how I now see myself living among men."

8. These things and also others which the Lord's servant saw, he would not tell to all men, everywhere slothful and careless of their life, but to those only who either were frightened for dread of torments, or delighted by the hope of everlasting joys; to whom he would with the love of piety shew and tell those things. There was a monk and mass-priest dwelling in the nighness of his cot, whose name was Hamgils, and evenly held the [priest]-hood with good deeds; who afterwards in Ireland sustained the utmost age of his life, in hermitage, with a little bread and cold water. He often went in to the same man, and by his earnest asking heard from him, what things he saw, when he was unclothed of his body; and by his unfolding and telling them also, the few which we here write came to our knowledge. He told also his vision to king Aldfrith, who was most learned in the holy scriptures, and he was so lustfully and so earnestly heard by him, that he was taken into the [before] mentioned monastery at his request, and shorn as a monk; and when the king came into those parts of the land, he often went in to him, because he would hear his words and his sayings. In the monastery at that time was an abbot and mass-priest of religious and moderate life, named Ethelwald, who afterwards, with deeds even worthy, of his degree, sat and held the bishop-seat of the church at Lindesfarne.

8. The man of God received in the same monastery a secret dwelling-place, that he there might freely praise and serve his Maker in constant prayers. And because the same place stood on the bank of the river, it was his wont, for the great love of cleansing (that is, chastising) his body, that he often went into the river, and there stood in psalm-singing and in prayers and abode fast sometimes up to the middle of his side, sometimes to the neck, and he sank himself and dived in the stream, as long as he seemed that he could bear it. And when he went thence to land, he never would put off his wet and cold garments, until they were warmed and dried from his own body. When, in the winter's tide, while the sticks of halfbroken ice were floating about him, which he himself often broke and mashed, that he might have a place in the stream to stand or to besink himself, men who saw it, said to him, "Why, it is a wonder, brother Drithelm," (that was the man's name,) "that in any wise thou canst bear so much sharpness of cold." He answered simply, for he was a man of simple wit and moderate nature; quoth he, "I have seen colder"; and when they said, "It is a wonder that thou wilt keep so sharp and so hard self-denial"; he answered, "I have seen harder and sharper." And thus, until the day on which he was called from the earth, with unwearied lust of heavenly goods, he swinked and tamed his old body amid daily fasting; and helped to the salvation of many men, both by words, and by the example of his life.

CHAPTER XIII.

That, against this, another coming to death saw brought to him by devils the book of his own sins.

1. Against this spell [or, as a contrast to this legend], there was a man in the land of the Mercians, whose visions and words, not his conversation and his life, did good to many men, but not also to himself. In the times of Kenred king of the Mercians, who got the kingdom after Ethelred, there was a man among the laity, a king's thane; but how much soever he was in liking to the king for the outer carefulness of worldly deeds, as much he was in misliking to himself for the inward carelessness of God's praise. The king often warned him that he should confess and amend, and forsake his sins and misdeeds, ere he, by the sudden oncoming of death, should lose all time of repentance and

amendment. And though he was often warned, yet he slighted the words of salvation which he taught him; but he promised that in afterfollowing time, when he was older, he would repent and confess his sins.

2. Then afterwards, among these things, he was suddenly touched and attacked by sickness, and soon fell a-bed, and soon began to be racked with sharp pain. Then the king went in to him, for he loved him much, exhorted and advised him, that he should then yet do repentance and confession of his sins, ere he died. He answered, and said, that he would not then yet confess his sins, but after he should rise from the sickness; lest his companions should lay it to him as a blame and a reproach, that for fear of death he had done those things, which in health he would not do. It seemed and appeared to himself, that he spoke boldly and stoutly; but he was wretchedly beguiled by the devil's wiles, as it was afterwards made known. When the illness waxed strongly, and weighed him down, the king went in again to see him and to teach him: then he cried out in a miserable voice, "What would you now, or why come you now hither? for you cannot over this day give me any help or comfort." Quoth the king, "O say not thou so: see that thou be in thy right wits." Quoth he, "I am not witless, but I see, and have before my eyes the worst witting in myself." The king asked him, what that was. Quoth he, "A little ere you came, two young men, fair and bright, came into this house to me, and sat by me, one at my head, another at my feet; then drew one of them forth a fair book and very small, and gave me to read. When I looked on the book, then found I there written all the good [things] which I ever did, but they were very few and small; then took they back the book from me, and said naught to me.

3. "Then came suddenly hither a great host of wicked ghosts, which were of a horrible countenance, and beset this house without, and sitting almost filled it within. Then one of them was of a dark countenance, and more frightful than the others, who had the first seat, and seemed and appeared to me to be their master. Then drew he forth a book of horrible appearance, huge bulk, and almost insupportable weight, gave it to one of his companions, and bade him bring it me to read. When I read the book, then found I written in it, in black and dismal staves, all

the sins that I ever committed ; and not only what I had sinned in work and in word, but even in the least thought. And then the master of the wicked ghosts said to the fair and bright men who sat by me : "Why sit ye here ? lo ! ye certainly know, that this is our man." They answered : "Sooth ye say, but take him, and lead him to the heaping of your damnation." With that word they instantly went from my sight. And then rose two of the dismal ghosts, having swords in their hands, and struck me, one on the head, another on the feet. And the wounds now with great torment are creeping into the inwards of my body ; and as soon as they come together, then I [shall] die, and the devils are ready waiting when they may snatch and drag me to the prison of hell."

4. When the wretched man then spoke thus in despair, then died he soon after in his sin, and the repentance which he for a little time delayed to do, with the fruit of forgiveness, he, undergoing punishment, shall do, even without fruit, to [all] eternity. And whereas he said, that he saw unlike books brought to him by the good ghosts, or by the bad, that was done through the high ordinance of Almighty God for this, that we should keep in mind that our deeds and our thoughts flow not asunder on the wind in idleness, but are all holden to the doom of the Supreme Judge, and will again be shown to us in the end, either by friendly angels, or by fiends. As to his saying that first the white angels brought forth the fair book, afterwards the devils the black [one], the angels, a very small [one], and these, one of huge bulk, that is to be understood, that in the first age of his life he did some good, but that he darkened and blotted out all that by his unright deeds and froward life. If he then on the other hand had taken care in his youth to correct the errors of his boyhood, and by his good deeds hide them from God's eyes, then might he have been added to the number of those of whom the psalm saith, *Beati quorum remissae sunt iniquitates, et quorum tecta sunt peccata*, "They are blessed whose iniquities are forgiven, and whose sins are covered." This spell I learned from the venerable bishop Peht-helm, and I have written and told it simply for the salvation of such as learn or hear it.

CHAPTER XIV.

That again another as he was dying saw the appointed place of his own punishment in hell.

1. I myself knew a brother, whom I would that I had never known, whose name I could also name, if that would do any good; he was set in a noble monastery, but he however lived his life ignobly. He was often reproved by the brethren and the elders of the place; and they warned and advised him that he should change his life to cleansing of his sins. And though he would not listen to them, yet he was patiently borne with by them all for the need of his outer (worldly) works, being singularly well skilled in smithcraft.[1] He was very much a slave to drunkenness, and many other indulgences of a loose life, and was wont rather to sit, and lie in his smithy day and night, than he would sing and pray in church, and, with the other brethren, hear the word of life and divine lore. Thence happened to him what some men are wont to say, "He that will not wilsomely go humbled into the door of the church, must needs be unwilsomely led condemned into the door of hell."

2. Then was the man stricken and attacked by a heavy illness, which waxed and became heavier, until he was brought to [his] last day. Then called he the brethren to him, and with great moaning, like [one] condemned, began to tell them, that he saw hell open, and Satan the old foe of mankind besunk into the grounds of hell. And he said that he saw there also Caiaphas the high priest, with the others, who slew the Lord Christ, beside him, given to the wreaking flames, in the neighbourhood of whom, quoth he, "Wo me wretched! I see made ready for me a place of everlasting forlornness."[2] When the brethren heard this, then began they earnestly to exhort and advise him, that he then yet being in the body should repent and confess his sins. He answered in despair, "I have not now (quoth he) time to change my life, when I myself see my doom decreed. When he then had thus spoken, he then, without the way-food of the soul's life, went out of the world; and his body was buried in the utmost spot of the monastery; and no man durst sing psalms or mass for him, nor even pray for him.

1. This term and the following "smithy" are not to be taken too strictly in the modern sense. The Latin would rather indicate that the man was a carpenter.
2. Perdition.

3. O, by how great a distance has God divided between light and darkness! The first and blessed martyr Stephen, when he was suffering death for the truth, saw heaven open, saw God's glory, and the Saviour standing on God's right [hand]; and, whither he himself was to come after death, thither he sent his mind's eye ere his death, that he the blithelier might suffer; and on the other hand [the] smith, of dark mood and deed, when his death drew nigh, saw hell open, and saw the devil's downputting and [that] of his afterfollowers. He saw likewise his own unblessed abode and prison, that amid such [things], despairing of salvation, he might here now the more miserably perish, but, to living men who learn these things, should leave a cause of salvation by his loss. This happened lately in the province of the Bernicians, and being published far and wide, called many forth to repent of their sins without delay, which I wish may be furthered by reading what I have written.[1]

CHAPTER XV.

That many churches in Ireland, by Adamnan's instructions, received the catholic [observance of] Easter.

CHAPTER XVIII.

Of Aldhelm, who made the book "On Virginity" and many other, and also that the South Saxons received as [their] own bishops Eadbert and Eolla, and the West-Saxons Daniel and Aldhelm, and of Aldhelm's writings.

1. Then (it came to pass) seven hundred and five winters after our Lord's incarnation, (that) Aldfrith, king of the Northumbrians, died, about twenty years of his reign, but one was not yet ended. His son Osric, a boy of eight years, got his kingdom, and held it eleven years. In the beginning of this king's reign died Heddi, bishop of the West-Saxons, and went to the heavenly life. He was a good and righteous man, and rather led the life of a bishop in the love of ghostly virtues, than was skilled in learning. Of this bishop, the venerable bishop Peht-helm, who, while yet a monk and deacon, was much time with his afterfollower Aldhelm, was wont to say, that on the spot on which the bishop died, for the merit of his holiness, many wonders of healing were wrought, and men of that province were wont to take the mould for ails and sicknesses, and put it in water, and

1. *Lit.* May be forth on learning our staves. 2. Ch. XVI and ch. XVII not mentioned.

by the tasting or sprinkling of the water, many sick men and also beasts became healthy : and that, for the away-taking of the holy mould, a great pit was there made. When he died, then was the bishopdom of that province dealt in two bishopshires ; one was given to Daniel, which he yet to-day governs, the other to Aldhelm, which he ably held and ruled four years. They were both of them enough skilled in church business, and in the knowledge of holy writ.

2. It is a token of this, that Aldhelm, when he was yet a masspriest and abbot of the monastery which they name Maldulfsbury, wrote a worthy book for his nation by the synod's command, against the error of the Britons, when they did not celebrate the right Easter at its own time, yea also many other things which they did against the purity and peace of the church. And he drew and led many of the Britons who were subject to the West-Saxons, to the right celebration of our Lord's resurrection, by the learning of these books : he likewise wrote a high and worthy book " De Virginitate ;" and on the example of Sedulius, by twofold work, he sang it in meter-verse, and set it in ready speech, or prose. He likewise wrote many other works, being every way a most learned man, in [his] words clean and shining, and in the knowledge of both liberal and ecclesiastical writings wonderfully skilled.

3. When he died, then Forth-here received the bishophood for him, and yet to day, quoth the writer, is living, who also was well skilled in holy writ. Whilst these men ministered the bishophood, it was set and decreed in synod, that the province of the South-Saxons should have [its] own bishop, and a bishopseat among their people ; they formerly belonged to the bishopshire of Winchester, over which Daniel was the bishop. Then was first hallowed as bishop to them Eadbert, who was abbot of the monastery of bishop Wilfrith of blessed memory, which is named Selesey. When he died, then Ealla got the bishoprick, and not many years after was taken away from this light, and the bishophood then stopped during many years.

---

1. Malmesbury.

CHAPTER XIX.

That Kynred king of the Mercians, and Offa, king of the East-Saxons, came to Rome in monastic habits, and these ended their lives; and of the life and death of the venerable bishop Wilfrith.

1. In the fourth year of Osred's reign, Kenred, who had nobly for some time ruled the kingdom of the Mercians, much more nobly forlet the government of the kingdom; for he came to Rome, and there was shorn and became monk in the times of pope Constantine, and abode at the seat of the blessed apostles, in prayers and fasts and almsdeeds until his last day. Then after him the kingdom of the Mercians was ruled by Keolred, the son of Ethelred, who had the same kingdom before Kenred. To Rome also came with him the son of Sighere, king of the East-Saxons whom we mentioned before, whose name was Offa; he was in his youth a man of a lovely age and fairness, and dear to all the nation, [as one who was] to have and hold their kingdom. He was of like devotion of mind to [that of] king Kenred, and forsook his wife, his lands, his kinsfolk, and his country, for the love of Christ, and for his gospels, that in this life he might receive a hundred-fold meed, and in the world to come, everlasting life. And as soon as he he came to Rome to the holy places, he was shorn, and, ending his life in monkhood, came to the sight of the blessed apostles, which with his mind he had long sought and wished.

2. Then in the same year in which these kings left Britain, the holy archbishop [1] Wilfrith, forty five years after he received the bishophood, closed his last day and departed, in the province which is called " In Undalum " [2]; and his body was put in a chest, and was carried north over the boundaries into his monastery, which is called " In Ripon," and was buried with the honour becoming so great a bishop, in the church of St Peter the apostle. Of the early state of this bishop's life, we shall *(must)* mention in few words, what things befel him. As he was a boy of good wit, and overstept his age by his ways of thinking and doing: and behaved himself so modestly and discreetly in all things, that he was deservedly loved and honoured by his elders (or superiors) as one of themselves. When he was waxen and had fourteen winters, then he preferred and loved monastic life before world-

---

1. *Lit.* "the high and holy bishop."—So, " high father," patriarch, " high angel," archangel, &c.
2. Supposed Oundle.

life. When he told this to his father, for his mother had died before, he then gladly granted and helped his will and his heavenly lusts, and ordered and advised him that he should earnestly fall to [and carry on] the wholesome beginnings. Then came he soon after to Lindesfarne isle, and gave himself into the service of the monks, and he then began carefully to learn, and to do, what he understood to belong to monastic purity and piety; and as he was of a sharp wit, he quickly learned his psalms and many other books. He was not yet indeed shorn, but however he was not less nor lower in the virtues of humility and obedience, than those who were older in the shearing;* for which he was loved with a right [and well earned] love, both by his elders, and by those of his own time of life.

3. When he then had served God in the monastery one year, then, the youth being of a skilful mind, he gradually learnt that it was not a perfect way of ghostly virtues, which had been told and given him by the Scots; [he] thought then and purposed in his mind, that he would come to Rome, and there see what ecclesiastic customs, or monastic customs were holden at the apostolic seat. When he then told the brethren that, then praised they his mind and his purpose, and urged and advised him to accomplish the journey, which he had loved in his mind. And he then quickly came to queen Eanfleda, for he was known to her, and by her counsel and support had been put in and joined to the foresaid monastery. [He] told her then that it was his lust and his will and his love, that ho should visit and seek the seat of the blessed apostles. The queen rejoiced at the young man's good purpose and will, [and] sent him then to Kent, to king Erconbert, who was her uncle's son, [and] begged that he would send him worshipfully to Rome. At that time, there in Kent, Honorius held the archbishophood, who was one of the disciples of the blessed pope St Gregory, and was a man highly instructed and skilled in ecclesiastical affairs. Whilst the young [man] staid a space with him, he [as being] of a quick mind diligently learnt those things which he there saw and beheld. Thither came also at the same time another young man, whose name was Biscop and his surname Benedict; he was of a noble

---

3. Had been shorn, or received into the order of monkhood, before him. "His elders" (in the next clause) *senioribus*, more aged,—ðam witum *Alf.* in an official sense, which is contradicted by the following *aequalibus*, "efenealdum," evenolds.

strain of the English nation; as we mentioned before, he likewise would go to Rome. To this man's fellowship the king then joined Wilfrith, and bade him lead him to Rome.

4. When they then came to Lyons, then was Wilfrith there held back by Dalfin, bishop of that city: Benedict stoutly went on the begun journey to Rome. Then began the bishop to be delighted with the young man's prudence, and his wise words, and the fairness of his looks, and gladness of his deeds, and steadiness of his thoughts, and he therefore gave and granted him abundantly all the things that he needed with his companions, so long as they were with him, and likewise offered him that he would give him a great part of the kingdom of Gaul to hold and to govern, and would give him his brother's maiden daughter to wife, and always love him as a son. Then he thanked him heartily for the kindness which he had shown him, when he was a stranger; and answered him, that he rather chose and loved other life than worldly life, and had therefore left his birth-land, and undertaken to go to Rome. When the bishop heard that, then he sent him with a guide to Rome, and well furnished him thither; and bade him, when he would return to his country, come to him, and he would furnish him well home.

5. Then he came to Rome, and there with daily earnestness engaged in prayers, and in the study of ecclesiastical affairs, as he had purposed in his mind; [and] came to the friendship of the holy and most learned man, archdeacon Boniface, who was also a (wise man⁴ and) counsellor of the apostolic pope, by whose instruction he learnt in order the four gospels,⁵ and the reckoning of right Easter, and many other things, which belong to ecclesiastical discipline, which he could not learn in his own country; and the same master gave him both books and lore. And when he had been earnestly busied there many months with those happy studies, then returned he into Gaul, to bishop Dalfin, his friend, and staid three years with him, and was shorn as a priest by him, and was had in so much love that he thought to make him his heir. But that, however, might not so be; for the bishop was snatched away by a bloody death, and Wilfrith was rather kept back as a bishop to the English nation.—Queen Baldhilda sent a great host, and bade slay the bishop. When he

---

4. Wita and geþeahtere. *Alf.* each usually rendered counsellor.
5. " Christ's books "—literally.

then was led to the spot where his head was to be struck off, then followed him Wilfrith [as] his priest and hand-thane, and wished to die together with him, though the bishop strongly forbade it him. But when the executioners learnt that he was a foreigner, and that he came from the English nation, they spared him then, and would not kill him with the bishop, though it was his wish.

6. Then he came back to Britain, and joined himself to the friendship of king Aldfrith. The king had learnt that he should always follow and love the right rules of God's church; and because he found Wilfrith rightly framed and wise, he soon gave and granted him ten households of land, in the place which is called Stanford, and after a short space gave him a monastery of thirty households, in the place which is called " In Ripon." Which place he had formerly given for building a monastery on, to the men who followed the lore of the Scots; but forasmuch as they, after a space, when the wish (and choice) was given them, would rather go from the place, than they would hold right Easters, and also receive other regular customs after the use of the Roman and apostolic church, he therefore gave the place to him, whom he saw skilled in better discipline and customs. At that time, by command of the foresaid king, was Wilfrith hallowed a mass-priest in the same monastery, by Aghilbert, bishop of the West-Saxons, whom we mentioned before; the king wished that a man of so much learning and piety should, by specially undivided fellowship, be his priest and teacher. Not a long while after, he sent him into the kingdom of Gaul, with the advice and consent of his father Oswy, [and] asked that he should be hallowed a bishop.

7. When he then had thirty winters, the same Aghilbert was at that time bishop of the city Paris, with whom came other eleven bishops to his hallowing, he was the twelfth: and they right worshipfully fulfilled the service. When he then was yet staying beyond sea, king Oswy bade hallow the holy man Keadda as bishop in York, as we mentioned before, and he worthily ruled and steered the church three winters; after which he went to his minstershire, which is in Lestingau. Then Wilfrith got the bishopshire of the whole province of the Northumbrians.

8. And after that, in the reign of king Egfrith, he was driven from his bishopshire, and other bishops hallowed for him, whom

we mentioned before. Then went he to Rome, and told his business before the apostolic pope. As soon as he went and stept up into ship, then blew a west wind and he was driven [so] that he came up into the land of the Friesians, and was worshipfully entertained by the barbarians and their king Eadghils. He soon preached to them and taught Christ's belief, and instructed many thousands of them by the word of truth, and washed them from the filthinesses of their sins by the bath of baptism; he first began the work of preaching Christ's gospel, which, after a space, the venerable servant of Christ, bishop Wilbrord, fulfilled with great wilsomeness and devotion; and he staid there happily and well [during] the winter, with the new folk which he had begotten; then he (trimmed and) prepared his journey and came to Rome, and when his business was thoroughly searched before pope Agatho and many others, he was, by all their doom, found unguilty, and, without crimes, clean of the things of which he had been accused and arraigned, and well worthy of his bishophood.

9. At the same time the same pope Agatho called together at Rome a synod of a hundred and twenty-five bishops against the heretics who published and taught one will and one working (to be) in the Lord Jesus; then the pope ordered to invite bishop Wilfrith also to the synod, and a seat was given him among the other bishops, and he was asked to tell his belief, and at the same time [that] of the isle, and of the nation, from which he came. Then he was found, along with his companions, orthodox in belief, and it was thought good, among other doings of the same synod, to insert in the Synod-writ, and thus write, about him: Wilfrith, God's beloved bishop of York, came to the apostolic seat about his business, and by the apostolic might was loosed and acquitted of things known and unknown, and sat in doom-seat in the synod, with a hundred and twenty-five [of] his fellow bishops, and, for all the north-deal of Britain, and the isle [of] Ireland, which are inhabited by the English nation, and Britons, and Scots and Picts, confessed, and with his handwriting confirmed, the true and orthodox belief.

10. After these things he returned to Britain, and brought the province of the South-Saxons over from the rites of idolatry to Christ's belief. And he likewise sent God's servants into the isle of Wight, and in the second year of king Aldfrith's reign, who

took the kingdom after Egfrith, he got his bishop-seat, and king Aldfrith invited him to him. After five years again he was accused by the same king and many bishops, and again driven from his bishopshire, and came to Rome again, and leave was given him, that he might shield and defend himself in the presence of his accusers. Many bishops sat there with John, the apostolic pope, and by all their doom, it was kithed and shown, that his accusers had in a great deal contrived against him and brought forward charges that were lies and falsehoods; and then the foresaid pope ordered to write a letter to Ethelred and to Aldfrith, kings of the English, in which he requested that they should at once make Wilfrith be received into his bishopshire, because he had been unlawfully deprived of it.

11. When he then was returning to Britain, and had come into the parts of the kingdom of Gaul, then was he suddenly touched and attacked by sickness, which waxed and became very sore, so that at last he could neither go, nor ride on a horse, but was borne on a bier by the hands of his men, and so was brought to Meaux, a city of Gaul, and there lay four days and four nights, as if a dead man, were it not that he shewed by a thin breathing only, that he was alive. When he had remained so without meat and drink, and without speech and hearing, full four days and nights, at last in the dawning of the fifth day, as if he awoke from a heavy sleep, he rose, and sat up, and opened his eyes, and saw about him bands of the brethren singing and weeping at the same time, and he some while sat and sighed. He asked then where Acca the mass-priest was; they soon called him, and he went in to him, and saw that he was better, and could speak, and he bowed his knees, and gave thanks to God, with all the brethren who were there within with him. And when they sat a while together, and with fear began to speak some things about the upper[1] dooms of God Almighty, the bishop bade the other brethren go out a while, and thus spoke to Acca the mass-priest: "There appeared to me," quoth he, " a little before, an awful sight, which I will tell and shew to you, and I command you to hide and keep it until I know what God wills, what is to become of me. A very bright and shining man in white garments came to me, and stood beside me, saying that he was Michael the high

---

1. Or "high,"—upplic (uply), above us, upward or upper, &c. It has been sometimes (in the foregoing pages) rendered sovereign, supreme, often "heavenly."

angel, 'And therefore am I sent to thee, that I may free and loose thee from death. The Lord has given thee life through the prayers and tears of thy disciples, and of thy brethren, and through the intercession of his blessed mother, the unspotted maiden saint Mary. Therefore I tell thee that thou shalt now be quickly healed of this sickness; but be thou ready; for after four years I will return and visit thee. Thou shalt come to thy country, and get back the most deal of thy goods, which were taken away from thee, and in a calm old age shalt end thy life.'"

12. Well! the bishop then quickly grew strong, and all his fellows were fain and gave God thanks for it, and came on the begun journey to Britain; and he gave the letter, which he brought from the apostolic pope, first to archbishop Bertwald to read, and next to Ethelred, who was formerly king, [and] was then abbot of Beardanea,[2] and they both gladly, and with one mind, helped him by the pope's behest. And Ethelred soon invited to him king Kenred, to whom he had given the kingdom of the Mercians, and begged and asked him, that he would be inwardly a friend to the bishop, and he was so. But Aldfrith, king of the Northumbrians, disdained to receive him, nor was he living a long time over that. Then it was brought about, after his son Osred got the kingdom, that a synod was called together, by the river Nid, and after some strife on either side, at last by the help of them all, Wilfrith was taken back into the bishophood of his church, and so, for four years, that is, until the day of his death, led his life in calm peace, and then with gladness ascended and entered the heavenly kingdom. He went forth [of this life] in his monastery, which he had in the province of Undalum, under the government of abbot Cuthbald; and, by the service of his brethren, was carried into his former monastery, which is called In Ripon, and was worshipfully laid and buried in the church of St Peter the apostle, by the altar, on the south, as we ere before said and mentioned.

CHAPTER XX.

That the religious abbot Adrian[3] was succeeded by Albinus; and, from bishop Wilfrith, Acca his mass-priest receives bishophood.

1. The next year after the death of the foresaid father, that is,

2. Beardsætena *Alf.*— the place not mentioned here by Bede.
3. Hadrianus in Bede.

the fifth year of king Oswy's reign, the venerable man abbot Adrian died, who was a fellow-worker in God's word with archbishop Theodore, of blessed memory, and was buried in his monastery, in the church of the blessed maiden St Mary, about one and forty winters after he was sent hither by pope Vitalian, with archbishop Theodore. Of the abbot's learning, and at the same time bishop Theodore's, among other witnessings, Albinus, the abbot's disciples who got the government of the monastery after him, says, that he was so well skilled in the study of the holy scriptures, that he knew the Greek tongue to a great extent, and Latin was as familiar to him [1] as English, which was kindly to him.

2. Then in Wilfrith's stead, Acca, his mass-priest, received the bishophood of the church at Hagustald: he was a most valiant man, and great before God and men, and he built his church, which is hallowed in honour of St Andrew, the apostle, and broadened and lengthened it with manifold comeliness and wonderful works. And he took great care, that he might get from every side most reliques of the blessed apostles and Christ's martyrs; and built altars to their honour, and wrought porches, and dealt them to the same end, within the walls of the same church. He likewise gathered histories of their suffering, together with other church-books, with great carefulness, and got there a great and noble library; as also he carefully prepared housel-vats and light-vats, and many other things of this kind, which belong to the furniture of God's house. He likewise brought thither a famous church-singer, who was named Mava, who had been taught song-craft in Kent by the afterfollowers of the disciples of the blessed pope St Gregory, and he had him twelve winters with him; and he both taught them the church-songs which they knew not before, and also those which they formerly knew, and which by long carelessness began to be forgotten, were by his lore renewed [and brought] to their former state. Bishop Acca himself too was a most skilful singer, and likewise most learned in holy writ, most clean in the acknowledging of right belief; and he was most heedful to hold the rules of the ecclesiastical canon, and from this he stopt not, until he received from God the meed of his pious devotion. He was first reared and taught from his boyhood, in the society of the

---

1. Natural, so "kindly death," *Ch.* mors naturalis.

holy Bosa, God's beloved bishop of York. He afterwards came to bishop Wilfrith, with the hope of a better pattern, and filled up all his age and his life in his service, until his death, with whom he also came to Rome, and there saw and learnt many profitable things of the laws of the church, which in his own country he could not, and which he held and fulfilled till his life's end.

CHAPTER XXI.
That abbot Keolfrith sent to the king of the Picts, named Naitan, high craftsmen, or architects, and at the same time an epistle about the holding of right Easter.

1. In these times Naitan, king of the Picts, who dwell in the north deal of Britain, was admonished by frequent meditation and learning of ecclesiastical writings, [so] that he forsook error, and agreed not to that [error] which till then was held in his nation, about the holding of right Easters; and taught himself and his nation to celebrate and observe the right set time of our Lord's resurrection. And that he might carry that through with the greatest authority, and fulfil it, he sought him help from the English nation, who, he well knew and wist, had learnt and received their religion at the example of the holy Roman and apostolic church.

2. He sent ambassadors to the venerable man, Keolfrith, who was abbot of the monastery, of the blessed apostles Peter and Paul, which is at Wire-mouth, by the river Tyne, in the place which is called " In Girwum" over which abbotdom he, Keolfrith, gloriously was, after Benedict, of whom we spoke before. The king begged that the abbot would send him (strengthening staves and writs, or) a letter of exhortation, by which he might more mightly shove off those, who should dare to hold and keep Easters out of their right time. He likewise sought and asked about the kind and right way of the shear [1] of God's servants, by which priests and God's servants should be marked and betokened. The king also asked him to send him a high craftsman of stone-work, (*an architect,*) that he might build a church after the Roman custom, and promised that he would then hallow a church in honour of the blessed Elder of the apostles, St Peter; and also promised that he himself, with all his nation, would always follow and hold

---
1. Or tonsure.

the custom of the holy Roman and apostolic church, " so far as we may best learn." The venerable abbot Keolfrith helped the king's pious wishes and boons, sent him a crafty workman, (whom he asked) to build a stone church, sent him also a letter and epistle about the holding of right Easters, and about the shear of God's servants, also other laws of God's church.

3. When the epistle was read before the king and many learned men, and carefully explained to him in his own tongue, by those who could understand it, it is said that he was very glad of his exhortation and lore, and rose off his seat, from the midst of his aldermen and counsellors, and bowed his knees to the earth, and gave thanks to God, that he had deserved to receive such a gift from the English nation; and thus spoke, " Well I wist and understood before, that this was the right observance of true Easters, but so clearly I now understand the law [1] of this time for holding Easter, that it seems altogether little and small, that I knew and understood before this. Therefore I now openly acknowledge and kythe [2] to you, who sit here present, that I will, with all my nation, ever hold this time of Easter, which I now understand and know [to be] right, and all priests and God's servants, who are in my kingdom shall take the "shear," which we hear to be full of all righteousness. And he then without delay, by his kingly authority, performed what he said; and soon sent through all his kingdom and commanded to write, and learn, and hold, through all the province of the Picts, the nineteenly rings [3] of right Easter; and ordered to abolish every where the erroneous rings of four and eighty years. Then were all the monks and priests shorn in the crown (or circular form) of St Peter's tonsure; and all the nation [now] set right was fain and glad to be subject, as it were, to the new disciplehood of the most blessed elder of the apostles, St Peter, and shielded by his protection.

CHAPTER XXII.
That the monks in the isle of Hii, with the monasteries subject to them, began to celebrate the orthodox Easter, under the preaching and teaching of Egbert.

1. Nor was [it] then after much space that the monks of the Scottish kin who dwelt in the isle of Hii, with the monasteries

1. Or reason, "riht," Ger. recht, law, right, reason.
2. Cause to know, make known, shew, &c.
3. Circles of 19 years.

which were subject to them, were, by the Lord's grace, brought to the regular custom of right Easters, and of the tonsure. [It] was about seven hundred and sixteen winters from our Lord's incarnation, in which king Osred was slain, and Kenred after him then undertook the steer⁴ (and rule) of the Northumbrian kingdom, when came to the isle of Hii from Ireland, the father and priest beloved of God, and to be named with all reverence, Egbert, the holy [man], whom we have often before mentioned, and was worshipfully and with great gladness received by them; for he was the sweetest and winsomest teacher, and of the things which he taught others to do, he himself was the most devout fulfiller and follower, and was gladly heard by them all, and by his pious and earnest exhortations, he changed the old custom and tradition of their elders, of whom may be said the apostolic word, "That they had zeal of God, but not after wisdom"⁵; and he warned and taught them that, after the apostolic and orthodox custom, they should hold and make the celebration of the greatest solemnity, as we have said, under the beacon and sign of the unending crown.⁶ It was, by a wonderful dispensation of the Divine Goodness, so brought about, that for as much as that nation had gladly, without envy, shewn and communicated the knowledge of divine truth, which it had learnt, to the English folks, itself also, after a space, through the English nation, came to a perfect rule of right life in those things in which they were wanting: so as the Britons on the contrary, who never would open and shew the knowledge of the Christian belief which they had, to the English nation; and then again when the English folks believed and were every way well instructed and taught in the rule of right belief, they now yet hold their old customs, and halt from the right paths, and shew their heads without the crown of St Peter's shear, and hold and celebrate Christ's festival of right Easter without the society of all God's churches.

2. The monks sitting in Hii received, through Egbert's lore, orthodox customs to live in, under abbot Dunchad, eighty winters after they sent bishop Aidan as a teacher to the English nation. The man of God, Egbert, abode thirteen years in the island, which he, by the light of a new grace, had hallowed to the society

---

4. That is, helm,—"steersman," man of the helm.
5. "Knowledge,'.—the literal meaning of "wisdom."
6. Or circle, the tonsure.

and peace of the church. And seven hunderd and twenty-nine winters after our Lord's incarnation, in which year was celebrated and observed our Lord's Easter day, that was on the eighth day of the kalends of May (*24th of April*), when he had then celebrated and honoured the same resurrection of our Lord with the solemnity of mass-songs, on the same day he went to the Lord and to the joy of the high festival, which he had begun with the brethren, whom he had converted to the grace of unity, [and which] he ended with the Lord and the holy apostles, and the other citizens of heaven; or, what is yet more true, which same he will not cease to celebrate and observe aye without end. It was a wonderful dispensation of Divine Providence, that the venerable man not only went from this world, to God the Father, at Easter, but also that Easter was celebrated on that day, on which it never before was wont to be celebrated in those places; and then the brethren were glad of the knowledge of the certain and orthodox Easter-tide; and rejoiced in the patronage of father who then went to the Lord, and through whom they were set right; and he rejoiced in this, that he had been held back in the body until he saw then his hearers receive, and with him have in honour, that Easter-day, which they always, ere that, had refused to receive; and thus certain of their correctness the venerable father rejoiced to see the day of the Lord, and he saw it, and was glad.

CHAPTER XXIII.

Of the death of bishop Tobias at Rochester, and of the venerable bishop[1] Egbert on the first day of Easter, and in the same year died Osric king of the Northumbrians. What the state is at present of the English (kin's) nation, yea eke of all Britain.

1. About seven hundred and twenty-five winters after our Lord's incarnation, which was the seventh year of Oswy, king of the Northumbrians, who got the kingdom after Kenred, then Wihtred son of Egbert king of Kent died on the ninth day of the kalends of May (*23d of April*), and left heirs to the kingdom, which he had thirty-four years and a half, his three sons, Ethelbert and Eadbert and Alric. The next year after that, Tobias, bishop of Rochester died, who was a man of much learning; he had been a disciple of archbishop Theodore of blessed memory, and

---

1. Egbert was not a bishop, *read*, priest.

of abbot Adrian, and therefore with the knowledge of ecclesiastical and general writings (literature), he likewise learned Greek, with Latin, so that they were as well known to him as his own speech in which he was born. He was buried in the porch of St Paul the apostle, which is in St Andrew's church, where he himself wrought a burial place. After him Eadulf took the bishop's ministry, whom archbishop Bertwald hallowed.

3. After these things, about seven hundred and twenty-nine winters after our Lord's incarnation, two stars appeared about the sun, which are in books named comets; and they stirred up much fear in the men who beheld and saw them. One of them went before the sun, in the morning, when it was upgoing; the other in the evening afterfollowed, when it was setting; as if they were prophets of bitter wo to the sun-rising (or east), and to its setting (or the west), [so] that they at each time, both in day and in night, betokened much evil to come to men. The light stood out from them as it were a fiery torch towards the north-deal of the world. The stars appeared in the month of January, and remained two weeks.

4. At that time soon after, the heaviest plague of the Saracene people wasted and forharrowed the kingdom of Gaul with sore and wretched slaughter, and they soon, after a short space, received a worthy punishment in the same province, and suffered for their faithlessness. The same year also the holy man of God, Egbert, as we formerly mentioned, went to the Lord on the same Easter-day; and soon over the Easter-tide, that is, the seventh of the ides (*the 9th day*) of May, Osric, king of the Northumbrians, went out of life, after he had held and steered the kingdom eleven years, and he wished and had deemed (and decreed) that Keolwulf should be king after him, and afterfollower of his kingdom; he was the brother of king Kenred, who had the kingdom before him. Of this king's reign both the beginning and forthgoing [1] were tossed and mingled by so many and so great stirrings of adverse things, that one cannot yet know what one can or should write, or what end sundry things are to have.

5. About seven hundred and thirty-one winters after our Lord's incarnation, archbishop Bertwald, wasted by long age, died on the fifth day of the ides (*9th day*) of January. He sat (or possessed) the bishop-seat thirty-seven years and six months and

---

1. Progress.

fourteen days; for whom, in the same year, was hallowed archbishop Tatwine, who was of the province of the Mercians; and was formerly a mass-priest in the monastery which is called Breodon. He was hallowed in Canterbury, by the venerable men, Daniel, bishop of Winchester, and Ingwald, bishop of London, and Aldwin, bishop of Litchfield, and Eadulf, bishop of Rochester, the tenth day of the month of June, being sunday. He was a man famous in religion and in prudence of wisdom, and likewise nobly instructed and skilled in holy writings.

6. At present the bishops of the churches in Kent are Tatwine and Eadulf; and Ingwald bishop of the East-Saxons; the bishops of the East-English are Aldbert and Hagolac; the bishops of the West-Saxons are Daniel and Forthhere; the bishop of the Mercians is Aldwin; and to the folks who dwell by west the Severn, Walstod is bishop; Wilfrid is bishop of the Whicks;[1] Kynebert is bishop of Lindesfarne; the bishopshire of the isle of Wight belongs to Daniel, bishop of Winchester; the province of the South-Saxons has stood many years without a bishop, and they seek the ministry of a bishop from the bishop of the West-Saxons; and all these provinces, and also the other south provinces, to the boundary of the river Humber, with their kings, are likewise subjected in obedience to Ethelbald, king of the Mercians.

7. Moreover [in] the province of the Northumbrians, over which king Keolwulf was in sovereignty, four bishops now have bishopshire; bishop Wilfrith, in the church of York; Ethelwald, in Lindesfarne; Acca, in Hagustaldsea; Peht-helm, in the place which is called at Whitern,[2] which place, the faithful folks being manifold, was newly raised to a bishopseat,[3] and he was the first bishop of the place. Likewise the Pictish kin, at this time, has peace and alliance with the English nations, and also rejoices to be partaking of the orthodox peace and truth with all God's church. The Scots who dwell in Britain were thankful with their [own] boundaries, and they contrive neither plots nor deceits against the English nation. But the Britons, though they, of a great deal, with inward hatred, have fought in a hostile manner against the English nation, and the state of the whole

---

1. Or Wiccii, *Huicciorum*, A. S. Hwicna,—nom. Hwican or Hwiccan.
2. White house, *Candida casa*, now Whithern, in the South-west of Scotland.
3. Eked or increased into a bishopstool, or episcopal throne.

orthodox church of God, both in the holding of unright Easters, and in unapproved customs, yet they have been withstood, both by divine and by human virtue, that they cannot, however, have nor accomplish their desire, and though they are in a great measure their own masters, they are, however, committed and subjected to thraldom of the English kin.

8. In this time of peace and tranquillity, now many in the province of the Northumbrians, both noble and ignoble, yearn more to give themselves and their children to monasteries, and to God's service, than they exercise worldly warfare. What end the thing is to have, the coming age will see and behold. This is now at present the state of all Britain, about two hundred and eighty-five years of the English kin's coming into the isle of Britain, and about seven hundred and thirty-one winters from our Lord's incarnation. In this Lord's eternal reign all the earth shall be glad; and while Britain equally rejoices in his belief, many isles shall rejoice, and shall confess the memory of his holiness.

9. These things concerning the history of the churches of the English nation, so [far] as I could know, from the writings of men of yore, or from the sayings of old men, or from my own knowledge, by the Lord's help, did ' I Bede, Christ's servant, and mass-priest of the monastery of the blessed apostles Peter and Paul, which is at Wire-mouth, and among the Girvii.

10. I was born in the sunder-land of the same monastery. When I was seven winters [old], then was I, by the care of my relations, given to the venerable abbot Benedict, to be fed and taught, and afterwards to Keolfrith; and afterwards led all the time of my life in the dwelling of the same monastery; and I gave all diligence to learn and to study the holy scriptures; and amid the holding of regular discipline, and the daily care to sing in church, it was always sweet and winsome to me, that I should either learn, or teach, or write. And then, in the nineteenth year, I received deaconhood, and in the thirtieth year priesthood, and both by the ministry of the venerable bishop John, through behest and command of abbot Keolfrith. From the time that I received priesthood, until nine and fifty winters of my age, I wrote and set (or composed) these books, for my own need, and [that] of my friends, out of the works of venerable fathers; and likewise added to the form of the sense and of ghostly interpretation:—

4. Made or composed.

11. First on the beginning of Genesis to Isaac's birth and the outcasting of Ishmael, I set four books.

Of the Tabernacle and its vats, and of priestly garments, three books.

On the first deal of Samuel, that is to the death of king Saul, four books.

Of the building of the Temple, and the allegorical explanation, two books.

Next On the book of kings, thirty questions.

On the proverbs of Salomon, three books.

On the song of songs, six books.

On Ezra and Nehemia, three books.

On the song of Abbacuc, one book.

On the book of the blessed father Tobias, of allegorical interpretation concerning Christ's church, one book.

On the gospel of Mark, four books.

On the gospel of Luke, six books.

Upon gospel homilies, two books.

On the apostle, whatever I found in the works of St Augustine, I wrote all in order.

On the acts of the apostles, two books.

On the seven canonical epistles, sundry books, (that is one book on each).

On the Revelation of St John, three books.

Of the six ages of the world, one book.

Of the dwellings of the children of Israel, one.

Of that which Isaias said, "And they shall be shut up there in prison, and after many days they shall be visited."

Of the right bissextile (or leap year), one book; of evennight (or the equinox), according to the explanation of Anatolius.

Of spells of holy men (legends of saints), one.

Books of the life and suffering of St Felix the confessor, Paulinus's books I turned from meter-work into prose.

The book of the life and suffering of Anastasius the martyr, which was badly translated out of Greek into Latin, and worse corrected by some unskilful person, I corrected so as I could to the sense.

I wrote the life of the holy father, and monk, and at the same time bishop, St Cathbert,—first in heroic meter, and after a space in prose.

The history (—spell) of the abbots of this monastery, in which I am glad to serve the Heavenly Goodness, Benedict, Keolfrith, and Whatbert, I wrote in two books.

The ecclesiastical history of our isle and nation I wrote in five books.

I composed a Martyrology concerning the festival days of holy martyrs, in which I carefully wrote all that I could find, not only on what day, but also by what kind of warfare, or under what judge, they overcame the world.

A hymn book in various meters.

A book of epigrams in heroic meter.

Of the nature of things, and of Times, sundry books (or, one book of each).

Again, of Times, one great book.

A book on orthography distinguished by the order of the stave-row (or alphabet).

A book of the metric art, and another added to it, viz a book of schemes and tropes,—of the figures and modes of expression in which the canon of holy scripture is written.

" And now I pray thee, good Saviour, as thou hast mildly given me to drink the words of thy knowledge, that thou also kindly grant, that I at last may come to thee, the well of all wisdom, and always appear before thy face."

(12. Moreover I humbly pray, &c.) See Address to King Keolwulf, § 3. (Page 202.) Misplaced here in A. S. MSS.

END OF BEDE'S ECCLESIASTICAL HISTORY

ADDITIONAL NOTES.

PAGE 207, *line* 15, *for* sown with the divine grace *&c. to* examples—*read* seen and pitied by the Divine Grace; and he soon began to imitate the example P. 217 Title of Ch. xix, *after* detained insert '. P. 233, *l.* 7, Legcaster *is now* Chester. P. 261, ch. v. § 2, "Learn" is often used for "read," and "stand on" for "be instant in." P. 265, § 3, *for* the Ireland, isle *r.* Ireland, the isle. P. 305, § 2, period 1, *after* truth *insert* '. P. 349 A.S. Poem, column 2, l, 2, *r.* ricaes, l. 6, gihuaes, N. 1, *add* See also p. 247, *l,* 15, " hailed and greeted." Ib. N. 6, *for* not mentioned *r.* though mentioned in the Preface, not quoted for this reading. P. 351, last l. *for* he *r.* the. P. 377, The note referred to regards the rendering of Bede's *catechizare* by cristnian, as Alfred has uniformly done. See p. 251, 8, & 32, and p. 377, 1, 3, 11. The course of instruction prescribed to candidates for baptism, was thought more likely to make them christians, than their formal submission to the sacramental rite. As these were christened before they were baptized, so there may have been many baptized, who never were christened.

P. 385, l. 15, *r.* " At Ættrecum."

The Translator, upon further consideration, does not wish the Note 4. p. 236, to be deemed a settlement of the question whether Menavian or Mevanian should stand in the text; though Alfred's Monige seems to vouch for the former.

KING ALFRED'S

ANGLO-SAXON VERSION OF BOETHIUS,

TRANSLATED INTO ENGLISH.

PREFACE.

The next work of King Alfred is an Anglo-Saxon version of a work entitled, *De Consolatione Philosophiæ*, which was written in the sixth century by Manlius Severinus Boethius, a Roman whose attainments and liberality had placed him among the most distinguished names, which grace the annals of the empire. He became known to Theodoric, king of the Ostrogoths, and was applied to by him for assistance in the regulation of his coinage, in order that forgery might be prevented, as he was justly celebrated for his scientific knowledge. His happiness was not confined to the favour of princes; he was also happy in his marriage with Rusticiana, the daughter of Symmachus; and he was moreover the father of two sons, who were elected consuls in the year 522. He is said to have reached the height of his prosperity, when, on the inauguration of his sons in the consulate, after pronouncing a panegyric on Theodoric, he distributed a largess to the Roman populace, in the games of the circus. But he was a remarkable instance of the uncertainty of earthly prosperity. His happiness was unexpectedly overcast; and he was suddenly hurled from the eminence he had attained. His unflinching integrity provoked enmity in the court of Theodoric and the boldness with which he pleaded the cause of Albinus, when accused of treason by an informer, appears to have been the ground on which he and his father-in-law, Symmachus, were charged with the intention of delivering Rome from the barbarian yoke which was then oppressing her. A sentence of confiscation and death was passed upon him, without his defence being heard, and he was for some time imprisoned in the baptistry of the church at Ticinum. During his confinement he wrote his treatise on the consolation of philosophy. His imprisonment, however, was not of very long continuance; for the sentence of death was after a few months carried into effect, although there is some doubt as to the manner in which it was executed.

From the absence of any direct reference to Christianity in his 'Consolation' it can scarcely be supposed that Boethius had embraced the Christian Religion: still, however, from the deep tone of piety which pervades the work, it is very evident that he was in no small degree influenced by its refreshing truths.

The version which King Alfred made, has been preserved to us in two very ancient manuscripts. One of these is in the Bodleian Library, in Oxford, and the other is in the Library of the British Museum, having been removed there with the other valuable books and manuscripts, which were saved in the fire which unfortunately destroyed a portion of Sir Robert Cotton's Library. This manuscript was so much injured as to be rendered almost useless; but through the skill and industry of the Rev Jas. Stevenson, assisted by the late John Holmes, esq., it has been made as perfect as the damaged state of the parchment would allow, and may now be read, in most parts, with the greatest ease. This manuscript contains the metrical version of Boethius, in addition to the prose, whilst that in Oxford contains nothing but prose. There are some variations in the texts of these MSS. and the reader will find this translation for the most part following the reading of the one in the Bodleian.

King Alfred entirely altered the arrangement of Boethius; for instead of dividing his work into four books, and subdividing each book into chapters, as his Author had done, he divided the whole work into forty two chapters, alluding occasionally to the books of the original.

Much of the work is in the form of a dialogue between Boethius and Wisdom, which is represented as visiting him in prison, and endeavouring to infuse comfort into his mind. The first six chapters of the Anglo-Saxon version comprise the chief part of the first book of Boethius, together with a short introduction. The next fifteen chapters contain the substance of the second book. The third book is translated in the following fourteen chapters. Four chapters and part of another, viz. part of chapter xl, are devoted to the fourth book, and the remaining portion of chapter xl, together with chapters xli and xlii, completes the whole. Although the work is altogether deeply interesting, yet the most striking portion will be found in the following chapters. In chapter xv there is a lively description of the golden age. In chapter xix the vanity of pursuing fame is pointed out. In chapter xxi the power and goodness of the creator in governing and upholding the universe are displayed. Chapter xxv contains a disquisition on natural disposition. The first part of chapter xxix describes the weakness and unhappiness of Kings; while the second part illustrates the condition of royal favourites by the treatment which Seneca and Papinian met with. Chapter xxx, part 2, declares the natural equality of mankind. Chapter xxxiii part 4, contains an address to God. Chapter xxxv, part 4, contains the fable of the giants warring against Jupiter, and the history of the tower of Babel; and Part 6 relates the story of Orpheus and Eurydice. Chapter xxxviii, part 1, gives the account of Ulysses and Circe. Chapters xl and xli, are devoted to an enquiry into divine predestination and human liberty. The last chapter treats of God and eternity.

King Alfred proposed, as he states, to render a correct translation of the Latin work of Boethius, but warming with his subject, he considerably enlarges on his author and displays to great advantage his own originality of thought. Indeed the great value of the present work arises from the insight it affords us into the mind and feelings of one, who was very far in advance of the age in which he lived; and who has ever since been regarded as a model of wisdom. The vicissitudes and hardships which King Alfred encountered would very naturally inspire him with a lively sympathy for a man, who suffered such great reverses as the noble Roman did; for in the sufferings of Boethius, and in the harassing cares which disturbed his mind, he would probably see a type of his own distractions and anxieties; and this would doubtless be a great inducement to overcome the difficulties which must have beset him in mastering a work which presented many difficulties to a mind very imperfectly educated, but endowed with a wonderful spirit for getting the better of them. The imperfection of King Alfred's early education will account for a few mistakes in names and historical facts. These however by no means lessen the value of the translation; and instead of wondering at their occurrence, one should feel surprised that they are not more numerous, and more important. The translation was made, as the Royal Author himself states, amid various and manifold worldly occupations which often busied him both in mind and body. "The occupations," said he, "are very difficult to be numbered which in his days came upon the kingdoms which he had undertaken to govern;" and on this account our wonder should be excited when we meet with literary attainments which in those days were rather to be sought for in the retirement of the cloister, than in the harass and dis_traction of a camp, ever moving and often in the immediate neighbourhood of piratical and cruel enemies.

For the first publication of King Alfred's version we are indebted to Mr Rawlinson, who in the year 1698 published at Oxford a very correct transcript of the Oxford manuscript which had been prepared for publication by Junius, and for which that eminent linguist had prepared the necessary types. This was merely the Anglo-Saxon text, without any translation. In the year 1829 a very beautiful edition was published by the late Mr Cardale together with an English translation. The Anglo-Saxon text having been taken from both of the existing manuscripts, gives a popular version, but not such a faithful one as is desirable in a work of this kind. In this, as well as in the other portions of King Alfred's works, the greatest fidelity has been observed in the translation.

Although differing in some passages the translator begs to acknowledge the assistance he has derived from Mr Cardale's labours, and to express his obligation for many acts of kindness which he received from that gentleman, whose friendship he had the happiness of enjoying many years.

KING ALFRED'S BOETHIUS.

PREFACE.

KING ALFRED was translator of this book, and turned it from book Latin into English, as it is now done. Sometimes he set word by word, sometimes meaning of meaning, as he the most plainly, and most clearly could explain it, for the various and manifold worldly occupations which often busied him both in mind and in body. The occupations are to us very difficult to be numbered which in his days came upon the kingdom which he had undertaken, and yet when he had learned this book, and turned *it* from Latin into the English language, he afterwards composed it in verse, as it is now done. And he now prays, and for God's name implores every one of those who list to read this book, that he would pray for him, and not blame him, if he more rightly understand it than he could. For every man must, according to the measure of his understanding, and according to his leisure, speak that *which* he speaketh, and do that which he doeth.⏋

TITLES OF THE CHAPTERS.

I.

First, how the Goths conquered the empire of the Romans, and how Boethius wished to deliver them, and Theodoric then discovered it, and gave orders to take him to prison.

II.

How Boethius in the prison was lamenting his hard lot.

III.

How Wisdom first came to Boethius in the prison, and began to comfort him.

IV.

How Boethius, singing, prayed and lamented his misfortunes to God.

V.

How Wisdom again comforted and instructed him with his answers.

VI.

How he related to him a parable of the sun, and of the other heavenly bodies, and of the clouds.

VII.

How Wisdom said to the mind, that nothing affected it more than *that* it had lost the worldly goods, which it before was accustomed to; and spoke to him a parable, how he should act if he should be their servant; and concerning the ship's sail; and how *he* wished to have the reward of all his good works, here in *this* world.

VIII.

How the Mind answered the Reason, and said it perceived itself every way culpable; and said it was oppressed with the soreness of trouble, so that it could not answer him. Then said Wisdom, this is still thy fault that thou art almost despairing; compare now the felicities with the sorrows.

IX.

Then began Wisdom again to speak a parable concerning the sun, how she outshines all other stars, and obscures them with her light; and how the raging of the wind troubles the placid sea.

X.

How Boethius said, he plainly perceived that it was all true that Wisdom said; and that the prosperity and the enjoyments which he formerly thought should be happiness, were nothing: and how Wisdom, that he might shew that he was happy, said that his anchor was still fast in the earth.

XI.

How Reason answered him and said, she thought she had in some measure raised him up, and almost brought him to the same dignity which he before had : and asked him, who had all that he would in this world : some have nobility and have not riches.

XII.

How Wisdom instructed him, that if he were desirous to build a firm house, he should not set it upon the highest hill-top.

XIII.

How Wisdom said that they might then argue more closely, because the instruction had in some measure entered into his understanding.

XIV.

How the Mind said, why should not fair land delight him? and how Wisdom asked, what of their fairness belonged to him?

XV.

How Reason said, how happy the first age was!

XVI.

How Wisdom said, that men would exalt themselves for power, to heaven : also concerning the power of Theodoric and Nero.

XVII.

How the Mind said, that power and covetousness never well pleased him; but that he toiled with reluctance.

XVIII. XIX.

Of Fame.

XX.

Of adverse fortune and of prosperous.

XXI.

Of the power of Almighty God, and how he governs all his creatures.

XXII.

How Wisdom and Reason had restored the Mind, both with profound argument and with pleasant song.

XXIII.

How Wisdom instructed the man who would sow fertile land, that he should first take away the thorns and the furze, and the useless weeds : and how he said, that if a person had tasted any thing bitter, honey-comb seemed the sweeter to him.

XXIV.
How men desire by different means to arrive at one happiness.

XXV.
How God governs all creatures with the bridles of his power; and how every creature tends towards its kind, and desires that it may come thither from whence it before came.

XXVI.
How Wisdom said, that men were able to *understand* concerning God, as in a dream, and *asked,* whether wealth could make a man so rich that he should not need more; and whether to Boethius all his condition were agreeable when he was most prosperous.

XXVII.
How dignity may do two things to the unwise, *who* is honoured by other unwise *persons;* and how Nonius was rebuked for the golden chair of state; and how every man's evil is the more public when he has power.

XXVIII.
Of Nero the Cæsar.

XXIX.
Whether the king's favour and his friendship are able to make any man wealthy and powerful: and how other friends come with wealth, and again with wealth depart.

XXX.
How the poet sung, that more men rejoiced at the error of the foolish people, than rejoiced at true sayings: that is, that they thought any one better than he was. Then do they rejoice at that which should make them ashamed.

XXXI.
How he shall suffer many troubles, who shall yield to the lusts of the body; and how any one may, by the same rule, say that cattle are happy, if they say that those men are happy who follow the lusts of their body.

XXXII.
How this present wealth hinders the men who are attracted to the true felicities, and how Wisdom is one single faculty of the soul, and is nevertheless better than all the faculties of the body, and though any one should collect together all these present goods, yet cannot he the sooner be so happy as he would, nor has he afterwards that which he before expected.

XXXIII.

How Wisdom, having taught the Mind the resemblances of the true felicities, would then teach it *the true felicities* themselves: also of the five objects of desire, namely, wealth, and power, and honour, and glory, and pleasure.

XXXIV.

How Wisdom, having explained what the highest good was, would then explain to him where it was: and how from the great good come the less.

XXXV.

How Wisdom instructed the Mind, that it should seek within itself what it before sought around it, and should dismiss vain anxieties as it best might: and how God directs all creatures, and all good things with the rudder of his goodness.

XXXVI.

How the Mind said to Wisdom, that it perceived that God said to it through him that which he said: and *asked*, why the good God suffers any evil to be: and how Reason desired the Mind to sit in her chariot, and she would be its guide: and how she said that will and power were two things; and that if to any man there were a deficiency of either of them, neither of them could without the other effect anything.

XXXVII.

Of proud and unjust rulers; and how man should have the crown at the end of the course: and how we should describe every man by the beast which he was most like.

XXXVIII.

Of the Trojan war: how Ulysses the king had two countries under the Cæsar: and how his thanes were transformed into wild beasts.

XXXIX.

Of right hatred, and of unright, and of just recompence: and how various punishments and manifold misfortunes come to the good, as they should to the wicked: and concerning the predestination of God, and concerning destiny.

XL.

How every fortune is good, whether it seem good to them, or whether it seem evil to them.

XLI.

How Homer the good poet praised the sun: and concerning freedom.

XLII.

How we ought with all our power to enquire after God! every one according to the measure of his understanding.

Chapter I.

At the time when the Goths of the country of Scythia made war against the empire of the Romans and with their kings *who* were called Rhadgast and Alaric[1] sacked the Roman city, and brought to subjection all the kingdom of Italy, which is between the mountains and the island of Sicily: and then after the before mentioned kings, Theodoric obtained possession of that same kingdom; Theodoric[2] was of the race of the Amali; he was a Christian, but he persisted in the Arian heresy. He promised to the Romans his friendship, so that they might enjoy their ancient rights. But he very ill performed that promise and speedily ended with much wickedness; which was, that in addition to other unnumbered crimes, he gave order to slay John the pope[3]. Then was there a certain consul, that we call heretoha, who was named Boethius.[4] He was in book learning and in worldly affairs the most wise. He then observed the manifold evil which the king Theodoric did against Christendom, and against the Roman senators. He then called to mind the famous and

---

1. Early in the fifth century, two immense armies of Goths under the command of Rhadgast and Alaric invaded Italy, and after laying the country in ruins as they advanced, sacked the city of Rome. They, however, soon retreated, partly through the defeats which they sustained from the forces of the Emperor Honorius and his allies, and partly through an unaccountable panic which pervaded the troops of the Gothic leaders.

2. Theodoric, king of the Goths, who had established themselves in Italy, and who are commonly called Ostrogoths, lived in the sixth century, and was remarkable for his wisdom and learning, but unhappily he imbibed the Arian heresy, which was prevalent at that time. He was however by no means disposed to promote his views by persecution, and even went so far as to behead one of his officers for becoming an Arian, saying, "If thou couldest not continue true to thy God, how canst thou prove faithful to me who am but a man?" The latter part of his life was stained by bloodshed, he having caused the death of Pope John, and condemned Boethius and his father-in-law Symmachus.

3. John, the first Pope who bore that name, was sent on an embassy by Theodoric to the Emperor Justin, at Constantinople, and on his return Theodoric confined him in a dungeon at Ravenna, where he died of want.

4. Boethius was a noble Roman, and was distinguished for his many and varied accomplishments. For some time he was in high favour with Theodoric; but in consequence of being detected in his correspondence with the Emperor Justin, at Constantinople, he was imprisoned with his father-in-law Symmachus, and after being confined six months, he was beheaded at Pavia.

the ancient rights which they had under the Cæsars, their ancient lords. Then began he to enquire, and study in himself how he might take the kingdom from the unrighteous king, and bring it *under* the power of the faithful and righteous men. He therefore privately sent letters to the Cæsar at Constantinople,[5] which is the chief city of the Greeks, and their king's dwelling-place, because the Cæsar was of the kin of their ancient lords: they prayed him that he would succour them with respect to their Christianity, and their ancient rights. When the cruel king Theodoric discovered this, he gave orders to take him to prison, and therein lock up. When it happened that the venerable man was fallen into so great trouble, then was he so much the more disturbed in his mind, as his mind had formerly been the more accustomed to worldly prosperity: and he then thought of no comfort in the prison: but he fell down prostrate on the floor, and stretched himself, very sorrowful: and distracted began to lament himself, and thus singing said:

CHAPTER II.

The lays which I, an exile, formerly with delight sung, I shall now mourning sing, and with very unfit words arrange. Though I formerly readily invented, yet I now, weeping and sobbing, wander from suitable words. To blind me these unfaithful worldly riches! and to leave me so blinded in this dim hole! At that time they bereaved *me* of all happiness, when I ever best trusted in them: at that time they turned their back upon me, and altogether departed from me! Wherefore should my friends say that I was a prosperous man? How can he be prosperous who in prosperity cannot always remain?

CHAPTER III.

1 When I, said Boethius, had mournfully sung this lay, then came there into me heavenly wisdom, and greeted my sorrowful mind with his words, and thus said: How! art not thou the man who was nourished and instructed in my school? But whence art thou become so greatly afflicted by these worldly cares? unless, I wot, thou hast too soon forgotten the weapons which I formerly gave thee. Then Wisdom called out and said, Depart now, ye execrable worldly cares, from my disciple's mind, for ye are the greatest enemies. Let him again turn to my precepts. Then came Wisdom near to my sorrowing thought, said Boethius,

---

5. The Cæsar here alluded to was the Emperor Justin.

and it so prostrate somewhat raised; then dried the eyes of my mind, and asked it with pleasant words, whether it knew its fosteri-mother. Thereupon when the mind turned, it knew very plainly its own mother that was the Wisdom that long before had instructed band taughtit. But it perceived his doctrine much torn and greatly broken by the hands of foolish people, and therefore asked him how that happened. Then answered Wisdom to him and said, that his scholars had thus torn him when they endeavoured to possess themselves of him entirely. But they gather much folly by presumption, and by annoyance, unless any of them to their amendment return.

2. Then began Wisdom to grieve for the frailty of the mind, and began to sing; and thus said: Alas! into how unfathomable a gulf the mind rushes when the troubles of this world agitate it. If it then forget its own light, which is eternal joy, and rush into the outer darkness, which is worldly cares, as this mind now does; now it knows nothing else but lamentations.

3. When Wisdom and Reason had sung this lay, then began he again to speak, and said to the mind: I see that there is now more need to thee of comfort than of bewailing.

4. Therefore, if thou wilt be ashamed of thine error, then will I soon begin to bear thee up, and will bring thee with me to the heavens. Then answered the sorrowing mind to him, and said, What! O what! are these now the goods and the reward which thou didst promise to the men who would obey thee? Is this, now, the saying which thou formerly toldest me that the wise Plato said, which was, that no power was right without right manners?[6] Seest thou now, that the virtuous are hated and oppressed because they would follow thy will: and the wicked are exalted through their crimes, and through their self-love? That they may the better accomplish their wicked purpose, they are assisted with gifts and with riches. Therefore I will now earnestly call upon God. He then began to sing, and thus singing said:

Chapter IV.

O Thou Creator of heaven and earth! Thou who reignest on the eternal seat! Thou who turnest the heaven in a swift course! Thou makest the stars obedient to Thee; and Thou makest the

---

6. This opinion of Plato was earnestly enforced by him in his dialogue de Republica.

sun, that she [7] with her bright splendour dispels the darkness of the swarthy night. So does also the moon with his pale light, which obscures the bright stars in the heaven; and sometimes bereaves the sun of her light, when he is betwixt us and her: and sometimes the bright star, which we call the morning star; the same we call by another name, the evening star. Thou who to the winter days givest short times, and to the summer's days longer! Thou who the trees by the stark north-east wind in harvest time of their leaves bereavest; and again in spring, other leaves givest, through the mild south-west wind! What! do all creatures obey Thee, and keep the decrees of Thy commandments, except man alone, who is disobedient? O Thou Almighty Maker and Governor of all creatures, help now Thy miserable mankind. Wherefore, O Lord, ever wouldest Thou that fortune should so vary? She afflicts the innocent, and afflicts not the guilty. The wicked sit on thrones, and trample the holy under their feet. Bright virtues lie hid, and the unrighteous deride the righteous. Wicked oaths in no wise injure men, nor the false lot which is with fraud concealed. Therefore almost all mankind will now wend in doubt, if fortune may thus change according to the will of evil men, and Thou wilt not control her! O my Lord! Thou who overseest all creatures, look now mercifully on this miserable earth, and also on all mankind; for it now all struggles in the waves of this world.

CHAPTER V.

Whilst the mind was uttering such sorrow, and was singing this lay, Wisdom and Reason looked on him with cheerful eyes; and he was nothing disturbed on account of the mind's lamentation, but said to the mind, As soon as I first saw thee in this trouble, thus complaining, I perceived that thou wast departed from thy father's country, that is, from my precepts. Thou departedst therefrom when thou didst abandon thy fixed state of mind, and thoughtest that fortune governed this world according to her own pleasure, without God's counsel, and his permission, and men's deserts. I knew that thou wert departed, but I knew not how far, until thou thyself toldest to me by thy lamentations. But though thou art now farther than thou wert, thou art not nevertheless entirely driven from thy country; though thou hast wandered therein.

---

7. In all the northern dialects sun is feminine, and moon is masculine.

Nor, moreover, could any other man lead thee into error, except thyself, through thine own negligence. Nor could any one thus believe it of thee, when thou wouldest call to mind of what families thou wert, and of what citizens, as to the world: or again spiritually, of what society thou wert in thy mind and in thy reason: that is, that thou art one of the just, and of those who will rightly, who are the citizens of the heavenly Jerusalem. Thence no man was ever driven unless he were willing, that is, of his *own* good will. Wherever he might be, he had this always with him: when he had this with him, wheresoever he might be, he was with his own kin, and with his own citizens, in his own land, when he was in the company of the just. Whosoever, then, is worthy of this, that he may be in their service, he is in the highest freedom. I shun not this inferior, and this unclean place, if I find thee well instructed. I am not desirous of walls wrought with glass, or of thrones ornamented with gold and with jewels; nor am I so desirous of books written with gold, as I am desirous of a right will in thee. I seek not here books, but that which books are profitable for, that I may make thy mind perfectly right. Thou complainedst of evil fortune, both on account of the height of unjust power, and on account of my meanness and dishonour: and also on account of the uncontrolled licence of the wicked, with respect to these worldly goods. But as very great trouble has now come upon thee, both from thine anger, and from thy sorrow, I may not yet answer thee before the time for it arrives.

2. For whatsoever any one begins out of season, has no good end. When the sun's brightness in the month of August hottest shines, then does he foolishly who will at that time sow any seed in the dry furrows. So also does he who will seek flowers in the storms of winter. Nor canst thou press wine at mid-winter, though thou be desirous of warm must.

3. Then spake Wisdom and said: May I now enquire a little concerning the fixedness of thy mind, that I may thereby discover whence, and how I may effect thy cure? Then answered the mind and said, Enquire as thou wilt. Then said Reason, Dost thou believe that fortune governs this world, or that aught of good can be thus made without the Maker? Then answered the mind and said, I do not believe that it could be made so full of order: but I know forsooth that God is Governor of his own work, and I never swerved from this true belief. Then answered Wisdom

again and said; About that very thing thou wast singing a little while ago, and saidst that every creature from God knew its right time, and fulfilled its right institution, except man alone. Therefore I wonder beyond measure what it can be, or what thou meanest, now thou hast this belief. We must, however, enquire still more deeply concerning it. I do not know very well about what thou still doubtest. Tell me, since thou sayest that thou doubtest not that God is Governor of this world, how he then would that it should be. Then answered the mind and said; I can scarcely understand thy questions, and yet thou sayest that I must answer thee. Wisdom then said; Dost thou think that I am ignorant of the severity of thy trouble that thou art encompassed with? But tell me, to what end does every beginning tend? Then answered the mind and said; I remembered it formerly, but this grief has deprived me of the recollection. Then said Wisdom; Dost thou know whence every creature came? Then answered the mind and said; I know that every creature came from God. Then said Wisdom; How can it be that now thou knowest the beginning, thou knowest not also the end? for grief may agitate the mind, but it cannot bereave it of its faculties. But I desire that thou wouldest inform me, whether thou knowest what thou thyself art. It then answered and said; I know that I am of living men, and rational, and nevertheless of mortal. Then answered Wisdom and said; Knowest thou anything else to say of thyself besides what thou hast now said? Then said the mind, I know nothing else. Then said Wisdom, I have now learned thy mental disease, since thou knowest not what thou thyself art: but I know how I must cure thy disease. For this reason thou saidest thou wert an exile and bereaved of all good, because thou knowest not what thou wert. Thou shewedst that thou didst not know to what end every beginning tended, when thou thoughtest that extravagant and reckless men were happy and powerful in this world: and moreover thou shewedst that thou didst not know with what government God rules this world, or how he would that it should be, when thou saidest that thou thoughtest that this inconstant fortune governs this world without God's counsel. But it was a very great peril that thou shouldest so think. Not only wast thou in immoderate trouble, but thou hadst well nigh altogether perished. Thank God, therefore, that He has assisted thee, so that I have not entirely forsaken thy mind. We have already the chief part of the materials for thy cure, now thou believest that fortune cannot of herself without God's counsel change this world. Now thou hast no need to fear anything, for from the little spark which thou hast caught with this fuel, the light of life will shine upon thee. But it is not yet time that I should animate thee more highly: for it is the custom of every mind, that as soon as it forsakes true sayings, it follows false opinions. From hence, then, begin to grow the mists which trouble the mind, and entirely confound the true sight, — such mists as are now on thy mind. But I must dispel them first, that I may afterwards the more easily bring upon thee the true light.

Chapter VI.

Look now at the sun and also at the other heavenly bodies; when the swarthy clouds come before them they cannot give their light: so also the south wind with a great storm troubles the sea, which before, in serene weather, was clear as glass to behold. When it is so mingled with the billows it is very quickly unpleasant, though it before was pleasant to look upon. So also is the brook, though it be strong in its right course, when a great stone rolling down from the high mountain falls into it, and divides it, and hinders it from its right course. In like manner does the darkness of thy mind now withstand my enlightened precepts. But if thou art desirous with right faith to know the true light, put away from thee evil and vain joys, and also the vain sorrow and the evil fear of this world; that is, that thou lift not up thyself with arrogance in thy health, and in thy prosperity; nor again, despair of any good in any adversity. For the mind is ever bound with misery, if either of these two evils reigns.

Chapter VII.

1. Then was Wisdom silent a little while, till he perceived the mind's thoughts. When he had perceived them, then said he, If I have rightly understood thy trouble, nothing affects thee more than this, that thou hast lost the worldly prosperity which thou formerly hadst, and now lamentest because it is changed. I know clearly enough that worldly goods with many an allurement very deceitfully flatter the minds which they intend at last utterly to betray; and then, at length, when they least expect it, scornfully leave them in the deepest sorrow. If thou now desirest to know whence they come, then mayst thou learn that they come from worldly covetousness. If thou, then, wilt know their manners,

thou mayest learn that they are not faithful to any man. Hence thou mayest understand, that thou hadst no felicity when thou hadst them; nor again, didst lose any, when thou didst lose them. I thought that I had formerly instructed thee, so that thou mightest know them : and I knew that thou despisedst them when thou hadst them, though thou didst use them. I knew that thou against their will didst often repeat my sayings. But I know that no custom can be changed in any man, without the mind being in some measure disquieted. Therefore thou art now moved from thy tranquillity.

2. O Mind, what has cast thee into this care, and into these lamentations ? Is it something which is unusual that has happened to thee, so that the same before ailed not other men ? If thou then thinkest that it is on thy account that worldly goods are so changed towards thee, then art thou in error : for their manners are such. They kept towards thee their own nature, and in thier changeableness they show their constant state. They were exactly when they most allured thee, such as they are now, though they flattered thee with false happiness. Thou hast now understood the unstable promises of this blind pleasure. These promises, which are now exposed to thee, are yet to many others concealed. Thou now knowest what manners worldly goods have, and how they change. If thou, then, art desirous to be their servant, and their manners are pleasing to thee, wherefore mournest thou so much ? Why changest thou not also with them ? But if thou wouldest avoid their deceits, then despise them, and drive them from thee, for they allure thee to thy ruin. The same *things* which have now occasioned to thee these lamentations, because thou hadst them, would have suffered thee to be in tranquillity if thou never hadst obtained them. The same *things* have now forsaken thee, of their own will, not of thine, which never forsake any man without *causing* sorrow. Do these things now seem to thee very dear, and very precious, which are neither constant to possess, nor yet easy to relinquish : but when they are departing from any one, he shall with the greatest sorrow of his mind relinquish them ? Since, then, thou canst not, according to thy wish, have them faithful to thee, and they will bring thee into mourning when they depart from thee ; for what else do they come, but for a token of care and unmixed sorrow ? The worldly goods are not alone

to be thought about which we at the time possess, but every prudent mind observes what end they have, and forewarns itself both against their threats, and against *their* allurements. But if thou choosest to be their servant, then oughtest thou willingly to bear whatever belongs to their service, and to their manners, and to their will. If thou, then, art desirous that they should on thy account assume other manners than their will and custom is, dost thou not, then, dishonour thyself, inasmuch as thou rebellest against the government which thou thyself hast chosen? and nevertheless thou canst not change their custom or their nature. Besides, thou knowest that if thou spreadest the sail of thy ship to the wind, thou then leavest all thy course to the power of the wind. So if thou hast given up thyself to the power of worldly goods, it is right that thou shouldest also follow their manners. Thinkest thou that thou canst turn back the revolving wheel when it moves in its course? No more canst thou alter the inconstancy of worldly prosperity.

3. I am still desirous that we should discover further concerning worldly goods. Why didst thou just now upbraid me, that thou hadst lost them on my account? Why dost thou complain against me, as if thou for my advantage wert deprived of thine own; either of thy riches, or thy dignity? both of which formerly came to thee from me, when they were lent to thee. Let us now speak before such judge as thou wilt; and if thou art able to prove that any mortal man possessed anything of this kind as his own, I will give thee again all that thou canst say was thine own. I received thee ignorant and uninstructed, when thou first camest to man's estate, and then taught and instructed thee, and imparted to thee wisdom, whereby thou obtainedst the worldly possessions which thou now sorrowing hast lost. Thou mayest, therefore, be thankful thou hast well enjoyed my gifts. Nor canst thou say that thou hast lost aught of thine own. Why complainest thou against me? Have I in any wise deprived thee of those thy gifts which came to thee from me? All true wealth and true dignity are mine own servants, and wheresoever I am, they are with me. Know thou for truth, if the riches, which thou art lamenting that thou hast lost them, had been thine own, thou couldest not have lost them. O how unjustly do many worldly men act towards me, in that I may not govern mine own servants! The heaven may bring light days, and again obscure the light with darkness: the year may bring

blossoms, and the same year take them away. The sea may enjoy calm waves; and all creatures may keep their custom and their will, except me alone! I alone am deprived of my manners and am doomed to manners foreign *to me*, through the insatiable covetousness of worldly men. Through covetousness have they deprived me of my name, which I should rightly have. This name I should rightly have, that I am wealth and dignity; but they have taken it from me, and in their pride they have kept me, and assigned *me* to their false riches: so that I may not with my *own* servants perform my service, as all other creatures may. My servants are wisdom, and virtues, and true riches. With these servants was always my delight: with these servants I am encompassing all the heaven, and the lowest I bring to the highest, and the highest to the lowest; that is, I bring humility to the heavens, and heavenly blessings to the humble. But when I ascend with my servants, then look we down on this stormy world, like the eagle, when he soars above the clouds, in stormy weather, that the storms may not hurt him. In like manner I am desirous, O Mind, that thou shouldest ascend to us, if thou art willing, on the condition that thou wilt again with us seek the earth for the advantage of good men. Dost thou not know my manners, how careful I always was concerning the wants of good men? Knowest thou how mindful I was of the necessity of Cæsar,[8] the Grecian king, when Cyrus, king of Persia, had seized him, and would burn him? When they cast him into the fire, I delivered him with heavenly rain. But thou, on account of thy virtue, wast over confident, and thoughtest that because of thy good intention nothing unjust could befall thee; as if thou wouldest have the reward of all thy good works in this world! How couldest thou dwell in the midst of the common country without suffering the same as other men? How couldest thou be in the midst of this changeable state, without also feeling some evil through adversity? What else do the poets sing concerning this world? What is there *peculiar* to thee that thou shouldest not change therewith? Why carest thou how it may change, when I am always with thee? This reverse was to thee *more tolerable, because this world's* goods did *not* too much delight thee, and that thou, moreover, didst not more confide *in* them.

8 This was Crœsus king of Lydia, who having been taken captive by Cyrus king of Persia and placed on a pile to be burned, is said to have been delivered from his danger by a shower of rain, which Apollo sent at his earnest intreaty. *Herod.* 1, 87.

4. Though to the covetous man come as many riches as there are grains of sand by the sea-cliffs, or stars which in dark nights shine; he nevertheless will not cease from complaints, so as not to lament his poverty. Though God fulfil the wishes of wealthy men with gold, and with silver, and with all precious things, nevertheless the thirst of their avarice will not be satisfied, but the unfathomable gulf will have very many waste holes to gather into. Who can give enough to the insane miser? The more any one gives to him, the more he covets.

5. How wilt thou now answer worldly goods, if they say to thee, Why blamest thou us, O Mind? Why art thou angry with us? in what have we offended thee? Indeed thou wast desirous of us, not we of thee! Thou didst set us on the seat of thy Maker, when thou didst look to us for that good which thou shouldest *have sought from* him. Thou sayest that we have betrayed thee; but we may rather say that thou hast betrayed us, since through thy desire, and through thy covetousness, the Maker of all creatures will abhor us. Thou art, therefore, more guilty than we, both on account of thine own wicked desire, and also because through thee, we cannot perform our Maker's will. For he lent us to thee, to be enjoyed according to his commandments, not to fulfil the desire of thine evil covetousness. Answer us now, said Wisdom, as thou wilt: we wait for thine answer.

Chapter VIII.

Then said the Mind, I perceive myself every way guilty: but I am so greatly oppressed with the soreness of this trouble, that I cannot answer. Then said Wisdom again, it is still thy fault that thou art almost despairing. But I am unwilling that thou shouldest despair: I would rather that thou wert ashamed of such error, for he who despairs is distracted, but he who is ashamed is in repentance. If thou now wilt call to mind all the honours in respect of this world, which thou hast had since thou first wert born, until this day; if thou wilt now reckon all the enjoyments against the sorrows; thou canst not easily say that thou art miserable and unhappy. For I took charge of thee young, inexperienced, and uninstructed, and adopted thee as my child, and taught thee by my discipline. Who can, then, say aught else, but that thou wert most happy when thou wert beloved by me, ere known; and sooner than thou knewest my discipline and my manners: and I taught thee young such wisdom as is to many other minds denied; and improved thee with my instructions until thou wert chosen *a judge?* If thou now sayest that thou art not happy, because thou hast not the temporary honours and the enjoyments which thou formerly hadst, still thou art not unhappy: for the sorrows wherein thou now art, will in like manner pass away, as thou sayest the enjoyments formerly did. Thinkest thou now that such change and such sorrow happen to thee alone, and that the like could happen to no other mind, either before thee or after thee? Or thinkest thou that to any human mind there can be anything constant, without change? Or if it for a time to any man firmly remain, death at least will take it away, so that it may not be where it before was. What are worldly goods but an emblem of death? For death comes for nothing else but that it may take away life. So also worldly goods come to the mind, in order that they may deprive it of that which is dearest to it in this world; that is, when they depart from it. Say, O Mind, whether thou judgest more wisely, seeing that nothing worldly can be constant and unchangeable, whether thou despisest them, and of thine own choice canst relinquish them without regret, so that thou canst abide it when they leave thee sorrowful?⁹

Chapter IX.

Then began Wisdom to sing, and sung thus: When the sun in the serene heaven brightest shines, then become dark all the stars, because their brightness is no brightness by reason of her. When the south-west wind gently blows, then grow very quickly field flowers; but when stark wind cometh *from the* north-east, then does it very soon destroy the rose's beauty. So often-times the north wind's tempest stirs the too tranquil sea. Alas! that there is nothing of fast-standing work ever remaining in the world!

Chapter X.

Then said Boethius: O Wisdom, thou who art the mother of all

---

9. This chapter ends abruptly, and is evidently incomplete.

virtues, I cannot gainsay or deny that which thou hast said to me, because it is all true: for I have now learned that those my felicities, and the prosperity, which I formerly thought should be happiness, are no happiness, because they so speedily depart. But this has most of all troubled me, when I most deeply think about that which I have clearly learned, that it is the greatest infelicity of this present life, that any one is first happy and afterwards unhappy Then answered Wisdom and Reason, and said, Thou canst not with truth accuse thy fortune and thy happiness, as thou supposest, on account of the false unhappiness which thou art suffering. It is a deception when thou imaginest that thou art unhappy. But if it has so much troubled thee, and made thee sad, that thou hast lost the false happiness; then may I plainly tell thee, that thou well knowest that thou hast still the greatest part of thy felicities which thou formerly hadst. Tell me now whether thou canst with justice complain of thy misfortunes, as if thou hadst altogether lost thy happiness, since thou hast yet kept entire everything most precious which thou wast anxious about? How canst thou, then, lament the worse and the more unworthy, when thou hast retained the more desirable? Thou knowest, however, that the ornament of all mankind, and the greatest honour yet lives, that is Symmachus, thy father-in-law. He is yet hale and sound, and has enough of every good; for I know that thou wouldest not be unwilling to give thine own life for him, if thou wert to see him in any difficulties. For the man is full of wisdom and virtues, and sufficiently free as yet from all earthly fear. He is very sorry for thy troubles, and for thy banishment. How! is not thy wife also living, the daughter of the same Symmachus? and she is very prudent und very modest. She has surpassed all other wives in virtue. All her excellence I may sum up to thee in few words; that is, that she is in all *her* manners like her father. She now lives for thee, thee alone: for she loves nothing else except thee. Of all good she has enough in this present life, but she has despised it all, beside thee alone. She renounces it all, because she has not thee. Of this alone she feels the want. Because of thy absence everything which she has seems naught to her. Therefore she is through love of thee wasted, and also dead with tears and with grief. What shall we say concerning thy two sons, who are noblemen, and counsellors? in whom is manifest the ability and all the virtues of their father, and of their grandfather, so far as young men may understand, that thou art as yet very happy, since thou still livest and art hale. This, indeed, is the greatest possession of mortal men, that they live and are hale: and thou hast yet in addition, all that I have already mentioned to thee. But I know that this is even more valuable than man's life: for many a man would wish that he himself should die, rather than behold his wife and children dying. Why toilest thou, then, in weeping without a cause? Thou canst not yet blame thy fortune, nor upbraid thy wife: nor art thou altogether brought to naught, as thou thinkest. No unbearable misery has yet befallen thee, thine anchor is still fast in the earth: that is, the noblemen whom we before mentioned. They suffer thee not to despair of this present life: and again, thine own faith, and the divine love and hope; these three suffer thee not to despair of the everlasting life. Then answered the sorrowful Mind and said; O that the anchors were so secure, and so permanent, both for God and for the world, as thou sayest! Then might we the more easily bear whatsoever misfortunes come upon us. They all seem the lighter to us, so long as the anchors are fast. But thou mayest nevertheless perceive how my felicities, and my dignity here in respect of the world are changed.

CHAPTER XI.

1. Then answered Wisdom and Reason, and said; I think I have in some measure raised thee up from thy sorrow; and almost brought *thee* to the same dignity which thou before hadst. Only thou art yet too full of what thou hast relinquished, and art therefore grieved. But I cannot endure thy lamentations for the little that thou hast lost. For thou always with weeping and with sorrow mournest if there *be* to thee a lack of anything desired, though it be of something little. Who was ever in this present life, or who is now, or who shall be yet after us, in this world, to whom nothing against His will may happen, either little or much? Very narrow and very worthless are human enjoyments; for either they never come to a man, or they never constantly remain there such as they first came. This I will hereafter more clearly shew. We know that some may have enough of all worldly wealth, but they have

nevertheless shame of the wealth, if they are not so noble in birth as they wish. Some are very noble and eminent on account of their birth, but they are oppressed and made sad by indigence and poverty, so that it were more desirable to them to be unnoble than so poor, if it were in their power. Many are, indeed, both full noble, and full wealthy, and are nevertheless very unhappy when they have either of these things; either when they have wives as yoke-fellows with them, or have not yoke-fellows. Many have married happily enough, but for want of children they leave all the riches which they amass to strangers to enjoy, and they are, therefore, unhappy. Some have children enough, but they are sometimes unhealthy, or evil, or worthless, or soon depart, so that the parents therefore mourn all their life. Hence no man can, in this present life, be altogether suited in respect of his fortune. Though he have nothing at all to sorrow about, this is able to make him sorrowful, that he knows not what is about to happen to him, whether good or evil, any more than thou knewest, and moreover he fears that what he then happily enjoys he may lose. Show me now any man of those who appear to thee the happiest, and who is most distinguished for the enjoyment of his desires. I tell thee at once that thou mayest observe that he is often immediately troubled for very trifling things, if anything happen to him against his will, or contrary to his custom, though it be ever so little; unless he may give his nod to every man to run at his will. Wonderfully little can cause the happiest man of all here in respect of the world, that he should think that his happiness is either much lessened, or entirely lost. Thou now thinkest that thou art very miserable, and I know that to many a man it would seem that he were raised to the heavens, if he had any part of thy felicities which thou hast still. Moreover, the place wherein thou art now detained, and which thou callest thy place of exile, is the country of the men who were born there, and also of those who by their own will dwell there. Nothing is evil until a man thinks that it is evil; and though it be now heavy and adverse, yet it will be happiness if he acts willingly, and patiently bears it. Scarcely any one is so prudent when he is in impatience, as not to wish that his happiness were destroyed. With very much bitterness is the sweetness of this world mingled. Though it seem pleasant to any one, he will be unable to hold it, if it begin to fly from him. Is it not, then, most resemble old men. Therefore I wonder why thou canst not

very evident how inconstant worldly goods are, when they are not able to satisfy the poor, inasmuch as he always desires something of that which he has not; neither do they always dwell with the patient and moderate.

2. Why seek ye, then, around you the happiness which ye have placed within you by the divine power? But ye know not what ye do: ye are in error. But I can with few words show you what is the root of all happiness: for which I know thou wilt strive until thou obtainest it: this then is good. Canst thou now discover whether thou hast anything more precious to thee than thyself? I think, though, thou wilt say that thou hast nothing more precious. I know, if thou hadst full power of thyself, thou wouldest then have something in thyself, which thou never with thine own consent wouldest relinquish, nor could Fortune take it from thee. Therefore I advise thee, that thou learn, that there is no happiness in this time of life. But learn that nothing is better in this present life than reason: because men cannot by any means lose it. Therefore that wealth is better which can never be lost, than that which may, and shall *be lost*. Is it not now clearly enough proved to thee, that Fortune cannot give thee any happiness? because each is insecure, both fortune and happiness; for these goods are very frail, and very perishable. Indeed every one who possesses these worldly goods, either knows that they are about to depart from him, or he is ignorant of it. If, then, he is ignorant of it, what happiness has he in riches, when he is so foolish, and so unwise as to be ignorant of this? But if he knows it, then he dreads that they may be lost; and also is well aware that he must leave them. Continued fear suffers not any man to be happy. If, then, any man cares not whether he have that wealth which he may not have, even when he has it, truly that is for little happiness or none which a man may so easily lose. I think, moreover, that I had formerly with sufficient clearness taught thee by many arguments, that the souls of men are immortal and eternal: and it is so evident that no man need doubt it, that all men end in death, and also their riches. Therefore I wonder why men are so irrational as to think that this life can make man happy whilst he lives, seeing that it cannot after it is ended make him miserable. But we certainly know of innumerable men, who have sought eternal happiness, not by this alone, that they chose the bodily death, but they also willingly submitted to

many grievous torments on account of the eternal life : those were all the holy martyrs.

Chapter XII.

Then began Wisdom to sing, and sung thus ; he prolonged with verse the speech that he before made, and said : He who will build a fine house must not set it upon the highest hill ; and he who will seek heavenly wisdom must not *seek* it with arrogance. And again, he who is desirous to build a firm house, should not set it on sand-hills. So also if thou art desirous to build wisdom, set it not on avarice. For as thirsty sand swallows the rain, so avarice swallows the perishable riches of this middle earth, because it is always thirsty after them. A house cannot stand long on the high mountain, if a very violent wind press on it; nor has it that which may stand on the thirsty sand for excessive rain. Thus also the human mind is subverted, and moved from its place, when the wind of strong afflictions agitate it, or the rain of immoderate care. But he who wishes to have eternal happiness, should flee from the dangerous splendour of this middle earth, and build the house of *his* mind on the firm rock of humility. For thirst dwells in the vale of humility, and in the mind of wisdom. Therefore the wise man ever leads all his life in joy unchangeable and secure, when he despises both these earthly goods, and also the evils, and hopes for the future, which are eternal. For God supports him everywhere, perpetually dwelling in the enjoyments of his mind ; though the wind of troubles, and the continual care of these worldly goods blow upon him.

Chapter XIII.

When Wisdom and Reason had thus sung this lay, then began he again to make a speech, and thus said ; Methinks that we may now argue more closely, and with profounder words ; for I perceive that my doctrine, in some degree, enters into thy mind, and thou understandest well enough what I say unto thee. Consider now what is thine own of all these worldly possessions and riches : or what of great price thou hast therein, if thou rationally examinest it. What hast thou from the gifts and from the riches which thou sayest fortune gives you, even though they were eternal ? Tell me now, whether in thy judgment this thy wealth is so precious to thee from its own nature. But I say to thee, that it is from its own nature, not from thine. If it, then, is from its own nature, and not from thine, why art thou ever the better for its good? Tell me what of it seems to thee most precious: whether gold, or what? I know, however, gold. But though it be gold, and precious, yet will he be more celebrated and more beloved who gives it, than he who gathers and takes it from others. Riches, also, are more honourable and more estimable when any one gives them, than they are when he gathers and keeps them. Covetousness indeed makes misers loathsome both to God and to men; and liberality always makes them estimable, and famous, and worthy, both to God and to the men whom they befriend. Since, then, wealth cannot be both with those who give it and with those who receive it, all wealth is therefore better and more precious given than held. If even all the wealth of this middle earth should come to one man, would not all other men be poor, except one? It is sufficiently evident that the good word and good fame of every man is better and more precious than any wealth; for this word fills the ears of all those who hear it, and yet is not the less with him who speaks it. His heart's recess it opens, and the locked heart of another it penetrates, and in the way between them it is not lessened, nor can any one with sword slay it, nor with rope bind; nor does it ever perish. But these your riches, if they were always yours, then does not the sooner seem to you enough of them; and if ye may not give them to other men, ye never the more therewith satisfy their want and their desire. Though thou divide them as small as dust, yet thou canst not satisfy all men equally: and when thou hast divided all, thou wilt then be poor thyself. Are the riches of this middle earth worthy of a man, when no one can fully have them? Nor can they enrich any man, unless they bring another to poverty. Does the beauty of gems attract your eyes to them, to wonder at them? I know that they do so. But the excellence of the beauty which is in gems is theirs, not yours. Wherefore I excessively wonder why the good of the irrational creatures seems to you better than your own good; why ye so immoderately admire gems, or any of the insensible things which have not reason; for they with no justice can deserve that ye should admire them. Though they are God's creatures, they are not to be compared with you. For either it is no good for yourselves, or at least for little good compared with you. We too much despise ourselves when we love that which is beneath us, in our own power, more than ourselves, or the Lord who made us, and gave us all good things. Do fair lands delight thee?

Chapter XIV.

Then answered the Mind to Reason, and said; Why should not fair land delight me? Is not that the fairest part of God's creatures? Full often we rejoice at the serene sea, and also admire the beauty of the sun, and of the moon, and of all the stars. Then answered Wisdom and Reason to the Mind, and thus said; What belongs to thee of their fairness? Darest thou to boast that their fairness is thine? No, no. Dost thou not know that thou madest none of them? But if thou wilt glory, glory in God. Dost thou rejoice in the fair blossoms of Easter, as if thou madest them? Canst thou then make anything of this kind, or hast thou any part in the work? No, no. Do not thou so. Is it through thy power that the harvest is so rich in fruits. Do not I know that it is not through thy power? Why art thou then, inflamed with such vain glory? or why lovest thou external goods so immoderately, as if they were thine own? Thinkest thou that fortune can cause to thee that those things should be thine own, which their own natures have made foreign to thee? No, no. It is not natural to thee that thou shouldest possess them; nor is it their nature that they should follow thee. But heavenly things are natural to thee, not these earthly. These earthly fruits are created for the food of cattle; and worldy riches are created for a snare to those men who are like cattle, that is, vicious and intemperate. To those moreover they come oftenest. But if thou wouldest have the measure, and wouldest know what is needful; then is it meat and drink, and clothes, and tools, for such craft as thou knowest, which is natural to thee, and which is right for thee to possess. What advantage is it to thee, that thou shouldest desire these present goods beyond measure, when they can neither help thee, nor themselves? With very little of them nature has enough. With so much she has enough, as we before mentioned. If thou givest her more, either it hurts thee, or at least it is unpleasant to thee, or inconvenient, or dangerous,—all that thou dost beyond measure. If thou beyond measure eatest or drinkest, or hast more clothes on thee than thou needest, the superfluity becomes to thee either pain, or loathing, or inconvenience, or danger. If thou think that wonderful apparel is any honour, then ascribe I the honour to the workman who made it, not to thee. The workman is God, whose skill I therein praise. Thinkest thou that the multitude of thy men can make thee happy? No, no. But if they are wicked, then are they more dangerous and more troublesome to thee, had than not had: for wicked thanes are always their lord's enemies. But if they are good and faithful to their lord, and sincere, is not that, then, their good, not thine? How canst thou, then, appropriate to thyself their good. If thou boastest of it, dost thou not boast of their good, not thine?

2. It is now plainly enough shewn to thee, that none of those goods is thine, which we have already spoken about, and thou didst think should be thine. If, then, the beauty and wealth of this world is not to be desired, why dost repine on account of what thou hast lost? Or wherefore dost thou long for what thou formerly hadst? If it is fair, that is of their own nature, not of thine; it is their fairness, not thine. Why then dost thou delight in their fairness? What of it belongs to thee? Thou didst not make it, nor are they thine own. If they are good and fair, then were they so made; and such they would be though thou never hadst them. Thinkest thou that they are ever the more precious, because they were lent for thy use? But because foolish men admire them, and they to them seem precious, therefore thou gatherest and keepest them in thy hoard. How, then, dost thou hope to have happiness from anything of this sort? Believe me now I say it unto thee, thou hast naught therefrom, except that thou toilest to avoid poverty, and therefore gatherest more than thou needest. But nevertheless I very well know that all which I here speak is contrary to thy will. But your goods are not what ye think they are; for he who desires to have much and various provision needs also much help. The old saying is very true, which men formerly said, that those need much who desire to possess much, and those need very little who do not desire more than is enough. But they hope by means of superfluity to satisfy their greediness, which they never do. I wot that ye think ye have no natural good or happiness within yourselves, because ye seek them without you, from external creatures. So is it perverted, that man, though he is divinely rational thinks that he has not happiness enough in himself, unless he collects more of irrational creatures than he has need of, or than is

suitable for him; whilst the irrational cattle are desirous of no other wealth, but think that sufficient for them which they have within their own skin, in addition to the fodder which is natural to them. Whatsoever, then, though little, ye have of divine in your soul, is the understanding, and memory, and the rational will, which makes use of them both. He, therefore, who has these three, has his Maker's likeness, as much as any creature can at all have its Maker's likeness. But ye seek the happiness of the exalted nature, and its dignity, from low and perishable things. But ye understand not how great injury ye do to God, your Creator. For he would that all men should be governors of all other creatures. But ye degrade your highest dignity below the meanest creatures of all; and thereby ye have shewn that, according to your judgment, ye make yourselves worse than your own possessions, when ye think that your false riches are your happiness, and are persuaded that all your worldly goods are superior to yourselves. So indeed it is, when ye so will!

3. It is the condition of the life of men, that they then only are before all other creatures, when they themselves know what they are, and whence they are: and they are worse than cattle when they will not know what they are, or whence they are. It is the nature of cattle that they know not what they are; but it is a fault in men that they know not what they are. It is therefore very plain to thee, that ye are in error, when ye think that any one can be made honourable by external riches. If any one is made honourable with any riches, and endowed with any valuable possessions, does not the honour, then, belong to that which makes him honourable? That is, to be praised somewhat more rightly. That which is adorned with anything else is not therefore fairer, though the ornaments be fair with which it is adorned. If it before was vile, it is not on that account fairer. Know thou assuredly, that no good hurts him who possesses it. Thou knowest that I lie not to thee, and also knowest that riches often hurt those who possess them, in many things: and in this chiefly, that men become so lifted up on account of riches, that frequently the worst man and the most unworthy of all, thinks that he is deserving of all the wealth which is in this world, if he knew how he might obtain it. He who has great riches dreads many an enemy. If he had no possessions he would not need to dread any. If thou wert traveling, and hadst much gold about thee, and thou then shouldest

meet with a gang of thieves, then wouldest not thou be anxious for thy life? If thou hadst nothing of this kind, then thou wouldest not need to dread anything, but mightest go singing the old adage, which men formerly sung, that the naked traveller fears nothing.' When thou, then, wert safe, and the thieves were departed from thee, then mightest thou scoff at these present riches, and mightest say, O how good and pleasant it is for any one to posssess great wealth, since he who obtains it is never secure!

Chapter XV.

When Reason had made this speech she began to sing, and thus said; O, how happy was the first age of this middle earth, when to every man there seemed enough in the fruits of the earth! There were not then splendid houses, nor various delicious meats, nor drinks; nor were they desirous of costly dresses, for they as yet did not exist, nor did they see or hear anything of them. They cared not for any luxury, but very temperately followed nature. They always ate once in the day, and that was in the evening. They ate the fruits of trees and herbs. They drank no pure wine, nor knew they how to mix any liquor with honey, nor cared they for silken garments of various colours. They always slept out, in the shade of trees. They drank the water of the clear springs. No merchant visited island or coast, nor did any man, as yet, hear of any ship-army, nor even the mention of any war. The earth was not yet polluted with the blood of slain men, nor was any one ever wounded. They did not, as yet, look upon evil-minded men. *Such* had no honour; nor did any man love them. Alas! that our times cannot now become such! But now the covetousness of men is as burning as the fire in the hell, which is in the mountain that is called Ætna, in the island that is called Sicily. The mountain is always burning with brimstone, and burns up all the near places thereabout. Alas! what was the first avaricious man, who first began to dig the earth after gold, and after gems, and found the dangerous treasure, which before was hid, and covered with the earth!

7. Cantabit vaacuus coram latrone viator.—*Juv.* x, 22.

Chapter XVI.

1. When Wisdom had sung this lay, then began he again to speak, and thus said: What more can I say to thee concerning the dignity, and concerning the power of this world? For power ye would raise yourselves up to heaven if ye were able. This is because ye do not remember nor understand the heavenly power and the dignity which is your own, and whence ye came. What, then, with regard to your wealth and your power, which ye now call dignity, if it should come to the worst men of all, and to him that of all is unworthiest of it, as it lately did to this same Theodoric, and also formerly to Nero the Cæsar, and moreover frequently to many like them? Will he not, then, do as they did, and still do? slay and destroy all the rich who are under or anywhere near him, as the flame of fire does the dry heath-field, or as the burning brimstone burneth the mountain which we call Ætna, which is in the island of Sicily? very like to the great flood which was formerly in Noah's days. I think that thou mayest remember that your ancient Roman senator, formerly in the days of Tarquin the proud king, on account of his arrogance, first banished the king's name from the city of Rome. And again in like manner the consuls who had driven them out, these they were afterwards desirous to expel on account of their arrogance; but they could not; because the latter government of the consuls still less pleased the Roman senators than the former one of the kings. If, however, it at any time happens, as it very seldom does happen, that power and dignity come to good men and to wise, what is there, then, worthy of esteem, except the good and dignity of him, the good king, not of the power? For power never is good, unless he is good who possesses it. Therefore, if power be good, it is the good of the man, not of the power. Hence it is, that no man by his authority comes to virtues and to merit; but by his virtues and by his merit he comes to authority and to power. Therefore is no man for his power the better; but for his virtues he is good, if he be good; and for his virtue he is deserving of power, if he be deserving of it. Learn, therefore, wisdom; and when ye have learned it, do not then despise it. Then I say to you, without all doubt, that ye may through it arrive at power, though ye be not desirous of power. Ye need not be anxious for power, nor press after it. If ye be wise and good, it will follow you, though ye

are not desirous of it.] But tell me now, what is your most valuable wealth and power which ye most desire? I know, however, that it is this life, and this wealth, which we before spoke about.

2. O, ye beastlike men, do ye know what wealth is, and power and worldly goods? They are your lords and your rulers, not ye theirs! If ye now saw some mouse, that was lord over mice, and set them judgments, and subjected them to tribute, how wonderful would ye think it! What scorn would ye have, and with what laughter would ye be moved! How much greater, then, is man's body compared with the mind? Indeed, ye may easily conceive, if ye will carefully consider and examine it, that no creature's body is more tender than man's. The least flies can injure it; and the gnats with very little stings hurt it: and also the small worms, which corrupt the man, both inwardly and outwardly, and sometimes make him almost dead. Moreover, the little flea sometimes kills him. Such things injure him both inwardly and outwardly. Wherein can any man injure another, except in his body? or again, in their riches, which ye call goods? No man can injure the rational mind, or cause that it should not be what it is. This is very evidently to be known by a certain Roman nobleman, who was called Liberius.[1] He was put to many torments because he would not inform against his associates, who conspired with him against the king, who had unjustly conquered them. When he was led before the enraged king, and he commanded him to say who were his associates, then bit he off his own tongue, and immediately cast it before the face *of the tyrant*. Hence it happened, that to the wise man, that was the cause of praise and honour, which the unjust king appointed to him for punishment. What is it, moreover, that any man can do to another, which he may not do to him in like manner? and if he may not, another man may. We have learned also concerning the cruel Busiris,[2] who was in Egypt. This tyrant's custom was, that he would very honourably receive every stranger, and behave very courteously to him when first he came. But afterwards, before he departed from him, he would be slain. And then it happened, that Hercules, the son of Jove, came to him. Then would he do to him as he had done to many a stranger before: he would drown him in the river which is called Nile. Then was he stronger, and drowned him very justly by God's

---

1. It is very doubtful who this Liberius was. Some affirm that Boethius is here referring to Zeno, who was put to death by Nearchus, while others maintain that he is speaking of Anaxarchus. 2. King of Egypt, said to have been son of Neptune and Lybia, and altogether a mythical personage. The cruelty attributed to him is said to have been perpetrated by the Egyptians at the tomb of Osiris, near which they sacrificed men. The whole statement, however, is contradicted by Herodotus.

judgment, as he many another before had done! So also Regulus,[3] the celebrated consul; when he fought against the Africans, he obtained an almost indescribable victory over the Africans. When he had grievously slain them, he gave orders to bind them, and lay them in heaps. Then happened it very soon that he was bound with their fetters. What thinkest thou, then? What good is power, when he *who possesses it* can in no wise, by his own strength, avoid suffering from other men the same evil which he before did to others? Is not power, then, in that case naught?

3. What thinkest thou? If dignity and power were good of its own nature, and had power of itself, would it follow the most wicked men as it now sometimes doth? Dost thou not know, that it is neither natural nor usual that any contrary thing should be mixed with other contrary, or have any fellowship therewith? But nature refuses it that they should be mixed together; still more that good and evil should be together. Hence it is very manifestly shewn to thee, that this present authority, and these worldly goods, and this power, are not good of their own nature, and of their own efficacy, nor have any power of themselves; since they are willing to cleave to the worst men, and permit them to be their lords. There is not, indeed, any doubt of this, that often the most wicked men of all come to power and to dignity. If power then were good of its own nature, and of its own efficacy, it never would be subservient to the evil, but to the good. The same is to be thought with regard to all the goods which fortune brings in this present life, both of talents and possessions: for they come to the most wicked. We very well know that no man doubts of this, that he is powerful in his strength, who is seen to perform laborious work: any more than if he be anything, any one doubts that he is so. Thus the art of musick causes the man to be a musician, and medical knowledge to be a physician, and rhetoric causes him to be a rhetorician. In like manner also the nature of things causes to every man, that good cannot be mixed with evil, nor evil with good. Though they are both in one man, yet is each in him separately. Nature will never suffer anything contrary to mix, for each of them rejects the other, and each will be what it is. Riches cannot cause the miser not to be a miser, or satisfy his boundless desires, nor can authority make its possessor powerful. Since, then,

---

3. Regulus committed very great devastations after landing in Africa, but not more than was usual with conquerors in those days: and when at length he was taken captive by the Carthaginians, and sent on an embassy to Rome, his patriotic advice to the Roman senate, and his sense of honour towards those who sent him, exposed him to a lingering and cruel death on his return to Carthage.

every creature avoids that which is contrary to it, and very earnestly endeavours to repel it, what two things are more contrary to each other than good and evil? They are never united together. Hence thou mayest understand, *that* if the goods of this present life through themselves had power of themselves, and were in their own nature good, then would they always cleave to him who did good with them, not evil. But whensoever they are good, they are good through the good of the good man, who works good with them, and he is good through God. If, then, an evil man has it, it is evil through the man's evil who doth evil with it, and through the devil. What good is wealth, then, when it cannot satisfy the boundless desires of the miser? or power, when it cannot make its possessor powerful, but the wicked passions bind him with their indissoluble chains! Though any one give to an evil man power, the power does not make him good nor meritorious, if he before were not; but exposes his evil, if he before were evil, and makes it then manifest, if it before were not. For though he formerly desired evil, he then knew not how he might so fully shew it, before he had full power. It is through folly that ye are pleased, because ye can make a name, and call that happiness, which is none, and that merit *which* is none; for they shew by their ending, when they come to an end, that neither wealth, nor power, nor dignity is to be considered as the true happiness. So is it assuredly to be said, concerning all the worldly goods that fortune brings, that there is nothing therein which is to be desired, because there is nothing therein of natural good which comes from themselves. This is evident from hence, that they do not always join themselves to the good, nor make the evil good, to whom they most frequently join themselves.

4. When Wisdom had thus made this speech, then began he again to sing, and thus said: We know what cruelties, and what ruins, adulteries, and what wickedness, and what impiety the unrighteous Cæsar, Nero, wrought. He at one time gave order to burn all the city of Rome at once, after the example that formerly the city of Troy was burned! He was desirous also to see how it would burn, and how long, and how bright, in comparison of the other; and besides gave order to slay all the wisest senators of the Romans, and also his own mother, and his own brother. He moreover slew his own wife with a sword. And for such things he was in no wise grieved, but was the blither and rejoiced at it!

And yet amid such crimes all this middle earth was nevertheless subject to him, from eastward to westward, and again from southward to northward; it was all in his power! Thinkest thou that the heavenly power could not take away the empire from this unrighteous Cæsar, and correct this madness in him, if he would? Yes, O yes, I know that he could, if he would! Alas! how heavy a yoke did he lay on all those who in his times were living on the earth! and how often his sword was stained with innocent blood! Was it not, then, sufficiently evident that power of its own nature was not good, when he was not good to whom it came?

Chapter XVII.

When Wisdom had sung this lay, he was silent, and the mind then answered and thus said; O Reason, indeed thou knowest that covetousness, and the greatness of this earthly power, never well pleased me, nor did I very much yearn after this earthly authority. But nevertheless, I was desirous of materials for the work which I was commanded to perform; that was, that I might honourably and fitly guide and exercise the power which was committed to me. Moreover, thou knowest that no man can shew any skill, or exercise or control any power, without tools, and materials. That is of every craft the materials, without which man cannot exercise the craft. This then, is a king's material and his tools to reign with; that he have his land well peopled; he must have bead-men, and soldiers, and workmen. Thou knowest that without these tools no king can shew his craft. This is also his materials which he must have beside the tools; provision for the three classes. This is, then, their provision; land to inhabit, and gifts, and weapons, and meat, and ale, and clothes, and whatsoever is necessary for the three classes. He cannot without these preserve the tools, nor without the tools accomplish any of those things which he is commanded to perform. Therefore I was desirous of materials wherewith to exercise the power, that my talents and fame should not be forgotten, and concealed. For every craft and every power soon becomes old, and is passed over in silence, if it be without wisdom; for no man can accomplish any craft, without wisdom. Because whatsoever is done through folly, no one can ever reckon for craft. This is now especially to be said; that I wished to live honourably whilst I lived, and after my life to leave to the men who were after me, my memory in good works.

Chapter XVIII.

1. When this was spoken, the mind remained silent, and Reason began to speak, and thus said; O Mind, one evil is very greatly to be shunned; that is, that which very continually, and very grievously deceives the minds of all those men, who are in their nature excellent, and nevertheless are not yet arrived at the roof of perfect virtue. This, then, is the desire of false glory, and of unrighteous power, and of unbounded fame of good works, among all people. Many men are desirous of power, because they would have good fame, though they be unworthy of it; and even the most wicked of all are desirous of the same. But he who will wisely and diligently enquire concerning fame, will very soon perceive how little it is, and how slender, and how frail, and how destitute of all good. If thou wilt now studiously enquire, and wilt understand concerning the circumference of all this earth, from the eastward of this middle earth to the westward; and from the southward to the northward, as thou hast learned in the book which is called Astrologium; then mayst thou perceive that it is all, compared with the heaven, like a little point on a broad board, or the boss on a shield, according to the opinion of wise men. Dost thou not know what thou hast learned in the books of Ptolemy, who wrote of the measure of all this middle earth in one book? Therein thou mightest see that all mankind, and all earth, do not occupy anywhere nigh the fourth part of this earth, which men are able to go over. For they cannot inhabit it all; some part for heat, some for cold; and the greatest part of it the sea has covered. Take, then, from this fourth part, in thy mind, all that the sea has covered of it, and all the sheards which it has taken from it; and all that fens and moors have taken of it; and all that in all countries lies waste; then mayest thou understand, that of the whole there is not more left for men to inhabit, than as it were a small enclosure. It is, then, in foolish labour that ye toil all your life, because ye wish beyond measure to spread your fame over such an enclosure as that is, which men inhabit in this world: almost like a point compared with the other! But what of spacious, or of great, or of honourable has this your glory, when ye think on the fifth part halved of land and desert; so is it narrowed with sea, with fen, and with all? Wherefore desire ye, then, too immoderately that ye should spread your name over the tenth part, since there is not more of it, with sea, with fen, and with all!

2. Consider also that in this little park, which we before have spoken about, dwell very many nations, and various, and very unlike both in the speech and in the manners, and in all the customs of all the nations which now very immoderately desire that ye should spread your name over. This ye never can do, because their language is divided into seventy-two; and every one of these languages is divided among many nations, and they are separated and divided by sea, and by woods, and by mountains, and by fens, and by many and various wastes, and impassable lands, so that even merchants do not visit it. But how, then, can any great man's name singly come there, when no man there hears even the name of the city, or of the country, of which he is an inhabitant? Therefore, I know not through what folly ye desire that ye should spread your name over all the earth! That ye cannot do, nor even anywhere nigh. Moreover thou knowest how great the power of the Romans was in the days of Marcus, the consul, who was by another name called Tullius, and by a third, Cicero.[4] But he has shewn in one of his books, that as then, the Roman name had not passed beyond the mountains that we call Caucasus, nor had the Scythians, who dwelt on the other side of those mountains, even heard the name of the city, or of the people; but at that time it had first come to the Parthians, and was there very new. But nevertheless it was very terrible thereabout to many a people. Do ye not then perceive how narrow this your fame will be, which ye labour about, and unrighteously toil to spread? How great fame, and how great honour dost thou think one Roman could have in that land, where even the name of the city was never heard, nor did the fame of the whole people ever come? Though any man immoderately and unreasonably desire that he may spread his fame over all the earth, he cannot bring it to pass, because the manners of the nations are very unlike, and their institutions very various; so that in one country that pleases best which is at the same time in another *deemed* most deserving of blame; and moreover worthy of great punishment. Therefore no man can have the same praise in every land, because in every land that pleases not which in another pleases.

3. Therefore every man should be well contented with this, that he be approved in his own country. Though he be desirous

---

[4]. Cicero shews in his "Somnium Scipionis," that the Romans occupied a comparatively small part of the earth, and that thereupon the glory of the Roman name was very limited in its extent

of more, he cannot, indeed, bring it to pass; because it is seldom that aught in any degree pleases many men; on which account the praise of a good man is frequently confined within the same country where he is an inhabitant; and also because it has often very unfortunately happened, through the misconduct of writers, that they from their sloth, and from negligence, and from carelessness, have left unwritten the manners of the men and their deeds, who in their days were most famous, and most desirous of glory. And even if they had written the whole of their lives, and of their actions, as they ought, if they were honest, would not the writings nevertheless wax old and perish, as often as it was done, even as the writers did, and those about whom they wrote? And yet it seems to you that ye have eternal honour, if ye can, in all your life, earn that ye may have good fame after your days! If thou now comparest the duration of this present life, and this temporal, with the duration of the never-ending life, what is it, then? Compare now the length of the time wherein thou mayest wink thine eye, with ten thousand winters; * then have the times somewhat of like, though it be little; that is, that each of them has an end. But compare these ten thousand years, and even more if thou wilt, with the eternal and the never-ending life; then wilt thou not find there anything of like, because the ten thousand years, though it seem long, will shorten: but of the other there never will come an end. Therefore it is not to be compared, the ending with the never-ending. Though thou reckon from the beginning of this middle earth to the end, and then compare the years with that which has no end, there will be nothing of like. So is also the fame of celebrated men. Though it sometimes may be long, and endure many years, it is nevertheless very short, compared with that which never ends.

· 4. And ye nevertheless care not whether ye do any good on any other account, than for the little praise of the people, and for the short fame which we have before spoken about. Ye labour for this, and overlook the excellencies of your mind, and of your understanding, and of your reason, and would have the reward of your good works from the report of strangers! Ye desire to obtain there the reward which ye should *seek* from God! But thou hast heard that it long ago happened, that a very wise man, and very

---

5. Northern nations reckon their years by winters, and the shorter divisions of time by night: a mode of reckoning which is still very common in this country, as instead of seven days, we say, se'nnight; and instead of fourteen days, we say fortnight.

noble, began to try a philosopher, and scoffed at him, because he so arrogantly lifted himself up and proclaimed this, that he was a philosopher. He did not make it known by any talents, but by false and proud boasting. Then the wise man would prove him, whether he were so wise as he himself thought that he was. He therefore began to revile and speak ill of him. Then the philosopher heard very patiently the wise man's words for some time. But after he had heard his reviling, he then defended himself against him very impatiently, though he before pretended that he was a philosopher, and asked him again, whether he thought him to be a philosopher or not. Then answered the wise man to him and said, I would say that thou wert a philosopher, if thou wert patient and able to be silent. How long was to him the fame which he before falsely sought? How did he not immediately burst because of one answer? What has it then availed the best men who were before us, that they so greatly desired vain glory and fame after their death? Or what does it profit those who now are? Therefore it were to every man more needful that he were desirous of good actions, than of deceitful fame. What has he from this fame, after the separation of the body and the soul? Do we not know, that all men bodily die, and yet the soul is living? But the soul goes very freely to the heavens, after it is set loose, and liberated from the prison of the body. It then despises all these earthly things, and rejoices in this, that it may enjoy the heavenly after it is taken away from the earthly. Then the Mind will itself be a witness of God's will.

Chapter XIX.

When Wisdom had made this speech, then began he again to sing and thus singing said, Whosoever desires to hear vain fame and unprofitable glory, let him behold on the four sides of him, how spacious the expanse of the heaven is, and how narrow the space of the earth is, though it seem large to us! Then may it shame him of the spreading of his fame, because he cannot even spread it over the narrow earth alone! O, ye proud, why are ye desirous to sustain with your necks this deadly yoke? or why are ye in such vain labour, because ye would spread your fame over so many nations? Though it even happen that the furthest nations exalt your name, and praise you in many a language; and though any one with great nobleness add to his birth, and prosper in all riches, and in all splendour, death, nevertheless, cares not for things of this sort, but he despises nobility, and devours the rich and the poor alike, and thus levels the rich and the poor.* What are now the bones of the celebrated, and the wise goldsmith, Weland?' I have therefore said the wise, because to the skilful his skill can never be lost, nor can any man more easily take it from him, than he can move the sun from her place. Where are now the bones of Weland; or who knows now where they were? or where is now the illustrious and the patriotic consul of the Romans, who was called Brutus? by another name Cassius? or the wise and inflexible Cato, who was also a Roman consul? He was evidently a philosopher. Were not these long ago departed? and no one knows where they are now. What of them is now remaining, except the small fame and the name written with a few letters? And it is yet worse, that we know of many illustrious and memorable men departed, of whom very few persons have ever heard. But many lie dead entirely forgotten! Though ye now think and desire that ye may live long here in the world, what is it to you, then, the better? Does not death come, though he come late, and take you away from this world? And what then does glory profit you? at least those whom the second death seizes, and for ever binds?

Chapter XX.

When Wisdom had sung this lay, than began he to speak, and thus said; Do not suppose that I too pertinaciously attack fortune. I myself have no dread of it, because it frequently happens that deceitful fortune can neither render aid to man, nor cause any injury. Therefore she is deserving of no praise, because she herself shews that she is nothing. But she reveals her fountain when she discloses her manners. I think, nevertheless, that thou dost not yet understand what I say to thee; for what I wish to say is wonderful, and I can hardly explain it with words as I would. It is, that I know that adverse fortune is more useful to every man than prosperous. For the prosperous always lies and dissembles that men may think that she is the true happiness. But the adverse is the true happiness, though to any one it may not seem

---

6. Pallida Mors æquo pulsat pede pauperum tabernas Regumque turres.—*Hor. Od.* 1, 4.
7. Weland was the Vulcan of northern mythology.

so, for she is constant and always promises what is true. The other is false, and deceives all her followers; for she herself shews it by her changeableness, that she is very unstable: but the adverse improves and instructs every one to whom she joins herself. The other binds every one of the minds which enjoy her, through the appearance which she feigns of being good; but the adverse unbinds, and frees every one of those whom she adheres to, in that she discloses to them how frail these present goods are. But prosperity goes confusedly as the wind's storm, while adversity is always faultless, and is saved from injury by the experience of her own danger. Moreover, the false happiness necessarily draws those who are associated with her from the true felicities by her flattery: but adversity often necessarily draws all those who are subjected to her, to the true goods, as a fish is caught by a hook. Does it, then, seem to thee little gain, and little addition to thy felicities which this severe and this horrible adversity brings to thee: that is, that she very quickly lays open to thee the minds of thy true friends, and also of thine enemies, that thou mayest very plainly distinguish them? But these false goods when they depart from thee, then take they their men with them, and leave thy few faithful ones with thee. How wouldest thou now buy, or when thou wert happiest, and it seemed to thee that fortune proceeded most according to thy will, with how much money wouldest thou then have bought, that thou mightest clearly distinguish thy friend and thy foe? I know, however, that thou wouldest have bought it with money that thou mightest well know how to distinguish them. Though it now seem to thee that thou hast lost precious wealth, thou hast nevertheless therewith bought much more precious, that is, true friends, whom thou art now able to distinguish and knowest what of them thou hast. But this is the most valuable wealth of all.

Chapter XXI.

When Wisdom had made this speech, then began he to sing. and thus singing said; There is one Creator beyond all doubt, and He is also Governor of heaven and earth, and of all creatures visible and invisible. He is God Almighty. Him serve all those *creatures* which serve, both those which have understanding and those which have not understanding; both those which know it that they serve him, and those which know it not. The same has appointed unchangeable customs and habits, and also natural agreement to all his creatures, when he would, and so long as he would, which now shall stand for ever. The motion of the moving creatures cannot be stayed, nor yet turned from the course, and from the order, that is set to them. But the Governor has so with his bridle caught hold of, and restrained, and admonished all his creatures, that they neither can be still, nor yet move further than he the space of his rein allows to them So has the Almighty God controlled all his creatures by his power, that each of them strives with another, and yet supports another, so that they cannot slip asunder, but are tnrned again to the same course which they before ran, and thus become again renewed. So are they varied, that contrary creatures both strive with each other, and also hold firm agreement with each other. Thus fire doth and water; and sea and earth; and many other creatures, which will ever be as discordant between themselves, as they are ; and yet they are so accordant, that not only they may be companions but moreover that even no one of them without another, can exist. But ever must the contrary the other contrary moderate. So has now the Almighty God very wisely, and very fitly appointed change to all his creatures. Thus spring and harvest. In spring it groweth, and in harvest it ripens. And again summer and winter. In summer it is warm, and in winter cold. So also the sun bringeth light days and the moon gives light in the night through the power of the same God. The same warns the sea that it may not overstep the threshold of the earth ; but he has so fixed their limits, that it may not extend its boundary over the still earth. By the same government is ordered a very like change of the flood and the ebb. This appointment then, he allows to stand as long as he wills. But when ever he shall let go the rein of the bridles with which he has now bridled the creatures, that contrariety which we before mentioned if he shall allow these to be relaxed, then will they forsake the agreement which they now keep, and strive, each of them with other, after its own will, and forsake their companionship, and destroy all this middle-earth, and bring themselves to naught. The same God joins people together with friendship, and unites families with virtuous love. He brings together friends and companions, that they faithfully hold their agreement and their friendship. O, how happy would this mankind be, if their minds were as right aud as established, and as ordered as the other creatures are! Here endeth the second consolation book of Boethius, and beginneth the third. Boethius was by another name called Severinus: he was a consul of the Romans.

Chapter XXII.

1. When Wisdom had sung this lay, then had he bound me with the sweetness of his song, so that I was greatly admiring it, and very desirous to hear him with inward mind; and immediately thereupon I spoke to him, and thus said; O Wisdom, thou who art the highest comfort of all weary minds! how hast thou comforted me, both with thy profound discourse, and with the sweetness of thy song! so much hast thou now corrected and overcome me with thy reasoning that it now seems to me, that not only am I able to bear this misfortuue, which has befallen me, but even if still greater peril should come upon me, I will never more say that it is without deserving: for I know that I were deserving of more and heavier. But I am desirous to hear something more of the medicine of these thy instructions. Though thou just now saidest that thou thoughtest that they would seem very bitter to me, I am not now afraid of them, but I am very anxious after them, both to hear, and also to observe; and very earnestly entreat thee, that thou wouldest perform to me, as thou a little while ago promisedst me. Then said Wisdom, I knew immediately, when thou didst so well keep silence, and so willingly heardest my doctrine, that thou wouldest with inward mind receive and consider it. Therefore I waited very well till I knew what thou wouldest, and how thou wouldest understand it; and moreover, I very earnestly endeavoured that thou mightest understand it. But I will now tell thee what the medicine of my doctrine is, which thou askest of me. It is very bitter in the mouth, and it irritates thee in the throat, when thou first triest it; but it grows sweet after it enters in, and is very mild in the stomach, and pleasant to the taste.

2. But when thou shouldest perceive whither I now design to lead thee, I knew that thou wouldest very anxiously tend thither, and be very greatly inflamed with that desire. For I heard what thou before saidest, that thou wert very desirous to hear it. Then

said the Mind, Whither wilt thou now especially lead me? Then answered Reason, and said; I propose that I should lead thee to the true goods, about which thy mind often meditates, and is greatly moved; and thou hast not yet been able to find the most direct way to the true goods, because thy mind was occupied with the view of these false goods. Then said the Mind, I beseech thee that thou wouldest shew me beyond all doubt, what the true happiness is. Then said Reason, I will gladly, for love of thee. But I must by some example teach thee some resemblance of the thing, till the thing be better known, that thou mayest know the true goods, aud forsake what is contrary to them, that is, the false goods: and then with the anxious thought of all thy mind, strive that thou mayest arrive at those goods which for ever remain.

Chapter XXIII.

1. When Wisdom had ended this discourse, then began he again to sing, and thus said; Whosoever is desirous to sow fertile land, let him first take away the thorns and the furze, and all the weeds which he observes to do injury to the field, in order that the wheat may grow the better. Also this example is to be considered, that is, that to every man honey seems the sweeter, if he a little before taste *anything* bitter. And again, calm weather is the more agreeable if it a little before be stark storms, and north winds, and much rain and snow. And more agreeable also is the light of the day, for the horrible darkness of the night, than it would be if there were no night. So is also the true happiness much the more pleasant to enjoy, after the calamities of this present life. And moreover thou mayest much the sooner discover the true goods, and arrive at the knowledge of them, if thou first rootest out from thy mind the false goods, and removest them from the ground. After thou then art able to discover those, I know that thou will not desire any other thing besides them.

Chapter XXIV.

I. When he had sung this lay, he ceased the song, and was silent awhile, and began to think deeply in his mind's thought, and thus said; Every mortal man troubles himself with various manifold anxieties, and yet all desire through various paths to come to one end: that is, they desire by different means to arrive at one happiness; that is, then, God. He is the beginning and the end of every good, and he is the highest happiness. Then said the mind, This, methinks, must be the highest good, so that man should need no other good, nor, moreover, be solicitous beyond that; since he possesses that which is the roof of all other goods, for it includes all other goods, and has all of them within it. It would not be the highest good, if any *good* were external to it, because it would then have to desire some good which itself had not. Then answered Reason, and said; It is very evident that this is the highest happiness, for it is both the roof, and the floor of all good. What is that, then, but the best happiness, which gathers the other felicities all within it, and includes and holds them within it; and to it there is a deficiency of none, neither has it need of any; but they all come from it, and again all *return* to it; as all waters come from the sea, and again all come to the sea! There is none in the little fountain which does not seek the sea, and again from the sea it returns into the earth, till it again comes to the same fountain that it before flowed from, and so again to the sea.

II. Now this is an example of the true goods, which all mortal men desire to obtain, though they by various ways think to arrive at them. For every man has natural good in himself, because every mind desires to obtain the true good; but it is hindered by the transitory goods, because it is more prone thereto. For some men think that it is the best happiness that a man be so rich that he have need of nothing more; and they choose their life accordingly. Some men think that this is the highest good, that he be among his fellows the most honourable of his fellows, and they with all diligence seek this. Some think that the supreme good is in the highest power. These desire, either for themselves to rule or else to associate themselves in friendship with their rulers. Some persuade themselves that it is best that a man be illustrious, and celebrated, and have good fame; they therefore seek this both in peace, and in war. Many reckon it for the greatest good, and for the greatest happiness that a man be always blithe in this present life, and follow all his lusts. Some indeed who desire these riches, are desirous thereof because they would have the greater power, that they may the more securely enjoy these worldly lusts, and also the riches. Many there are of those who desire power, because they would gather over much money ; or again, they are desirous to spread the glory of their name.

3. On account of such and other like frail and perishable advantages, the thought of every human mind is troubled with solicitude and with anxiety. It then imagines that it has obtained some exalted good when it has won the flattery of the people : and methinks that it has bought a very false greatness. Some with much solicitude seek wives, that thereby they may, above all things have children, and also live happily. True friends then, I say, is the most precious thing of all these worldly felicities. They are not indeed to be reckoned as worldly goods, but divine ; for deceitful fortune does not produce them, but God, who naturally formed them as relations. For of every other thing in this world man is desirous, either that he may through it attain to power, or else some worldly lust : except of the true friend, whom he loves, sometimes for affection, and for fidelity, though he expect to himself no other rewards. Nature joins and cements friends together with inseparable love. But with these worldly goods and with this present wealth, men make oftener enemies than friends. By these and by many such things it may be evident to all men, that all the bodily goods are inferior to the faculties of the soul; we, indeed, think that a man is the stronger, because he is great in his body. The fairness, moreover, and the vigour of the body rejoices, and delights the man, and health makes him cheerful. In all these bodily felicities men seek simple happiness, as it seems to them. For whatsoever every man chiefly loves above all other things, that he persuades himself is best for him, and that is his highest good. When, therefore, he has acquired that, he imagines that he may be very happy. I do not deny that these goods, and this happiness are the highest good of this present life. For every man considers that thing best which he chiefly loves above other things and therefore he supposes that he is very happy, if he can obtain what he then most desires. Is not now clearly enough shewn to thee the form of the false goods, that is, then, possessions, dignity, and power, and glory, and pleasure ? Concerning pleasure, Epicurus the philosopher, said, when he inquired concerning all those other goods, which we before mentioned ; then said he, that pleasure was the highest good, because all the other goods which

we before mentioned, gratify the mind, and delight it, but pleasure alone chiefly gratifies the body only.

4. But we will still speak concerning the nature of men, and concerning their pursuits. Though, then, their mind and their nature be now dimmed, and they are by that fall sunk down to evil, and thither inclined, yet they are desirous, so far as they can and may, of the highest good. As a drunken man knows that he should *go* to his house, and to his rest, and yet is not able to find the way thither, so is it also with the mind, when it is weighed down by the anxieties of this world. It is sometimes intoxicated and misled by them, so far that it cannot rightly find out good. Nor yet does it appear to those men that they mistake aught who are desirous to obtain this, that they need labour after nothing more. But they think that they are able to collect together all these goods so that none may be excluded from the number. They, therefore, know no other good than the collecting of all the most precious things into their power, that they may have need of nothing besides them. But there is no one that has not need of some addition, except God alone. He has of his own enough, nor has he need of anything, but that which he has in himself. Dost thou think, however, that they wrongly imagine that that thing is best deserving of all estimation, which they may consider most desirable? No, no. I know that it is not to be despised. How can that be evil, which the mind of every man considers to be good, and strives after, and desires to obtain! No, it is not evil; it is the highest good. Why is not power to be reckoned one of the highest goods of this present life? Is that to be esteemed vain and useless, which is the most useful of all these worldly things, that is power? Is good fame and renown to be accounted nothing! No, no. It is not fit that any one account it nothing: for every man thinks that best, which he most loves. Do we not know that no anxiety, or difficulties, or trouble, or pain, or sorrow is happiness? what more then need we say about these felicities? Does not every man know what they are, and also know, that they are the highest good? And yet almost every man seeks in very little things the highest felicities: because he thinks that he may have them all, if he have that which he then chiefly wishes to obtain. This is, then, what they chiefly wish to obtain, wealth and dignity, and authority, and this world's glory, and ostentation, and worldly lust. Of all this they are desirous, because they think that through

these things they may obtain that there be not to them a deficiency of anything wished: neither of dignity, nor of power, nor of renown, nor of life. They wish for all this, and they do well that they desire it, though they seek it variously. By these things we may clearly perceive, that every man is desirous of this, that he may obtain the highest good, if they were able to discover it, or knew how to seek it rightly. But they do not seek it in the rightest way. It is not of this world.

Chapter XXV

When Wisdom had made this speech, then began he again to sing, and thus said: I will now with songs declare how wonderfully the Lord governs all creatures with the bridles of his power; and with what order he establishes and regulates all creatures, and how he has restrained and bound them with his indissoluble chains, so that every creature is kept within bounds with its kind, the kind that it was fashioned to, except men, and some angels, who sometimes depart from their kind. Thus the lion, though she be very tame, and have fast chains, and greatly love, and also fear her master; if it ever happen that she tastes blood, she immediately forgets her new tameness, and remembers the wild manners of her parents. She then begins roaring, and to break her chains; and bites first her leader and afterwards whatsoever she may seize, both of men and of cattle. So do also wood-fowls. Though they be well tamed, if they return to the woods, they despise their teachers, and remain with their kind. Though their teachers then offer them the same meats with which they before grew tame, they then care not for those meats, so that they may enjoy the wood. But it seems to them pleasanter that the weald resound to them, and they hear the voice of other fowls. So is it also with trees, whose nature it is to stand up high. Though thou pull any bough down to the earth, such as thou mayest bend, as soon as thou lettest it go, so soon springs it up, and moves towards its kind. So doth also the sun. Though she after mid-day sink and incline to the earth, again she seeks her kind, and departs by unknown ways to her rising, and so hastens higher and higher, until she comes so far up as her highest nature is. So doth every creature. It tends towards its kind, and is joyful if it ever may come thereto. There is no creature formed which desires not that it may come thither, whence it before came : that is, to rest and tranquillity. The rest is with God, and it is God. But every creature turns on itself like a wheel : and so it thus turns that it may again come where it was before, and be the same that it was before, as often as it is turned round *may be* what it before was, and may do what it before did.

Chapter XXVI.

1. When Wisdom had sung this lay, then began he again to speak, and thus said : O, ye earthly men, though ye now make yourselves like cattle by your folly, ye nevertheless can in some measure understand as in a dream, concerning your origin, that is God. Ye perceive the true beginning and the true end of all happiness, though ye do not fully know it. And nevertheless, nature draws you to that knowledge, but very manifold error draws you from that knowledge. Consider now, whether men can arrive at the true goods, through these present goods; since almost all men say that he is happiest who possesses all these earthly goods. Can, then, much money, or dignity, or all this present wealth, make any man so happy, that he may need nothing more ? No, no. I know this, that they cannot. Why, is it not, then, from this very clear, that these present goods are not the true goods, because they cannot give what they promise ? But they pretend *to do* what they are not able to fulfil, when they promise to those who are willing to love them the true felicities; and tell lies to them more than they perform to them; for they are deficient in more of these *felicities* than they possess of them. Consider, now, concerning thyself, O Boethius, whether thou wert ever aught uneasy *when thou wert most prosperous?* or whether there were ever to thee a want of anything desired, when thou hadst most wealth ? or whether thy life were then all according to thy wish ? Then answered Boethius, and said, No, O no! I was never yet at any time of so even mind, as far as I can remember, that I was altogether without care : that I was so without care I had no trouble : nor did all that I experienced ever yet please me, nor was it ever with me entirely as I wished, though I concealed it. Then answered Wisdom and said, Wast thou not, then, poor enough and unhappy enough, though it seemed to thee that thou wert rich, when thou either hadst that which thou wouldest

CHAPTER XXVI.

not, or hadst not that which thou wouldest? Then answered Boethius, and said, All was to me as thou hast said. Then said Wisdom, Is not every man poor enough in respect of that which he has not, when he is desirous to have it? That is true, said Boethius. Then said Wisdom, But if he is poor, he is not happy, for he desires that he may have what he has not, because he wishes to have enough. Then said Boethius, That is all true which thou sayest. Then said Wisdom Hadst thou not, then, poverty when thou wert richest? Then answered I, and said, I know that thou sayest truth, that I had it. Then said Wisdom, Does it not appear to thee, then, that all the riches of this middle-earth are not able to make one man wealthy? so wealthy that he may have enough and may not need more? And nevertheless they promise it to every one who possesses them. Then said I, Nothing is truer than that thou sayest.

2. Then said Wisdom, But why, then, art thou not an assenter to this? Canst thou not see every day that the stronger take riches from the weaker? Wherefore else in every day such sorrow, and such contentions, and meetings, and judgments; except that every one demands the spoil which is taken from them, or again exacts that of another? Then answered I, and said, Thou arguest rightly enough: so it is as thou sayest. Then said he, On these accounts every man has need of help in addition to himself, that he may keep his riches. Then said I, Who denies it? Then said he, If he had nothing of that which he fears he may be obliged to lose, then he would not have occasion for any more help than himself. Then said I, Thou sayest truly. Then retorted Wisdom sharply and said; O how inconsistent in every man's custom and every man's will, does that thing appear to me, which I will now mention; that is, that from whence they persuade themselves that they shall become happier, they from thence become poorer and weaker! For if they have any little, then it behoves them to cringe for protection to those who have anything more. Whether they need, or whether they need not, they yet crave. Where, then, is moderation, or who has it, or when will it come, that it may entirely drive away miseries from the wealthy? The more he has, the more *men* he must cringe to. Do the rich never hunger, nor thirst, nor become cold? But I suppose thou wilt say, that the rich have wherewith they remedy all that. But though thou say so, riches cannot altogether remedy it, though they somewhat may.

For it behoves them every day to add, what man every day lessens; because human want, which is never satisfied, requires each day something of this world's wealth, either of clothing, of meat, of drink, or of many things besides. Therefore, no man is so wealthy that he needs not more. But covetousness neither knows limit nor ever is bounded by necessity: but desires always more than it needs. I know not why ye confide in these perishable riches, when they are not able to remove your poverty from you, but ye increase your poverty whenever they come to you.

3. When Wisdom had made this speech, then began he again to sing, and thus singing said: What profit is it to the rich miser, that he gathers an infinite quantity of these riches, and obtains abundance of every kind of jewels: and though he till his land with a thousand ploughs; and though all this middle-earth be subject to his power, he will not take with him from this middle-earth any more of it than he brought hither.

Chapter XXVII.

1. Two things may dignity and power do, if it come to the unwise. It may make him honourable and respectable to other unwise persons. But when he quits the power, or the power him, then is he to the unwise neither honourable nor respectable. Has, then, power the custom of exterminating vices, and rooting them out from the mind of great men, and planting therein virtues? I know, however, that earthly power never sows the virtues, *but collects and gathers vices; and when it has gathered them,* then it nevertheless shows, *and* does not conceal them. For the vices of great men many men see; because many know them, and many are with them. Therefore we always lament concerning power and also despise it, when we see that it cometh to the worst, and to those who are to us most unworthy. It was on these accounts that formerly the wise Catulus was angry, and so immoderately censured Nonius the rich,[1] because he observed him to sit in an ornamented chair of state. It was a great custom among the Romans that no others should sit therein, except the most worthy. Then Catulus despised him, because he should sit therein; for he knew him to be very unwise, and very intemperate. Then began

---

8. Nonius having been created a curule magistrate by Julius Cæsar, of which he appears to have been unworthy, Catulus indignantly exclaimed, Quid est Catulle, quid moraris emori? Sella in curuli struma Nonius sedet!

Catulus to spit upon him. Catulus was a consul in Rome: a very wise man. He would not have despised the other so greatly if he had not possessed any rule or any power.

2. Canst thou now understand how great dishonour power brings on the unworthy, when he receives it? For every man's evil is the more public when he has power. But tell me now, I ask thee Boethius, why thou hadst such manifold evil, and such great uneasiness in authority, whilst thou hadst it? or why thou again didst unwillingly relinquish it? Dost thou not know that it was for no other reason but that thou wouldest not in all things be conformable to the will of the unrighteous king Theodoric; because thou didst find him in all respects unworthy of power, very shameless, and unrelenting, without any good conduct? For we cannot easily say that the wicked are good, though they may have power Yet thou wouldst not have been driven from Theodoric, nor would he have despised thee, if his folly, and his injustice had pleased thee, as well as it did his foolish favourites. If thou, now, shouldest see some very wise man, who had very excellent dispositions and was nevertheless very poor, and very unhappy, wouldst thou say that he were unworthy of power, and of dignity? Then answered Boethius, and said, No, O no! If I found him such, I would never say that he were unworthy of power and of dignity. But methinks that he would be worthy of all that is in this world. Then said Wisdom, Every virtue has its proper excellence; and the excellence and the dignity which it has, it imparts immediately to every one who loves it. Thus wisdom is the highest virtue, and it has in it four other virtues of which one is prudence, another temperance, the third is fortitude, the fourth *is* justice. Wisdom makes his lovers wise and worthy, and moderate, and patient, and just; and he fills him who loves him, with every good quality. This they cannot do who possess the power of this world. They cannot impart any virtue through their wealth, to those who love them, if they have it not in their nature. Hence it is very clear that the rich in worldly wealth have no proper dignity: but the wealth is come to them from without, and they cannot from without have aught of their own. Consider now, whether any man be less honourable because many men despise him; but if any man be the less honourable, then is every foolish man the less honourable the more authority he has, to every wise man. Hence it is sufficiently clear that power and wealth cannot make its possessor the more honourable. But it

makes him the less honourable when it comes to him, if he were not before virtuous. So is also wealth and power the worse, if he be not virtuous who possesses it. Each of them is the more worthless, when they meet with each other.

3. But I may easily instruct thee by an example so that thou mayest clearly enough perceive that this present life is very like a shadow, and in that shadow no man can attain the true felicities. How thinkest thou, then? If any very great man were driven from his country, or goeth on his lord's errand, and so cometh to a foreign people, where no man knows him, nor he any man, nor even knows the language, thinkest thou that his greatness can make him honourable in that land? But I know that it cannot. But if dignity were natural to wealth, and were its own; or again wealth were the rich man's own, then could not it forsake him. Let the man who possessed them be in whatsoever land he might, then would his wealth and his dignity be with him. But because the wealth and the power are not his own, therefore they forsake him and because they have no natural good in themselves, therefore they go away like shadows or smoke. Yet the false opinion, and the imagination of foolish men persuades them that power is the highest good. But it is entirely otherwise. When the great are either among foreigners, or in their own country, among wise men, then either to the wise, or to the foreigners, is his wealth for naught, when they learn that they were chosen for no virtue, but through the favour of foolish people. But if they in their power, had anything of proper, or natural good, then would they have that with them, even if they should lose the power. They would not lose the natural good, but that would always follow them, and always make them honourable, let them be in whatsoever land they might.

4. Now thou mayest understand that wealth and power cannot make any man honourable in a foreign country. I wot, however, thou mayest think that they always can in their own country. But though thou mayest think it, I know that they cannot. It was formerly through all the territories of the Romans, that consuls, and judges, and the treasurers who kept the money, which they were every year to give to the soldiers, and the wisest senators had the greatest honour. But now, either none of these exists, or they have no honour, if any one of them exists. So is it with respect to every one of those things which have not in themselves

proper and natural good. One while it is to be censured, another while it is to be praised. But what of delightful or useful appears to thee then, in wealth, and in power, when they have enough of nothing, nor have anything of proper good, nor can give anything durable to their possessors?

Chapter XXVIII.

When Wisdom had made this speech, then began he again to sing, and thus said: Though the wicked king Nero decked himself with all the most splendid clothes, and adorned himself with gems of every kind, was he not nevertheless, to all wise men loathsome, and unworthy, and full of all vice and debauchery? Yet he enriched his favourites with great riches; but what was *it* to them the better? What wise man could say that he was the more honourable when he had enriched him?

Chapter XXIX.

1. When Wisdom had sung this lay, then began he again to speak, and thus said; Dost thou think that the king's familiarity and the wealth and the power which he gives to his favourites, can make any man wealthy or powerful? Then answered I, and said, Why cannot they? What in this present life is pleasanter and better than the king's service, and his presence: and moreover wealth and power? Then answered Wisdom, and said; Tell me now, whether thou hast ever heard, that it always remained to any one who was before us? or thinkest thou that any one who now has it can always have it? Dost thou not know that all books are full of examples of the men who were before us, and every one knows concerning those who are now living, that from many a king power and wealth go away, until he afterwards becomes poor? Alas! is that, then, very excellent wealth, which can preserve neither itself, nor its lord, so that he may not have need of more help, lest they should both be lost? But is not this your highest felicity, the power of kings? And yet if to the king there be a want of anything desired, then that lessens his power, and increases his misery. Therefore these your felicities are in some respects infelicities! Moreover kings, though they govern many nations, yet

they do not govern all those which they would govern; but are very wretched in their mind, because they have not some of those things which they would have : for I know that the king who is rapacious has more wretchedness than power. Therefore a certain king[1] who unjustly came to empire, formerly said, O, how happy is the man, to whom a naked sword hangs not always over the head, by a small thread, as to me it ever has yet done! How does it now appear to thee? How do wealth and power please thee, when they are never without fear, and difficulties, and anxieties? Thou knowest that every king would be without these, and yet have power, if he might. But I know that he cannot: therefore I wonder why they glory in such power. Does it seem to thee that the man has great power, and is truly happy, who always desires that which he cannot obtain? Or thinkest thou that he is really happy who always goes with a great company? Or again, he who dreads both him that is in dread of him, and him that is not in dread of him? Does it seem to thee that the man has great power who seems to himself to have none, even as to many a man it seems that he has none, unless he have many a man to serve him? What shall we now say more concerning the king, and concerning his followers, except that every rational man may know that they are full miserable and weak? How can kings deny or conceal their weakness, when they are not able to attain any honour without their thanes' assistance?

2. What else shall we say concerning thanes but this, that it often happens that they are bereaved of all honour, and even of life, by their perfidious king? Thus we know that the wicked king Nero would hate his own master, and kill his foster-father, whose name was Seneca.[1] He was a philosopher. When, therefore, he found that he must die, he offered all his possessions for his life, but the king would not accept of it, or grant him his life. When he learned this, he chose for himself the death that they should let him blood from the arm, and they did so. We have also heard that Papinianus[2] was to Antoninus the Cæsar, of all his favourites the most beloved, and of all his people had the greatest power. But he gave order to bind and afterwards to slay him. Yet all men know that Seneca was to Nero, and Papinianus to Antoninus the

---

9. Dionysius the elder, tyrant of Syracuse.

1. Seneca is called the foster-father of Nero, because he was his tutor and instructor.

2. Papinian was highly esteemed by Marcus Antoninus, and it was Caracalla who put him to death.

worthy, and the most dear: and they had the greatest power both in their court and elsewhere, and nevertheless without any guilt they were destroyed! Yet they both desired most earnestly that the lords would take whatsoever they had, and let them live, but they could not obtain it: for the cruelty of those kings was so severe, that their submission could naught avail, nor indeed would their high-mindedness, howsoever they might do, have availed them either, but they were obliged to lose life. For he who does not take timely care for himself, will at length be destitute. How doth power and wealth now please thee, now thou hast heard that a man neither can have it without fear, nor can part with it, though he wish? What did the crowd of friends avail the favourites of those kings, or what avails it to any man? For friends come with wealth, and again with wealth go away, except very few. But the friends who before for wealth's sake love any one, go away afterwards with the wealth, and then turn to enemies. But the few, who before loved him for affection, and for fidelity, these would nevertheless love him, though he were poor. These remain to him. What is a worse plague, or greater hurt to any man, than that he have in his society, and in his presence, an enemy in the likeness of a friend?

3. When Wisdom had made this speech, then began he to sing, and thus said: Whosoever desires fully to possess power ought to labour first that he may have power over his own mind, and be not indecently subject to his vices; also let him put away from his mind unbecoming anxieties, and cease from complaints of his misfortunes. Though he reign over the middle earth, from eastward te westward, from India, which is the south-east end of this middle earth, to the island which we call Thule,[1] which is at the north-west end of this middle earth, where there is neither night in summer, nor day in winter; though he rule over all this, he has not the more power, if he has not power over his mind, and if he does not guard himself against the vices which we have before spoken about.

Chapter XXX.

1. When Wisdom had sung this song, then began he again to make a speech, and said; Worthless and very false is the glory of

[1]. Thule is supposed to have been Iceland, but it is very questionable what locality is indicated by this name.

this world! Concerning this a certain poet formerly sung.* When he contemned this present life he said, O glory of this world! Alas! why do foolish men call thee with false voice, glory, when thou art none! For man more frequently has great renown, and great glory, and great honour, through the opinion of foolish people, than he has through his deservings. But tell me now, what is more unsuitable than this; or why men may not rather be ashamed of themselves, than rejoice, when they hear that any one belies them? Though men even rightly praise any one of the good, he ought not the sooner to rejoice immediately at the people's words. But at this he ought to rejoice, that they speak truth of him. Though he rejoice at this, that they spread his name, it is not the sooner, so extensively spread, as he persuades himself for they cannot spread it over all the earth, though they may in some land; for though it be heard in one, yet in another it is not heard. Though he in this land be celebrated, yet is he in another not celebrated. Therefore is the people's esteem to be held by every man for nothing: since it comes not to every man according to his deeds, nor, indeed, remains always to any one. Consider first concerning birth; if any one boast of it, how vain and how useless is the boast; for every one knows that all men come from one father, and from one mother. Or again concerning the people's esteem, and concerning their applause. I know not why we rejoice at it. Though they be illustrious whom the vulgar applaud, yet are they more illustrious, and more rightly to be applauded who are dignified by virtues. For no man is really the greater, or the more praiseworthy for the excellence of another, or for his virtues if he himself has it not. Art thou ever the fairer for another man's fairness? A man is full little the better, though he have a good father, if he himself is incapable of anything. Therefore I advise that thou rejoice in other men's good, and their nobility; so far only that thou ascribe it not to thyself as thine own. Because every man's good, and his nobility is more in the mind than in the flesh. This only, indeed, I know of good in nobility, that it shames many a man, if he be worse than his ancestors were; and therefore he strives with all his power, to reach the manners of some one of the best, and his virtues.

2. When Wisdom had finished this speech, then began he again to sing about the same and said; Truly all men had a like begin-

2. Euripides in Andromache.

ning, for they all came from one father, and from one mother: they are all, moreover, born alike. That is no wonder, because one God is father of all creatures: for he made them all, and governs them all. He gives light to the sun, and to the moon, and places all the stars. He has created men on the earth, joined together the soul and the body by his power, and made all men equally noble in their original nature. Why do ye then lift up yourselves above other men, on account of your birth, without cause, since ye can find none unnoble,[2] but all are equally noble, if ye are willing to remember the creation, and the Creator, and moreover, the birth of every one of you? But true nobility is in the mind, not not in the flesh, as we have before said. But every man who is altogether subject to vices, forsakes his Maker, and his first origin and his nobility, and thence becomes degraded, till he is unnoble.

Chapter XXXI.

When Wisdom had sung this lay, then began he again to make a speech, and thus said: What good can we say of the fleshly vices? for whosoever will yield to them shall suffer great anguish and many troubles. For intemperance always nourishes vices, and vices have great need of repentance, and repentance is not without sorrow and without anguish. Alas! how many diseases, and how great pain, and how great watching, and how great sadness has he who possesses wicked lust in this world? And how much more thinkest thou they shall have after this world *as the* retribution of their deserts? even as a woman brings forth a child, and suffers much trouble, after she formerly has fulfilled great lust. Therefore I know not what joy the worldly lusts bring to their lovers. If any one say that he is happy who fulfils all his worldly lusts, wherefore will he not also say that the cattle are happy, for their desire is extended to no other things but to gluttony and to lust? Very pleasant is it that a man have wife and children. But nevertheless many children are begotten for their parents' destruction. For many a woman dies by reason of her child before she can bring it forth. And we have also learned that formerly a most unusual

---

2. Unnoble, It has been necessary to invent a word to express the meaning of the original. Ignoble would convey a very false impression of what is meant, both here and in other passages.

and unnatural crime happened, that the children conspired together and lay in wait for the father. And moreover, what was worse, we have heard long ago in ancient histories, that a certain son[3] slew his father. I know not in what manner, but we know that it was an inhuman deed. Besides every one may know how heavy trouble to a man is the care of his children. I need not, however, say that to thee, for thou hast experienced it of thyself. Concerning the heavy care of children, said my master Euripides, that it sometimes happened to the unhappy that it would be better for him that he had not children, than that he had.

2. When Wisdom had ended this speech, then began he again to sing, and thus singing, said; Alas! the evil desire of unlawful lust disquiets the mind of almost every living man. As the bee shall perish when she stings anything angrily, so shall every soul perish after unlawful lust, unless the man turn to good.

Chapter XXXII.

1. When Wisdom had sung this lay, then began he again to speak, and thus said: Therefore there is no doubt that this present wealth obstructs and hinders those men who are intent upon the true felicities: and it can bring no one where it promised him, that is, to the highest good. But I can in a few words declare to thee with how many evils these riches are filled. What meanest thou, then, by covetousness of money? When thou no how else canst acquire it, unless thou steal it, or take *it* by force, or find *it* hid; and wheresoever it increases to thee, it decreases to others. Thou wouldest, then, be illustrious in dignity? But if thou wilt have this, then must thou very meanly and very humbly flatter him who is able to help thee thereto. If thou wilt make thyself greater and more honourable than many, then must thou suffer thself to be inferior to one. Is not this, then, somewhat of misery, that a man so anxiously cringe to him who has the power of giving to him? Of power thou art desirous? But thou never obtainest it without danger, on account of foreigners, and still more on account of thine own men and kindred. Of glory thou art desirous? But thou canst not have it without care: for thou shalt have always something adverse and inconvenient. Thou wouldst, then, enjoy immoderate lust? But then thou art desirous to despise God's servants, inasmuch as thy vile flesh has the mastery of thee, not

[3] Œdipus slew his father Laius

thou of it. How can any man conduct himself more wretchedly than when he subjects himself to his vile flesh, and will not to his rational soul? If, then, ye were greater in your body than the elephant, or stronger than the lion, or the bull, or swifter than the tiger, that wild beast: and if thou wert of all men the fairest in beauty, and then wouldest studiously seek after wisdom until thou couldest perfectly understand it; then mightest thou clearly perceive that all the powers and the faculties which we have before spoken about, are not to be compared with any one of the faculties of the soul. Indeed wisdom is one single faculty of the soul, and yet we all know that it is better than all the other faculties which we have before spoken about.

2. Behold now the wideness and the firmness and the swift course of this heaven. Then may ye understand that it is absolutely nothing, compared with its Creator, and with its Ruler. Why then suffer ye it not to warn you that ye should not admire and praise that which is less perfect, that is, earthly wealth. Even so the heaven is better and higher and fairer than all which it includes, except men alone; so is man's body better and more precious than all his possessions. But how much thinkest thou then the soul better and more precious than the body? Every creature is to be honoured in its measure and *always the highest in the greatest degree; therefore* is the heavenly power to be honoured, and to be admired, and to be adored above all other things. The beauty of the body is very fugitive, and very frail, and very like the flowers of the earth. Though any one be as fair as Alcibiades, the noble youth, was, if any one be so sharp-sighted that he can see through him, as Aristotle the philosopher said that wild beast was, which could see through everything, both trees, and even stones; which wild beast we call lynx; if, then, any one were so sharp-sighted that he could see through the youth whom we have before spoken about, then would he not appear to him so fair within as he outwardly seemed. Though thou seem fair to any one, it is not the sooner so; but the imperfection of their eyes hinders them, so that they cannot perceive that they behold thee outwardly, not inwardly. But consider now carefully, and enquire rationally, what these fleshy goods are, and these felicities, which ye now immoderately desire. Then may ye clearly understand that the fairness of the body and its strength, may be taken away by three days' fever. I therefore say to thee all that I have before said to thee, because I would openly prove to thee

in the conclusion of this chapter, that all these present goods cannot perform to their lovers that which they promise them, that is the supreme good which they promise them. Though they collect together all these present goods, they have not the sooner perfect good therein, neither can they make their lovers as wealthy as they wish.

3. When Wisdom had ended this speech, then began he again to sing, and thus singing said : Alas! how grievous and how dangerous the error is, which seduceth miserable men, and leads them from the right way! The way is God. Do ye seek gold on trees? I know, however, that ye seek it not there, neither find ye it : for all men know that it grows not there, anymore than jewels grow in vineyards. Do ye set your net on the highest hill, when ye are minded to fish? But I know that ye set it not there. Do ye carry out your hounds and your net into the sea, when ye wish to hunt? I think, however that ye then place them upon hills and in woods. Truly it is wonderful that diligent men know that they must seek on the sea-shore, and on river banks both white jewels and red, and gems of every kind : and they know also in what waters, and in what rivers' mouths they must seek fishes, and they know when they must seek all this present wealth, and incessantly seek it. But it is a very miserable thing, that foolish men are so destitute of all judgment that they know not where the true felicities are hid, nor indeed have they any desire to seek them : but think that in these frail and perishable things they can find the true happiness, that is God! I know not how I can their folly all so plainly declare, and so greatly censure as I would, for they are more miserable, and more foolish, and more unhappy than I can explain. Wealth and honour they desire, and when they have it, then think they, so ignorant! that they have the true happiness.

Chapter XXXIII.

1. Enough I have now declared to thee concerning the resemblances, and concerning the shadows of the true happiness. But if thou canst now clearly understand the resemblances of the true happiness, then afterwards it is necessary that I shew thee itself. Then answered I, and said ; Now I plainly perceive that there is not enough of every good in these worldly riches, nor is perfect

power in any worldly authority; nor is true dignity in this world; nor are the greatest honours in this world's glory; nor is the highest pleasure in the fleshly lusts. Then answered Wisdom, and said: Dost thou fully understand why it is so? Then answered I, and said; Though I understand it in some measure, I would nevertheless learn it more fully, and more distinctly from thee. Then answered Wisdom, and said: It is sufficiently clear that good is single and inseparable, though foolish men divide it into many, when they, erring, seek the highest good in the worse creatures. But dost thou think that he has need of nothing more, who has the greatest power in this world? Then answered I again, and said: I do not say that he has need of nothing more, for I know that no one is so wealthy, that he needs not some addition. Then answered Wisdom, and said: Thou sayest rightly enough. Though any one have power, if another have more, the weaker needs the aid of the stronger. Then said I, it is all as thou sayest. Then said Wisdom, though any one call power and abundance two things, it is nevertheless one. Then said I, So I think. Then he said, Thinkest thou now that power and abundance is to be despised? or again more to be esteemed than other goods? Then said I, No man can doubt of this, that power and abundance is to be esteemed. Then said he, Let us now, if it so seem to thee, make an addition to the power and the abundance; let us add dignity thereto, and then account the three as one. Then answered I, and said, Let us do so, for it is true. Then said he, Does the assemblage of these three things then seem to thee worthless and ignoble, when the three are united together: or whether again does it seem to thee, of all things the most worthy and the most noble? If thou knewest any man who had power over everything, and had all dignity, even so far that he needed nothing more, consider now, how honourable and how eminent the man would seem to thee; and yet though he had the three, if he were not celebrated, then would there nevertheless be to him a deficiency of some dignity. Then said I, I cannot deny it. Then said he, Is it not then sufficiently clear that we should add celebrity to the three, and make the four as one? Then said I, That is proper. Then said he, Dost thou think that he is blithe who has all these four? The fifth is bliss, and *that any one* may do whatsoever he will, and need nothing more than he possesses. Then said I, I can never imagine if he were such, and had all this, whence any trouble should come to him. Then said he, But it must then be considered that the five things which we have before spoken about, though they are separately named in words, that it is all one thing, when they are collected together, that is, power, and abundance, and glory, and dignity, and bliss.

2. These five things, when they are all collected together, then, that is God. For all the five no human being can fully have, while he is in this world. But when these five things, as we before said, are all collected together, then is it all one thing, and that one thing is God; and he is single and undivided, though they before were in many, separately named. Then answered I, and said, Of all this I approve. Then said he, Though God be single and undivided, as he is, human error divides him into many by their vain words. Every man proposes to himself for the supreme *good*, that which he chiefly loves. Then one loves this, and one another thing. That, then, is his good, which he chiefly loves. But when they divide their good into so many parts, then find they neither good itself, nor the part of good which they chiefly love. When they add it all together, they then have neither all of it, nor the part which they separated therefrom. Therefore every man finds not what he seeks, because he seeks it not rightly. Ye seek where ye cannot find when ye seek all good in one good. Then said I, That is true. Then said he, When the man is poor he is not desirous of power, but wishes for wealth, and flies from poverty. He labours not for this, how he may be most illustrious; nor moreover, does any one obtain that which he labours not for. But he labours all his life for wealth, and foregoes many a worldly pleasure, in order that he may acquire and keep wealth, because he is desirous of that above all things. But if he obtain it, he then thinks that he has not enough unless he have also power besides: for he thinks that he cannot keep the wealth without power. Nor moreover does there ever seem to him enough, until he has all that he desires. For wealth desires power, and power desires dignity, and dignity desires glory. After he is full of wealth, it then seems to him that he may have every desire if he have power; and he gives all the wealth for power, unless he is able to obtain it for less; and foregoes every other advantage, in order that he may attain to power. And thus it often happens, that when he has given all that he had for power, he has neither the power, nor moreover, that which he gave for

it, but at length becomes so poor, that he has not even mere necessaries, that is, food and clothing. He then is desirous of necessaries, not of power. We before spoke of the five felicities, that is wealth, and power, and dignity, and glory, and pleasure. Now have we treated of wealth, and of power : and the same we may say of the three, which we have not treated of ; that is, dignity and glory, and pleasure. These three things, and the two which we before named, though any man think that in any one soever of them he can possess full happiness, it is not the sooner so, though they hope for it, unless they have all the five. Then answered I, and said, What ought we, then, to do ? Since thou sayest that we cannot in any one soever of these have the highest good and full happiness ; and we do not at all think that any one soever of us can obtain the five altogether. Then answered he, and said : If any one desire that he may have all the five, then desireth he the highest felicities : but he cannot fully obtain them in this world. For though he should obtain all the five goods, it nevertheless would not be the supreme good, nor the best happiness, because they are not eternal. Then answered I, and said, Now I perceive clearly enough that the best felicities are not in this world. Then said he, No man needs in this present life to seek after the true felicities, nor think that here he can find sufficient good. Then said I, Thou sayest truly.

3. Then said he, I think that I have said enough to thee about the false goods. But I am desirous that thou shouldest turn thy attention from the false goods; then wilt thou very soon know the true goods, which I before promised thee that I would shew thee. Then said I, Even foolish men know that full goods exist, though they may not be where they suppose them. Thou promisedst me a little while ago, that thou wouldest teach me them. But of this I am persuaded, that that is the true and the perfect happiness which can give to all its followers permanent wealth, and everlasting power, and enduring dignity, and eternal glory, and full abundance. And moreover I say, that is the true happiness which can fully bestow any of these five : because in every one of them they all are. I say these words to thee, because I am desirous that thou shouldest know that the doctrine is well fixed in my mind; so fixed, that no man can draw me aside from it. Then said he, O child, how happy art thou that thou hast so learned it ! But I am desirous that we should still enquire after that which

is deficient to thee. Then said I, What is that, then? Then said he, Dost thou think that any of these present goods can give thee full happiness? Then answered I, and said, I know nothing in this present life that can give such. Then said he, These present goods are images of the eternal good, not full good, because they cannot give true good, nor full good to their followers. Then said I, I am well enough assured of that which thou sayest. Then said he, Now thou knowest what the false goods are, and what the true goods are, I would that thou shouldest learn how thou mayest come to the true goods. Then said I, Didst thou not formerly promise me that thou wouldest teach it me? and I am now very anxiously desirous to hear it. Then said he, What ought we now to do, in order that we may come to the true goods? Shall we implore the divine help as well in less as in greater *things*, as our philosopher Plato said? Then said I, I think that we ought to pray to the Father of all things: for he who is unwilling to pray to him, will not find him; nor moreover will he pursue the right way towards him. Then said he, Very rightly thou sayest; and began then to sing, and thus said:

4. O Lord, how great and how wonderful thou art! Thou who all thy creatures visible and also invisible wonderfully hast created, and rationally governest them! Thou who times from the beginning of the middle earth to the end, settest in order, so that they both depart and return! Thou who all moving creatures according to thy will stirrest, and thou thyself always immoveable and unchangeable remainest! For none is mightier than thou, nor any like thee! No necessity taught thee to make that which thou hast made, but by thine own will, and by thine own power, thou madest all things, though thou needest none of them. Very wonderful is the nature of thy good, for it is all one, thou and thy goodness. Good is not come to thee from without, but it is thine own. But all that we have of good in this world is come to us from without, that is, from thee! Thou hast no envy to anything, because no one is more skilful than thou, nor any like thee; for thou by thy sole counsel hast designed and wrought all good. No man set thee an example, for no one was before thee, who anything or nothing might make. But thou hast made all things very good and very fair, and thou thyself art the highest good and the fairest. As thou thyself didst design, so hast thou made this middle earth, and dost govern it as thou wilt; and thou thyself dost distribute

all good as thou wilt. And thou hast made all creatures like to each other, and also in some respects unlike. Though thou hast named all these creatures *separately* with one name, thou hast named them all together, and called *them* world. Nevertheless that one name thou hast divided into four elements. One of them is earth; another, water; the third *is* air; the fourth fire. To every one of them thou hast set its own separate place, and yet every one is with other classed, and peaceably bound by thy commandment; so that none of them should pass over another's boundary, and the cold suffer by the heat, and the wet by the dry. The nature of earth and of water is cold; the earth is dry and cold, and the water wet and cold. But the air is distinguished that it is either cold, or wet, or warm. It is no wonder: because it is created in the midst between the dry and the cold earth, and the hot fire. The fire is uppermost over all these worldly creatures. Wonderful is thy counsel, which thou hast in both respects accomplished; both hast bounded the creatures between themselves, and also hast intermixed them: the dry and the cold earth under the cold and the wet water; that the soft and flowing water may have a floor on the firm earth, because it cannot of itself stand: but the earth holds it, and in some measure imbibes, and by that moistening it is lightened, so that it grows and blossoms, and produces fruits. For if the water moistened it not, then would it become dry, and would be driven by the wind like dust or ashes. Nor could anything living enjoy the earth or the water, or dwell in either for cold, if thou didst not a little mix them with fire. With wonderful skill thou hast caused it, that the fire burns not the water, and the earth, when it is mixed with both: nor again, the water and the earth entirely extinguish the fire. The water's own region is on the earth, and also in the air, and again above the sky. But the fire's own place is above all visible worldly creatures; and though it is mixed with all elements, nevertheless it cannot altogether overcome any one of the elements, because it has not leave from the Almighty. The earth, then, is heavier and thicker than other elements, because it is lower than any other creature except the sky: for the sky extends itself every day outwardly, *and* though it approaches it nowhere, it is in every place equally nigh to it, both above and beneath. Every one of the elements which we formerly spoke about, has its own region separately, and yet is every one mixed with another; because no one of the elements can exist without another, though it be imperceptible in the other. Thus water and earth are very difficult to be seen or to be perceived by ignorant men in fire, and yet they are nevertheless mixed therewith. So is there also fire in stones, and in water, very difficult to be seen, but it is nevertheless there. Thou hast bound the fire with very indissoluble chains, that it may not come to its own region, that is, to the greatest fire, which is over us; lest it should forsake the earth, and all other creatures should perish by excessive cold, if it should altogether depart. Thou hast established earth very wonderfully, and firmly, so that it does not incline on any side, nor stand on any earthly thing; nor does anything earthly hold it, that it may not sink: and it is not easier for it to fall downwards than upwards. Thou also movest the threefold soul in agreeing limbs, so that there is not less of the soul in the least finger than in all the body. I said that the soul was threefold, because philosophers say that she has three natures. One of these natures is, that she has the power of willing; the second is, that she is subject to anger; the third, that she is rational. Two of these natures beasts have, the same as men. One of them is will, the other is anger. But man alone has reason, and not any other creature. Therefore he has excelled all earthly creatures by thought, and by understanding. For reason should govern both will and anger, because it is the peculiar faculty of the soul. So hast thou created the soul that she should always turn upon herself, as all this sky turns, or as a wheel turns round, enquiring about her maker, or about herself, or about these earthly creatures. When she enquires about her maker, then she is above herself; but when she enquires about herself, then is she in herself. And she is beneath herself when she loves these earthly things and admires them. Thou, O Lord, hast given to souls a dwelling in the heavens, and on them thou bestowest worthy gifts; to every one according to its deserving, and causest them to shine very bright, and yet with very varied brightness; some brighter and some less bright, even as the stars, every one according to its desert. Thou, O Lord, bringest together the heavenly souls, and the earthly bodies, and unitest them in this world. As they from thee came hither, so shall they also to thee hence tend. Thou filledst this earth with various kinds of animals, and afterwards didst sow it with various seed of trees and plants! Grant now, O Lord, to our minds, that they may ascend to thee through these difficulties of this world; and from these occupations come to thee; and *that* with the open eyes of our mind, we may see the noble fountain of all goods. That art thou! Grant to us, then, sound eyes of our mind, that we may fix them on thee; and drive away the mist that now hangs before the eyes of our mind, and enlighten the eyes with thy light: for thou art the brightness of the true light; and thou art the soft rest of the just, and thou wilt cause that they shall see thee. Thou art of all things the beginning and the end. Thou supportest all things without labour. Thou art both the way, and the guide, and the place that the way leads to. All men tend to thee!

Chapter XXXIV.

1. When Wisdom had sung this lay, and this prayer, then began he again to speak, and thus said: I think that it is now in the first place necessary, that I shew thee where the highest good is, now I have already shewn thee what it was; or which was the perfect good. One thing I would first ask thee; whether thou thinkest that anything in this world is so good, that it can give thee full happiness? For this reason I ask thee, because I am unwilling that any false resemblance should impose upon us for the true happiness. For no man can deny that some good is the highest; as it were a great and deep fountain and from *which* many brooks and rivers flow. We therefore say concerning any good, that it is not full good, because there is in it a deficiency of something; and yet it is not entirely without *good*, for every thing comes to naught if it has no good in it. Hence thou mayst learn, that from the greatest good come the less goods; not from the less the greatest, any more than the rivers may become a fountain. But the fountain may become a river, and yet the rain comes again to the fountain! So every good comes from God, and again to him; and he is the full and perfect good, which is not deficient in any will. Now thou mayest clearly understand that this is God himself. Why canst thou not imagine *that* if nothing were full, then would nothing be *deficient, and if nothing were deficient, then would nothing be* full? Therefore is anything full because some is deficient; and therefore is anything deficient because some is full. Everything is fullest in its proper station. Why canst thou not then conceive that if in any of these earthly goods there is a

deficiency of any will, and of any good, then is some good full of every will, and is deficient in no good ? Then answered I, and said : Very rightly and very rationally thou hast overcome, and convinced me ; so that I cannot contradict, or even imagine *any-thing* contrary to it : but that it is all even as thou sayest.

2. Then said Wisdom, Now I would that thou shouldest consider studiously until thou discover where the full happiness is. Dost thou, then, not know that all mankind is unanimously consenting that God is the origin of all goods and the ruler of all creatures ? He is the highest good, nor do any men doubt it, for they know nothing better, nor indeed, anything equally good. Therefore every argument informs us and all men acknowledge the same, that God is the highest good ; for they shew that all good is in him. For if it were not so, then he would not be that which he is called. Or if anything were more ancient, or more excellent, then would that be better than he. But because nothing was more ancient than he, nor more excellent than he, nor more precious than he, therefore is he the origin, and the source and the roof of all goods. It is sufficiently evident that the perfect good was before the imperfect. This *then* is to be acknowledged, that the highest good is fullest of every good, that we may not speak *longer* about it than we need. The same God is, as we before said, the highest good, and the best happiness since it is evidently known that the best felicities are in no other things but in God. Then said I, I am convinced *of it*.

3. Then said he, I beseech thee that thou wouldest rationally understand this, that God is full of all perfection, and of all good and of all happiness. Then said I, I cannot fully comprehend why thou again sayest the same thing which thou saidest before. Then said he, For this reason I say it to thee again, because I am unwilling that thou shouldest suppose that God, who is the Father and Origin of all creatures ; that the supreme goodness of him of which he is full, came to him from without. Nor moreover am I willing that thou shouldest suppose that his good and his happiness were one thing, and himself another. For if thou thinkest that the good which he has, came to him from without, then would that thing from which it came to him, be better than he, if it were so. But it is very foolish, and a very great sin, that any one should thus think of God; or moreover think that anything was before him, or better than he, or like him. But we must be

convinced that God is of all things the best. If thou, then, believest that God is like as it is among men, *that* one thing is the man, that is soul and body, *and* another is his goodness, which God joins, and afterwards holds together and regulates : if thou believest that it is so with God, then must thou of necessity believe that some power is greater than his, which may join together what belongs to him, as he does what appertains to us. Besides, whatsoever is distinct from another thing is one, *and* the thing another, though they be together. If, therefore, anything is distinct from the highest good, then that is not the highest good. It is however, great sin to imagine concerning God, that any good can be external to him, or any separated from him ; because nothing is better than he or equally good with him. What thing can be better than its Creator ? Therefore I say with right reason, that that is the highest good in its own nature, which is the origin of all things. Then said I, Now thou hast very rightly instructed me. Then said he, But then I before said, that the highest good, and the highest happiness were one. Then said I, So it is. Then said he, What shall we then say ? What else is that but God ? Then said I, I cannot deny this, for I was before convinced of it.

4. Then said he, Perhaps thou mayest more clearly apprehend it, if I again give thee some instance. If, therefore, two goods existed, which might not be together, and were nevertheless both good, would it not then be sufficiently evident that neither of them was the other ? Therefore the full good cannot be divided. How can it be both full and deficient ? Hence we say, that the full happiness and good are one good, and that is the highest. They can never be separated. Must we not, then, necessarily be convinced that the highest happiness and the supreme divinity are one ? Then said I, Nothing is more true than that. We are not able to discover anything better than God. Then said he, But I would still prepare thee by some example, so that thou mayest not find any way of escaping ; as the manner of philosophers is, that they always wish to declare something new and extraordinary, that they may thereby awaken the mind of the hearers.

5. Have we not already proved that happiness and the divinity were one ? He, then, who has happiness has both in having either. Is he not, then, full happy ? Knowest thou not, moreover, what we say, that any one is wise who has wisdom ; and righteous, who has righteousness ? So we also say that that is God which has

goodness and happiness : and every happy man is a God. And yet there is one God, who is the stem and foundation of all goods, and from him cometh all good ; and again, they tend to him, and he governs all. He is, moreover, the origin and foundation of all goods which proceed from him. Thus all the stars are lighted and made bright by the sun : some, however, more brightly, some less brightly. So also the moon gives light in such measure as the sun shines upon him. When she shines upon him all over, then is he all bright. When I heard this speech, I was astonished, and greatly afraid, and said : This is, indeed, a wonderful and delightful, and rational argument which thou now usest. Then said he, Nothing is more delightful or more certain than the thing which this argument is about, and which we will now speak of ; for methinks it good that we add it to the preceding. Then said I, What is that ?

6. Then said he, Thou knowest that I before said to thee, that the true happiness was good ; and from the true happiness come all the other goods which we have before spoken about, and again *return* to *it*. Thus from the sea the water enters into the earth, and then becomes fresh. It then comes up through the fountain, then runs to the brook, then to the river, then along the river till it returns to the sea. But I would now ask thee how thou hast understood this discourse. Whether thou thinkest that the five goods which we have often before mentioned, that is power, and dignity, and glory, and abundance, and pleasure ; I would know whether thou thoughtest that these goods were members of the true happiness, as there are many members in one man, and yet all belong to one body, or whether thou thoughtest that any one of the five goods constituted the true happiness, and then the four *other* goods were its good, as soul and body constitutes one man, and the one man has many members, and nevertheless, to these two, that is to the soul, and to the body, belong all these goods of the man, both ghostly and bodily. This, then, is the good of the body, that a man be fair, and strong, and tall, and broad, and many other goods in addition to these ; and yet it is not the body itself, because if that loses any of these goods ; it is nevertheless what it was before. Then the good of the soul is prudence, and temperance, and patience, and justice, and wisdom, and many like virtues ; and nevertheless the soul is one *thing*, and its virtues are another. Then said I, I wish that thou wouldest speak to me more plainly

about the other goods which belong to the true happiness. Then said he, Did I not say to thee before that the happiness was good? Yes, said I, thou saidest that it was the supreme good. Then said he, Art thou now convinced that power, and dignity, and glory, and abundance, and pleasure, and happiness, and the supreme good, that these are all one, and that one is good? Then said I, How shall I deny this? Then said he, Which dost thou then consider these things to be; members of the true felicities, or the felicity itself? Then said I, I now perceive what thou wouldest know. But I rather wish that thou wouldest inform me somewhile concerning it, than that thou shouldest enquire of me. Then said he, Canst thou not imagine that if the goods were members of the true happiness, they would then be in some degree separated as the members of a man's body are in some degree separated. But the nature of the members is that they constitute one body, and yet are not altogether alike. Then, said I, Thou needest not labour more about that. Thou hast clearly enough proved to me that the goods are in no wise separated from the true happiness. Then said he, Very rightly thou understandest it, now thou understandest that the goods are all the same that happiness is, and happiness is the highest good: and the highest good is God; and God is ever one, inseparable. Then said I, There is no doubt of this. But I wish that thou wouldest now inform me of something unknown.

7. Then said he, it is now evident that all the goods which we have before spoken about, belong to the highest good; and therefore men seek sufficient good when they consider that *which they seek*, the highest good. Therefore they seek power, and also *the* other goods, which we before mentioned, because they think that it is the highest good. Hence thou mayest know that the highest good is the roof of all the other goods which men desire and covet. For no man covets anything but good, or something of that which resembles good. They are desirous of many a thing which is not full good, but it has, nevertheless, something of resemblance to good. Therefore we say that the highest good is the highest roof of all goods, and the hinge on which all good turns; and also the cause on account of which man does all good. For this cause men covet every one of the goods which they covet. This thou mayest very plainly perceive hereby, that no man desires the thing which he desires, nor that which he does, but

that which he thereby earns. For he thinks that if he obtain *his* desire, and accomplish that which he has resolved, that then he shall have full happiness. Dost thou not know that no man rides because he lists to ride, but rides because he by riding obtains *some earning ?* Some by their riding earn that they may be healthier; some earn that they may be more active; some that they may come to one of the places which they are then hastening to. Is it not, then, sufficiently clear to thee, that men love nothing more earnestly than they do the highest good; because everything which they desire or do, they do for this reason, that they would have the highest good thereby? But some of them err in thinking that they can have full good and full happiness in these present goods. But the full happiness and the highest good is God himself, as we have often said before. Then said I, I cannot imagine how I can deny this. Then said he, Let us, then, relinquish this discourse, and be so far secure; since thou hast so fully learned that God is ever inseparable, and full good; and that his good and his happiness came to him from nowhere without, but was always in himself, and now is, and for ever shall be.

8. When Wisdom had ended this discourse, then began he again to sing, and thus said; Well, O men, well! Let every one who is free aspire to this good, and to these felicities. And whoever is now bound with the vain love of this middle earth, let him seek freedom for himself, that he may arrive at these felicities. For this is the only rest of all our labours; the only haven which is ever calm after all the storms and billows of our labours. This is the only place of peace, and the only comfort of the wretched, after the calamities of this present life. But golden stones, and silver, and gems of every kind, and all this present wealth, neither enlighten the eyes of the mind, nor improve their sharpness for the contemplation of the true happiness; but rather blind the eyes of the mind than sharpen them. For all the things which give pleasure here in this present life are earthly, and therefore fleeting. But the wonderful brightness which brightens all things, and governs all, wills not that souls should perish, but wills to enlighten them. If, then, any man may behold the brightness of the heavenly light with the clear eyes of his mind, then will he say that the brightness of the sun-shine is darkness, to be compared with the eternal brightness of God.

9. When Wisdom had sung this lay, then said I, I am convinced

CHAPTER XXXIV.

of that which thou sayest, for thou hast proved it by rational discourse. Then said he, With how much money wouldest thou have bought, that thou mightest know what the true good was, and of what kind it was? Then said I, I would rejoice with excessive gladness, and I would buy with countless money, that I might see it. Then said he, I will then teach it thee. But this one *thing* I enjoin thee: that thou, on account of this instruction, forget not what I before taught *thee*. Then said I, No, I will not forget it Then said he, Did we not before say to thee, that this present life which we here desire, was not the highest good; because it was varied, and so manifoldly divided, that no man can have it all, so that there be not to him a lack of something? I then taught thee that the highest good was there, where the goods are all collected as if they were melted into one mass. Then is there full good, when the goods which we before spoke of, are all collected into one good. Then is there a deficiency of no good. Then the goods are all in unity, and the unity is eternal. If they were not eternal, then would they not be so anxiously to be desired. Then said I, That is proved, nor can I doubt it. Then said he, I have formerly proved to thee, that that was not full good, which was not all together: because that is full good which is all together, undivided. Then said I, So methinks. Then said he, Dost thou think that all the things which are good in this world, are therefore good, because they have something of good in them? Then said I, What else can I think; is it not so? Then said he, Thou must however believe that unity and goodness are one thing. Then said I, I cannot deny this. Then said he, Canst thou not perceive, that every thing is able to exist, both in this world, and in the future, so long as it remains unseparated, but afterwards it is not altogether as it was before? Then said I, Say that to me more plainly; I cannot understand after what thou art enquiring. Then said he, Dost thou know what man is? Then said I, I know that he is soul and body. Then said he, But thou knowest that it is man, while the soul and the body are unseparated. It is not man after they are separated. So also the body is body while it has all its members; but if it lose any member, then it is not all as it before was. The same thou mayest conceive with respect to every thing; that nothing is such as it was, after it begins to decay. Then said I, Now I know it. Then said he, Dost thou think that there is any creature which of its will desires not always to be, but of its own will desires to perish?

10. Then said I, I cannot find any living thing which knows what it wills, or what it wills not, which uncompelled chooses to perish. For every thing, of such as I deem living, desires to be hale and to live. But I know not concerning trees, and concerning herbs, and concerning such creatures as have no souls. Then smiled he and said, Thou needest not doubt concerning these creatures any more than about the others. Canst thou not see that every herb and every tree will grow best in that land which suits it best, and is natural and habitual to it : and where it perceives that it may soonest grow and latest fall to decay ? Of some herbs, or some wood, the native soil is on hills, of some in marshes, of some on moors, of some on rocks, of some on bare sands. Take, therefore, tree or herb, whichsoever thou wilt, from the place which is its native soil and country to grow in, and set it in a place unnatural to it, then will it not grow there at all, but will wither. For the nature of every land is, that it should nourish herbs suitable to it, and suitable wood. And so it does : protecting and supporting them very carefully, as long as it is their nature that they should grow. What thinkest thou ? Why should every seed grow in the earth, and turn to germs and to roots in the earth, except because they endeavour that the trunk and the head may the more firmly and the longer stand ? Why canst thou not understand, though thou art not able to see it, that all that part of the tree which grows in twelve months, begins from the roots and so grows upwards into the trunk, and afterwards along the pith, and along the bark to the head ; and afterwards through the boughs, until it springs out in leaves, and in blossoms, and in fruits ? Why canst thou not understand, that every living thing is inwardly softest, and unbroken hardest ? Moreover thou mayest observe how trees are outwardly clothed and covered with bark, against the winter, and against the stark storms ; and also against the heat of the sun in summer. Who can refrain from admiring such works of our Creator, and still more the Creator ? And though we admire him, which of us can declare worthily our Creator's will and power ? How his creatures grow and again decay, when the time thereof comes ; and from their seed become again renewed, as if they were then newly created ? What they then again are, and also in some measure alone are, such they ever shall be, because they are every year newly created.

11. Dost thou now understand that *even* inanimate creatures would desire to exist for ever, the same as men, if they could? Dost thou understand why fire tends upwards and earth downwards? Wherefore is it, but because God made the station of one up, and of the other down? For every creature chiefly tends thither, where its station and its health especially is, and flies from what is contrary, and disagreeing, and unlike to it. Stones, because they are of immoveable and hard nature, are difficult to divide, and also with difficulty come together, when they are divided. If thou cleavest a stone, it never becomes united together as it before was. But water and air are of a somewhat softer nature. They are very easy to separate, but they are again soon together. The fire, indeed, cannot ever be divided. I just now said, that nothing of its own will would perish; but I am *speaking* more about the nature than about the will, for these sometimes are differently inclined. Thou mayest know by many things that nature is very great. It is through mighty nature that to our body comes all its strength from the food which we eat, and yet the food goes out through the body. But nevertheless its savour and its virtue enter every vein: even as any one sifts meal: the meal comes through every hole, and the bran becomes separated. So also our spirit is very widely wandering, without our will, and without our power, by reason of its nature, not by reason of its will; that happens when we sleep. But cattle, and, also other creatures seek that which they desire, more from nature than from will. It is unnatural to every thing that it should desire danger or death, but still many a thing is so far compelled that it desires both of them; because the will is then stronger than the nature. Sometimes the will is more powerful than the nature, sometimes the nature overcomes the will. Thus lust does. It is natural to all men, and yet its nature is sometimes denied to it through the man's will. All the desire of propagation is from nature, not from will.

12. By this thou mayest plainly know, that the Maker of all things has imparted one desire and one nature to all his creatures, that is, that they would exist for ever. It is natural to every thing that it should desire to exist for ever: so far as it can and may retain its nature. Thou needest not doubt concerning that which thou before didst question, that is, concerning the creatures which have no souls. Every one of the creatures which have souls, as

well as those which have not, desires always to exist. Then said I, Now I understand that about which I before doubted; that is, that every creature is desirous always to exist, which is very clear, from the propagation *of them*. Then said he, Dost thou then understand, that every one of the things which perceives itself to exist, desires to be together, whole and undivided; because if it be undivided then it is whole? Then said I, that is true. Then said he, that all things have one will, that is, that they would exist for ever. Through this one will they desire the one good which for ever exists, that is God! Then said I, So it is. Then said he, Thou mayest then plainly perceive that it is on account of a thing good in itself, that all creatures and all things desire to possess *it*. Then said I, No man can more truly say; for I know that all creatures would flow away like water, and keep no peace, nor any order, but very confusedly dissolve and come to naught, as we before said in this same book, if they had not one God, who guided, and directed, and governed them all. But now, since we know that there is one Governor of all things, we must needs be convinced, whether we will, or whether we will not, that he is the highest roof of all goods. Then he smiled upon me and said, O, my child, how truly happy art thou, and how truly glad am I, on account of thine understanding! Thou hast very nearly discovered the truth; and the same that thou before saidest thou couldst not understand, of that thou hast now been convinced. Then said I, What was that which I before said, I knew not? Then said he, Thou saidest that thou knewest not the end of every creature. But know now that that is the end of every creature which thou thyself hast already named, *that is good*. To this all creatures tend. They have no good besides this to seek, nor can they discover anything either above or beyond *it*.

Chapter XXXV.

I. When he had ended this discourse, then began he again to sing, and thus said; Whosoever is desirous to search deeply with inward mind after truth, and is unwilling that any man, or anything should mislead him: let him begin to seek within himself that which he before sought around him; and let him dismiss vain anxieties as he best may, and resort to this alone, and say to his own mind, that it may find within itself, all the goods which it seeks outwardly. Then may he very soon discover all the evil and vanity which he before had in his mind, as plainly as thou canst behold the sun. And thou wilt know thine own mind, that it is far brighter, and lighter than the sun. For no heaviness of the body, or any fault can wholly take away from his mind wisdom, so that he have not some portion of it in his mind; though the sluggishness of the body, and *its* imperfections often prepossess the mind with forgetfulness, and affright it with the mist of error, so that it cannot shine so brightly as it would. And nevertheless a grain of the seed of truth is ever dwelling in the soul, while the soul and the body are united. That grain must be excited by enquiry and by instruction if it shall grow. How then can any man wisely and rationally enquire if he has no particle of wisdom in him? No one is so entirely destitute of wisdom that he knows no right answer when any one enquires. Therefore it is a very true saying that Plato the philosopher said. He said, Whosoever is forgetful of wisdom, let him have recourse to his mind: then will he there find the wisdom concealed by the heaviness of the body, and by the trouble and occupation of his mind.

2. Then said I, I am convinced that it was a true saying, which Plato said. But hast thou not again twice reminded me of the same argument? First thou saidest that I had forgotten the natural good which I had within myself, through the heaviness of the body. At another time, thou saidest to me, that thou hadst discovered that it seemed to myself that I had altogether lost the natural good which I should have within myself, through the immoderate uneasiness which I had on account of lost wealth. Then said he, Since thou now rememberest the words which I said to thee, in the first book, thou mayest by those words clearly enough call to mind what thou before saidest thou wert ignorant of. Then said I, What was that? What did I say that I was ignorant of? Then said he, Thou saidest in that same book, that thou knewest that God governed this middle earth; but thou saidest that thou couldest not discover in what manner he governed it, or how he governed it. Then said I, I very well remember mine own folly, and I have already acknowledged it to thee. But though I know it in some measure, I would yet hear more concerning it from thee. Then said he, Thou formerly hadst not any doubt that God ruled and governed all the middle earth. Then said I, Nor do I now doubt it, nor ever shall doubt it. I

will moreover, at once tell thee by what I was first convinced of it. I perceived that this middle-earth was composed of very many and various things. and very firmly cemented and joined together. If these, such contrary creatures, had not been united and reduced to order, then they would never have been formed nor joined together: and if he had not bound them with his indissoluble chains, then would they all be dissolved. Neither would their station and their course be formed so wisely, and so orderly, and so suitably in their places, and in their times, if one unchangeable God did not exist. Good, therefore, directed whatever is. This I call God as all creatures call *it*.

3. Then said he, Since thou hast so clearly understood this, I need not now greatly labour, in order that I may instruct thee further, concerning good; for thou art now almost come into the city of the true happiness, which thou some time ago couldest not discover. But we must nevertheless consider what we have already proposed. Then said I, What is that? Then saidhe, Have we not before agree agreed that sufficiency was happiness, and happiness, God? Then said I, So it is as thou sayest. Then said he, God needs no other help besides himself to govern his creatures with, any more than he before needed for the creation: for if he had need of any help in any thing, then would he himself not have sufficiency. Then said I, So it is as thou sayest. Then said he, By himself he created all things and governs all. Then said I, I cannot deny it. Then said he, We have before shewn to thee, that God was of himself good. Then said I, I remember that thou so saidest. Then said he, Through good, God created every thing, for he governs by himself all that, which we before said was good: and he is the only stable governor, and pilot, and rudder: for he directs and rules all creatures, as a good pilot *steers* a ship. Then said I, Now I confess to thee that I have found a door, where I before saw only a little chink, so that I scarcely could see a very small ray of light in this darkness. And yet thou hadst before pointed out to me the door, but I could not ever the more discover it, though I groped for it whereabout I saw that little light twinkle. I said to thee some time ago, in this same book, that I knew not what was the beginning of all creatures. Thou didst then inform me that it was God. Then again I knew not concerning the end, until thou hadst told me that it was also God. Then said I to thee, that I knew not how he governed all these creatures, but thou

hast now explained it to me very clearly, as if thou hadst opened the door which I before sought. Then answered he me and said, I know that I before reminded thee of this same argument, and now methinks that thou understandest, as the later, so the better concerning the truth. But I would yet shew thee some example as manifest as that was, which I before mentioned to thee. Then said I, What is that?

4. Then said he, No man can doubt this, that by the proper consent of all creatures, God reigns over them, and bends their will conformably to his will. By this it is very evident that God governs everything with the helm, and with the rudder of his goodness. For all creatures naturally of their own will endeavour to come to good, as we have often before said in this same book. Then said I, Indeed I cannot doubt it, for God's power would not be entirely perfect if creatures obeyed him against their will : and again, the creatures would not be worthy of any thanks, or any honour, if they unwillingly obeyed their Lord. Then said he, There is no creature which attempts to contend against its Maker's will, if it desire to retain its nature. Then said I, There is no creature which contends against its Maker's will except foolish man : or again, the rebellious angels. Then said he, What thinkest thou ? If any creature determined that it would contend against his will, what could it do against *one* so powerful as we have proved him ? Then said I, They cannot do anything, though they will it. Then wondered he, and said, There is no being which can or will oppose so high a God! Then said I, I do not imagine that there is anything which opposes, except what we before said. Then smiled he, and said, Be assured that that is the highest good which so powerfully does everything, and has created all things, and so widely over all extends, and so easily without any labour disposes everything. Then said I, I well liked what thou before saidest ; and this pleases me still better, but I am now ashamed that I did not know it before. Then said he, I wot thou hast often heard tell in old fables,[1] that Jove, the son of Saturn, should be the highest god above other gods ; and he should be the son of heaven, and should reign in the heavens ; and the giants should be the sons of earth, and should reign over the earth, and then they should be as if they were sisters' children, for he should be the son of heaven, and they of earth. Then should it appear to the giants

---

1. This portion is entirely the production of King Alfred, who has considerably enlarged on a passing allusion of Boethius.

that he possessed their kingdom. Then were they desirous to break the heaven under him. Then should he send thunders and lightnings, and winds, and therewith overturn all their work, and slay them. Such fictions they invented, and might easily have related true history if the fictions had not been more agreeable to them, and yet very like to these. They might have related what folly Nimrod the giant wrought. Nimrod was the son of Cush; Cush was the son of Ham; *and* Ham of Noah. Nimrod gave order to erect a tower in the field which is called Shinar, and in the country which is called Dura, very near to the city, which men now call Babylon. They did it for these reasons, that they wished to know how high it was to the heaven, and how thick the heaven was, and how firm, or what was over it. But it happened, as was fit, that the divine power dispersed them before they could complete it, and overthrew the tower, and slew many a one of them, and divided their speech into seventy-two languages. So happens it to many of those who strive against the divine power. No honour accrues to them thereby, but that is diminished which they had.

5. But see now whether thou art desirous that we should still seek after any argument further, now we have discovered what we before sought. I think, however, if we again strike our words together, there may spring out some spark of truth of those things which we have not yet observed. Then said I, Do as thou wilt. Then said he, No man doubts that God is so mighty that he is able to work whatsoever he will. Then said I, No man doubts this who knows anything. Then said he, Does any man think that there is aught which God cannot do? Then said I, I know that there is nothing which he cannot do. Then said he, Dost thou imagine that he can do any evil? Then said I, I know that he cannot. Then said he, thou sayest truly, for it is nothing. If evil were anything, then could God do it. Therefore it is nothing. Then said I, Methinks thou deceivest and deludest me, as any one does a child: thou leadest me hither and thither in so thick a wood, that I cannot find the way out. For thou always, on account of some small matter, betakest *thyself* to the same argument, and again leavest that before thou hast ended it, and beginnest a fresh one. Therefore I know not what thou wouldest. Methinks thou revolvest about some wonderful and extraordinary argument concerning the oneness of the divine nature. I remember that thou formerly madest to me a wonderful speech, wherein

CHAPTER XXXV.

thou toldest me, that it was all one, happiness and the highest good : and saidest that the felicities were fixed in the highest good, and the highest good was God himself, and he was full of all happiness. And thou saidest that every happy man was a God. And again thou saidest, that God's goodness, and his happiness, and himself, that this was all one, and was consequently the highest good : and to this good all creatures which retain their nature tend and are desirous to come. And moreover, thou saidest that God governed all his creatures with the rudder of his goodness : and also saidest that all creatures of their own will, uncompelled, were subject to him. And now at last thou saidest, that evil was nothing And all this thou hast proved for truth very rationally, without any ambiguity. Then said he, thou saidest just now that I deceived thee : but methinks I have not deceived thee, but have stated to thee a very long and wonderful argument very rationally, concerning that God to whom we some time ago prayed ; and I still intend to teach thee something unknown concerning the same God. It is the nature of the divinity to be able to exist unmixed with other beings, without the help of other beings, in such a way as nothing else is capable of. No other thing is able to exist of itself. Thus formerly Parmenides, the poet, sung,² and said ; the Almighty God is Ruler of all things, and he alone remains unchangeable, and governs all changeable *things*. Therefore thou needest not greatly wonder, when we are enquiring concerning what we have begun, whether we may prove it with fewer words, or with more. Though we should produce many and various examples and fables, yet our mind always hangs on that which we are enquiring after. We do not betake ourselves to examples and fables, for love of fictitious speeches, but because we desire therewith to point out the truth, and desire that it may be useful to the hearers. I called to mind just now some instructions of the wise Plato,² how he said, that the man who would relate a fable, should not choose a fable unlike the subject of his discourse. But hear now patiently what I shall further say, though it formerly appeared to thee unprofitable, whether the end may better please thee.

6. He began then to sing, and said, Happy is the man who can

---

2. Parmenides was a distinguished Greek philosopher, and flourished about the same time as Socrates : and like other philosophers of that period, expressed his notions in poetry. The poem here alluded to was entitled, "On Nature."

The passage here alluded to was the remark made by Plato in his Timæus, viz. that Discourses, in those matters of which they are the interpreters, should always have a certain relationship to the subject.

behold the clear fountain of the highest good, and can put away from himself the darkness of his mind! We will now from old fables relate to thee a story: It happened formerly that there was a harper, in the country called Thrace, which was in Greece. The harper was inconceivably good. His name was Orpheus. He had a very excellent wife, who was called Eurydice. Then began men to say concerning the harper, that he could harp so that the wood moved, and the stones stirred themselves at the sound, and wild beasts would run thereto and stand as if they were tame; so still, that though men or hounds pursued them, they shunned them not. Then said they, that the harper's wife should die, and her soul should be led to hell. Then should the harper become so sorrowful that he could not remain among other men, but frequented the wood and sat on the mountains both day and night, weeping and harping, so that the woods shook and the rivers stood still, and no hart shunned any lion, nor hare any hound; nor did cattle know any hatred or any fear of others, for the pleasure of the sound. Then it seemed to the harper that nothing in this world pleased him. Then thought he that he would seek the gods of hell, and try to soften them with his harp, and pray that they would give him back his wife. When he came thither, then should there come towards him the dog of hell, whose name was Cerberus; he should have three heads; and began to wag his tail and play with him for his harping. Then was there also a very dreadful gate-keeper, whose name should be Charon. He had also three heads, and he was very old. Then began the harper to beseech him that he would protect him while he was there, and bring him thence again safe. Then did he promise that to him, because he was desirous of the unaccustomed sound. Then went he further, until he met the grim goddesses, whom the common people call Parcæ, of whom they say, that they know no respect for any man, but punish every man according to his deeds; *and* of whom they say, that they controul every man's fortune. Then began he to implore their mercy. Then began they to weep with him. Then went he further, and all the inhabitants of hell ran towards him, and led him to their king; and all began to speak with him, and to pray that which he prayed. And the restless wheel which Ixion, the king of the Lapithæ, was bound to for his guilt, that stood still for his harping. And Tantalus the king, who in this world was immoderately greedy, and whom that same vice of greediness followed there, he became quiet. And the vulture should cease, so that he tore not the liver of Tityus the king, which before therewith tormented him. And all the punishments of the inhabitants of hell were suspended, while he harped before the king. When he long and long had harped, then spoke the king of the inhabitants of hell, and said, Let us give the man his wife, for he has earned her by his harping. He then commanded him that he should well observe that he never looked backward after he departed thence, and said, if he looked backwards, that he should lose the woman. But men can with great difficulty, if at all, restrain love. Wellaway! what! Orpheus then led his wife with him, till he came to the boundary of light and darkness. Then went his wife after him. When he came forth into the light, then looked he behind his back towards the woman. Then was she immediately lost to him! This fable teaches every man who desires to fly the darkness of hell, and to come to the light of the true good, that he look not behind him to his old vices, so that he practise them again as fully as he did before. For whosoever with full will turns his mind to the vices which he had before forsaken, and practises them, and they then fully please him, and he never thinks of forsaking them; then loses he all his former good, unless he again amend it. Here ends the third book of Boethius, and begins the fourth.

Chapter XXXVI.

1. When Wisdom had very delightfully and wisely sung this lay, then had I as yet some little remembrance in my mind of the sorrows which I formerly had, and said, O Wisdom, thou who art the messenger, and forerunner of the true light, how wonderful methinks *is* that which thou declarest to me! Therefore I am persuaded that all which thou before saidest to me, God said to me through thee. And I also knew it before in some measure, but this sorrow had distracted me, so that I had entirely forgotten it. And this besides is the chief part of my unhappiness, that I wonder why the good God should suffer any evil to exist; or if it yet must *exist*, and he wills to permit it, why he then does not speedily punish it. Indeed thou mayest thyself know that this is to be wondered at. And also another thing seems to me even a greater wonder, that is, that folly and wickedness now reign over all the middle earth, and wisdom and also other virtues have no praise

nor any honour in this world, but lie despised like dirt on a dung hill; and in every land wicked men are now honoured, and the good have manifold punishments. Who can forbear lamenting and wondering at such a marvel, that ever such evil should take place under the government of Almighty God, when we know that he sees it, and wills all good. Then said he, If it is as thou sayest, then is this more dreadful than any other prodigy, and is endless wonder, most like to this; that in a king's court gold and silver vessels should be despised, and men should esteem wooden *ones.* It is not as thou supposest. But if thou wilt call to mind all that which we have before said, then, with the help of God, concerning whom we are now speaking, thou wilt be able to understand that the good are always powerful, and the wicked have no power and that virtues are never without praise, or without reward; nor are vices ever unpunished; but the good are always happy, and the wicked unhappy. I can shew thee very many examples of this, which may encourage thee, so that thou mayest not know what thou any longer shouldest lament. But I will now teach thee the way which will lead thee to the heavenly city whence thou formerly camest, since thou knowest through my instruction, what the true happiness is, and where it is. But I must first give wings to thy mind, that it may the sooner raise itself up, before it begins to fly on high: in order that it may, sound and untroubled, fly to its native country, and leave behind it every one of the troubles which it now endures. Let it sit in my chariot and be conducted in my path; I will be its guide.

2. When Wisdom had ended this speech, then began he again to sing, and said; I have very swift wings, so that I can fly over the high roof of heaven. But I must furnish thy mind with wings that thou mayest fly with me; then mayest thou look down upon all these earthly things. When thou art able to fly over the sky thou mayest behold the clouds under thee, and mayest fly over the fire which is between the sky and the air; and mayest go with the sun between the stars, and then be in the sky, and afterwards near the cold star which we call Saturn's star. It is all icy. It wanders above other stars, higher than any other heavenly body. After thou art elevated far above it, then wilt thou be above the swift sky, and wilt leave behind thee the highest heaven. After this thou mayest have thy portion of the true light. There reigns

one king, who has power over all other kings. He regulates the bridle, and the rein of all the circuit of heaven and earth. The only judge is stedfast and bright. He directs the chariot of all creatures. But if thou ever comest into the path, and to the place which thou hast now forgotten, then wilt thou say; This is my proper country; hence I formerly came, and hence was I born: here I will now stand fast: I will never go hence. But I wot, if it ever happen to thee, that thou wilt or must again explore the darkness of this world, then wilt thou observe unjust kings, and all the proud rich to be very feeble, and very wretched exiles: the same whom this miserable people now most dreads!

3. Then said I, O Wisdom, great is that, and wonderful, which thou dost promise: and I moreover doubt not that thou canst perform it. But I beseech thee, that thou wouldest not any longer hinder me, but teach me the way, for thou mayest perceive that I am desirous of the way. Then said he, Thou must first understand that the good always have power, and the wicked never *have* any nor any ability; for none of them comprehends that good and evil are always enemies. If, therefore, the good always have power, then the wicked never have any, because good and evil are entirely contrary. But I would inform thee somewhat more distinctly concerning each of them, that thou mayest the better believe what I shall sometimes tell thee, concerning the one, and sometimes concerning the other. There are two things which every man's intention requires, that is, will and power. If therefore there is to any man a deficiency of either of the two, he cannot with the other effect anything. For no one will undertake what he is unwilling, unless he needs must: and though he fully wills he cannot *perform it*, if he has not power of that thing. Hence thou mayest clearly know, when thou seest any man desirous of that which he has not, that to him power is wanting. Then said I, That is true: I cannot deny it. Then said he, But if thou seest any one who can do what he desires to do, then there is no doubt to thee, that he has power. Then said I, I have no doubt of it. Then said he, Every man is powerful so far as he exercises power; he has no power when he does not exercise power. Then said I, Of that I am convinced. Then said he, Canst thou now call to mind what I before told thee, that is, that the mind of every man desires to arrive at the true happiness, though they pursue it differently? Then said I, That I remember; it is clearly

enough proved to me. Then said he, Dost thou remember that I before said to thee, that it was all one, good and happiness? He who seeks happiness seeks good. Then said I, I have *it* sufficiently fixed in *my* memory. Then said he, All men, both good and evil, desire to come to good, though they desire it variously. Then said I, that is true which thou sayest. Then said he, it is sufficiently evident that good men are good because they find good. Then said I, it is evident enough. Then said he, the good obtain the good which they desire. Then said I, So methinks. Then said he, the wicked would not be wicked if they found the good which they desire; but they are wicked because they do not find it; and they do not find it because they do not seek it rightly. Then said I, So it is as thou sayest. Then said he, therefore there is no doubt that the good are always powerful, and the wicked have no power, because the good seek good rightly, and the wicked wrongly. Then said I, He who thinks that this is not true, then believes he no truth.

4. Then said he, Whether dost thou think? if two men are going to one place, and have equally great desire to arrive there, and one has the use of his feet, so that he may go where he will, as it were natural to all men that they could, and the other has not the use of his feet, that he can go, and yet is desirous to go, and begins to creep the same way, whether of the two dost thou think the more powerful? Then said I, there is no comparison. He is more powerful who goes, than he who creeps, because he can more easily come whither he will than the other. Say what else thou wilt, every man knows that. Then said he, in like manner it is with the good and with the wicked. Each of them desires naturally that he may come to the highest good. But the good is able to come whither he desires, because he desires it rightly, and the wicked cannot come to that which he desires, because he seeks it wrongly. I know not but thou mayest think differently. Then said I, I do not think at all differently from what thou sayest. Then said he, Very rightly thou understandest it; and that is also a token of thy health, as it is the custom of physicians to say, when they see a sick man, if they perceive in him any healthy token. Methinks now that thy nature and thy habit contend very powerfully against error.

5. I have now found that thou art prompt to understand my doctrine: therefore I am desirous to collect for thee many argu-

ments and many examples, so that thou mayest the more easily understand what I am about to say. Observe now how feeble wicked men are when they cannot come thither, where *even* irrational creatures are desirous to come: and how much more feeble they would be if they had no natural inclination to it. Behold with how heavy a chain of folly and unhappiness they are bound! Even children, when they can first go, and also old men, as long as they can go, are desirous of some honour, and some praise. Children ride on their sticks, and play at various sorts of play, wherein they imitate old men. But the unwise are not willing to attempt anything from which they may expect to themselves praise or rewards. But *they* do what is worse; *they* run erring hither and thither under the roof of all things; and that which irrational creatures know, unwise men do not know. Therefore the virtues are better than the vices. For every man must be convinced, whether he will, or whether he will not, that he is the most powerful who is able to arrive at the highest roof of all things, that is God; whom nothing is above, nor anything beneath, nor about, but all things are in him, and in his power. God is greatly to be loved. Didst thou not before say, that he was most powerful in walking, who could go if he would to the end of this earth, so that no part of this earth were beyond it? The same thou mayest conceive with regard to God, as we before said; that he is most powerful who can come to him, because he no where beyond that can come.

6. From all these arguments thou mayest understand, that the good are always powerful and the wicked are destitute of all power and all ability. Why then thinkest thou that they forsake virtues and follow vices? But I suppose thou wilt say, that it is through ignorance that they are not able to distinguish them. But what wilt thou then say is worse than this ignorance? Why do they suffer themselves to be ignorant? Why will they not enquire after virtues, and after wisdom? But I know that drowsiness oppresses them, and overcomes them with sloth, and covetousness blinds them. We have before said, that nothing was worse than ignorance. But what shall we now say, if the intelligent have vices, and will not enquire after wisdom and after virtues? I know, however, that thou wilt say, that luxury and intemperance oppress them. But what is weaker than the man who is utterly subdued by the frail flesh, unless he afterwards desist and contend against

vices as he best may? But what wilt thou say if any creature will not contend against *them*, but with full will forsakes all good and does evil, and is nevertheless intelligent? I say that he is feeble, and moreover altogether nothing. For whosoever forsakes the universal good of all goods, without doubt he is nothing. But whosoever desires that he may be virtuous, desires that he may be wise. Whosoever, then, is virtuous, is wise, and he who is wise, is good: he then who is good, is happy; and he who is happy, is blessed; and he who is blessed, is a God, so far as we have before mentioned in this same book. But I rather think that foolish men will wonder at that which I have just now said, that is, that wicked men were nothing; because there is a greater number of them than of the others. But though they never believe it, yet it is so. We can never reckon the wicked man pure and sincere, any more than we can call or esteem a dead man living. Nor indeed is the living better than the dead, if he repent not of his evil. But he who lives recklessly, and will not preserve his nature, is not he nothing?

7. I think, however, thou wilt say that this is not altogether so likely, because the wicked can do evil though he cannot *do* good and the dead do neither. But I say to thee, that the power of the wicked does not come from any virtues, but from vices. But if the evil were always good, then would they do no evil. It is not from power that any one is able to do evil, but it is from weakness. If that is true, which we some time ago asserted, that evil is nothing, then he works nothing who works evil. Then said I, Very true is that which thou sayest. Then said he, Did we not prove before that nothing was more powerful than the highest good? Then said I, So it is as thou sayest. Then said he, Yet it cannot do any evil. Then said I, That is true. Then said he, Does any one think that any man can be so powerful that he is able to do all that he wills? Then said I, No man thinks it, who has his senses. Then said he, But wicked men nevertheless can do evil. Then said I, O that they were not able! Then said he, It is evident that they can do evil, and cannot *do* any good. That is because evil is nothing. But the good, if they have full power, are able to do whatsoever good they will. Therefore full power is to be reckoned among the highest goods, for both power, and the other goods and excellencies which we long ago mentioned, are fixed in the highest good. As the wall of a house is fixed both

to the floor, and to the roof, so is every good fixed in God, for he is both the roof and floor of every good. Therefore is the power that man may do good, ever to be desired: for that is the best power, that any one is able and willing to do well, whether with less means or with greater, whichsoever he may have. For whosoever wills to do good is desirous to have good, and to be with good. Therefore is Plato's saying very true, which he said, The wise alone can do the good which they desire : the wicked can only attempt what they desire : I know not, however, but thou wilt say, that the good sometimes begin what they cannot accomplish. But I say that they always accomplish it. Though they may not perfect the work, they have nevertheless full will, and the sincere will is to be reckoned for the perfect work. Therefore they never fail of rewards either here or there, or both. If the wicked have will to work what they list, though it is not now perfect, they lose not also the will, but have its punishment either here, or elsewhere, or both. So greatly does the evil will control them. For this reason they cannot obtain the good which they desire, because they seek it through this will, *and* not through the right way. The evil will has no fellowship with happiness. When Wisdom had finished this speech, then began he again to sing and thus said :

Chapter XXXVII.

1. Hear now a discourse concerning proud and unjust kings, whom we see sitting on the highest thrones; who shine in clothes of many kinds, and are surrounded by a great company of their thanes, who are adorned with belts and golden-hilted swords, and with manifold weapons, and terrify all mankind with their greatness. And he who governs them, regards neither friend nor foe any more than a mad hound; but is inconceivably lifted up in his mind, through unbounded power. But if any man should strip off from him the clothes, and deprive him of the retinue and the power, then wouldest thou see that he is very like to any one of those, his thanes, who serve him, unless he be worse. And moreover, if by chance it happen unto him, that he at any time is deprived of the retinue and of the clothes, and of the power, then it seems to him that he is brought to prison, or to chains. Because from excess, and from immoderate clothing, and from dainty food,

and from various drinks of the cup, the fury of lust is excited, and disquiets their minds very greatly : then increases also arrogance and wickedness; and when they are offended, then is their mind scourged with the heat of anger, until they are distracted with unhappiness, and so enslaved. After this takes place, the hope of revenge begins to deceive them, and whatsoever his anger wills, his recklessness promises him. I said to thee long before, in this same book, that all creatures were naturally desirous of some good ; but unjust kings can do no good, for the reason I have now given thee. That is no wonder, for they subject themselves to all the vices which I have already named to thee. *Every one of them* therefore necessarily must *submit* to the judgment of the lords to whom he has already subjected himself ; and what is still worse, that he will not even strive against them. If he were willing to attempt it, and then were able to persevere in the contest, then would he be free from his guilt.

2. When Wisdom had sung this lay, then began he again to speak, and thus said ; Seest thou in how great and in how deep and in how dark a sink of vices the unwilling are involved, and how the good shine brighter than the sun ? For the good are never destitute of the rewards of their good, nor the wicked ever of the punishments which they deserve. Everything which is done in this world has recompence. Let any one work what he may, or do what he may, he will ever have that which he earns. Moreover it is not unmeet, as was formerly the custom of the Romans, and still is in many nations, that man should have a golden crown, at the end of some course. Many people come thereto and all run equally ; those who have confidence in their running, and whichsoever arrives first at the crown, then may he have it to himself. Every one desires that he may first arrive, and have it, but nevertheless it falls to one. So does all mankind in this present life,—runs and hastens, and is desirous of the highest good. But it is offered to no one man, but is *offered* to all men. Therefore it is needful to every one that he strive with all his power after the reward. Of the reward no good man is ever deprived. A man cannot rightly call himself good, if he be destitute of the highest good, for no good servant is without good rewards. Let the wicked do what they may, the crown of good reward will always be possessed by the good for ever. The evil of the wicked cannot deprive the good of their good, and of their excellence. But if they had that good

from without them, then might some one deprive them of it; either he who formerly bestowed it, or another man. But a good man then loses his rewards when he forsakes his good. Understand, then, that to every man his own good gives good reward: that good which is in himself. What wise man will say, that any good man is destitute of the highest good, for he always labours after it? But meditate thou always on the great and the fair reward, for that reward is above all other rewards to be loved; and add that reward to the before-mentioned goods, which I formerly recounted to thee in the third book. When they are added together, then mayest thou perceive that happiness and the highest good are all one, and that is God. And then thou mayest also perceive that every good man is happy, and that all happy men are gods, and have eternal reward of their good!

3. Therefore no wise man needs to doubt that the evil have also eternal recompence of their evil, that is, eternal punishment. Though thou mayest think that any of them is happy here, in respect of the world, he nevertheless has always his evil with him, and also the recompence of the evil, *even* whilst it gives him pleasure. There is no wise man who is ignorant that good and evil are always discordant between themselves, and always are at variance in their wishes. And as the goodness of the good is his own good, and his own reward, so is also the evil of the wicked his own evil and his reward, and his own punishment. No man if he has punishment, doubts that he has evil. What! do the wicked think that they are exempted from punishments, and *yet* are full of all evil? Not only are they foul, but almost brought to nothing. Understand, therefore, from the good, how great punishment the wicked always have; and hear, moreover, an example, and well retain those which I before mentioned to thee. Whatsoever has unity, that we say exists while it remains together; and this unity we call good. Thus a man is a man whilst the soul and the body are together. But *when they are separated* then is he not that which he was before. The same thou mayest conceive concerning the body, and concerning its limbs. If any of the limbs is off, then is it not full man as it was before. So if any good man depart from good, then is he not any more fully good, if he altogether depart from good. When it happens that the wicked leave off what they before did, *they* are not what they before were. But when men forsake good and become wicked, then are they nothing

but a resemblance; so that one may see that they formerly were men, but they have lost the best part of humanity, and kept the worst. They forsake the good of their nature, that is, human manners, and have nevertheless the likeness of man while they live.

4. But as the goodness of men raises them above human nature so far that they are named Gods; so also their wickedness depresses them below human nature, so far that they are called evil, which we say is nothing. Therefore if thou shouldest meet a man so debased, that he is turned from good to evil, thou canst not rightly name him man, but beast. If, then, thou observest with respect to any man, that he is a rapacious man and a spoiler, thou shouldest not call him a man, but a wolf. And the fierce *man* who is a brawler, thou shouldest call a hound, not a man. And the deceitful, crafty *man*, thou shouldest call a fox, not a man. And the immoderately proud and angry *man* who has great malice, thou shalt call a lion, not a man. And the dull *man* who is too slow thou shouldest call an ass more than a man. And the excessively timid *man* who is more fearful than he needs, thou mayest call a hare more than a man. And to the inconstant and the light thou mayest say, that they are more like the wind or restless birds, than modest men. And to him whom thou observest that he is lying in the lusts of his body, *thou mayest say*, that he is most like to fat swine, which always desire to lie in foul mire, and will not wash *themselves* in pure water; but if they sometimes rarely are made to swim, then cast they *themselves* again into the mire and wallow therein. When Wisdom had ended this speech, then began he again to sing, and thus said.

Chapter XXXVIII.

1. I can relate to thee from ancient fables a story very like to the subject which we have just now spoken about. It happened formerly, in the Trojan war, that there was a king whose name *was* Ulysses,[1] who had two countries under the Cæsar. The countries were called Ithaca and Retia, and the Cæsar's name was Agamemnon. When Ulysses went with Cæsar to the battle, he had some hundred ships. Then were they some ten years in that war. When the king again returned homeward from the Cæsars and they had conquered the land, *he* had not more ships

---

3. Ulysses is called by Boethius, Neritius Dux, this name being derived from Nerites, a mountain in Ithaca. King Alfred evidently mistook his author's meaning, and considered Retia, or Neritia as a distinct country over which Ulysses ruled.

than one; but that was *a ship* with three rows of oars. Then opposed him a great tempest and a stormy sea. *He* was then driven on an island out in the Wendel sea[4]. Then was there the daughter of Apollo, the son of Jove. Jove was their king, and pretended that he should be the highest god, and that foolish people believed him, because he was of royal lineage, and they knew not any other God at that time, but worshipped their kings for Gods. Then should the father of Jove be also a god, whose name was Saturn; and likewise all his kindred they held for Gods. Then was one of them the Apollo, whom we before mentioned. Apollo's daughter should be a goddess, whose name was Circe. She, they said, should be very skilful in sorcery; and she dwelt in the island on which the king was driven, of whom we before spoke. She had there a very great company of her servants, and also of other maidens. As soon as she saw the king driven *thither*, whom we before mentioned, whose name was Ulyses, then began she to love him, and each of them the other beyond measure; so that he for love of her neglected all his kingdom, and his family, and dwelt with her until the time that his thanes would no longer remain with him; but for love of their country, and on account of exile, determined to leave him. Then began false men to work spells. And they said that she should by her sorcery overthrow the men, and cast them into the bodies of wild beasts, and afterwards throw them into chains and fetters. Some, they said, she should transform to lions, and when *they* should speak, then they roared. Some should be wild boars, and when they should lament their misfortune, then they grunted. Some became wolves. These howled when they should speak. Some became that kind of wild beast that man calls tiger. Thus was all the company turned into wild beasts of various kinds; each to some beast except the king alone. Every meat they refused which men eat, and were desirous of those which beasts eat. They had no resemblance of men either in body or in voice, yet every one knew his mind, as he before knew *it*: That mind was very sorrowful through the miseries which they suffered. Indeed the men who believed these fictions, nevertheless knew that she by sorcery could not change the minds of men, though she changed the bodies. How great an excellence is that of the mind in comparison of the body! By these *things* and the like, thou mayest learn

4. The Wendel sea was probably the whole of the Mediterranean sea, or that part of it called the Adriatic.

that the excellence of the body is in the mind; and that to every man the vices of his mind are more hurtful. *Those* of the mind draw all the body to them, and the infirmity of the body cannot entirely draw the mind to it.

2. Then said I, I am convinced that that is true which thou before saidest, that is, that it would not be unfit that we should call evil-willing men cattle, or wild beasts, though they have the resemblance of man. But if I had such power as the Almighty has, then would I not let the wicked injure the good so much as they now do. Then said he, It is not permitted to them so long as thou supposest. But thou mayest be assured that their prosperity will very soon be removed, as I will shortly inform thee, though I have not leisure now on account of other discourse. If they had not the vain power which they think they have, they would not have so great punishment as they shall have. The wicked are much more unhappy when they are able to accomplish the evil which they list, than they are when they are unable to do it, though these foolish men do not believe it. It is very wicked that any man wills evil, and it is still much worse that he is able to do it: for the evil will is dispersed like incense before the fire, if man is not able to accomplish the work. But the wicked have sometimes these misfortunes; one is, that they will evil; the second, that they are able *to do it:* the third, that they accomplish it. For God has decreed to give punishments and miseries to wicked men for their wicked works. Then said I, So it is as thou sayest; and yet I would wish, if I might, that they had not the unhappiness of being able to do evil. Then said he, I think, however, that that power will be lost to them sooner than *either* thou or they would expect. For nothing is of long duration in this present life, though it seem to men that it be long. But very frequently the great power of the wicked falls very suddenly, even as a great tree in a wood makes a loud crash when men least expect: and through fear they are always very miserable. But if their wickedness makes them miserable, is not then the long evil always worse than the short? Though the wicked never died, I should still say that they were most miserable. If the miseries are all true, which we long ago discoursed about, that the wicked should have in this world, then is it evident that those miseries are infinite, which are eternal. Then said I, that is wonderful which thou

sayest, and very difficult to be understood by foolish men. But I nevertheless perceive that it appertains well enough to the discourse which we were before holding. Then said he, I am not now speaking to foolish men, but am speaking to those who desire to understand wisdom: for it is a token of wisdom that any one is willing to hear and understand it. But if any of the foolish doubt any of the reasonings which we have already uttered in this same book, let him shew, if he can, some one of the arguments which is either false, or inapplicable to the subject about which we are enquiring: or thirdly, let him then understand and believe that we argue rightly. If he will do none of these *things*, then he knows not what he means.

3. But I can still teach thee another thing, which to foolish men will seem more incredible, and is nevertheless suitable enough to the argument which we are holding. Then said I, What thing is that? Then said he, It is this, that those wicked persons are much happier who in this world have great misery, and manifold punishments, for their evil, than they are who have no suffering and no punishment in this world for their evil. Let no one, however, think that I speak thus because I would reprove vices and praise virtues and by the example urge and persuade men to good conduct through fear of punishment; but I speak it still more for other reasons. Then said I, For what other reasons wouldest thou speak it, except what thou hast just mentioned? Then said he, Dost thou recollect what we before said, that is, that the good always had power and happiness, and the wicked never had either? Then said I, That I remember. Then said he, But what thinkest thou if thou seest any man very unhappy, and yet perceivest something of good in him; is he as unhappy as the man who has no good *in him*? Then said I, He appears to me happier who has something *of good*. Then said he, But what then dost thou think concerning him who has no good, if he has some addition of evil? He, thou wilt say, is still more unhappy than the other, through the addition of evil. Then said I, Why should not I think so? Then said he, Consider that it so appears to thee, *and* understand with inward mind that the wicked have always something of good among their evil, that is, their punishment, which we may very easily and justly reckon to them as good. But those whose evil is all unpunished in this world, have an evil heavier and more dangerous than any punishment in this world is; that is, that

their evil is unpunished in this world, which is the most evident token of the greatest evil in this world, and of the worst recompense after this world. Then said I, I cannot deny this. Then said he, Therefore the wicked are more unhappy, because their wickedness is undeservedly forgiven them, than they are if their wickedness is recompensed according to their deserts. Therefore it is right that evil should be inflicted on the wicked, and it is wrong that they should be suffered to go unpunished. Then said I, Who denies this? Then said he, No man can deny that every thing is good which is right, and everything evil which is wrong. Then said I, I am very much troubled with their discourse, and wonder why so righteous a judge should bestow any unjust gift. Then said he, Wherefore sayest thou that? Then said I, Because thou before saidest that he did wrong, inasmuch as he left the wicked unpunished. Then said he, That is his glory that he is so bountiful, and bestows so abundantly. It is a great gift that he waits till the wicked are sensible of their evil and turn to good. Then said I, Now I understand that it is not an eternal gift which he gives to the wicked, but is rather the delay and waiting of the highest Judge. On account of *his* waiting and forbearance, methinks he is the more contemned; and yet this argument pleases me well enough, and seems to me like enough to what thou before saidest.

4. But I beseech thee, now, that thou wouldest tell me whether thou thinkest that the wicked have any punishment after this world; or the good any reward for their goodness? Then said he, Did not I say to thee before, that the good have recompence for their goodness, both here and for ever; and the wicked also have recompence for their evil, both here and also for ever? But I will now divide the wicked from the wicked in two parts. For one part of the wicked shall have eternal punishment, because they have deserved no mercy; *and* the other part shall be cleansed and proved in the heavenly fire, as silver here is, because it has some deserving of some mercy, wherefore it may come after these troubles to everlasting honour. Still I could instruct thee more both concerning the good and concerning the evil, if I now had leisure. But I fear that I should neglect what we were before seeking after, that is, that we would argue so that thou mightest perceive that the wicked have no power, nor any honour, either in this world or in that to come. For formerly this appeared to thee the worst of all things, that thou thoughtest they had too much; and thou always

Boethius. Otho A.17. Fol. 99.   Pl. IV

To face Ch. XXI

ðonne þu his loca[...] [...]s þe ðæs biht... þios [...] hleo... ni[h]te ðio[...] hion [...] ... [...] þa ablindan mod [...] [...] mæ[...] se ræd [...]s... ælfred ge[...] to donne þio ðæs hi mote bion un[...]nod. þon[...]... ne ly... sce[...]pian [...]... æ þu lon[g]e oð his þ iuht [...] [...]n... þenað on hiora unnettan [...]... [...] [...]æ[...] ðæm þe ic nat hu [...] me æhst toðæm ðy þysu [...] þu nyst þe ðæt me ne sp... r þilce nystþe to ðæm ac ic s[...] to þe forðæm þu ioh hafst f[...] ne ðæt me isþ[...]or spinæd on ðæm srope þonne hi don ne þilæce [...] hi ðsnsh[...] ic læt... nu to þinu dome ma þonne to hiora forðæm hi [...] lociað mid b[...]n eagum on þæs [...] lican ðincg þi him liciað [...] þus se on þæs lichoman. æþu... [...] hpilum beryrlyt mid oðne [...]n on þa hlyronlican þincg mid oð[...] þu locast nu git on þæs [...]lican [...] ðæm enað þu ðæt sun þinc mon... blind sra hi rin[...] sr nan mon n em[...]

didst lament that they were not always punished: and I always said to thee that they never are without punishment, though it appear not so to thee. But I know, however, that thou wilt lament that they have so long time permission to do evil; and I have always said to thee, that the time is a very little while; and I now say to thee, that the longer it is, the more unhappy they are; *and* it would be to them the greatest unhappiness of all, that the time continued till doomsday. And I said to thee also, that they would be more unhappy if their evil were unjustly passed over, than they would be if their evil were justly punished. Yet it so happens, that thou thinkest those who have impunity are happier than those who are punished.

5. Then said I, Nothing ever appears to me so true as thy arguments appear to me at the times when I hear them. But if I turn myself to the judgment of this people, they not only are unwilling to believe this thy doctrine, but they will not even hear it. Then said he, That is no wonder. Thou knowest that the men who have unsound eyes cannot very easily look at the sun when she shines brightest, nor indeed do they choose to look on fire, or anything bright, though the apple *of the eye* be left. In like manner the sinful minds are blinded by their evil will, so that they are not able to behold the light of bright truth, which is the highest wisdom. But it is with them as with the birds and the beasts which can see better by night than by day. The day blinds and darkens their eyes, and the darkness of the night enlightens them. Therefore the blinded minds think that this is the greatest happiness, that a man should be permitted to do evil, and his deed should be uupunished. For they are not desirous to enquire after every instruction, until they know what is right, but turn to their evil will and seek after it. Therefore I know not to what purpose thou teachest me to the foolish men who never enquire after me. I never speak to them, but I speak to thee, because thou art inclined to seek after me, and labourest more in the pursuit than they do. I care not what they judge. I approve thy judgment more than theirs, for they all look with both eyes, as well with the eyes of the mind, as with *those* of the body, on these earthly things which excessively delight them. But thou alone sometimes lookest with one eye on the heavenly things, *and* with the other thou lookest as yet on these earthly *things*. For the foolish think that every man is as blind as they are, and that no man is able to see what

ithey cannot behold. Such folly is most like *to this*; that a child should be born full sound and full healthy, and so flourishing in all excellencies and virtues during childhood, and afterwards throughout youth, that he becomes capable of every art; and then a little before his middle age, *he* should become blind in both eyes; and also the eyes of the mind should become so blinded, that he remembers nothing which he ever before saw or heard: and nevertheless he should think that he is so capable of everything as he was *when* most capable: and should think that it is with every man as it is with him; and that it seems to every man as it seems to him. But though he were so foolish as to think so, should we all think as he thinks? I think, however, that he should not. But *I* wish to know what thou thinkest concerning the men of whom we before said, that it appeared to us that they were more like wild beasts than men? How much wisdom had they? Methinks, however, they have none.

6. I would now utter to thee a true observation, but I know that this people will not believe it; that is, that those *persons* whom men injure are happier than those are who injure them. Then wondered I at this, and said, I wish that thou wouldest explain to me how it can be so. Then said he, Dost thou understand that every evil-willing man, and every evil-doing *man* is deserving of punishment? Then said I, Clearly enough I understand that. Then said he, Is he not then evil-willing and evil-doing who injures the innocent? Then said I, So it is as thou sayest. Then said he, Dost thou think that they are miserable and unhappy who are deserving of punishment? Then said I, I not only think it, but I know *it* very well. Then said he, If thou wert now to judge, which wouldest thou judge more deserving of punishment, him who injured the innocent, or him who suffered the injury? Then said I, There is no comparison. I would fain help him who was innocent, and oppose him who injured him. Then said he, then in thy opinion, he *is* more miserable who does the evil than he who suffers it. Then said I, This I believe, that every unjust punishment is the evil of him who inflicts it, not of him who suffers it: therefore his evil makes him miserable. And I perceive that this is a very just observation which thou now makest, and very like to those which thou madest before; but I nevertheless know, that this people will nos think so.

7. Then said he, Thou understandest it well. But advocates

now-a-days plead for those who have less need *of it*. *They* plead for those who are injured, and do not plead for those who do the injury. It were more needful to those who injure others, *who are* innocent, that some one should plead for them before the magistrates, and pray that as great hurt might be done to them as they had done to other innocent *persons*. As the sick man has need that some one should lead him to the physician, that he may cure him; so has he who does evil, that some one should lead him to the magistrates, that they may cut off and burn his vices. I do not say that it is wrong that men should help the innocent and defend him, but I say that it is better that we should accuse the guilty; and I say that the defence does no good either to the guilty or to him who pleads for him, if they wish that their evil should not be punished in proportion to its guilt. But I know that if the guilty had any spark of wisdom, and in any measure knew *it*, they would make amends for their crimes by punishment, which might be inflicted on them here in this world. They would not then say that it was punishment, but would say that it was their purification and their amendment, and would seek no advocate, but they would cheerfully suffer the magistrates to punish them according to their own will. Hence no wise man ought to hate any one. No one hates the good except the most foolish of all. Nor is it right that we hate the wicked, but it is more right that we have mercy on him. This, then, is mercy to them, that we punish their vices according to their deservings. No one ought to afflict a person grievously sick, but we should lead him to a physician, that he may cure him. When Wisdom had finished this discourse, then began he again to sing, and thus said:

Chapter XXXIX.

1. Wherefore vex ye your minds with evil hatred, as waves through the wind agitate the sea? Or wherefore upbraid ye your fortune, that she has no power? Or why cannot ye wait for natural death, when he every day hastens towards you? Why cannot ye observe that he seeks every day after birds, and after beasts and after men, and forsakes no track till he seizes that which he pursues? Alas! that unhappy men cannot wait till he comes to them, but anticipate him as wild beasts wish to destroy each other. But it would not be right in men, that any one of them should hate

another. But this would be right, that every one of them should render to another recompense of every work according to his deserts : that is, that we should love the good, as it is right that we should do ; and should have mercy on the wicked, as we before said ; should love the man, and hate his vices, and cut them off as we best may.

2. When he had sung this lay, then was he silent for some time. Then said I, Now I clearly understand that true happiness is founded on the deservings of good men, and misery is founded on the deservings of wicked men. But I will yet say that methinks the happiness of this present life is no little good, and its unhappiness no little evil. For I never said, nor heard of any wise man who would rather be an exile and miserable, and wandering and despised, than wealthy and honourable and powerful, and eminent in his own country. For they say that they can the better make their wisdom perfect and preserve it, if their power be ample over the people that are under them, and also in some measure over those who are in the neighbourhood round about them ; because they are able to repress the wicked, and promote the good. For the good is always to be honoured, both in this present life, and in that to come ; and the wicked, whom man cannot restrain from his evil, is always deserving of punishment both in this world, and in that to come. But I very much wonder why it should so fall out, as it now often does ; that is, that various punishments and manifold misfortunes come to the good, as they should to the wicked ; and the blessings which should be a reward to good men for good works, come to wicked men. Therefore I would now know from thee, how that course of events were approved by thee. I should wonder at it much less, if I knew that it happened by chance, without God's will, and without his knowledgs. But the Almighty God has increased my fear, and my astonishment, by these things. For he sometimes gives felicities to the good, and infelicities to the wicked, as it were right that he always did. Sometimes again he permits that the good have infelicities, and misfortunes in many things ; and the wicked have happiness '; and it frequently happens to them according to their own desire. Hence I cannot think otherwise but that it so happens by chance unless thou still more rationally shew me the contrary. Then

---

5. The prosperity of the wicked caused a perplexity to the royal Psalmist, and almost shook his confidence in God's superintending providence, until, as he tells us, he was further instructed on this subject. See Psalm lxxxiii.

answered he, after a long time, and said, It is no wonder, if any one think that something of this kind happens undesignedly, when he cannot understand and explain, wherefore God so permits. But thou oughtest not to doubt that so good a Creator and Governor of all things, rightly made all that he has made, and rightly judges and rules *it* all, though thou knowest not why he so and so may do.

3. When he had made this speech, then began he to sing, and said : Who of the unlearned wonders not at the course of the sky and its swiftness : how it every day revolves about all this middle earth ? Or who wonders not that some stars have a shorter circuit than others have, as the stars have which we call the waggon's shafts ? They have so short a circuit because they are so near the north end of the axis, on which all the sky turns. Or who is not astonished at this, except those only who know it, that some stars have a longer circuit than others have; and those the longest which revolve mid-ward about the axis, as Boötes does ? And *that* the star Saturn dares not come where it was before, till about thirty winters? Or who wonders not at this, that some stars depart under the sea, as some men think the sun does when she sets ? But she nevertheless is not nearer to the sea, than she is at midday. ! Who is not astonished when the full moon is covered over with darkness ? Or again that the stars shine before the moon and do not shine before the sun ? At this, and many a like thing, they wonder, and wonder not that men and all living creatures have continual and useless enmity with each other. Or why wonder they not at this, that it sometimes thunders, and sometimes begins not ? Or again at the strife of sea and winds, and waves, and land ? Or why ice is formed, and again by the shining of the sun returns to its own nature ? But the inconstant people wonders at that which it most seldom sees, though it be less wonderful; and thinks that that is not the old creation, but has by chance newly happened. But they who are very inquisitive, and endeavour to learn, if God removes from their mind the folly with which it was before covered, then will they not wonder at many *things* which they now wonder at.

4. When Wisdom had sung this lay, then was he silent a little while. Then said I, So it is as thou sayest. But I am still desirous that thou wouldest instruct me somewhat more distinctly concerning the thing which has chiefly troubled my mind, that is,

what I before asked thee. For it was always hitherto thy wont that thou wouldest teach every mind abstruse and unknown things. Then began he to smile, and said to me, Thou urgest me to the greatest argument and the most difficult to explain. This explanation all philosophers have sought, and very diligently laboured about, and scarcely any one has come to the end of the discussion. For it is the nature of the discussion, and of the enquiry, that always when there is one doubt removed then is there an innumerable multitude raised. So men in old tales say, that there was a serpent which had nine heads, and whenever any one of them was cut off, then grew there seven from that one head. Then happened it that the celebrated Hercules came there, who was the son of Jove. Then could not he imagine how he by any art might overcome them, until he surrounded them with wood, and then burned *them* with fire. So is this argument which thou askest about: with difficulty comes any man out of it, if he enter into *it*. He never comes to a clear end unless he have an understanding as sharp as the fire. For he who will enquire concerning this ought first to know what the simple providence of God is, and what fate is, and what happens by chance, and what the divine knowledge is, and the divine predestination, and what the freedom of men is. Now thou mayest perceive how weighty and difficult all this is to explain. But I will nevertheless endeavour to teach thee a little of it, because I have conceived it to be a very powerful remedy for thy sorrow, if thou learn something of this, though it be long for me to teach. For it is near the time when I had intended to begin other work, and I have not yet finished this; and methinks, too, thou art rather weary, and these long discourses appear to thee too lengthy, so that thou art now desirous of *my* songs. I know, too, that they give thee pleasure. But thou must nevertheless bear *with me* for some time. I cannot so readily sing it, nor have I leisure, for it is a very long argument. Then said I, Do as thou wilt.

5. Then began he to speak very far about, as if he intended not that discourse, and nevertheless approached thitherward, and said, All creatures, visible and invisible, still and moving, receive from the immoveable, and from the stedfast, and from the singly-existing God, order, and form, and measure; and therefore it was so ordained, because he knew wherefore he made all that he made. Nothing of that which he has created is useless to him. God dwells

always in the high city of his unity and simplicity. Thence he distributes many and various measures to all his creatures, and thence he governs *them* all. But that which we call God's providence and foreknowledge is *such* while it is with him in his mind, before it is fulfilled, *and* so long as it is designed, but after it is fulfilled then we call it fate. Hence may every man know that these are both two names and two things, providence and fate. Providence is the divine intelligence which is fixed in the high Creator, who foreknows all, how it shall come to pass before it happens. But that which we call fate is God's work, which he every day works, both what we see and what is invisible to us. But the divine providence restrains all creatures, so that they cannot slip from their order. Fate, then, distributes to all creatures, forms, and places, and times, and measures. But fate comes from the mind, and from the providence of Almighty God. He therefore works after his unspeakable providence whatsoever he wills.

6. As every artificer considers, and makes out his work in his mind, before he executes it, and afterwards executes *it* all : this varying fortune which we call fate, proceeds after his providence and after his counsel, as he intends that it should be. Though it appear to us complicated, partly good, *and* partly evil, it is nevertheless to him singly good, because he brings it all to a good end and does for good all that which he does. Afterwards, when it is wrought, we call it fate; before, it was God's providence, and his predestination. He therefore directs fortune, either through good angels, or through the souls of men, or through the life of other creatures, or through the stars of heaven, or through the various deceits of devils; sometimes through one of them, sometimes through them all. But this is evidently known, that the divine predestination is simple, and unchangeable, and governs everything according to order, and fashions everything. Some things, therefore, in this world are subject to fate, others are not at all subject to it. But fate, and all the things which are subject to it, are subject to the divine providence. Concerning this I can mention to thee an example, whereby thou mayest the more clearly understand which men are subject to fate, *and* which are not. All this moving and this changeable creation revolves on the immoveable, and on the stedfast, singly-existing God; and he governs all creatures as he at the beginning had, and still has determined.

7. As on the axle-tree of a waggon the wheel turns, and the axle-tree stands still, and nevertheless supports all the waggon, and regulates all *its* progress ; the wheel turns round, and the nave *being* nearest to the axle-tree goes much more firmly, and more securely than the fellies do; so that the axle-tree may be the highest good, which we call God, and the best men go nearest to God, as the nave goes nearest to the axle-tree; and the middle class *of men* as the spokes. For of every spoke one end is fixed in the nave, and the other in the felly. So is it with respect to the middle class of men. One while he meditates in his mind concerning this earthly life, another while concerning the heavenly : as if he should look with one eye to the heavens, *and* with the other to the earth. As the spokes stick, one end in the felly, *and* the other in the nave, *and* the spoke is midward, equally near to both, though one end be fixed in the nave *and* the other in the felly ; so are the middle class of men in the middle of the spokes, and the better nearer to the nave, and the most numerous class nearer to the fellies. *They* are nevertheless fixed in the nave, and the nave on the axle-tree. But the fellies depend on the spokes, though they wholly roll upon the earth. So do the most numerous class of men *depend* on the middle class, and the middle class on the best, and the best on God. Though the most numerous class turn all their love towards this world, they are not able to dwell there, nor do they come to anything, if they are not in some measure fastened to God, any more than the fellies of the wheel can make any progress if they are not fastened to the spokes, and the spokes to the axle-tree. The fellies are farthest from the axle-tree, therefore they go the most roughly. The nave goes nearest to the axle-tree, therefore it goes the most securely. So do the best men. As they place their love nearer to God, and more despise these earthly things, so are they the more free from care, and are less anxious how fortune may vary, or what it may bring. Provided the nave be always thus secure, the fellies may rest on what they will. And yet the nave is in some measure separated from the axle-tree. As thou mayest perceive that the waggon is much longer secure which is less separated from the axle-tree, so of all men those are most untroubled with the difficulties either of this present life, or of that to come, who are fixed in God ; but as they are farther separated from God, so are they more troubled and afflicted both in mind and in body. Such is what we call fate.

CHAPTER XXXIX.

8. With respect to the divine providence, as argument and reasoning is, compared with the intellect, and such the wheel is, compared with the axle-tree. For the axle-tree regulates all the waggon. In like manner does the divine providence. It moves the sky, and the stars, and makes the earth immoveable, and regulates the four elements, that is, water, and earth, and fire, and air. These it tempers and forms, *and* sometimes again changes their appearance, and brings *them* to another form, and afterwards renews *them*: and nourishes every production, and again hides and preserves *it* when it is grown old, and withered; and again discovers and renews *it*, whensoever he wills. Some philosophers however say, that fate rules both the felicities and the infelicities of every man. But I say, as all Christian men say, that the divine predestination rules over him, not fate. And I know that it decrees everything very rightly; though to unwise men it does not appear so. They think that every thing which fulfils their desire is God. It is no wonder, for they are blinded by the darkness of their sins. But the divine providence understands every thing very rightly, though it seems to us, through our folly, that it goes wrongly; because we cannot perfectly understand it. He however, ordains all very rightly, though to us it sometimes does not appear so.

9. All men, the good as well as the wicked, seek after the highest good. But the wicked are unable to come to the high roof of all goods, for this reason, that they do not seek after it rightly. I know, however, that thou wilt on some occasion say to me, What injustice can be greater, than *that* he should permit it to come to pass, as it sometimes does, that to the good unmixed evil happens in this world, and to the wicked unmixed good, and at other times both mixed, as well to the good as to the wicked? But I ask thee whether thou thinkest that any man is so discerning, that he is able to know aright, what he is, so that he may be neither better nor worse than he thinks him? I know however, that they cannot. Yet it is very often improperly the custom for some persons to say that *a man* is deserving of reward *while* others say that he is deserving of punishment. Though any one may observe what another does, he cannot know what he thinks. Though he may know some *part* of his disposition, yet he cannot *know* it all. I can, moreover, relate to thee an example whereby thou mayest more clearly understand *this*, though unwise

men cannot understand it. That is, Why does the good physician give to this healthy man mild and sweet drink, and to another healthy *man* bitter and strong ? And sometimes also to the sick ; to one mild : to another strong : to one sweet ; to another bitter ? I know that every person who is unacquainted with the art will wonder at it, why they do so. But the physicians wonder not at it, because they know what the others are ignorant of. For they know how to discover, and distinguish the infirmity of each of them; and also the arts which should be *used* with respect to it. What is the health of souls but virtue ? or what is their infirmity but vices ? Who then is a better physician of the soul than he who made it, that is, God ? He honours the good and punishes the wicked. He knows what each is deserving of. It is no wonder, because he from the high roof sees it all ; and thence disposes and metes to each according to his deserts.

10. This, then, we call fate, when the wise God who knows every man's necessity, does or permits anything which we expect not. And yet I may give thee some examples in few words, so far as human reason is able to understand the divine nature. That is, then, that we sometimes know man in one wise, *and* God knows him in another. Sometimes we judge that he is the best, and then God knows that it is not so. When anything comes to any person, either of good or of evil, more than it appears to thee that he deserves, the injustice is not in God, but the want of skill is in thyself, that thou canst not rightly understand it. Yet it often happens that men know a man in the same manner that God knows him. It often happens that many men are so infirm both in mind and body, that they cannot of their own accord do any good, or avoid any evil ; and are moreover so impatient, that they cannot with resignation bear any troubles. Therefore it often happens that God, through his mercy, wills not to impose on them any intolerable affliction, lest they should forsake their innocence and become worse, if they are moved and troubled. Some men are full virtuous in all virtue, and full holy and righteous men. Then seems it to God unjust that he should afflict such ; and moreover death, which is natural to all men to suffer, he makes more tranquil to them than to other men : as formerly a certain wise man [1] said, that the divine power saved his darlings under the

---

1. See Psalm xvii. 8. " Keep me as the apple of an eye," &c.

shadow of his wings, and protected them as carefully as man does the apple of his eye. Many so earnestly endeavour to please God, that they desire of their own accord to suffer manifold troubles, because they desire to have greater honour, and greater fame, and greater dignity with God, than those have who live more pleasantly.

11. Frequently also the power of this world comes to very good men, in order that the power of the wicked may be overthrown. To some men God gives both good and evil mixed, because they earn both. Some he bereaves of their wealth very soon, when they first are happy, lest through long felicities *they should too much exalt themselves and thence become proud. He permits some* to be vexed with severe trouble, that they may learn the virtue of patience by the long affliction. Some fear difficulties more than they need, though they may easily bear them. Some purchase the honourable fame of this present life by their own death, because they think that they have no other price worthy of this fame, except their own life. Some men were formerly unconquerable, so that no one could overcome them with any torment. These set an example to their successors, that they should not be overcome by torments. In these it was evident that they, for their good works, had the strength that man might not overcome them. But the wicked, for their evil works, have been punished beyond measure, in order that the punishments might restrain others from daring to do so, and also might amend those whom they then afflict. It is a very clear token to the wise, that he ought not to love these worldly goods immoderately, because they often come to the worst men. But what shall we say concerning the present wealth, which often comes to the good? What is it else but a token of the future wealth, and a beginning of the reward which God has decreed to him for his good disposition? I suppose also that God gives felicities to many wicked men, because he knows their nature and their disposition *to be* such, that they would not for any troubles be the better, but the worse. But the good physician, that is, God, heals their minds with the wealth, until they learn whence the wealth came to them, and *the man* obeys him, lest he take away the wealth from him, or him from the wealth, and turns his manners to good, and forsakes the vices and the evil which he before through his troubles did. Some indeed are the worse if they have wealth, because they become proud on account of the wealth, and enjoy it without moderation.

12. To many men also these worldly felicities are therefore given, that they may recompence the good for their good, and the wicked for their evil. For the good and the wicked are ever at variance with each other, and also sometimes the wicked are at variance between themselves; and moreover, a wicked man is sometimes at variance with himself. For he knows that he does amiss, and bethinks himself of the retribution, and yet will not cease therefrom, nor indeed suffer himself to repent of it; and therefore through perpetual fear he cannot be reconciled with himself. Frequently it also happens that the wicked forsakes his evil for hatred of some other wicked man, because he would thereby upbraid the other, by avoiding his manners. *He* labours, then, about this as he best may; that *is*, he takes care to be unlike the other; for it is the custom of the divine power to work good from evil. But it is permitted to no man that he should be able to know all that God has decreed, or indeed to recount that which he has wrought. But in these *things* they have enough to understand that the Creator and the Governor of all things, guides and rightly made, all that he made, and has not wrought, nor yet works any evil, but drives away every evil from all his realm. But if thou wilt enquire concerning the supreme government of the Almighty God, then wilt thou not perceive evil in anything, though it now seems to thee that here is much in this middle earth. Since it is just that the good have good reward for their good, and the wicked have punishment for their evil; that is, no evil which is just, but is good. But I perceive that I have wearied thee with this long discourse, wherefore thou art now desirous of *my* songs. And now accept them, for it is the medicine and the drink which thou hast long wished for, that thou mayest more easily receive the instruction.

13. When Wisdom had ended this speech, then began he again to sing, and thus said: If thou desirest with pure mind to understand the supreme government, behold the stars of the high heaven. The heavenly bodies preserve the ancient place in which they were created: so that the fiery sun does not touch that part of the heaven in which the moon moves; nor does the moon touch that part in which the sun moves, so long as she is therein. Nor does the star, which we call Ursa, ever come into the west, though all other stars go with the sky, after the sun to the earth. It is no wonder, for it is very near to the upper end of the axis. But the star,

which we call the evening star, when it is seen westwardly, then betokens it the evening. It then goes after the sun into the earth's shade, till it runs off behind the sun, and comes up before the sun. Then we call it the morning star, because it comes up in the east, and announces the sun's approach. The sun and the moon have divided the day and the night very equally between them, and they reign very harmoniously through divine providence, and unweariedly serve the Almighty God till doomsday. God does not suffer them to be on one side of the heaven, lest they should destroy other creatures. But the peace-loving God regulates and adapts all creatures when they exist together. Sometimes the wet flies *from* the dry. Sometimes he mingles the fire with the cold. Sometimes the light and bright fire goes upwards, and the heavy earth is stationed beneath by the king's command. The earth brings yearly every fruit, and every production; and the hot summer dries and prepares seeds and fruits; and the fruitful harvest brings ripe corn. Hails, and snows, and frequent rain moisten the earth in winter. Hence the earth receives the seed, and causes it to grow in spring. But the Creator of all things nourishes in the earth all growing fruits, and produces *them* all; and hides when he will, and shews when he will, and takes away when he will. While the creatures obey, the Supreme Creator sits on his throne. Thence he guides with reins all creatures. It is no wonder; for he is King, and Lord, and Fountain, and Origin, and Law, and Wisdom, and righteous Judge. He sends all creatures on his errands, and he commands *them* all to come again. If the only stedfast king did not support all creatures, then would they all be dissolved and dispersed, and all creatures would come to naught. But they have in common one love in serving such a Lord, and rejoice because he rules over them. That is no wonder, for they could not else exist, if they served not their author. Then ceased Wisdom the song, and said to me:

Chapter XL.

1. Dost thou now perceive whither this discourse tends? Then said I, Tell me whither it tends. Then said he, I would s a, that every fortune is good, whether it seem good to men, or whether it seem evil to them. Then said I, I think that it perhaps may be

so, though it sometimes appears otherwise to us. Then said he, There is no doubt of this, that every fortune which is just and useful is good; for every fortune, whether it be pleasant, or whether it be unpleasant, comes to the good for this reason, that it may do one of two *things*, that it may either admonish him, in order that he should do better than he did before; or reward him because he before did well. And again, every fortune which comes to the wicked, comes on account of two things, whether it be severe, *or* whether it be pleasant. If severe fortune come to the wicked, then it comes for retribution of his evil, or else for correction, and for admonition, that he should not do so again. Then began I to wonder, and said, This is a perfectly right explanation which thou givest. Then said he, it is as thou sayest. But I am desirous, if thou art willing, that we should turn ourselvss a little while to this people's speech, lest they say that we speak above man's comprehension. Then said I, Speak what thou wilt.

2. Then said he, Dost thou think that that is not good which is useful? Then said I, I think that it is. Then said he, Every fortune is useful which does either *of two things*, either instructs or corrects. Then said I, That is true. Then said he, Adverse fortune is good for those who contend against vices, and are inclined to good. Then said I, I cannot deny it. Then said he, What thinkest thou concerning the good fortune which often comes to good men in this world, as if it were a fore-token of eternal blessings? Can this people say that it is evil fortune? Then smiled I, and said, No man says that, but *every one* says that it is very good, as it moreover is. Then said he, What thinkest thou of the more invisible fortune which often threatens to punish the wicked? Does this people think that this is good fortune? Then said I, They do not think that this is good fortune, but think that it is very miserable. Then said he, Let us beware that we think not as this people think. If we in this respect think what this people think, then shall we forsake all wisdom and all righteousness. Then said I, Why shall we ever the more forsake them? Then said he, Because vulgar men say that every severe and unpleasant fortune is evil. But we should not believe it, since every fortune is good, as we before said, whether it be severe, *or* whether it be pleasant. Then was I afraid, and said, That is true which thou sayest. I know not, however, who dares to mention it to foolish men, for no foolish man can believe it.

CHAPTER XL.

3. Then replied Wisdom sharply, and said, Therefore no wise man ought to fear or lament in whatever wise it may happen to him, or whether severe fortune or agreeable may come to him, any more than the brave man ought to lament about this, how often he must fight. His praise is not the less; but the opinion is, that it is the greater. So is also the wise *man's* reward the greater if more adverse and severe fortune come to him. Therefore no wise man should be desirous of a soft life, if he make account of any virtues, or any honour here in this world, or of eternal life after this world. But every wise man ought to contend both against the severe fortune and against the pleasant, lest he, through the pleasant fortune should be presumptuous, or through the severe, despair. But it is necessary for him that he seek the middle way between the severe fortune and the agreeable; that he may not desire more agreeable fortune or greater security than is fit; nor again, too severe *fortune*, because he is unable to bear excess of either. But it is in their own power which of them they will choose. If, therefore, they desire to find the middle way, then ought they themselves to moderate to themselves the pleasant and the prosperous fortune. Then will God moderate to them the severe fortune, both in this world and in that to-come, so that they may easily bear *it*.

4. Well, O wise men, well! Proceed ye all in the way which the illustrious examples of the good men, and of the men desirous of honour, who were before you, point out to you. O ye weak and idle! why are ye so useless, and so enervated? Why will ye not enquire about the wise men, and about the men desirous of honour, what they were who were before you? And why will ye not, then, after ye have found out their manners, imitate them as best ye may? For they strove after honour in this world, and sought good fame by good works, and set a good example to those who should be after them. Therefore they now dwell above the stars, in everlasting happiness, for their good works.] Here ends the fourth book of Boethius, and begins the fifth.

5. When Wisdom had ended this discourse, then said I, Very right is the doctrine. But I would now remind thee of the manifold instruction which thou before promisedest me concerning the predestination of God. But I wish first to know from thee whether that be aught, which we often hear, that men say concerning some things that it will happen by chance. Then said he, I would

rather that I hastened towards this, that I might perform to thee, what I before promised thee, and might teach thee as short a way as I shortest might find, to thy native country. But this is so far out of our way, out of the way which we intended to travel, that it would be more expedient to return and understand what thou before askedst me. But I *also* fear I should lead thee hither and thither in paths out of thy way, so that thou mightest not again find thy way. It is no wonder if thou shouldest grow weary, if I lead thee beside the way. Then said I, Thou needest not fear that; but I shall be very glad if thou leadest me whither I desire thee. Then said he, I will instruct thee by discourses, as I always did; and I will say to thee, that it is naught that men say, that anything may happen by chance. Because everything comes from certain things, therefore it has not happened by chance : but if it had come from nothing, then it would have happened by chance.

6. Then said I, But whence came the name first ? Then said he, My beloved Aristotle has explained it in the book called Physica. Then said I, How has he explained it ? Then said he, Men said formerly, when anything happened to them unexpectedly, that it happened by chance ; as if any one should dig the earth and find there a hoard of gold, and then say that it had happened by chance. I know, however, that if the digger had not dug the earth, or man had not before hid the gold there, then he would not have found it. Therefore it was not found by chance. But the divine predestination instructed whom he would, that he should hide the gold, and afterwards whom he would, that he should find it.

7. Then said I, I perceive that this is as thou sayest; but I would ask thee whether we have any freedom or any power what we may do, *and* what we may not do ? *or whether* the divine predestination, or fate, compels us to what they will ? Then said he, We have much power. There is no rational creature which has not freedom. Whosoever has reason is able to judge and discern what he ought to desire, and what he ought to shun. And every man has this freedom, that he knows what he wills, *and* what he wills not. And yet all rational creatures have not equal freedom. Angels have right judgments and good will ; and whatever they desire they very easily obtain, because they desire nothing wrong. There is no created being which has freedom and reason, except angels and men. Men have always freedom ; the more as they

lead their mind nearer to divine things: and *they* have so much the less freedom, as they lead the will of their mind nearer to this worldly honour. They have not any freedom when they, of their own accord, subject themselves to vices. But as soon as they turn away their mind from good, so *soon* do they become blind with folly. But one Almighty God exists in his high city, who sees every man's thought, and discerns his words, and his deeds, and renders to every one according to his works. When Wisdom had made this speech, then began he to sing, and thus said:

Chapter XLI.

1. Though Homer, the good poet, who with the Greeks was the best, he was Virgil's master; Virgil was with the Latin men the best, though Homer in his poems [1] greatly praised the nature of the sun and her excellencies, and her brightness, yet she cannot shine upon all creatures, nor those creatures which she may shine upon, can she shine upon all equally, nor shine through *them* all within. But it is not so with the Almighty God, who is the Maker of all creatures. He beholds and sees through all his creatures equally. Him we may call without falsehood the true sun.

2. When Wisdom had sung this lay, then was he silent a little while. Then said I, A certain doubt has troubled me. Then said he, What is that? Then said I, It is this, that thou sayest God gives to every one freedom as well to do good as evil, whichsoever he will; and thou sayest also, that God knows everything before it comes to pass; and thou sayest also, that nothing comes to pass unless God wills and permits it; and thou sayest that it must all proceed as he has ordained. Now I wonder at this, why he permits that wicked men have the freedom that they may do either good or evil, whichsoever they will, since he before knows that they will do evil. Then said he, I can very easily answer thee this enquiry. How would it please thee if there were some very powerful king, and *he* had not any free man in all his realm, but all men slaves? Then said I, I should not think it at all right, or moreover suitable, if men in a state of slavery should serve him. Then said he, How much more unnatural would it be if God had not in all his kingdom any free creatures under his power? Therefore he created two rational creatures free, angels and men. To

these he gave the great gift of freedom, that they might do either good or evil, whichsoever they would. He gave a very sure gift, and a very sure law with the gift, to every man, until his end. That is the freedom, that man may do what he will; and that is the law which renders to every man according to his works, both in this world and in that to come, good or evil, whichsoever he does. And men may attain through this freedom whatsoever they will, except that they cannot avoid death. But they may by good works delay it, so that it may come later: and moreover, they may sometimes defer it till old age, if they do not cease to have good will to good works, that is, good. Then said I, Well hast thou set me right in the doubt, and in the trouble wherein I before was, concerning freedom. But I am still disquieted with much more trouble, almost to despair. Then said he, What is this great disquiet? Then said I, It is concerning the predestination of God. For we sometimes hear say that everything must come to pass as God at the beginning had decreed, *and* that no man can alter it. Now methinks that he does wrong when he honours the good, and also when he punishes the wicked, if it is true that it was so ordained to them that they could not do otherwise. In vain we labour when we pray, and when we fast, or give alms, if we have not therefore more favour than those who in all things walk according to their own will, and run after their bodily lust.

3. Then said he, This is the old complaint, which thou hast long bewailed, and many also before thee; one of whom was a certain Marcus, by another name Tullius, and by a third name he was called Cicero, who was a consul of the Romans. He was a philosopher. He was very much occupied with this same question; but he could not bring it to any end at that time, because their mind was occupied with the desires of this world. But I say to thee, if that is true which ye say, it was a vain command in divine books which God commanded, that man should forsake evil and do good: and again, the saying which he said, *that* as man labours more, so shall he receive greater reward. And I wonder why thou shouldest have forgotten all that we before mentioned. We before said, that the divine predestination wrought all good and no evil; nor decreed to work, nor ever wrought any. Moreover, we proved that to be good, which to vulgar minds seemed evil: that is, that man should afflict or punish any one for his evil. Did we not also say in this same book, that God had decreed to give freedom to

men, and so did; and if they exercised the freedom well, that he would greatly honour them with eternal power; and if they abused the freedom, that he would then punish them with death? He ordained that if they at all sinned through the freedom, they afterwards through the freedom should make amends for it by repentance; and that if any of them were so hard-hearted that he did not repent, he should have just punishment. All creatures he had made servile except angels and men. Because the other creatures are servile, they perform their services till doomsday. But men and angels who are free, forsake their services. How can men say that the divine predestination had decreed what it fulfils not? Or how can they excuse themselves that they should not do good, when it is written, that God will requite every man according to his works? Wherefore, then, should any man be idle, that he work not? Then said I, Thou hast sufficiently relieved me from the doubting of my mind, by the questions I have asked thee. But I would still ask thee a question, which I am perplexed about. Then said he, What is that? Then said I, I am well aware that God knows everything beforehand, both good and evil, before it happens, but I know not whether it all shall unchangeably happen which he knows and has decreed. Then said he, It need not happen unchangeably. But some of it shall happen unchangeably, that is, what shall be our necessity, and shall be his will. But some of it is so arranged, that it is not necessary, and yet hurts not if it happen; nor is there any harm if it do not happen. Consider, now, concerning thyself, whether thou hast so firmly designed anything, that thou thinkest that it never with thy consent may be changed, nor thou exist without *it*. Or whether thou again in any design art so inconsistent, that it aids thee, whether it happen, or whether it happen not. Many a one is there of the things which God knows before it may happen, and knows also that it will hurt his creatures if it happen. He does not know it because he wills that it should happen, but because he wills to provide that it may not happen. Thus a good pilot perceives a great storm of wind before it happens, and gives orders to furl the sail; and moreover, sometimes to lower the mast, and let go the cable, if it before beat against the adverse wind, *and so* provides against the storm.

4. Then said I, Very well hast thou assisted me in this argument; and I wonder why so many wise men have so greatly laboured with the question, and found so little certain. Then said

he, What dost thou so greatly wonder at, so easy as it is to understand? Dost thou not know that many a thing is not understood according as it is, but according to the measure of the understanding which enquires after it? Such is wisdom, that no man in this world can comprehend it such as it is. But every one strives according to the measure of his understanding, that he might comprehend it if he could. But wisdom is able to entirely comprehend us such as we are, though we cannot entirely comprehend it such as it is. For wisdom is God. He sees all our works, both good and evil, before they are done, or even thought of. But he does not compel us the more, so that we necessarily must do good, nor prevent us from doing evil, because he has given us freedom. I can also shew thee some examples, whereby thou mayest more easily understand this discourse. Thou knowest that sight and hearing and feeling perceive the body of a man, and yet they perceive it not alike. The ears perceive that which they hear, and yet they perceive not the body altogether such as it is. The feeling may touch it, and feel that it is a body, but cannot feel whether it be black or white, fair or not fair. But the sight in the first instance, as the eyes look thereon, perceives all the form of the body. But I would still give some explanation, that thou mayest understand that which thou wert wondering at.

5. Then said I, What is that? Then said he, It is that the same man perceives in separate ways what he perceives in others. He perceives it through the eyes separately; through the ears separately; through his imagination separately; through reason separately: through intelligence. Many living creatures are unmoving, as for instance, shell-fishes are, and have, nevertheless, some portion of sense, for they could not otherwise live, if they had no particle of sense. Some can see, some can hear, some *can* feel, some *can* smell. But the moving beasts are more like to men, because they have all which the unmoving have, and also more: that is, that they resemble men; love what they love; and hate what they hate; and fly from what they hate, and seek what they love. But men have all that we before mentioned, and also in addition thereto, the great gift of reason. But angels have intelligence. On this account are the creatures thus formed, that the unmoving may not exalt themselves above the moving, or strive with them; nor the moving above men; nor men above the angels; nor the angels against God. But it is wretched that the greatest part of men do

not look on that which is given them, that is, reason; nor regard that which is above them, that is, what angels and wise men have, namely, intelligence. But most men imitate cattle, inasmuch as they follow worldly lusts, like cattle. But if we had any portion of undoubting intelligence, as angels have, then might we perceive that that intelligence is much better than our reason. Though we contemplate many things, we have little understanding free from doubt. But to the angels there is no doubt of any of the things which they know; therefore is their understanding as much better than our reason, as our reason is better than the understanding of cattle is, or any portion of that intellect which is given them, either to prone [1] cattle, or to those not prone. But let us now elevate our minds, as we highest may, towards the high roof of the supreme intelligence, that thou mayest most readily and most easily come to thine own country, whence thou before camest. Then may thy mind and thy reason see plainly that which it now doubts about, in everything, both concerning the divine foreknowledge, which we have often discoursed about; and concerning our freedom; and concerning all things.

6. When Wisdom had ended this speech, then began he to sing, and thus said; Thou mayest perceive that many an animal moves variously upon the earth, and *they* are of very dissimilar form, and go differently. Some lie with their whole body on the earth, and so go creeping, because neither feet nor wings support them; and some are two-footed, some four-footed, some flying, and all, nevertheless, are inclined downwards towards the earth, and there seek either what they list, or what is needful for them. But man alone goes upright. This betokens that he ought more to direct his thoughts upwards than downwards, lest the mind should be inferior to the body. When Wisdom had sung this lay, then said he:

Chapter XLII.

Therefore we ought with all our powers to enquire concerning God, that we may know what he is. Though it may not be our lot that we should know what he is, we ought, nevertheless, according to the measure of understanding which he gives us, to strive

---

1. By Prone Cattle are meant those animals which have their faces turned towards the earth.

after it: for, as we have already mentioned, man must know every thing according to the measure of his understanding, since we are not able to know everything such as it is. Every creature, however, whether rational or irrational, testifies this, that God is eternal. For never would so many creatures, and so great, and so fair, submit themselves to an inferior being, and to less power, than they all are, nor indeed, to equally great. Then said I, What is eternity? Then said he, Thou askest me about a great *thing*, and difficult to understand. If thou wouldest understand it, thou must first have the eyes of thy mind clean and clear. I cannot conceal from thee anything which I know. Knowest thou that there are three things in this middle earth? One is temporary which has both beginning and end; and I nevertheless know nothing of that which is temporary, neither its beginning nor its end. Another thing is eternal, and has beginning. and has no end; and I know when it begins, and I know that it never will end : that is angels, and men's souls. The third thing is eternal, without end and without beginning, that is, God. Between the three is very great dissimilarity. If we should enquire into the whole of it, then should we come late to the end of this book, or never! But one thing thou must necessarily first know, why God is called the highest eternity. Then said I, Why? Then said he, Because we know very little of that which was before us, except by memory and by enquiry; and still less of that which shall be after us. That alone is truly present to us, which at the time is; but to him all is present, both what was before, and what now is, and what after us shall be; it is all present to him. His riches increase not, nor moreover do they ever diminish. He never recollects anything, because he never forgets anything. He neither seeks nor enquires after anything, because he knows it all. He searches for nothing, because he has lost nothing. He preserves not anything, because nothing can fly from him. He fears nothing, because he has none more powerful, nor indeed any like *him*. He is always giving, and nothing of his ever decreases. He is always Almighty, because he always wills good, and never any evil, where is not need to him of anything. He is always seeing, he never sleeps. He is always equally gracious. He is always eternal, for the time never was when he was not, nor ever will be. He is always free : nor is he compelled to any work. By his divine power, he is everywhere present. His greatness no man can measure; yet this is not to be understood bodily, but spiritually, even as wisdom is, and righteousness, for he is that himself. But what are ye then proud of, or why lift ye up yourselves against so high power? For ye can do nothing against him. For the Eternal and the Almighty always sits on the throne of his power. Thence he is able to see all, and renders to every one with justice according to his works. Therefore it is not in vain that we have hope in God; for he changes not as we do. But pray *ye* to him humbly, for he is very bountiful, and very merciful. Lift up your minds to him, with your hands, and pray for that which is right and is needful to you, for he will not refuse you. Hate, and fly from evil as ye best may. Love virtues, and follow them. Ye have great need that ye always do well, for ye always in the presence of the Eternal and Almighty God, do all that ye do. He beholds it all, and he will recompense it all. Amen.]

[O Lord God Almighty, Creator and Ruler of all creatures, I beseech thee by thy great mercy, and by the sign of the holy cross and by the virginity of Saint Mary, and by the obedience of Saint Michael, and by the love of all thy saints, and their merits; that thou wouldest direct me better than I have done towards thee; and direct me to thy will, and to my soul's need, better than I myself know; and make steadfast my mind to thy will, and to my soul's need; and strengthen me against the temptations of the devil, and remove from me impure lust and all unrighteousness; and defend me against mine enemies, visible, and invisible: and teach me to do thy will, that I may inwardly love thee before all things, with pure mind, and with pure body: for thou art my Creator and my Redeemer, my Help, my Comfort, my Trust, and my Hope. To thee be praise and glory now and for ever, world without end. Amen.]

Errata.—Page 516, line 12, for 'he' read 'we.'   Page 518, line 12, for 'said,' read 'saw.' last line, for ' lxxxiii. ' read ' lxxii.'

THE WORKS

OF

KING ALFRED THE GREAT:

Volume II.—Part ii.

THE WORKS

OF

KING ALFRED THE GREAT:

Volume II.—Part ii.

THE WORKS

OF

KING ALFRED THE GREAT:

Volume II.—Part ii.

I.

KING ALFRED'S
𝔥𝔞𝔫𝔡-𝔟𝔬𝔬𝔨.

ASSER, the king's biographer, asserts, that it was the 11th of November, (St Martin's day, as it appears, either in 886 or 887) when Alfred began himself to write. He had desired his instructor to notice every sentence or date, which he wished to commit to memory. But the royal pupil was so eager, and the extracts from the various books they read together became so numerous, that the little book soon grew to the form and size of a Psalter. The king continually carried it with him, night and day, and therefore called it his *hand-boc* (manual).[1]

As no traces of it have been found since the middle of the 12th century, we can only guess, that it contained passages of the Latin authors, which the king and Asser had read together, before the former began to translate them. But a few other scanty extracts, of no mean interest, have been preserved by two important historians, who must have used either the original itself or a copy of it.

1. FLORENCE OF WORCESTER writes in his Genealogies:[2]

After this reigned Kenter two years, as it is found in the *Sayings of King Alfred*; but, according to the English Chronicle, his son Æscwine reigned for about three years.

---

[1]. Quem Enchiridion suum, id est MANUALEM LIBRUM, nominari voluit, eo quod ad manum illum die noctuque solertissime habebat. Asser. See vol. 1, page 100 of this work.

[2]. FLORENT. WIGORN. in Mon. Hist. Brit. p. 641. Deinde Kenfus [Kenterus] duobus annis secundum DICTA REGIS ALFREDI, juxta Chronicam Anglicam vero filius ejus Æscwinus fere tribus annis regnavit.

2. William of Malmsbury states in his life of Aldhelm, the poet and bishop of Sherburne:[3]

Whoever refers to the *handbook of King Alfred*, will find there, that Kenterus, the father of the blessed Aldhelm, was not the brother of king Ina, but connected with him by the nearest relationship.

3. The same historian describes the style of Aldhelm's poetry with the words of king Alfred:[4]

Being so highly learned, he yet did not neglect the songs of his native tongue; so much so, that on the testimony of *Alfred's book*, which I have mentioned before, nobody had been equal to him at any time in English poetry, in composing as well as singing or reciting it appropriately. At last, *Alfred* mentions, that a popular song, which is still sung in the streets, was composed by Aldhelm, adding the reason why such a man occupied himself with things, which appear to be frivolous. The people at that time being half barbarians and caring very little about church-sermons, used to run home immediately after mass had been chanted. For this reason the holy man would stand on the bridge, which connects the town with the country, and would meet them on their way home like one, whose profession is the art of singing. Having done so more than once, he obtained the favor of the people, who flocked round him. Mixing by this device by-and-by the words of Holy Scripture with his playful ditty, he led the people back to a proper life. For, if he had preferred to act severely and by excommunication, he would never have gained anything by it.

There is scarcely a reason to doubt, that the *Dicta regis Alfredi* and the *Liber manualis* which William of Malmesbury elsewhere[5] calls *handboc* by its Saxon name, were the same memorandum-book, which must have been extant at the time, when Henry I and Stephen reigned over England. It was unquestionably written in Saxon and contained important infor-

---

3. Will. Malmesb. Vita Aldh. ap. Wharton, Angl. Sac. II, p. 3. Qui enim legit MANUALEM LIBRUM REGIS ELFREDI reperiet Kenterum beati Aldhelmi patrem non fuisse regis Inae germanum, sed arctissima necessitudine consanguineum.

4. Will. Malmesb. Vita Aldh: ap. Wharton, Angl. Sac. II, p. 5. Literis itaque ad plenum instructus, nativae quoque linguae non negligebat carmina; adeo ut, teste LIBRO ELFREDI, de quo superius dixi, nulla unquam aetate par ei fuerit quisquam, poesim Anglicam posse facere, tantum componere, eadem apposite vel canere vel dicere. Denique commemorat ELFREDUS carmen triviale, quod adhuc vulgo cantitatur, Aldhelmum fecisse; adjiciens causam qua probet rationabiliter tantum virum his quae videntur frivola institisse; populum eo tempore semi-barbarum, parum divinis sermonibus intentum, statim cantatis missis domos cursitare solitum; ideoque sanctum virum super pontem qui rura et urbem continuat, abeuntibus se opposuisse obicem, quasi artem cantandi professum. Eo plus quam semel facto, plebis favorem et concursum emeritum. Hoc commento sensim inter ludicra verbis scripturarum insertis, cives ad sanitatem reduxisse; qui si severe et cum excommunicatione agendum putasset, profecto profeciasset nihil.

5. De gest. reg. Angl. II, 4, liber proprius, quem patria lingua HANDBOC, id est manualem librum, appellavit.

mation about the early history of the kingdom of Wessex during the 7th and 8th centuries, about Alfred's own ancestors, and that holy man and poet, whose powerful influence upon his rude countrymen was so highly appreciated by the great king.

Alfred was a true friend of historical lore, and it is very probable, that he intended to use these collections for the history of his own country either in his translations of the Latin authors or in an original work. Since all researches to recover some more traces of the Manual have been in vain, its loss will be ever deplored by all, who care for Saxon England and its greatest king.[6]

[6]. In the catalogue of the library of a Norman monastery, preserved in Ms. Bodl. 163, fol. 251, of the time of Henry I, occurs a book under the title, ALFREDI REGIS LIBER ANGLICUS.

AN ESSAY

ON

The Geography of King Alfred the Great,

Taken from his A. S. Version of Orosius:

CONTAINING

ALFRED'S DESCRIPTION OF EUROPE IN THE 9TH CENTURY,

AND HIS ACCOUNT OF

THE VOYAGES OF OHTHERE AND WULFSTAN INTO THE WHITE AND BALTIC SEAS:

BY

R. T. HAMPSON ESQ.

AUTHOR OF "*Medii Ævi Kalend.*" "*Origines Patriciæ,*" &c.

ESSAY ON

KING ALFRED'S GEOGRAPHY,

AND THE NORTHERN VOYAGE OF

OHTHERE AND WULFSTAN.

1. It is justly remarked by the Rev. Dr Bosworth, among the notes to his translation of the Anglo-Saxon OROSIUS, that the geographical notices, relating to Europe, in Section X of the version, are invaluable, " as being the only account of the Germanic nations, written by a contemporary, so early as the ninth century." The same opinion has been formed of it by men of erudition on the continent, particularly in Germany, Denmark, and Sweden ; and the names of Porthan, Raske, Dahlmann[1] and others, who have translated Alfred's " precious fragment of antiquity,'" and investigated the geographical problems which it presents, will ever be associated with that of the truly great monarch of England. I cannot but remember the disappointment, which I experienced, on examining with attention M. D'Anville's learned disquisition on the foundation of the states of Europe as geographically situated before the French revolution at the close of the last century, at finding that this distinguished geographer made no reference to a work, in which Europe in the 9th century, when we first behold the germs of future empires and kingdoms, was already sketched with the vivacity of an actual map.[3] He shews no sign of a knowledge, that there existed such a record of the physical appearance of the continent, and yet, although he might never have seen the Latin translation of the two northern voyages in Alfred's Orosius, in Sir John Spelman's *Vita Ælfredi*, he could scarcely have been ignorant of Hakluyt's Voyages, where

---

[1] Professor Dahlmann, Forschungen auf den Gebiete der Geschichte, Altona, 12mo, 1822.—Prof. Raske, Afhandlinger, Köbenhavn, 8vo, 1834.

[2] Le Comte J. Gräber, La Scandinavie Vengée. p. 36.

[3] D'Anville, Etats formés en Europe après la Chûte de l'Empire Romaine en l'Occident, Paris, 4to, 1774.

they are inserted. It is very true, that D'Anville chiefly occupied himself with Germania and Europe South of the Danube, but one of the Voyagers mentions places on the German shores of the Baltic, about which there was a difficulty, well deserving of elucidation, and he describes very curious customs in the present Pomerania of Prussia.

Owing to the neglect of Saxon literature, which seems to have been one consequence of the destruction of the monastic libraries, so pathetically bewailed by John Bale, about the reign of Edward VI, and also to the superior claims of the treasures of Greece and Rome, no attention appears to have been bestowed, for a long time, on the works of the illustrious Alfred, before the insertion in Hakluyt, in the 16th century, of the narrations, personally and colloquially communicated to the king by the voyagers, Ohthere and Wulfstan.[4] The English versions and notes in that collection of voyages are said to have been written by Lambarde, a learned antiquary and a successful cultivator of Anglo-Saxon literature, who is well known as the author of *Eirenarchia*. Nearly a century afterwards, Sir John Spelman obtained a Latin translation of the northern voyages from certain scholars of Oxford, "Oxonienses Alumni," and either he or they endeavoured to pursue the course and ascertain the places named by Ohthere and Wulfstan.[5] Another century elapsed before the value of these relics of antiquity interpolated by Alfred in the Spanish historian began to be appreciated by the learned. The publication of the whole of the Anglo-Saxon version of this work, with an English translation by the Hon. Daines Barrington, in 1773, seems to have conveyed the information to the public, that, besides these precious voyages, there was an original description, at a very interesting epoch, of that vast portion of Europe, which, from remote antiquity, had been comprised under the general name of Germania. Judge Barrington, a man of great erudition, and well versed in old English and Romance, or ancient French, literature, was not, however, perfectly competent to accomplish the task, which he undertook as a labour of love. Besides frequently mistaking the sense of his author, he has injudiciously adapted some conjectural emendations, and given others. That such a process, well execu-

[4] Hakluyt, Principal Navigations, Voiages, &c. of the English Nation, Vol. I, p. 4, Ed. 1598, fol.
[5] Spelman, Vita Ælfredi Magni, Append. VII. 1678.

ted by means of the two ancient MSS. Lauderdale and Cotton might not be advantageous to students, it would, perhaps, be bold to say, but the person who undertakes the emendations of ancient authors, though profoundly skilled in their languages, encounters the risk of making them say what they never intended. The judge enriched his translation with geographical notes of much research supplied to him by the celebrated Swedish circumnavigator and naturalist J. Reinhold Forster, the associate of Captain James Cook. A map of Europe also prepared by M. Forster accompanied the work. M. Forster's errors are chiefly attributable to the faulty translation by Barrington, but he is surely not to be blamed if his conjectures respecting the sites of places, of which the names had long been forgotten, or had become completely disguised in the vicissitudes of times and nations, are not always happy. Subsequently Forster revised his notes, and corrected the more considerable of his wanderings under the guidance of a flickering light.[6]

After Forster, Langebek, about 1773, inserted the Anglo-Saxon voyages in his collection of Danish historians and others, apparently from Barrington's publication. That he was not an inattentive editor appears from his suggestion, that the name *Cyningesheal* had been corrupted in the Anglo-Saxon MS. into *Sciringesheal*,[7] respecting which Dr Bosworth has removed all uncertainty.

In 1807, Dr Ingram the compiler and translator of the Anglo-Saxon Chronicles, on assuming the chair of Anglo-Saxon professor in the university of Oxford, published a new translation of Alfred's geography of Europe, with numerous explanatory notes,[8] for the most part valuable as well as curious, but, strange to say, he has preserved Barrington's original mistakes of proper names for ordinary words, when a little research among the Latin writers of this age would have shown him that Alfred's *æfeldan* were not "heath-fields" in Jutland, but the Heveldi, a warlike tribe of Slavons on or near the banks of the Havel; and that *wylte* were not "wilds, wealds, wolds," but the Wilti, Wilzi, Weleti, or Welatabi, appellations which in the Latin Chronicles of the times

---

6 History of Discoveries and Voyages in the North, Ed. 1786.
7 Langebek, Scriptorum Rerum Danicarum.
8 Inaugural Lecture, p. 72, 4to, 1807.

about the ninth century, denote another fierce and celebrated tribe of Slavons in the vicinity of the former.

On the continent, as before observed, Sprengel, Porthan, Raske, and Dahlmann have closely investigated the tracts of Ohthere, and Wulfstan, and the statements of Alfred. They have cleared away many of the difficulties, which remained, but in several instances, they ventured on the last resource of a faithful illustrator of the literary relics of antiquity. Where their researches have not rendered them successful in establishing the identity of names and places, they have substituted their own conjectures.

II. It will be the object of the present inquiry to endeavour to ascertain the position of the chief places, named in Alfred's geographical delineation, without violence to the text of the Saxon MS. in the Cotton library. That there are serious errors in the Greek and Latin names of places and persons, towards the middle of the codex, is incontestible, and it is equally clear, that they are attributable, not to the royal translator, but to the penman, who wrote the codex after him. Though this is true, it by no means follows, that he should be as faulty in names, with which, we may presume, if he were a Saxon,[9] he was more familiar, than with those which occur in the account of Alexander's Asiatic conquests, and in some other places. Indeed, it seems that great reliance may be placed upon this important portion of the manuscript, except in one solitary instance, where, by a slight slip of the pen, either in ignorance or inattention, an Anglo-Saxon *s* has become an *r*, as plainly appears from the sense of the context.[10]

9 It is by no means certain, that the Saxon remains in England are in the hand writing of Saxons. For the most part, the mechanical execution of the MSS. is very neat, and may be termed beautiful. It was stated some years ago in the *Athenæum*, as a proof of learning at an early period among the Irish, that the Saxon MSS. were the work of Irish monks. The fact, if true, proves nothing more than their skill in that kind of penmanship, which consists in carefully drawing the outlines of letters upon vellum, and then filling them up with ink colours, by the process which boys in writing schools contemptuously call painting letters. One thing is certain, that some of the MSS. have been written or painted by persons, who had no knowledge of the language, or at least, whose acquaintance with it was very imperfect. It is not unusual to find several words run together as if they were a single word, and often a word of significance is enclosed between the end of the preceding and the beginning of the following, as if the strange compound were one word. The same observation applies to the Latin MSS of the Saxons and to the Greek and Latin passages inserted in their vernacular compositions. Examples of this sort of blundering may be seen in the curious Greek Symbolum in Saxon letters, of which Suicer has given a corrected copy in the second volume of his Thesaur. Antiquit. Eccles.

10 Dr Bosworth, Translation, B. I, ch. 1, § 18.

With the intention of adhering to that which is my original, I am precluded from classifying the different peoples of Europe according to their races, Finns with Finns, Slavons with Slavons, and Teutons with Teutons, because that method will demand too many repetitions to follow Alfred in the course taken by himself; for it must be borne in mind, that for the purpose of his description of Europe, he stations himself on a particular spot, whence, as from a centre, he surveys the countries around him and indicates their situation relatively to each other and to his centre. In like manner, we are constrained to place ourselves on the deck with Ohthere or Wulfstan, and to observe the direction of his hand, as he names the places by which the vessel is sailing. Were we to do otherwise, we should soon be obscured in a mist of doubt, and wrecked in a sea of conjecture. By adopting this method we shall find, that Alfred is exact in his cardinal points, and that he does not miss the bearing of his places, as supposed first by Forster, and afterwards by Rask and Dahlman, who have led themselves into error by considering Alfred to have described the situation of all his places from one and the same spot, where he commenced. There are, however, plain indications that, having filled up a circle, he removed to another centre, until he completed his Germania.

III. What is Alfred's Germania? Professor Rask wishes to exclude from it all Scandinavia, or to consider the whole of a vast region as Gothic. We have to attend to Alfred's boundaries,[11] in order to understand what he considered to be Germania. He has supplied the demarcation of Germania on the north, which Strabo, Tacitus, and later of the ancient writers did not clearly define, left but in vague and imaginary traditions respecting the Hyperboreans. He has understood, and is probably right, that the term Germania comprehended all Europe between the Danube and the extreme north or Frozen ocean, and included a vast region of which very little was previously known beyond the Eastern or Baltic Sea. Alfred's description seems too clear to admit dispute. The words material to the question are these :

11 He calls them *land gemære*, which judge Barrington, with a laudable desire to render Saxon in English words of Saxon origin, translates *land marks*; but *mær*, though perhaps not elsewhere preserved in the same sense among the remains of Anglo-Saxon, appears to be allied to the Lithuanian *miera*, a measure, Polish, *miara*, and Latin *meare*, in the primary sense of measuring out a road. All these are related to the Sanskrit root *ma*, to measure.—See Dr Pott's Etymologische Forschungen, 1, 194, 5, Lemgo, 8vo, 1813.

"From the river Tanais westward to the Rhine, which springs from the Alps, and then runs right northwards on the sea's arm which lies around Britain—

— "And again south to the river Danube whose source is near the Rhine, and afterwards runs eastward against Greece, and out into the Wendel, or Vandal Sea,[12]" near the Mediterranean and Adriatic Gulf—

— "And northward to the ocean [13] which is called Cwen Sea, now the White Sea. Within this are many nations and it is all called Germania."

If the Cwen Sea can be identified with the Baltic, M. Rask's hypothesis, that Scandinavia is not comprised in Alfred's Germania, is an established truth; but it will be found from another part, that, in common with the Germans and Northmen, Alfred

---

12 He invariably names this sea the *Wendel Sea*. Vindelicus Sinus occurs in Orosius for the Adriatic, probably so called from the Illyrian Vindelici. Adam of Bremen speaks of the *Mare Wendile*, meaning the northern *Sinus Venedicus* of the ancients. "Hæc est strata Ottonis Cæsaris usque ad mare novissimum Wendile, quod usque in hodiernum diem ex victoria regis *Ottinsund* appellatur." Page 130.

The Baltic may have been called the Venedic Gulf from the Veneti or Wenden on the German coast; but some of these Slavonians occupied the northern portion of Jutland, and Adam takes their station to be an island, though only a small peninsula, formed between the Lüm Fiord on the south, and Leigestrup on the north. He names this peninsula now called Vendsyssel, and Funen, Wendila: "Finni insula est non modica post eam, quæ Wendila dicitur in ostio Barbari occurrens." p. 132. Before the 5th century, the "Wendla leod," (*Beowulf*, l. 193) or Vandals, had established themselves in Andalusia and Africa. Their seats in the north gave names to the Venedicus Sinus, which Ortelius understands to be that part of the Baltic which is between Prussia, Livonia and Sweden. "Hæc (Gothia) in Venedico sinu ante Chersini ostia jacet, mater Gepidarum, Rugiorum, Vandalorum, Longobardorum, Herulorum, Turcilingorum, Hunnorum, Vinnulorum, Visigothorum, Ostrogothorum, et Gothorum: Infesta et formidata terris nomina." Fortunately we shall have little to do with them. Morisot, Orbis Maritim. l. I, c. 36, p. 258, 9. All over the north, traces of the Vandals are found in the names of cities and districts.

13 The name of ocean in Alfred is *garsecg*, which I always thought to be *gars ecg*, quasi *geardes ecg*, the border or boundary of the land, until I saw in Mr Kemble's note to Beowulf, the derivation *gar secg*, a man armed with a spear, a term referring, he supposes, to some ancient myth. It is certainly possible, that the northmen had a myth similar to that of Neptune with his trident; but it does not seem likely that a poetical or mythological fiction should have furnished the name of the ocean. Undoubtedly our forefathers believed with others still older than themselves, that the earth was a vast plain encompassed by boundless waters: καὶ τὰς Ἡρακλείους στήλας, ὧν ἔξω περιῤῥεῖ τὴν γῆν ὁ ὠκεανός. Aristot. de Mundo, 3. There seems to be little hazard in referring *gar* or *geard*, whence we have *earth*, which is still pronounced *yarth* in Lancashire, to the Gothic *gards*, a house, connected with *gairdan*, to gird, or encircle, in the same language. All these words have the latest signification of inclosure, whether we see them in the form of *gard*, a city, a *yard* or a *garden*, Fr. *jardin*, and I must still believe *garsecg* to be the water boundary of the earth, or, more literally, the edge of the earth defined by the ocean, and so at length, the ocean itself.

gives the name of East Sea to the Baltic in order to distinguish it from the German Ocean, which was the West Sea; and from Ohthere, that he sailed northward from Halogaland in Norway round the North Cape, and along the coast, until he came to a sea running southward into the continent, which he names the Cwen Sea. Consequently, Alfred's Germania extended from the Don on the East, to the German Ocean and the Rhine on the west; and from the Danube, on the south, to the frozen Ocean and the White or Cwen sea, on the north. This definition is so clear, ample, and comprehensive, that we cannot but wonder how so learned a man as Rask, believed that he excluded Scandinavia.

IV. It will now be necessary to place ourselves in each of Alfred's centres of observation, and to accompany him just as he removes himself. His first position is that part of Europe eastward of the Rhine, which in the middle ages was known as Francia Orientalis or eastern Frankland,—the Frankland of the Northmen. At an early period, the term *Franci*, A.-Sax. *Francan*, O. Germ. *Vranken*," denominated a number of tribes, to whom the Romans gave distinct appellations. Schildius quotes an ancient Itinerary Table, containing the following gentile names: —" Chauci, Ampsivarii, Cherusci, Chamavi, qui et Franci"; and lower down he found FRANCIA, which he prints in large characters." It is probable that the tribes thus designated were formed into a league or confederacy similar to that of the Alemanni; but the Franci Orientales, the East Franks of Alfred, comprised also

---

14 It is the name of the country rather than of the people:

Gab her ihme dugidi	*He gave to him nobles,*
fronisc githigni	*pleasing co-thanes,*
stuel hier in Vranken	*a throne here in Frankland.*

SONG ON HLUDWIG'S VICTORY OVER THE NORTHMEN IN 882.

Liess der heidena mann	*He allowed the heathen men*
ober sie lidan	*upon them to be led,*
thiot Vrancono	*the people of Franks*
mannon sin diono.	*to serve with his men (soldiers).*

SAME, ST. 4.

15 Joh. Schild. De Caucis, l. 1, c. 7, p. 48. Lugd. Batav. 1649. It scarcely deserves to be mentioned that there is a short decree of a king of the Franks, in the name of the Franks, commanding the Sicambri to be called Franks for the future. The marginal date, "Anno Mundi 3949," throws a doubt on the authenticity of this instrument, but there is a probability, that some anonymous king of the Franks may have issued such an order after the Christian era. Goldasti Constit. In perial. t. I, p. i, p. 3.

the Bructeri, Sicambri, Attuarii, and Salii. The first mention of the Franks, according to M. D'Anville, occurs in Vopiscus, where that writer is speaking of their defeat near Maience by Aurelian, in the middle of the third century. In 272, Probus repressed the incursions of the Franks, and is said to have been the first emperor who adopted the surname of Francicus. In the 4th century, the name of Francia was given to the country extending from the Rhine to the Weser, and bounded beyond the latter river by Thuringia. Charlemagne farther enlarged this country, and extended Francia from the Saxe to the Danube, and from the Rhine on the west, to the Sala on the east where it enters Thuringen.[16] The Latin addition of Orientalis is probably a translation of the German, and with it had reference to the Frankish settlements in Gaul. Franconofurt is stated in the Annals of Fulda to be the metropolis of the eastern kingdom, "—principalis sedes orientalis regni." D'Anville judiciously observes, that we are not to be surprised at finding Francia Orientalis employed to denominate all Germany; for princes who have reigned there without descending from Charlemagne, have been styled " Reges Francorum Orientalium"; and that it is only since the 13th century, that the name of Francia, previously used in the title of the ancient Frank monarchy, was insensibly lost to it, and used only for the French kings of what had been Francia Orientalis.[17]

Alfred assigns to the east Franks the same situation as Eginhard the secretary of Charlemagne. On a loose computation, for there can be little expectation of certainty in such matters, they appear at this time to have occupied about three thousand square miles.

The etymology of the word Frank, at one time synonymous with freeman, and among us a title of minor nobility, franklin, and in France denominating a species of fief, has been much disputed. It certainly means free only inasmuch as a Frank was free. The Sanskrit *prangch,* does not distinguish them from the other immigrants from Asia. Eccard believes the name to be formed from Urac, as Warangus from Varegus, and he cites the Anglo-Saxon wræc, "latro, exul, ein avanturier, pyrata," to explain Wargus and Urac.[18] Warangus is very probable when

---
16 Eginhard, Vita Karoli Magni.
17 D'Anville, Etats formés en Europe, p. 18.
18 Barker's Germany of Tacitus, c. 39, n. 4. p. 75.

taken in the sense of a military freebooter, when piracy and rapine were deemed honourable occupations. He observes that Snorro uses Fracoland.¹ Both Frackland and Frankariki occur in Iceland Sagas²; and the anonymous author of a manuscript Icelandic and Latin dictionary in the British Museum, gives "*Frackland*, Franconia; item Gallia, vulgo Franka rike; incolæ hic olim Frackar.³

V. Standing on the territory of the East Franks, Alfred places Suabia on their south, across the Danube, and on their South East the Bavarians, to whom he assigns the part which is called Regensburh, still called in modern German, Regensburg, which is situated at the influx of the rivers Danube and Regen, whence the name. In English maps of Germany, it is named Ratisbon, from an older Ratispona, or Radisbona in the Latin Chronicles.

1. The names *Swœfas* in Anglo Saxon, *Schwæbe* in modern German, and *Suevi* in the Roman writers, are too obviously identical to call for remark; but the people so designated, anciently occupied several parts of the continent at the same time.⁴ Their appellation was generic, like that of the body of distinct tribes, who composed the Allemannic confederacy, and the name Suevi was frequently interchanged with that of Allemanni.⁵ Forster observes that the part of Europe indicated by Alfred, and forming a portion of the modern Schwæbe or Suabia was called Allemannia⁶ from the time of Caracalla; but here were also the Catti or Chatti, who, as Tacitus states, composed but one nation or tribe. If we are to dwell on this circumstance, we shall, perhaps, find reason to conclude, either that they were a part of the Suevi, or that they were forced northward, when the Hermanduri took possession of the seats evacuated by the Suevi

---

1 Catal. Theot.   2 Norna, Geats Saga, capp. 3, 4.
3 Ayscough's Collect. MSS. Cod. 4880.
4 Nunc de Suevis dicendum est, quarum non una, ut Chattorum Tencterorumve, gens: majorem enim Germaniæ partem obtinent, propriis adhuc nationibus nominibusque discreti, quanquam in commune *Suevi* vocarentur.—De Mor. Germ. 38. Ed. E H. Barker, 1835. They were probably the Σκουηοι of Strabo, l. vii. whose territories stretched from the Rhine to the Elbe, and of whom a part lived on the other side of the latter river.
5 Suevia, hoc est, Alemannia—Suevorum, hoc est, Alemannorum.—Paul. Warnefrid. de Gest. Longobard. l. II, c. 15. l. III. c. 18. Lugd. Bat. 12mo 1595. Dio Cassius calls them Αλαμβαννοι which in a name almost universally considered to be Germanic, has a very Keltic sound and appearance; for *bann*, in Armoric, is a province, and *alban*, whence *Albani*, is the upper part, while *all mann* is a foreigner, as in the French law phrase *droit d'aubain*, in which aubain is a stranger, who has not been naturalised in the country, in which he resides.

in the Hercynian Forest. The composition of this great league gives probability to the usual derivation of Allemanni, from *all* and *man* in the Teutonic dialects, and if so, it is but a common word appropriated for a gentile appellation; nevertheless, by an extension of the idea common to all ancient and warlike people, the word *man* denotes a soldier, a hero, while *all* was a strengthening augment, so that Allemanni may equally have been an appellation prompted by military vanity. The name, however, is the direct progenitor of the French name of Allemagne applied to the whole of Germany, while the more ancient term designated what is now only a province. The French suggests another Teutonic derivation perfectly conformable to the usage of rude barbarians, and significant of their own opinion of their strength and prowess. Of this name, however, Dr Bosworth has given an account, which will, no doubt, be deemed satisfactory. At all events, it proves that as early as the 6th century, it was believed to relate to the union of many nations. He cites Agathias a Greek writer of that time, who relying on Asinius Quadratus, an Italian, but a careful historian of Germany, says that the Alamanni, Αλαμαννοι, are collected from various nations, and signify that fact in the term by which they denominate themselves.[6] It is more to our purpose to know, that this name is much more ancient, for we are told that a king of the Allemanni in 366 was taken and hanged by the Avari, under Valentinian and Valens.[7]

The Allemannic Confederacy sustained a severe defeat from Hludwig, (Chlodovæus of the Latins, and Clovis of the old French writers; now Louis) and his Franks, at a place called Tolbiac, now Zulpich, near the heights of Cologne, between the Meuse and the Rhine. We may, perhaps, regard this as their principal station. Afterwards they were subjects of Theodoric, king of Austrasia, a name which has direct reference to East Frankland. This monarch was the son of Hludwig. The complete subjugation of the Allemanni was effected by Theodebert, son of Theodoric, and thenceforth Allemannia was a province of the Frankish monarchy, forming a duchy in Suevia, part of Helvetia, and the country of the Grisons.[8]

[6] Dr Bosworth, Origin of the German and English Languages, Sect. VIII, p. 120, note.—As usual, Professor Pott of Berlin exhausts this subject. Etymologische Forschungen II. 523,4.
[7] Ammian. Marcellin. l. XXVII, c. 3, p. 270.
[8] D'Anville, p. 14.

2. Bavaria, on the south east of the east Franks, was considered a part of Slaviana, and by Adam of Bremen is named Beguaria.[9] In much the same manner, Alfred calls the inhabitants Bægǒware, and from some form of the word of this kind, we have the modern German Bayern, Bavaria; but the people themselves were a portion of the Boii, distinguished by mediæval writers with the termination *ar—er—wer—vir*, denoting man, an inhabitant, from another division of the Boii called Boiohemi, who occupied what is now Bohemia. The Boii succumbed to the Marcomanni, under their king Marobudus, in the time of Augustus, and thus their country, Boiohemum, was placed under the rule of the conquerors. From the name of these new occupants of the territory, anciently held by the Boii, Mark, or March-men, i. e. men of the marches or borders, it is probable, that the conquerors came from the mountains which form the boundaries of Boiohemum. However this may be, it is very probable, that the Boioarii or Bægǒware, were those Boii, who then abandoned their seats. That they did so appears from Tacitus, in whose days the Marcomanni were on this spot.[1]

Theodoric, king of the Ostrogoths, is supposed to have taken possession of Rhætia, and a part of Boioaria, for after his death in 526, his son Theodoric king of Austrasia, who was living in 534, aggrandised himself in that country, the first of the laws of which is attested and authorised in his name. In 594 or 596 it was in the power of Childebert, king of the Franks, when he appointed Thessilo or Tassilo 1 to be king of the Bajoarii.[2] Charles Martel led an army into the country in 725, and also in 728, according to the testimony of the Annalists, but as its name does not occur in the partition of the provinces of the Franks between Pepin and Charlemagne, the sons of Martel, we cannot affirm, that Bavaria was entirely subjugated. It is styled a duchy of the Franks under Ogdilo, " dux Bajoariorum," in 743, when a papal legate, charged with an interdict of all war against Ogdilo,

---

9 Longitudo (Slavianæ) autem illa videtur, quæ initium habet ab nostra Hammaburgensi parochia, et porrigitur in orientem, infinitis auctis spaciis, usque in Beguariam, Ungriam, et Græciam.—Ad. Brem. Hist. Eccles. p. 46. Lugd. Batav. 8vo, 1595.

1 Juxta Hermunduros Narisci, ac deinde Marcomanni et Quadi agunt.—Tacit. de M. Germ. 42.

2 His diebus Tassilo, rex Bajoariorum, a Hildeberto constituitur, qui mox, Sclavis superatis, magnam exinde prædam deportavit.—Hermann. Contract. ad ann. 594, 5. Paul. Warnefried gives the date 596.

received for answer, that Bajoaria and her people belonged only to the empire of the Franks.³ Had a similar spirit of manly independence been manifested by the immediate descendents of these warriors, the arrogance of overweening bishops of Rome would not so often have plunged Europe into war, and prolonged the night of ignorance and barbarism to the 16th century. The conclusion from the answer seems to be that the country was then subdued. Tassilo II, the son of Ogdilo, rendered homage to Pepin in 757, and to Charlemagne in 781. After this he appears to have rebelled against the latter monarch. A long decree of the year 788 issued by Charlemagne and his nobles assembled at Ingelheim is extant among the imperial constitutions, collected by Goldast. The "oratores Boiorum," who were introduced, accused him of inciting the Huns and Avares against Charlemagne, and Tassilo, who is here called Thessalonus, was convicted of high treason according to the Salic Law and adjudged to suffer death, and Boiaria was awarded to the king.⁴ Theodo, his son, was made a priest or monk, and Lytopyrga, (a Greek translation of Friburga the wife of Thessalon) was commanded to reside in a convent of nuns; for the above mentioned orators accused her of instigating her husband to his disloyalty. Though some of his party were exiled, he himself seems to have evaded all punishment, for after his duchy had been committed to the administration of counts,⁵ he was pardoned by Charlemagne in 794, and retired to a monastery. Ludovic or Hludwig, the stammerer, gave Bavaria as a kingdom to his son of the same name, who, having had Germany on succeeding his father, is surnamed the Germanic. In 920, Bavaria once more became a duchy, apparently in consequence of the rebellion of Arnulf against Henry III in 918, when it was " Boiariæ regnum locupletissimum " in an imperial diploma.⁶ Regensburh appears to have been called " Reginum, urbs Bojoiariæ " in the Annales Rerum Francorum. Ratispona is found in Mediæval Chronicles,

---

3 Bajoariam Bajoariosque ad Francorum imperium pertinere.—Annal. Metens. ad ann. 143. Ogdilo is named again as " Dux Bajoariorum," in 748. Annal. Eiginhardi ad ann. eund.

4 Secundum legem itaque Salicam ex veteri instituto Thessalonus crimine læsæ majestatis reus peractus, capitali supplicio condemnatur, Boiaria Regi adjudicatur.—Goldasti Constitutiones Imperial. t. I, par. i. p. 18. Francofurt. fol. 1713.

5 Neque provincia quam tenebat Tassilo, ulterius duci, sed comitibus, ad regendum data est.—Eginhard.

6 Goldast, ut supra, p. 211.

and Cluver has "Ratisbona, vulgo Regensburg." According to him, this city was the seat of the counts, who governed Bavaria, and Munich was that of its dukes.'

The river Leck separated Boioaria from Suevia, and it is still the common boundary of Suabia and Bavaria. On the east, Boiaria was bounded by the Ems: on the north, it extended beyond the Danube, and included the district of Egra, which is united to Bavaria at the present day.

VI. Alfred, still pointing from the seat of the East Franks, places the Bohemians directly to the east of them; on the north east, were the Thuringians; on the north the Old Saxons, and on the north west, the Frieslanders.

1. The Bohemians of old have already been mentioned as the probable relations of the Bavarians, who were displaced by the Marcomanni. Tacitus notices that the name of Boiemi preserves the memory of its ancient occupants.[8] Our Alfred calls the inhabitants Beme, which is not very unlike the German Böhmen. The Marcomanni, who had expelled the Boii, were themselves displaced by the Czechi, a Slavonic tribe from the northern shores of the Black Sea. In the time of Charlemagne, the country was governed by Slavonic dukes, when that monarch, in 805, sent an army under his son Charles, who depopulated the whole territory, and slew Lechi, its sovereign. In 904 we find the emperor Ludwig IV enacting favourable customs in the *Leges Portoriæ* then passed, for the Venedi who came to Boiemia for the purpose of merchandise, and also the Venedi, dwelling in Boiaria.' The name of the country, it is scarcely necessary to say, denotes the *home* of the Boii.

In the beginning of the 10th century, territories, which in Alfred's age, were alternately governed by kings, dukes, and counts, appear to have been settled under dukes, for so the rulers are styled in their attestations of the " Statuta et Privilegia Ludorum Equestrium" of the emperor Henry I in 938.

2. The Thuringi, mentioned as the Thyringas by Alfred and

---

7 Introd. Geogr. l. III, c. II, p. 136.
8 Manet adhuc Boiemi nomen, significatque loci veterem memoriam, quamvis mutatis cultoribus.—De M. G. 28.
9 Eodem anno misit imperator exercitum suum cum filio suo Carolo, in terram Sclavorum, qui omnem eorum terram depopulatus, ducem eorum, nomine Lechonem, occidit.— Annal. Caroli Mag. ad ann. 805.
1 Goldast. Const. Imper. I. i. p. 210, n. 6.

the contemporary author of Widsith's geographical catalogue,[2] are said to have originally been a branch of the Dacian Goths settled on the banks of the Niester. They were conjoined in the 4th century with the Victophali and Thaiphali, nations from Scythia.[3] These people appear to have crossed the Danube, and constituted a single province. Ammianus Marcellinus represents the Gothic Thervingi as governed by Judges.[4] The mention of such names as Ermanrichus and Athanaricus among them is almost conclusive of their Gothic extraction.[5] It is very probable, that as the Latin writers constantly confounded the title, philologically equivalent to their rex—*reg-s*—*rek-s*, in Goth *reiks*, O. Germ. *richi*, A.S. *rice*, O. Norse *rick-r* with the personal name, these judges, who were celebrated for military talent and prowess, were kings and generals, like the kings and dukes under the Frank monarchs.

The presence of the Thervingi in the part of Germany, which Alfred indicates, and which still continues to be Thuringia, or the Thüringische Kreis, must be ascribed to some considerable emigration. Their Dacian neighbours appear to have accompanied them, for we find, nearly adjoining the Thuringians, both Ostphali and Westphali:

—Westfalos vocitant in parte manentes
Occidua, quorum non longe terminus amne
A Rheno distat. — Saxo Poeta, de Vita Kar. Magni, ad an. 772.

The termination of these names, *phal, fal,* has given some trouble to those who have sought for a knowledge of the people designated with them. Forster supposes them to have been Saxons; "When the Franks," he says, "had conquered France, the Saxons took possession of their seats even to the Rhine; and those of them who lived on the west shores of the Weser were called Westphali from the old word *fahlen, wahlen, dwalen,* to dwell, because they really were to the west; those who were to the east of the Weser, bore the name of Ostphali, i. e. the east-

---

[2] Incip. Wid sið maðelode, &c. Addit. MSS. Brit. Mus. Cod. 9067. fol. 84b—85b.

[3] Provincia trans Danubium facta in his agris, quos nunc Thaiphali tenent, et Victiphali, et Theruingi.—Eutropius, l. VII.

[4] Athanaricus ea tempestate (A. D. 366) judicem potentissimum—coegit in fugam.—Judicesque etiam nunc eligunt, diuturno bellandi usu spectatos.—Amm. Marcell. l. XXVII. c. 5, p. 377. l. XXXI. c. 2. p. 478.

[5] Ermenrichi nobilissimi regis.—Ib. l. XXI. c. 3. Doctus Athanaricus Thervingorum judex.—Ib. l. XXXI. c. 3. p. 479.

dwellers, and part of them extending to the north along the Weser, were the Angrivarii or Angrii." Yet M. Forster has just mentioned the Thaiphali and Victophali, who occur elsewhere in Europe before the Frank conquest of Gaul. Another derivation, from the old Swedish *fala*, a field or plain, is inapplicable to the latter names, which are Scythian. It seems to belong to a root which is common to Teutonic, Slavic, and Keltic, and which, besides giving rise to designations of peoples and countries, as Wales, Welsh, Gallia, Walloon, Γαλαται, appears in the low Latin *wallus*, a stranger. What was East Frankland, Francia Orientalis, was known as Valland to the Scandinavians, who also gave the same name to Italy.

Theodoric, king of Austrasia, the son of Ludwig or Chlodovæus, conquered the country of the Thuringians, when the Saxons were rewarded for their assistance on this occasion, with the possession of Nord Duringen, or the portion of Thuringia separated from the rest by the river Unstrut, which enters the Sala on its left. From this territory the Saxons preceeded, who accompanied the Longobards into Italy, when their evacuated seats were filled with the Suevi whom Lothaire and Sigebert expelled; and, according to D'Anville, a canton on the left of the Sala, below the Unstrut, was known in the middle ages as Suavia. In a donation of certain privileges in mines by Charlemagne, " Terræ Saxonum et Thuringorum Dominator," in 746, he confers on his sons, Charles and Ludoic, the hereditary right of seeking and digging for gold, silver, and all other metals in the tract, now called Thuringer Wald, or Thuringian Wood, which is defined to be 20 miles in length and 10 in breadth,[1] or about 66 by 33 English, which gives upwards of 2100 square miles. Charlemagne commemorates his subjugation of the Saxons in 777 in a confirmation of the privileges, apparently claimed on that occasion by his Frank and German nobles.[2] This expression seems to deny the Franks to be Germans. When he and Pepin[3] and others use the

[1] Paul, Warnefied, l. I. c. 4.
[2] Tractum regionis in *Saltu* nostro *Thuringiaco* ad 20 milliaria in longitudine et 10 in latitudine jure hereditario possidendum et facultatem damus in territorio districti illius dominatione's quærere et fodere aurum argentumque, atque omnia metalla uti debeatis et possitis. — Goldasti Constit. Imperial. I. i. 17. This diploma is better evidence of the antiquity of the name, Der Thuringer Wald, than the existence of gold and silver mines.
[3] Goldast: III. i. p. 120.

style, "Rex Francorum et Longobardorum," we understand the reason.

In the tenth century, among the dukes and princes of the empire who attested the Statutes of Henry 1, in 938, are John Palatine of Thuringia, and Reiner, provincial count of this province, which in the 11th century was governed by a count from whom descended Ludwig III, who was created Landgrave of Thuringia, in the 12th, the title applying more particularly to the Southern division.

The Angarii, who have been incidentally mentioned, occupied a canton, which separated the West and East Fali, having the Franks to the South, the ocean towards the north and Thuringia to the east. They are considered by the anonymous Saxon writer of the metrical life of Charlemagne, to have made the third branch of his countrymen. Having named the two Fali, he says:

> Inter prædictos media regione morantur
> Angarii populus Saxonum tertius, horum
> Patria Francorum terris sociatur ab austro,
> Oceanoque eadem conjungitur ex aquilone.   Ad ann. 772.

Tacitus says that the Chamavi and Angrivarii, occupied the seats of the Bructeri, near the Tencteri, after they had been nearly extirpated by their neighbours, yet these Angrivarii, in the numerous transitions from place to place, which occurred in those ages, may have removed to this position and have become the Angarii. The celebrated Saxon duke Witekind or Witechind, who long opposed the arms of Charlemagne against the Saxons, governed Angria in 785, according to the inscription on his tomb in Engern, which seems to preserve the ancient name of the people, who probably were eventually absorbed into the tribes whom they separated.

3. The appellation of Old Saxons is obviously employed by Alfred, to distinguish the Germanic Saxons from his own countrymen,[4] and he unquestionably means all the branches of the Saxons occupying the territory between the Eyser and the Weser. Three of these branches have here been separated on account of the ancient conjunction of the two principal with the Thuringii on the banks of the Danube. These people seem to have been the

[4] Paul. Warnefried, l. 1. 9. D' Anville is of opinion that it was the Saxons of Thuringia, who followed the Longobards.

van of the great immigration from Asia, which drove the Kelts to the West of Europe. By the addition of *Eald* old, he in all likelihood points more particularly to the Saxons, called Angli, who occupied Anglen to the south east part of the present duchy of Schleswig. It is the maritime part, or Lower Saxony, and includes all the coast from the Eyder to the Rhine, that is, from Schleswig to Holland, this district seems to have been denominated from a word in the language of the natives, allusive to the chief occupation of the people, who lived by fishing in the sea, when they were not engaged in piracy.[6] *Angel* an angle or hook, is an apparatus for fishing. But the Saxons are found on the Elbe in the time of Ptolemy, A. D. 90, and here it is that the country once called Anglen, whose people in conjunction with the Werini or Warini, established the code of laws, which bears the names of each,[7] was more generally understood by the designation Anglia in the Latin writers. As to their partners in legislation, it is probable that their appellation was early absorbed, like that of the Angarii into the denomination of a more considerable people. This early situation on the corner formed by the Elbe with the German Ocean, seems to denote, as just observed, that they formed the foremost of the columns in the Teutonic invasion, and renders probable Colonel Tod's opinion that the Saxons were originally the Asiatic people indifferently named Sakas and Sakasenas,[8] both in Sanskrit denoting powerful.

The Werini or Warini are unquestionably the Varini of Tacitus, who names the "Angli et Varini," after the Aviones and others, all of whom had rivers and forests. The Varini appear to have resided about the river Warna, the months of which give name to Warnemunde in Lower Saxony and Duchy of Mecklenburg, and not improbably Wern in the circle of Westphalia held

[6] G. Waller of Gottenburg, Travels through the country of the Anglo-Saxons, during the years 1805-6-7. Dr Aikin's Athenæum. 111. 115. The diploma of Charlemagne for the creation of the bishopric of Bremen in 788, mentions particularly the northern part of Saxony as possessing abundance of fish, "Septentrionalem Saxoniæ partem, quæ est piscium ubertate ditissima, et pecorum alendis habetur aptissima." Schildius, de Caucis, l. 1. c. 4. p. 25.

[7] Leges Anglorum et Werinorum, in the large collection of German and Latin Chronicles of Brunswick—Scriptores Rerum Brunsw. 4 tom. fol.

[8] Travels in Rajasthan. He does not seem to have been aware that Sakasena is a compound; *sak*, power, and *sena*, an army, in Sanskrit. This derivation seems much more probable than those from *sassen*, to sit or dwell, *saks* and *seax*, a knife, a short sword, &c. The latter belong to Witechind the Annalist.

some of the Varini.¹ Whether Brunswick denote the wic or vyk of the Varini I cannot determine. In 593, Theodoric, king of the Romans, required the assistance of the kings of the Burgundii, Herculi (Heruli), Varini, and Turugi, against his rival the king of the Franks. The missive commences with a sentiment worthy of a good monarch in a more enlightened age,—" Princeps absque justicia nil aliud profecto est, quam gentium latro publicus.² A law of Charlemagne concerning travelling merchants, speaks of the parts of Saxony up to Bardenwich, and Laurialum— Werinheri.³ The Anglo-Saxon author of the Traveller's Song found Billing chief of the Wernas (" Billing Wernum," l. 50) and Eccard, in a note on the Reudigni of Tacitus, speaks of Weigria and the neighbourhood, as a large space towards the Baltic, between the Angles and the Varini.⁴ It is nevertheless more than probable from their joint code of laws, that they were intimately connected.

Ptolemy's position of the Saxons is on the right hand of the Elbe at its mouth, and he attributes to them some islands adjoining the continent. From this quarter the hordes of Saxon pirates issued, who infested the shores of Gaul and Britain. To these Saxons Pliny's description of the vessels used by the German sea-robbers relates.⁵ They were trunks of single trees excavated, and some were large enough to hold thirty men. Instead of these canoes Apollinaris Sidonius in the 5th century attributes to them coracles or leathern canoes :

—cui pelle salum sulcare Britannum
Ludus, et assuto glaucum mare findere limbo."

That they occupied a long line of sea coast in the 4th or 5th century, appears from the *Notitiæ Romanæ*, where the shores of Belgium and Armorica, as also that of Britain, which is opposite Gaul, are designated *Littus Saxonicum*; but when Boniface, bishop of Maience, in the middle of the 8th century, calls Britain

1 See infra and Procopius in the note.
2 Goldast. I. i, 13.
3 Capitul. Caroli M. c. 7.
4 In Barker's Germania of Tacitus, cap. 39, n. 4.
5 Germaniæ prædones singulis singulis arboribus cavatis, quarum quædam et triginta homines ferunt,—Plin. l. xvi. c. 40. In three long ships, says Paul Warnefried, the Saxons invaded England, about the year 430.— De Gestis Longobard. l. xiv., and in two such ships, Ragnar Loðbrog invaded Northumbria : Enn betra er ad hallda langskipum til hafna enn knorum.—Saga of Ragnar L. c. 14.

Saxoniam Transmarinam, he unquestionably alludes to it as Saxon England.⁶

It is not certain whether the Saxon territory were enclosed within its first limits, when the Britons summoned the Saxons and Angles to defend them against the Picts or Scots, about 428, or whether it had then been extended beyond the Elbe. Adam of Bremen, indeed, speaks of the Saxons as having originally their seat about the Rhine, and being called Angli, of whom a part expelled the Romans from Britain.⁷ As he wrote six hundred years after the event, he has, perhaps, mistaken the occupants of that part of Littus Saxonicum for Angli, or the Angli really had become possessed of the country near the Rhine; but the testimony of Ptolemy to their occupancy near the Elbe so early as 90 is sufficient. We have it from a subsequent passage in Adam, and from Witechind, that a part of the Saxons obtained North Thuringia for assisting the king of Austrasia in his conquest of the whole of that country, as before mentioned. In 553, Hlothaire, king of the Franks, subdued the rebellious Saxons with a great slaughter near the Weser;⁸ which not improbably prepared the survivers for their great migration, in 560, when twenty thousand of them, with their wives and children, accompanied Alboin, king of the Longobards, in his expedition to Italy.⁹ It may be inferred, that they were a populous nation from the anonymous Saxon, who wrote the life of Charlemagne in the reign of Charles the Fat, and who assigns them a territory, at that time extending towards the ocean on the north, to the Rhine on the South, where they were named the Westfali. Their eastern limit, occupied by the Ostfali, otherwise called Osterliudi, reached the confines of the Slavic tribes in the angle of the Weissel or Vistula and the Baltic:

————regionem solis ad ortum
Inhabitant Osterliudi, quos nomine quidam
Ostvalos alio vocitant, confinia quorum
Infestant conjuncta suis gens perfida Sclavi.
POETA SAXO ad ann. 772.

6. Bonifac. ep. Moguntini Epist. ad Zachariam papam.
7 Saxones primo circa Rhenum sedes habebant, et vocati sunt Angli, &c. Altera pars Thuringiam oppugnans tenuit eam regionem.—Hist. Eccles. Bremens. p. 6.
8 Hlotarius Francorum rex Saxones rebellatis juxta Wiseram fluvium magna cæde domuit.—Marcellin. Comes in Chron. a dann. 553.
9 Supra vi. 2.

Frequent hostilities arose between the Saxons and the Franks, but Charlemagne finally subdued the former and blended them with the empire.[1] With this arrangement, however, they were not satisfied, for under the emperor Ludovic, whom the French term Louis le Debonnaire, they obtained permission to return to their former abodes, part of which on the East they found occupied by the North Albingi, whose capital was Hammaburg, now Hamburg, and whom some have considered to be a tribe of Saxons. It was necessary to notice these changes, for Mr Forster states that the position, which Alfred assigns the Old Saxons, is their ancient seat on the East of Elbe; but without confining them to this narrow space, Alfred is perfectly consistent and correct in stating them to be north of the East Franks. He gives no other indication of their geographical position.

4. The Frieslanders are placed by Alfred to the north west of the East Franks, where they had been found by Ptolemy, who states that the Frisii held the parts above the Bructeri, adjacent to the ocean, up to the river Amisia [2] which is now the Eems. Here they are also found in the Annals and Chronicles of the middle ages, and here they continue almost a solitary instance of immobility amidst the numerous and frequent vicissitudes of situation, experienced by the other people of Europe. It is not improbable, that they partook of the noble character, which Tacitus gives to their next neighbours, the Chauci, north of the space now denominated Holland, though a part of the latter, the Chauci Majores, lay between the Elbe and the Weser. Without being powerless, they were contented and peaceable, never provoking wars by rapine.[3] Of such a people we may not expect to find many notices in monkish chronicles. A record, which though unquestionably of high antiquity, is rendered doubtful by its marginal date, "Ann. Christi 11," states that Clogis I king of the Franks, in the 10th year of his reign, created his second son

---

1 According to the Frank Annals, for 804, all the Saxons, with their wives and children, living across the Elbe and in Wihmuodi, were sent by Charlemagne into Frankland, and their vacated seats given to the Slavic people named Abotriti.—Æstate in Saxonicum ducato exercitu, omnes qui trans Albiam et in Wihmuodi habitabant Saxones cum mulieribus et infantibus transtulit in Franciam, et pagos transalbinos Abotrides dedit,—Annal. Rerum Francorum, ad ann. 804. So also Eiginhard at this year.

2 $T\eta\nu$ δε παρωκεανιτην κατεχουσιν ὑπερ μεν τους Βρουκτερους οἱ Φρεισιοι, μεχρι του Ἀμισιου ποταμου. Ptol. l. II.

3 De Mor. Germ. 35.

Phrisus duke of Phrisia, to repel the incursions of the Ambrians and Orchadians; and that afterwards he permitted the Phrisians to raise Phrisus to the rank of king, so that all future kings should be subject to the Franks, paying to them an annual tribute of 240 oxen, 20 talents of pure butter, and 3000 royal cheeses.⁴ Some such agreement may have been made during the progress of Charlemagne or his sons, but unfortunately Melchio Goldast, who has copied it, scarcely ever indicates his authorities Under Claudius, Drusus the first Roman who reached the northern ocean, having crossed the Rhine, subdued the Frisians, erected immense works, which were still called *Drusinæ* in the second century,⁵ and advancing thence across a lake which is not named, but which may have been the mouth of the Weser, against the Chauci (Majores?) he was imperilled by the ebb of the tide which left his ships on dry land.⁶

In 728 Charles Martel subdued the Frisians and reduced their country to a duchy of the Frank monarchy, their leader Ratbod taking refuge among the Danes. Mention is made of the duchy of Frisia in 839 when it extended to the Meuse.⁷ The Danes and Normans in the same century were masters of the country, and so continued until the 10th century, when the Frisians expelled them, and Charles the Simple, as prince of Austrasia, in 913, extended the dominion of Diedrick, count of Friesland, beyond the Rhine. In 938 we find on the same diploma, "Arnoldus II comes Flandriæ," "Arnoldus comes Hollandiæ," and "Theodoricus II comes Hollandiæ."⁸ Probably the second Arnold was count, earl, or graaf of Frisia; for a Diederik was the first "Graaf van Holland," and in this century too, which, in 38 years, gives a Diederik II.⁹ A canal called Kinnen, which gives name to the district of Kinnenser Land, separated what is properly Holland from West Friesland. The oldest Dutch writers in their own language give the name of Ollant to the former; but Hol-

---

4 Caseorum Regalium tria millia.—Constit. Imper. I. i. 3.
5 Sueton. Claud. I.
6 Ες την Χαυκιδα δια της λιμνης εμβαλων, εκινδυνευσε, των πλοιων επι της του ωκεανου παλιρροιας επιξηρου γενομενων. Dio Cass. l. 54.
7 Ducatus Fresiæ usque ad Mosam. Annal. Sci Bertini ad ann. 839.
8 Goldast. 1. i. 215.
9 Jan Wagenaar, Vaderlandsche Historie de Vereenijde Nederlanden, 11 Afd. s. 51. Amsterdam 8vo. 1792.

land is probably the true denomination, for *hol land* signifies low, or rather hollow, that is, concave land.

VII. After the mention of Friesland, we have from Alfred the following: " From thence north west is the country called Angle and Zealand, and some part of Denmark."

Mr Forster, probably not observing that Alfred refers the position of the Angles to that of the East Franks, thinks that " it is very probable that this point of the compass must be wrong in the original, or that the good king must be mistaken," and he observes that " Angle is to the north East of Old Saxony, together with Sillende or Zealand and part of Denmark." When the Old Saxons occupied both sides of the Elbe, the Angels and Denmark lay directly to the north of them between the degrees of longitude 9 and 10 from Greenwich, and $26\frac{1}{2}$ and $27\frac{1}{2}$ from Ferro, while the East Franks lay from 7 to $11\frac{1}{2}$ or thereabouts; but certainly far enough in this direction to reconcile Alfred's geography with the true position of Angle and Denmark, without having to advert to the occupation of the sea coast by the Angli south of that which is deemed their proper country. If Sillende be Zealand, which appears probable from similarity of sound, the compass is still right as regards the north from the East of the East Franks, and we cannot expect the nicety of the 19th century from an island monarch statesman and warrior of the ninth. The marvel is that he did so much and so well in matters which are not often usual to persons in his station and difficulties.

1. According to Professor Dahlmann, two tribes of Angles are mentioned: the Angles of the old times, who embraced the middle station, and the Angles who before their migration to Britain were seated at Schleswig, in Jutland, Funen and the smaller islands on the left of the great gulf in Cattegat and the East Sea. This is shown at the conclusion of Ohthere's voyage, where the remark, that " The Angles dwelt on the land before they came hither" is evidently inserted by the Anglo-Saxon translator.[1] By this Saxo Grammaticus is justified in placing Dan and Angle at the head of Danish history. Danes and Angles were the old inhabitants of the land now called Denmark. Those in the east as far as Schonen and Halland; these in the

---

[1] There appears to be no just reason to suppose that Ohthere, a man of importance and manifestly a traveller, did not speak Anglo Saxon to " his hlaforde," king Alfred. The difference between old Norrsk and the Saxon is not such as to present any difficulty.

west, the boundaries of the Great Belt. But in Alfred's time, the western lands were no longer named from the Angles; for after the great migration to Britain, the Danes had entered, and were there called south Danes with the common appellation, which they had received from the English. We would rather set the west Danes in opposition to the east Danes, and this opposition certainly appears in the Anglo-Saxon,[1] but at one time, the ancient Danes were confounded with the idea of the powerful people of the Scandinavian continent, which goes far up into the north, of whom Ptolemy knew the Danes, and, therefore, saw in those Danes, who had occupied the seats of the recently emigrated Angles, the offspring of the north, who had become Southlanders. At that time, the situation and name of Angles were limited to a small south Danish country, probably not larger than that which extends from Schlei northwards as far as Flendsburg. It still bears the name. That the land was preeminently called Denmark, and formed a kingdom, which lay partly on the Scandinavian continent (Halland and Schonen) and partly on the islands of Zealand, Fiona, Falster, Seland, and Langaland, is granted at the end of the voyage of Ohthere and beginning of that of Wulfstan.[2]

It is a remark of Dr Ingram, that Alfred is the earliest writer who uses the name, Dena-mark, the country of the Danes; but *mark*, as before observed in speaking of the Marcomanni, who took possession of the lands belonging to the Boii, is a boundary, the march of our own language, when we speak of the lords of the welsh marchers, or lords marchers. In the ancient Sagas, Jutland is Reidgotaland[4] as well as Jötaland, which was sometimes used to designate Finnland.[5] As to the distinction between the east and west Danes in Beowulf, remarked by M. Dahlmann, it does not seem to be of much moment, since we have equally the south and west Danes, besides the Hring and Gar Danes in the same composition.[6] The Geata leod, people of the Geats,

---
2 See that highly imaginative fiction, called Beowulf, edited by Thorkelin, II, 31 and 32. Dahlmann.
3 Dahlmann, Forschungen, &c. pp. 431, 432.
4 Hervarar Saga, XI Kap.
5 Jotland, hodie Jylland, (evidently an error of the scribe in the Icelandic MS. for Jytland; interdum Finnland.—Icelandic and Lat. Dict. MS. Aynscough's Collect. Cod. 4880, Brit. Mus. The latter is the Totunheimur of Hervarar Saga, the home or region of Eotenas of the Saxons, the Jutes of the Scandinavians, and the Goths of southern Europans.
6 In Mr Kemble's excellent edition of this poem, the several epithets will be found in the lines numbered as follows,

Jutes, or Goths, also perhaps in the peninsula, may subsequently have given rise to the name of Jutland, Julland and Jytland, as well as to the more ancient appellation of Reid-Gota-Land. With this variety, we may conclude, that the Danes were anciently distinguished by their situation according to the cardinal points of the compass, just as we might distinguish them by merely signifying their situation, and not regarding them as politically separated in that manner, while Ring and Gar Danes may really denote clans. As to the rest, Geat, Got, Jot or Jut, which are found in Pliny's Cod-anus Sinus, they are the generic denomination of both the Danes and a part of the Swedes of ancient times.

An observation by Prof. Dahlmann respecting the old name of Reidgotaland, deserves notice. He says that Ohthere mentions Jutland, and Sellende, and that, as he was wanting a common name, probably Funen, Fiona, might be included in that of Jutland, and that perhaps hence came the old distinction of the Island of Jutland, and Reit Jutland, i. e. continental Jutland. And perhaps, it may be explained, for the Jutish law of king Waldemar II was valid not only in the whole of Jutland at first, but also in Funen.[7] The Icelandic *reid* denotes riding, and used with the name of a place may be equivalent to our riding of a county, as the ridings of Yorkshire for instance, signifying a division, probably such as might be traversed on horseback in a day. This observation is made, not to controvert Dahlmann, but to endeavour to show that Olaus Verelius had some ground for conjecturing *reid,* in Reidgotaland, was intended to mean *equitatio.*[8]

East Dene 779, 1225, 1650.
West   763, 3456.
North   1650.
South   921, 3988, &c.
Hring   232, 2559, 3555.
Gar   1195.

There may be other places which have been overlooked.

7 Dahlmann, Forschung. p. 436.

8 See Dr Bosworth's note 56 sect. 8, p. 15. where we have Hreth Goths—the fierce, i.e. warlike Goths.

"Ryding in Yorkshire is a third part of the county, being of vast extent, and called rydings, shires, hundreds, and wapentakes, which were formerly set out *per ambulationem,* as bounding them by processions made on foote. This being of so vast extent, was performed by processions made on horseback, including divers hundreds and shires, and so thereupon take upon them the name of ryding, scil. West Ryding, East Ryding, South Ryding."—Dr Kuerden (i. e. Jackson of Cuerden) 4to MS. fol. 358. Chetham Library, Manchester; a MS. of the 17th century, part of an intended History of Lancashire, of which one vol. is in the Brit. Museum, and four or five in the Herald's College, all in MS

2. Hitherto there has been no difficulty in determining the places named in the Anglo-Saxon, but now we have Sillende, which, as Dahlman observes, we naturally suppose at first to be the island of Zealand. This island however lies to the north east of Angle and old Saxony, and to the direct north of the utmost eastern limit attained by the eastern Franks in the 9th century.

Alfred names Sillende thrice; and in this place, according to its connection with Angle and part of Denmark ("sume dæl Dena"), it seems to be also a part of Jutland; but at the end of Ohthere's voyage, it twice occurs in such a manner, that it can denote only the island of Zealand. We do not find errors in the description of Europe, in regard to countries, about which no doubt can possibly be entertained, and, therefore, we have a probable reason for placing confidence in the royal geographer where we are unable to confirm his statements from ancient writings. It is possible that a portion of Jutland, whose Danish and Jutish inhabitants were variously denominated in one and the same Anglo Saxon work, may have been designated by a name resembling Sillende.

Since Professor Dahlmann has taken pains with this difficulty, it may be well to accept his assistance. The following translated extract is the purport of what he says respecting Sillende, under the title "Sillende-Hetvare."

"What the word Sillende signifies occasions uncommon difficulty. One naturally thinks of the island of Zealand at first, but it is also clear, when it is first named by Alfred, it is not suitable. He gives it as the lands which are on the borders of the Saxons: how could the island called Zealand, be named with them, when, also, it nowhere lies seaward opposite to the Saxons? and, at all events, how could it be placed towards the north west? Truly, king Alfred deviates somewhat from the true situation of the countries of the world in his account of the nations in the east sea, seeing that he places the north somewhat too far towards the north east (Porthan), by which the Cimbrian peninsula seems to be on the north west of the Saxons, for it lies on the north of the Shem, and the land of the Obotriti in the north; but never can Zealand appear in a north western direction. Besides, when Ohthere, at the end of his account, mentions Sillende, he by no means names it as an island, and it does not suit that of Zealand. There is no question that he chose the broad sea course of the great Belt. It was the nearest for his object Hadeby, and hence probably it was the common one to the Norwegians,[9] and only when he took the course could it be said, that in the last two days of his voyage, he had the islands belonging to Denmark on his larboard side. Porthan first clearly acknowledged that Zealand could not be intended, and that Sillende should be in the southern part of the Cimbrian Peninsula; and that the present men of Sleswick should have filled up the middle spaces which the Friesians here, and the Angles there, left vacant. Still, however, a number of the Danes (sum dæl Dena) found a place here, provided that Jutland be not understood in this case. Ptolemy also adduces the Sigulonians among many nations of the Cimbrian Chersonesus, which can be placed here,[1] and a Frankish annalist of the century of Alfred describes the warriors, who, after the passage of the Eider, came into the Danish land, and into a district called Sinlende.[2] Who will say whether this signifies Südland, the first germ of the appellation of South Jutland or Schleiland? If the latter be adopted, then probably the Hetvarians of the Anglo-Saxon poem of Beowulf, for the greater part imaginary, can be appealed to and serve as an explanation.[3]

We are not here called upon to discuss the question of the Hetvare. But with respect to the objection, that Ohthere does not mean Zealand by Sillende, it may be answered that if he sailed through the Skiöldungahaff, coasting the southwest of Scandinavia, then Gotland or Jutland, and next Sillende or the island of Zealand, did lie, as he says, on his starboard, or right, before he came to Hæthe. There will thus appear to have been an island and a part of Jutland, to which the same name of Sillende has been negligently applied in the Anglo-Saxon."[4]

---

9 Rask maintains as an undisputed thing, that in the olden time the traffic of the Norwegians was through the Great Belt. I admit that we swerve from the demonstrating passages, and besides I have not been able to find any proof in the History of Commerce by Suhn, G. L. Baslen, and the valuable Dissertations on the Sound Toll. (Dissertations, Vol. II). *Dahlmann.*

1 Ptolem. Geogr. Ed. 1805. p. 53.
2 Vita Hlud. p. 563.
3 Dahlmann, Forsch. pp 437—439
4 Its name in the preface of Saxo Grammaticus is Sialandia: in the prose Edda, Sælun *Fab.*2. As to its signification, there are two old explanations: by some it is called Sæd

This reasoning is very ingenious, but it fails to convince me; and I hold with Forster and Dr Bosworth (p. 3 n. 16, p. 15 n. 56) that Sillende can be only Zeeland; but it is impossible to deny that there is a clerical error in the MS. If we take the eastern limit of Francia Orientalis, Zealand lies directly to the north, and if, which seems to be the meaning, we take Friesland ("From thence, &c." p. 3) it lies to the north east, and it is also north east of the Saxons. So far it is evident we have west for east. But accompanying Ohthere, we shall be satisfied of the identity of Sillende and Zealand. Omitting, at present, what is said of Sciringesheal, where the voyager first mentions Sillende, we find him stating, that two days before he came to Haddeby on the coast of Schleswig, he had Julland, Zealand, and many islands on his right. If, then, he sailed from some part called Sciringesheal, which is supposed to be about the southern extremity, he would necessarily throughout the voyage to Haddeby have Julland and Zealand on his right, for they would lie to his north. All the difficulty, and it is by no means inconsiderable, if reliance be placed upon the Saxon scribe, who has blundered most egregiously in a vast number of places, arises from the substitution of *west* for *east* in the compound with *north*.

VIII. In the Anglo Saxon, it is said after "some part of Denmark," that "to the north are the Afdrede, and north east are the Wylte, who are called Hæfeldan."

1. If Forster, Porthan, and Dahlmann are right in computing Alfred's indications of the geographical site of a country from the place last named, he must be in error with respect to the Afdrede, or Apdrede, as he elsewhere calls the same people, who are the Obotriti and Abotritæ of the Latin writers, and whose territory was the northern part of the present duchy of Mecklenburg in the west of Swedish Pomerania, extending from about $11\frac{1}{2}$ to $12\frac{1}{2}$ longitude from Greenwich, being there bounded by the wide mouths of a river on each side.[1] They were, therefore

land, the land of seed; by others, Seeland, from the surrounding sea.—Ælnoth de Vita Cnuti, p. 17.

[1] Apud Michlinburg, civitatem Obitritorum.—Ad. Brem. p. 110. Helmold also speaks of their "civitas Mikilinburg," and D'Anville and others suppose that the Abotriti had a city so called. But civitas may mean a state, and Michelinburg may have been a large castle which left its name to the duchy. Certainly there is no other trace of a city which was so stu rd in the territory of these people. Besides they were Slavons, while Michilenburg is German, and both Adam and Helmold wrote when the country was possessed by Germans.

on the south east of Angle and some part of Denmark; but at this time, a portion of the Obotriti occupied the seats of the Saxons across the Elbe and in a place named Wihmuodi² in the district of Bremen, on the Wirra.³ This, however, cannot be his meaning, for they would be eastward. The situation given to the Obotriti and Wilti is true only in regard to the East Franks, whose eastern extremity, or what is thought to be probably so, is south of the Obotriti. Very great nicety cannot be expected, when nations were in continual motion, and writers neither were exact, nor, if they wished to be, were possessed of the means. We shall soon find that Alfred abandons this post of observation.

The Abotriti were a Slavic people, who appear to have divided themselves at an unknown period; for besides these on the shores of the Baltic, there was a nation also called both Abotriti and Obotritæ, on the banks of the Danube. The latter, in 824, sent a deputation to the emperor Hludwig, better known as Louis le Debonnaire. According to Eiginhard, who records this mission, they were commonly called Prædecenti, and inhabited Dacia, adjacent to the Danube; and on the confines of the Bulgarians. It would appear from the different situations, some very remote from each other, in which we find people of the same name, the loss of gentile appellations, once familiarly mentioned in ancient compositions, such as the Sagas, Beowulf, the Scop's Tale or Traveller's song, and others, and also in medieval chronicles, that at one time, commencing before the Christian era, and not ending exactly with the establishment of the Frank monarchy, the vast plains and forests of Germania were continually traversed by restless hordes of wanderers, some of whom must have separated from the parent stock, and either they or their kindred have been immerged and lost to knowledge in other tribes. The 9th century appears to be that in which the principal or strongest of nomadic tribes and portions of tribes began to find stations, or attempted to establish themselves in permanent resting places. It is on this account, and the success which attended many of their efforts, that the Geography of our

2 Supra, VI, 2, n. 2.
3 In a præcept of Charlemagne respecting provincial tributes issued in 788, we have the words—" in Vuigmodia in loco Bremon vocato super fluvium Viraam—" and again " Huic parochiæ decem pagos subjecimus, quos etiam adjectis eorum antiquis vocabulis et divisionibus, in duas redigimus provincias, his nominibus appellantes, Vigmodiam et Lorgoe."—Goldast. Const. Imperial. t. III,. p. iii, p. 137.

great Alfred is particularly valuable to Europeans. Oriental antiquaries might also find it interesting. The descendants of those who were once the Heneti, a people of Paphlagonia, have now their chief seats in Magdeburg and Venice, are found in the neighbourhood of the Bothnic Gulf and north Jutland, in the central parts of Europe, are known to have penetrated into Africa, and have left traces of their presence in Spain.

With respect to the southern branch of the Obotriti, D'Anville observes: "I shall not conjecture that Bodrog, the name of a district in Lower Hungary between the Danube and the Teisse, may have come from these Abotrites; but then, I find the denomination of Præden in that of Pardan, which is preserved in a canton of the Banat of Temeswar." The northern Abotriti, as has been mentioned, surrendered to Charlemagne, and assisted him in his expedition against the Saxons on the north of the Elbe, whose lands were abandoned to them, and who, in the 10th century, obtained permission to return to their ancient abodes, were probably the two races intermingled and the Abotritic name became lost as that of an existing people. According to D'Anville, that name once extended up the Elbe to the south, and to the little river Pene towards the east. As the Peene, which empties itself into the Frische or Stelliner Haff, rises in Mecklinburg, the tract described is of considerable extent.

2. The Wylte, who are called Hæfeldan, were another of the numerous tribes of Slavons, settled in this part of the Baltic coast. Their country in Alfred's time was what now is Swedish Pomerania, on the east of the Abotrites. The anonymous Saxon poet, who wrote towards the end of the 9th century, describes their situation with more particularity than Alfred:

> Gens est Slavorum Wilti cognomine dicta,
> Proxima litoribus quæ possidet arva supremis,
> Jungit ubi oceano proprios Germania fines.

They were a very warlike people, and strenuously opposed the arms of Charlemagne by whom they were finally subjugated in 789.[1] A chronicle of that age states that king Charles [2] marched again through Saxony until he came to the Slavi, who are called

1 Saxo Poeta, Vita Karoli Magni, ad ann. 789.
2 Tunc Carlus rex iterum per Saxoniam pervenit usque ad Sclavos, qui dicuntur Wilti, et venerunt reges terræ illius, cum rege eorum Tragivite ei obviam, etc. Annal. Laurisham. ad ann. 789.

Wilti; that kings of that land, with their king Tragwit, came to meet him, and that, having solicited peace, they surrendered all their lands into his power. These kings were probably chiefs, who had elected one of their number to be a war king like the guð cyningas of the Saxons, and other Teutonic peoples. Tragevit appears to be the Teutonic translation of a Slavic name. At all events, it admits of a natural explanation in the dialects of the former. How long they had occupied the territory, which Charlemagne then annexed to the empire, we do not learn, but there they were found by Ptolemy, who names them Βελτοι, and we know from another source, that their name, at an early period, was communicated in regular form to their country, Wilcia,³ from *wylk*, a wolf, the singular of *wilzi*, whence, or from Weleti come the Wilti and Wiltzi.⁴ Eiginhard, at the year 822, claims the name Wilsi as German, and says that in their own language they called themselves Welatabi.

A reviewer of Paul Joseph Schafarjk's Slavonian Antiquities has the following remarks on this people and their name :—

"Of all the Polabian Slavonians the Weleti were the most celebrated, both for their numbers and for the persevering courage with which they defended their nationality against the Germans. Their primitive site appears to have been in the vicinity of Wilno, though Ptolemy assigns them a district (Veltæ) in Prussian Pomerania, between the Vistula and the Niemen They were early conspicuous for their warlike habits, which were such as to draw upon them from the other Slavonians the appellation of Wolves, which gave rise to the fable related by Herodotus, which that historian treats as absurd, as a matter of fact, of a northern tribe annually transformed into these predatory beasts. Similar epithets were frequent among the Slavonians, who even now call the Turks Viper; and the Kerrods, from their predatory habits, still bear that of Wolves. The appellation may have been originally an honourable one, as it must be borne in mind, that in the primitive simple state of society, physical force was considered in the light of a prime virtue. From the Slavonian word for wolf, *wilk*, sing. *Wilzi*, plu., Greek *lykos*, Latin, *lupus*,

---

3 Eo anno fuit dominus rex Karolus in Wineta pervenitque in Wilciam, — Annal. Petav. ad ann. 789.

4 Karolus rex pergit in Sclavos qui dicuntur Wiltezi—Ann. Sangall. Breves ad ann. 789. This date is corrected to 792 by some one, who did not agree with the commencement of the Christian era, then universally adopted.

Lithuanian *lut, liat*, ferocious, are derived the words, Wilzi, Wilzen, Lutici, and Weleti, Woloti, Welatabi, &c. from *welot wolot*, signifying a giant; all which are indicative of the reckless courage for which the Weleti were distinguished. When their fame spread over Europe during the middle ages, the Germans and Scandinavians, invented marvellous tales concerning them, and finally declared them to be a nation of sorcerers. A sword that worked wonders was called from their name walsung, welsung, welsi.[1] Their sway extended from the shores of the O'st Sea, which was called after them Wildamor (the sea of the Weleti) and their capital city was the famed Vinetha, in Slavonian Wolin (Julinum ?) situated at the mouth of the Oder. According to Venantius Fortunatus, and to Beda, the Weleti penetrated, between 560 and 600, into Batavia, and settled near the city of Utrecht, which from them was called Wiltaburg, and the surrounding country, Wiltenia. Being separated from the other Slavonians by the German nations, the Weleti were unable long to preserve their independence, and in the course of time, either lost their nationality altogether, or ultimately rejoined their countryman. Unquestionable proofs, however, of their having settled in the Netherlands exist in the names of the cities evidently, as Wiltsween in Holland, Wiltenburgh near Utrecht &c. and in such purely Slavonian names as Kamens Sweta, Widenitz Hudnin, Zevola, Wispe or Wespe, Slota, &c. It is the opinion of German historians and of M. Safarik himself, that a body of Weleti or Wilti settled in our country of Wiltshire, where they arrived after the Anglo-Saxons. And some English authors derive the inhabitants of Wiltshire from a colony of Belgæ, who migrated from Wiltorica." *For. Quar. vol.* 26, *p.* 27.

Some corroboration of the settlement of Wilti in England is obtained from the Anglo Saxon name of the people of Wiltshire. They are invariably called Wilsætan, that is the Wilt-settlers. In all other cases the termination was *ware*, as Cantware, the Kent-men or people.

2. Adam of Brem. (pp. 47. 48) names the Hæfeldan as the Heveldi, among the Slavonic tribes between the Elbe and the Oder,

[1] To what the reviewer says it may be added that the *Volsunga Saga*, in which we have the fable of some men who transformed themselves into wolves, derives its title from the same source. The story occupies the 17th chapter headed Sigmundur og Sinfiotle verda ad Ulfum. It deserves no farther notice here.

but he does not seem like Alfred to have been aware that they were a detachment from the Wilti, or rather, were Wilti so named from their seat on the banks of the Havel.

IX. In the next geographical notice, Alfred seems to change his station, and no longer to refer to the East Franks, or he becomes less careful of preserving the relation of countries to the cardinal points of the compass. He directs attention in the first place to what is now called Pomerania, which lies to the north east of the probable limits of Francia Orientalis towards the east. His words are rendered thus:

"To the east of them is the country of the Wends, who are called Sysyle; and extending south east over some part of the Moravians, have, to the west of them, the Thuringians and Bohemians, and some part of the Bavarians."

1. Such are precisely the sites of Thuringia, Bohemia and Moravia in respect to Pomerania, and Silesia, but he seems by the name of Sysyle, the Siusli of the Latin writers, to mean all the Slavonic tribes, who occupied the present Ober and Nieder Lausitz, and part of the Middle Mark. The Slavoni appear to have had two generic appellations, Slavi and Venedi with its numerous variations in orthography, according to the language, in which the latter name occurs. Alfred's words give the impression that he considered all the tribes in this part of the continent to be indifferently named Neuds, and Suisli. The people who were commonly distinguished as Slavi Suisli, were very widely spread. Professor Dahlmann says in a note on the name, "The Sjusli belonged to the Servian Slavi, and were found among the Meissnischians, as well as in other places." We seem to find them in conjunction with the Vends in the peninsular tract on the north of Jutland, between the Shagensian promontory on the north and Lincil gulf on the South. This detachment from the main of Jutland, was called Vendsussel, and in Icelandic, Vendilsyssla. Mr R. Forster has the following remarks. "The name of Sysele or Sysyle is very little known in history, unless the name be preserved in the lately published Obotritic monuments, where on the sacred caduceus, fig. 23 a, the following Runic characters are engraved, namely *Shesil*. The *Annales Fuldenses* mentions, in the year 874, the revolt of the Sorbi and Suisle; perhaps the latter may be our Sysele. In the ode of Harald the Valiant, among the Five pieces of Runic Poetry;

Harald says 'My ships have made the tour of Sicily;' which I suspect to be our Sysele.

The Syslo kynd of an ancient Saga, preserved by Snorre, and relating to Yngvar a questionable king of Sweden as early as 545, are most likely a portion of the Sjusli, who had penetrated into Eistland or Esthonia, the northern part of Liefland or Livonia. Here it is said that Yngvar was slain by the Syslo kind, and buried:

that stoc upp	*It is reported*
at Yngvari	*that the race of the Syslo*
Sysla kynd	*had deprived*
um so at hefthi	*Yngvar of his light.*
oc lios—[3]	[Ynglinga saga, c. 16.]

It is surprising that Forster, a Swede and a man of learning, should entertain this strange supposition. The conquest of Sicily by the Northmen is a well known event, and he might have found it in the Norman history by our Salopian countryman, Orderic Vital. Had he consulted the Runic itself, instead of the *Five Pieces* which are English translations apparently of Latin versions that are not always correct, he would have found that Harald wrote Sikeley—Sicilia.

The word *Slowa* or *Slava*, conveying an idea of glory or nobility, gave rise to the generic appellation of the people who were known to the Greeks as the Ενετοι, of which the Romans made Venedi, Veneti, and the like. Western writers in the middle ages took the national name, and added a c to the s, as if they pronounced *Shlavi*, and the Italians actually wrote *Schiavi—Schlavi*. The French wrote *Sclavons*, whence they made *esclave*, the original of our *Slave*, and thus a word chosen from their own language by a brave and gallant people to claim the respect due to them, is now a term of reproach and misfortune.

Among the Greeks, it was believed from ancient tradition that the 'Ενετοι, who probably had the digamma, Fενετοι, or aspirated the E. initial letter, 'Ενετοι,—Heneti,—Veneti, came from Paphlagonia into Illyria[3]; whence, after they had spread themselves over Panonia and the coasts of the Adriatic, these were distinguished as Ιλλυριων Ενετοι, just as we find Slavi Sorabi, Slavi Behemani, according to the country which they occupied. From Illyria a part of them passed on northward, some settling on the route, and others advancing to the Baltic. "What is most ac-

[3] See Homer. Il. 2, 851.

knowledged," says Strabo, "is that the Heneti were the most celebrated tribe of the Paphlagonians, of whom was Pylæmenes; and that most of them followed him on warlike expeditions; but on losing their leader at the capture of Troy, passed over into Thrace, and after wandering about, arrived in what is now Henetica," or Venetia. This tradition was known to Quintus Curtius, who observes that some believe the Venetians to have taken their origin from the Paphlagonian Heneti. That they were an Asiatic people,[4] there can be no reasonable doubt. The affinity of the Slavic dialects with the Sanskrit is not less marked than that of the Teutonic, and as to the Greek name of the alleged Paphlaginian tribe, which rambled into Europe, it seems to be nothing more than a very slight variation of the name Hindü.

It is certain that the Iavons arrived in Europe at a very early period, and that they settled at an unknown time in various parts from the South to the Baltic, that part from which the Greeks obtained amber in the days of Herodotus; and it is no improbable presumption that they were Slavons by whom it was furnished to his countrymen. On the Adriatic, they engaged in war with Philip, and afterwards with Alexander the Great, who reduced them; but soon after his death, they recovered their liberty. The Romans next invaded their territory, and called it the province of Illyria, comprehending Thrace and Dacia. According to Jornandes the Slavi were called Venedi, and Pliny says that they lived about the banks of the Vistula. Ptolemy places them on the Eastern shore of the Baltic, which he calls the Venedan Gulf, and Procopius says that "formerly the Slavons and Antæ had the same name; both were called Spori because they lived in a scattered manner ($\sigma\pi o\rho a\delta a$) in isolated huts, and they occupy for the same reason a large extent of territory.

In this scattered manner the Servians build their villages at the present day. The villages of Servia stretch far up into the gorges of the mountains, into the valleys formed by the rivers and streams or into the depths of the forests. Sometimes, where consisting of forty or fifty houses, they spread over a space as extensive as that occupied by Vienna and its suburbs. The dwellings are isolated at a distance from one another, and each contains within itself a separate community. The real house is a room enclosed by loam

[4] Qu. Curt. lib. III.

walls and covered with the dry bark of the lime, having the hearth in the centre.

Jornandes says that Dacia is on the left side of the Alps (Carpathian) in which from the source of the Vistula to the north, through an immense extent of country, exist the nations of the Winidi. Although their names vary in various tribes and places, they call themselves Slavi and Antæ. This Antæ is no doubt intended for *Ενετοι*. He also states that they have the three names Venedi, Antæ, and Slavi.

I have ventured an opinion that *Ενετοι* is slightly varied from Hindû, and certainly there is no improbability in a belief that Hindûs migrated to Paphlagonia. The mythology of the Slavons is that of Hindustan; Brahma, Vishnu, and Seva are represented by the Slavonian Perun, Volos, and Kolida. They hold the doctrine of the immortality and transmigration of the soul, and a more decided proof of conformity with India exists in the rule which forced the widow on the burning pile with her husband. Perun, the god of thunder, Volos, god of flocks, Kolida, god of festivals, were worshipped by the eastern Slavonians. And the common people now in many parts of Poland and Russia call Christmas Kolida, as the festival of that god was celebrated on the 24th of December. The Slavonians of the Baltic acknowledged two principles, good and bad; the former Biel Bog or white god, and the second Cherni Bog, the black god. Other deities were Porenut, who had four faces, and a fifth on his breast, supposed to be the god of the seasons; Poreoit represented with five hands; Rughevi, supposed to be god of war with seven faces, seven swords at his side, and an eighth in his hand. These three gods were in the isle Rugen, the last asylum of Slavonian idolatry. It is worthy of observation that many of them have the figure of a beetle on them, which will appear to denote an Egyptian origin—the Scarabæus.

The god Poreit is strongly suggestive of Prithivi the earth, a form or power of Vishnu; their goddess of pleasure and love is supposed to be Leljo. The gul, goul, ghoul, of Asia is revived in the Vampyre, which is common in Slavic nations.

2. Alfred's Wineda Land, or country of the Wends, since he says that they are also called Siusli, extended from the Baltic coast constituting the northern boundary of Pomerania, which has its other boundaries formed by the Oder and one of its branches, to the Carpathian Mountains, which are the southern limit of Silesia

It is not improbable that he also included the Lusitzis on the west or the north west of Silesia in the same term. If so, Wineda Land contained the modern Pomerania, Nieder Lausitz, and Silesia.

3. The Slavi Behemani, who appear as the Behemas in the Anglo Saxon, and the Bægŏware or Bavarians, are most probably two branches of the ancient Boii, who in the time of Augustus, submitted with their leader Marobudus to the Marcomanni. These Boii are said to have been Gauls, and therefore, Kelts : yet Mr Forster adduces a people whom he calls Slavi Behemani. On this point Adam of Bremen speaks doubtingly. He would consider Slaviana ten times larger than his Saxony, particularly if he may add Bohemia, and the Poles across the Oder, because they differ in neither habit nor language. Subsequently he seems to include the Bohemians among the Slavi, and this may possibly have been the author who has furnished Mr Forster with the term.

The meaning of the Teutonic termination of Bohemia, the house of the Boii, suggests a belief that this country was their chief or first settlement in Germany proper. In like manner Bægŏ-ware, Ba-varians, of one of which the modern German Bayern is a corruption, that is men of the Boii, would appear to point to an emigration from Bohemia to the South. We have no historical proof of such an occurrence, which, however, was usual enough with other nations, and we know that the Boii retreated from the Marcomanni. We shall presently find that D' Anville, who states that the name of Boioaria extended under the Frank empire to the Alps, is confirmed by king Alfred. According to D' Anville the Leck bounded this country on the side of Suevia as it still separates Bavaria from Suabia. On the other side, what was Boioaria extended to the river Ems, *Anisus*, a little beyond the present limits of Bavaria, encroaching on what was Austria. It was the frontier of the Avares or Abares. That the tract at the north of the Danube between Franconia and Bohemia, still comprised in Bavaria, was part of the ancient Boivaria seems probable. It contained the part in the district of Egra, which is now annexed to Bohemia. This part was denominated "Nortgowe" in the will of Charlemagne, 806. Nord Gau, or the northern Canton, agrees with the situation of this part.

D' Anville has collected some particulars of the mediæval history of Bavaria. There is reason to believe that Theodoric, king of the Ostrogoths, in Italy, having acquired Rhetia, occupied a part of Boioaria. It was probably after his death in 526, that Theodoric, king of Austrasia who lived in 534, made acquisitions in the same country, where the first of the laws is authorised in his name. Charles Martel invaded it in 725 and 728. As, however, we do not find Boioaria in the partition of the provinces between Pepin and Carloman, sons of Charles Martel, we cannot infer that this country was entirely subjugated. That was effected by the defect of king Odilon; and we read in the Annals of Metz, at the year 743, that a papal legate, charged with an interdict of all war against Odilon, received for answer that Boioaria and the Boioarians belonged to the emperor of the French (Franks; there were no French until long afterwards). Tassilo, son of Odilo, rendered homage to Pepin in 757, and to Charlemagne in 781. Despoiled of his duchy in 788, the government of the country was entrusted to his counts. Louis le Debonnaire gave Boioaria under the title of a kingdom to his son Louis the Germanic. Bavaria subsequently again became a dukedom, and finally, for the second time a kingdom.

The Moravians, whom Alfred designates Maroaro, occur in the next division of the present arbitrary sections of his geography:

" To the south of them, on the other side of the river Danube is the country Carinthia, (lying) south to the mountains called the Alps. To the same mountains extend the boundaries of the Bavarians, and of the Suabians; and then to the East of the country, Carenthia, beyond to the desert, is the country of the Bulgarians; and East to them the land of the Greeks; and on the East of Maroaro, is Wisle land; and to the east of them are the Dacians."

1. The situation of Carinthia is still south of the Alps. Mr Forster's note on the Anglo-Saxon name, Carendre, deserves transcription: " Carendre is the name, by which king Alfred probably calls the Sclavi Carenthani or Carentani; at present their country is the duchy of Carinthia, or Cærenthen. Formerly, in Strabo's time, the Carni lived there, *l*. VIII. Whether they were of Teutonic offspring, or one of those Gallic tribes, who settled here with the Scordisi and Boii, cannot be easily ascertained. From the neighbourhood of the Sarmatæ in Pannonia, and from the affinity of the name of Carni with Crain, which in the Sclavonic language signifies a limit, I suspect the Carni were Sarmatians, and continued to live in these parts, till by length of

time they were called Carni and Carinthi, and at last their name was changed into Carentani. This opinion may be further proved from the name of the duchy of Crain, which lies next to Carinthia, and which preserves the Sclavonic name of Crain, though it is called by the Latin writers Carniola (Paul Warnefrid, *Hist. Longob. l.* VI. c. 12.) This country was always considered as the boundary of Pannonia, Germany and Italy. Even in the later ages, there was established a marquisate of the Winedi, or, as it is commonly called, the Windische Marck, *i. e.* Limes Venedicus, or March Sclavonic. The Sclavonic nations frequently employed the word *crain* for a limit. Thus the Ukraine in Russia served as a barrier against the Tartars. In Great Poland is a tract situated along the New Marck of Brandenburg and Lilesia, called Krania, because it marks the limits of the above countries. It is, therefore, highly probable, that the Carendre or Sclavi Carentani, are derived from the ancient Carni, and had formerly the name of Crain, an account of their limitary situation. The Alps were no doubt the strongest barriers for all nations; these begin in this part called Crain, and were called by Strabo and other writers Alpes Carnicæ."

Carinthia, Carniola, and Stiria had been detached from the marquisate of Friuli in Italy by Louis le Debonnaire, in order to comprise it to his kingdom of Germany. Arnulf, natural son of Carloman, the eldest son of Louis the Germanic, was created duke of Carinthia as having commanded those provinces before he succeeded the emperor Charles the Fat in Germany. Otho the Great, in 951, invested his brother Henry, duke of Bavaria, with Carinthia united to the marquisate of Venetian Lombardy. On the erection of Austria into a duchy, that of Carinthia was detached from Bavaria, and by default of dukes on this part, Carinthia and Upper Carniola were united to Austria, when the emperor Rodolf of Hapsburg with the consent of the imperial states conferred it on his son Albert.

Professor Dahlmann seems to have mistaken Alfred's westen, wastes or deserts, to the East of Carinthia, for the name of a people, since he observes that they have nothing to do with the Wustians, descendants from the Avarian kings, annihilated by Charlemagne. Alfred, however means the desolate tract, on the north of the Drave, and eastward of Clagenfurt, the capitol of Carinthia.

2. Since Alfred places Bulgaria to the east of the wastes above mentioned, it is probable, that anciently there were two divisions of the people, one of which was seated on the Danube next to Dacia, which is the present Moldavia; the other appears to have been those who are sometimes called Belo-Chroati. We certainly find Bulgarians named as conterminous with the inhabitants of Dacia. They are believed to have taken the name from their original seats on the Volga. Sixty miles south west of the Russian city of Kazan, between the rivers Volga, Kazna, and Saniara, occurs Bulgursk, where, says Mr Forster, Peter the Great, when in 1722, as he was going on his Persian expedition found a great many old buildings and sepulchral monuments in ruins with ancient inscriptions in various characters and languages, chiefly Pannonian. Abulfedah, who died in 1345, mentions, in his great geographical work, the town of Bolar or Bolgar as not far from the Atol or Etol i. e. the Volga. The Persian geographer, Nasir Eltusi, who wrote between 1258 and 1266, and Ulughrbegh, the grandson of Timerling, who wrote in 1437, both mention Bolgar. The name of the nation is certainly derived from Volga, beyond which the Bolgari or Wolgari lived; for so it ought to be spelled because the later Greeks pronounced the *B* like a *W*. The Herns, who became powerful towards the end of the 4th century, expelled them from their seats in Bulgaria beyond the Volga. One body of them settled between the Cuphis or Cuban, the Tanais, and the Atal or Volga, and another on the Weissel or Vistula, near the Congobardi, who were then in the neighbourhood of Dacia.

There is nothing to be added to Mr Forster's account of the Sarmatic Bulgari. After their expulsion, their country was occupied by the Hunnic tribes, who obtained the name of Bulgari, though they were of a different race; the Onoguri and Cuturguri were chiefly those tribes who were called Bulgari, because they had taken possession of ancient Bulgaria. One of their chiefs Culratus is mentioned by Theophanes; he came into Bulgaria or Masia on the Dane, and shook off the yoke of the Avari. Two of his sons returned to Bulgaria in 667. Probably in the 9th century the Bulgari occupied many of the seats of the Avari; for Charlemagne had so much weakened them that their country was then considered a waste, till in the year the Madgiari, or present Hungarians, united with the remains of the Avari, and erected a new kingdom. This, at the same time, is a proof of the date, when Alfred wrote his geographical accounts as he mentions the desert between Carenthia and Bulgaria, which must have been before 899 when the Hungarians made the first invasion of Bulgaria and Pannonia. About fifty years after this, the emperor Constantine Porphyrogenitus wrote his book De Administratione Imperii, which was in 939.

3. Moldavia appears to have retained the ancient name of Dacia in Alfred's time. He does not seem to have been aware, that a portion of his Afdrede or Obotrites near the Elbe, occupied seats in Dacia adjacent to the Danube, and near the Bulgarians.

Dacia, east of Wisleland, appears to denote Moldavia and New Servia, for on the shore of the Lake Mæotis, now the sea of Azof, the Getæ were seated, and Alfred tells us that the Dacians were formerly Goths. The error, if it be one, which confounds the Getæ of Dacia with the Goths is more ancient than Alfred, and was embraced by his own Orosius. We find on their side Jornandes, Procopius, Jerome, Spartian, Claudian, John the Goth (Joannes Gothus), and Jos. Scaliger, who are in opposition to Herodotus, Strabo, and Stephanus. The latter demonstrate, that the Getæ were Thracians, and, therefore, a different people from either the Germans or Kelts.

4. By Wisleland, Alfred beyond all doubt means Weissel or Vistula land, but then he places it to the east of Moravia, which he has already occupied with Bohemia. The river itself takes its rise in Silesia and no part of it is found on the east of Moravia. Had he described Vistula to be to the north east of Moravia, we should have understood, with Mr Forster, that the country intended was Poland, of which Silesia formed a part in early ages. It is very embarrassing, but professor Dahlmann affords us no assistance. If, at this time, the South Eastern boundary of Silesia was formed by the small branch of the Oder which flows from the mountains on the confines of Silesia and Moravia, then a portion of the south of Poland with a part of the Carpathian mountains which are a source of streams tributary to the Vistula, may be admitted, though really north east, to be east of Moravia in an ancient and rude state of geographical knowledge. We cannot expect minute accuracy respecting countries, which were comparatively unknown in the extreme west.

5 It may be remarked that Alfred, in relating from Orosius

that Philip, on his return from his conquest in Scythia, was wounded in an engagement with the Triballi, says that a Cwene shot him through the thigh. The Cwenas of the geography occupied a country not far from the frozen Ocean, and cannot be supposed to have descended to the confines of Scythia and Mysia; but on the hypothesis that Mægdha Land was the Land of Maids or Women, and almost a synonyme with the Northern Cwena Land, or country of women, there is no difficulty in believing that the Mazovians joined the Triballi as allies against Philip, and that Alfred called one of them a Cwene in consequence of the name of his country. It is to be observed also, that he has just before spoken of the Triballi as "other Scythians" On the whole, the opinion, that Mægdhaland and Mazovia are the same tract of country, seems to be confirmed by these incidents, which are unconnected with the geographical account.

That the Greeks made any mistakes about the Amazons may be doubted, for having derived the foreign name from their own language, they invented a fable in support of their theory. A true mistake, however, appears respecting another northern people, who inhabited Kuennaland, the present Cajania, between the Gulf of Bothnia and the White Sea. By an equivoque common to the Norsk and Anglo-Saxon, Kuena Cwena, probably Chuna or Hun, in the first instances signifies a woman, and this equivoque occasions the informants of Adam of Bremen to tell him of a nation of Amazons on the Baltic, whose country was called the land of women, and who conceived by tasting water.

5. The Srupe or Servians have already been mentioned in noticing another branch of Slavons, whose appellation seems to have had as much claim to designate the whole race as Slavi, Slavons, and Slavonians. This branch of a widely extended and even scattered people, was known in the middle ages as the Sorbi and Scravi, and as the Scravi and Soravi. They occupied Lusatias, or Lausitz Misnia, part of Brandenburg and Silesia below Glogau; their capital was Soraw, and it still exists in the circle of Upper Saxony and in Lusatia, near the river Bober, about 30 miles to the north east of Gorlitz. In 640, the Servians, having obtained license from the emperor Heraclius, built the city of Servia on the banks of the Danube. About 806 Charlemagne conquered the Sorabi in the vicinity of the Elbe on the north, where they were separated from Thuringia by the Sala. The

government was given to a count, who ruled in Thuringia, and mention occurs of a Dux Sorabici Limitis in 848 and 872; and when Otho, eldest son of the emperor Henry I, was Duke of Thuringia in 938, one of his nobles was Artuvinus, Dux Surbenus. In the 11th century Vladimir assumed the title of king of Servia. Afterwards, under Tzedomil, the Servians submitted to the authority of Rome, and leagued themselves with its emperors against Comnenus, the Greek emperor, in consequence of which he marched upon Servia in 1151, subdued its inhabitants and led their king Tzedomil into captivity. These were the Danubian Servians. Those of the north retired into Bohemia about the middle of the 12th century, being then assailed by Henry the Lion, duke of Saxe, and Albert the Bear, count of Anania, on whom Conrad II conferred the marquisate of Brandenburg.

Dr Bowring has the following interesting remarks on the ancient Servians, and their peculiar name:

"In the middle of the 7th century, a number of Servian tribes stretched themselves along the Sava and the Danube down to the Black Sea, and founded at different times no less than six separate kingdoms,—that of Bulgaria and Croatia, Servia, Srb, Bomia, Slavonia, and Dalmatia. Under the name of *Srb*, the four last of these nations must be considered as comprised. Their irregular history it is not easy to trace. Slavonian writers are disposed to represent the Mæstidæ, who made an incursion into Italy during the age of Claudius, A.D. 276, as synomymous with the Sarmatæ; and Kepitar (a high authority) has gathered much evidence to prove that the dialect spoken to the east of Sparta is of Slavonian origin. Leake has remarked that many of the names of places in the Morea are Slavonic—Kastunika Σηλαβοχωρὶ, and it is notorious that the language of several of the islands of the Grecian Archipelago, Hydra, for example, is Slavonic.—The original meaning of the word *Srb* it is not easy to fix. Some derive it from *srp*, a sickle; others from *sibir, sever*, the north; some from the Latin *servus*, but Dobrowsky says, Significatum radicis *srb*, consultis etiam dialectis omnibus, nondum licuit errare (Instit. Ling. Slav. p. 154)."

From Slavonic of the south-east spring the Russian, Bulgarian, Servian, Dalmatian, and Windenic forms of language. The Lorabic is found in Lusatia, Posen and Wenden, and in old Slavonic a translation of the Sacred Scriptures was made at an early period

Sir Isaac Newton attributes it to Cyrillus, who accompanied Methodius among the Slavons in their different settlements in Europe, and converted them to Christianity in Alfred's century, when the germs of the Russian empire first appeared.

XI. On the north east of Moravia we are introduced to the Dalmatians, on whose east are the Horithi; and, says Alfred, "on the north of the Dalmatians are the Servians, and on the west, the Suisli: on the north of the Horiti is Mægdhaland, and north of Mægdhaland are the Sarmatians."

1. As Dalmatia proper lies far to the south of Moravia, too far, by four or five degrees, to admit the possibility of a mistake, we are to conclude, that a band of the Slavi Dalamense were found in the ninth century in the situation indicated. Mr Forster finds that they formerly inhabited Silesia, from Moravia as far as Glogau, along the river Oder. Professor Dahlmann speaks of them as lying south west of the Sjusli, also among the Meisnisehias and a part of Lausitia.

A missive of king Theodoric, king of the Goths, about 497 is extant in Goldast. It directs Simeon V, or one count, perhaps a graff, or fiscal judge, with this name, to make enquiries through the Dalmatic province respecting the *siliquaticum*, which was a species of tribute or duty imposed upon all saleable goods, and also respecting the truth of iron mines in the warren of Dalmatia (in Dalmatiæ cuniculo), where, it is observed, the softness of the earth produces the hardness of the iron, and is heated in the fire that it may be passed into hardness: such appears to be the meaning of his words.

2. The branch of the Dalmatians on the north east of Moravia, had the Horithi on the east, and Mægdhaland was between them and the Sarmatians on the north. The name Horithi or Horiti has been very perplexing to most of the learned who have investigated the geography of Alfred; but the necessity of re peating their ingenious conjectures is happily obviated by Mr S. W. Singer, who adduces a passage, which shows that a branch of the Chroats may very well have been in the part, where Alfred places his Horiti. There is nothing remarkable in either the migration or dispersion of a nation in this century, which witnessed Saxons on the Elbe, and Saxons on the north eastern confines of Moravia; Obotrites on the coast of the Baltic, and Obotrites on the northern banks of the Danube.

3. Mægthaland, or more correctly according to the Anglo Saxon orthography, in which the *d* is an aspirate, Mægdhaland, is still more enbarrassing than were the Horiti. The term signifies the country of the Mægdhs; we may, therefore, reject the supposition of the learned Professor Rask, that the word is mægth, a province, tribe, nation, and that it stood for Gardariki, or Russia. But if the question be, what are the Mægdhs, the only answer is that mægdh is a maid, or virgin, and Mægdha Land, the country of maids, or unmarried women, denoting, as professor Dahlmann believes, Amazon's Land. Of this last, this Greek name, the memory seems to have been preserved in that of Mazow, Latinized Mazovia, in Poland, precisely where, with Alfred's words, we should place his Land of Maidens.

It would be an easy though pedantic task, to collect what ancient authors have said of the Amazons, yet so much as may tend to show that among the places assigned for their station, Mazovia is not unlikely to have been one, may be permitted.

According to Herodotus (IV, 110), the Amazons from the river Thermodon, invaded Scythia, where they resided, he says, in his own time. Though Diodorus Siculus (II, 45) says that they carried their arms beyond the Tanais, and subdued Thrace, and there leaves them, Justin (II, 4) traces them as Herodotus had done already, into Scythia, Pliny (VI, 7) and Pomponius Mela (I, 19) are both agreed in placing a Sauromatic nation of Gynæcocratumeni, whose first seats were in the neighbourhood of Lake Mæotis, on the banks of the Tanais. The description of them that they were one nation of several peoples, and several names, taken in connection with their residence in these parts, appears to indicate the Slavonic tribes, of whom some ancient term denoting the whole has been tortured by the Greeks, after their usual fashion, into Amazons; and having thus formed a new word, they also found its derivation in their own language to denote a people without breast, which would almost naturally suggest the wild fables, which they relate of a nation of female warriors, who lived in celibacy. Bopp produces the Russian word, my' zj, man, the husband, and Dr. Aug. Friedr. Pott, of Berlin thinks $Aμαζονες$, the pretended breastless, is probably formed from the Zend, *a* priv. *masya*=man=husband, and *amasya*, a woman without husband. It may account for the Greek name of the people about whom so many fables are reated, and who occupy parts which were wholly unknown to the ancients, who liberally peopled those in the north with Hippodes, or men with the feet of horses, and others whose ears covered the nakedness of their bodies. The old Sagas stock trackless marshes, mountains, and forests, with giants, dwarfs, elves, trolls and ovættir, a sort of spectres, and the household, or rather tenthold tales of the Tartars place the very same creations of wild fancy in the boundless steppes which the foot of man has not crossed.

XII. In placing Sarmatia to the north of Mazovia, for no other part answers so well to Alfred's Mægdhaland, he must have considered a portion of the Prussians, or the inhabitants of the present Prussia, to be Sermende or Sarmatians, whom he continues up to the Riphæan mountains.

1. To the East of the East Sea, he places the Osti and Obotrites. By the former, he means those inhabitants of Pomerania, who were known to the Romans as the Æstyi, or Æsti, a name which appears to be philologically the same, and to denote a people to the East. On the north, the Osti or Easterns, have the same arm of the sea, the Winedas and the Burgundians, and on their South the Heveldi.

The Winidas are so called by Jornandes, and the name of Wenden is familiar in Brandenburg, Pomerania, and Lusatia, at the present time.

2. Mr Forster is strongly of opinion, that the Burgundians are the inhabitants of Bornholm, which Wulfstan calls Burgendaland. He says that they were formerly a nation in the north of Germany, mentioned by Pliny, III, 28, belonging to the Wandali or Vandali.

I find nowhere else these names Borgendaholm and Borgenda-Land; but Borgund was the name of a Norwegian island, while the name of Bornholm variously occurs as Boreholm, Bureholm, Boringholm, and Borgholm. The reasoning above, however, is satisfactory.

XIII. Ohthere's personal exploration of the north western and northern coasts to see how the land looked (*sceawode*) due north, and whether any man abode to the north of his habitation, is the earliest recorded voyage undertaken in the pure spirit of philosophical inquiry. The object was noble, and the result, considering the paucity of means at his command, is satisfactory. We have, very fairly described, the situation of what is now known as the

North Cape, and the declension of the land towards the southeast as far as the White Sea, apparently until this time unknown to all Europeans but Finnish hunters and fishermen.

A few observations may be conveniently made on the people with whom the two travellers met, without constraining ourselves to accompany them from sea to sea, and port to port.

1. He dwelt northmost of all the Northmen, that is, of all the Norwegians of that time; for he himself finds Finns and others more northward. Halgoland, little known in the south, was one of those places which popular superstition taking "omne ignotum pro magnifico," invested with a sacred character.

2. "For three days."—Distances were computed by time as among southern mariners. Mr Forster endeavours to turn the circumstance to useful account, and if the method could be depended upon, we certainly might employ it in determining the voyage to Sciringsheal, and from that to Haddeby, and perhaps also ascertain the position of Wulfstan's Truso. Forster shows that a day's sail with the ancient Greeks was 10,000 stadia, which, he says, is above 100 sea miles. But there can be no certainty in this method, and we must depend upon other aids. Ohthere after sailing six days, found himself at a bend of the land directly east. He had manifestly arrived at the termination of the sea-coast, and in fact, become the first discoverer of the North Cape. On a rough calculation, he had sailed 417 statute miles and proceeded at a rate of less than 70 miles a day. A Saga, of which I forget the name, records an expedition to Valland, or Frankland, in order to plunder a tomb. The pirates occupied five days in sailing from the south of Norway to the nearest point, by which they could advance directly to their destination by land. From the Naze to the mouth of the Weser is about 277 miles, so that these people made way about 55 miles a day. Everything is quite clear from his arrival at this bend. He waits for a right north wind, which, though the coast does not bend to the direct south, would serve his purpose, and he states that he does not know whether it were the land or the sea which bent. He was yet a stranger to the place. In five days he comes to a great river, which is clearly the entrance of the White Sea. The distance pretty well agrees with the probable rate of 60 miles a day. But what places it beyond question is, that the land was all inhabited, and the people were Biarmians.

3. Than the Biarmians and their country Biarmaland no places or people in the north are more frequently mentioned in the Sagas. They had the reputation of possessing much gold; but whether "gull" is to be understood of the metal or wealth in general, is doubtful. At all events, the pirates often found their way to Biarmaland. On this country Dr Bosworth's note (42, p. 9) is abundantly explanatory of its situation. The notice of it in the old MS. Icelandic and Latin Dictionary, so often cited, is to the same effect, but with the additional information that Biarmaland was also called Dvina, from the river of that name.

4. Besides Finns who visited the North Sea for the purposes of hunting and fishing, Ohthere speaks of Terfinns and Scride Finns; and he makes an observation of no little value to those who contend that the Biarmians are also Finns. The country occupied by the several bodies of people, who all take the general name of Finn, with a distinctive addition to each, is stated in round numbers to be more than 100 miles in length and ninety in breadth. These are Swedish miles, and represent a square of 157.114 of our miles. What is more certain is that they occupy Lapmark, as well as Finnmark, and that the Swedes distribute the former into dioceses or governments, which they name Uma Lapmark, Pitha Lapmark, Ula Lapmark, Torne Lapmark, and Kimi Lapmark. There are of the people the Siofinns or Sea Finns, who live solely on fish, and Laplanders, subjects of Russia, from Finnmark and the castle of Wardhuys near North Cape, to the White Sea. Belonging to Sweden is the tract inhabited by Laplanders called Trennes and Pihinieni, called by the Russians Trachana Voloch, or according to Pontanus, Terschana Voloch. In the Trennes we seem to have the Terfinns of Alfred, while Pihinieni is probably the vernacular name of the Finn.

The name of the Scride-finns, which presents no difficulty to a modern ear and pen, was very troublesome to writers at one time. Both the meaning and orthography are given in Dr Bosworth's note (37, p. 7). Warnefried believes that they received their name from their manner of leaping with a piece of wood bent like a bow, when they were in pursuit of wild beasts. Adam of Bremen says that on the confines of the Swedes or Northmen to the North dwell the Scritefinns who are said to surpass wild beasts in running. Their largest city is Halsingaland, and Halsingaland is a region. To make a brief description of Sueonia or Sweden, it has the Goths and their city Scaranen on the west; on the north the Wermilians with the Scritefinns: from the South it has the length of the Baltic sea: there is the great city Sictena; and to the east it touches on the Riphæan mountains, where are Amazons, Cynocephali and Cyclopes.

5. Three kinds of deer are mentioned by Ohthere among his own property, wild, tame, and decoy deer, which are valuable to the Finns for taking the wild deer. These he calls "stæl hranas." The translation decoy deer, has the advantage of being more intelligible than the mere Saxon word *Stale*, which, however, is not entirely obsolete as a noun, signifying anything offered to allure, and so, a decoy. Iu this sense it is used by Shakspeare—

> *Katherine.*—I pray you, sir, is it your will
> To make a stale of me among these mates?
> Taming of the Shrew, I, 1.

At stœla, in Icelandic, has the meaning to conceal the intention.

6. In the seventh section (p. 13) we have a fuller account of the situation of Cwena Land and its inhabitants; and if again noticed it is chiefly to say that the range given to Cwena Land from Norway to the White sea, including Finnmark on the north, in note 36, p. 6, is certainly correct, and reconciles the apparent differences among old writers of the north, who sometimes, in speaking of Kuenna Land, assigned situations to it according to that part of the extensive region, bearing the name, which they had particularly in view. Malte Brun's story of Adam of Bremen, of whom we know little more than his book, and the Quaines, mentioned to him by a king of Sweden (Dr Bosworth, p. 6, n. 36), does not make him so guilty of absurdity as the French geographer imagines. He had the belief of most of the people in the north to keep him in countenance. Quaine is nothing more than a variety *Kuen, cwen*, both of which not only denominate a country, but signify a woman. Adam's Terra Feminarum is a translation of a current name, and when universal credit was given to tales of trolls, ovættir, eotenas,

> And Cannibals that each other eat,
> The Anthropophagi, and men whose heads
> Do grow beneath their shoulders,

was more than matched by the Greek belief in Amazons.

Besides this Terra Feminarum, which is seen, in a passage just cited, not to be intended for the country of the Amazons, we have the Smameyland of the old Sagas, in reference to a very large tract in the same regions, and often appearing to denote Biarmaland, Cwenaland, and a part of the eastern coast at the entrance of the Cwen or White Sea, if not extending even as far as the Ural mountains in the South East.

Of Smameialand the Icelandic MS. dictionary says, after the name so written, " Smaojeda, ortum versus a Biarmia ad Mare Glaciale contra Nova Zembla."

The position assigned to Smameialand nearly corresponds with that of the Samoiedes at the present time on and to the west of the Ural Mountains, and north of the modern government of Perm, which is believed to receive its name from the ancient Biarmia. Ohthere found the Biarmians in a close proximity to the Cwen Sae. Samoiedes have been found to the north of Archangel, and in a Saga much more ancient than the dictionary, the nation called the Smameyar are said to inhabit the parts about a promontory which lies out at and which appears to be the peninsula now called Candenos at the entrance of the White sea. It does not appear very improbable that Biarmians Lappons and the northern Finns are all Samoiedes, differently denominated according to localities. Ohthere found a remarkable resemblance between the languages of the Finns and the Biarmians. The Finns, as before said, not Finns but Sooma-laimen, the dwellers on marshes, and the first word of this name is manifestly mistaken and corrupted into the Icelandic Smameiar.

7. Ohthere says, after stating that none abode to his north: " There is a port on the south of the land which is called Sciringsheal that no man could sail in a month, if he anchored at night, and every day had a fair wind. All the while he must sail near the land. On his right is first Iceland, and then the islands which are between Iceland and this land. Then this land continues till it comes to Sciringsheal; and all the way on the left is Norway."

There are few passages of antiquity more embarassing than the present, and no doubt much of the difficulty arises from our own ignorance; but it is possible that mistakes have been made by transcribers. Ohthere leaves Halogaland in Latitude 65, and the first object on his right is Iceland, written Iraland in the MS.

This in fact would be Iceland and no other island, nor where he was in the north sea could he well think of Ireland, hidden from him by England, and far to his south west. Then occur on the right the islands between Iceland and this land. What land? He manifestly means the Faroe, and Shetland islands and the Orkneys, which are actually between Iceland and Scotland, or Britain, but not between Ireland and Norway. Here "this land" is that in which he then was relating his voyage.

From Halogaland to the South of " this land," his own Norway, we may roughly reckon 12 degrees, which at 69.5 miles to the degree will give 834 miles sailed in the days of a month keeping in-shore with a fair wind. Then in 14 days at the probable rate of 60 miles a day, he would arrive at some port west of the Naze. This he calls Sciringesheal, and there was actually a place in Westford, called Skiringssaal, (*saal=heal*) in the *Ynglinga Saga*. This evidence of identity seems to outweigh Professor Dahlmann's objection, that the latter was not a port. But do we know that our ancient mariners, gliding along coasts, and in a manner making their course parallel with all its indentations, in small vessels, attached the same idea to a port that we do? That, as far as I have been able to discover, was a port, which received them at the end of their voyage, or which sheltered them from tempest, provided it were inhabited. Admitting that Skiringssaal was not exactly on the shore, still it would afford the mariner the means of signifying his landing place. But in opposition to conjecture, Ohthere calls his Sciringes heal a port, and for such it must be received.

8. He then proceeds to state that a broad sea, too broad to be seen over, runs up into the land and that Jutland is opposite, and then Zealand.

These indications perfectly agree with a Sciringesheal on the south of Norway-Julland and then Zealand opposite, and this Sciringesheal may be the Skiringesheal on the west of the bay of Christiana. It seems unnecessary to quote Professor Dahlmann's objection on this occasion, since the weightiest is, that the place so named was not a port. To the present purpose it is quite sufficient that Ohthere believed it to be a port.

9. In five days he sailed to the port called Haddeby, of which the identity with the Saxon Hæth, or Hæthe, is very satisfactorily established by Dr Bosworth (note 57, p 15.) Does he now speak

of five days and nights, or of two or of three days' actual sailing? At 83 miles a day he would attain it in two days and a half, and at 60 in a little more than three days: either allowing him to discontinue sailing as in proceeding from Halogaland.

XIV. Wulfstan's voyage to another quarter necessarily brings us to an acquaintance with other peoples and places, and particularly islands which might not otherwise have entered into Alfred's account of the continent, his principal object. His port of departure was that Hæthe, which puzzled translators and annotators before Dr Bosworth. The Icelanders call Haddeby in Schleswig Heidabær, and Heidabyr, names by which they also designate Schleswig; "hodie Slesvik, villa ad fines Holsatiæ et sinum amnemque Eliam."

Truso, which has been another difficulty, seems more probably to be Drausen than the present Dirchsau, because, according to the only person who names it, Truso stood on the shore of a lake, which we knew to be the Frische Haffe, while Dirchsau was out of Wulfstan's course and 30 miles inland. In the seven days' voyage to this place which did not include sailing at night, Wulfstan's rate was nearly 90 miles. Herodotus [l. iv.] quoted by Dr Arbuthnot assigns 700 stadia or 84.5 English miles for a day's sailing, and for the night 500 stadia, or 70.5 miles, which, the latter remarks, making in 24 hours 155 English miles, seems too long. In computing the probable rate of Ohthere's voyage at 60 miles a day of 12 hours, though it would hardly be so long, allowance was made for his following the line of a coast totally unknown to him.

The Land of the Burgundians, in this voyage, certainly belonged to those Burgundians of whom a part passed at a very early period to the continent of Germania, and again into Gaul (Supra xii, 2) Gothland, another of Wulfstan's islands, has one town, Visby Wisbuy, in Latin Visburgum, which was anciently celebrated for its power, splendour and magnitude. It was also a famous mart, raising its head above the Pomeranian Wineta and Julinum of which so much is said in the medieval writings of the north. Wisby has the reputation in Sweden of having given the first laws to navigation. Very near this city are numerous rocks carved in Gothic (Runic?) characters; some particulars of the history of Gothland or rather of Wisby, after the beginning of the 13th century, have been collected by zealous antiquaries. The islanders themselves call the name not Gothland, or Gutland, but Guland; nevertheless these gentlemen, arguing from Gothlandia in the Latin writers, maintain that it was peopled by Goths.

Wulfstan's Estan or Estas, for the declension is not very clear, were in all probability a Vandalic people, and we have already seen that at least a part of the inhabitants were Slavonian Sjusli. Tacitus, who assigns his Æstii the same situation as Wulfstan gives to Eastland, remarks that they have the rites and habits of the Suevi, but that their language is nearer to the British. We may well believe him to have been little versed in Slavonic and Keltic, but he has made a distinction from Teutonic, which no doubt he had observed, and which shows that they were a different people, though without strong affinities to the Kelts. Zeiller without citing his authority pronounces them to be of uncertain origin, but nevertheless Germans, who having abandoned their ancient seat on the Rhine, long before Cæsar, removed into Sarmatia.

It is remarked by Wulfstan that in Eastland there are many towns and in every town a king. The European title of king was not anciently one denoting great power or magnificence, since it was freely attributed to any chief person,—the head of a village, the holder of a ness or promontory, the captain of a piratical boat, such as that of king Half or Alf with his crew of twelve men. In Curland another division of Liefland, those of the husbandmen who are rich and free men, and who have one hundred serfs, are still called kings. Wulfstan's kings may have been the most considerable man in each wick, or borough as he calls it, and performing functions in the manner of a magistrate.

The Esthonians did not brew ale, he says, but they had mead enough. Respecting these very ancient names of fermented liquors it may be remarked that ale, which has been ignorantly derived from the Saxon *ælan* to inflame, is in that language ealoth where the *ea=o* long of the Gothic. With *l* it is found in Άλωας an epithet of Ceres, as goddess of αλωαι cornfields, and in αλφιτον barley. It is not improbably related to the Old Norse *ala,* and the Latin, *al*-ere, to nourish, whence *ali*-meant.

Mead, the wine of honey, is not only a very ancient word, but one widely diffused. *Medo,-u,* etymologically is identical with *mel* honey; O. H. Germ. metu; Lithuanian medus; Lettic, the language probably spoken by the Esthonians meddus; Slavonic

God! to the worship of the religious, that those men that are the most religious are the worthiest,; very many a man pretends that he is a religious teacher, because he desires to have much of the world's honour. Of them Christ himself cried out, and thus said; " They seek that one should greet them the first, and honour them in the market-places and at feasts, and that they recline foremost at the evening meals, and that they seek the chief seats at meetings." For that with arrogance and pride they enter upon the honours of the pastor's duties, they cannot with moderation fulfil their ministrations and be teachers of lowly-mindedness. But the tongue is confounded in the teacher's office, when it one thing learneth but another teacheth. With such men the Lord contended by means of his prophet, and blamed them in such wise when he said, " They have reigned, though not of my wish : they were princes, and I knew them not." When, then, they reign, they reign of their own authority, not by (the authority of) the most high Judge— therefore they are not supported by any prop of the Divine power, and are not chosen for any ability; but by their own appetite they are puffed up, so that they, though so worthless, seize the teacher's office rather than deserve it. These, then, the same eternal and secret Judge lifteth up as if he knew them not, and permitting them, he forbears from their condemnation in his patience, and though they may perform many wondrous works in their condition, again, when they come to him he will say, " Depart from me, ye unrighteous workers, I know not who ye are." Again he reproved them through the prophet for their want of learning, when he said, " The shepherds had no understanding; they had my laws and have not known me." He that knows not God's commandments, is unknown of God. The same thing also saith St Paul, Whoso knows not God, God knows not him. Unwise teachers come for the people's sins; for that often for the teacher's unwisdom the hearers fare ill, and often for the teacher's wisdom unwise hearers are defended. If, then, both be unwise, then is to be brought to mind what Christ himself said in his gospel; he said, " If the blind leadeth the blind, they fall both into the pit." Concerning the same the psalm-minstrel said : " Let their eyes be darkened that they may not see, and let their back be continually bent." He said not this because he wished or desired it for any persons, but he prophesied, in the way that it should come to pass : but that the eyes are the teachers, and that the back is the hearers; for the eyes are in the forward and upward part of the body, and the back goes after everything: so the teachers go before the folk, and the folk go after. When therefore the eyes of the teacher's mind, whose duties are to go before with good examples, are darkened, then the people will bend their backs to many heavy burdens.

Chap. II.

That the learned, who are not willing so to live as they have learned in books, should not undertake the honour of the teacher's office.

Many wise teachers, also, by their modes of living, contend against the spiritual commandments, which they teach with their words, when they live in one wise and in another teach. Often when the pastor walks in ways of danger, the herd, that is unwary, falls. Of such herdsmen the prophet said, "Ye have trodden down the grass of God's sheep, and ye have disturbed their water with your feet, although ye have drunk it beforehand, undisturbed." So then the teachers drink water very clear, when they learn the divine wisdom, and also when they teach it; but they disturb it with their own evil habits, when the folk take example after their evil habits, not after their teaching. Though then the people may thirst after instruction, they may not drink it, but it is disturbed by this, that the teachers do one thing and teach another. Of them the Lord said again through the prophet, "Evil priests are the destruction of the folk." No man injures the holy congregation more than those that undertake the name and the order of the holy condition, and then do wickedly; for no man dares to reprove these, though they may become guilty, but sins are greatly extended by these means, that they (who commit them) are so honoured. But they themselves would flee the burthens of so great guilt, who were unworthy of it, if they with the ears of their hearts would hear, and earnestly think upon that saying of Christ, when he said, He that deceiveth any of these little ones, it were better for him that some ass-mill were tied to his neck, and so he were cast away to the sea's bottom." By the mill is signified the circuit of this world, and also man's life and his labour, and by the sea's bottom their end and the last judgment. When the mill is turned round, then the man is ended. When the great mill is turned round, then this world is ended. He, then, that comes to the holy condition, and then with evil examples, either of words or works, brings others into error; it were better for him that he should have ended his life in a lesser condition, and in earthly occupations; for if any one does well in this, he will have a good reward of it, if he does evil, he will suffer less punishment in hell, if he comes thither alone, than he will (do) if he shall bring others with him.

Chap. III.

Of the burthens of the ruler's office and how he shall overlook all hardships, and how he shall be frightened for every ease.

Therefore have we said this in a few words, that we would make known how great is the burthen of the teacher's office, lest that any of those that may be unworthy of it, should dare to undertake it, lest, through the coveting of the world's honour, they obtain the leadership of perdition. Very aptly James the Apostle restrained them, when he said, "Brethren, let there not be of you too many masters." For the Mediator himself of God and men, that is Christ, fled from the receiving of an earthly kingdom, even he who oversteps all the wisdom of the upper spirits, and before the world's ages reigned in the heavens. It is written in the gospel, "The Jews came, and would make him by force a king;" when the Saviour knew that, he passed by them and hid himself, Who might easily give counsel to men, without guilt, but he that created them? He did not flee the kingdom because that any man was better worthy of it, but he wished to give us an example that we should not so greatly covet it, and he also would suffer for us. He would not be a king, and by his own will he came to the rood-gallows. The dignities of the kingly state he refused, and the punishment of the most ignominious death he chose, for this, that we, who are his limbs, may learn from him, that we flee from the flatteries of this world; and also in order that we should not fear its terrors and its horrors, and that for the truth we should love labour and dread ease, and for this cause eschew it, for that on account of prosperity man is often puffed up with pride, and then difficulties through sorrow and through cares cleanse him and humble him. In a prosperous state the mind becomes up-heaved and in difficulties, though it was erst upheaved, it becomes humbled. In prosperity a man forgets himself; in affliction he shall bethink himself, though he be unwilling. In a state of security man often omits to do good; in trouble he often amends the evil that he formerly did.

Very often a man is made submissive to the discipline of adversity though before he was unwilling to be so to his teachers' manners and doctrines. But although afflictions then correct and instruct him, soon, if he comes into power, for the reverence of the people he is turned to pride, and becomes accustomed to vain glory. Thus Saul the king; first he shunned the kingdom and counted himself very unworthy of it; but, as soon as he took upon himself the rule of the kingdom, he rose into arrogance, and was displeased with the same Samuel, who had formerly brought him to the kingdom, and moreover had consecrated him, for that he (Samuel) told him his faults before the people, in that he could not, just before, controul their will; and when he would go from him he then caught him and rent his garment, and dishonoured him. So also David, who full nigh in all things pleased God, as soon as he had not the burthens of so many difficulties, he was wounded with pride, and he made that known in a very cruel manner by slaying Uriah his own faithful servant, on account of a shameless passion for his wife. The same, too, who had formerly spared many evil men who had offended against himself, became afterwards so immoderately greedy of the good man's death without any guilt or any opposition to him. The same David, who forbore so, that he did not do any evil to the king, who had brought him into such harsh banishment, and who had often driven him away from his native soil, when he had him completely in his power in the cave, took a lap of his garment as a token that he had power over him; but, nevertheless, he let him go, on account of his old pledges. The same David exposed his army to great danger, and sent many into exile, when he plotted concerning his faithful servant that was guiltless. His guilt would have drawn him very far away from the number of all holy men, if on the other hand again labours and adversities had not preserved him.

Chap IV.

And how often the business of power and of government rends the mind of the ruler.

Very often the manifold care of those that undertake teachership troubles the heart, and when the mind is divided into many parts, it is in every one of these the more unsteady, and also the more unprofitable. Of them Solomon the wise said, " My son, distract not on too many things thy mind and thy work likewise." For that often, when a man gives up the awe and the resolution which he by right should have within him, his mind allures him to very many an unprofitable work; he is careful about them, and is very mindful of them; and forgets himself when he binds his mind to those unprofitable works more than needs. It is with him as with the man that is busied in a journey with other affairs until that he knows not whither he formerly wished to go; and he cannot think what is lost to him in the delay with which he mars the time, and how greatly he sins in this. Hezekiah, king of the Israelites, did not think that he sinned, when he led the foreign ambassadors into his treasure-house, and shewed them his gold hoard: but he nevertheless experienced the anger of God in the harm that came to his son after his days; and nevertheless he thought it was no sin. Often when it happens to any one, that he doeth anything glorious and wonderful, and when those that are subject to him, wonder at him and commend him, then he is lifted up in his mind, and he fully provokes the anger of his judge against him, though he may not display it in evil works, yet nevertheless by self-love the judge is urged to anger, and the judge who knows every thought will also judge the thought. We can conceal our thoughts and our will from men, but we cannot from God. Moreover, the king of the Babylonians was very much lifted up in his mind on account of his power, and of his success, when he made joy of the great work, and fairness of the city, and he preferred himself in his thoughts to all other men; and he tacitly said in his mind, " How is not this now the great Babylon that I have myself built for a royal seat, and for majesty, for beauty, and glory to myself, by mine own might and strength." That silent voice, the unseen judge very quickly heard, and answered him very manifestly by the punishments with which he very quickly avenged it.

That loftiness he discovered and rebuked when he cut him off from the worldly kingdom, and turned him to irrational cattle, and so, changing his mind, he joined him to the field-going beasts, and so, by the severe judgment he lost his humanity. The same who weened that he was over all other men,—to him it happened that he himself knew not whether he was a man. Yet nevertheless though I now account this, I speak not ill of a great work nor of rightful power, but I reprove that a man for this should be lifted up in his mind, and I would strengthen the weaknesses of the heart, and controul the wills of the unworthy, in order that none of them may dare to seize, in such a careless way, on rule and on the teacher's office, lest they go into such a dangerous path, who cannot stand without quaking in an even field.

Chapter V.

Of those that may be useful in the office of elder, by their example and abilities, and then, for their own ease, shun it.

And many are honoured with great gifts of many powers and faculties, for that they should teach many and for the need of others they receive such like gifts, that is they hold their bodies clean from sinful pleasures: the second is, that they are strong in the strength of abstinence: the third is, that they are filled with the sweetmeats of learning; the fourth is, that they are in troublesome things and in every weariness—patient: and in forbearance —humble; the fifth is, that they have activity and boldness that they can have power; the sixth is, that they are courteous; the seventh is, that they are austere and strict for righteousness. To those then who are like this, and have such an employment enjoined upon them, and they refuse it, it often happens that they are bereaved of the gifts that God gave them for the sake of many men, and not for theirs alone, When they exclusively think how they themselves should become most perfect, and care not what other men's affairs come to, they by this bereave themselves of the good, which they desire exclusively to have. Of such men Christ in his Gospel said, " No man shall light a candle under a bushel," and again he saith to Peter the apostle, "Peter, lovest thou me?" He said " Thou knowest that I love thee," and then said the Lord, " Feed then my sheep, if thou lovest me." If then the feeding of the sheep is a sign of love, why then does he to whom God gives such abilities, refuse to feed his flock, unless that he wishes to say that he does not love the Lord and the High Shepherd of all creatures? Of him had Paul the apostle said, If Christ died for all, then all men become dead. What is then better, the while that we live, than that we live not to the lusts of our flesh, but to the commands of Him who for us was dead and afterwards again arose? Of this saith Moses: If any one die and beget no child, if he leave a brother, let him take to his wife, if he then a child thereby beget, then let him produce it for the brother that is dead, who erewhile had her. But if he will refuse his wife, then let her spit in his face, and let his relation unshoe his one foot, that men may afterwards call his town the town of the unshod. This was a right judgment under the old law, and it is now to us a parable. The brother that was first dead betokeneth Christ. He shewed himself after his resurrection and said, "Go and make known to my brethren, that they come to Galilee, there shall they see me." He died as if he died without children, for he had not yet filled up the number of his chosen. So, as under the old law it was bidden the living brother to take the dead brother's wife, so it is proper that the care of the holy church, which is the congregation of Christ's folk, should be enjoined on him that may have sufficient power over it, and knows how to give good counsel to it. If therefore any one renounces it, then it is proper that the wife should spit in his face, that is, that the congregation of the people should reprove him equally as if they spat into his face. For that, as he will neither give that which God has given him, nor help the people with that with which He hath helped him, so is it proper that the holy congregation should reprove the good of every one of those that desires to have it, as good for himself alone, and is unwilling to assist others: he shall rightly be unshod of one foot, and men shall call him, in reproach, the unshod one. Of these, said Christ in his gospel, "Shoe your feet, that ye may be ready to go the way of peace, after the commandments of my books." If then we have as much care and as great anxiety for our neighbours as for ourselves, then we shall have both feet shod very irreproachably: if, however, we disregard our neighbour's advantage, and think about our own separately, then shall our one foot be very disgracefully unshod. There are many men, as we have said before, who are honoured with many great gifts from God, and then are led on by a yearning for meditations upon God's wisdom alone, and therefore avoid the useful obedience of teaching, and are not willing to think upon this ; how they may be most useful to their neighbours, but love secret places, and fly from the faces of men. If, therefore, God will very rightly and strictly judge men, and they honour him not for his mild-heartedness, then are they guilty of as many crimes as they had the power of controulling by their doctrines and examples, if they had been willing to be among men. What do those think who shine in works of this kind, and that may in this way be serviceable to their neighbours ? why should they better trust in the merits of their secresy and solitude than this ; how they should most help other men ? Lo ! the only begotten Son of God went forth from the bosom of his Father to our presence, that He might help us.

Chapter VI.

Of those that for lowly-mindedness flee the burthens of the teacher's office; but they rightly are lowly, who do not strive against the divine judgment.

There are many that flee from it for lowly-mindedness alone, for that they are unwilling that men should raise them up above those that seem to them better than themselves. There is, however, no doubt of this, if lowly-mindedness of this kind is begirt with other good habits, that is, before the eyes of God, true lowly-mindedness, when a man does not for wilfulness withstand the useful works which he is bidden to undertake. It is not true lowly-mindedness, if a man understands that this is God's will, that he be over others, that he then gainsay. But let him be subject to God's will and judgement, and forsake the vices of self-will, when he is convinced, and it is declared to him, that it may be useful to others in those things, which are then enjoined upon him. In his mind he shall flee from it, though for obedience he shall undertake it.

Chapter VII.

That often the teacher's office is verry blamelessly wished for, and also many are very blamelessly driven to it.

Nevertheless many persons very blamelessly desire office and authority (elderdom), and many are also very blamelessly driven to it. That we can understand very clearly if we recollect the two prephets whom God would send forth to teach : the one offered himself of his own will for the teaching and for the journey ; the other, for the dread that he felt lest he might not do it so worthily, refused him—that was Jeremiah. When He would send him, then he prayed with lowliness of mind, that he would not send him, and said " Alas, alas, alas ! Lord, I am a child, what can I speak ?" But Isaiah, when the Lord asked whom he might send, then quoth Isaiah, " I am ready, send me." Look now, how unlike a speech out of these two men's mouths, but it was from a very like will, for that it flowed from one well : though it flowed into two [streams] nevertheless the spring was true love about which we have two commandments : the first is that we love God, the second that we love our neighbour. For love, Isaiah wished how he might be most useful to his neighbours in this life of hardship, and for that he wished the ministry of the teacher's office. Jeremiah, however, desired to join himself continually to the love of his Maker and for this he gainsaid and was unwilling that he should be sent to teach. That same thing that he blamelessly dreaded to undertake, the other very praise-worthily desired. The one feared that he should lose in speaking, the treasures which he had the power of thinking on in silence ; the other feared that he might discover by his silence that he was silent with some harm, where he might cry aloud with advantage, if he laboured about it earnestly. But it is our duty to think very deeply about both of these men, for that he who there gainsaid did not fully gainsay, and he that wished to be sent saw before that he was cleansed through the coals of the altar, lest any one, uncleansed, should dare to undertake so great a holiness of the pure ministry of the priesthood ; or, again, any one should dare, under colour of lowly-mindedness, proudly to gainsay as if he feigned lowly-mindedness, and nevertheless acted for vain glory, if the grace from on high chooses him. But for that it is very difficult for any man to know when he is made clean, he may, therefore, with the greater security decline the ministry. Nevertheless let him not decline too obstinately, as we have said before, when he understands the heavenly will that he should do it. Both of these things Moses fulfilled, when he refused elderdom or authority, he both would and would not, and nevertheless, for lowly-mindedness, [he] consented. We know that he would not have been humble if he undertook the office of leader to such an innumerable people without awe, and again, he would have been arrogant, if he refused to be submissive to his Creator. But both of these things he did, for lowly-mindedness and for obedience. He considered himself and then it seemed to him that he could not do it, but nevertheless he consented, for he had confidence in the power of him that commanded it him. Moreover, the holy man knew that he had God's help, and yet nevertheless he feared to undertake the office of guide to the people. But now the foolish do not fear, on account of their own faults, to be over others, and they cannot gather from such an example how great a sin and how great a danger it is! God himself persuaded Moses into the office, yet nevertheless was afraid; and now such wretched men try and court—they would undertake the honour (worship) and also the burthens. And those that are oppressed with their own burthens, so that they have no power to stand are willing gladly to undertake those of other men, and without any necessity they bow their shoulders under other men's burthens in addition to their own. He cannot bear his own, and yet would have more.

Chapter VIII.

Of those that wish to undertake bishophood, how they grasp at the saying of the apostle Paul to support their wishes.

But those that desire to grasp at such an employment, make an excuse for their covetousness by the saying in which Paul said " He that wisheth bishophood, wisheth a good work."

If however, he praised and recommended it to men, he hath again controuled the wish for it when he said, " It becometh a bishop that he be blameless." And there above is told what sort of person he must be if he is irreproachable. With one sentence he exhorted, with another he terrified, as if he openly said, " I commend that ye seek, but learn that ye may know what it is: but if ye take no care to measure yourselves of what sort ye are, as ye raise yourselves into an higher office, so you make your blameworthiness more manifest and widely notorious. In this way the great artist by exhorting pushes on and by terrifying controuls the arrogance of his hearers with the reproof that he may bring them into life. It is also to be considered that in the times in which the bishophood was so praised, whosoever undertook it undertook martyrdom. In those times it was to be praised that one should wish for bishophood when there was no doubt that through it he should come to heavy martyrdom. It is a token that a man held the bishophood in an orderly manner, that he ended it in good works; for it is said, " He that wishes for bishophood, wisheth a good work." He therefore that does not, for the desire of such work, seek the bishop's office, is a witness to himself that he desires glory to himself. He therefore not only does that evil, that he does not love holy ministrations, but he altogether despises them, and when he endeavours to attain to the honour of the employment, his mind is fed with the meditation of the desire of other men's subjection and with his own pride, and he is glad of this, how men shall praise him. Then he uplifts his heart for that and he rejoices for the weight of the flowing wealth. He feigns humility, and therefore seeks this world's gain. Under the pretext by which he should check vain glory he adds to it: when he should scatter his gains, he gathers them. When his mind thinks to lay hold on humility for its own exaltation, what he shews without, he changes within.

CHAPTER IX.

That the mind which wishes to be before others, deceives itself when it thinks to work good works, and flatters other men if they have world's honour, and will then uplift itself after he has it.

But when he wishes to undertake the honour and the authority he thinks in the surface of his mind that he shall work many a good work therein, and he thinks with inward mind that he desires the office for glory and for pride. They however meditate and consult in their mind's rind to work many a good work, but in the pith is another thing hid. For in his outward mind he lies to himself about himself concerning the good works—feigns that he loves that which he does not love. This world's glory he loves, and he feigns as if he shunned and dreaded it. When he wishes in his mind that he should reign, he is much afraid and very modest, when he has that which he would have, he is very bold. When he is seeking it he dreads that he may not come to it, and, soon as he comes to the honour, so seems to him that he who gave it him owed it him, as a necessary debt, and brooks the spiritual benefice in a worldly manner, and forgets very quickly what he before religiously thought. How may it be without that, that the mind which before was led from its wont for the desire of the world's honour, that it be not turned back when it has that which it formerly desired ? for soon will the mind's eyes be turned back to the works which it formerly wrought. But let each man think before how profitable he is, and how obedient to those whom he then with right should obey, in the things which he then does; then may he know by that if he shall have a higher office, whether he then may do that which he thinks beforehand that he would do ; for seldom does a man learn humility in great power, if he formerly in a less office was proud and reckless. How may he then flee praise and glory when he is exalted, who coveted them before when he was without [them] ? How can he be without covetousness when he must think about many men's sustenance, if he would not when he might think about his own alone ? Let him take heed lest his own thought beguile him ; lest he trust that he will do well in the greater office if he would not in the less, for in a higher office a man oftener loses a good custom than he learns it therein, if he had it not before in a less office, and in more leisure. Very easily may an unlearned ship-steerer rightly steer in a smooth sea; but the learned trusts not to himself in the rough sea and in the great storms. What then is the rule and authority [of a pastor] but the mind's storm, which is always striking the ship of the heart with squalls of the thoughts ? and it is dragged hither and thither into very narrow bays of words and works, as if it were broken among great and many rocks.

2. What is now more to be spoken about this, but that he who is known to have the virtues which we mentioned above, undertake [the office] if he needs shall, and he who is not such, come not thereto, though he be compelled. Let him who is striving in such virtues and merits as we spoke of before, and then too strongly refuses the eldership, beware that he do not knit the received money in the napkin, about which Christ spoke in his gospel; that is, that he tie not up God's gifts, which he has received, both in abilities and in goods, in the skirt of his sloth, and that he do not for his laziness hide them, lest it be afterwards punished to him. But let those who are empty of such gifts, and yet covet the elder- ship, beware that by their unright example they hinder not those who go into the right way towards the kingdom of heaven, as did the Pharisees : they neither would themselves go into the right way, nor let others [go into it]. About such a thing as this, it is

to be considered and meditated, that he who undertakes bishophood undertakes the folk's infirmities, and must go through the land as the 'leech' among sick men's houses. If he then has not yet renounced his own evil habits, how may he leech other men's minds, when he bears many open wounds in his own? That leech is much too bold and too shameless who goes among other men's houses leeching, and has on his own face open wounds unleeched.

Chapter X.
What sort of person he shall be who shall come to rulership.

But all powers should draw to bishophood the man who dies in many sufferings of his body, and lives spiritually, and cares not for this world's prosperity, nor dreads any adversity of this world, but loves God's will only. It becomes such a mind that he, neither for weakness of body nor for the world's reproach alone, strive against the office, nor should he be coveting other men's goods, but be liberal of his own; and let his breast always be for piety inclined to forgiveness, though never more than is becoming for righteousness. Nor shall he do aught unlawful, but that which other men do unlawfully, he shall weep for as his own guilt. Their infirmities he shall suffer in his heart, and of the good of his neighbours he shall be as fain as of his own. His works shall be of such worth that other men may imitate them. He shall toil so to live as he may moisten the dried hearts with the flowing waves of his love. He shall learn that he be accustomed to continual prayers until he know that he may obtain from God what he desires: as if it were said to him, " Now thou calledst me; now I am here." What wantest thou now? if some guilty man comes and begs one of us to lead him to some powerful man, and intercede for him, when he is angry against him; if he then is not known to me, nor any man of his household, I will very soon answer him and say, " I cannot plead that cause; I am not so well acquainted with him." If we then are ashamed to speak of such a thing to unknown men, how then dare we speak of such a thing to God? or how dare he seize on the office that he should plead to God for other men, who knows not himself [to be] acquainted with God through his life's earning? Or how dares he seek reconciliation for other men, and knows not whether reconciliation has been made for himself; he may dread that, for his own sins, he works more wrath. We all know by men, he who bids the man intercede for him with another, with whom he (the other) is also angry, he irritates the angry mind, and stirs a worse anger. Let those consider that, who then yet covet this world, and take heed that by their intercession they stir not a heavier anger of the strict Judge. Let them beware, when they covet so great rule, that they become not rulers to the perdition of their subjects.

Let every man, therefore, carefully examine himself, lest he should dare to undertake the instruction of the people, while any evil habit reigns in him. Let not him desire to be an intercessor for other men's guilt, who is defiled by his own.

These ten chapters of King Alfred's version of *Gregory's Pastoral Care* are sufficient to shew the character of the work. Even if it were desirable to translate the whole, a great impediment to our doing so would be the nature of some parts of it, far too indelicate for modern general perusal, though quite of a piece with other treatises on points which in former times it was not thought unbecoming of the Church to handle.

The translation here printed is from the pen of the late lamented Rev. H. W. Norman, whose high Anglo-Saxon knowledge was cut short by an early death. The hand of the original translator being still, the translation has received the revision of that able scholar, Mr. Thomson, whose help has been felt in many other parts of the work.   J. A. G.

A
Modern English Version
OF
KING ALFRED'S
BLOSSOM-GATHERINGS FROM SAINT AUGUSTINE.

KING ALFRED'S PREFACE

[*The manuscript begins so abruptly, that there is ground for believing the beginning to have been lost.*]

. . . . gathered me then javelins,[1] and 'stud-shafts,' and 'lay-shafts,' and helves to each of the tools which I could work with, and 'bay-timbers,' and 'bolt-timbers,' and to each of the works that I could work, the comeliest trees, by the deal that I might bear. Neither came I with a burthen home, for I did not wish to bring all the wood home, if I might bear it all. In every tree I saw something which I needed at home; therefore I advise every one who is able and has many wains, that he trade to the same wood where I cut the stud-shafts, there fetch more for himself, and load his wains with fair rods, that he may wind many a neat wall, and set many a comely house, and build many a fair town, of them; and thereby may dwell merrily and softly, both winter and summer, so as I now yet have not done. But he who taught me, to whom the wood was agreeable, [even] he may make me to dwell more softly in this temporary cottage; by this way, the while that I am in this world, and also in the everlasting home which he has promised us through Saint Augustine, and Saint Gregory and Saint Jerome, and through many other holy fathers; as I believe also that for the merits of all those he will both make this way more convenient than it was ere this, and especially enlighten

---

1. Kigelas, unaccountably made "rigelas" by Junius, and quoted Rigelas by Wanley, and Lye or Manning; but "cigel" *jaculum* occurs elsewhere. Stud, a prop—Lay-shafts, beams to lie in a horizontal posture; Bay, or bow-timbers, to be bent into curves; Bolts, to be set upright as standards, in buildings.

the eyes of my mind so that I may search out the right way to the everlasting home and to the everlasting glory, and to the everlasting rest, which is promised us through those holy Fathers. Be [it] so.

2. It is no wonder, though men 'swink'[2] in timber-working, and in the out-leading and in the building; but every man wishes, after he has built a cottage on his lord's lease, by his help, that he may sometimes rest him therein, and hunt, and fowl, and fish, and use it in every way to the lease, both on sea and on land, until the time that he earn bookland and everlasting heritage through his lord's mercy. So do the wealthy Giver, who wields both these temporary cottages and the everlasting homes, may he who shaped both, and wields both, grant me that I be meet for each, both here to be profitable, and thither to come.

3. AUGUSTINUS, bishop of Carthage, wrought two books about his own Mind. The books are called SOLILOQUIORUM, that is, of his mind's musing and doubting; how his Reason answered his Mind, when the mind doubted about anything, or wished to know anything which it could not clearly understand before.[3] Then said he, his mind went oft asking and searching out various and rare things, and most of all, about himself, what he was; whether his mind and his soul were deadly and perishing, or it were aye-living and eternal; and again, about his good, what it was, and what good was best for him to do, and what evil to 'forlet.'

4. AUGUSTINE. Then answered me something I know not what, whether myself or another thing, nor know I whether it was within me or withont; but of which I soothly ween, that it was my Reason, and then it said to me, "If thou have any good 'herd,' who well knows to hold that which thou gettest and committest to him, shew him to me; but if thou have none so prudent, seek him till thou find him; for thou canst not both always sit over that which thou hast gotten, and also get more." Then quoth I, "To whom else will I commit what else I get, but to my memory?"[4] R. Is thy memory so strong that it may hold everything which thou thinkest and commendest to it to hold? A. No, oh no; neither mine nor

2. Part of the word has been torn off,—the translator supposes it to have been swinke (swince, or swinco). The Junian transcript, swilce.
3. Here ends King Alfred's Introduction.
4. Instead of "Then quoth it," "Then quoth I," as in the A. S.—R. and A. here mark the speakers, as in the Latin—Ratio, (Reason) and Augustinus.

any man's memory is so strong that it may hold everything that is committed to it. R. Commit it then to letters, and write it; but methinks, however, that thou art too unhale, that thou canst not write it all; and though thou were altogether hale, thou wouldest need to have a retired place, and leisure from every other thing, and a few known and able men with thee, who would not hinder thee anything, but help thy ability. A. I have none of those, neither the leisure, nor other men's help, nor so retired a place that might suit me for such a work; therefore I know not what I shall do. R. I wot not, then, aught better than that thou pray. Make thy wish to God, the Saviour of mind and body, that thou may thereby get health, and what thou wishest. And when thou hast prayed, write then the prayer, lest thou forget it, that thou be the worthier of thy ability. And pray in few words deeply, with full understanding. A. I will do as thou teachest me.

5. O Lord, who art the Maker of all creatures, grant me first that I may know thee rightly and distinctly, and that I may earn that I be worthy that thou for thy mercy redeem and deliver me. I call to thee, Lord, who wroughtest all that else could not be made, nor even abide without thee. I call to thee, Lord, who leavest none of the creatures to become to naught. To Him I call, who wrought all the creatures beautiful, without any matter. To thee I call, who never wroughtest any evil, but every good work wroughtest. To Him I call, who teacheth to a few wise men that evil is naught. Lord, thou who hast wrought all things worthy and nothing unworthy; to thee is no creature untoward; though any one will, it cannot, for thou hast shapen them all orderly and peaceable and harmonious, and none of them can altogether 'fordo' another. But always the beautiful beautifieth the unbeautiful. To Thee I call, whom everything loveth that can love, both those which know what they love, and those which know not what they love. Thou who hast shapen all the creatures without any evil, very good,—thou, who wilt not altogether shew thyself openly to any but them who are cleansed in their mind,—I call to Thee, Lord, for thou art Father of soothfastness, and wisdom, and true life, and of the highest life, and of the highest blessedness, and of the highest brightness, and of the understanding's light.—Thou, who art Father of the Son, who has awakened and yet wakens us from the sleep of our sins, and warneth us that we come to thee, —To thee I pray, Lord, who art the highest soothfastness, and for

thee is sooth all that sooth is. I pray to thee, Lord, who art the highest wisdom, and through thee are wise all they that are wise. I pray to thee, Lord, who art right life, and through thee live all they that live. Thou art the highest blessedness, and for thee are blessed all they that are blessed. Thou art the highest good, [and for thee is good all that good is,] and beautiful. Thou art the understanding's light; through thee man understands. I pray to thee, Lord, who wieldest all the world; whom we cannot know bodily, neither by eyes, nor by smell, nor by ears, nor by taste, nor by touch; although such laws as we have, and such customs as we have, we took from thy kingdom, and from thy kingdom we draw the example of all the good that we do. For every one falls who flees from thee, and every one rises who turns to thee, and every one stands who abides in thee; and he dies who altogether forsakes thee, and he quickens who comes to thee; and each of them,* and he lives indeed who thoroughly abides in thee. None forsakes thee that is wise, and none seeks thee but the wise, and none altogether finds thee but the cleansed. That is, that a man is lost, that a man forsakes thee. He who loves thee seeks thee; he who follows thee has thee. The truths which thou hast given us awaken us from the sleep of our sins. Our hope heaves us up to thee. Our limbs, which thou hast given us, fasten us to thee. Through thee we overcome our foes, both ghostly and bodily. Thou who art a free giver, come to me, and have mercy on me; for thou hast bestowed on us great gifts, that is, that we shall never altogether perish, so that we become to naught.

6. O Lord! thou who warnest us that we should watch, thou hast given us reason, that we may discern and distinguish good and evil, and flee the evil. Thou who hast given us the power that we should not despond in any toil nor in any inconvenience it is no wonder, for thou very well rulest, and makest us well serve thee. Thou hast well taught us that we may understand that that was strange to us and transitory, which we looked upon as our own, that is worldly wealth, and thou hast also taught us to understand that that is our own, which we looked upon as strange to us; that is, the kingdom of heaven, which we then disregarded. Thou who hast taught us that we should do naught unlawful, and hast also taught [us] that we should not be sorrowful though our substance waned to us. Thou who hast

---

5. Some error or omission in the MS.

taught us that we should subject our body to our mind. Thou who didst then overcome death when thou thyself didst arise, and also wilt make all men arise. Thou who honourest us all to thee, and cleansest us from all our sins, and justifiest us, and hearest all our prayers. Thou who hast made us of thy household, and who teachest us all righteousness, and always teachest us good. and always doest us good, and leavest us not to serve an unrighteous lord, as we formerly did. Thou callest us to our way, and leadest us to the door, and openest to us, and givest us the bread of everlasting life, and the drink from life's well. Thou who threatenest men for their sins, and teachest them to deem right dooms, and to do righteousness.

7. Thou hast strengthenest in, and yet strengthened our belief that the unbelieving may not mar and hinder us. Thou hast given us, and yet givest, the understanding, that we may overcome the error of those [who teach that] men's souls have no recompense, after this world, of their earnings either of good or of evil, whichsoever they here do; Thou who hast loosed us from the thraldom of other creatures. Thou always preparest everlasting life for us, and preparest us also for the everlasting life.

8. Come now to my help, thou who art the only, eternal, and true God of Majesty, the Father, the Son, and the Holy Ghost, without any jarring or change, and without any need or unmight, and without death. Thou who always dwellest in the highest brightness, and in the highest steadiness; in the highest unanimity and in the highest sufficiency: for to thee is no want of any good; but thou always abidest thus full of every good unto eternity. Thou art Father and Son and Holy Ghost.

9. Thee serve all the creatures which thou hast shapen; to thee is every good soul subject; by thy behest the heaven turneth and all the stars keep their run: by thy behest the sun brings light by day, and the moon [brings] light at night. By their likeness thou steerest and wieldest all this world, so that all creatures change as day and night. Thou rulest the year, and riddest the change of the four tides, that is, Lent, and Summer, aud Harvest and Winter; of which each changes with another, and turns so that each is again evenly that which it was before, and there where it was before: and so change all the stars (*planets*), and turn in the same wise; and again the sea and rivers. On the same wise turn all creatures; some change in another wise, so that the same

come not again there where they formerly were, altogether so as they formerly were, but others come for them; as leaf on trees and apples, and grass, and worts, and trees, grow old and sear; and others come, wax green and grow and ripen; for that they again begin to wither. And so all beasts and fowls, so as is now long to reckon all to thee. Yea even men's bodies grow old; as other creatures grow old; but as they formerly live more worthily than trees or beasts, so they also shall arise more worthfully on doom's day, so that never after shall the bodies end nor wax old: and though the body was formerly rotten, yet was the soul always living since it was first shapen.

10. And all the creatures about which we are speaking that they seem to us unharmonious and unsteady—they have however some deal of steadiness, for they are bridled with the bridle of God's commandments. God gave freedom to men's souls, that they might do either good or evil, whether they would: and promised good [as a] reward to the well doing, and evil to the evildoers. With God is prepared the wellspring of every good to us which we have; He shields us against all evils. Nothing is above him: but all things are under him, or with, or in him. He wrought man to his likeness; and every man who knows himself, knows that this is all sooth.

11. To that God I call, and say, Hear me! hear me, O Lord, for thou art my God, and my Lord, my Father, and my Maker, and my Governor, and my hope, and my substance, and my worship, and my house, and my birth-land, and my health and my life. Hear, hear me, Lord, thy servant! Thee few understand. Thee alone I love over all other things: thee I seek; thee I follow; thee I am ready to serve; under thy government I wish to abide for thou alone reignest. I pray thee, that thou command me that which thou wilt. But heal my eyes, and upon [them], that I may see thy wonders; and drive from me folly and pride; and give me wisdom, that I may know thee: and teach me whither I should look to thee: that I may there behold thee; then believe I that I shall gladly do that which thou commandest me.

12. I beseech thee, thou merciful, well-willing, and well-working Lord, that thou receive me, thy runaway; for I was formerly thine and then fled I from thee to the devil, and fulfilled his will; and much misery I suffered in his service. But if it now seems to thee, as to me it seems, long enough I have suffered the pains, which I

now awhile have suffered, and have longer than I ought served thy foes, whom thou hast in bonds ; long enough have I been in the reproach and the shame which they brought on me. But receive me now, thy lonely servant ; for I am come fleeing from them. Lo ! they took me before I had fled from thee to them. Give me never again to them now [that] I have sought thee ; but open thy door and teach me how I shall come to it. I have naught to bring thee but a good will ; for I myself have naught else ; nor know I aught better than that. I love the heavenly and the ghostly over this heavenly, as I also do, good Father, for I know naught better than that.

13. But I wot not how I shall now come to thee unless thou teach me ; but teach me it and help me. If by faith they find thee, who find thee, give me then faith. If by any other craft they find thee who find thee, give me that craft. If by wisdom they find thee, who find thee, give me then wisdom ; and increase in me the hope of the everlasting life, and thy love increase in me. O how wonderful is thy goodness, for it is unlike all goods. I desire to come to thee, and all that I have need of on the way I desire from thee, and chiefly that without which I cannot come to thee if thou forsake me : for through thee I . . . . . . But I wot though, that thou wilt not forsake me, unless I forsake thee : nor will I also forsake thee, for thou art the highest good. There is none who rightly seeks thee that he finds thee not. He alone seeks thee aright whom thou teachest aright, that they may seek thee, and how they shall seek thee. Well, O good Father, well deliver me from the error in which I have erred till this, and yet err in ; and teach me the way in which no foe may find [me] ere I come to thee. If I love naught over thee, I beseech thee that I may find thee ; and if I immoderately and unlawfully desire anything, free me of that, and make me worthy that I may see thee.

14. Thou best Father, and thou wisest, I commend to thee my body, that thou hold it hale. I wot not, though, what I there ask, whether I ask [what is] profitable or unprofitable to myself, or to the friends whom I love, and [who] love me. Nor wot I this, how long thou wilt hold it hale ; therefore I commit and commend it, for thou knowest better than I know what I need ; therefore I pray thee, that thou always teach me the while that I am in this body, and in this world ; and help me that I may always search out the counsel that is likeworth [1] to thee and best and rightworth to me for this life.

15. And now yet, over all other things, I most earnestly pray

---

1. Worthy to be liked.

thee, that thou altogether convert me to thee, and let nothing overcome me on this way, so that I may not come to thee ; and cleanse me the while that I am in this world, and make me humble.² Give me ....³ Make me discreet and righteous, and forethoughtful, and perfect. And, O God, make me a lover and a finder of thy wisdom. And make me worthy that I be dwelling in thy blessed kingdom. Be it so!

16. (Then, quoth I,) Now I have done as thou advisedst me; now I have prayed, as thou advisedst me. Then answered me my reason, and quoth : R. I see that thou hast prayed ; but say now what thou desiredst, or what thou wouldest have. A. I would understand and know all what I now sang. R. Gather, then, from all those things, about which thou hast sung, that which seems to thee to be most needful to thee, and most profitable to be known, and clothe it then with few words, and tell it me. A. I will tell thee soon. God I would understand, and my own soul I would know. R. Wouldest thou know aught more ? A. Many things I wish to know, which I know not; I wish not, however, to know anything more earnestly than this. R. Search after it then, and seek what thou askest ; and tell me first what thou most intimately knowest, and say then to me, " Enough known to me will God and my soul be, if they shall be as known to me as this thing." A. I wot nothing so known to me as I would that God were. R. What must we do, then, if thou knowest not the measure ? Thou shouldest know when it seemed to thee enough ; and if thou ever shouldest come to that, that thou then shouldest not go over that, but shouldest seek elsewhat, lest thou shouldest desire anything above measure. A. I know what thou wouldest, I should shew thee by some example, but I cannot, for I know nothing like God, that I can say to thee, " Thus certainly would I know God as I know this thing." R. I wonder at thee, why thou sayest that thou knowest nothing like God, and even yet knowest not what he is. A. If I knew aught like him, I would love that very vehemently. But since I know nothing like him, I love nothing but him and my own soul ; and yet I know not what either of them is.

17. R. Thou sayest that thou lovest nothing but God and thy soul. If, then, that is so, dost thou then love no other friend ? A. Why, if I love a soul should I not love my friend ? has not he a soul ? If thou lovest thy friend for this, that he has a soul, why lovest

2. Literally, unmoody. 3. Sile me ofer eds. What the two last words mean is doubtful.

thou not then each thing that has a soul; why lovest thou not mice and flies? A. I love not them, for they are fleshly beasts, not men. R. How, have not thy friends bodies, as beasts [have]? A. I love them not for that, but because they are men, and have reason in their mind, which I love. Yea, even in manners, those whom I hate, I hate [them] because they turn the good of reason into evil; for each of these is left free to me, both to love what is good, and to hate what is evil. Therefore I love every one of my friends, some less, some more; and each of them whom I love more than another, I love him so much more than the other, as I understand that he has a better will than the other, and a will to make his reason more profitable.

18. R. Well enough thou understandest it, and right enough. But if any one should now say to thee, that he could teach thee how thou mayest understand God so clearly, that he were as [well] known to thee as is to thee now thy servant Alipius, would there then in that seem to thee enough? or how much wouldest thou thank him for it? A. "Thank," I would say; not the more, however, would I say "Enough." R. Why? A. Alipius is more known to me than God, and yet I know him not so well as I would. R. Look now that thou desire not above measure, now thou measurest them together, wouldest know God so as Alipius. A. No, I make them not the more alike, though I name them together. But I say that a man oft knows more about the higher [things] than about the lower. I know now about the moon how it will fare tomorrow, and other nights; but, which is lower, I know not what I shall eat tomorrow.

19. Wotst thou then yet enough about God, if he is so known to thee, as is now the journey of the moon, in which constellation it now is, or into which it is going thence? No, but would that he were more known to me. The moon I see through my eyes; but to me [it] is unknown, that God will not, for some hidden things which we know not, turn it in other wise; then shall I be marred of that which I now ween that I wot about it; but I would so know about God, in my reason and in my mind that nothing could mar me, nor bring me into doubting. Believest thou that I can make thee more witting about God than thou now art about the moon? A. Yea, I believe it; but I would rather that I wist it; for we believe every thing that we know, and many things which we believe, we know not.

20. R. Methinks that thou believest not the outer wits, neither the eyes, nor the ears, nor the smell, nor the taste, nor the touch, that thou through them canst understand so clearly that which thou wouldest, unless thou understand it in thy mind, through thy reason. A. That is sooth: I believe them not. R. Whether wouldest thou then know thy servant, about whom we formerly spoke, by the outer wits, or by the inner? A. I know him now as I can know him from the outer wits; but I wished that I knew his mind from my mind; then I should know what faith he had towards me. R. Can a man know everything but that with the mind? Can a man know otherwise than with the mind? A. Methinks not that I can so know it as I would. R. Then knowest thou not thy servant? A. How can I know him and wot not whether I know myself? It is said in the law, that a man shall love his neighbour as himself; how wot I then how I ought to love him, if I wot not whether I love myself? I wot that he does the same by me.

21. R. Why directest thou me to the outer senses, if thou would know God with the inner, as if thou wouldest see him bodily, as thou formerly saidest that thou saw the moon? I wot not how profitable thou directest me thither: I cannot show it to any outer senses. But tell me whether it would seem enough to thee, if thou knew God so as Plato or Plotinus knew him? A. I dare not say that, that there would seem to me enough in that; for I wot not whether there seemed enough to them in that which they there know. I wot not, however, [if] it seemed to them, that they needed to know more of it; and so as they formerly seemed to me. When I prayed, me thought that I understood not so fully that which I asked as I would; but I could not however forbear, that I should not speak about [it] so as methought I durst, and so as I weened that it was.

22. R. Methinks now that it seems to thee that it is one thing that a man knows, another, that a man most soothly weens. A. Yea, so methinks; therefore I would now that thou explain to me what is between them, or what a man certainly knows. R. Wotest thou that thou learnedest the craft which we call Geometry; in which craft thou learnedst painted on a sphere or on an apple or on an egg, that thou mightest by the painting understand the revolution of this globe, and the path of the constellations? Wotest thou now what thou learnedest in the same craft, by a line drawn

along the middle of the sphere? Wotest thou now that to thee was there shewn the places of the twelve constellations, and the path of the sun? A. Yea, enough well I wot what the line betokens. R. Dreadest thou not now the academic philosophers, who said that nothing ever was certain without a doubt, now thou sayest that thou hast no doubt of this? A. No, I dread naught much by myself, for they said that no man ever was wise; therefore I am naught ashamed though I were not; for I wot that I am not yet wise. But if I ever become as wise as they are, then will I do as they teach, until I will say that I know without doubt that which methinks I know. R. I gainsay that naught that thou do so. But I would wit now thou sayest that thou knowest about the line which was painted on the sphere on which thou learnedest about the revolution of this globe, [I wish to know] whether thou also knowest about the sphere on which the line was drawn? A. Yea, both of them I wot; no man can mistake that.

23. R. Whether learnedest thou by the eyes, or by the mind? A. By both I learned it: first, by the eyes, and afterwards by the mind; the eyes brought me into the understanding; after I understood it, I left off the looking with the eyes, and thought; for it seemed to me that I could think much more than I could see of it, after the eyes had fastened it to my mind; as a man brings a ship over sea. When he then comes to land, then leaves he the ship to stand; for it seems to him then that he can go more easily without it than with it. Easier it seems to me, however, to go with a ship on dry land, than it seems to me to learn any craft with the eyes without the reason, though the eyes must sometimes help thereto. R. For these things it is needed that thou look with the mind's eyes right to God, as right as the ship's anchor-string is stretched right from the ship to the anchor; and fasten the eyes of thy mind on God, as the anchor is fastened on the earth. Though the ship be out on the sea, among the billows, it will be sound [and] untobroken, if the string holds out, for the one end of it is fast in the earth, and the other in the ship. A. What is that which thou callest the mind's eyes? R. Reason, besides other crafts. A. What are those other crafts? R. Wisdom, (or knowledge,) and humility, and wariness, and moderation, and righteousness, and mercy, discretion, steadiness, and well-wishing, cleanness, and continency. With these anchors thou shalt fasten the string on God, which shall hold the ship of thy mind.

24. A. The Lord God do me all as thou teachest me. I would if I might : but I cannot understand how I may get the anchors, or how I may fasten them, unless thou more clearly teach me. R. I can teach thee. But first I should ask thee, how many of this world's lusts thou hast forsaken for God. After thou then hast told me that, then I can tell thee without every doubt, that thou hast gotten so many of the anchors as thou hast forsaken of the lusts in the world. A. How can I forsake that which I wot and know, and from childhood have been wont to, and love that which is unknown to me but by sayings? I ween, however, that if that were as known to me which thou now tellest me of, as is to me that which I see here, that I would love that and despise this. R. I wonder why thou speakest so. Think now, if thy Lord's errand-writ and his in-seal' come to thee, canst thou say that thou canst not understand him by that, nor canst know his will? If thou then sayest that thou canst know his will therein, say then whether it seems righter for thee that thou follow his will, or [that] thou follow the wealth which he has given thee before, besides his friendship. A. Whether I will or nill, I must needs say right, unless I will lie. If I then lie, then God wot that; therefore I dare say no other but sooth so far as I can know. To me it seems better that I forsake the gift and follow the giver, who is Steward of each to me, both of the wealth and of his friendship, unless I may have both, if I might both have the wealth and also follow his will.

25. R. Full rightly thou hast answered me. But I would ask thee, whether thou ween that thou mayest have all that which thou now hast with thy lord's friendship. A. I ween not that any man is so foolish that he weens that. R. Enough rightly thou understandest it. But I would wit whether it seemed to thee, about that which thou hast, whether it were temporary or everlasting. A. Never weened I that it was everlasting. R. What weenest thou about God, and about the anchors, of which we spoke before, whether they be like these, or everlasting? A. Who is so mad, that he dare say that God is not everlasting? R. If He then is everlasting, why then lovest thou not the everlasting Lord more than the temporary? Lo! thou wotest that the Everlasting will not go from thee, unless thou go from Him; and thou needs shalt from the other whether thou will or thou nill. Either thou shalt leave him, or he thee. I hear, however, that thou lovest him very

---

3. Errand-writ *letter*, in-seal *envelope*. See *Thorpe's Laws*, &c. p. 227, N.

strongly, and also dreadest and well dost; [1] very rightly and very discreetly thou dost. But I wonder why thou dost not much more love the other, who gives thee both this world-lord's friendship, and his own, and everlasting life after this world. The Lord is Governor of you both, both of thee and of the lord whom thou there so immoderately lovest. A. I own to thee that I would love Him over all other things if I could understand and know Him as I would. But I can understand very little of Him, or naught, and yet at those times that I think carefully of Him, and any sharpness of feeling comes to me about the everlasting life, then I love naught of this world's life over that, nor even like it.

26. Dost thou now wish that that thou may see, and clearly understand Him? A. I have no wish over that. R. Keep, then, his commandments. A. What commandments? R. Those which I formerly told thee. A. But they seem to me very heavy, and very manifold. R. Naught seems to me heavy which a man loves. A. To me no toil seems heavy, if I see and have what I toil after; but the doubting works the heaviness. R. Enough well thou takest up the speech, and enough rightly thou understandest it. But I may say to thee, that I am thy mind's reason which speaks to thee, and I am the discourse, which it is meet for me rightly to explain to thee,—that thou shalt see God with the eye of thy mind, as clearly as thou now seest the sun with the eyes of the body.

27. God Almighty foryield thee; I have much thank, that thou promisest me, that thou wilt so clearly shew it me, uncouth though I were, and then uncome-to,) [2] that I may more clearly see Him, if I first see Him, so as I now see the sun, so clearly as I would see it. I wot full little the better what the sun is, though I look on it each day; methought it good, however, that I might see God as clearly. R. Think now very carefully on that which I formerly said to thee. A. I will as I most carefully may. R. Know that first certain, that the mind is the soul's eye, and that thou shalt also know; the other is, that a man see that which he looked after.[3] . . . . The fourth is, that which a man would see. Every man who has eyes first looks at that which he would see,

---

5. Weldest. MS.
6. Something seems omitted here.

till the time that he has beheld it; when he then has beheld it, then he sees it. But thou must know, that I who now speak to thee, am Reason, and I am to every human mind in the stead in which the looking is to the eyes. The eyes of each body behove to have three things in themselves, (therefore asks that which it seeks, and would draw to it;) one is, that thou hast and brookest and lovest that which thou formerly hopedst. A. O! shall a ever come to that which I hope for, or that ever come to me which I wish. R. Put now love [as the] third besides belief and hope; for no soul's eyes are full-hale, at least to see God with, without these three.

28. A. The sight, then, is understanding: if it then has hale eyes, that is, a hale understanding,, what then is wanting to it, or what more needs it? R. The soul's looking is reason and meditation; but many souls look with these, and yet see not that which they wish; for they have not full hale eyes. But he who wishes to see God, shall have his mind's eyes hale; that is, that he have fast belief, right hope, and full love. If he then has all these, then has he a blessed life, and everlasting. The sight by which we shall see God is understanding; the understanding is between two things; between that which understands and that which is there understood, and is fast on both; as love is between the lover and that which he there loves; on each it is fast, as we formerly spoke about the anchor-string, that the one end was fast on the ship, the other on the land.

29. If it then again shall ever happen, that I may see God, as thou now hast taught me that I should look towards him, do I need all the three things of which thou formerly spokest, that is, belief, hope, and love? R. What need will then be of belief, [or of hope,] when a man sees that which he formerly believed, and has that which he formerly hoped? But love shall never be waned, but shall be very much eked when the understanding shall be fastened on God, nor of love shall ever be an end. "Omni consummatione vidi finem: latum mandatum tuum nimis." That is, Of every worldly thing I see an end; but of thy commandments I never see an end. That is love, about which he prophecied. But thou the soul be ful-framed, and full clean, (the) while (that) it is in the body, it cannot see God so as it wishes, for the body's heaviness and trouble, but with much toil, through belief, and hope, and love; which are the three anchors that hold the ship of the

mind amid the dread of the waves. The mind, however, has much comfort in that which it believes and well knows ;—that the mischances and unhappiness of this world are not everlasting ; as the ship's master, when the ship sits most inconveniently at anchor, and the sea is roughest, then knows for certain that mild weather is to come.

30. Three things are needful to the eye of every soul : one is, that it shall be hale ; another, that it look towards that which it would see ; a third, that they may see that which they look towards. To these three is need of God's help, for a man can neither do good nor any thing without His help. Therefore he is much to be entreated, that he be always helping ; for it is that, that he instigate us, and persuade us, that we first be well willing, and then [that he] work with us that which he will, until the time that we full-frame [1] it with him ; and especially that he [work] with us as with some wielded tools, as it is written, that with every well-worker God will be a with-worker. We know that no man can work aught good, unless God work with him ; and yet no man shall be idle, so that he begin not something by the might which God gives him. A. A right way thou teachest me ; now I wot what I ought to do ; but I wot not whether I can or cannot. R. Thou must not forthink thee [or lose heart,] though thou cannot be full soon come to that which thou wishest. Who may ever in a little time learn any craft, either less or more, who should [learn] the craft ? To thee is the craft of all crafts, which is, that a man search after God, and look towards him, and see him.

31. A. Well thou teachest me ; but I remember that thou formerly promisedst me, and very fain I abide the promise ; that was, that thou promisedst me that thou wouldest teach me that I might see God with the eye of my mind as clearly as I now see the sun with the eye of my body. R. Well thou remindest me. I will perform to thee what I promised thee. Think now that thou canst see with thy body's eye three things in the sun : one is, that it is ; another, that it shines ; a third, that it enlightens many things with its shine.

32. All those things which are bright, when the sun shines on them, shine against it ; each by its measure ; but those which are dull shine not against the sun ; though it shines on them ; but the

---

1. Or perfect—fulfremian to "fulframe," or perfect.

sun shines, however, on them, although whoso looks against it he cannot altogether see it such as it is. All this thou mayest think about God, and also much more : He is the high sun ; He is always shining [and enlightening], from his own light, both the sun which we see with [our] bodily eyes, and all the creatures, both ghostly and earthly. Therefore he seems to me a very foolish man, who wishes to understand him altogether such as he is, (the) while (that) we are in this world. Lo! I ween that no man is so foolish as to be therefore sorry, though he cannot see and understand this sun (which we look on with our bodily eyes) altogether such as it is. But every one is fain of what at the least he can understand by the measure of his understanding. Well does he who wishes to understand the Everlasting and Almighty Sun ; but he does very foolishly if he wishes to understand Him altogether while he is in this world.

33. A. Very wonderfully and very truly thou teachest, and very well thou hast comforted me, and brought me into good hope. But I ask that which thou formerly promisedst me. R. Two things I promised thee which I would do for thee, and teach thee ; that is, that thou shouldest understand God and thyself. But I would know how thou wouldest understand that, whether thou wouldest know of untried belief, or tried. A. I would know it tried, for I wot naught of it fastly. R. That is no wonder ; for I have not yet told thee in the wise in which thou mayest know it tried ; for there is yet something which thou must know before; that is, first, whether we be hale. A. Thou must know whether thou find any health either in me, or in thee, or in us both. It becomes thee to teach, me to listen; and it becomes me to answer that which I understand, by the measure of my understanding, if I understand aught of it; but if I understand naught, then ought I to grant that, and leave it to thy doom.

34. Wishest thou to know more than about God, and about thyself ? A. I acknowledge to thee that I now wish nothing more earnestly; but I dare not promise that I shall wish naught else but that; for to me it is very dark, though something comes to mind to me, of which methinks nothing can hinder me that I shall not further and fulfill it, then comes another thing which seems to me more right and more reasonable; then I forsake that which I formerly thought enough, and therefore sometimes it befalls me that something is so fast in my mind, that I think that I shall never

while I am living, let it go; then comes, however, to me, some trouble, which so busies me, that I neither can leave it nor can fulfill it, though I cannot think of any better. But three things have most troubled me; one is, that I dread that I shall part with my friends whom I most love, or they with me, either for life or for death. Another is, that I dread sickness, either known or unknown. A third is, that I dread death.

34. I hear now what thou most lovest after thy own soul,[1] and after God; that is, first, the life of thy friend, and thy own health, and thy own life. Of these five things thou dreadest that thou shalt lose some one, for thou lovest them all very strongly: if thou loved them not, thou wouldest not dread that thou shouldest lose them. A. I grant that which thou sayest to me. R. Therefore methinks that I see thee very sorrowful and very troubled in thy mind, because thou hast not such health as thou hadst, nor hast thy friends with thee, all so one-minded and so harmonious, as thou wouldest; methinks also no wonder, though thou art sorrowful for that. A. Rightly thou understandest it, I cannot gainsay that. R. But if it shall ever happen that thou understand thyself [to be] full hale and full strong, and have all thy friends with thee, both in mind and in body, and in the same work, which best listeth thee to do, wilt thou then be aught blithe? A. Yea, O yea, if it should suddenly happen, I should not know anywhere on earth how I would begin.

35. R. Hast thou not, then, yet every trouble, both of mind and body, now [that] thou hast these two; that is, immoderate sorrow? Wert thou forinwardly foolish when thou wishedst that thou shouldest with such eyes see the High and Everlasting Sun? A. Now thou hast altogether overcome me, that I wot nowhere on earth what deal of health I have, nor what deal of unhealth. R. That is no wonder; no man has so hale eyes that he can anywhile look at this sun, which we see here, and especially so much the less if he has unhale [eyes]. But they who have unhale eyes can be more easily in darkness than in light. Methinks, however, that thou thinkest that thou hast hale eyes; thou thinkest of the health of thy soul's eyes, but thou thinkest not of the great light which thou wishest to see. Be not angry with me, though I ask thee, and try thee; for I must needs do that. Methinks that thou understandest not thyself. A. I am not a whit angry with thee;

---

1. Gewitte, wits, wit or knowledge; but "soul" is more suitable to the context.

but I am fain of that which thou sayest; for I wot that thou seekest my good.

36. Wishest thou any wealth. A. I long ago thought that I should despise it. I have now three and thirty winters. I had one less than twenty, when I first thought that I should not at all love it too much. Though enough should come to me, I should not be full immoderately fain of it, nor brook it; nor even toil to hold more than I could moderately live by, and have and hold the men on, whom I must feed, and that which is there over, I think to deal as orderly as I most orderly can. R. Wishest thou any worship? A. I own to thee that I wished that, until I now of late became very weary.

37. Wishest thou not a fair wife, and modest, and well learned, and of good manners, and well subject to thy will, and who had very great substance, and did not in any things busy thee, nor hinder thee from enjoying leisure at thy will? A. Dost thou not praise her too much to me, that I may aye the more wish her? For to me seems naught worse for him who would serve God, than to have a wife; though somebody has said, that it is better to have [one] for the begetting of children : I, however, have said, that it is better for priests not to have than to have : therefore I thought that I should have none : for I would be the freer to serve God. R. I hear now that thou dost not think of having a wife. But I would wit whether thou have any love or lust of any uncleanness? A. Why askest thou me after that? I do not now desire it; but if ever it comes into my desire, I dread it as the adder. My desire of it is, the longer the less, and ever the more I desire to see the light, the less I lust after these things.

38. R. How about meat? how much dost thou desire that? A. I have no desire of those meats which I have; but I desire those which I have thought right to eat, when I see them. What will I say more, either about meat or about drink, or about bathing, or about wealth, or about worship, or about any worldly lusts? I desire none of them aught more than I needs must have to the health and strength of my body, [and] may hold; but I need much more for the wants of those men of whom I must take care, which I also wish, and needs must. R. In right thou art. But I would wit whether thy old craving and the appetite be altogether plucked up and rooted out of thy mind, or if it may yet grow? A. About what sayest thou this? R. I say [it] about the things which thou

formerly saidst to me that thou hadst resolved to forsake, and wouldest not for any things return to them again : that is, pride, wealth, too great worship, and immoderately rich and soft life : and therefore now ask I thee, whether either for the love of them, or for the love of any thing, thou wilt seek to them again. I heard before that thou saidest that thou lovedst thy friends, after God and thy own soul, over all other things ; now I would wit whether thou for their love wouldest undertake these things ? A. I will undertake it all again for their love, though I like it not full well, if I cannot otherwise have their fellowship.

39. R. Full discreetly thou answerest me, and full right. But I understand, however, that the worldly lusts are not altogether rooted out from thy mind, though the graf is rid ;[1] for the roots can sprout thence again. I reckon not that, however, to thee for any guilt ; for thou wilt not undertake it for the love of the things, but for the love of the thing which it is more right for thee to love than that. I never ask about any man what he does ; but I ask thee now yet, why thou lovest thy friends much, or what thou lovest in them, or whether thou lovest them for themselves, or for some other things ? A. I love them for friendship and for fellowship ; and those, however, above all others, who make the most help to me, to understand and to wit, reason and wisdom, most of all about God, and about our souls ; for I wot that I can more easily search after [these things] with their help than without.

40. R. But how then, if they will not search after that which thou searchest ? A. I will teach them that they will. R. But how then, if thou cannot, and they are so reckless, that they love another thing more than that which thou lovest, and say that they cannot or will not ? A. I will have them, however ; they will be profitable to me in some things, and I also to them. R. But how then, if sickness of the body hinder and lett thee ? A. That is sooth. I nothing dread sickness, however, were it not for three things ; one is heavy sore ; another is death ; a third, that I may not seek, or at least not find, that which I wish, as it lately did to me. Tooth-ache hindered me from all learning ; it did not, however, withdraw me altogether from the remembrance of that which I had formerly learnt. I ween, if I certainly understood that which I wish to understand, that the ache would seem to me very little or else nothing, over the belief. I wot, however, that many

---

1. What 'graf' and 'gerid' mean, is not clear.

a pain is stronger than tooth-ache; though I never suffered any stronger.

41. I have learnt that Cornelius Celsus told in his books, that in every man wisdom was the highest good, and sickness the greatest evil; the saying seemed to me very sooth. About the same things the same Cornelius has said, " Of two things we are what we are, that is, of soul and of body; the soul is ghostly, and the body earthly; of the soul the best craft is wisdom, and of the body the worst thing is unhealth. This also seems to me not false."

42. R. Have we not now clearly enough shewn that wisdom is the highest good; and is it not now without all doubt that it is for every man the best craft, and the best work, that he search after wisdom, and that he love it, where he finds it? But I would that we now sought who should be the lovers of this wisdom. Wotest thou not now that every man who loves another, likes better to clap and kiss the other on the body than where clothes are between. I understand now that thou lovest wisdom so much, that thou wishest to know and feel it naked so well, that thou wouldest not that any cloth were between; but will very seldom shew himself so openly to any man. In the times when he will shew any limb so bare, then shews he it to few men. But I wot not how thou canst take it with gloved hands. Thou must also put bare body towards it, if thou wilt feel it.

43. But tell me if thou lovedest any comely woman very immoderately over all other things, and she then fled thee, and would not love thee on any other condition, but that thou wouldest leave every other love for the love of her alone, wouldst thou then do as she wished? A. Alas! alas! thou thinkest me too hard. Didst thou not formerly consent that I should love nothing over wisdom? and I consented to that; and thou saidest then, however, whosoever loved anything for the sake of some other thing, that he loved not that which he there loved, but that through which he loved the thing, and [which] he thought to come to; therefore I said that I loved wisdom for no other things, but for itself. All this world I love, each thing by the deal by which I understand it to be profitable, and especially those things most which help me to wisdom; and those things I also dread most to lose. I love nothing else however, in that wise in which I love wisdom each of the things which I most love, while I love it most I give

it to no man but to myself, except wisdom. It I love over all other things; and yet I would give it to every other man, of my own will, that every man who was in this world might love it and search after it, and also find it, and afterwards brook it; for I wot that each of us would love another so much more as our will and our love were more in one.

43. R. How, said I not before, that he who would feel a bare body must feel it with a bare [one]? And I say also; if thou wilt see wisdom itself so bare that thou shalt let no cloth between thy eyes and it, nor even any mist; to that thou canst not however in this present[life] come, though I teach thee, and though thou wish it. Therefore no man ought to mistrust, though he have not so hale eyes as he who can look sharpest: since he who can look sharpest of all, cannot, however, see the sun such as it is, while he is in this present life. No man however has so unhale eyes, that he may not live by the sun, and use it if he can see anything, unless he be stark-blind.[2]

44. I can also teach thee other examples about wisdom. Think now whether aught many men should seek the king's home where he then is in town, or his moot or his host, or whether does it seem to thee, that they all come thither on one way? I ween however, that they come on many ways: some from very far, and have a very long way, and very evil, and very difficult, some have a very long [one] and very straight, and very good, some have a very short [one,] and yet crooked, and narrow, and foul; some have a short [way], and smooth, and straight; and yet they all come to one lord, some more easily some more uneasily, neither come they alike easily thither, nor are they alike easily there. Some are in more honour and in greater ease than others some in less: some fullnigh without; but that only which he loves. So it is also by wisdom, every one who wishes him and is careful of him may come to him and abide in his house-hold and live by him; though some of them magnify him, some hate [him]; as every king's home [is]; some are in bower, some in hall, some in court, some in prison; yet all live by his favour, as all men live under one sun, and by its light see that which they see. Some look very sharply and very clearly: some hardly see aught; some are stark-blind, and yet make use of the sun. But as this seen sun enlightens the eyes of our body, so enlightens Wisdom our

2. Stare blind, MS., which might be retained.

mind's eye, that is our understanding; and as the body's eyes are haler, so they take in more of the sun's light. So it is also by the mind's eye, that is understanding: as it is haler, so it can see more of the Everlasting Sun, that is, Wisdom.

45. Every man who has hale eyes, needs no other guide or teacher to see the sun, but that health. If he has hale eyes, he can look for himself on the sun; but if he has unhale eyes, then needs he that one teach him that he look first on the wall, then on gold, then on silver, then he may more easily look on the fire, before he look against the sun. After he has learned that his eyes do not shun the fire, then let him look on the stars, and on the moon, then other sunshine, before he look on [the sun] itself. And so likewise by the other sun, about which we spoke before, that is Wisdom. He who would see it with his mind's eye must begin by very little, and then by little and little climb nigher and nigher, and stepmeal, as if he were climbing on a ladder, and would be up on some sea-cliff; if he ever then come up on the cliff, then may he look both over the shore, and over the sea, which is then beneath him, and also over the land which was above him. But if it seems so to us, let us pray here daylong, and search even to morrow after the same that we formerly searched [after]. A. No, oh no! but I humbly pray thee, that thou be not weary, nor leave the speech there, but say yet somewhat more clearly about it, that I may more openly understand something about this wisdom; and command me what thou wilt, I will undertake it, if it is meet for me. R. I wot naught to command thee, of which thou hast more need for the craft which thou wishest to know, than that thou despise as thou most strongly canst the world's honours, and especially the immoderate and unlawful: for I dread that they bind thy mind to them, and catch it with their snare, as a man catches fowls, so that thou may not go about that which thou wishest. And if it shall ever happen, that thou canst so clean forsake them, that thou shalt have no wish for them, then I can tell thee forsooth, believe me if thou wilt, that in the same time, thou shalt know all that thou now wishest to know, and shalt have all that thou wishest to have.

46. A. When will that be? I believe not that it will ever be, that I shall have no wish for this world's glory, unless one thing happen, that is, that I see the glory which thou promisest me. When I wot not though it should like me so well, that I should not wish

this world's glory. R. Methinks now, that thou hast aught directly answered; methinks that thou speakest likess as if thy eyes said to thy mind, " We will never shun the darkness of the night, ere we can see the sun itself." Thus methinks the eyes do, if they shun the dole of the sun's light which they can see· It cannot befall even the halest of all eyes, that they may hence from this world see the sun itself; by which thou mayest think that thou oughtest not to sigh though thou canst not, with thy mind's eye, see Wisdom naked such as he is : for this thou never canst the while thou art in the darkness of thy sins. But use the wisdom which thou hast, be fain of the dole which thou canst understand, and strive earnestly after more. Wisdom himself knows what thou art worthy of, how much he may show himself to thee. Nothing is worse in the man, than ween he that he is worthy of that of which he is not. The leach wot better than the sick man, whether he can cure him or not; or whether he can cure him by mild treatment or by strong. Therefore thou must not weep too much nor sigh too much after aught. The eyes of thy mind are not at all so hale as thou weenest. A. Be still, oh be still! do not vex me, nor increase my sorrow. I have enough else though thou eke it not, Thou seekest it sometimes so high, sometimes so deep, that I understand that I am not such as I weened; but I am ashamed now that I weened that which was not. Sooth enough thou hast said. The Leach whom I wish to heal me knows how hale eyes I have. He knows what he is willing to shew me. To him I entrust myself, and to his well-willingness I commend me; do he has he will. To him I call that he raise my mind to him. I will never more say that I have hale eyes ere I see Wisdom himself.

47. R. I wot no better rede for thee, than thou formerly saidest. But let be the weeping and the sorrow, and be moderately blithe. Thou wert formerly too immoderately sorrowful; for sorrow hurts both the mind and the body. A. Thou wouldest moderate my weeping, and my sorrow; and I know not any bounds of my miseries and unhaps. Thou biddest me leave off sorrowing, lest I be the weaker either in mind or in body, and I find strength neither in mind nor in body; but am full nigh out of my mind; but I beseech thee if thou in any wise canst, that thou lead me into some shorter way, some deal nigher that light of understanding

which I long wished, and could not yet come to, unknown though I be afterwards ashamed that I look back towards the darkness which I formerly wished to forsake; if I aye come nigh to the light.

48. R. Let us end this book now here rightly, and say in another book a shorter way if we may. A. No, ah no: let us not leave yet this book, ere I can more clearly understand that which we are about. R. Methinks that I must do as thou askest me: something draws me on, I wot not what it is, I ween that it is the God whom thou searchest after. A. Thank be to him who advises thee, and also to thee, if thou hearest him. Lead me whither thou wilt, I will follow thee, if I may. R. Methinks that thou wishest yet to know the same thing that thou formerly wouldest about God, and about thy soul. A. Yea, this I wish. R. Dost thou not wish aught more? Dost thou not wish to know soothfastness? A. How can I without soothfastness know aught sooth or what wilt thou say that God is, without soothfastness? for we are wont to read in the Gospel that Christ said that he was the way, and soothfastness and life.

49. R. Right thou sayest. But I would wit whether it seems to thee that it is all one—sooth and soothfastness? A. Two things methinks that they are: as there are two things [of which] the one is wisdom, the other is that which is wise; and again by cleanness, (or chastity,) cleanness is one thing, that which is clean is another. R. Whether seems to thee then better, sooth or soothfastness? A. Soothfastness; for all that is sooth is from soothfastness sooth; and each one that is clean, is for cleanness clean; and he that is wise is for wisdom wise. R. To God [be] thank that thou so well understandest it? But I would wit what thou weenest, if a wise man were dead, whether wisdom were then dead? or again, if a clean man were dead whether cleanness were then dead, or if a soothfast man were dead, whether sooth [fastness?] were then dead? A. No, ah no, that may not be.

50. R. Well thou understandest it. But I would wit whether thou ween that wisdom is then gone, or cleanness or sooth-fastness, when the man goes away; or whence they formerly came, or where they are, if they are; or whether they be bodily or ghostly? For of that a man has no doubt, that each thing that is, is somewhere. A. O deep is the asking, and winsome to wit, to him who may wit it; what is wanting to him who knows that. R. Canst

thou know the righteous [man], and the unrighteous? A. Yea by some deal,—not however, so as I would. But I wish to know that which thou formerly askedst.

51. R. I wonder why thou hast so quickly forgotten what thou hast now a little before acknowleged that thou knewest. Saidest thou not before, that thou knewest that soothfastness yea was, though the sooth-fast [man] went away? and now thou sayest "If it be." A. The same I say yet, that I wot that it is, hough the soothfast [man] goes away. R. Every [thing] that is, easily is that, while it is: But what thou callest soothfastness, that is God. He aye was and aye shall be, undeadly and everlasting. This God has all crafts in him, sound and full meet. He has shapen two everlasting creatures, that are angels and men's souls, to whom He has given some deal of everlasting gtfts, such as now wisdom is, and righteousness and many other which to us seems long to reckon. To angels he has given by their capacity; and to men's souls he gives, to each by their capacity of such gifts. Such gifts they need never lose, for they are everlasting And he gives also to men many and diverse good gifts in this world, though they are not everlasting, yet they are stalworth while we are in this world. Understandest thou yet that souls are undeadly? If thou have understood it, hide it not from me but grant it; if it be elsewhat, tell it me.

52. A. Thanks to God for the share that I wot! I will now study it, and hold it as carefully as I can, If I doubt of any thing, then will I shew it thee soon. R. Cleave fast to God, and betake thyself wholly to God; aud wish not too much for thy own will over his: but be his man, not thy own: and grant that thou art his servant: then will he raise thee for that always nigher to himself and nigher; and will let naught be adverse to thee. If he, however, shall permit that aught adverse shall come though to thee, then shall that be for thy good, though thou be not able to understand it. A. That I hear, and that I believe, and this love I will follow as I best can, and [will] pray God that I may be able to perform it, as thou long before hast taught me; teach me if thou wilt. R. Do that to me first, and tell me again after thou hast studied this, what thou likest of this; and if thou doubt aught about any of these things, then tell thou me that.

HERE END THE BLOSSOMI OF THE FIRSTS BOOK:

HERE BEGINNETH THE GATHERING OF THE BLOSSOMS OF THE
SECOND BOOK.

1. A. Oh! long have we now been at leisure, and we have not searched after that which thou formerly promisedst me. R. Let us better it; let us take [it] in the beginning of another book. A. Let us [do] that. R. Let us believe that God is in our help. A. Willingly would I believe it, if I had power: but methinks that belief is not in our power in the measure which we there seek, unless God give it us. R. Both belief and all the goods that we shall have; therefore I wot not what we can do at all without his help. I advise thee however that thou begin it; pray in few words, as thou most inwardly canst, and ask that which is most needful to thee.

2. A. "Lord Lord, thou who abidest always unchangeable, give me the two things which I have always wished; that is that I may know Thee and myself."

3. Now I have done as thou advisedst me; now I have prayed R. I hear what thou wouldest wit; but I would wit first from thee, whether thou wist without doubt, whether thou were or not were: or whether thou lived, or not lived. A.—The two things which I certainly know. R. What more wishest thou to know? A. Whether I be undeadly. R. I hear that thou wouldest alway live. A. That I grant. R. Shalt thou then know enough, if I make thee know that thou mayest always live? A. That is a very good desire: say however, what I asked after, whether I should be aye living; and then I would wit whether I, after the parting of the body and the soul, should aye know more than I now wot of all that which I now have long wished to know; for I can understand naught better in a man than that he know, and naught worse than that he not know.

4. R. Now I wot all what thou wouldest. One is that thou wouldest be; another, that thou wouldest live; a third, that thou wouldest know. And I wot also why thou wouldest those three things,—therefore thou wouldest be, that thou wouldest live; and therefore wouldest thou live, that thou wouldest know. And hose three things I hear that thou certainly knowest. Thou

knowest that thou art, and thou knowest that thou livest, and thou knowest also that thou knowest somewhat, though thou knowest not all that thou wouldest. A. That is sooth. Those three things I wot, and those three things I would. I would be, because I would live. What would I care whether I were if I lived not? or what would I care for life, if knew I naught. R. Now I hear that thou lovest all that thou lovest for these three things—thou lovest that, that thou art, because thou wouldest live; and therefore wouldest thou live, because thou wouldest know. By that I understand that thou lovest wisdom over all other things, which methinks is thy highest good. A. Sooth thou sayest [to] me. What is wisdom else but the highest good? or what is the highest good but that each man in this world by so much love God as he loves wisdom, whether he love much or love it little, or love it middling? By the deal he love God by which he loves wisdom.

R. Enough rightly thou hast understood it. But I would that we went back where we formerly were. Thou knowest that thou art, and also knowest that thou livest, and knowest that thou knowest somewhat, though thou knowest not so mnch as thou wouldest; and a fourth thing which thou wouldest know, that is whether these three things were all everlasting or were not: or whether any [one] of them were everlasting; or if they were all everlasting, whether any of them after this world, in the everlasting life, either waxed or waned. A. All my yerning thou hast understood very rightly. R. About what doubtest thou now? Didst thou not formerly grant that God was everlasting and Almighty, and had made two rational and everlasting creatures as we formerly said, that is, angels and men's souls, to whom he has given everlasting gifts, which gifts they need never let go? If thou now rememberest this and believest this, then wotst thou without doubt that thou art, and ever shalt be, and ever shalt live, and ever shalt know somewhat, though thou shalt not know all that thou wouldest.

6. Now thou knowest about the three things after which thou askedst, that is, I. whether thou aye shouldest be, II. whether thou aye shouldest know somewhat: III. whether thou after the parting of the body and the soul, shouldest know more than thou now knowest or less. After the fourth we must yet search, now thou knowest these three until thou know that also.

7. A. Very orderly thou settest it forth. But I will yet however say, what I there firmly believe, about what I there yet doubt I doubt naught about God's everlastingness, and about his almightiness ; for it cannot be otherwise of the trinity and unity, which was without beginning, and is without end ; therefore I cannot elsehow believe, for He has shapen so great and so many, and so wonderfully seen creatures ; and steers them all, and keeps them all within bounds and onewhile clothes them with the winsomest beauties, another while again unclothes, and unbeautifies them. He governs the kings who have the most power on this world; who like all men are born, and eke like other men die whom he lets reign while he will. For such and many such [things] I wot not how I can doubt of his everlastingness ; nor eke of the life of our souls, do I now the more doubt aught, but I doubt yet about their everlastingness, whether they be aye living.

8. R. About what doubtest thou there ? Are not all holy books fulnigh full about the nndeadliness of the soul ? But methinks now that too long to reckon all, and too wearisome for thee to hear. A. I have heard a good deal of it, and I also believe it ; but I wish rather now to hear it than to believe it. R. I wonder why thou yearnest so strongly and so certainly to know what no man in this prison of this present life ever could certainly know, as thou wishest, though many earned that they in this present life understood it more clearly than many others. By the sayings of there and of truthfnl men, never can any man, ere the soul is parted from the body, understand all that he would know ; nor even then yet, before doomsday, so clearly as would, Although the holy fathers, who were before us, very certainly knew about that which thou formerly askedst ; that is, about the undeadliness of men's souls, which was very clear in this that they naught doubted, when they despised this present life* ...... were parted and how they suffered the greatest pains in this world; that they might afterwards have the greater need in the everlasting life ; though the sayings of such men ought to give that when we cannot understand it so clearly as we would ; although about the undeadliness of the soul, if thou dost not yet grant it, I shall make thee understahd it, and I shall also make thee ashamed that thou so slowly understandest it. A. Do, oh do make me ashamedof that.

9. R. Lo, I wot that thou hast the Master now to day whom

6. Something omitted.

thou believest in all things better than thyself; and so hath many a servant who has a less powerful master than thou hast; and I wot that thou hast also many a friend whom thou well enough lovest, though thou believest him not at all so well as thou dost thy Master. How seems it to thee now if thy master tell thee some spell which thou never heardest? or says to thee that he has seen somewhat which thou hast never seen? does it seem to thee that thon wouldest aught doubt at his saying, because thou hast not thyself seen it? A. No, oh no; there is no story so incredible if he tell it that I will not believe it. Yea, even many companions I have, if they tell me anything, which they have themselves seen or heard. I believe it all as well as if I had myself seen or heard it. R. I hear that thou believest thy lord, better than thyself and thy companions equally well as thyself. Thou dost very right and very reasonably, when thou hast so good faith in them. But I would that thou told me whether seems to thee Honorius the son of Theodosius wiser or truer than Christ the son of God? A. No, oh, no; nor anywhere nigh but methinks it hard that thou comparest them together Honorius is very good, though his father was better; he was very pious and very constant, and very rightly of my master's kin; and so is [he] who there yet lives. Them I will honour, as a man ought a worldly master, and the others whom thou formerly spokest about, as their masters, and as a man ought [to honour] that King who is the Maker and Governor of all kings and of all creatures.

10. R. Now I hear that the Almighty God is more highly esteemed by thee than Theodosius, and Christ, the son of God, more than Honorius, the son of Theodosius. I blame thee not for loving both, but I advise thee to love the higher Masters more, for they know all that thou wishest, and can [do] all that they will. A. It is all sooth that thou sayest, all that I believe. R. Now I hear that thou believest the higher Master more. But I would wit whether it seemed to thee that thy worldly masters had wiser and more truthful ministers than the higher masters had. Believest thou now thyself and thy companions more than the apostles who were Christ's own ministers? or [than] the patriarchs, or the prophets, through whom God himself spoke to his folk that which he would? A. No, ah no; I believe not us so well, nor anywhere nigh so (well) as them.

R. What spoke God then after, or what said he soothlier through his prophets, to his folk, than about the undeadliness of souls? Or what said the apostles and all the holy fathers, if they said not about the everlastingness of souls, and about their undeadliness? Or what meant Christ, when he said in his gospel, "The unrighteous shall go into everlasting pains, and the righteous into everlasting life"? Now thou hearest what Christ said, and his ministers; and I heard that thou doubtedst naught about the sayings of Honorius, and of his ministers; why doubtest thou then about the sayings of Christ the son of God, and about those of the higher ministers, which they themselves spoke who have said to us more of such words than we can reckon; and by many examples and tokens have confirmed it to us? Why canst thou not then believe all these, and saidest before that thou wert their man? A. So I say yet; and say that I believe them, and well wot that it is all sooth, that god has said to us either through himself or through them; there is more of them both in holy book than I can reckon. Therefore I am ashamed now, that I ever doubted about it: and I grant that I am very rightly overcome, and I shall alway be much fainer when thou overcomest me with such things than I ever was when I overcome another man. All this I wist though before; but I forgot it, as I dread also that I shall do this I wot too that I had so clean forgotten it, that I should never have remembered it if thou hadst not told me clearer examples both about my master, and about many proverbs.

12. R. I wonder why thou ever couldest ween that about men's souls, that they were not everlasting; for thou well enough wittest that it is the highest and the best of all God's creatures: and thou wotest also well enough, that he leaves no creature to go away so that it should become as naught, not even the unworthiest of all. But he beautifies and clothes all creatures, and again unbeautifies and unclothes them; and again renews them; moreover they all so change that they go, and anon come back, and return to the same beauty, and the same winsomeness for the children of men, in which they were before Adam sinned. Now, thou mayest hear, that no creature goes so clean away, that it comes not back, nor so clean perishes, that it does not become somewhat. But why weenest thou, since the weakest creatures go not wholly away, that the best creature should altogether go away? A. Oh! I am beset with wretched forgetfulness

somewhat. But why weenest thou, since the weakest creatures go not wholly away, that the best creature should altogether go away? A. Oh! I am beset with wretched forgetfulness, that I could not remember it, so known as it formerly was to me. Methinks now that thou hadst clearly enough explained it to me by this one example, though thou had told me no more.

13. R. Seek now in thyself the examples and the tokens, and know well that which thou formerly wouldest know, which I explained to thee by the outer examples. Ask thy mind, why it is so wishing and so careful to know what formerly was before thou wert begotten, or even before thy elder father was born; and ask it also why it knows what is now present to it, and it sees and hears every day; or why it wishes to know that which shall be after us. Then ween I that it will answer thee, if it is discreet, and see, that it therefore wishes to know that which was before us, because it always was after God had created the first man: and it therefore strives towards that which it formerly was, [and] to know that which it formerly knew, though it is now kept down by the burden of the body, that it cannot know what it formerly knew. And I ween that it will tell thee, that it therefore knows that which it here sees and hears, because it is here in this world. And I ween that it will say that it therefore wishes to know what shall be after our days, because it knows that it shall aye be. A. Methinks now that thou hast clearly enough said, that each man's soul aye is and aye shall be, and aye was since God in the beginning made the first man.

14. R. There is no doubt that souls are undeadly; believe thine own reason and believe Christ, God's Son; and believe all his Hallows; for they were very unlying witnesses; and believe thine own soul, which alway says to thee through its reason, that it is in thee; it says too that it is everlasting, for it wishes everlasting things. It is not such a foolish creature that it would seek that which it could not find, or wish that which it had not, or belonged not to it. Leave off now the unright doubting; enough clear it is that thou art everlasting and shalt aye be. A. That I hear; and that I believe and well know; and I am so fain of it, as I never was [of anything]. Now I hear that my soul is everlasting and shall aye live; and all that my mind and my reason have gathered of good crafts, the mind shall ever have them. And I hear also that my wit [or knowledge] is everlasting. But I wish yet

to know about that knowledge, what I formerly asked—whether after the parting of the body and the soul it should wax or wane or stand still, or should so do as it here doth in this world, one while wax, another while wane? I wot now that the life shall aye be, and the wit, but I dread that it be in that world as it is here on children. I ween not that the life there shall be without witting, the more than it is here in children, then there will be too little winsomeness in that life.

15. I hear now what thou wouldest wit; but I cannot tell it thee by few words. If thou wilt openly wit it, then must thou seek it in the book which we call *De videndo Deo*. This book is called in English, " Of the sight of God."—But be now of good mood, and study what thou hast now learned: and let us both pray Him that he help us; for he promised that he would help every one who called to him and wished aright; and he promised without any doubt, that he would teach us after this world, that we might full certainly know full wisdom 'and full soothfastness; which thou mayest hear more openly in the book which I formerly named to thee *De videndo Deo*.

HERE END THE BLOSSOMS OF THE SECOND BOOK WHICH WE CALL SOLILOQUIORUM.

16. A. Now thou hast ended the speeches which thou hast gathered out of his book, and hast not yet answered me about that [which] I now last asked, that was about my witting.— I asked thee whether, after the dealing of the body and the soul, it should wax or wane, or do both, as it here doth? R. How said I not to thee before, that thou must seek it in the book which we then spoke about? Learn the book, then shalt thou find it there. A. It is not meet for me now to study all that book, but I would that thou [told] me.[1]

17. [The wicked see] the glory of the good, that their own torments may seem to them the greater, because they would not, by the advice of their fathers, earn the same honour, while they were in this world. And the good see also their torments, to the end that their own glory may seem to them the greater. The

---

1. MS. þou me þæt wulder &c. without any break; but there is manifestly some omission here and also much inaccuracy and confusion.

evil see God, as the guilty man who is condemned [for treason] against some king, and sees him and his darlings; then seems to him his punishment the greater; and also the king's darlings see [his] punishment, therefore their own honour seems to them the greater. No man, however, should ween that all those who are in hell have the like torment, nor [that] all those who are in heaven have the like glory; but every one has by his own earning either pain or glory, whichever he is in. The like have their like. It is also not to be weened that all men have like knowledge in heaven; but each by the measure after which he here earneth: as he here more strongly toils and more strongly yearns for knowledge and righteousness, so he (there] has the more of it, and also more honour, and more glory.

18. Has it now yet been enough clearly told thee about knowledge and about the sight of God? A. Yea; enough well I believe that we need not lose aught of the knowledge which we now have, though the soul and the body part from each other; but I believe that our knowledge shall then be very much increased, though we cannot know all ere doom's day that we would know, But I believe that after doom's day nothing shall be hidden from us, neither what is in our days, nor what was before us, nor what shall be after us. Thou hast told me many examples, and I have myself seen in holy writings more than I can tell, or even remember. Thou hast also shown me so unlying witnesses, that I can do no other but needs must believe them; for if I believe no weaker testimony, then shall I know very little or nothing.

19. What wot I but that I wish that we knew abont God as clearly as we would; but the mind is " heavied" [2] and busied by the body so that we cannot with the mind's eyes see anything such as it is, any more than sometimes thou canst see the sun's brightness, when the clouds shoot between it and thee, although it shines very bright there where it is: even where no cloud is between thee and it, thou canst not see it full clearly such as it is, because thou art not there where it is; neither thy body, nor thy bodily eyes can come anywhere nigh it, nor therenigh. Nor even the moon, which is nigher us, we cannot see such as it is,

---

2. Weighed down, 'gehefigod.'

We know that it is broader than this earth, although it seems to us at times not broader than a shield, on account of the distance.

19. [R] Now thou hast heard that neither can we from this world with the mind's eye see anything altogether so as it is; but from the deal which we see of it we ought to believe the deal which we see not. But it is promised us, without any doubt, so [soon] as we are out of this world, and the soul is let out of the prison of the body, that we shall know every thing that we wished to know, and much more than all the old men, the wisest of all, can know in this world.

20. And after doom's day, it is promised that we may see God all openly such as he is, and aye after know him, as truly as he now knows us. We shall never after have a want of any knowledge. Nothing will He hide from us, who lets us know Himself, but we shall then know all that we now wish to know, yea that too which we have no wish to know. All we shall see God, both they who are here worst, and they who are here best. All the good shall see him for comfort and gladness and honour and blessedness and glory; and the evil shall see him as well as the good: to them however, for torment; because they could or might have seen in this world;[3] or whether they had any remembrance of the friends whom they left behind them in this world.—(Then answered he his own thoughts and said.)

21. A. Why weenest thou that the good deceased, who have full freedom, and know all that they wish to know both in this present life, and in that to come,—why weenest thou that they have no remembrance of their friends in this world?—when the evil rich [man], who [was] in hell's torments, dreaded for his friends the evil pains which he had earned? That was he of whom Christ said in his gospel, that he prayed Abraham that he would send Lazarus the beggar to him, that he with his little finger might drip some water on his tongue, and thereby cool his thirst. Then said Abraham, "Nay, my child, nay; but remember that thou withheldest every benefit from him when ye were both in the body, and thou hadst every good, and he had every ill: he may not now the more do thee any benefit than thou wouldest [then do] him. Then quoth the rich [man], Since it cannot be, send him to my five brothers that are yet on earth, where I was, that he may tell them in what torments I am and

3. Something omitted here.

teach them to guard themselves against that, that they come not hither? Then quoth Abraham, "Nay, nay: they have the books of holy fathers with them on earth; let them learn in these and believe them; for if they believe not them, neither will they believe Lazarus, though he come to them."

23. Now may ye hear that both the good deceased and the evil know all that is done in this world which they are in. They know the most deal, though they shall not know it all ere doom's day; and they have very great remembrance in that world, of their kinsmen and their friends; and the good help the good, and each of them another by the deal that they can. But the good will not help their evil friends, because they will not forsake their evil, the more than Abraham would help the rich man, though he was of his own kin; because he understood that he was not so humble to God, as by right he should.

24. The evil then can [do] no good either to their friends or to themselves; for they formerly were in no help either to themselves or to their friends who were gone forth [of life] before them, when they were in this world: but it shall be with them then as it is with those men who here are brought into some king's prison, and can every day see their friends, and ask about them that which they will, and yet cannot be for any good to them; no more will they, nor can they to them. Therefore have the evil the more torment in the world to come, that they know the honour and the worship[4] of the good; and also the more that they remember the honour which they (themselves) had in this world.

24. The good then who have full freedom, see both their friends and their foes, as here great men see often together both their friends and their foes; alike they see them, and alike they know them, though [alike] they love them not. And again the righteous after they are off this world, remember very often both the good and the evil which they had in this world, and rejoice very greatly that they forsook not their Lord's will,—neither in easy things nor in mysterious, while they were in this world; as if a great man in this world have driven one of his darlings from him; or he have been forced away from him against the will of them both, and then have many pains and many mishaps in his exile, and come however to the same lord whom he was formerly

---

4. Worth-ship or dignity.

with, and be there much more honourable than he formerly was; then he remembers the unhappiness which he had in his exile, but is, however, not the unblither.

26. But I myself have seen, or [have believed] that which less trustworthy men have told me, than those were, who have said that which we are now about. How must I not needs (do) one of two things, either believe some man or none? Methinks that I now know who built the city Rome, and also many other things which were done before my days, all (of) which I cannot reckon. I wot not thereby who built the city that I myself saw it; nor even wot I of what kin I am, nor who was my father or mother, but by hearsays. I wot that my father begot me, and my mother bore me, [but] I wot it not by that, that I myself saw it, but for that, that it was told me. It was not told me however by any so soothfast men as they were who told that which we have now been long searching, after, and yet I believe it; therefore he seems to me a very foolish man and inexcusable, who will not eke his knowledge the while that he is in this world, and always wish and will that he may come to the everlasting life where nothing shall be dark or unknown.

HERE END THE SAYINGS WHICH KING ALFRED GATHERED OUT OF THE BOOK WHICH WE CALL IN LATIN [*De videndo Deo?*].

THE LAWS
OF
KING ALFRED THE GREAT.

In the two volumes of *Ancient Laws and Institutes of England* published by the Record Commissioners, and edited by B. Thorpe, are found the Laws of Alfred *Ælfredes Domas*, comprising the Laws of Ine a former king of Wessex, and followed by a copy of the treaty of peace between Alfred and Guthrum in the year 878. It is th opinion of Mr Thorpe that the manuscripts, where these so occur, were wr.tten for the use of the West-Saxon kingdom, whilst another collection, with the Institutes of Offa in like manner appended, was destined for the inhabitants of Mercia.

How far King Alfred himself may have been the author of these laws, it is impossible to say: but we may reasonably conjecture that a king, so devoted to books and so anxious for the improvement of his people—and that people so illiterate—would be likely to take an active part in constructing a body of laws for the guidance of his subjects. For this reason we have thought proper to include these laws among the works of this great king, and to present them not in a free version, like that which is found in the Laws and Institutes, but in a version so literal that the philological reader who may choose to compare it with the original text will be astonished and pleased to observe how nearly we still speak in the language of our forefathers who lived more than a thousand years ago.
J. A. G.

ÆLFREDE'S DOOMS.

The Lord was speaking these words to Moyse, and thus quoth; I am the Lord thine God. I led thee out of the Ægyptians' lands, and of their bondage.

1. Love thou not other strange gods over me.

2. Call not thou mine name in idleness, for that thou art not guiltless with me, if thou in idleness callest mine name.

3. Mind that thou hallow the rest-day. Work you six days, and on the seventh rest you. For that in six days Christ wrought heavens and earth, seas, and all shapen things that in them are, and rested him on the seventh day: and for that the Lord hallowed it.

4. Honour thine father and thine mother that the Lord gave thee: that thou be the longer living on earth.

5. Slay thou not.

6. Commit thou not adultery.

7. Steal thou not.

8. Say thou not leasing[1] witness.

9. Wish not thou thy neighbour's goods with unright.

10. Work thou not to thyself golden gods or silvern.

✗ 11. These are the dooms that thou shalt set them. If any one buy a Christian theow [bondsman], be he theow to him six years: the seventh be he free unbought. With such clothes as he went in with such go he out. If he himself have a wife, go she out with him. If, however, the lord gave him a wife, go she and her bairn the lord's. If then the theow say, " I will not [go] from mine lord, nor from mine wife, nor from mine bairn, nor from mine goods: bring him then his lord to the temple's door, and drill through his ear with an awl, to token that he be ever since a theow.

12. Though any one sell his daughter to theowdom, let her not be all such a theowen, as other women. Nor may he sell her out among strange folk. But if he reck not of her—he that bought her, let her [go] free among strange folk. If, then, he allow his son with [her] to cohabit, let him do to her marriage-gifts, and look he that she have clothes, and what is the worth of her maid-

---

1. Mr Thomson says that 'nane o' your leasing' is a common phrase in Scotland.

hood, that is the dowry; give he her that. If he do to her none of these things, then be she free.

13. The man that wilfully slays another man, let him suffer death. He, however, that slays him needfully, or unwillingly, or unwilfully, so as God may have sent him into his hands, and he has not lain in wait for him, be he worthy of his life and lawful boot, if he seek a shelter. But if any one of presumption and wilfully slay his neighbour through guile, lug thou him from mine altar, to the end that he suffer death.

14. He that slays [strikes] his father or his mother, he shal suffer death.

15. He that steals a free man, and he sells him, and it be proved on him, that he may not clear himself, suffer he death.

16. If any one slay his neighbour with stone or with fist, and he may go out though by a staff, get him a leech, and work his work the while that he himself may not.

17. He that smites his own theow-man or his woman, and he be not the same day dead, though he live two nights or three, he is not all so guilty, for that it was his own fee. If however he be dead the same day, then sit the guilt on him.

18. If any one, in strife, hurt a breeding wife, let him make boot for the hurt as the doomers appoint him. If she be dead, let him pay soul with soul.

19. If any one out-do other his eye, let him give his own for it; tooth for tooth, hand for hand, foot for foot, burning for burning, wound for wound, læl for læl.[1]

20. If any one smite his theow or his theowen the eye out, and he them make one-eyed, free he them for that. If he then strike out a tooth, do he the like.

21. If an ox gore man or wife that they be dead, be he with stones warped off, and be not his flesh eaten. The lord be guiltless, if the ox were goring two days before, or three, and the lord

---

1. Læl: *see* JAMIESON.

wist not of it; if however he wist of it, and he would not tine him in, and he then slew man or wife, be he with stones destroyed, and be the lord slain, or the man paid for, as the witan find to be right. If he gore son or daughter, be he worthy of the same doom. If he however gore theow or theow-mennen, let thirty shillings of silver be given to the lord, and be the ox destroyed with stones.

22. If any one delve a water pit, or untine a tined one, and tine it not again, let him pay for such neat as therein fall, and let him have the dead one.

23. If an ox wound other man's ox, and he then be dead, let them sell the ox; and have the worth in common, and eke the flesh so of the dead one. If the lord however wist that the ox were goring, and would not hold him in; let him give another ox for it, and have for himself all the flesh.

24. If any one steal other's ox, and slay or sell him, give he twain for it, and four sheep for one. If he have not what he may give, be he himself sold for the fee.

25. If a thief break man's house by night, and he be there slain, be he not of manslaughter guilty. If he doeth this since [after] sun-rise, he is guilty of manslaughter; and he then himself shall die, unles he were a needs doer. If with him quick be found what he before stole, by twofold let him pay for it,

26. If any one harm another man's vineyard, of his acres or aught of his lands, let him make boot as men value it.

27. If fire be kindled 'ryht' to burn, let him then make boot for the mischief who the fire tinded.

28. If any one trust feé to his friend, if he himself steal it, pay he for it twofold. If he know not who stole it, let him clear himself that he there no fraud committed. If however it were quick [live] cattle, and he say that the army took it, or that it died of itself, and he have witness, he need not pay for it. If he, however, have no witness, and he believe him not, let him then swear.

29. If any one deceive an unwedded woman, and sleep with

her, let him pay for her, and have her to him afterwards to wife. If, however, the woman's father will not sell her, let him give money according to her dowry.

30. The women that are wont to receive enchanters, and conjurers, and witches, let thou not them live.

31. And let him that lies with neat [cattle], suffer death.

32. And let him that sacrifices to the gods, unless to God alone, suffer death.

33. Comers from afar and strangers vex thou not, for that ye were strangers [long] ago in the Egyptians' land.

34. The widows and the step-children scathe ye not, nor harm them any where. If, however, ye do otherwise, they cry to me, and I hear them, and I then slay you with mine sword, and I so do that your wives be widows, and your bairns be step-children.

35. If thou give money to borrow to thine comrade that will dwell with thee, press thou him not as a " niedling," and oppress him not with the interest.

36. If a man have not but a onefold garment wherewith to cover him or to wear, and he give it to pledge, ere the sun goes to set, give it him back. If thou doest not so, then calleth he to me, and I hear him : for that I am very mild-hearted.

37. Revile not thou thine Lord ; nor curse thou the lord of the folk.

38. Thine tithe-monies and thine first-fruits of going and growing [things], give thou to God.

39. All that flesh that wild deer leave, eat ye not that, but give it to the hounds.

40. A leasing man's word reck thou not to hear, nor his dooms allow thou, nor no witness after him say thou.

41. Wend thou not thyself to the folk's unwise and unrigh will, in their speech and cry, beyond thine right [reason ?] and to the learning of the unwisest : nor allow them.

42. If to thee be come other man's stray cattle into thy hand, though it be thine foe, make it known to him.

43. Doom [judge] thou very evenly; doom thou not other doom to the wealthy, other to the poor; nor other doom to the more loved, other to the more loathed, doom thou not.

44. Shun thou aye leasings.

45. A sooth-fast [righteous] man and unguilty, slay thou him never.

46. Take thou never meed-monies, for they blind full oft wise men's thoughts; and turn aside their words.

47. To the stranger and out-comer [comer from abroad], let thou nothing uncouthly with [against] him, nor oppress thou him with no unright.

48. Swear ye never under heathen gods; nor in none things call ye to them.

49. These are dooms that the Almighty God himself was speaking to Moses, and bade him to hold, and, since the Lord's one-begotten son, our God, that is, healing Christ, on middle earth came, he quoth that he came not these biddings to break nor to forbid, but with all good to eke them, and mild-heartedness and lowly-mindedness to learn. Then after his throes [sufferings], ere that his apostles were gone through all the earth to learn [teach], and then yet that they were together, many heathen nations they turned to God. While they all together were, they send errand-doers to Antioch and to Syria, Christ's law to learn [teach]. When they understood that it speeded them not, then sent they an errand-writing to them. This is then that errand-writing that the apostles sent to Antioch, and to Syria, and to Cilicia, that are now from heathen nations turned to Christ.

The apostles and the elder brethren wish you health. And we make known to you, that we have heard that some of our fellows with our words to you have come, and bade you a heavier wise [way or law] to hold, than we bade them, and have too much misled you with manifold biddings, and your souls more perverted than they have righted. Then we assembled us about that, and to us all it seemed good, that we should send Paul and Barnabas, men that will their souls sell [give] for the Lord's name. With them we sent Judas and Silas, that they to you the ilk [same] may say. To the Holy Ghost it was thought and to us, that we none burden on you should not set, over that to you was needful to hold, that is then, that ye forbear that ye devil-gilds [idols] worship. and taste blood and things strangled, and from fornication, and that ye will that other men do not to you, do ye not that to other men.

From this one doom a man may think that he should doom [judge] every one rightly : he need keep no other doom-book. Let him think [take care] that he doom to no man that he would not that he doom to him, if he sought doom over him.

Since that, it happened that many nations took to Christ's faith ; there were many synods through all the middle earth gathered, and eke throughout the English race, they took to Christ's faith, of holy bishops', and eke of other exalted witan [wise men]. They then set forth, for their mild-heartedness, that Christ learned [taught], at almost every misdeed, that the worldly lords might, with their leave, without sin, at the first guilt, take their fee-boot that they then appointed ; except in treason against a lord, to which they durst not declare no mild-heartedness, for that the God Almighty doomed none to them that slighted him, nor Christ God's son doomed none to him that sold him to death, and he bade to love a lord as himself. They then in many synods set a boot for many misdeeds of men ; and in many synod books they wrote, here, one doom, there, another.

I then, Alfred king, gathered these together, and bade to write many of those that our foregoers held,—those that to me seemed good : and many of those that seemed not good, I set aside with mine witan's counsel, and in other wise bade to hold them : for that I durst not venture much of mine own to set in writing, for that it was unknown to me what of this would be liking to those that were after us. But those that I met with either in Ine's days mine kinsman, or in Offa's, king of Mercia, or in Æthelbryte's that first took baptism in the English race,—they that seemed to me the rightest, I gathered them herein and let alone the others.

I then, Ælfred, king of the West Saxons, shewed these to all mine witan, and they then said that that all seemed good to them to hold.

OF OATHS AND OF WEDS.

1. At first we learn [teach] that it is most needful that every man warily hold his oath and his wed. If any one is forced to whether [either] of these in wrong, either to lord treachery [treachery against a lord], or to any unright help, that is then righter to belie than to fulfil. If he however pledge that that to him is right to fulfil, and belie that, give he with lowly-mindedness his weapon and his goods to his friends to hold, and be forty nights in carcern [prison] in a king's town; suffer there as the bishop assigns him; and his kinsmen feed him, if he himself have no meat. If he have no kinsmen, or have no food, let the king's reeve feed him. If one should compel him, and he else will not, if they bind him, forfeit he his weapons and his inheritance. If one slay him, let him lie without amends. If he outflee ere the time and one take him, let him lie forty nights in prison, as he ere should [should at first]. If however he escape, let him be looked on as a runaway and be excommunicated of all Christ's churches. If, however, there be another man's suretyship, let him make boot for the breach of suretyship, as the right [law] may direct him; and for the pledge-breaking as his shriever [confessor] may shrive [appoint] him.

OF CHURCH SOCNS.

2. If any one, for whatever guilt, seek any of the minister-homes to which king's farm belongs, or other free family household of monks independant of the king, that is worthy of respect, let him have three nights' space to save himself, unless he will plead. If any one in this space harm him with slay [blow] or with bond or wound him through, let him make boot for each of these in right fashion, both with were and with wite; and to the brother-hood a hundred and twenty shillings to boot for the church-frith, and let him not have prejudiced his own.

OF BAIL-BREAKING.

3. If any one break the king's bail, let him make boot for the charge in right [legal] wise: and for the bail-breaking with five pounds of mere pennies [pure coin?]. For an archbishop's bail-breaking, or his protection, let him make boot with three pounds; for another bishop's or alderman's bail-breaking or protection, let him make boot with two pounds

OF TREACHERY AGAINST A LORD.

✗ 4. If any one is treacherous about the king's life, through himself or through protecting exiles or his men, be he liable in his life and in all that he owns. If he will prove himself true let him do that by the king's were-gild. So we eke appoint for all ranks both churl and earl. He that is treacherous about his lord's life, be towards him liable in his life and all that he owns; or by his lord's were prove him true.

OF CHURCH FREEDOM.

5. Eke (also) we appoint to every church that a bishop has hallowed, this freedom; if a foe-man flee into them, that for seven nights no man drag him out. But if any one do so; be he liable of the king's 'mund-byrde' and of the church-freedom; more if he there *mare of-gefo*, if he, for hunger, may live; unless he himself *ut feohte*. If the household (of monks) have more need of their church, let them hold him in another house, and that not have however more doors than the church. Let the church-elder see that men during this space of time do not sell [give] him meat. If he himself will reach out his weapons to his foes, let them hold him thirty nights, and let them tell of him to his kinsman. Eke church-frith is; if any man seek a church for any of those crimes that were not ere revealed, and there confess himself in God's name, be it half forgiven. He that stealeth on Sunday night, or at Yule (Christmas) or at Easter, or on Holy Thursday, and on Going-days (Rogation days) for each of them we will there be twain-boot, as on Lenten fast.

OF CHURCH STEALING.

6. If any one thieve aught in a church let him pay the one-gild, and the wite as to the one gild will befall, and slay man the hand off that he did it with. If he will lose the hand, and man will grant him that, pay (yield) he as to his wer befalls.

OF THAT A MAN FIGHTS IN THE KING'S HALL.

7. If any man in the king's hall fight, or draw out his weapon and man take him; be that in the king's doom, whether death or life, as he may be willing to give him. If he escape, and man take him again, let him pay for himself according to his were-gild and make boot for the guilt, whether were or wite, as his own merit (deserves.)

Of fornication with a nun.

8. If any one lead out a nun from a minster, without the king's leave or the bishop's, let him sell [give] a hundred and twenty shillings, half to the king, and half to the bishop and to the church's lord, that owns the nun. If she live longer than he that led her out, let her not have aught of his property. If she give birth to a bairn, let not that have of the property more than the mother.

If men slay her bairn, let him yield to the king the mother's kindred's deal (share), to the father's kindred let man give their share.

Of slaying a child-bearing woman.

9. If a man slay a wife with bairn, when the bairn is in her, let him pay for the woman full gild, and bairn, according to the father's kindred's were, half a gild.

Always be the wite 60 shillings until the one-gild arise to 30 shillings. Since it has arisen to that, then be the wite 120 shillings. Ago [formerly] was for a gold-thief, and for a mare-thief, and for a bee thief, and many wites more than others; now are all alike, except for a man-thief 120 shillings.

Of a twelve-hynde man's wife's adultery.

40. If a man lie with a twelve-hynde man's wife, let him make boot 120 shillings for the were. To a six-hynde man let him give boot an hundred shillings. To a churlish man let him make boot 40 shillings.

Of taking hold of a churlish woman.

11. If a man take hold of a churlish woman's breast, let him make boot to her with five shillings. If he overthrow her and do not lie with her, let him make boot with 10 shillings. If he lie with her, let him make boot with 60 shillings. If other man lay with her before, then be the boot half that. If a man accuse her, let her exculpate herself with 60 hides, or forfeit with half the boot. If to a more nobly born woman this befal, let the boot increase according to the were.

Of wood-burning.

12. If a man other's wood burneth or heweth unleaved (without leave,) let him pay for every great tree with five shillings, and then, for each, be they as many as of them may be, with five pence and 30 shillings to wite.

IF A MAN BE FELLED AT COMMON WORK.

13. If a man at common work fell another unwillingly, let them give the tree to the kindred and let them have it ere 30 nights off the land, or he take it, who owns the wood.

OF DUMB MEN'S DEEDS.

14. If a man be dumb or deaf born, that he may not his sins say out or confess, let the father make boot for his mideeds.

OF THE MEN THAT FIGHT BEFORE A BISHOP.

15. If a man fight before an archbishop or draw out his weapon, let him make boot with 50 shillings. If before another bishop or an alderman this happen, let him make boot with 100 shillings.

OF THE CASE THAT A MAN DRIVES OFF A MARE'S FOAL OR A COW'S CALF.

16. If a man steal a cow or a stud-mare, and drive off the foal or the calf, let him pay with a shilling, and for the mothers by their worth.

OF THE CASE THAT ONE COMMITS AN INFANT TO ANOTHER.

17. If any one commit to another his infant and he decease in the keeping, let him that feeds him clear himself of treachery if any one accuse him of aught.

OF SEIZING HOLD OF A NUN.

18. If any one, with desire to cohabit, seize a nun, either on her raiment or on her breast, without her leave, be it twain-boot. as we ere found [before decided] about lay-men. If a wedded woman commit adultery, if she be churlish, with 60 shillings let boot be made to the surety; and that be in live goods, cattle-goods, and let man give no man for that. If she be a six-hynde, let him pay 100 shillings to the surety. If she be a twelve-hynde, 120 shillings let him make boot to the surety.

OF THOSE MEN THAT LEND THEIR WEAPONS FOR MEN-SLAYING.

19. If any man lend his weapon to another, that he may slay a man with [it], they may join themselves together, if they will, for the were. If they will not join together, yield [pay he that

lent the weapon, a third deal [share] of the were, and of the wite a third share. If he will clear himself, that he wish not deceit in the loan: that he may do. If a sword-whetter take other man's weapon to furbish, or a smith a man's material, let both give it back sound, as whether [either] of them before took it, unless either of them had before agreed that he should not hold it 'angild.'

OF THOSE WHO COMMIT THEIR CATTLE TO MONKS WITHOUT LEAVE.

20. If a man entrust cattle to another man's monk without the monk's lord's leave, and it escape him, let him forfeit it that before owned it.

OF THE FIGHTING OF PRIESTS.

21. If a priest slay another man, warp man to hand all that he at home bought, and the bishop unhood him: then let man give him from the minster, unless the lord will settle for the were.

OF CONFESSION OF DEBT.

22. If a man at folk-meeting reveal a debt to the king's reeve and afterwards will withdraw from it, let him fix it on a righter hand [person], if he may [can]. If he cannot, let him lose his angild and take to the wite.

OF A DOG'S SLITTING [TEARING].

23. If a hound [dog] slit or bite a man, at foremost misdeed pay 6 shillings, if he give him meat, at after turn [next time] 12 shillings; at the third, 30 shillings. If at either of these misdeeds the hound escape, go this boot, whether or no, forth. If the hound work more misdeeds, and he have [keep] him, let him make boot the full were; both wound-boot, and as he works [for whatever he may do].

OF CATTLE'S MISDEEDS.

24. If a neat wound a man, warp that neat to hand, or make composition.

OF THE RAPE OF A CHURL'S MAID.

25. If a man forces a cohabitation with a churl's maid, let him make boot to the churl with five shillings, and 60 shillings for wite. If a theow-man force a theow-woman to fornication, let him make boot with his membrum virile.

OF THE RAPE OF AN UNWINTERED [YOUNG] WOMAN.

26. If a man forces an unwintered woman to cohabit, be that as the boot of a full-aged man.

OF KINLESS MEN.

27. If a man kinless of father's kin fight, and slay a man, and then if he have mother's kin, give they a third share of the were, a third share his gild brethren ; for a third share let him flee. If he have no mother's kin, let his gild brethren pay half, for half let him flee.

OF SLAYING A MAN SO SITUATED.

28. If a man slay a man so situated ; if he have no kinsman, let them pay half to the king, half to the gild-brethren.

OF SLAYING A TWO-HYND MAN WITH A BAND OF ROBBERS.

29. If a man with a band of robbers slay an unsinning two-hynd man, let the confessor of the slaying pay, be it were and wite ; and every man that was of the party, pay 30 shillings for robber-boot.

OF A SIX-HYND MAN.

30. If it be a six-hynd man, let each man pay for robber-boot 60 shillings, and the slayer, were and full wite.

OF A TWELVE-HYND MAN.

31. If he be a twelve-hynd man, let each of them pay 120 shillings, and the slayer, were and wite. If a band do this, and afterwards will off-swear it [swear that they did not do it], let them accuse them all ; and then all pay the were at common hand, and all one wite, as to the were belongs.

OF FOLK-LEASING WORKERS.

32. If a man work folk-leasing [be guilty of slander], and it become fixed on him, with no lighter thing let him make boot than that men cut his tongue off, which men must redeem at no undearer [cheaper] worth than men have valued at the were.

OF PLEDGES BY GOD.

33. If any one accuse another of a God-borh, and will complain that he has not fulfilled any of those that he gave him, let him give the fore-oath in four churches, and the other, if he will clear himself, in twelve churches do he that.

OF CHAPMEN

34. Also it is to chapmen laid down; the men that they lead up with them, that they bring before the king's reeve at the folk-meeting and reckon how many there are, and let them take the men with them that they may afterwards bring to right [justice] at the folk-meeting: and when there is need to them of more men up with them to have on their journey, let them always tell as oft as need is to them, in the meeting's witness, to the king's reeve.

OF BINDING A CHURLISH MAN.

35. If a man bind a churlish man unsinning, let him make boot with ten shillings. If a man swinge [scourge] him, with twenty shillings let him make boot. If he lay him in prison, with 30 shillings let him make boot. If he shear [shave] him in insult to [like] a 'homila,' with 10 shillings let him make boot. If he shear him unbound, to a [like] priest, with 30 shillings let him make boot. If he shear off the beard, with 20 shillings let him make boot. If he bind him, and then shear him to a priest, let him make boot with 60 shillings.

OF SPEAR-CARELESSNESS.

36. Also is decreed, if a man have a spear over his shoulder and a man stake himself on it, that he pay the were without the wite. If he stake himself before his eyes, that he pay the were. If a man accuse him of wilfulness in the deed, let him clear him according to the wite; and with that let the wite abate. And let this be if the point be three fingers over the hindward shaft; if they be both alike [level], point and handward part, be that without danger.

OF A HOUSEHOLD-ROLL.

37. If a man will from one household-roll seek a lord in another household-roll, let him do that with the alderman's witness

that he before followed in his shire. If he do it without his witness, let him that feeds him as his man, pay 120 shillings to wite. Let him deal, however, the half to the king in the shire that he before followed, half in that that he cometh into. If he hath done any evil where he before was, let him make boot for it, that before took him as his man, and to the king 120 shillings for wite.

OF THE CASE THAT A MAN FIGHT BEFORE AN ALDERMAN AT THE MOTE.

38. If a man fight before a king's alderman in the mote, let him make boot were and wite, as it may be right; and before this, 120 shillings to the alderman for wite. If he disturb the folk-mote with weapon-drawing, 120 shillings to the alderman for wite. If aught of this befal before a king's alderman's younger, or a king's priest, 30 shillings to wite.

OF FIGHTING A CHURLISH MAN'S HOUSE-FIGHT.

39. If any one fight in a churlish man's house, with 6 shillings let him make boot to the churl. If he draw his weapon and fight not, be it half of that. If either of these happen to a six-hynd man, let it arise threefoldly according to the churlish boot; to a twelve-hynd man twofoldly, according to the six-hynd boot.

OF BURH [HOUSE]-BREAKING.

40. The king's burh-breaking is 120 shillings. An archbishop's, ninety shillings. Another bishop's and an alderman's, 60 shillings. A twelve-hynd man's 30 shillings. A six-hynd man's, 15 shillings. A churl's fence-breaking, 5 shillings. If aught of this happen when the army is out [away on duty], or in lent-fast, be it two boot. If a man put down holy right in the folk without leave, let him make boot with 120 shillings.

OF BOOK-LANDS.

41. The man who has book-land, and his kinsman left [it] him, then set we that he must not give it from his kindred, if there be writing or witness that it was forbidden by those men that at first gained it, and by those that gave it him that he so might not; and that, then, let him declare, on the king's and on the bishop's witness, before his kinsman.

Of feuds.

42. Also we bid; the man that wits [knows] his foe to be at home sitting, that he fight not ere that he bid [demand] right of him. If he have might that he beride his foe, and beset him within, let him hold him seven nights within and not fight against him, if he will abide within. And then, about seven nights, if he will go on hand [surrender], and give up his weapons, let him hold him 30 nights sound, and let him warn his kindred and his friends of him. If he however, flee into a church, let it then be according to the holiness of that church, as we before above said. If he, however, have not might, that he may besiege him within, let him ride to the alderman and bid help of him. If he will not help him, let him ride to the king ere he fight. Likewise also, if a man come upon his foe, and he did not before know him to be fast at home; if he will give up his weapons, let men hold him 30 nights and warn his friends of him, if he will not give up his weapons, then may he fight on him [attack him]. If he will go on hand [surrender himself] and give up his weapons, and any one, over that, fight on him, let him pay both were and wound, as he may do, and wite, and forfeit his kinmanship. Also we quoth [say], that a man might fight with [on the side of his] lord without feud if a man fight against the lord; so might the lord fight for his man. After the same wise, a man might for his born kinsman, if a man attack him in wrong, except with his lord: that we allow not. And a man might fight without feud, if he meet another at [with] his own wife, in tined [closed] doors, or under one covering, or with his daughter own-born, or with his sister own-born, or with his mother that was given to his father for his lawful wife.

Of mass-day festivals.

43. To all free-men let these days be given, save to theow-men and hired work-men; 12 days at Yule (Christmas), and the day that Christ overcome the devil and Saint Gregory's memorial day, and 7 days at Easter and 7 days after, and one day at St Peter's tide and St Paul's and in harvest the full week ere St Mary's mass, and at All-Hallows' celebration one day and 4 Wednesdays on 4 ember weeks. To all theow-men, be it given those to whom it may be most agreeable to give, whatever any man give them for

God's name, or they on any of their while-sticks [bits of time] may learn.

OF A HEAD-WOUND.

44. For a head-wound, to boot, if the bones be both pierced, let men give him 30 shillings. If the outer bone be pierced, give 15 shillings to boot.

OF A HAIR-WOUND.

45. If in the hair be a wound an inch long, let him give one shilling to boot. If before the hair be a wound an inch long, twain shillings to boot.

OF STRIKING OFF AN EAR.

46. If a man strike him other an ear off, give 30 shillings to boot. If the hearing stand off [be gone] that he may not hear, give 60 shillings to boot.

OF A MAN'S EYE-WOUND AND OTHER MIS-LIKE [VARIOUS] LIMBS.

47. If a man strike out a man's eye, let the man pay him 60 shillings, and 6 shillings and 6 pennies and a third part of a penny to boot. If it be in the head, and he may not see naught with [it], let the third part of the boot stand.

48. If a man strike off to another the nose, let him give him boot with 60 shillings.

49. If a man strike out to another the tooth in the fore of his head, let him make boot for that with 8 shillings. If it be the cheek-tooth, give 4 shillings to boot. A man's tusk be'th [is] 15 shillings worth.

50. If a man fore-slayeth [strikes in front] a man's cheeks, that they be broken, let him make boot with 15 shillings. A man's chin-bone, if it be broken, let a man pay 12 shillings to boot.

51. If a man's throat-bowl [wind-pipe] be pierced, let him make boot with 12 shillings.

52. If a man's tongue be done out of his head by another man's deeds, that be like as eye-boot.

53. If a man be wounded on the axle [shoulder], that the lith

[limb]-juice out-flow, let him make boot with 30 shillings.

54. If the arm be broken above the elbow, there shall be 15 shillings to boot.

55. If the arm-shanks be both broken, the boot be 30 shillings.

56. If the thumb be off-struck, for that shall be 30 shillings to boot.
If the nail be off-struck, for that shall be 5 shillings to boot.

57. If the shooting-[fore-] finger be off-struck, the boot be 15 shillings : his nails be 4 shillings.

58. If the middle-most finger be off-struck, the boot be 12 shillings ; and his nail's boot be 2 shillings.

59. If the gold-[ring] finger be off-struck, for that shall be 17 shillings to boot : and his nails 4 shillings to boot.

60. If the little finger be off-struck, for that shall be to boot 9 shillings, and one shilling his nails, if he be off-struck.

61. If a man be on the riff [belly] wounded, let man give him 30 shillings to boot, if he be thorough wounded; at whether mouth [for either opening] twenty shillings.

62. If a man's thigh be pierced, let man pay 30 shillings to boot if it be broken, the boot also be 30 shillings.

63. If the shank be pierced beneath the knee, there shall be 12 shillings to boot, if he be broken beneath the knee, pay him 30 shillings to boot.

64. If the mickle [great] toe be off-struck, pay him 20 shillings to boot ; if it be the after [next] toe, 15 shillings to boot pay him man ; if the middle-most toe be off-struck, there shall be 9 shillings to boot ; if it be the fourth toe, there shall be 6 shillings to boot : if the little toe be off-struck, pay him 5 shillings.

65. If a man be wounded in the genitals to the excess that he may not beget a bairn, let boot be made to him for that with 80 shillings.

66. If to a man be the arm, with hand, with all cut off before

the elbow, let boot be made for that with 80 shillings. For every wound before the hair, and before the sleeve, and beneath the knee, the boot is two shot [parts] more.

67. If the loin-breadth is smitten, there shall be 60 shillings to boot ; if it is pierced, pay 15 shillings to boot : if it is through pierced, then shall there be 30 shillings to boot.

68. If a man is wounded in the axle [shoulder], make boot with 80 shillings, if the man be quick [alive].

69. If a man maim outwardly the hand of another, let him pay him 20 shillings to boot, if a man may heal him ; if it half fly away, then shall be 40 shillings to boot.

70. If a man maim another's rib within a whole hide, let him pay 10 shillings to boot; if the hide be broken, and men take out the bone, let him pay 15 shillings to boot.

71. If a man strike a man's eye, or his hand, or his foot off, there goeth like boot to all ; 6 pennies and 6 shillings and 60 shillings and a third part of a penny.

72. If a man's shank be struck off at the knee, then shall be 70 shillings to boot.

73. If a man maim the shoulder of another, let the man pay him 20 shillings to boot.

74. If a man break it in [within,] and men take out the bone, let the man pay for this to boot 15 shillings.

75. If a man break the great sinew, if a man may leech it, that it be whole, let him pay 12 shillings to boot. If the man be halt for the sinew's wound and man may not heal him, let him pay 30 shillings to boot.

76. If a man break the small sinew, let the man pay him 6 shillings to boot.

77. If a man break the tendons of another upon the neck, and wound them so sorely that he may not use them, and nevertheless live so shent [illtreated] ; let the man pay him 100 shillings to boot unless the witan allow to him one righter and more.

OF INE'S DOOMS.

I, Ine, with God's gift, West-Saxons' king, with the thought [counsel,] and with teaching of Kenred mine father and of Hedde mine bishop, and of Eorkenwold mine bishop, with all mine aldermen and the most famous witan of mine people, and eke a mickle gathering of God's servants, was searching of [about] the health of our souls and of the steadfastness of our kingdom, that the right law and right king's dooms through our folk were [might be] fastened and trimmed [confirmed], that none of the aldermen nor our subjects after them turn aside these our dooms.

Of God's servants' rule.

1. First, we bid that God's servants hold their right rule in right. After that, we bid that all the folk's law and dooms be thus holden.

Of children.

2. Let a child be baptized within 30 nights. If it be not so, let him give boot 30 shillings. If it however be dead without baptism, let him give boot for it with all that he owns.

Of sunday-works.

3. If a theowman work on Sunday by his lord's behest, be he free, and the lord pay 30 shillings for wite. If however the thew work without witness, let him suffer in his hide [or hide-gild]. If however the freeman that day work without his lord's behest, let him forfeit his freedom or sixty shillings, and a priest be two-fold guilty.

Of church scots.

4. Let church-scots be given at Saint Martin's mass. If any one do not follow that, be he liable for 60 shillings, and give to twelve-fold for the church-scot.

Of church socns.

5. If any one be guilty of death, and he run into a church, let him have his life, and give boot as the right may direct him. If any one forfeit his hide, and run into a church, be the swingeing [whipping] forgiven him.

Here follow about thirty pages of King Ine's Laws; after which are found two copies of the treaty between King Alfred and Guthrum. As these differ in some material points, we give them in parallel columns.

ALFRED AND GUTHRUM'S PEACE.

This is that peace that Alfred king and Guthrum king and all the witan of Angle-kind, and all the people that in East-Anglia be have all ordained and with oaths fastened [confirmed], for themselves and for their descendants, both for born and for unborn, who of God's mercy reck or of ours.

1. First about our land-marks; up on the Thames, and then up on the Lea; and along the Lea unto its source; then on right to Bedford; then up on the Ouse unto Watling Street.

2. That is then: if a man become slain, we value all even [equally] dear, English and Danes, at eight half-marks of unsodden [pure] gold, except the churl that sits on gavel-land and their liesings: they are eke [equally] dear either at two hundred shillings.

3. And if a man accuse a king's thane of man-slaying, if he dare clear himself, do he that with twelve king's thanes. If man accuse that man, that is of less power than the king's thane, clear he him with eleven his likes [equals]; and with one king's thane.

And so in whatever suit that may be for more than four mancuses. And if he dare not, let him requite it threefold, as man it may value.

This is that peace that Alfred king and Guthrum king and all the witan of Angle-kind and all the people that in East Anglia be, spoke and have sworn to, both for themselves and for their offspring.

1. First about their land-marks, along the Thames, then up on the Lea; along the Lea unto its source; then on right to Bedford; then up on on the Ouse unto Watling Street.

2. And they spoke: if a man become slain, we value all even [equally] dear, English and Danes, at eight half-marks of unsodden [pure] gold, except the churl that sits on gavel-land and their lysings: they are eke [equally] dear: either at two hundred shillings.

3. And if a man accuse a king's thane of man-slaying and he dare clear himself, do he that with twelve king's thanes; and if man accuse that man, that is of less power, clear him eleven his likes [equals] and one king's thane.

OF WARRANTERS.

4. And that every man wit [know] his warranter for men, and for horses, and for oxen.

5. And we all ordained on that day that men swore the oaths, that neither bond nor free might into the army fare [go] without leave, nor none of them than may to us. If then it happen that for need any of them will have traffic with us, or we with them, with cattle and with goods, that is to be allowed in this wise; that men give hostages to pledge peace and to evidence that man know that man has a clean back [has acted honestly].

4. And they all ordained when man swore the oaths, that neither we might fare [go] into the army without leave, nor none of them than may to us: unless man give between [mutually] sureties and hostages to pledge peace, and to evidence that man goes with right, if that happen that any of us to other goes with cattle and with goods.

KING ALFRED'S PREFACE

TO

The Anglo - Saxon Version

OF

GREGORY'S DIALOGUES.

The Saxon version of Gregory's Dialogues is understood to have been made at Alfred's request, by Werfrith bishop of Winchester, who was one of the king's academy of learned men. The preface, written by Alfred himself, and consisting of a few lines only, completes the works of a king, whose fame rests even more on his intellectual than on his military superiority to the rude age in which he lived.

Ic Ælfrede gyfendum Criste mid Cynehades mærnesse geweorðað hæbbe cuðlice ongiten, and þurh haligra boca rædunge oft gehyred, þæt us an God swa micele healicnesse woruld geðingða forgifen hæfð. Is seo mæste þearf þæt we hwilon ure mod geliðian and gebigian to ðam Godcundum and gastlicum rihte, betweoh þas eorðlican carfulnesse; and ic forþam rohte and wilnode to minum getrywum freondum þæt hy me of Godes bocum be haligra manna þeawum and wundrum awriton þas æfter-fyligendan lare; þæt ic þurh þa mynegunge and lufe getrymmed on minum mode hwilum gehicge þa heofenlican þing betweoh þas eorðlican gedrefednysa. Cuðlice we magon nu æt ærestan gehyran hu se eadiga and se Apostolica þer Scs Gregorius spræc to his Diacone þam wæs nama Petrus, be haligra manna þeawum and life, to lare and to byrne eallum þam þe Godes willan wyrceað and be be him silfum þisum wordum; and þus cwæð.

I, Alfred, by the grace of Christ with royal dignity endowed, have truly understood, and through reading of holy books often heard, that to us one God so much greatness of worldly things hath given. *There* is the greatest need that we for a time should soften and bend our mind to divine and spiritual services, amid this earthly care : and I therefore sought and desired my true friends, that they for me from God's books, concerning the manners and miracles of Holy men would write the following doctrine; that I through this admonition and love being confirmed in my mind, for a time may study these heavenly things amid these earthly troubles. Truly we may now at first hear how the blessed and apostolic man Saint Gregory spake to his deacon, whose name was Peter, concerning the manner and life of holy men, for instruction and example to all those, who perform the will of God: and he of himself in these words *spake*, and thus quoth.

CONTENTS OF THE THIRD VOLUME.

King Alfred's Hand-book.	5
Essay on the Geography of King Alfred the Great, taken from his Anglo-Saxon Version of Orosius: containing Alfred's Description of Europe in the Ninth Century, and his account of the voyages of Ohthere and Wulfstan into the White and Baltic seas.	9
Anglo-Saxon Version of Gregory's Pastoral Care	64
A Modern English Version of King Alfred's Blossom-gatherings from Saint Augustine	80
The Laws of King Alfred the Great.	119
King Alfred's Preface to the Anglo-Saxon Version of Gregory's Dialogues	140

**DO NOT REMOVE
OR
MUTILATE**

Check Out More Titles From HardPress Classics Series In this collection we are offering thousands of classic and hard to find books. This series spans a vast array of subjects – so you are bound to find something of interest to enjoy reading and learning about.

Subjects:
Architecture
Art
Biography & Autobiography
Body, Mind &Spirit
Children & Young Adult
Dramas
Education
Fiction
History
Language Arts & Disciplines
Law
Literary Collections
Music
Poetry
Psychology
Science
…and many more.

Visit us at www.hardpress.net

Im TheStory
personalised classic books

"Beautiful gift.. lovely finish. My Niece loves it, so precious!"

Helen R Brumfieldon

★★★★★

UNIQUE GIFT

FOR KIDS, PARTNERS AND FRIENDS

Timeless books such as:

Alice in Wonderland • The Jungle Book • The Wonderful Wizard of Oz
Peter and Wendy • Robin Hood • The Prince and The Pauper
The Railway Children • Treasure Island • A Christmas Carol

Romeo and Juliet • Dracula

Highly Customizable | Change Books Title | Replace Characters Names with yours | Upload Photo (for inside page) | Add Inscriptions

Visit
Im TheStory.com
and order yours today!